Energy Policy Design in the Eastern Mediterranean Basin

This book explores energy consumption and thermal comfort in the social housing sector in the Eastern Mediterranean basin.

This book presents a novel methodological framework for the optimisation of post-war social housing developments in the Eastern Mediterranean climate. The authors draw on semi-structured interviews to present evidence on in situ thermal sensation and provide the results of walk-through and walk-in thermographic surveys to highlight building-fabric performance and highlight anomalies in the building envelopes. The authors go on to show how this data-informed retrofit design solution can be applied to reduce household energy consumption, increase awareness of domestic energy use and inform effective policymaking decisions in energy use in the Eastern Mediterranean basin, including the development of Energy Performance Certificate schemes.

This book will be of great interest to students and scholars of energy policy, energy efficiency and planning. It will also assist architects, building engineers and other practitioners in closing the gap between the current understanding and the actual performance of existing residential building stocks in the Eastern Mediterranean basin.

Bertug Ozarisoy is an architect and expert in building energy modelling both in the UK and Cyprus. His research focuses on understanding the theory between architecture and energy-policy design in conjunction with exploring the impact of passive-cooling systems on domestic energy use and households' thermal comfort. Dr Ozarisoy has an intensive 10 years' experience in teaching, research and architectural practice. He was initially involved in the BSc (Hons) in Construction Management programme at the University of East London (UEL) between September 2016–2018. He has developed teaching skills to demonstrate significant intellectual input to the students' technical drawings and monitor their learning adaptability and integration to the 'Construction Technology and Materials' module. He authored over 35 journals and conference papers relevant to the building engineering field and assisted with research projects in the Sustainable Development of the Built Environment (SDBE) and Sustainable Development Goals (SDGs) in Europe. Dr. Ozarisoy is a Lecturer in Technology in the School of Built Environment and Architecture, in London South Bank University (LSBU). He is a co-author of the book 'Transgressive Design Strategies for Utopian Cities: Theories, Methodologies and Cases in Architecture and Urbanism which has been published in Routledge Research in Architecture series by Taylor & Francis. Currently, he continues his research on the development of neutral adaptive thermal comfort benchmarking to contribute to the American Society of Heating, Refrigerating and Air-Conditioning Engineers (ASHRAE) Global Thermal Comfort Database II with the team of international experts in thermal comfort studies.

Hasim Altan is Professor of Sustainable Design and Architectural Engineering in the College of Architecture and Design (COAD) at Prince Mohammad bin Fahd University (PMU), Khobar, Dhahran, Saudi Arabia. He is a Chartered Architect (RIBA) and a Chartered Engineer (CIBSE) with over 20 years of academic and practice experience in the field of Architecture, Engineering and Construction (AEC) in the Built Environment in the UK, Europe, the Middle East and North Africa (MENA) regions. Prof. Dr Altan sits on a number of editorial boards and reviews project proposals for the European Commission, UK Research Councils and Qatar National Research Fund (QNRF) by the Qatar Foundation. Since 2004, he has, singly or jointly, secured and directed 32 research grants worth over £21 million. He is a founding member of the International Network on Zero Energy Mass Custom Home (ZEMCH), which has so far organised nine international conferences, several design workshops and numerous technical visits. As well as having supervised 17 successful PhD theses (11 as first supervisor) and over 80 Masters dissertations (MSc, MArch and MEng), he has published over 300-refereed international journal and conference papers, technical reports, edited/authored books and chapters, and editorials in related fields.

Routledge Explorations in Energy Studies

Perspectives on Energy Poverty in Post-Communist Europe
Edited by George Jiglau, Anca Sinea, Ute Dubois and Philipp Biermann

Dilemmas of Energy Transitions in the Global South
Balancing Urgency and Justice
Edited by Ankit Kumar, Johanna Höffken and Auke Pols

Assembling Petroleum Production and Climate Change in Ecuador and Norway
Elisabeth Marta Tómmerbakk

International Law and Renewable Energy Investment in the Global South
Avidan Kent

Local Energy Governance
Opportunities and Challenges for Renewable and Decentralised Energy in France and Japan
Edited by Magali Dreyfus and Aki Suwa

Local Energy Communities
Emergence, Places, Organizations, Decision Tools
Edited by Gilles Debizet, Marta Pappalardo and Frédéric Wurtz

Building Resilient Energy Systems
Lessons from Japan
Jennifer F. Sklarew

Regulatory Support for Off-Grid Renewable Electricity
Edited by Ngozi Chinwa Ole, Eduardo G. Pereira, Peter Kayode Oniemola and Gustavo Kaercher Loureiro

Northern Indigenous Community-Led Disaster Management and Sustainable Energy
Ranjan Datta, Margot Hurlbert and William Marion

Energy Policy Design in the Eastern Mediterranean Basin
A Roadmap to Energy Efficiency
Bertug Ozarisoy and Hasim Altan

For more information about this series, please visit: www.routledge.com/Routledge-Explorations-in-Energy-Studies/book-series/REENS

Energy Policy Design in the Eastern Mediterranean Basin

A Roadmap to Energy Efficiency

Bertug Ozarisoy and Hasim Altan

Routledge
Taylor & Francis Group
LONDON AND NEW YORK

earthscan
from Routledge

First published 2024
by Routledge
4 Park Square, Milton Park, Abingdon, Oxon OX14 4RN

and by Routledge
605 Third Avenue, New York, NY 10158

Routledge is an imprint of the Taylor & Francis Group, an informa business

British Library Cataloguing-in-Publication Data
A catalogue record for this book is available from the British Library

ISBN: 978-1-032-49304-6 (hbk)
ISBN: 978-1-032-49305-3 (pbk)
ISBN: 978-1-003-39309-2 (ebk)

DOI: 10.4324/9781003393092

Typeset in Times New Roman
by Deanta Global Publishing Services, Chennai, India

Access the Support Material: www.routledge.com/9781032493046

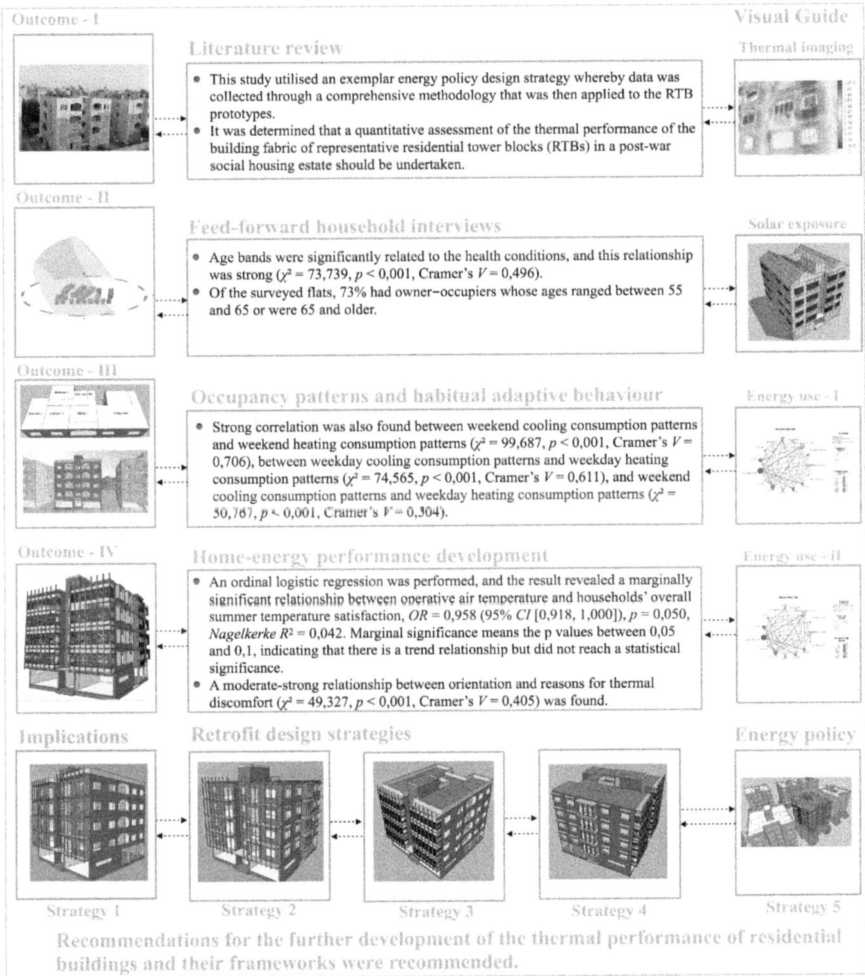

Graphical Abstract: Step-by-step development of methodological framework in energy-policy design.

To my family, for their unconditional support and my aunt Dt. Serife Gurkan for her sponsorship throughout my research journey and academic career. I would like thank my aunt Sevilay Salkok and my mother Ayse Ozarisoy for their continuous support at the time of writing this book and a new start of lectureship in the School of Built Environment and Architecture at London South Bank University (LSBU) in London, United Kingdom.

Dr Bertug Ozarisoy

Contents

Figures

Preface

Efforts to retrofit post-war residential buildings have gained increasing momentum in the last several years, especially after the European Union (EU) called for a zero-carbon emission target by 2050. While many scholars have published works on the topic of upgrading the thermal performance of buildings in many aspects, including considering occupants' habitual adaptive behaviours on home-energy performance and thermal comfort, few have approached this topic from the time-limited, output-driven perspective of conducting a longitudinal field survey through adopting the socio-technical-systems (STS) design approach. Numerous field studies have found that occupants' thermal comfort varies with local climate conditions. However, there is no generally recommended acceptable comfort range for multi-family residential buildings, nor are there specific adaptive thermal comfort prediction methods, particularly for Eastern Mediterranean countries.

This study aims to fill a research gap in the area of developing an evidence-based framework for energy policy decision-making mechanisms related to the integration of the Energy Performance of Building Directives (EPBD) at the level of conceptual and nationwide implementation schemes. The objective of this study is to focus on the interaction of policymaking and underlying determinant factors with socio-cultural and contextual factors. The primary research question addressed is: What is the most effective and universally applicable energy-policy framework to implement the EPBD mandates recommended by the EU and to improve the energy efficiency of existing housing stock in Northern Cyprus (NC)?

This study presents a novel methodological framework for the optimisation of post-war social housing developments in the Eastern Mediterranean climate. It was developed according to in situ measurements of building-fabric thermal structures to assess robust energy performance evaluation and certification schemes in the residential sector. The study examines how this specific area of energy policy and regulation is carried out through use of an exploratory case study approach that analyses nationally representative archetype buildings in a post-war social-housing estate in the coastal city of Famagusta, Northern Cyprus. First, an empirical framework was developed to integrate the STS approach and to provide data about households through field interviews to better understand socio-demographic characteristics, energy use and thermal comfort; for this survey, 118 flats were successfully recruited during the summer of 2018. Second, an in vivo experience of householders' thermal-sensation votes was assessed to predict individual aspects of adaptive thermal comfort and its relevance to overheating. Third, in situ measurements were employed, including recordings of household indoor air temperatures integrated with thermal-imaging surveys and heat-flux measurements of building-fabric elements, along with a concurrent *on-site* monitoring of environmental conditions and a review of household energy bills to accurately determine actual energy use. Furthermore, this study explored the uncertain input parameters for building-energy simulations that quantitative modelling has adopted to measure dynamic thermal simulation findings in conjunction with occupants' socio-demographic characteristics, occupancy patterns, household sizes and *on-site* monitored environmental conditions. Finally, evidence-based passive-cooling retrofit design strategies were developed to assess energy performance of the archetype buildings and test feasible retrofitting interventions.

The study set out to design and execute three main research outputs. First, a novel framework combining assessment methodology with existing benchmark criterion of thermal comfort was developed. The results of environmental monitoring findings showed the typically warm conditions of the environment during the survey period in summer. The maximum indoor and outdoor air temperatures peaked at 34.10 and 36°C, respectively. Additionally, it was recorded that, during *on-site* environmental monitoring period, the external temperatures were above 23°C for 95% of the time. The occupants' thermal-sensation votes indicated that the 'neutral' temperature was 28.5°C, and the upper limit of the comfort range in warm indoor air temperature conditions was 31.5°C. This suggests that, in hot and dry climates in which thermally uncomfortable indoor environments occur, particularly in summer, occupants appear to tolerate a warmer condition than at other high and medium altitudes.

Second, a novel building diagnostic and thermal performance-oriented approach was proposed. The findings explored thermal anomalies resulting from air infiltration through building fabric, a lack of natural ventilation through living spaces and excessive heat gains through sizeable and glazed areas. On a typical hot summer day, the internal temperatures of the simulated condominiums remained high throughout the day and night, ranging from a minimum of 28.5°C to a maximum 36.5°C. There was a difference of +5°C between the actual and the simulated-and-predicted operative air temperatures and the 36.5°C upper thermal-comfort threshold identified in the building-energy-simulation analysis; this is +3.5°C higher than the recommended thermally acceptable threshold for hot Mediterranean climates in the summer.

Third, a building-energy-simulation framework was developed. The results revealed that in a non-retrofitted building, cooling and heating comprised the greatest proportion (73%) of total energy consumption. Applications for six passive-cooling design strategies were analysed, and after the life-cycle cost assessment of each was considered, off-site modular building applications were developed. After building optimisation, approximately 81% of savings related to cooling consumption were achieved, which suggests that design, ventilation and servicing strategies combined with passive shading systems can improve the energy efficiency and indoor air quality of residential buildings, as recommended by the EPBD.

Famagusta, Cyprus
Dhahran, Saudi Arabia

Dr Bertug Ozarisoy
Prof. Dr Hasim Altan

Acknowledgements

Firstly, we would like to express our sincerest gratitude to the Graduate School at the University of East London (UEL) for offering a research environment for Dr Ozarisoy to pursue his PhD research at the School of Architecture, Computing and Engineering. Special thanks go to Prof. Verity Brown and Dr Mihaela Anca Ciupala for their continuous support throughout his research journey in the UK.

Secondly, we would like to acknowledge and thank the following people whose help and encouragement made it possible for Dr Ozarisoy to receive a supportive and rigorous research culture during the course of his PhD research. They are Dr Thomas Rusbridge, Dr Sahar Zahiri and Dr Wei Shi.

Most of all we want to thank Dr Ozarisoy's aunt Dt. Serife Gurkan for her never-ending love, support and understanding throughout his research work. Nevertheless, the continued support and encouragement of his family has given him the strength to strive for excellence and personal growth and hopefully this handbook is a tiny reflection of both. I would like to say my thanks to the Sustainable Environment and Energy Systems (SEES) Graduate Program at the Middle East Technical University. We would like to thank the School of Built Environment and Architecture in London South Bank University (LSBU), London, United Kingdom for giving Dr Ozarisoy an interactive research environment to pursue this novel research in energy efficiency studies.

Last but not least, we would like to thank Taylor & Francis for giving us the opportunity to publish this handbook.

Thanks to all.

Dr Bertug Ozarisoy
Prof. Dr Hasim Altan

Nomenclature and Abbreviations

A	Area (m^2)
°C	Degree Celsius
Clo	Insulation value of clothing
C_v	Air permeability coefficient
CV	Coefficient of variation (%)
df	Degree of freedom
E	Energy (kWh/m^2)
f	Frequency
F	Fuel (MJ)
f_c	Correction factor of thermal mass
$f_{shading}$	Envelope shading reduction factor
G_{value}	Solar energy transmittance
GWH	Giga-watt hour
h	Equation parameter
H	Height (m)
h^{-1}	Air infiltration rate
m	Mass (kg)
M	Mean
M	Thermal conductivity coefficient (kJ/m^2K)
$\mathbf{m^2}$	Square meter
$\mathbf{m^3}$	Cubic meter
met	Metabolic activity
MJ	Mega-joule
N	Number of data
N_s	Number of total simulations
p	Significant level
P-**set**	Subject respondents
P-**test**	Parametric (analysis)
q	Heat flux (W/m^2)
Q_{glass}	U-value of windows (W/m^2K)
Q_{op}	Operative air infiltration threshold (°C)
r	Density (kg/m^3)
R	Heat absorptivity coefficient (m^2K/W)
r	Number of elementary effects per parameter

r^2	Coefficient of determination
$RC_{façade}$	Thermal resistance of façade (m^2K/W)
RC_{floor}	Thermal resistance of floor (m^2K/W)
RC_{roof}	Thermal resistance of roof (m^2K/W)
s	Thickness (m)
sf	Solar fraction factor
T	Temperature (°C)
t	Time(s)
T_a	Indoor air temperature (°C)
$T_{ed} - 1$	Daily mean external temperature for previous day (°C)
T_{ed}	Daily mean external temperature (°C)
T_{ground}	Ground temperature (°C)
T_{int}	Indoor zone temperature (°C)
T_m	Mean air temperature (°C)
T_{max}	Maximum temperature (°C)
T_o	Outdoor air temperature (°C)
$T_{o/u}$	Total over/underheating hours
T_{op}	Operative air temperature (°C)
T_{pma}	Prevailing mean outdoor air temperature (°C)
$T_{rm} - 1$	Running mean temperature for previous day (°C)
$T_{rm} - 2$	Daily mean external temperature for two days ago (°C)
T_{rm}	Running mean temperature (°C)
T_{set}	Setpoint zone temperature (°C)
T_{upp}	Upper limit of threshold temperature (°C)
T_{wall}	Envelope zone temperature (°C)
U	Heat loss coefficient (W/m^2K)
V	Wind speed (m/s)
W	Width (m)
W	Wind velocity (m^2s)
W_s	Monthly average wind speed (m/s)
y	Statistical variable

Abbreviations

.epw	EnergyPlus Weather (file format)
.gbxml	Green Building extensible markup language
.xml	Extensible markup language (file format)
A/C	Air conditioning
AMY	Actual meteorological year (weather file)
ANOVA	Analysis of variance
ASHRAE	American Society of Heating, Refrigerating and Air-Conditioning Engineers
ASTM	American Society for Testing and Materials
BEM	Building-energy modelling
BES	Building-energy simulation

BIM	Building-information modelling
BPE	Building-performance evaluation
BPS	Building-performance simulation
BS	British Standards
CEA	Cyprus Electricity Authority
CEN	Comité Européen de Normalisation
CFD	Computational fluid dynamic
CIBSE	Chartered Institution of Building Services Engineers
CO_2	Carbon dioxide
CSV	Comma-separated values (plain-text file)
CY	Cyprus
DBT	Dry-bulb temperature
DECC	Department of Energy and Climate Change
DTS	Dynamic thermal simulation
EA	Electricity Authority
ECM	Energy conservation measures
EEG	Energy-efficiency gap
EEM	Energy-efficiency measure
EN	European Norm
EPBD	Energy Performance of Buildings Directives (standards)
EPC	Energy performance certificate
EU	European Union
EUI	Energy use intensity
FLIR	Forward-looking infrared radiometer
GA	Genetic algorithms
GBS	Green Building Studio (Autodesk®)
GHG	Greenhouse gas
GIS	Geographic Information Systems (software tool)
GNP	Gross national product
HSI	Heat-stress index
HSRS	Health and Safety Rating System
IES	Integrated Environmental Solutions (energy-simulation tool)
IHG	Internal heat gain
IPCC	Intergovernmental Panel on Climate Change
IPMVP	International performance measurement and verification protocol
IR	Infrared radiometer
IRT	Infrared radiometer thermography
LCCA	Life-cycle cost assessment
MANOVA	Multivariate analysis of variance
MET	Metabolic equivalent
MFH	Multi-family house
MkWh	Million kilowatt-hours
MM	Mixed-mode (ventilation)
MO	Multi-objective
NC	Northern Cyprus

NV	Natural Ventilation
nZEB	nearly zero energy building
NZEB	Net zero energy building
OP1	Low occupancy
OP2	Moderate occupancy
OP3	High occupancy
OT	Operative air temperature
PCDS	Passive-cooling design strategies
PMV	Predicted mean vote
POE	Post-occupancy evaluation
PPD	Predicted percentage of dissatisfied
RA	Regression analysis
RC	Resistance capacitance
RESNET	Residential Energy Services Network
RH	Relative humidity
RHI	Relative humidity index
RoC	Republic of Cyprus
RQ	Research question
RTB	Residential tower block
SAP	Standard assessment procedure
SAR	Suggested acceptable range
SCAT	(EU) Smart Controls and Thermal Comfort
SD	Standard deviation
SFH	Single-family house
SME	Small and medium enterprise
SP	Set point
SPSS	Statistical Package for Social Sciences (Version 25.0 software)
STS	Socio-technical systems
TL	Turkish Lira
TMY	Typical meteorological year
TPV	Thermal-preference vote
TRNSYS	Transient System Simulation Tool
TRY	Test reference year (weather file)
TSV	Thermal-sensation vote
UCR	United Cyprus Republic
UCTCEA	Union of Cyprus Turkish Engineers and Architects
UHI	Urban heat island (effect)

Superscripts/Subscripts

act	Actual
adj	Adjacent
air	Indoor air
amb	Ambient
av	Average

e	East (building envelope)
eff	Effective
eq	Equivalent
ext	External (ambient air temperature)
in	Indoor
int	Internal
losses	Losses to ambient temperature
min	Minimum value
max	Maximum value
n	North (building envelope)
nom	Nominal
opt	Optimal
percap	Per capita
ppm	Parts per million
pred	Predicted
rad	Radiation
s	South (building envelope)
sim	Simulation
t	Top
tot	Total
w	West (building envelope)

Greek Symbols

γ	Linear correlation coefficient
$\propto_e$	Absorptivity of external surface
Δ	Difference, variation
ΔT	Time step(s)
β	Energy performance coefficient
μ	Mean value
θ	Opening/closing windows and doors (°)
ρ	Air density (m^3/kg)
ω	Weight of objective function

Köppen Climate Classifications

Aw	Tropical wet and dry or savanna
Bsh	Semi-arid
BSk	Cold semi-arid
BWh	Hot desert
Cfa	Humid subtropical
Cfb	Temperate oceanic
Csa	Subtropical
Dfb	Warm summer humid continental

Data Captions

Introduction

Problem Statement

Achieving zero-carbon targets plays a vital role in reducing the impact of greenhouse gas emissions. Societies, either developed or developing, are not dealing with the demand on consumer's energy use—in the design and procurement of the built environment set by many European laws to reduce energy use and cut CO_2 emissions by 2020 to 80% of those in 1990 levels or by the UK Climate Act to reduce CO_2 emissions to 30% by 2050. Many government initiatives at different levels globally are urgently seeking effective solutions to the problems emanating from the rising energy bills globally. Developing the energy and simulation framework plays an important role in the buildings' retrofitting to bridge the knowledge gap between education and practice to improve awareness in energy conservation within the EU-27 members which could be achieved by bringing effective control mechanism in the residential sector. There is not any set of agenda or rules to identify baseline scenario in energy use nor to set an effective guidance nor a roadmap in order to imply the Energy Performance of Buildings Directive (EPBD) in the residential sector available in the Northern Cyprus (NC) due to the restrictions imposed by being a 'de facto' state. This study proposes that sustainable energy-efficiency schemes could be implemented at the local and regional level consistently with national and European energy policies within the technical framework of EPBD for the Cypriot context while assessing occupants' thermal comfort concurrently. To accomplish this, local planning strategies, initiatives and sustainable development goals (SDGs) could be integrated into the decision-making process for increasing awareness in domestic energy use across the sectors. The present study demonstrates a novel statistical method to improve energy efficiency of housing stock in the Eastern Mediterranean climate.

Aims and Objectives

The study addresses the question of whether the thermal-comfort field studies should continue to search for methods to predict neutral thermal-comfort levels or shift the focus toward other applicable adaptive thermal-comfort models that optimise indoor air temperature and consequently lead to a greater human physical body adaptation and a lower dependence on air conditioning systems for space

DOI: 10.4324/9781003393092-1

cooling or intensive energy use. A further study aim is to fill the knowledge gap on thermal comfort of occupants, as this topic had not been addressed by previous scholars at the time of developing the energy-policy design. This is the main research gap identified by this empirical study and is presented extensively through the development of adaptive thermal-comfort thresholds. This study presents the importance of a human-based approach involving features such as users' behaviours on energy use and their thermal-comfort preferences to fill a current knowledge gap in existing building-energy simulation studies. One of the reasons for this gap is that most previous studies in energy research have neglected to explore occupants' thermal comfort while undertaking building-energy optimisation studies in warm and humid climate.

The energy-efficiency gap and the absence of any verified database to assess occupants' thermal comfort accurately were delineated at the beginning of this study to clarify the research hypothesis and provide the rationale behind the development of effective energy simulation framework by considering users' interactions in the energy calibration model. This research focuses on the development of a novel energy simulation framework which could lead to offer feasible retrofitting design solutions. Hence, the study findings could benefit policymakers seeking to devise and implement energy-saving measures and efforts to retrofit existing housing stock in warm and humid climates.

Methodology

First, the most up-to-date globally available studies were reviewed, and extensive additional literature was conducted in four main query terms as follows: energy use, thermal comfort, climate change, energy policy to support the grounds for the energy and simulation framework were developed.

Second, the national representativeness of the housing typology was selected for the present study. Additionally, the statistical data analysis method was applied to develop the energy policy implications. Research methods that were applied to develop the thermal-comfort assessment criteria were investigated, and technical information related to various research instruments that were used during the field-survey investigation were identified. To accomplish this, feed-forward household interviews were conducted.

Third, occupants' energy-consumption patterns and different types of domestic appliances were investigated. The primary aim is to identify actual household energy use, which was further validated with the building-energy simulations. Correlation statistical analyses were conducted to fully validate the questionnaire-survey findings. To further validate these findings, an Analysis of Variance (ANOVA) statistical model was performed; this was conducted to demonstrate households' in vivo experiences to articulate the energy calibration framework that was based on statistical findings.

Fourth, household thermal comfort was more fully investigated. According to the environmental measurements' findings when the questionnaire survey was administered, an inclusive human-based approach was utilised to fully develop the adaptive thermal-comfort criteria for the Cypriot climate. The aforementioned *on-site* observations were bolstered with photographic documentation of the field-survey set-up. Additionally, histograms of the statistical findings would effectively demonstrate the environmental monitoring findings, so these graphs were designed. Descriptive statistics, a correlation analysis and a regression forecasting analysis of the environmental inputs gathered through the various environmental research instruments were conducted to further develop and explain the thermal-comfort theory.

Fifth, the building-energy performance evaluation and energy model calibration analyses are intended to identify the current building-fabric thermal performance. The concept of energy simulation framework was articulated within the development of energy calibration model in the area of applied energy, and detailed illustrations of the walk-through and walk-in thermal-imaging surveys also were included. Anecdotally, in earlier thermal-comfort studies that used the energy-simulation tool, scholars failed to use evidence-based thermal-comfort parameters gathered through a longitudinal field survey; in this proposal the real-time assessment criteria as it related to the statistical findings were explored, and environmental parameters associated with measurements were recorded when the subject participants were recruited to validate the infrared radiometer thermography (IRT) survey findings.

Sixth, a discussion related to industry benchmarks and existing adaptive thermal-comfort studies were presented to explain the statistical stem-flow bar charts that were included, and the actual household energy bills were fully explored via a statistical analysis. A solar exposure analysis was used in conjunction with the Integrated Environmental Solution (IES) simulation tool to conduct a comparative analysis to validate the IRT-survey findings, and extensive illustrations of the solar exposure analysis were presented. Furthermore, dominant representative occupancy profiles were developed according to the data collected in the course of the questionnaire survey.

Lastly, evidence-based retrofitting design strategies were presented, and the implications thereof were discussed, and the building-energy simulations and retrofitting design strategies were explored. To confirm the findings of the building-energy simulations, a validation study of the actual household energy bills was conducted, and the findings were delineated. Additionally, the statistical method (i.e., predictions) was implemented to increase the sample size and further confirm the energy reliability of the archetype buildings that were selected for this study and to demonstrate the validity of the implementation of EPCs by considering occupants' thermal comfort.

A flow chart of the passive-cooling design strategies (PCDS) that was developed as an outcome of the study was created to demonstrate the contribution thereof to the body of knowledge, and a schematic illustration of the six passive-cooling design strategies and the energy effectiveness thereof was also presented; this schematic illustration is, which has been completely neglected by previous scholarly work. Because this is an exemplar pilot study model for future retrofitting endeavours for the social-housing stock in NC and other EU member states, extensive depictions of the PCDS were included to provide guidance to government institutions.

Contribution to Knowledge

The most significant contributions this study makes to the literature are as follows: (i) Use of household's user data to discover the thermal-comfort zone. This is a novel approach not previously used. (ii) A model to enable evidence-based design decisions for retrofit of buildings. The study findings will be gathered via a thermal-comfort survey and in situ measurements of households where there is not any sufficient data available for the summer period to measure the impact of climate change and its influences on households' TSVs. The present study is the very first of its kind to consider the social sciences (i.e., household socio-demographic characteristics and cultural assets), building and environment (i.e., adaptive thermal comfort via in vivo experiences recorded during the longitudinal field survey) and applied sciences (i.e., bridging the energy performance gap to develop effective retrofitting energy-policy designs); this is fully clarified in 'Methodology' section. Factual information gathered throughout the present study is laid out, and the study contributions to the ASHRAE Global Thermal Comfort Database II record version 2.1 were included with the research findings to develop a roadmap to EU countries. It should be noted that the findings of this project are helpful in continuing to define the Republic of Cyprus's (RoC) energy network in subsequent research, which were accompanied by an analysis of built-fabric thermal performance of archetype buildings in four different climatic characteristics/locations both in rural and urban areas across the island.

Novelty of the Study

The novelty of the study is to combine three elements when researching buildings: social survey data with measured building parameters and modelled outcomes. The attempt to integrate socio-demographic information about the occupants with technical–physical parameters and outcome is also an important under-investigated topic in Energy Modelling, Simulation and Prototyping. This book provides a novel solution and engagement with developing state-of-the-art thermal-comfort evaluation criteria which aid to provide background data for the global databases. In this research context, no existing energy policy agenda was set by any type of public initiatives nor government organisations that apply energy performance certification schemes of increasing awareness to any sectors, whether considering the necessity of any benchmarking criterion to assess occupants' thermal comfort in such a comprehensive way. This pilot project seeks to demonstrate to ascertain quota sampling criteria in research methods that how representative housing typology identified to be exemplar studies and how the relevant training has set to inform decision-making process in energy policy in accordance with changing climate conditions. This helps to build the picture of current conditions of energy-efficiency awareness in selected case study buildings. Furthermore, the knowledge and practice developed throughout the project process could benefit the community and the country (including the RoC) at the wider scale, and the capacity-building process could directly benefit vulnerable households in their everyday lives and professionals in their practices who have lack of resources to access relevant energy-efficiency training.

Outcomes and Implications

As an outcome of the study, the main research outputs present the development of a new methodological design approach that demonstrates the conceptual workflow by presenting the main findings to the government, stakeholders, non-governmental organisations (NGOs). The simulation model is calibrated with on-site measurements, which contributed to the credibility and accuracy of performance simulation. To avoid research bias and to demonstrate the most appropriate method of design selected for the study, a top-down energy-policy framework is also discussed to identify both the benefits and limitations of the socio-technical systems (STS) approach in conjunction with building physics. This is the contribution that the present study makes to the applied energy field; thus, this research is executed to design an energy policy for the EU-27 member states. The output of this present study could be donated to the EU Horizon 2030 research project as an open-source policy guidance.

The implications of the present study are two-fold: the knowledge and practices developed throughout the research process could benefit Cyprus and the Cypriot community, including the RoC, and the capacity-building process could directly benefit the everyday lives of social-housing residents and help researchers with limited resources who are engaged in the development of thermal-comfort thresholds for benchmarking. Moreover, the level of awareness and understanding of energy-efficiency measures, both in the current construction process and as it relates to demands on the households' energy use, and the impact of energy usage on the environment are all addressed in the present study.

As of the writing of this proposal, there are no existing energy efficiency, retrofitting and energy-consumption awareness policies in the Eastern Mediterranean region, the study outcomes present a roadmap to improve and enhance the procurement of effective energy-efficiency subsidisation schemes of existing housing development estates and demonstrate how the NC and RoC governments can use these findings to accelerate policymaking decisions. Furthermore, this study contributes to the EU's energy-policy framework, because public agencies and institutions (i.e., non-profit organisations) could be able to use the findings to determine and prioritise the types of dwellings for which greater energy savings can be obtained and invest in effective measures that could provide energy-efficiency awareness information to households through economic viability studies.

1 Energy Policy in the Eastern Mediterranean Climate

Introduction

The concept of retrofitting is an important milestone in the evolution of upgrading the energy efficiency of residential buildings. A significant proportion of the social-housing stock in south-eastern Europe is obsolete in this area, and occupants who represent different socio-demographic profiles require in-depth study (Fokaides et al., 2017; Nematchoua et al., 2021).

Various policy instruments have been introduced to retrofit existing social-housing stock, but many have failed to acknowledge the significance of occupancy patterns in relation to energy use (Santin, 2011). To address the diversity of each European Union (EU) nation and the variances of the housing typologies thereof, the Energy Performance of Buildings Directive (EPBD) schemes were influenced by many factors, including the diversity of the thermal properties of buildings, the range of occupant behaviour, energy-governance structures and energy-subsidisation goals and schemes adopted by EU countries (Cristino et al., 2021); this is why there are neither stringent building regulations nor any type of control mechanism to determine the effectiveness of energy-efficient subsidisation schemes in Northern Cyprus (NC) and the Republic of Cyprus (RoC) (Evcil & Vafaei, 2017). This resulted in a shortfall between the full potential of EPBD implementations and awareness of the adoption of energy-efficiency measures (EEMs); in the residential sector, this knowledge gap is referred to as the 'energy-efficiency gap' (Fokaides et al., 2014; Nabitz & Hirzel, 2019).

Several scholarly research endeavours have investigated associations between governmental policies on thermal retrofitting and current energy-efficiency awareness related to the energy use in residential buildings for the development of socio-technical systems (STS) approach in buildings' retrofitting, specifically that of EU countries (Brimicombe & Li, 2007; Bertoldi & Mosconi, 2020; Morton et al., 2020; Thonipara et al., 2019). A lack of control mechanisms and implementation frameworks arose due to the variety of European laws that were enacted in each country, which took the political agendas and international relations of each EU member state into consideration; this led to a communication gap between policy design and community-level energy-subsidisation schemes (Arbolino et al., 2019; Buessler et al., 2017; Haley et al., 2020).

Government initiatives in Cyprus, which is an EU member state, and NC, which is not an EU member state, have attempted to alleviate the burden of the existing

DOI: 10.4324/9781003393092-2

housing stock by changing the legislative framework to adopt the EPBD guidelines and nearly zero-energy building (nZEB) schemes to upgrade the thermal efficiency of existing building stock (Dascalaki et al., 2016; Kylili et al., 2014; Spyridaki et al., 2020). Such legislative frameworks were not devised, however, by taking occupants' habitual adaptive energy-use behaviour into consideration, which would have led to more effective guidelines for the reduction of energy consumption and the optimisation of occupant thermal comfort in the residential sector (Hamborg et al., 2020; Cyprus Electricity Authority of Northern Cyprus, 2020a.). Furthermore, the RoC government promoted a multilateral agreement with the EU for implementing energy-efficient systems and other retrofitting interventions that will improve the thermal efficiency of existing housing stock (Panayiotou et al., 2013; Cyprus Electricity Authority of Northern Cyprus, 2020b). This transformational technology and the associated legislation have not been implemented to adopt the European International Organisation for Standardisation benchmark legislation within the development of the STS approach in energy use (Baldoni et al., 2019). There is currently no legislative procedure in NC to assess the energy performance of buildings to provide an internationally recognised energy performance certificate (EPC) scheme that can be applied to any type of housing stock.

Several studies recommended a territorial approach to improve energy-subsidisation programmes associated with the economy and implement EPCs that are related to a building life cycle cost assessment (LCCA), and a review of the feasibility of optimisation studies was also suggested to provide a roadmap to stakeholders and policymakers (Barone et al., 2019; Gaspar, 2017; Renner & Giampietro, 2020); these studies asserted that the selection of archetype buildings and nationally representative household population would facilitate the development of a bottom-up energy-policy framework across all EU member states. As such, the present study considers the Cypriot housing stock, which was not accurately demonstrated in the TABULA/EPISCOPE[1] project developed under the *Horizon 2030* framework; this study was the first to identify social-housing stock as representative building typologies to address the energy-efficiency gap and provide accurate primary data sources to this national online database platform, which is required for the energy-governance development of each EU member state.

Another technical constraint is the lack of available primary databases to record the impact of EPCs on home-energy performance and household energy bills; this dearth of data is evident in many areas, such as legislation and regulations for issuing EPBDs and relevant training materials, which include the development of software tools and an online open-source platform to disseminate the outcomes of each country (Ballarini et al., 2014; Cozza et al., 2020). In this regard, there is a growing body of literature that recognises the importance of the integration of EU mandates, because the representativeness of housing stock in NC was not thoroughly classified, primarily because the housing typology classification was based on a random selection of case study buildings for an archetype analysis of local initiatives and energy agencies. Because of this challenge, a comprehensive energy performance evaluation of housing stock can only be conducted at the building level; as such, there is an urgent need for effective nationwide implementation of EPCs and other control mechanisms to achieve policy targets and additional actions related to future holistic retrofitting efforts for urban neighbourhoods, all of which must put into place by stakeholders and government initiatives in NC.

The EPBD developed guidelines for each EU member state, including the RoC, but as of the date of conceptualisation of this research, these recommendations have not been implemented; thus far, the authorities have failed to comply with the EU's *Horizon 2030* recommendations, and an effective methodological framework based on studies that represent the housing stock and households has not yet been developed. The present study fills this energy-governance gap and creates a roadmap to upgrade the energy efficiency of the housing stock and increase household energy-efficiency awareness; the effect of the absence of retrofit policy design remains unclear and further research is required. The present study provides a new methodological framework to develop EPC implementation strategies in the Cypriot context, according to the recommendations put forth in the EPBD mandates as part of the EU energy policy. The main aim of this research is to fill the knowledge gap in the area of an evidence-based framework for energy-policy decision-making mechanisms related to the integration and implementation of the EPBD regulations at the conceptual and national levels. The objectives are threefold:

1. To examine the significance of occupancy patterns and habitual adaptive household behaviour on home-energy performance by conducting feed-forward interviews with social-housing occupants;
2. To investigate overheating risks and occupant thermal comfort within representative residential tower blocks (RTBs) and subsequently provide primary data sources to build future performance evaluation studies; and
3. To develop and test the applicability of building-energy simulation (BES) on base-case RTB prototypes to demonstrate a design method based on comprehensive accounting of energy governance in the EU and to examine the energy-policy framework at the European level and the development of a holistic retrofitting agenda for all EU member states.

The present study focuses on socio-cultural issues deemed to be the most relevant to efforts to improve the thermal efficiency of residential buildings; a number of significant, difficult-to-quantify home-energy-performance factors that are often under-emphasised in energy policy, such as the ingrained energy-use habits of different households and the socio-demographic characteristics and degree of thermal discomfort thereof, can facilitate the development and implementation of energy-efficiency schemes, which is why an STS approach that simultaneously considers multiple factors is an effective means to address the energy-efficiency gap (EEG). In line with this objective, the present research adopts an STS conceptual framework that concurrently considers retrofitting-related social and technical factors to improve the likelihood of adopting long-term holistic retrofitting schemes that will enhance the energy performance of the domestically built environment.

Development of Evidence-Based Energy-Policy Design

The research questions (RQs) in the present study focused on domestic-energy use and occupant thermal comfort in purpose-built RTBs to determine what information was necessary to properly calibrate building energy performance, to provide guidelines, tools and policy implications to improve the energy efficiency of post-war social-housing estates in NC. The primary RQ that was addressed was: What is the most effective and universally applicable energy-policy framework to implement the EPBD mandates recommended by the EU and improve the energy efficiency of existing housing stock in NC?

The following RQs are outlined to develop a bottom-up energy-policy framework to upgrade the thermal efficiency of the existing Cypriot housing stock:

- **RQ 1:** Which household socio-demographic characteristics and home-energy performance factors influence household energy use?
- **RQ 2:** Which occupant energy-consumption behaviours have an impact on the energy performance of social-housing estates?
- **RQ 3:** How do environmental factors affect occupants' thermal comfort?
- **RQ 4:** How will this study contribute to and inform the design of nZEBs in EU countries?

Investigating current design methods while developing the STS design approach resulted in energy-policy frameworks and regulations that will enable NC, the RoC and other EU member states to properly address the EEG. To achieve these targets, the present study sought to address the outlined RQs in three conceptual frameworks: First, to analyse the manner in which EPCs can be utilised as energy-planning tools by calculating and verifying average energy consumption; second, to examine the current state of existing research into the validity of EPCs as an effective policymaking tool to accelerate the transformation of post-war social-housing stock into low-energy dwellings; and third, to investigate the technical constraints of building regulations and thermal properties of RTB prototypes in energy performance developments between NC and EU countries when devising and implementing a universal energy-policy directive.

Socio-technical Systems Approach

An STS approach was used as a theoretical framework to integrate household socio-demographic characteristics related to energy use, the thermal conductivity level of buildings and environmental factors; and to address the question of how different contexts influence the development of energy-efficiency strategies. Drawing on this approach, the present study investigated domestic-energy use and indications of how much is being used thereof in base-case RTBs to improve the energy efficiency of existing social-housing stock.

It should be noted that the present study focuses on the STS research design approach to integrate a multidisciplinary study into a methodology for building-energy simulation studies. The choice of focus was intentional in light of the fact that decisions associated with post-war social-housing development estates, which seek to improve the energy efficiency of existing housing stock were generally made according to assumptions, overlay general studies or forecasting scenarios that fail to consider human-based factors in building-energy modelling (BEM) stage.

The implications of the present study were exploratory in nature and used a human-based empirical design approach that specifically targeted household energy-use characteristics, the overheating risk of different occupied spaces and the impact thereof on occupant thermal comfort. To fulfil the study research, aim and objectives, the conceptual framework placed social-household occupants at the centre who were influenced by three determinant factors—socio-demographic characteristics, environmental conditions and building-thermal properties.

This model illustrates the manner in which the STS conceptual framework can be adopted to address the EEG, as opposed to measures that simply targeted Famagusta households. Without considering the significance of occupancy patterns on energy use, the empirical studies aim to address that vulnerable neighbourhoods steeped in energy poverty may not be as effective.

The STS model clearly demonstrates that without an understanding of household socio-demographic characteristics, empirical studies conducted to develop the potentialities of the STS approach have found to be an appropriate method of design to overcome issues in the EEG (Cockbill et al., 2020; GuerraSantin et al., 2017). As such, the variants in the model are interlinked (i.e., the inner circle), and they affect home-energy performance (i.e., the outward-moving arrows and dashed outer circle). By investigating the factors that were outlined in the model, all obtained data were concurrently analysed feed-forward, then embedded into each other to inform policymaking decisions related to energy use (Sovacool et al., 2020).

The STS approach can be found in previous scholars' work in central European countries and few studies that considered council estates in the United Kingdom, but no other studies adopted the STS and investigated household energy use, occupancy patterns and their degree of thermal discomfort in Eastern Mediterranean Europe have been considered (Anderson et al., 2020; Johnstone et al., 2020). Hence, this empirical study is the first to examine the applicability of the STS approach while taking household cultural values, norms and social assets into account.

Contribution to Knowledge

The main contribution to the body of knowledge is the integration of data to identify the empirical analysis of the STS conceptual framework to develop a new

Table 1.1 The Impact of Key Research Areas to the Contribution to Knowledge

Key Concepts	*Contributions*
Energy policy	• EU energy governance by integrating EPCs into building energy performance development of social-housing stock
Thermal comfort	• Donation of the neutral adaptive thermal comfort identified by a thermal-comfort survey of the Cypriot context to the *American Society of Heating, Refrigerating and Air-Conditioning Engineers* (*ASHRAE*) Global Thermal Comfort Database II • Donation of the neutral adaptive thermal comfort identified for the Cyprus climate to the EU *Smart Controls and Thermal Comfort* (*SCAT*) online database • Dissemination of the optimum thermal-comfort level thresholds that were developed as a result of a field investigation in the Eastern Mediterranean climate and can be applied to the European Norm *EN 15251* standards—which are related to indoor environmental input parameters associated with the design and assessment of building energy performance and address indoor air quality, the thermal environment, lighting and acoustics—as an updated methodological framework
Energy use	• Integration of the archetype housing stock into the EU's *Horizon 2030 TABULA/EPISCOPE* national database
Building-energy simulation	• Development of energy-assessment methods for archetype housing stock and analytical BEM with integrated human-based data from the questionnaire survey to demonstrate a policy design tool to the applied sciences field in energy use

method of design for the EPBD mandates that can be applied to the universal databases, as listed in Table 1.1.

Contribution to Socio-technical Systems Conceptual Framework Development

The present study provides new insights into the EU energy governance and presents the outcome of comprehensive methodology developed by adopting the STS design approach, which is not found in other EU countries' holistic retrofitting projects. Hence, this is the first study to be adopted and developed in the Eastern Mediterranean climate of Cyprus. Thus, the findings should make an important contribution to the research subject of energy policy in the development of retrofitting schemes.

One of the unique features of the research technique developed in the present study is that it adopts the STS approach to create a novel methodological workflow to assess domestic-energy use and thermal comfort, neither of which is well defined in traditional building physics nor in regression-based forecasting for policymaking decisions. As a result, the building-performance evaluation (BPE) remains largely unpredictable when considering real-life occupant energy-use experiences. Moreover, an evidence-based STS approach was developed for the present study to determine the feasibility of the retrofitting design interventions when human-based considerations, including in situ measurements to assess occupant thermal comfort were recorded during the survey, are factored into the BES model.

While the present study makes several important original contributions to EEGs, the retrofitting interventions developed herein may not be economically feasible with current energy-efficiency policy targets, even though the applicability of the research context and the recently recommended EPBD objectives from the EU may lead to an increased demand for domestic-cooling options. As such, it can be asserted that the economic and environmental benefits are mutually supportive of one another and that addressing current design methods related to thermal comfort, overheating risk and building optimisation will eventually lead to a win-win situation.

Contribution to Global Thermal-Comfort Database

Numerous field studies have found that occupant thermal comfort varies with the local climate. There is no generally recommended acceptable comfort range for multi-family houses (MFHs), however, nor are there specific thermal-comfort prediction methods, particularly in Eastern-Mediterranean EU countries. The present study addresses the question of whether the thermal-comfort field studies (ASHRAE (American Society of Heating, Refrigerating and Air-Conditioning Engineers) Global Thermal Comfort Database II) should continue to search for methods to predict neutral thermal-comfort levels or shift the focus toward other applicable adaptive thermal-comfort models that optimise indoor air temperature and consequently lead to a greater human physical body adaptation and a lower dependence on air condition systems for space cooling or intensive energy use.

The study findings gathered via a longitudinal thermal-comfort survey and in situ measurements of households where there is not any data available for the Cypriot context will contribute to the ASHRAE Global Thermal Comfort Database II.[2] Notably, the most up-to-date representative sample that considered thermal comfort in buildings was developed by Zhang et al. (2014); the results were available on the ASHRAE Global Thermal Comfort Database II universal online platform, an open-access site for scholars. The regression forecasting of neutral adaptive thermal comfort could provide a universally accepted benchmarking criterion for the baseline scenario development on thermal comfort in the Mediterranean region.

The *EN 15251*[3] guidelines were last updated in 2007; the present study contributes to the development framework of *EN 15251* with such a methodology. One of the main reasons is that a statistical tool was used for the purpose of regression forecasting to validate the field-survey findings and identify neutral adaptive thermal-comfort thresholds. To obtain accurate data and eliminate research bias, discrepancies in the findings of the regression-forecasting analysis and limitations related to the adoption of several thermal-comfort assessment benchmark criteria, the present study employed all applicable methodologies currently available to ensure that the results of this field investigation would be accurate and suitable for inclusion in the EU's *SCAT*[4] database.

Contribution to Energy Performance Evaluation Studies

To address the knowledge gap of current building-diagnostic design methods, the present study delineates the development of a novel methodological framework based on an empirical case study approach that utilises a field survey, infrared-radiometer-thermography (IRT) and numeric experiments to calibrate BES procedures.

In this exploratory case study, an IRT survey and in situ measurements of environmental conditions were concurrently carried out in vivo with a questionnaire survey that was distributed to the households; household energy bills were obtained from the Cyprus Electricity Authority (CEA) to verify the data derived from the BES analysis. This is the first study to use energy-simulation studies as diagnostic tools to examine the existing post-war social-housing stock in NC and the RoC. This conventional building-diagnostic method was adopted to verify building-thermal properties and the impacts thereof on overheating risks and occupant thermal comfort. The aim was to obtain human-based results in the BES to prove that the end result of energy performance analysis is not based on forecasting scenarios, but rather on actual household information related to occupancy patterns and home-energy performance factors embedded in the BES to design effective retrofitting strategies that will improve the thermal efficiency of the existing housing stock.

Contribution to Building-Energy Simulation Research

The present study is the first to target and conduct BES procedures on existing Cypriot social-housing stock. A BES analysis was integrated into the implementation of EPCs because of the reliable assumptions thereof to assess the energy performance of case study RTBs. The energy-simulation inputs seek to identify the impact of household occupancy patterns and habitual adaptive behaviour on home-energy performance to provide a basis for the information that is needed to properly calibrate the building-energy performance of targeted households. It also envisages demonstrating that occupants' real-life energy-use experiences have had a significant impact on calibrating domestic-energy use to simultaneously identify discrepancies between the actual and predicted energy use on the dynamic energy-simulation platform.

This is the first BES prototype model to demonstrate results obtained by a field-study investigation to develop a set of simulation input parameters that are needed for dynamic thermal simulations (DTS). These were evidence-based conclusions, but an examination of design methods that were recommended for BPE studies in the available exemplar projects confirmed that a BES is a steady-state analysis that is premised on testing the thermal efficiency of energy-efficient materials and building technologies without considering human-based data in the model. As such, the present study was developed according to human-based BES input parameters obtained from the questionnaire survey, in situ measurements, the IRT survey and environmental monitoring of the project site to demonstrate real data for energy-use policymaking decisions. This conceptual framework can be applied to efforts to implement the EPBD mandates and to demonstrate the exemplary development framework, policy and regulations as it relates to the social-housing stock of NC and other EU member states.

Cyprus as a Case Study

Context

Cyprus is situated in the north-eastern area of the Mediterranean Sea between latitudes 34′ 33″ and 35′ 41″ north and longitudes 32′ 15″ and 34′ 35″ east (Makri, 2018). It is located approximately 40 miles north of Turkey, 60 miles east of Syria, 250 miles south of Egypt and 300 miles west of the Greek islands, as shown in Figure 1.1(a). The island has an area of 9.251 km^2 (Zittis et al., 2020); it is the third-largest island in the eastern portion of the Mediterranean Sea. This location has four distinct topographical characteristics—semi-mountainous (Zone 1), coastal (Zone 2), mountainous (Zone 3) and inland (Zone 4)—all of which give rise to varied climate conditions, as shown in Figure 1.1(b) (Katsanos et al., 2016).

An exploratory case study approach was undertaken in the coastal city of Famagusta, which is directly connected to an intercontinental body of water, the Mediterranean Sea, as shown in Figure 1.1(c). Famagusta is an exposed frontline city that has been subjected to frequent changes in its construction industry in the last three decades as a result of policy gaps in town planning and building regulations. This coastal city, a map of which is shown in Figure 1.1(d), is an exemplar model for rapid urbanisation processes in evolving high-density, post-war social-housing estate developments that failed to consider the local climate and geographic topographical conditions of construction project sites in urban territories, as shown in Figure 1.1(e).

Figure 1.1(f) illustrates the Famagusta city centre, which is dependent on a continuous, densely populated area that the rapid construction of medium-rise residential tower block (RTB) development was continued by the small-and-medium enterprise (SMEs) after 1998 when the government's social-housing scheme ended. In the early 1950s, the urban agglomerations of Famagusta included approximately 34,000 units, which was the highest amount of residential stock built in Cyprus from 1960 to 1974.[5] The Famagusta population in 1973 was 38,960,[6] including remote rural locations, and the overall island population was 146,740 (Oktay, 2002; SPO, 2009).

Notably, a continual urbanisation process commenced in the mid-1980s in the form of high-density urban blocks, as shown in Figure 1.1(g); this is due to the growth of local population as a consequence of housing demands from the displaced Turkish and Greek Cypriot communities,[7] which lead to an expansion of the boundaries to rural regions and agricultural lands (Pulhan & Numan, 2005). This territory is currently characterised by an endlessly fragmented, repetitive stream of purpose- or self-built residential areas and privately owned construction company-built mass housing estates for which no bioclimatic design features were considered (Ozay, 2005). This rampant construction activity is continuing up until today. There the SMEs[8] are building housing estates in exactly the same method of construction as the government's social-housing schemes in the mid-1980s and early

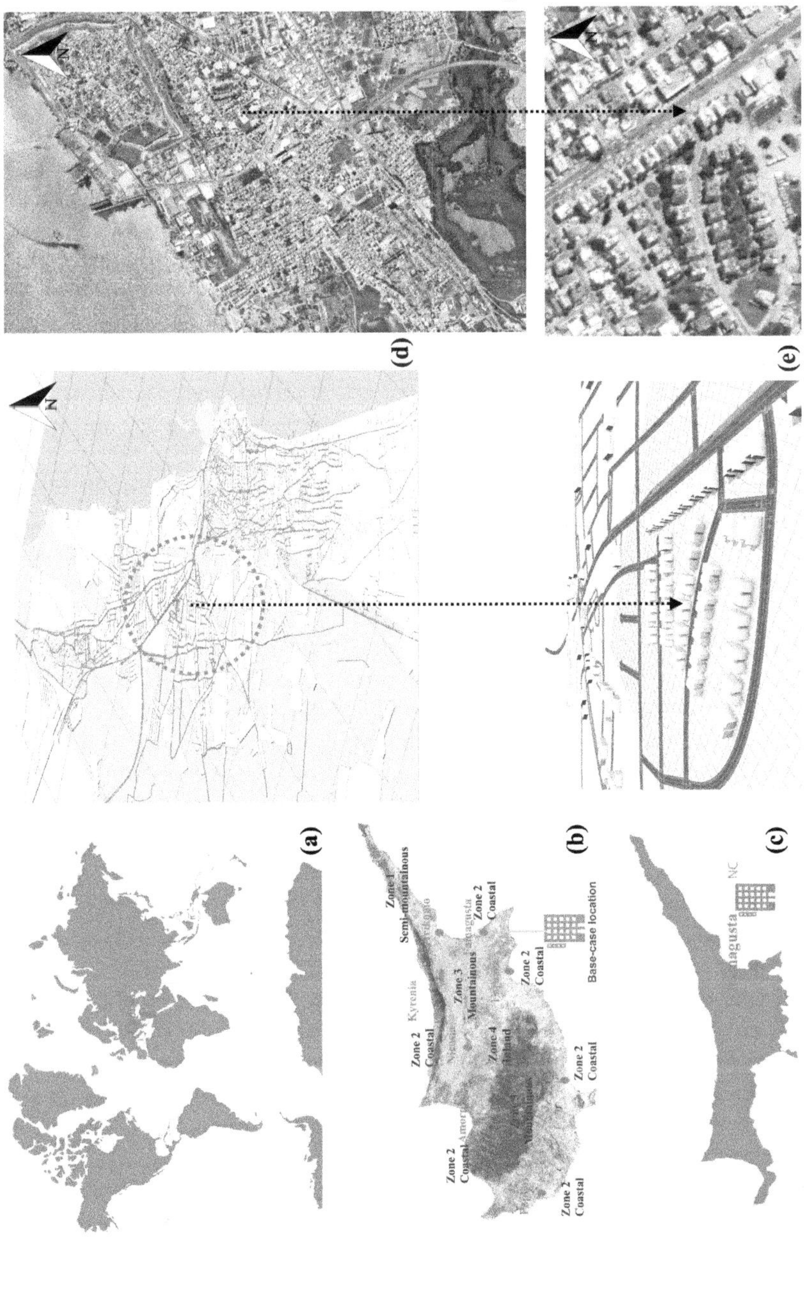

Figure 1.1 (a) Cyprus geographic position and (b) geological characteristics; (c) Northern Cyprus; (d) Famagusta vulnerable neighbourhood; (e) 3D model of medium-rise RTBs; (f) residential area urban tissue; and (g) base-case morphology characteristics.

1990s without considering any type of effective ventilation strategies nor households' thermal comfort; hence, no lessons have been learnt from this poor construction practice during this 30 year period of time. The coastal city of Famagusta was chosen for the present study because no research project has been undertaken in the RoC or in other EU countries that concurrently involves households and the domestic built environment related to retrofitting existing housing stock[9]. The main aims of this endeavour were to remedy the knowledge gap and apply the findings of the present study to the creation of a bottom-up design approach to develop effective policymaking decisions related to energy use.

Climate

Cypriot climates are determined by geographical positions in the north-east corner of the Mediterranean Sea, the morphological characteristics of ground plains and the meteorological variations of the region (Zachariadis & Hadjinicolaou, 2014; Cyprus Meteorological Service, 2020). According to the Köppen-Geiger[10] climate classification system, Cyprus has climate characteristics that are typical of the Mediterranean region. Köppen-Geiger climate data show that the overall climate type for Cyprus is subtropical (*Csa*) and partly semi-arid (*Bsh*) in the northeast part of the island (Kottek et al., 2006); this means that Cyprus is hot and dry during the summertime.

In Cyprus, the average yearly temperatures range from a maximum of 20°C to a minimum of 13.7°C. The average relative humidity (RH) ranges from 84% at 05:30 hours to 78% at 11:30 hours (Cyprus Meteorological Office, 2020). The average rainfall is 417 mm and there is bright sunshine for 3,000–3,100 hours each year. The hottest summer month is August with a maximum of 28.7°C and minimum of 19.7°C average monthly temperatures and a maximum of 37.5°C and minimum of 21.7°C absolute temperatures; during this period, the average RH was 89% at 05:30 hours and 81% at 11:30 hours. Alternately, with a maximum of 17.7°C and minimum of 5.5°C average monthly temperatures and a maximum of 19.8°C and minimum of 4.7°C absolute temperatures, January is the coldest month; the average RH was 82% at 05:30 hours and 78% at 11:30 hours.

It should be noted that winds in Eastern Mediterranean are mostly westerly or south-westerly in the winter and north-westerly or northerly in the summer. In Cyprus, the minimum and maximum wind speeds in December are 2.98 m/s and 6.16 m/s, respectively; while in the month of June, they tend to be 3.75 m/s and 7.0 m/s, respectively (Cyprus Meteorological Office, 2020).

It should be mentioned here that winds significantly increase in the months of April, October and November and are relatively slow in August; higher wind speeds are higher during the months when the weather is becoming warmer, and the wind can then be used to improve occupants' thermal comfort (Pyrgou et al., 2020). During the other months of the year, wind-speed levels are close to the abovementioned figures due to relatively mild temperatures. Even though prevailing winds are from the north-east, the most consistent wind directions are from the south-west and west.

The case study location also highlights the fact that prevailing south-western winds are capable of changing RH rates along the southern coastline by as much as 90% in the summertime, particularly during the evening hours; it is therefore reasonable to assert that the cooling effect of the prevailing winds affects the thermal-comfort conditions of buildings and significantly decreases space-cooling demands (Giannakis et al., 2016).

Solar-radiation statistics reveal that most regions of the island have 75% average bright sunshine hours during the period when the sun is above the horizon (Constantinidou et al., 2019). Notably, a horizontal surface over Cyprus at the top of the atmosphere typically receives 4.7 k Wh/m^2 per day in December and 11.6 k Wh/m^2 per day in June. Due to the island's geographical location, the data demonstrate that during the cloudiest months of December and January, the average duration of sunshine is 5.5 hours, while this figure reaches an average of 12 hours a day in the summer.

Notably, the psychometric chart can be utilised to plot the temperature and RH occurring over a period of 2,385 hours of 8,760 hours in accordance with the annual weather-climate data that is generated from the Energy Plus[11] weather database. This illustrates different comfort-index parameters that are represented by specific zones on the psychometric chart. Furthermore, the percentage of hours that fell into different design strategy zones offers a relative understanding of the solar-irradiance factor and thermal-absorptivity levels of building envelopes.

A climatological analysis of the research context reveals that hot, dry summers and moderate, wet winters are the primary climate characteristics for Cyprus and have a direct impact on annual cooling and heating demands due to the need for space conditioning in the summer and winter (Giannakopoulos et al., 2016; Katsanos et al., 2018). A time-plot series of dry-bulb temperature (DBT) data and a 3D representational chart thereof demonstrate the effect of high temperatures on building-envelope absorptivity levels; this was utilised as a reference source to determine the thermal vulnerability of Cypriot housing stock (Desougus et al., 2013).

Famagusta demonstrates mild Mediterranean climate characteristics. Maximum DBT can reach as high as 42°C in the summer; and minimum DBT can drop down to 6°C in the winter (Cyprus Meteorological Office, 2020). Mean-minimum DBT varies from 6.8 to 22.3°C, and mean-maximum DBT varies from 16.3 to 33.3°C.[12] As can be seen, there is an opportunity to use natural convection to optimise indoor air temperatures during the midseason (i.e., mean 26°C; DBT > 6°C), and also during the winter season if the internal gains are high (i.e., mean 26°C; DBT > 12°C); when mean ambient air temperature is high in the summer, this index is low, which suggests alternative cooling strategies are needed to maintain indoor air temperatures within a comfortable range.

Energy Consumption

In Cyprus, electricity is derived from fuel oil; this is the most expensive form of energy production (Pulhan et al., 2020). Eurostat data demonstrates energy-dependency rates for all EU member states between 2008 and 2018. The lowest energy-dependency rates in 2018 were recorded for Estonia, Denmark, Romania and Sweden; Malta, Luxembourg and Cyprus were almost entirely dependent on primary energy imports, with dependency rates between 92.4% and 97.8% (Eurostat, 2018). Due to its geographic location and energy governance, Cyprus was the third-highest energy importer.[13]

According to the Ministry of Agriculture and Energy Statistics (2019), 43.34% of diesel fuel was imported to respond to growing energy demands for central electric units. These results indicate that energy consumption in NC was dominated by oil products, which produced 80% of the total energy; the remaining 20% of production was from coal, an energy source used for cement production and in other heavy industries, and solar energy. Because of the absence of regulatory bodies and NC's status as a *de facto* state, energy conservation was not a priority for the authorities or government initiatives, and total energy consumption rose by approximately 4.5% each year in the period of 1983–2004, with a significant increase in 2005 that was the result of a property boom in the early 2000s (Katircioglu et al., 2014). This exponential rise in energy consumption gained momentum in 2017 due to high demand in the RTBs. The 2018 Cyprus Electricity Authority (CEA) statistics indicated that the residential sector consumed 230,367 M kW h (i.e., million kilowatt-hours) in 2003; this figure rose to 377,971 M kW h in 2017 (Cyprus Electricity Authority, 2018).

In 2018, the CEA stated that there were no grid connections going to and from the island, so the Eastern Mediterranean island of Cyprus could not trade electricity with surrounding countries. It was estimated that during the period of 2020–2025, renewable energy sources will comprise 20% of the total electricity generation. At the same time, the 2019 annual CEA report suggested that the remainder of the necessary electricity could be generated from fossil-fuelled power plants, the majority of which burn heavy fuel oil and to a lesser extent, diesel fuel.

Increasing energy demand in NC is primarily due to economic growth and higher-quality living standards; the absence of regulatory bodies in the area of energy governance makes implementing EPBD mandates problematic (Celik et al., 2017). This energy-policy gap caused all sectors to be dependent on imported oil products to meet energy demands. The 2019 CEA Annual Report revealed that the power plant system in NC is isolated, resulting in significant barriers related to upgrading energy networks that have caused high energy costs (CEA, 2020a). To fully understand current energy consumption and the impact of construction activity on domestic-energy use, the CEA report in 2020 highlights the greatest energy consumption from among the building stock in NC.

The CEA report in 2020 demonstrates the overall energy consumption in NC between 2010 and 2020; this timeframe was selected because residential buildings and apartment projects gained momentum during this period as a consequence of demand on the property market by foreign investors. This rapid construction activity led to a sharp increase in the number of energy consumers. As is shown in the graph, energy consumption in dwellings continued to increase, followed by commercial buildings.

According to the 2020 *CEA Annual Report*, dwellings consumed 375,617 M kW h in 2010, and this amount increased to 528,231 M kW h in 2020; notably, data related to social support revealed that households consumed 2,023 M kW h in 2020 and 3,246 M kW h in 2020. There was a notable increase in low-income consumers, whose energy bills were paid by government social service programmes; the findings revealed that 2% of the energy consumers were vulnerable households living in energy poverty. This energy-consumption index was used as a baseline to validate the type of energy consumer groups in the social-housing development estates in Famagusta.

Regarding energy consumption, the CEA Annual Report in 2020 shows that 48% was consumed by residential buildings, followed by 41% of commercial, 10% of industrial and 2% of households with social beneficiaries[14] by the government. These figures lead to an important conclusion, namely that the thermal conductivity level of building properties could be the cause of high energy consumption.

The CEA Annual Report in 2020 demonstrates the overall percentages of energy consumers between 2017 and 2019. This timeframe was chosen because most of the 2–5-storey medium-rise RTBs and 5–23-storey high-rise buildings were constructed between 2017 and 2019 (SPO, 2020). According to the 2020 housing statistics, a significant increase in the number of flat units was recorded; approximately 90,000 units were completed in five major cities in NC, and there was a total of 37,458 energy consumers; this growth led to increased energy consumption during this same period.

The residential sector in NC accounted for 38% of the overall energy consumption between 2017 and 2019; within this same timeframe, a majority of the NC housing stock was constructed and 38% of the 2–5-storey RTBs in Famagusta were completed. This is nationally representative of the overall social-housing stock in the urban and suburban territories in NC. To develop the socio-technical systems (STS) conceptual framework, a social-housing estate located in Famagusta was chosen for an exploratory case study approach. One of the primary reasons for this is that the social-housing estate that will be investigated was the first to be built with random orientations of the RTBs, which did not consider any type of environmental design principles during the decision-making process.

It should be noted that this layout for social-housing estates was used as an exemplar development project under the governmental social-housing scheme in the mid-1980s and early 1990s, because it was affordable and practical to accommodate a large number of residents in a short period of time, which indicates that the government took a decisive role in replicating this same housing project in four other major cities in NC. It should also be highlighted that this social-housing project was not limited to Famagusta households; it was also representative of the entire social-housing stock in NC. Notably, terraced houses were built under the governmental social-housing scheme concurrently with medium-rise RTBs, but only a limited number were constructed, because construction materials for these structures were more expensive; hence, the government offered less-affordable options to social-housing residents. This is why medium-rise RTBs were the subject of the present study.

In summary, these indicators reveal the determinant factors for the selection of Famagusta as a case study location and medium-rise RTBs as archetype buildings to develop an evidence-based STS framework for policymakers. Additional details related to the selection of a case study location and archetype buildings are discussed in Chapter 2.

Rationale for the Present Study

Northern Cyprus (NC) is marked by a lack of construction standards, codes of practice and building regulations associated with a thorough investigation of the building-energy performance of existing housing stock, which does not help to resolve the issue of high energy demand in the residential sector. Debates on the energy performance of social housing in EU member states have revealed considerable shortcomings in the integration of current design methods that concurrently assess building overheating risks and optimise occupants' thermal comfort to develop an effective conceptual framework for each member state that considers variations in climate characteristics, building codes and regulations and household types during the decision-making process.

The importance of developing an evidence-based energy-policy framework to assess robust energy performance evaluation and certification schemes in Eastern Mediterranean EU countries has not yet been addressed. A theoretical investigation of the STS design model and the integrity thereof in a multi-criteria decision-making process have gained momentum in research endeavours related to energy and the social sciences. A thorough empirical analysis of the energy-planning systems and energy-efficiency investments was the result of strategic policies and political issues that arose because of multidisciplinary research and was developed within the scope of the EPBD mandates. To address the knowledge gap in current energy-efficiency frameworks, the present study adopted the STS design approach to develop a new adaptation of building-energy performance assessment criteria and to identify the neutral thermal-comfort thresholds of households through a longitudinal field survey.

The Theory of Socio-technical Systems Approach

The theoretical foundation of the socio-technical systems (STS) approach dates to the 1950s when Jay W. Forrester first introduced a new method of design that bridged engineering and management (Forrester, 1961); this theory was then developed and applied by a group of researchers from the Massachusetts Institute of Technology (MIT). Forrester defines STS as 'a way of combining all available information including the written description and personal experience with computer simulation to yield a better understanding of social systems' (Forrester 1976). The rationale of the present study is to provide a detailed record of the development of an STS conceptual framework.

What Forrester developed in the 1950s was an early stage of an economic modelling and forecasting design approach that could be applied to other disciplines (Forrester, 1994); this method of design re-emerged in the 1970s to become an approach commonly applied by scholars both for research and for developing energy forecasting scenarios for policymakers (Forrester, 1971). In 1975, Forrester explained the constraints of the method he had developed and reported on its limitations after two decades of experimenting with his own methodological approach in system dynamics (SD) (Forrester, 1998).

First, Forrester (1975) outlined that he found there to be a failure to develop adequate sampling to represent the loop structure that makes up economic systems: this was due to the discrepancies detected when analysing closed loops in purpose-built experimental analyses, which led to changes in the loop structure and the overlapping of multiple datasets and time constraints when undertaking energy modelling simulations. He also found that shortcomings of the STS approach include an inability to include flows of goods, issues with secondary data sources of information, and the fact that labour-intensive work is required to identify each parameter to be correctly included in simulation models (Forrester, 2003). Finally, the STS model is constrained by not being able to produce a null result, if, for instance, there isn't enough data for the model to work (Forrester, 2009). Additionally, the STS model is that it cannot conduct an analysis that recognises its own failure to forecast economic analysis in the field of business and management (Forrester, 2013).

It should also be noted that one of the constraints of the early-stage STS model was a restriction in building-energy models: these were constrained by their capacity for manipulating numerical data. These technical constraints caused research bias and manipulation in many scientific papers that were published at the time. In this same 1975 work, Forrester stresses that the early stage of the STS model predominantly relied on only undertaking multiple regression analysis for obtaining coefficients for equation models that define behavioural analysis in the SD approach. Forrester also noted that the early STS model showed a lack of representativeness in identifying assumptions related to the behavioural models developed by scholars (Forrester et al., 1976).

Later, after identifying the above shortcomings in the early models developed between 1946 and 1976, Forrester revised his theory and in 1998 published an instruction manual entitled 'Designing the Future' to provide a new approach to understanding the efficacy of variables included in energy simulation for forecasting energy-policy design scenarios (Forrester, 2016). In this 1998 manual, Forrester proposes a series of new methods of design that incorporate (i) dynamic structure; (ii) information flows; (iii) benchmarking; (iv) non-linear systems; (v) differential equations; (vi) discontinuous changes in variables; (vii) model complexity; (viii) representativeness and integration with evidence-based data collection; and (ix) a workflow for coefficient accuracy. A review of these step-by-step development stages demonstrates that Forrester provided advancements in his technique, and with these improvements considered, it can be said that Forrester provided a significant contribution with his article entitled 'Industrial Dynamics: A Major Breakthrough for Decision Makers' in the *Harvard Business Review* in 1958.

Ansari and Seifi (2013), Oladakun and Odesola (2015) and Wolstenholme (1990) all indicate that Forrester's developed multidisciplinary SD approach has become a powerful and well-established methodology and tool for energy forecasting modelling and for understanding the integration of attitudes in the development of parametric energy models. Coyle (1977), conversely, criticises the STS approach. Coyle stresses the definition of the STS conceptual framework in his criticism, saying that it

> deals with the time-dependent behaviour of managed systems with the aim of describing the systems and understanding through qualitative and quantitative models how information feedback governs STS's behaviour and designing robust information feedback structures and control policies through simulation and optimisation.
>
> (Coyle, 1977)

According to Coyle, the STS dynamic model offers new insight into the mixed-method design where the data was fed by in vivo experiences or real-time historic data series integrated into energy modelling. In light of this, Coyle argues that the STS conceptual framework consists of complex parameters and that it requires further experimental validation techniques to provide reliable outputs in the decision-making process.

In 2007, Forrester reviewed the past 50 years of experimental studies conducted within the STS conceptual framework since he developed the field of system dynamics, and provides guidance for the next 50 years. In this latest work, Forrester stresses that

> a model can be useful if it represents only what we believe to be the nature of the system under study … we are forced to commit ourselves on what we believe is the relative importance of various factors. We shall discover inconsistencies in our basic assumptions … Through many of these we learn.
>
> (Forrester, 2007)

In light of this statement, it can be understood that there will be a high likelihood of identifying discrepancies in datasets when predicting energy and economic models. Despite the shortcomings of his approach, Forrester highlights the advantages of adopting the STS conceptual framework and integrating the systems dynamic approach in the matter of exploring statistical analysis in the building engineering field, as shown in Figure 1.2.

In the same 2007 paper, Forrester outlines the advantages of using the STS conceptual framework based on a review of the past 50 years of experimental studies and their outcomes, and provides nine main conclusions about STS, which are outlined in the following paragraphs.

(i) Forrester finds that the integration of STS provides a clear description of the methodological approach used by scholars. Using STS also enables them to improve shortcomings in their models so that they can integrate a comprehensive methodological framework to conduct their experiments accurately.

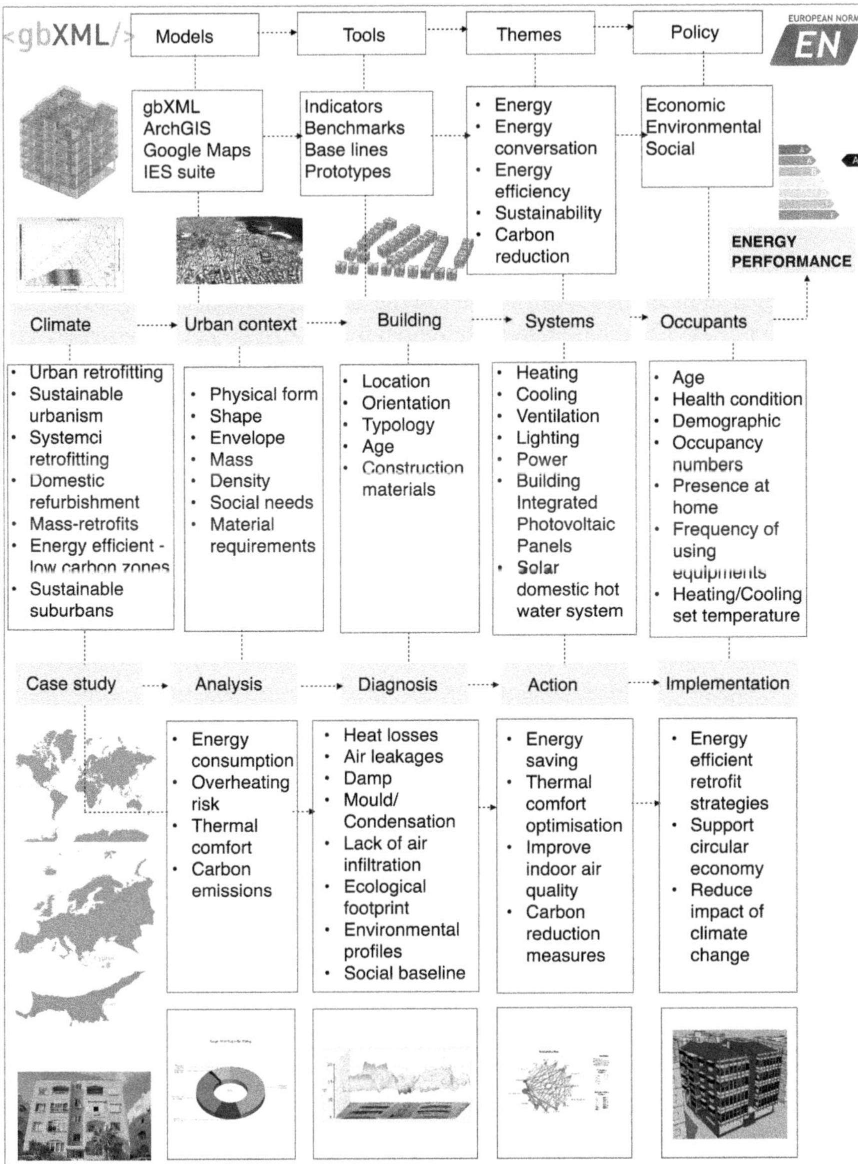

Figure 1.2 Steps for developing an evidence-based energy-policy framework that considers the effects of household adaptive behaviour on home energy performance.

(ii) Forrester indicates that STS provides a compact model that can demonstrate how inaccuracies are resolved in a model and how researchers can deal with complex parameters in their own fields.
(iii) STS provides a reduction in the time constraints of energy modelling approaches where it requires the inclusion of time-series data for the validation of research outcomes.
(iv) Forrester (2007) argues that STS requires generic models, and while researchers set out the baseline model for benchmarking assessments, the descriptive assessment of results is required to interpret the findings of research outcomes.
(v) Forrester indicates that the attributes of the developed models require the integration of evidence-based datasets so that the system model allows researchers to generate more realistic assumptions while developing energy-policy design scenarios. At the same time, Forrester stresses that energy-policy design scenarios should be tested with dependent variables that are gathered through survey sampling to validate research outcomes.
(vi) Forrester (2007) recommends that energy-policy design scenarios require policies that support criticism by applicable theories. One of the reasons for this is that the STS model can be applied to multidisciplinary studies.
(vii) Forrester discusses the difference between current and past studies so that the developed STS design approach can demonstrate the inaccuracies and shortcomings of each experimental model. This technical aspect can also provide a guide to future scholars in thoroughly identifying their own knowledge gaps while designing a comprehensive methodological framework for their own studies.
(viii) Forrester clearly outlines that the STS model examines developed energy design policies by including households' in vivo experiences in energy use, and he also highlights that this developed STS design approach provides a way to reduce any research bias while conducting the statistical analysis.
(ix) Forrester outlines the STS model and provides a reliable methodological design approach for researchers to deal with research bias and develop evidence-based energy models for SD in the engineering field.

After reviewing all these advantages, Forrester (2007) states that as the STS conceptual framework has developed over time, it has enabled researchers to continue to use similar design approaches in their own fields without the need for applying new advances in system dynamics. Therefore, Forrester indicates that if researchers decide to use the STS conceptual framework, a high quality of work is required to determine realistic assumptions in the decision-making process. Forrester stresses that if scholars fail to apply all these approaches under the framework of STS, they should not be criticised as they may not have had the opportunity to receive the education to fully train themselves in the engineering field.

In his paper entitled 'System Dynamics—The Next Fifty Years,' Forrester (2007) outlines guidelines for researchers for the next 50 years of integrating the STS design approach and strongly recommends that researchers consider the complexity of the STS design. To reduce shortcomings in SD, Forrester indicates that more established energy models should be set out in accordance with the research hypotheses so that the results can generate effective energy-policy design mechanisms for stakeholders. Forrester also indicates that the main advantage of integrating STS is that it leads to a non-linear relationship and multi-loop feedback system in the SD approach, which in turn enables researchers to go beyond the established settings when conducting experimental analysis. Finally, Forrester notes that the STS design approach will always remain complex and may be difficult for scholars to understand and apply to their own methodologies.

In summary, the STS conceptual framework provides a multidisciplinary modelling approach. It is a widely accepted well-known theory that has been widely applied by scholars in many fields to develop evidence-based energy design scenarios. Balnac et al. (2009) refer to STS as the common approach in energy and environment. Morecroft (1988) and Milstein et al. (2010) indicate that STS allows researchers to conduct evidence-based longitudinal studies to assess energy consumption. The STS approach has also been widely used by Davis and Durbach (2011), Motawa and Banfill (2010) and Dyner et al. (1998) in the development of other energy-efficiency decision-making criteria. These studies highlight the importance of the effective applications that could be developed through the identification of the 'energy-efficiency gap': this theory should be further developed by other scholars to fill knowledge gaps due to changes in energy building regulations and to tackle climate change. Forrester (2007) also mentions that the integration of STS is not only limited to conducting experimental studies in energy efficiency.

In the present study, the STS design approach is adopted and further developed in view of the technical constraints and strengths indicated by Forrester in 2007. The present study consists of a comprehensive methodology used to gather data on household energy-efficiency awareness in order to optimise thermal comfort within the integration of conventional thermal-comfort assessment indicators for benchmarking. The present study examines households' subjective attitudes through thermal sensation votes gathered through a questionnaire survey and assesses household energy use by establishing an energy-simulation approach in the Eastern Mediterranean climate of Cyprus. This subject can be accepted as applicable to an STS design model, and the research can be applied to develop further guidance for energy-efficiency research.

In the present study, the use of the STS model allows the researchers to apply a comprehensive method of design to their own studies in the building engineering field; this use of the STS model could have long-term implications for building-energy performance development. Table 1.2 delineates the critical evaluation of the STS approach and its impact on developing an effective method of design in retrofitting energy-policy design. Additionally, Forrester (2007) indicates that the use of the SD approach enables scholars to achieve reliable energy-policy measures by simplifying the complex parameters in multilinear loop systems. This enables scholars to provide energy design implications for policymakers, including economic feasibility and forecasting scenarios to foresee the cost-effectiveness of energy-efficient design scenarios in the residential sector.

Table 1.2 Evaluation of the STS Concept in Key Research Areas

STS Concepts	*Benchmarking Indicators*	*Occupants' Behaviour*	*Thermal Comfort*	*Overheating Risk*	*Energy Modelling*
Occupants (Users and aspects)–Data functional inputs	**People detection**				
	Presence of users	√	■	Δ	Δ
	Average count of users	Δ	Δ	⊕	Δ
	Actual count of users	√	√	√	√
	Occupants' position in a room	Δ	√	⊕	⊕
	Ability to analyse each user data	■	Δ	Δ	√
	Behavioural pattern				
	The behaviour of occupant in space	√	Δ	⊕	⊕
	Configuring occupancy patterns	Δ	⊕	√	√
	The different modes of users	Δ	■	Δ	Δ
	The usual actions occur by user	Δ	■	Δ	Δ
	Metabolic activity (*met*) level	√	√	√	√
	Clothing insulation (*clo*) level	√	√	√	√
	Thermal sensation	■	■	Δ	√
	Comfort temperature degree need	⊕	⊕	Δ	■
	Predicted mean vote	■	■	Δ	√
	Predicted percentage of dissatisfied	Δ	Δ	√	√

(*Continued*)

Table 1.2 (Continued)

STS Concepts	*Benchmarking Indicators*	*Occupants' Behaviour*	*Thermal Comfort*	*Overheating Risk*	*Energy Modelling*
Technical parameters	**Green resilient design**				
	Increase airtightness	⊕	Δ	Δ	■
	Adjust glazing by orientation	■	Δ	√	■
	Apply passive solar design	⊕	■	Δ	■
	Provide thermal mass	⊕	⊕	■	√
	Use high-transmittance glazing	⊕	⊕	⊕	√
	Sustainability				
	Combine vernacular design practices with modern materials	Δ	■	■	Δ
	Use locally available materials	Δ	⊕	⊕	√
	Orient building to optimise wintertime solar gain	Δ	√	⊕	√
	Block unwanted solar gain	Δ	Δ	Δ	√
	Energy-policy design				
	Technology maturity	⊕	⊕	⊕	■
	Efficiency	Δ	Δ	Δ	Δ
	Distribution grid availability	■	■	Δ	√
	Reducing peak demand	√	⊕	√	√
	Energy input–output ratio	Δ	⊕	■	Δ
	Technical feasibility	■	⊕	√	⊕
	Local technical knowledge	⊕	⊕	⊕	■

(*Continued*)

Table 1.2 (Continued)

STS Concepts	*Benchmarking Indicators*	*Occupants' Behaviour*	*Thermal Comfort*	*Overheating Risk*	*Energy Modelling*
Systems modelling	**Building conditions and climate data**				
	Weather data	Δ	√	√	√
	Natural daylighting information	⊕	⊕	⊕	√
	Natural ventilation information	■	■	Δ	√
	Occupancy schedules	Δ	Δ	■	■
	Miscellaneous parameters				
	Space principles	Δ	■	Δ	√
	Geo-fencing upon users' habits	Δ	Δ	⊕	■
	Lighting schedules	√	Δ	Δ	Δ
	Use of appliances	⊕	⊕	⊕	■
	Air flow				
	Outside temperature	√	√	√	√
	Operative air temperature	Δ	⊕	⊕	■
	Demand response	■	Δ	Δ	■
Legend: (*Assessment criteria*)	√ Meet criterion ■ Knowledge gap Δ Meet criterion with expectations ⊕ Does not meet criterion				

This section has reviewed the power of the STS design approach and its implications for the development of energy-policy design scenarios. Robert et al. (1983), Richardson (1996) and Ranganath and Rodrigues (2008) suggest that the inclusion of problem identification, system conceptualisation, reliable energy modelling for simulations, analysis of SD model behaviour, energy performance evaluation, policy analysis, and improvement and policy implementation processes should be considered when conducting any kind of experimental analysis using the STS conceptual framework. These scholars also stress that the energy-efficiency gap should be addressed if scholars are able to apply the theory of STS in their research hypothesis. This is the reason that the aim of the present study is to investigate the significance of energy efficiency in filling the knowledge gap in energy use. The following section discusses the terminology of the energy-efficiency gap and its implications for the development of energy-policy design scenarios.

Theory of the Energy-Efficiency Gap

This section reviews the theoretical and empirical research studies that have been aimed at identifying terminology around the energy-efficiency gap (EEG). For this analysis, first the most widely accepted well-known EEG terminology is defined and then critical analysis is undertaken to provide a guide to the changing notions around EEG as it relates to political events, changing climate conditions and ongoing trends in energy efficiency. Figure 1.3 demonstrates the stages of development in energy-policy design scenarios that affect EEG in the residential sector.

The conventional terminology of EEG was defined by Jaffe and Stavins: 'The energy-efficiency gap is described as the gap that exists between the current or expected future energy use of homes and the optimal current or future energy use' (Ozarisoy & Altan, 2018). Ozarisoy and Altan then further describe the EEG in order to provide a foundation of theoretical information to guide policymakers in the implementation of energy-policy design in the residential sector. However, the starting point of a well-established meaning for EEG dates to the 1970s. A pilot study project entitled 'Drivers and Barriers to Improving Energy Efficiency and Reducing CO_2 Emissions in the Private Housing Sector' states that in the United Kingdom little action had been taken towards energy conservation through the method of considering existing housing stock that was built in the United Kingdom pre-1973 (Altan, 2004). This pilot study demonstrated the relevance of the rapid increase in energy prices in the 1970s.

Altan (2004) recommends that in energy-efficiency studies aiming to identify the EEG, international attention should be given to the energy conservation of households and the habitual adaptive behaviours of households. Following the study conducted by Altan, Pelenur (2013) presented a study outlining the importance of analysing households' socio-demographic characteristics alongside barriers to the adoption of domestic-energy efficiency measures in large UK cities. The aim of the study was to better understand the EEG and to improve the effectiveness of future energy-efficiency initiatives. This study shows distinct differences to the

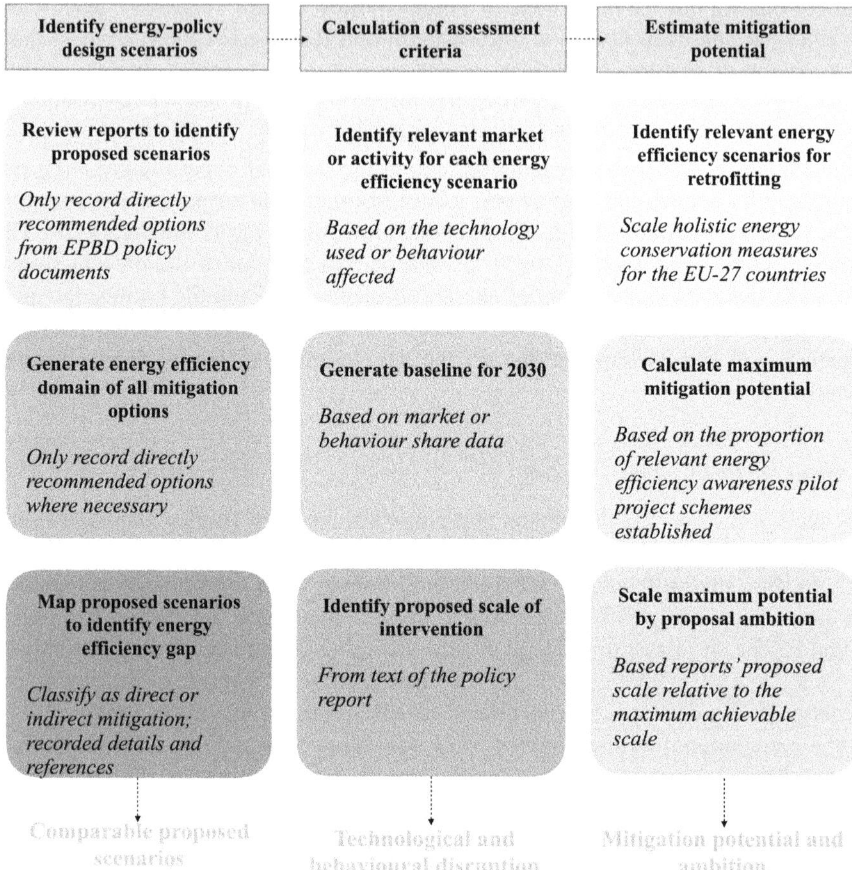

Figure 1.3 Procedure of energy-efficiency implementations recommended by the Energy Performance of Buildings Directive (EPBD) under the Horizon 2030 framework.

pilot study conducted by Altan (2004) in terms of researching a tool for the identification of the EEG.

Pelenur (2013) investigated the type of methodological advances required in order to improve household energy-efficiency awareness in Cardiff and Manchester, while Altan (2004) developed a novel study to examine the energy-efficiency standards, CO_2 emissions and energy ratings of the existing housing stock in Sheffield. Both of these studies predominantly focused on a regional scale, on interviewing households, on modelling existing housing stock to understand households' energy use behaviour and on analysing energy-efficiency standards, particularly examining the worst housing conditions in the United Kingdom.

In the last 70 years, there has been a rapid increase in world energy use, partly because of the availability of easily extractable fossil fuels (coal, gas and oil), though awareness of the limited nature of these reserves has existed since the 1970s. While industrialised nations depend heavily upon fossil fuels for their industrial processes, developing nations also desire to increase their technological capabilities and their use of energy in various forms. Although it is unlikely that the world will completely run out of fossil fuels in the next 50 years, the majority of easily extractable reserves are located in a small part of the world and the prices are due to increase. This significant energy crisis in the 1970s opened a pathway for scholars and policymakers to find alternative practical solutions for improving energy efficiency in housing. From the 1970s up to the present, scholars in many fields have conducted both theoretical and experimental studies to identify the knowledge gap in energy-efficiency research.

Pelenur and Cruickshank (2012) indicate that the EEG is a well-researched topic across a wide range of disciplines in terms of both the availability of previously developed energy-efficiency studies and its popularity amongst scholars for developing energy-efficiency design scenarios in both the UK and EU-27 countries.

To identify the feasible integration of the EEG into energy research, Ozarisoy and Altan (2017a) describe four diverse disciplinary approaches that can help scholars develop an STS conceptual framework without altering the conventional definition of the EEG: (i) conventional and behavioural economics, (ii) technology, (iii) adoption attitude-based decision-making, and (iv) social and environmental psychology. Wilson and Dowlatabadi highlight that there are theoretical preferences across different conventional traditions in energy efficiency, and that can lead to a research gap that allows the integration of the STS conceptual framework when developing energy design policy.

Weber (1997) stresses that the energy-efficiency gap is a complex issue, where technical, institutional, organisational and behavioural barriers all play a significant role during the decision-making process and that all these aspects are interconnected. In light of this complexity, Pelenur and Cruickshank (2012) form a new outline of the causes of EEGs: these scholars describe the EEG problem formulation from an interdisciplinary perspective that offers a general overview for improving energy-efficiency awareness (specifically in UK households).

Conversely, Ozarisoy and Altan (2018) argue that the reason for the EEG is a lack of transparent information about the strength of implementing energy-efficient technologies. They posit that uncertainty regarding the up-front costs of adopting energy-efficient materials and also inaccuracies in the calculation of discount rates by households has led to a negative impact on implementing energy-efficient retrofit decisions. Ozarisoy (2022) clearly outlines that the constraints of the EEG are interconnected with household attitudes regarding energy use, the financial burden of implementing energy-efficient technologies and a lack of awareness around energy conservation.

Pelenur (2013) also stresses that one of the main constraints of the EEG is that many stakeholders did not accept householders as rational actors at the time of developing energy-efficiency scenarios. Ozarisoy (2022) indicates that household interaction with energy is subjective and energy-use behaviour is generally left to chance. Although Ozarisoy highlights the importance of effective control mechanisms for regulating energy incentives and subsidisation schemes, most scholars have failed to address this knowledge gap by considering households' in vivo experiences of energy use. This concern in EEG research has been investigated by many scholars, but so far none of them has been able to define this aspect of EEG enough to use it to inform policymaking decisions regarding energy use. The aim of the present study is therefore to apply scientific insights to an energy engineering problem, specifically to an investigation of Cypriot post-war social housing, using householders as demographic variables who are associated with empirically identifiable barriers to affecting the implementation of evidence-based retrofit design solutions. Table 1.3 delineates the critical evaluation of the EEG and its impact on key research areas discussed in Chapter 2.

Many field studies conducted by scholars from different climate zones across the globe have investigated correlations between households' habitual adaptive behaviours and their socio-demographic variables (Pelenur, 2010; Pelenur and Cruickshank, 2013). These studies highlight that household behaviour is one of the factors that can affect the EEG.

Pelenur (2013) suggests that the forces behind EEGs can be further identified through comprehensive research on both the psychological and sociological aspects of households. These are factors that require further investigation in terms of their relationship to the EEG, and this is a knowledge gap that other scholars have failed to fill with previous multidisciplinary studies. After thoroughly reviewing other pilot studies, the present study finds that researching the EEG can be integrated with the STS conceptual framework in order to provide reliable research outputs in energy policy. The present study therefore reviews previous scholars' work to discuss the strength of EEG theory.

The importance of identifying the EEG began at the policy level with the regulatory innovation introduced by Directive 2010/31/EU (Bertoldi and Mosconi, 2020). This policy regulation is also known as the Energy Performance of Buildings Directive (EPBD). The EPBD has become a mandatory policy regulation to assess the energy performance of buildings through a multi-decade process. After the implementation of the EPBD, most scholars have changed their research focuses to conducting comprehensive research studies aimed at improving the energy efficiency of existing housing stock. The outcome of EPBD implementation has been a positive impact on integrating the concept of the EEG as an energy-policy tool.

Ozarisoy (2022) indicates that there is a strong correlation between the rationale of the EPBD and the subject matter of the EEG. Ozarisoy stresses that the EPBD has had a linear effect on improving energy-efficiency awareness across households. Bracke et al. (2016) indicate that EPBD implementation, when considering the EEG, could provide an effective mechanism for establishing policy tools and supporting non-governmental organisations (NGOs) to further develop energy-subsidisation schemes. Ma et al. (2012) note that the presence of the EPBD mandates has opened a new pathway for an evolutionary process of methodological approaches in the building engineering field. Tian (2013) highlights that the implementation of the EPBD has enforced households' need to apply for energy performance certificates (EPCs) for their buildings, which in turn has enabled people to

Table 1.3 Evaluation of the EEG in Key Research Areas

Energy-efficiency gap	*Benchmarking Indicators*	*Occupants' Behaviour*	*Thermal Comfort*	*Overheating Risk*	*Energy Modelling*
Energy efficiency	Embodied energy in construction materials	Δ	⊕	⊕	√
	Embodied energy in materials for maintenance	Δ	Δ	⊕	Δ
	Efficient HVAC distribution systems	■	■	Δ	√
	Energy performance	⊕	■	Δ	■
	Water heating system (solar/any)	Δ	Δ	√	√
	Energy-efficient equipment	⊕	⊕	Δ	√
	Energy metering	⊕	⊕	√	√
	Efficient lighting system	Δ	Δ	⊕	√
	Thermal efficiency of building system	⊕	⊕	⊕	√
	Good fenestration design	■	■	■	■
	Air infiltration	⊕	⊕	Δ	√
Energy-policy design	GHG emissions from energy use	Δ	Δ	⊕	Δ
	Primary energy uses per capita	⊕	Δ	Δ	⊕
	Annual energy consumption per capita	⊕	⊕	Δ	⊕
	Ratio of energy-related jobs to population	⊕	⊕	⊕	⊕
	Active public participation	⊕	Δ	Δ	■
	Household energy intensity	Δ	Δ	√	√
	Share of household income spent on fuel and electricity	⊕	⊕	Δ	⊕
	Awareness raising campaigns on energy issues	⊕	⊕	⊕	⊕
	Local authority advice	⊕	⊕	⊕	⊕
	Assistance to the citizens on energy use	⊕	⊕	⊕	⊕

(*Continued*)

Table 1.3 (Continued)

Energy-efficiency gap	*Benchmarking Indicators*	*Occupants' Behaviour*	*Thermal Comfort*	*Overheating Risk*	*Energy Modelling*
Energy optimisation	**Optimisation**				
	Construction cost & energy	Δ	Δ	■	√
	Thermal & lighting performance	Δ	Δ	⊕	√
	Life cycle cost	Δ	Δ	■	■
	Thermal performance	Δ	■	Δ	⊕
	Solar energy utilisation	Δ	Δ	Δ	Δ
	Specify reflective, high-emissivity roofing	Δ	Δ	⊕	√
	Provide operable windows	⊕	⊕	■	■
	Retrofitting				
	Post-occupancy evaluation	√	√	⊕	√
	Energy audit	√	⊕	■	√
	Building commissioning	Δ	Δ	⊕	⊕
	Life cycle assessment	Δ	Δ	■	Δ
	Cost analysis	⊕	⊕	Δ	Δ
	Energy benchmarking	⊕	⊕	■	■
	ASHRAE guidelines	Δ	Δ	Δ	Δ
	Measurement and verification	⊕	⊕	■	■

(*Continued*)

Table 1.3 (Continued)

Energy-efficiency gap	*Benchmarking Indicators*	*Occupants' Behaviour*	*Thermal Comfort*	*Overheating Risk*	*Energy Modelling*
Affordable and clean energy # SDG Call 7	**Energy planning**				
	Energy produced from resources	√	√	⊕	Δ
	Level of energy distribution	⊕	⊕	Δ	Δ
	Raise of energy-efficiency awareness	⊕	⊕	⊕	⊕
	Supporting energy initiatives	⊕	■	⊕	■
	Clean energy research & development	⊕	■	⊕	⊕

better understand the energy performance of their buildings (Davis & Durbach, 2010). This is because the concept of the EEG has a direct impact on understanding energy efficiency and assessing the energy performance of existing housing stock (Motawa & Oladokun, 2015).

Hitchcock (1993) states that 'households' can be viewed as systems being defined by both physical and social variables for developing evidence-based energy design solutions. It should be noted from the above scholars' statements that the implementation of the EPBD mandates in both Central Europe and in the Eastern Mediterranean region of the EU has had a positive effect in increasing households' awareness of energy use, but there are still shortcomings in implementing energy-efficient technologies, particularly as the human behaviour factor has largely been neglected by scholars (De Dear & Brager, 2001; Gonzales-Cacenas et al., 2020). Knight et al. (2022) stress that the EEG has been debated for decades by scholars because they are still questioning whether or not investing in energy efficiency is worth it. Reviewing all these views on the EEG, it appears that scholars do not agree on a single research pathway for determining the EEG (Dyner et al., 1995).

A review of other scholars' work in the EEG field is necessary for integrating the STS conceptual framework into EEG research to avoid research bias and provide reliable energy-efficiency measures. All the referred pilot studies conducted extensive research to understand the factors that create the EEG. Despite constraints reported by earlier studies after the implementation of the EPBD, there is great potential for considering the EEG when taking into account energy efficiency, energy performance development and energy-policy design.

The starting point for the present study was the human-based data that enabled a triangulation of the findings from the collected data, which were further enriched and verified by a field investigation. To ensure a systematic analysis of the key aims and objectives, this study adopted a mixed-method research design approach by conducting a building-energy performance evaluation with the use of dynamic thermal modelling and simulations, which was then validated by a comprehensive questionnaire survey, thermal imaging and in situ measurements of the base-case prototype RTBs in the post-war social-housing development estate in NC. In general, each phase was carried out in a sequential order to facilitate a discussion of the literature review that was conducted as part of the main research scope. Table 1.4 outlines the development of a novel STS conceptual framework.

The Concept of Statistical Representativeness

In order to provide a background analysis for developing the concept of statistical representativeness, this section presents a review of selected theoretical information and exemplar pilot projects and their applicability. Table 1.5 delineates the original research articles that were reviewed to identify the most appropriate concept of statistical representativeness for the present study (see Appendix A).

Hu and Kohler-Hausmann (2020) highlight the importance of the integration of the STS approach into using the conceptual analysis of sampling size to test associations gathered through various experimental statistical analyses. Chasalow

Table 1.4 Step-by-Step Development of STS Conceptual Framework

STS DevelopmentStructure	*Guidance to Develop a Methodfor Current Design Approach*
Step 1:Literature review	To undertake a literature review based on selected key terms—'overheating risk,' 'thermal comfort,' 'occupant behaviour and energy modelling' and 'building-energy simulations'—to address the knowledge gap in the field of energy efficiency and to develop a new design method for the STS approach.
Step 2:Questionnaire survey	To conduct a questionnaire survey that will assess household energy performance and the energy-use patterns of occupants prior to and following the energy-saving measures implemented in the selected archetype buildings.
Step 3:Thermal-comfort survey	To make recommendations that will support successful delivery of current and future policy schemes related to retrofitting efforts for existing residential buildings that take occupant thermal comfort into consideration to promote evidence-based retrofitting interventions.
Step 4:Measurements and monitoring	To concurrently conduct in situ measurements and on-site monitoring through semi-structured interviews with households to assess the degree of overheating risk that they experienced and to thoroughly identify their thermal-comfort preferences.
Step 5:Building-energy modelling	To model and simulate the base-case representative RTBs to test the current energy performance of the structures before implementing retrofitting design strategy phases for energy policy. In line with the overheating and thermal-comfort assessments, the CIBSE *TM59 Design Methodology for the Assessment of Overheating Risk in Homes*, which was embedded in the building modelling simulation phase of the present study.
Step 6:Building-performance evaluation	To test the validity of environmental monitoring and modelling outcomes in the IES software suite by using actual meteorological year (AMY) weather files, occupancy patterns and the occupants' habitual adaptive behaviours and window-opening schedules in the summer.
Step 7:Retrofitting policy design	To develop a novel design guideline for retrofitting efforts in post-war housing stock and to demonstrate the feasibility of implementing passive-cooling design systems and energy-consumption-reduction measures during pre- and post-retrofitting phases.

and Levy (2021) discuss the STS approach providing a multidisciplinary integrated conceptual framework that enables both statisticians and engineers to interrogate taken-for-granted terms and categories while developing benchmarks in energy-policy design (Owen et al., 2007). These studies indicate that representativeness of

Table 1.5 Reviewing the Concept of Representativeness in Statistics

References	*Concept(s)*	*Method(s)*	*Outcome(s)*
Chasalow and Levy (2021)	Law, social and behavioural sciences	● Stratification of population sample size ● Generalisability of research findings	Equal representation of each subgroup of the user population was recommended
Hirsch and O'Donnell (2017)	Education, social and behavioural sciences	● A multiple-choice test-based survey was distributed ● Descriptive statistics ● 4 × 2 chi-square test of independence	A unique set of test questions to identify students who hold common representativeness was developed
Schmill et al. (2014)	Global change sciences (i.e., human factors, climate, remote sensing)	● Pearson's chi-square tests ● Heat mapping ● Histograms ● Kullback-Leibler *f*-divergence test ● Multivariate analysis	Implementing a variety of methods for making assessments about the representativeness of a collection of case studies across the globe
Schouten et al. (2009)	Social and behavioural sciences	● Population R-indicators ● Chi-square statistics used to test independence and goodness of fit ● Logistic regression models	A mathematically rigorous definition and perception of representative response was developed

sampling size shows differences between one pilot study and another due to demographic structures, geography and the political conditions of each research context.

Chasalow and Levy (2021) explain their own representativeness concerns while developing a novel methodological framework for representativeness in statistics, politics and machine learning. In this theoretical study, these scholars contribute a sense of the variety of meanings and values associated with representativeness in order to prove the validity of chosen sampling sizes. Chasalow and Levy indicate that they did not select a large sampling to develop their own representative study. In their pilot research project, these scholars predominantly focused on sampling in Europe and the United States more than in other parts of the world. According to Chasalow and Levy, it is difficult to identify the limitations of their own selected sampling size representativeness because of the geographical extent of their research context. To avoid a research bias and provide a generalisation of their research findings, their study set out to offer reliable and statistically representative sampling criteria that would allow the targeted reader group to understand their research outcomes (Shaughnessy, 1977; Roberts, 1978).

Garett (1942), Jensen (1926), Kruksal and Mosteller (1980) and McNemar (1940) all discuss the issue of how to check a particular sample for representativeness. Kiaer (1976) states that 'the representative method can be applied in several ways.' To explain this claim, Kiaer develops two different sample types. His first method is an arbitrary filtering of the variables gathered from the sampling. Kiaer explains that this selection should be done in a 'haphazard or random way' to avoid giving preference to subject respondents in certain occupations or belonging to particular social strata (Ryan, 1976). This method of selection highlights that the representativeness of sampling size results from the absence of selective discretion. His second method involves allocating representativeness in a mechanical procedure that can provide a feasible method of design to undertake statistical analysis faster and provide an opportunity to detect discrepancies in the sample (see Appendix A).

In previous studies that develop the concept of statistical representativeness of sampling size, one of the main strengths of the selection of a random sampling method is that it enables the use of all available data to ensure a proportionate match on known relevant variables (see Appendix B). This was proven by Kiaer in 1976 in a population study that consisted of surveyors in rural areas and used census data to allocate counts per country and then selected districts within the countries to 'represent the main industry groups within the country as well as its various geographic conditions' (Kiaer, 1976). This method of design demonstrates that it can be applied to choose a single geographic domain to develop the concept of statistical analysis by integrating census data and applying outcomes to other geographic domains that have been shown to have similar demographic structures, political assets and cultural norms.

Hirsch and O'Donnell (2001) used a 4 × 2 chi-square test of independence to determine whether performance on a test was dependent on students' experience. For the statistical analysis, Cramér's V was chosen to measure the association between variables; this study reported findings with low p-values by selecting the conventional measurement of $p < 0.001$. Shaughnessy (1992) and Konold (1991) identified a knowledge gap for overestimating students' understanding of probability by using applicable test instruments to identify the representativeness of a sample size. This also creates some concern about the consistency, reliability and calculation of adequate sampling size for statistical analysis.

Hirsch and O'Donnell (2001) have developed a scientific method of design that measures the reliability of datasets and the applicability of concepts of statistical design to provide an understanding of the conceptual change that can have a long-term impact on conceptual-level analysis. Schmill et al. (2014) developed a theory of analytics for assessing global representativeness in social science studies to guide future scholars that were aimed at addressing sampling bias and providing a public domain for similar pilot projects. This pilot study aimed to reduce the gap between local and global researchers in providing analytical methods of design that could help scholars assess the representativeness of sampling size and assist in correcting any bias in the interpretation of statistical findings. Schmill et al. (2014) recommend the chi-square test as the most appropriate statistical method that allows scholars to apply it to their own hypothesis testing. In the Schmill study, Pearson's chi-square tests were used for testing the independence of two samples using a model function defined over a contingency table of observed versus expected values.

Schmill et al. (2014) clearly highlighted that the chi-square test is useful in computing representativeness, which gives the degree of extent for the global representativeness of case studies included in the dataset. Schmill et al. also indicate that the chi-square analysis is the standard and most applicable practice in many disciplines and it allows researchers to provide a reliable result without requiring any research limitations at the time of addressing their own research hypotheses. However, Schmill et al. recommend that the chi-square test is not an applicable test for sample sizes of less than 50, or when the expected frequency for more than one category is less than 5. These statistical criteria provide a reasonably representative sample size that should be considered to prevent any research bias. Schmill et al. (2014) also indicate that Fisher's exact test can help in cases where there is an expected frequency of zero to avoid any research bias in relatively small sample sizes.

The concept of using a statistical method allows researchers to avoid research bias while undertaking multinominal logistic regression analysis to determine benchmarking criteria for their own research hypothesis. Schouten et al. (2009) have developed benchmarks for the representativeness of survey responses in order to reduce the risk of non-response when developing a statistical dataset extracted from field-survey responses. Schouten et al. propose that the R-indicator, which is related to Cramér's V, be used as a measure for the association between response and non-response variables. Their study indicates that the R-indicator was selected as a lack-of-association measure for a given sampling size. Schouten et al. highlight that for assessment of the R-indicator, the weaker the association the better; this implies that there is no evidence related to the issue of no-response rate and this issue has not affected the composition of the observed data.

Little and Rubin (2002) describe the concept of representative response as closely related to missing-data mechanisms, such as Missing-Completely-at-Random

(MCAR), which is a standard method of design applied to multidisciplinary studies globally. Schouten et al. (2009) stress that the applicability of the MCAR test should be considered for longitudinal field surveys, particularly where the target group is householders, to provide a statistically representative sample size. Schouten et al. also indicate that chi-square test statistics are often used to test independence and goodness of fit for exploring discrepancies between any survey items and the missing-data mechanism.

To prove the representativeness of a sample size, Schouten et al. (2009) developed a benchmarking criterion where researchers can apply chi-square statistics to χ in order to measure the reliability between true response behaviour and the response behaviour that is expected when the response is independent of χ. This concept of statistical benchmarking criteria indicates that Cramér's V is an association measure that enables a transformation of chi-square test statistics to the [0, +1] interval. It should be noted that Cramér's V provides a universal design approach to other researchers that they can apply to test associations gathered through longitudinal field surveys.

Goodchild et al. (2017) and Marsh Bella and McDonald (1988) indicate that there are many applicable association measures developed by earlier statisticians to identify the representativeness of sample sizes. Therefore, these scholars recommend that R-indicators have a strong relation to response parameters. Goodman and Kruksal (1979) outline that R-indicators are for measuring in a multivariate setting to avoid any discrepancies at the time of undertaking statistical analysis.

To test the reliability of their statistical analysis, Schouten et al. (2007) conducted logistic regression models to predict the type of responses expected. In a further study conducted by Schouten et al. (2009), the researchers developed an advanced indicator to identify the concept of statistical representativeness of sample sizes. In this pilot study, the researchers found that the field-survey approach gave more accurate results regardless of the limitation of only being able to recruit relatively small sample sizes. As an outcome of this pilot study, Schouten et al. (2009) recommend that in multinominal logistic regression models, variables give a significant contribution at the 5% level, and where this cannot be done, these variables should be excluded from the sampling size.

In conclusion, the reviewed papers inform us about the theoretical aspects of the development of relevant statistical backgrounds globally. Through the review of these papers, it was found that Cramér's V tests allow researchers to measure associations gathered through longitudinal field surveys, thus allowing researchers to develop an evidence-based benchmarking criterion. While this section discusses theoretical information around the concept of statistical representativeness, further exemplary pilot studies are reviewed and discussed.

References to the Works of Other Scholars on Representativeness

This section presents a review of pilot studies that have examined different methods in statistics to avoid research bias and develop a reliable concept of statistically representative sampling sizes (see Appendix C). This section supports the selection criteria of conventional statistical analysis for non-parametric or parametric tests and also provides guidance to readers developing their own statistical methods in the building engineering field. Table 1.6 delineates the original research articles that were reviewed to understand the development of a statistically representative population sample.

Beresewicz (2017) developed a two-step procedure to measure the representativeness of internet data sources. In this study, Beresewicz focuses on representativeness and non-sampling errors to avoid any research bias while developing the dataset for parametric analysis. Several types of surveys and their pros and cons are also discussed. Beresewicz's analysis is in line with the survey recommendations. The study stresses that a self-selection survey can provide a true response and can also avoid any bias in research outcomes.

On the contrary, Kruksal and Mosteller (1980) argue that there is no straightforward definition of a statistically representative sample size. These scholars tabulate a list of definitions used in the conventions of statistical dataset preparation and interpretation, as follows: (i) unjustified obtained data, (ii) absence of dependent variable, (iii) lack of population sample, (iv) typical archetypes, (v) general representativeness of sample population, (vi) clarification of vague terms, (vii) dominant representativeness of targeted population sample, (viii) precise estimation obtained from a precise population sample, (ix) reasonable fraction of a population sample for a particular purpose. Kruksal and Mosteller claim that all these stated types of population samples could be counted as representative samples.

Beresewicz (2017) discusses the importance of selection of actual data to avoid any errors during the data preparation stage; his study implements a referred statistical convention to measure the representativeness of sampling size by using both individual and aggregated data. As an outcome of this pilot study, Beresewicz recommends that to assess the representativeness of new data sources, the time series of historical data should be considered by future scholars. He also suggests that data collated over time may reveal similarities to existing data sources.

To follow this recommendation, in the present study, the time-of-day factor was used to present in situ measurements of environmental parameters in order to foresee the benchmark indicators when undertaking the building-performance evaluation. The statistical convention Beresewicz developed proved to be an appropriate statistical convention to use in this study.

Bertino (1998) defines the representativeness of a random sample as 'the degree of capacity of the sample to demonstrate the typical or dominant characteristics of the targeted sample population.' In light of this theory, Bertino conducted an empirical study to measure the representativeness of a sample population to provide a reliable source for inferential purposes. In this experimental study, Cramér's *V* statistical method was used to identify measures for the observed values. The study set out to assess the degree of efficiency of several conventional techniques (i.e., power function, coverage probabilities) in order to support the representativeness function of the selected sample population. Bertino conducted hypothesis testing to measure the sample population and to remunerate the representativeness

Table 1.6 Reviewing Pilot Studies to Develop the Concept of Representativeness in Statistics

References	*Concept(s)*	*Method(s)*	*Outcome(s)*
Beresewicz (2017)	Business, economics and information technology	• Self-selection survey • Domain-level data • Deterministic and probabilistic approaches	Advantages and disadvantages of measuring representativeness by using individual and aggregated data is outlined
Bertino (2006)	Statistics	• Power function and coverage probabilities used to calculate representative population sample size • Cramér–von Mises criterion	The utilisation of the representativeness function in many standard statistical constraints is outlined through experimental statistical techniques
Marsh et al. (1988)	Statistics	• Goodness-of-fit indicators • Stand-alone indexes • Incremental-fit indexes	Guidance on the effects of sample size and data set on the fit indexes distributed
Barratt et al. (2017)	Social and behavioural sciences	• Web-survey method • Global drug survey developed • Descriptive statistics • Identification of continuous and categorical variables • Adjusted R-square for the probabilistic analysis	Opt-in web surveys of hard-to-reach populations are an efficient way of gaining in-depth understanding of stigmatised behaviours and are appropriate
Grillone et al. (2020)	Business, economics and information technology	• General sample-based R-indicators	Probability-based samples are more representative
Li and Brimicombe (2008)	Geo-information and statistics	• Small area population modelling approach was adopted • The raw datasets of local scenarios were cleaned and then checked with each other in order to control data quality	The findings were implemented to support local social infrastructure planning in the Thames Gateway London boroughs in the UK

(Continued)

Table 1.6 (Continued)

References	*Concept(s)*	*Method(s)*	*Outcome(s)*
Li and Brimicombe (2008)—continued	Geo-information and statistics	• Average-weighted distance by small area geography method was applied • Regression analysis conducted to explore the effect size of an average-weighted Euclidean and network distance	The Euclidean distance approach has less computational load and is generally applicable, particularly where rapid 'what-if' analyses are required for decision support in a planning context
Brimicombe and Mungroo (2018)	Health, geography and social sciences	• Locally available secondary data sources • Welch's two-sample *t*-test • Correlation-tree analysis • Euclidean distance method	Visualisation map to demonstrate the distances between GP practices by using the conventions of various statistical methods could provide an effective mechanism for policymaking decisions

index, which can be used in a similar design approach to the Cramér–von Mises test.

Marsh et al. (2006) developed a novel goodness-of-fit index in a confirmatory factor analysis to assess the effect of sample size. In this pilot study, observed variables were selected to provide a background for multivariate distribution. Marsh et al. considered large sample sizes to include for their statistical analysis. To assess the degree of associations in large sample sizes, in this pilot study the chi-square test was chosen because this method of design can be applied to testing the efficiency of the goodness-of-fit base of the stratified data on a large sample size while interpreting statistically significant chi-square outcomes.

To prove the empirical analysis developed by Marsh et al. (2006), the present study examines a theory developed by Forrester (1992). This is in order to understand how the present study has been impacted by previous scholars' statistical methods in terms of applicability and in terms of bringing theory into practice to enable the development of benchmark criteria and energy-policy implications in the residential sector. Forrester states that 'sacrificing the power of a test by utilising small sample sizes simply blinds the researcher to significant differences between a model and the data' (Forrester, 1992). To avoid this mistake, the present study aims to avoid bias and develop a set of methods as outlined by Bertino (2006).

Marsh et al. (2006) indicate that the interpretation of Cramér's V findings will generally fall between 0 and +1, but their experimental study shows that it is also possible to detect negative findings for relatively small sample sizes. Marsh et al. report that higher values reflect more reliable outcomes for all benchmarking indexes and most outputs are positively intercorrelated. This finding may support the hypothesis testing model developed by Bertino (2006) discussed earlier. Marsh et al. discuss the indexes used to calculate what sample size is adequate to conduct a relevant statistical analysis. To this extent, no absolute criterion has been found to be acceptable for sample limitation. Bentler and Bonett (1980) found that $N = 90$ was an acceptable minimum population size to conduct their parametric analysis, while Forrester (1992) found that $N = 200$ was an acceptable sample size. The variance in these studies shows that there have been many acceptable conventional theories developed by previous researchers, and an inability to apply conclusions to other scholars' research hypotheses may be due to both the constraints and strengths of analytical methods and the implications of individual studies. Table 1.7 delineates the strengths and constraints of using both individual and domain data at the time of developing a statistically representative population sample size.

Barrat et al. (2017) conducted a global drug survey in order to determine a representative sample. Their data was gathered through a call-back survey. To identify the representativeness of this global database, Barrat et al. discuss the theory of representativeness developed by Kruksal and Mosteller between 1979 and 1980, discussed earlier. Barrat et al. also highlight that the representativeness of a sampling size may show differences due to the research hypotheses of each survey and the response rate of sampling to be included in the dataset.

Table 1.7 Strengths and Constraints of Measuring Representativeness in Statistics

Aggregation Level	*Strengths*	*Constraints*
Individual data	1. Measuring representativeness at any level 2. Detection of the selection mechanism 3. Control over data processing and cleaning 4. Linkage with units or objects from statistical and non-statistical data sources 5. Assessment of uncertainty of estimates	1. Limited access to individual data 2. Time-consuming data cleaning process 3. Linkage uncertainty 4. Linkage may be legally prohibited or impossible
Domain data	1. Alternative when individual data is not available 2. Overall information about consistency with official and non-official data 3. May provide a general overview of the data without time-consuming data cleaning processes 4. May indicate whether the use of such data is possible for official statistics	1. Limited possibilities of measuring representativeness and the selection mechanism 2. Requires historical time-series data for comparison 3. Requires harmonisation with available domain-level data 4. Lack of a measure of uncertainty of estimates

Source: Pelenur (2013).

Gabe (2016) argues that a household survey with 100 variables will create weights on variables that can be matched to population distributions. In line with this theory, Barrat et al. (2017) prove that for the statistical representativeness of household surveys, a minimum of $N = 100$ is required to provide reliable research outputs.

In the 2017 global drug survey conducted by Barrat et al., age was pre-coded as a categorical variable with indicators for categories of participant age as follows: 15–19, 20–24, 25–34, 35–44, 45–54, 55–64, 65–74 and 75+. However, the sample from the Australian database used the age factor as a continuous variable, and the researchers gathered the continuous variable from the Australian context as a categorical variable. This present study shows a similar design approach in terms of exploring households' socio-demographic characteristics: the conceptual data preparation strictly considered age as a categorical variable, but the gathered information from households was numeric and was counted as a continuous variable to understand the standard deviation (SD) and mean of the selected household populations.

Cornesse and Bosnjak (2018) investigated an association between survey characteristics and representativeness in order to provide a reliable conceptual framework to conduct an appropriate statistical test. This pilot study also referred to the previous experimental analysis conducted by Kurksal and Mosteller (1980). One of the main parallels is that these studies refer to the success and also reliability of survey estimates as mirroring the 'true' parameters of a target population. Ozarisoy and Altan recommend that random survey sampling is an applicable method of design to develop the convention of statistical analysis.

Ozarisoy and Altan (2017b) recommend that a mixed-mode survey can increase the representativeness of sample size and enable researchers to conduct statistical analysis in accordance with their research hypotheses. Fincham (2008) identifies the term 'auxiliary data,' by which he means combining all available data from both respondents and non-respondents to enhance post-survey adjustments and provide an effective method of design for the data preparation stage.

Dubois and Meier (2016) and Caro and Sendra (2021) argue that accurate identification of aggregated data shows limitations for constructing sampling from data, survey pro-data and data linked to survey data, when considering a particular population sample. One of the main constraints is the lack of aggregated data available on municipality and district levels to construct accurate and reliable datasets that can represent collated data on a national level.

Schouten et al. (2009) highlight the importance of using representative sample-based R-indicators to measure the effect sizes between dependent and independent variables to identify the national representativeness of sample sizes and their effects on a developed research hypothesis. To support this theory, Brimicombe and Cafe (2012) stress the importance of using logistic regression models of propensity to identify accurate effect-size measures for parametric tests. These studies predominantly discuss the concept of statistically representative sample sizes and how this concept enables researchers to decide on appropriate statistical methods of design for their statistical analyses.

After a thorough review of these pilot research projects, this present study finds the assessment using global representativeness of heat mapping to foresee global patterns conducted by Schmill et al. (2014) to be one of the best exemplar studies. It provides a synthesis of pilot studies and brings the findings of local case studies out by demonstrating globally representative sample sizes in the public domain. The technical effectiveness of this study is due to the use of Pearson's chi-square tests to measure the independence of two samples. Additionally, the study uses a function defined over a contingency table of observed versus expected values. This selected conventional method of design enables the researchers to set a common design approach that can be applied by other scholars when developing nationally representative sample sizes.

Another pilot study, conducted by Schouten et al. (2009), clearly outlines the benchmarking indicators for the representativeness of survey responses; the study stresses the use of R-indicators related to Cramér's V measures for the association between dependent and independent variables. To this extent, Schouten et al. recommend that random sampling surveys require the use of well-known chi-square statistics because of the need to use the independence test and goodness of fit. These technical details relate to the development of conventional statistical analysis and can provide reliable effect-size measures.

Ozarisoy and Altan (2017b) and Ozarisoy (2022) discuss the effectiveness of the integration of administrative datasets by using limited geographic regions to develop an appropriate method of design for statistical analysis. This convention enables researchers to conduct population modelling in agreement with frequently updated regional administrative datasets. In line with this concept of statistical detail, Li and Brimicombe (2008) conducted a scenario-based, small-area population model for social infrastructure planning in London. This study set out to investigate the population of each individual borough to propose effective solutions for modelling multiple data sources and included a wide range of local administrative datasets applied to small-area geography. By contrast, the pilot studies conducted by Schmill et al. (2014) and Schouten et al. (2009) discuss the applicability of the development of a universal design approach to provide more reliable outputs for their own statistical analyses.

In the study conducted by Li and Brimicombe (2008), a small area of a particular location was selected intentionally by collecting secondary data resources from administrative datasets to conduct statistical analysis for modelling-proposed design scenarios. In such manner, the selection of a particular case study location and conducted statistical analysis could be applied to the other regional pilot studies that aim to integrate particular households, demographics and cultural assets for their own scenario-based modelling approaches.

Li and Brimicombe (2011) investigated a new variable for spatial accessibility measurement in social infrastructure planning. In this study, UK census data was used to develop their statistical analysis. For the concept of statistical representativeness, an average-weighted distance method was applied by selecting small-area geography. The London Borough of Haringey and the Uttlesford district were selected as case study locations and the Euclidian distance method was applied to measure network distances for regression analysis. To understand the method of design applied by Li and Brimicombe, we looked back at the theoretical study conducted by Chasalow and Levy (2021) on the representativeness in statistics, politics and machine learning, and found that a representative method of stratification could be applied at the time of developing a dataset where the data gathered from municipalities or local administrative resources enables the generalisation of the research outputs for decision-making criteria.

Brimicombe and Mungroo (2018) conducted a statistical analysis to explore geographical variation in general practice (GP) drug prescriptions for schizophrenia and similar psychoses in England. This pilot study used monthly files on GPs' prescribing practices in England, which were downloaded from the National Health Service (NHS) digital database. This data was then aggregated by the 326 local authorities in England. Brimicombe and Mungroo used the Euclidian distance method by using GP survey postcode data to measure the effect-size differences between urban and rural locations.

According to the benchmark indicators for the representativeness of survey responses, Schouten et al. (2009) recommend that the concept of representative response be closely related to missing-data mechanisms, such as MCAR, and their theoretical study also suggests that randomly sampling criteria by using a population sample to conduct statistical analysis is the most appropriate statistical method of design.

In conclusion, the pilot studies conducted by Li and Brimicombe (2008, 2011) and Brimicombe and Mungroo (2018) highlight that the selection of particular small-area geographies, such as local case study locations in a given country, requires a representative sampling criterion to develop a feasible and nationally representative statistical analysis. While, conversely, Schmill et al. (2014) and Barratt et al. (2017) discuss the efficacy of developing globally statistically representative datasets by using survey samples gathered through random sampling data collection instruments.

With these methods in mind, the present study aims to use the method of small-area geography by undertaking a questionnaire survey to develop a statistically representative sample size; findings are supported by census data and national housing survey datasets to avoid any research bias and provide applicability of research outcomes to other EU-27 countries when developing evidence-based energy-policy design scenarios.

Sample Size Calculation Criteria

This section reviews other scholars' work in multidisciplinary studies on determining the applicable method of design for establishing sampling size. This section also reports on the statistical representativeness of sample size to provide background information on the identification of margin of error; this enables the study to provide acceptable and more reliable benchmarking criteria. To calculate sample size criteria, first, the margin of error was calculated using an online calculator[15] in accordance with the suggested conventions in statistical analysis. After a thorough calculation of the sampling criteria, power estimator analyses were conducted in order to establish the validity of Fisher's exact tests and Pearson's correlation tests.

The online calculator findings report that—with the confidence level set at 95%, sample size set at 100, population proportion set at 50% and population size set at 1,440—the margin of error is 9.46%. This means that there is a 95% chance that the real values are within ±9.46% of the measured/surveyed value. In this study, the margin of error was found to be 9.46%. However, the conventional recommendation for a margin of error calculation is that it should be 5% with a population proportion set at 50%. Many scholars indicate that 5% is the generally accepted benchmark criterion for developing a statistical analysis. The reason for this 5% threshold is that it is necessary to interpret statistical findings and explore their impact on the outcome of research projects. For example, the traditionally acceptable interventions of the Fisher's exact test and Pearson's correlation analysis findings require the identification of a 5% threshold level in order to provide a reliable statistical interpretation and level of frequency to determine the significance of the statistical findings.

In the present study, the margin of error was found to be 9.46% and this is not within the traditionally acceptable threshold limit. However, many scholars indicate that a threshold level in the 10–20% range can be accepted to demonstrate the statistical representativeness of sample size. Table 1.8(a) and (b) introduce other scholars' works that contain sampling size criteria within the range of 10%–20%. After thorough analysis of previous scholars' work on the identification of a sufficient sample size, it appears that some studies recommend a margin of error between 10% and 20% as a traditional threshold level in the building engineering field. This is the reason that, in the present study, the identified 9.46% margin of error is considered to provide a reasonably acceptable sample fraction for undertaking statistical analysis.

On further questioning, the identified 9.46% margin of error, an a priori power analysis using G*Power 3.1.9 was conducted to determine the minimum sample size. With the power set at 0.08, the alpha level set at 0.05, a moderate effect size of 3.5 (odds ratio) and the proportion of the control group at 0.5, results indicate that

Table 1.8(a) Reviewing the Theoretical Approach in Representativeness

References	*Concept(s)*	*Method(s)*	*Outcome(s)*
Al-Momani (2000)	Construction management	• Descriptive statistics • Bar-chart representation • Regression analysis	Guidance to help construction managers in establishing reliable evaluation criterion
Owen et al. (2006)	Social and behavioural science	• Exploratory factor analysis • Descriptive statistics • -Missing data and outliers tests conducted • Data missing at random (MAR) • Confirmatory factor analyses—cross-validation technique	Exploratory and confirmatory factor analyses formed the central portion of this reappraisal of the psychometric properties developed The conducted questionnaire survey could be successfully shortened from 27 to 14 items
Saka and Chan (2020)	Architectural engineering and design management	• A pilot survey was carried out by administrating the questionnaire proforma • Descriptive statistics • Mann–Whitney *U* test	Guidance on knowledge, skill and functionality requirements for quantity surveyors in building information modelling

Table 1.8(b) Reviewing the Theoretical Approach in Representativeness (Continued)

References	*Concept(s)*	*Method(s)*	*Outcome(s)*
Willcoxon and Chatham (2006)	Business management and social science	• Longitudinal survey • Descriptive statistics • Pearson's correlation analysis	Guidance on testing the accuracy of the representativeness of sample size selected to develop effective policymaking decisions
Borrego et al. (2009)	Education and building engineering	• Descriptive statistics • Chi-square test • Pearson's correlation • ANOVA • MANOVA	Guidance on the applicable representative sampling criteria Evaluation criteria for quantitative, qualitative and mixed-methods research

a total of 104 participants would be needed in order to reach an adequate sample size for running cross-tabulations using Fisher's exact tests, as shown in Figure 1.4(a). This sample size was also sufficient when running the correlation analysis, as shown in Figure 1.4(b).

In the present study, both the conventional online calculator and power analysis were used. One of the reasons for this was to provide an exact clarification regarding the power of the sampling size because the sufficiency of sampling size plays an important role in explaining the significance of research outcomes. Previous scholars' work indicates that using the online calculator may lead to inaccuracies because the researcher may have misinterpreted the population. To avoid any research bias, the present study also conducted a power analysis to foresee the impact of the population size for interpreting the statistical analysis.

Theoretical information on power analysis recommends that the acceptable threshold level should be 80% in order to determine statistical findings. This means that the use of Fisher's exact test and Pearson's correlation analysis could provide effective and more reliable research outcomes at the time of developing an evidence-based energy-policy design.

To develop the concept of statistical representativeness of sample size, the present study reviews other scholars' work to provide evidence-based statistically representative sampling criteria that set out to determine the threshold range between 10% and 20% used by previous scholars. This review aims to demonstrate that a margin of error between 10% and 20% can be an applicable threshold level in the building engineering field. Table 1.8(a) and (b) delineate the review of exemplar studies.

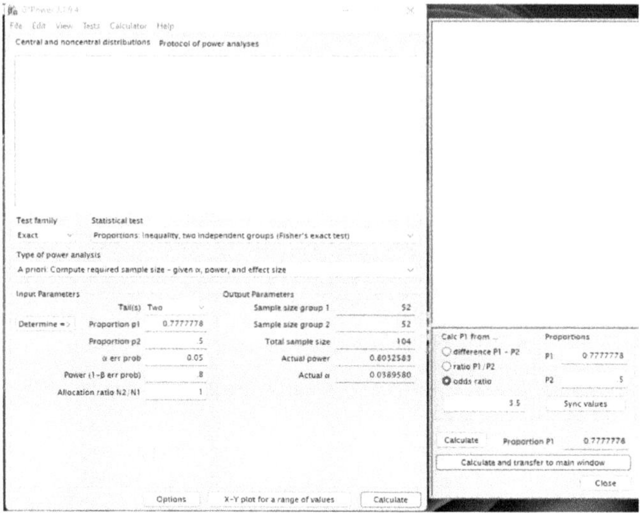

(a)

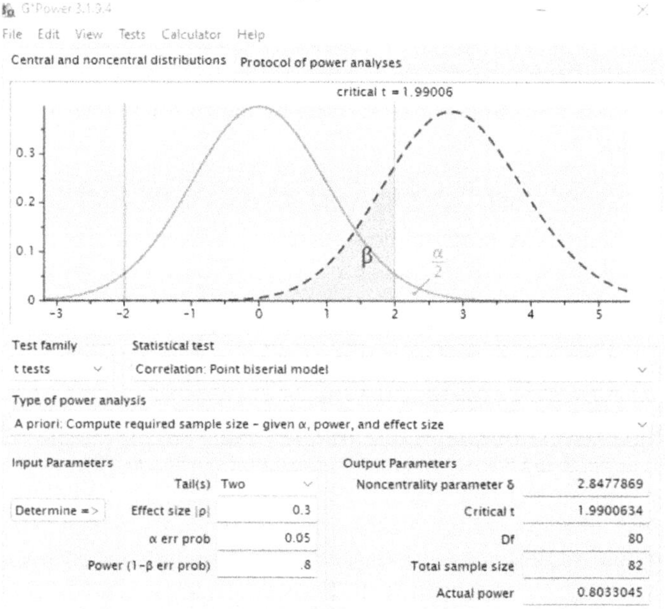

(b)

Figure 1.4 (a) The step-by-step calculation to prove the validity of using Fisher's exact test; (b) the step-by-step calculation to prove the validity of using correlation analysis. G*Power is a tool used to compute statistical power analyses for many different *t*-tests, *F*-tests, *z*-tests and χ^2-tests. G*Power can also be used to compute effect sizes and to graphically display the results of power analyses. *Source*: https://www.psychologie.hhu.de/arbeitsgruppen/allgemeine-psychologie-und-arbeitspsychologie/gpower

Al-Momani (2000) conducted a survey of 130 public projects constructed in different regions of Jordan between 1990 and 1997. To provide a roadmap for policymakers, descriptive statistics, correlation coefficients and linear regression analysis were used to measure the effectiveness of the selected sampling size on the research outcomes.

Owen et al. (2006) developed a psychometric re-evaluation of the Women in Science Scale to determine an exploratory factor analysis. In this pilot study, 1,439 middle and high school students were recruited to participate in the statistical analysis. In the questionnaire survey proforma, 27 items were asked of the participants to explore the correlations between dependent and independent variables.

In this pilot study, Owen et al. asked the students to circle a number on a 6-point Likert scale that reflected their true feelings for each item. The response format ranged from Strongly Agree (1) to Strongly Disagree (6), with no option of a neutral response. The variables that were set out to measure the students' responses on the Likert scale were included as 'ordinal' to run an appropriate statistical analysis. Owen et al. used the factor analysis method as their main conceptual method of design to generate research outcomes in accordance with their research hypotheses. In this pilot study, every confirmatory factor analysis (CFA) was inspected for potential multivariate outliers, defined as those with significance ($p < 0.001$). One-way analysis of variance (ANOVA) was used to probe the multivariate results. Table 1.9 demonstrates the lists of variable scaling requirements for several widely used statistical procedures.

Saka and Chan (2020) conducted a longitudinal survey on the knowledge, skill and functionality requirements for quantity surveyors in the building information modelling (BIM) environment, using a case study in Delphi. A pilot survey was carried out by administrating a questionnaire to 25 target experts, including researchers and practitioners. While the chosen sampling size was relatively small, the questionnaire survey items were sufficient to gather data that was representative of the sampling size of the study. In the Saka and Chan study, the statistical

Table 1.9 Selecting a Statistical Procedure Based on Variable Scaling

	Scale of Criterion	
Scale of Predictor	*Categorical*	*Continuous*
Categorical	Logistic regression or log-linear analysis	ANOVA
Continuous	Logistic regression or discriminant analysis	Ordinal logistic regren (OLS)
Categorical or continuous	Logistic regression	Ordinal logistic regression (OLS) with dummy coding

Note: The table is not meant to be exhaustive. When faced with all categorical variables, for example, a chi-square test of independence could be applied. However, log-linear analysis is preferable due, in part, to its ability to include interaction terms in the model.
Source: Adapted from Konold et al. (1990).

methods of analysis used to determine the significance of questionnaire survey items include the Cronbach's alpha reliability test, mean score ranking, the Mann–Whitney *U* test and quartile deviation. Notably, the power analysis test was conducted to test the effect size of the sampling survey recruited for the study. It was found that the value ranges from 0 to 1 and a value of at least 0.7 was an acceptable threshold level to conduct the statistical analysis.

Willcoxon and Chatham (2006) investigated profiling information technology (IT) managers' personality and behavioural characteristics to outline significant differences. The questionnaire survey was conducted with 130 IT senior managers to develop a statistically representative sample size; multiple surveys with relatively large indicators related to each survey item were then distributed to target groups. This method of design allowed Willcoxon and Chatham to analyse the statistical findings within a margin of error between 10% and 20% to provide a reliable benchmarking criterion.

To provide an evidence-based theoretical approach for the use of a margin of error in the 10%–20% range, Borrego et al. (2009) outlined a set of guidelines for scholars in engineering education to develop quantitative, qualitative and mixed-methods analyses by considering the significance of the benchmarking criterion for each discipline in the engineering field.

For undertaking ordinal logistic regression analysis, Schumacker (2017) describes a logistic regression coefficient to be estimated and then interpreted as the increase in the log odds of the outcome per unit increase in the value. Table 1.10 demonstrates the interpretation of the odds ratio recommended by Schumacker.

According to Borrego et al. (2009), in any type of engineering field, descriptive statistics should be conducted in the case of research topics about which little is known. This is also known as the deterministic approach, as it does not address any relationships between variables or groups. However, Borrego et al. recommend that for hypothesis testing, researchers should seek to examine the relationships between and among various indicators to report statistically significant findings.

To conduct an accurate correlation analysis between variables, Li and Yao (2021) outline a required conventional method of design, as shown in Table 1.11.

It should be stressed that the identification of the accurate variable type plays an important role in testing associations between study variables. According to Borrego

Table 1.10 Selecting a Statistical Procedure Based on Variable Scaling

Effect-Size Range	*Description*
OR = 1	(a)The effect size/variable does not affect the odds of the outcome
OR > 1	(b)The effect size/variable is associated with higher odds of the outcome
OR < 1	(c)The effect size/variable is associated with lower odds of the outcome

Source: Schumacker (2017).

Table 1.11 Identification of the Appropriate Use of Variables

Variables	*Analyses*	*Predictive Analyses*
Categorical	(d)Contingency tables, chi-square	(e)Logistic regression, discriminant analysis
(f) Continuous (i.e., scale, ordinal, ratio)	(g)ANOVA, MANOVA, *t*-tests, Pearson's correlation	(h)Linear regression, multiple linear regression

Note: This table only includes statistical analyses used to examine relationships between variables in the engineering field.
Source: Adopted from Li and Yao (2021).

et al. (2009), there is a strong association between variable type and the convention of the statistical method chosen for analysis. Borrego et al. also highlight the importance of using the appropriate design type and the relevant interpretation of each statistical analysis to provide reliable research outcomes, as shown in Table 1.12.

According to Creswell and Clark (2007), a researcher-adapted mixed-methods study involves the collection and analysis of both quantitative and qualitative data in a single study to interpret statistical analysis in accordance with conventional methods (i.e., Cramér's V and Phi test, Pearson's correlation, chi-square test, Fisher's exact test). Their conventions for undertaking a mixed-methods research design are presented in Table 1.13. To develop statistically representative research outcomes related to households' socio-demographic characteristics and their habitual adaptive behaviour on home energy performance, Cramér's V tests were applied by using both chi-square and Fisher's exact tests (see Appendix D).

Table 1.12 Applied Convention to Undertake a Mixed-Methods Research Design

Design Type	*Timing of Quan and Qual Phases*	*Relative Weighting of Quan and Qual Components*	*Mixing—When Quan and Qual Phases Are Integrated*	*Notation*
Triangulation	Concurrent	Equal	During interpretation or analysis	QUAN + QUAL
Embedded	Concurrent or Sequential	Unequal	One is embedded within the other	QUAN (qual) or QUAL (quan)
Explanatory	Sequential, quan then qual	Usually quan is given priority	Phase 1 informs phase 2	QUAN > qual
Exploratory	Sequential, qual then quan	Usually qual is given priority	Phase 1 informs phase 2	QUAL > quan

Abbreviations: quan = quantitative; qual = qualitative
Source: Adopted from Creswell and Clark (2007).

Table 1.13 Qualitative and Quantitative Research Criteria

Quantitative Research Criteria	*Qualitative Research Criteria*
Validity: project and instruments measure what is intended to be measured	(j) **Credibility:** establishing that the results are credible or believable
(k) Generalisability: results are applicable to other settings, achieved through representative sampling	(l) **Transferability:** applicability of research findings to other settings, achieved through limited description
(m) Reliability: findings are replicable or repeatable	(n) **Dependability:** researchers account for the ever-changing context within which the research occurs
(o) Objectivity: researcher limits bias and interaction with participants	(p) **Reflexivity:** researchers examine their own biases and make them known

Source: Adopted from Borrego et al. (2009).

Borrego et al. (2009) stress that using the triangulation design method plays a crucial role in any type of engineering research in order to validate survey findings from any type of data collection method (e.g., in situ measurements, on-site environmental monitoring, energy modelling). Borrego et al. also discuss the strengths and constraints of both quantitative and qualitative research methods, as shown in Table 1.13.

Borrego et al. (2009) state what is one of the main reasons for the margin of error being set at 5% to identify whether a gathered sample size is sufficient or not. However, many scholars have adopted a mixed-methods research design approach to represent statistical findings, and in these scholar's engineering studies, a margin of error can be acceptable within the 10%–20% threshold level. This means that in the engineering field, it is not necessarily compulsory to use the conventional method that is applied when using the online sampling calculator tool (see Appendix E).

In summary, this section demonstrates the significance of identifying statistically representative sampling criteria for benchmarking evaluation studies by considering several multidisciplinary studies' findings and providing a general overview of the subject matter. The present study concludes that scholars should use the power estimator analysis method to identify a sufficient sampling size before determining what type of statistical method should be applied in accordance with their questionnaire survey items. It should also be noted that this present study recommends that scholars in the building engineering field use both the online sample size calculator tool and undertake the power analysis method concurrently to avoid any research bias when interpreting statistical findings, particularly in energy research.

Selection Criteria for Thermal-Comfort Assessment

This section reviews previous scholars' thermal-comfort assessment criteria to provide thorough guidance for the development of 'neutral' adaptive thermal-comfort thresholds in the Eastern Mediterranean climate of Cyprus. Scholars have applied and developed different methods of design to measure occupants' thermal sensation in order to identify their predicted mean vote (PMV), but none of these scholars have clarified the differences between the selection of thermal sensation as either an ordinal or continuous variable type, or they haven't accurately undertaken parametric statistical analysis in the building engineering field.

In the present study, throughout the development stages of the statistical analysis, it was found that the differences between ordinal and continuous variable types of thermal sensation should be addressed. This is supported by the conventional methods of design applied by previous studies on thermal comfort, as listed in Table 1.14.

Many scholars have debated the identification of accurate statistical analysis criteria for the convention of the initial thermal-comfort assessment scale that was developed by Nicol in 2017 (Nicol, 2017). This assessment used a 7-point Likert scale and was later applied and proved by Fanger in the 1970s (Fanger, 1970); it has since become the widely used conventional method of design, and was applied, among others, by Griffiths in the 1990s (Griffiths, 1990; Nicol, 2004). Its scale was also made popular by Nicol in the 2000s, and since then many top-notch scholars in thermal-comfort research, such as Brager in 2008, de Dear and Brager in 2001, have continued developing this reliable thermal-comfort assessment criterion based on the conventional methods of design applied and developed by previous scholars.

de Dear and Brager in 2001, as well as their colleagues in thermal-comfort studies, established the ASHRAE Global Thermal Comfort Database I and II. This open-source international global database allows researchers to identify the appropriate method of thermal-comfort assessment criteria for their studies (i.e., using thermal sensation as either an ordinal or a continuous variable) (de Dear & Brager, 2001).

Rupp et al. published an article in 2021 entitled 'The Impact of Occupants' Thermal Sensitivity on the Adaptive Thermal Comfort Model.' In this paper, 107,583 samples were extracted from the ASHRAE Global Thermal Comfort Database II to conduct a regression analysis using a p-value of <0.001 to determine the significance factor within the variables. Rupp et al. (2021) used the [−3, +3] thermal-comfort assessment criteria as a continuous variable to run a statistical analysis with in situ measurements (i.e., indoor operative temperature, indoor air temperature) (Smith et al., 1995; Tian et al., 2018).

The thermal sensation variable is represented in the continuous variable formatting style [−3, +3] which was identified by Wang et al. (2018). The Wang study discusses the uncertainty of subjective thermal-comfort measurement criteria to provide guidance to scholars in thermal-comfort studies (see Appendix F). Many scholars have applied different measurement criteria by using the point ranking of the Likert scale assessment that was developed between 1936 and 2016.

Wang et al. (2018) stress that the use of different measurement criteria in thermal-comfort studies has led to misunderstandings when interpreting the findings in accordance with statistical conventions. To avoid any further misunderstanding by

Table 1.14 Worldwide Studies on Thermal-Comfort Assessment

References	*Sample Size*	*Statistical Method*	*Thermal-Comfort Assessment*
Rupp et al. (2021)	Data extracted from the ASHRAE Global Thermal Comfort Database II (n = 107,583)	Regression coefficient	Griffiths constant/ occupant's thermal sensitivity theorem applied
Wang et al. (2018)	Three different experiments conducted in the climate chamber by using a discrete scale of 2 votes per subject, a discrete scale of 5 votes per subject and a continuous scale for thermal sensation and satisfaction with 5 votes per subject	• Frequency statistics • Normalised standard uncertainty • Descriptive statistics • Box plot distribution • Bar-chart distribution	Humphreys and Nicol's (2002) theorem was applied by investigating subject respondents' PMV and PPD
Haldi and Robinson (2008)	- A dataset of some 5,908 entries from 60 participants was used - The dataset was built on a comprehensive longitudinal field survey conducted during the warm summer of 2006	• Histograms were used for the distribution of temperature measurements in the database • Logistic regression techniques were used • G-statistics differences were reported by using Nagelkerke's statistical tradition	Nicol and Humphreys's (2004) theorem was applied to assess occupants' thermal-comfort votes
Haghighat and Donnini (1998)	A total of 877 subjects participated in the questionnaire survey during the summer and winter of 1996	• Descriptive statistics • Pearson's correlation coefficient • Bar-chart diagram distribution	ASHRAE Standard 62-89R and ASHRAE Standard 55-92 were used for the benchmarking criteria
Brager et al. (2004)	A total of 1,000 survey responses were integrated into the dataset	• Descriptive statistics • Scatter plot diagrams • Bar-chart distribution • Linear regression analysis • Histograms	ASHRAE RP-884 and ASHRAE RP-1161 datasets were used for the benchmarking criteria

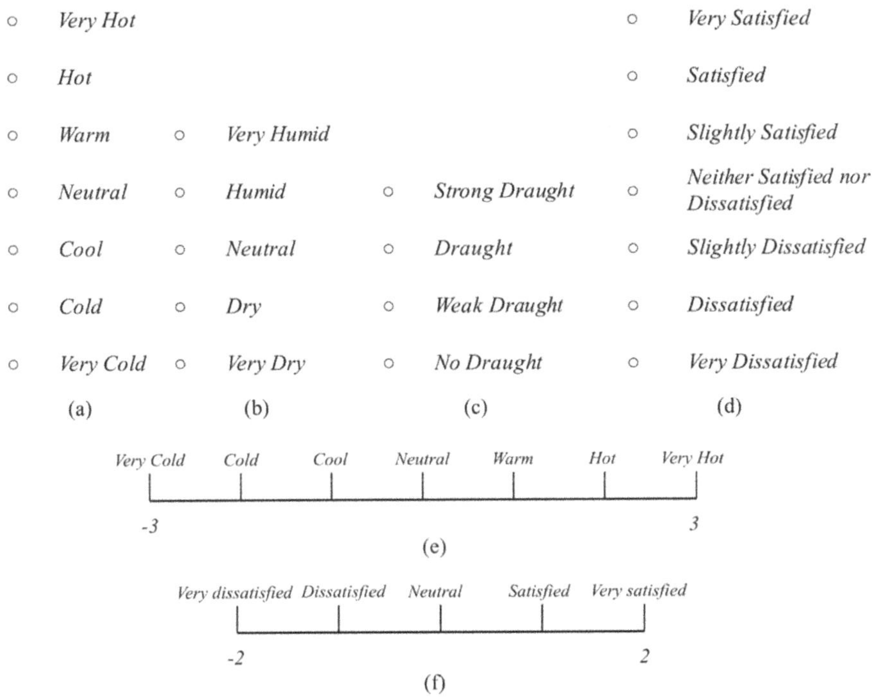

Figure 1.5 Thermal sensation scale on the questionnaire. (a) 7-point discrete thermal sensation scale; (b) 5-point discrete humidity sensation scale; (c) 4-point discrete draught sensation scale; (d) 7-point discrete thermal sensation scale; (e) 7-point continuous thermal sensation scale; (f) 5-point continuous thermal sensation scale. ***Source*:** Wang et al. (2018).

scholars who are not experts in thermal-comfort studies, Wang et al. (2018) recommend the most appropriate thermal sensation assessment criteria to be that shown in Figure 1.5.

Wang et al. (2018) used a climate chamber to control thermal variables and determine the most appropriate design for their thermal sensation scale. They provide a list of the acceptable variable types to be used when assessing any type of variable related to thermal-comfort studies, which is shown in Table 1.15.

Haldi and Robinson (2008) conducted a longitudinal field survey to assess occupants' thermal comfort. They conducted a multiple logistic regression analysis to identify neutral adaptive thermal comfort; the assessment criteria were presented by using the thermal scale band [−3, +3]. Another pilot study was conducted by Haghighat and Donnini (1998) to investigate the psycho-social factors affecting occupants' thermal sensation by using in situ measurements of indoor air environment conditions. Haghighat and Donnini used descriptive statistics to report the monitored indoor air environment conditions by using the continuous variable type. Haghighat and Donnini also used Pearson's correlation analysis to measure

Table 1.15 Variables for Thermal-Comfort Assessment

Subjective Thermal Indicators	*Points on Rating Scale*	*Subjective Rating Scale*
Thermal sensation	Fig. 1.15(a)	Discrete
Humidity sensation	Fig. 1.15(b)	Discrete
Draught sensation	Fig. 1.15(c)	Discrete
Thermal satisfaction	Fig. 1.15(d)	Discrete
Thermal sensation	Fig. 1.15(a)	Discrete
Thermal satisfaction	Fig. 1.15(d)	Discrete
Thermal sensation	Fig. 1.15(e)	Continuous
Humidity sensation	Fig. 1.15(b)	Discrete
Draught sensation	Fig. 1.15(c)	Discrete
Thermal satisfaction	Fig. 1.15(f)	Continuous

Source: Adapted from Wang et al. (2018).

occupants' thermal sensations and the measured/recorded variables for their statistical analysis. In their study, occupants' thermal sensation was coded by using the conventional tradition of [−3, +3] parameters. Additionally, Haghighat and Donnini (1998) presented the questionnaire survey items set out as ordinal variables in bar-chart formatting to demonstrate the survey findings according to their research hypothesis.

De Dear and Brager (2002) conducted a longitudinal survey by using a sample size of 105 for the warm season and 93 for the cool season to assess occupants' thermal sensation. By using this method, they were following a similar method of design to that developed by Haghighat and Donnini (1998) to report on-site measurement findings by using the environmental monitoring dataset as a continuous variable and occupants' thermal sensation votes coded as a continuous variable ranging between −3 and +3 for accuracy in their linear regression analysis.

The present study follows the conventional method of design that was developed and conducted by previous scholars. To identify the neutral adaptive thermal-comfort thresholds in the Eastern Mediterranean climate of Cyprus, the present study codes thermal sensation as [−3, +3] and conducts a Pearson's correlation analysis.

In this study, for exploring the relationships between the in situ measurements of environmental conditions and occupants' thermal sensation votes in order to calculate the acceptable 'neutral' thermal-comfort threshold level, the present study uses the [−3, +3] assessment criteria. According to Wang et al. (2018) thermal sensation variables can also be used as an ordinal variable type for thermal-comfort studies. This is the reason that the present study coded the variables that were asked of the subject respondents on a 7-point Likert scale as ordinal variables and conducted the Fisher's exact test for the statistical analysis. It should be noted that the present study adopted and applied the most recommended tradition in thermal-comfort studies to provide a universal design approach to contribute to the ASHRAE Global Thermal Comfort Database II (see Appendix G).

Book Content

The contribution of this book is a detailed record of the development of an STS conceptual framework. The novel methodological workflow was developed through a comprehensive, interdisciplinary study that informed the applicability of evidence-based retrofitting interventions as energy-policy design tools, and the case study RTB prototypes delineated in the present study will serve as examples in the development of future BES studies in academia and in practice. The chapters that comprise this book will guide the reader through a journey of research that inevitably leads to the conclusions in the final chapter, as listed in Table 1.16(a) and (b).

Table 1.16(a) The Narrative Structure of the Chapters

Chapters	*Descriptions*
Chapter 1	• It describes the knowledge gap and outlines the research aim, objectives and questions that informed every stage of the STS conceptual framework and the integration thereof into the existing body of knowledge and highlights the novelty of the study. • Information regarding the research context is presented to demonstrate the validity of the nationally representative archetype housing stock in NC and the household population that were selected for the present study.
Chapter 2	• It details a literature review of overheating risk of buildings and thermal-comfort studies across the globe in an effort to provide a comprehensive understanding of occupants' habitual adaptive behaviour on energy use. • The barriers to and motivation for the adoption of EEMs are also presented, followed by a comprehensive review of the literature related to the developed energy-policymaking framework and retrofitting schemes for existing housing stock that addresses current thermal-comfort design methods, overheating risks and BES procedures. • It describes the mixed-method research design that was utilised to study the internal, intrinsic motivation embedded in the context of the present study, specifically household socio-demographic characteristics and the influences thereof on thermal discomfort. • The rationale for each of the case study selections is then given, and the relevance thereof on the framework development for future energy policy is explained, and finally, the research limitations are outlined.
Chapter 3	• It reports the collated data from the feed-forward interviews with households to develop an evidence-based energy-policy framework to assess robust energy performance evaluations and certification schemes. • The RQs related to gender, age, socio-economic position, level of education, tenancy situation, employment status and health conditions of household members, the aim of which was to establish each participant's capacity to provide quality information for this research, are included and analysed. • The chapter concludes with a synthesised variation of the results and recommendations intended to help NC, the RoC and other EU member states address the EEG.

Table 1.16(b) The Narrative Structure of the Chapters (Continued)

Chapters	*Descriptions*
Chapter 4	• It presents the field-study findings on the effect of occupancy patterns and habitual household behaviour on home-energy performance. • Household socio-cultural contextual factors are described based on the survey data, particularly those that are related to energy-use awareness and home-energy systems, after which qualitative findings related to household feedback that are structured according to the conceptual framework are presented.
Chapter 5	• It presents the results of a longitudinal field study that assessed household thermal comfort within the framework of the development of adaptive thermal-comfort theories by previous scholars. • It describes the discourse on numeric experiments conducted to avoid risk of bias on the subject respondent's TSVs and thermal-preference votes (TPVs), and the impact thereof on understanding the correlations between the reaction of the human body and the built environment. • It identifies, in detail, a methodological framework for conducting a field investigation by including human data in the regression-forecasting analysis to develop an empirical case study approach.
Chapter 6	• It presents a novel methodology that was developed according to the in situ measurements of the building-fabric thermal performance to assess as-built energy models of case study RTBs. • The BES studies were investigated according to the recommended international benchmarks and criteria to assess overheating risks and occupant thermal comfort by taking the real-life household energy-use experiences into consideration.
Chapter 7	• It seeks to corroborate the empirical model by integrating the findings from the questionnaire survey and energy-assessment analyses to feed BES procedures. • The degree of overheating in each occupied space is discussed and evaluated in terms of impact of orientations and floor-level differences. Building-energy performance is then validated by running a DTS to develop a reliable assessment of the overall energy end-uses for space conditioning to optimise occupant thermal comfort. • It discusses the uncertain input parameters for the BES that quantitative modelling adopted for the energy assessment of dynamic thermal simulation findings in conjunction with occupants' socio-demographic characteristics, occupancy patterns, household size and environmental conditions recorded. • It presents the DTS analysis of six passive-cooling design strategies were developed, including the LCCA impact of households' energy use also was discussed.
Conclusion	• It makes conclusions based upon the observations of the preceding chapters. It also delineates implications for long-term holistic retrofitting programmes and policy design for evidence-based retrofitting design interventions with the implementation of the EPBDs in NC and other EU countries at the household levels and building levels.

Notes

1 The European EPISCOPE project provides a nationally representative online database to provide transparent, effective, energy-efficient retrofitting processes in the European housing sector: https://episcope.eu/welcome.
2 The ASHRAE Global Thermal Comfort Database II: http://www.comfortdatabase.com.
3 European standard EN 15251: https://standards.cen.eu/dyn/www/f?p=204:110:0::::FSP_PROJECT,FSP_ORG_ID:24552,6138&cs=1AAF5A672C76C7DC4F78CCAAE6304DE5D.
4 EU Project Smart Controls and Thermal Comfort: https://cordis.europa.eu/project/id/JOE3970066.
5 Data represents number of housing units built on Famagusta shoreline; this area is currently fenced off and closed for human habitation due to the 1974 division of the island. In literature, this city is also known as 'Varosha,' which translates to 'ghost town'; and it was the centre of international trade and tourism until 16 August 1974. The Turkish military currently controls this territory, which opened to pedestrians on 8 October 2020. Notably, this territory plays a prominent role in the negotiations and peace talks in international affairs of Cyprus.
6 This census data was recorded on 1 April 1973 before the outbreak of civil war on 20 July 1974. The data detailed the island's overall population and included all ethnic groups: Greek, Turkish, Maronite, Armenian, British and others. Data were extracted from the distribution of population by location during census years and is available in a reference document that was published in 1983 by the Chamber of Commerce and Industry.
7 As a result of the outbreak of intercommunal fighting, the Green Line that divided communities in Nicosia was established. Currently, this physical line still divides the northern and southern territories in the RoC.
8 SMEs in NC are predominantly regulated by family-owned or privately owned construction companies. The 1998 withdrawal of social-housing schemes led to increased demand for construction projects built by the SMEs.
9 The United Cyprus Republic (UCR), which is what the new proposed state of Cyprus will be called, is comprised of a set of institutions that were inspired by convocational models drawn from EU member states. Currently, unification negotiations continue in an effort to determine which constitutional arrangements would allow the two communities to live together in amity when the physical division of the island is ended.
10 World Köppen-Geiger climate classification data was reviewed; dataset is available to researchers.
11 Energy Plus is an open-source whole building-energy simulation program which is compatible with the weather data for more than 2,100 locations in the Energy Plus weather (i.e., .epw) format. Weather datasets available at https://energyplus.net/weather.
12 Data obtained from the Meteorological Office in NC: http://kktcmeteor.org.
13 Statistical data extracted from 2018 Eurostat data represent the RoC's energy-dependency rate. The energy network between the RoC and NC was connected to feed-in tariff due to power-cutting issues that were the result of increasing space-cooling and space-heating demands. According to the biliteral agreement, the entities are only allowed to share electricity.
14 According to the State Planning Organisation statistics in 2020, 2% of the NC population were social beneficiaries. This proportional percentage represents the vulnerable population who were given income benefits and received a monthly stipend of 3,500 TL between January of 2020 and March of 2021. At the time that this book was written, there was a 4,400 TL stipend on 31 March 2021, which was just after the second national lockdown that lasted from 27 January 2021 to 22 February 2021. Data was utilised in the present study as a baseline to identify the vulnerable population in the social-housing estate.
15 *Source*: https://www.calculator.net/sample-size-calculator.html.

References

Al-Momani, A. H. (2000). Construction delay: A quantitative analysis. *International Journal of Project Management*, *18*(1), 51–59. https://doi.org/10.1016/S0263-7863(98)00060-X

Altan, H. (2004). *Energy efficiency in housing: Drivers and barriers to improving energy efficiency and reducing carbon dioxide emissions in private sector housing*. PhD Thesis, University of Sheffield. Retrieved May 10, 2019, from http://isni.org/isni/0000000134185603

Anderson, B., Rushby, T., Bahaj, A., & James, P. (2020). Ensuring statistics have power: Guidance for designing, reporting and acting on electricity demand reduction and behaviour change programs. *Energy Research and Social Science*, *59*. https://doi.org/10.1016/j.erss.2019.101260

Ansari, N., & Seifi, A. (2013). A system dynamics model for analyzing energy consumption and CO_2 emission in Iranian cement industry under various production and export scenarios. *Energy Policy*, *58*, 75–89. https://doi.org/10.1016/j.enpol.2013.02.042

Arbolino, R., Boffardi, R., & Ioppolo, G. (2019). The effectiveness of European energy policy on the Italian system: Regional evidence from a hierarchical cluster analysis approach. *Energy Policy*, *132*, 47–61. https://doi.org/10.1016/j.enpol.2019.05.021

Baldoni, E., Coderoni, S., D'Orazio, M., Di Giuseppe, E., & Esposti, R. (2019). The role of economic and policy variables in energy-efficient retrofitting assessment: A stochastic life cycle costing methodology. *Energy Policy*, *129*, 1207–1219. https://doi.org/10.1016/j.enpol.2019.03.018

Ballarini, I., Corgnati, S. P., & Corrado, V. (2014). Use of reference buildings to assess the energy saving potentials of the residential building stock: The experience of TABULA project. *Energy Policy*, *68*, 273–284. https://doi.org/10.1016/j.enpol.2014.01.027

Balnac, K., Bokhoree, C., & Bassi, A. (2009). A system dynamics model of the mauritian power sector. *Proceedings of the 27th International Conference of the System Dynamics Society*, *21*.

Barone, G., Buonomano, A., Calise, F., Forzano, C., & Palombo, A. (2019). Building to vehicle to building concept toward a novel zero energy paradigm: Modelling and case studies. *Renewable and Sustainable Energy Reviews*, *101*, 625–648. https://doi.org/10.1016/j.rser.2018.11.003

Barratt, M. J., Ferris, J. A., Zahnow, R., Palamar, J. J., Maier, L. J., & Winstock, A. R. (2017). Moving on from representativeness: Testing the utility of the global drug survey. *Substance Abuse: Research and Treatment*, *11*. https://doi.org/10.1177/1178221817716391

Beręsewicz, M. (2017). A two-step procedure to measure representativeness of internet data sources. *International Statistical Review*, *85*(3), 473–493. https://doi.org/10.1111/insr.12217

Bertino, S. (1998). A measure of representativeness of a sample for inferential purposes. *International Statistical Review*, *74*(2), 149–159. https://doi.org/10.1111/j.1751-5823.2006.tb00166.x

Bertino, S. (2006). A measure of representativeness of a sample for inferential purposes. *International Statistical Review*, *74*(2), 149–159. https://doi.org/10.1111/j.1751-5823.2006.tb00166.x

Bertoldi, P., & Mosconi, R. (2020). Do energy efficiency policies save energy? A new approach based on energy policy indicators (in the EU Member States). *Energy Policy*, *139*. https://doi.org/10.1016/j.enpol.2020.111320

Bonett, D., & Wright, T. (2000). Sample size requirements for estimating Pearson, Kendall and Spearman correlations. *Psychometrika*, *65*(1), 23–28.

Borrego, M., Douglas, E. P., & Amelink, C. T. (2009). Quantitative, qualitative, and mixed research methods in engineering education. *Journal of Engineering Education*, *98*(1), 53–66. https://doi.org/10.1002/j.2168-9830.2009.tb01005.x

Bracke, W., Laverge, J., Van Den Bossche, N., & Janssens, A. (2016). Durability and measurement uncertainty of airtightness in extremely airtight dwellings. *International Journal of Ventilation*, *14*, 383–393. https://doi.org/10.1080/14733315.2016.11684095

Brager, G., Paliaga, G., & De Dear, R. (2004). UC Berkeley envelope systems title operable windows, personal control and occupant comfort. *Permalink*. https://escholarship.org/uc/item/4x57v1pf; www.ashrae.org

Brimicombe, A., & Cafe, R. (2012). Beware, win or lose: Domestic violence and the World Cup. *Significance*, *9*(5), 32–35. https://doi.org/10.1111/j.1740-9713.2012.00606.x

Brimicombe, A. J., & Li, Y. (2007). Improving geocoding rates in preparation for crime data analysis. *International Journal of Police Science & Management*, *9*(1), 80–92. https://doi.org/10.1350/ijps.2007.9.1.80

Buessler, S., Badariotti, D., & Weber, C. (2017). Evaluating the complex governance arrangements surrounding energy retrofitting programs: The case of collective ownership buildings in France. *Energy Research and Social Science*, *32*, 131–148. https://doi.org/10.1016/j.erss.2017.05.007

Caro, R., & Sendra, J. J. (2021). Are the dwellings of historic Mediterranean cities cold in winter? A field assessment on their indoor environment and energy performance. *Energy and Buildings*, *230*. https://doi.org/10.1016/j.enbuild.2020.110567

CEA - Cyprus Electricity Authority of North Cyprus. (2018). *Annual report of financial resources and economic indicators on energy in Northern Cyprus*. Retrieved February 2021.

CEA - Cyprus Electricity Authority of North Cyprus. (2020a). *Annual report of energy consumer statistics*. Retrieved February 2021, from https://www.kibtek.com/statistikler/

CEA—Cyprus Electricity Authority of North Cyprus. (2020b). *Annual report of energy indicators*. Retrieved February 2021, from https://www.kibtek.com/statistikler/

Çelik, T., Kamali, S., & Arayici, Y. (2017). Social cost in construction projects. *Environmental Impact Assessment Review*. Advance online publication. https://doi.org/10.1016/j.eiar.2017.03.001

Chasalow, K., & Levy, K. (2021). Representativeness in statistics, politics, and machine learning. In *FAccT 2021 - Proceedings of the 2021 ACM conference on fairness, accountability, and transparency* (pp. 77–89). Association for Computing Machinery, Inc. https://doi.org/10.1145/3442188.3445872

Cockbill, S. A., Mitchell, V., & May, A. J. (2020). Householders as designers? Generating future energy services with United Kingdom home occupiers. *Energy Research and Social Science*, *69*. https://doi.org/10.1016/j.erss.2020.101615

Constantinidou, K., Zittis, G., & Hadjinicolaou, P. (2019). Variations in the simulation of climate change impact indices due to different land surface schemes over the Mediterranean, Middle East and Northern Africa. *Atmosphere*, *10*(1, 20–27).

Coyle, R. G. (1977). *Management system dynamics*. Chichester: Wiley.

Cozza, S., Chambers, J., & Patel, M. K. (2020). Measuring the thermal energy performance gap of labelled residential buildings in Switzerland. *Energy Policy*, *137*. https://doi.org/10.1016/j.enpol.2019.111085

Creswell, J. W. and Plano Clark, V. L. (2007). *Designing and conducting mixed methods research*. New York: SAGE Publications Inc.

Cristino, T. M., Lotufo, F. A., Delinchant, B., Wurtz, F., & Faria Neto, A. (2021). A comprehensive review of obstacles and drivers to building energy-saving technologies and their association with research themes, types of buildings, and geographic regions.

Renewable and Sustainable Energy Reviews.Elsevier Ltd. https://doi.org/10.1016/j.rser.2020.110191

Cyprus Meteorological Service. (2020). *Meteorological statistical data for cyprus; the annual report*. Nicosia, Cyprus: Department of Meteorology. Retrieved October 3, 2020.

Dascalaki, E. G., Balaras, C. A., Kontoyiannidis, S., & Droutsa, K. G. (2016). Modeling energy refurbishment scenarios for the Hellenic residential building stock towards the 2020 & 2030 targets. *Energy and Buildings*, *132*, 74–90. https://doi.org/10.1016/j.enbuild.2016.06.003

Davis, S., & Durbach, I. (2010). Modelling household responses to energy efficiency interventions via system dynamics and survey data. *ORiON*, *26*(2). https://doi.org/10.5784/26-2-88

Davis, S., & Durbach, I. (2011). Modelling household responses to energy efficiency interventions via system dynamics and survey data. *ORiON*, *26*(2). https://doi.org/10.5784/26-2-88

De Dear, R., & Brager, G. S. (2001). The adaptive model of thermal comfort and energy conservation in the built environment. *International Journal of Biometeorology*, *45*(2), 100–108. https://doi.org/10.1007/s004840100093

De Dear, R. J. and Brager, G. S. (2002). Thermal comfort in naturally ventilated buildings: Revisions to ASHRAE standard 55. *Energy and Buildings*, *34*(6), 549–561.

Desogus, G., Di Pilla, L., Mura, S., Pisano, G. L., & Ricciu, R. (2013). Economic efficiency of social housing thermal upgrade in Mediterranean climate. *Energy and Buildings*, *57*, 354–360. https://doi.org/10.1016/j.enbuild.2012.11.016

Dubois, U., & Meier, H. (2016). Energy affordability and energy inequality in Europe: Implications for policymaking. *Energy Research and Social Science*, *18*, 21–35. https://doi.org/10.1016/j.erss.2016.04.015

Dyner, I., Smith, R. & Pena, G. (1995). System dynamics modelling for energy efficiency analysis and management. *Journal of Operational Research*, *46*, 1163–1173.

Dyner, I., Smith, R., & Pena, G. (1998). System dynamics modelling for energy efficiency analysis and management. *Journal of the Operations Research*, *46*, 1163–1173

Eurostat. (2018). *Energy production and imports: Distribution of energy dependency rate for all products in EU-27 member states*. Retrieved January 2021, from https://ec.europa.eu/eurostat/statistics-explained/index.php?title=Energy_production_and_imports#More_than_half_of_EU_energy_needs_are_covered_by_imports

Evcil, A., & Vafaei, L. E. (2017). A comparative survey of the energy performances of dwellings across Cyprus. *Energy and Buildings*, *148*, 15–22. https://doi.org/10.1016/j.enbuild.2017.05.008

Fanger, P. O. (1970). *Thermal comfort analysis and applications in environmental engineering*. Copenhagen: Danish Technical Press.

Fincham, J. E. (2008). Response rates and responsiveness for surveys, standards, and the journal. *American Journal of Pharmaceutical Education*, *72*(2), 1–3.

Fokaides, P. A., Christoforou, E. A., & Kalogirou, S. A. (2014). Legislation driven scenarios based on recent construction advancements towards the achievement of nearly zero energy dwellings in the southern European country of Cyprus. *Energy*, *66*, 588–597. https://doi.org/10.1016/j.energy.2013.12.073

Fokaides, P. A., Polycarpou, K., & Kalogirou, S. (2017). The impact of the implementation of the European Energy Performance of Buildings Directive on the European building stock: The case of the Cyprus Land Development Corporation. *Energy Policy*, *111*, 1–8. https://doi.org/10.1016/j.enpol.2017.09.009

Forrester, J. W. (1961). *Industrial dynamics*. Cambridge, MA: MIT Press.

Forrester, J. W. (1971). *Industrial dynamics*. Cambridge, MA: MIT Press.
Forrester, J. W., Mass, N. J., & Ryan, C. J. (1976). The system dynamics national model: Understanding socio-economic behavior and policy alternatives. *Technological Forecasting and Social Change*, *9*(1–2), 51–68. https://doi.org/10.1016/0040-1625(76)90044-5
Forrester, J. W. (1992). Policies, decisions and information sources for modeling. *European Journal of Operational Research*, *59*(1), 42–63. https://doi.org/10.1016/0377-2217(92)90006-U
Forrester, J. W. (1994). System dynamics, systems thinking, and soft OR. *System Dynamics Review*, *10*(2–3), 245–256. https://doi.org/10.1002/sdr.4260100211
Forrester, J. W. (1998). *Designing the future by designing the future* (pp. 1–11). Sevilla: Universidad de Sevilla.
Forrester, J. W. (2003). Dynamic models of economic systems and industrial organizations. *System Dynamics Review*, *19*(4), 329–345. https://doi.org/10.1002/sdr.284
Forrester, J. W. (2007). System dynamics: A personal view of the first fifty years. *System Dynamics Review*, *23*(2–3), 345–358. https://doi.org/10.1002/sdr.382
Forrester, J. W. (2009). *Learning through system dynamics as preparation for the 21st century working in K-12 education to develop systems citizens permission granted for copying and for electronic distribution for non-commercial educational purposes* (pp. 1–24). www.clexchange.org
Forrester, J. W. (2013). Economic theory for the new millennium (2003). *System Dynamics Review*, *29*(1), 26–41. https://doi.org/10.1002/sdr.1490
Forrester, J. W. (2016). Learning through system dynamics as preparation for the 21st century. In*System dynamics review*. John Wiley and Sons Ltd. https://doi.org/10.1002/sdr.1571
Forrester, J. W., Mass, N. J., & Ryan, C. J. (1976). The system dynamics national model: Understanding socio-economic behavior and policy alternatives. *Technological Forecasting and Social Change*, *9*(1–2), 51–68. https://doi.org/10.1016/0040-1625(76)90044-5
Gabe, J. (2016). An empirical comparison of voluntary and mandatory building energy performance disclosure outcomes. *Energy Policy*, *96*, 680–687. https://doi.org/10.1016/j.enpol.2016.06.044
Garrett, H. E. (1942). The representativeness of a sample. *The American Journal of Psychology*, *55*(4), 580–581. http://www.jstor.org/stable/1417131
Gaspar, A. R. (2017). A review on current advances in the energy and environmental performance of buildings towards a more sustainable built environment. *Renewable and Sustainable Energy Reviews*. Advance online publication. https://doi.org/10.1016/j.rser.2017.04.027
Giannakis, E., Bruggeman, A., Poulou, D., Zoumides, C., & Eliades, M. (2016). Linear parks along urban rivers: Perceptions of thermal comfort and climate change adaptation in Cyprus. *Sustainability (Switzerland)*, *8*(10). https://doi.org/10.3390/su8101023
Giannakopoulos, C., Psiloglou, B., Lemesios, G., Xevgenos, D., Papadaskalopoulou, C., Karali, A., … Loizidou, M. (2016). Climate change impacts, vulnerability and adaptive capacity of the electrical energy sector in Cyprus. *Regional Environmental Change*, *16*(7), 1891–1904. https://doi.org/10.1007/s10113-015-0885-z
Gonzalez-Caceres, A., Lassen, A. K., & Nielsen, T. R. (2020). Barriers and challenges of the recommendation list of measures under the EPBD scheme: A critical review. *Energy and Buildings*. Advance online publication. https://doi.org/10.1016/j.enbuild.2020.110065
Goodchild, B., Ambrose, A., & Maye-Banbury, A. (2017). Storytelling as oral history: Revealing the changing experience of home heating in England. *Energy Research and Social Science*, *31*, 137–144. https://doi.org/10.1016/j.erss.2017.06.009

Griffiths, I. D. (1990). Thermal comfort in buildings with passive solar features: Field studies. *Report to the Commission of the European Communities*, EN3S–090.

Grillone, B., Danov, S., Sumper, A., Cipriano, J., & Mor, G. (2020). A review of deterministic and data-driven methods to quantify energy efficiency savings and to predict retrofitting scenarios in buildings. *Renewable and Sustainable Energy Reviews*. Advance online publication. https://doi.org/10.1016/j.rser.2020.110027

Guerra-Santin, O., Boess, S., Konstantinou, T., Romero Herrera, N., Klein, T., & Silvester, S. (2017). Designing for residents: Building monitoring and co-creation in social housing renovation in the Netherlands. *Energy Research and Social Science*, *32*, 164–179. https://doi.org/10.1016/j.erss.2017.03.009

Haghighat, F., & Donnini, G. (1998). Impact of psycho-social factors on perception of the indoor air environment studies in 12 office buildings. *Building and Environment*, *34*(4), 479–503. https://doi.org/10.1016/S0360-1323(98)00034-1

Haldi, F., & Robinson, D. (2008). On the behaviour and adaptation of office occupants. *Building and Environment*, *43*(12), 2163–2177. https://doi.org/10.1016/j.buildenv.2008.01.003

Haley, B., Gaede, J., Winfield, M., & Love, P. (2020). From utility demand side management to low-carbon transitions: Opportunities and challenges for energy efficiency governance in a new era. *Energy Research and Social Science*. Advance online publication. https://doi.org/10.1016/j.erss.2019.101312

Hamborg, S., Meya, J. N., Eisenack, K., & Raabe, T. (2020). Rethinking resilience: A cross-epistemic resilience framework for interdisciplinary energy research. *Energy Research and Social Science*, *59*. https://doi.org/10.1016/j.erss.2019.101285

Hirsch, L. S., & O'Donnell, A. M. (2001). Representativeness in statistical reasoning: Identifying and assessing misconceptions. *Journal of Statistics Education*, *9*(2). https://doi.org/10.1080/10691898.2001.11910655

Hitchcock, G. (1993). An integrated framework for energy use and behaviour in the domestic sector. *Energy Build*, *20*, 151–157. https://doi.org/10.1016/0378-7788(93)90006-G

Hu, J. and Kohler-Hausmann, I. (2020). What's sex got to do with machine learning? In *Proceedings of the 2020 conference on fairness, accountability, and transparency (Barcelona, Spain) (FAT* '20)*. New York, NY: Association for Computing Machinery, p. 513. https://doi.org/10.1145/3351095.3375674

Jensen, A. (1926). Report on the representative method in statistics. *Bulletin de l'Institut international de statistique*, *22*(1), 359–438.

Johnstone, P., Rogge, K. S., Kivimaa, P., Fratini, C. F., Primmer, E., & Stirling, A. (2020). Waves of disruption in clean energy transitions: Sociotechnical dimensions of system disruption in Germany and the United Kingdom. *Energy Research and Social Science*, *59*. https://doi.org/10.1016/j.erss.2019.101287

Katircioglu, S. T., Feridun, M., & Kilinc, C. (2014). Estimating tourism-induced energy consumption and CO_2 emissions: The case of Cyprus. *Renewable and Sustainable Energy Reviews*. Advance online publication. https://doi.org/10.1016/j.rser.2013.09.004

Katsanos, D., Retalis, A., & Michaelides, S. (2016). Validation of a high-resolution precipitation database (CHIRPS) over Cyprus for a 30-year period. *Atmospheric Research*, *169*, 459–464. https://doi.org/10.1016/j.atmosres.2015.05.015

Katsanos, D., Retalis, A., Tymvios, F., & Michaelides, S. (2018). Study of extreme wet and dry periods in Cyprus using climatic indices. *Atmospheric Research*, *208*, 88–93. https://doi.org/10.1016/j.atmosres.2017.09.002

Kiaer, A. N. (1976). *Den repræsentative undersøgelsesmethode = The representative method of statistical surveys*. Oslo: Aschehoug.

Knight, P., Biewald, B., & Takahashi, K. (2022). The cost of energy efficiency programs: Estimates from utility-reported datasets. *Energy, 239*. https://doi.org/10.1016/j.energy.2021.122448

Konold, C., Pollatsek, A., Well, A. D., Hendrickson, J., & Lipson, A. (1990). The origin of inconsistencies in probabilistic reasoning of novices. Presented at the third international conference on teaching statistics, Dunedin, New Zealand.

Kottek, M., Grieser, J., Beck, C., Rudolf, B., & Rubel, F. (2006). World map of the Köppen-Geiger climate classification updated. *Meteorologische Zeitschrift, 15*(3), 259–263. https://doi.org/10.1127/0941-2948/2006/0130

Kruskal, W., and Mosteller, F. (1980). Representative sampling, IV: The history of the concept in statistics, 1895–1939. *International Statistical Review/Revue Internationale de Statistique, 48*(2), 169–195. http://www. jstor.org/stable/1403151

Kylili, A., Fokaides, P. A., Christou, P., & Kalogirou, S. A. (2014). Infrared thermography (IRT) applications for building diagnostics: A review. *Applied Energy*. Advance online publication.https://doi.org/10.1016/j.apenergy.2014.08.005

Li, X., & Yao, R. (2021). Modelling heating and cooling energy demand for building stock using a hybrid approach. *Energy and Buildings, 235*. https://doi.org/10.1016/j.enbuild.2021.110740

Li, Y., & Brimicombe, A. J. (2008). Scenario-based small area population modelling for social infrastructure planning (pp. 2–7).

Little, R. J. A., & Rubin, D. B. (2002). *Statistical analysis with missing data* (2nd ed.). New York: Wiley.

Ma, Z., Cooper, P., Daly, D., & Ledo, L. (2012). Existing building retrofits: Methodology and state-of-the-art. *Energy and Buildings, 55*, 889–902. https://doi.org/10.1016/j.enbuild.2012.08.018

Makri, A. (2018). *Cyprus asserts itself as regional hub for climate-change research news.* Nature Publishing Group. https://doi.org/10.1038/d41586-018-05528-9

Marsh, H. W., Balla, J. R., & McDonald, R. P. (1988). Goodness-of-fit indexes in confirmatory factor analysis: The effect of sample size. *Psychological Bulletin, 103*(3), 391–410. https://doi.org/10.1037/0033-2909.103.3.391

McNemar, Q. (1940). Sampling in psychological research. *Psychological Bulletin, 37*(6), 331–365. https://doi.org/10.1037/h0063476

Milstein, B., Homer, J., & Hirsch, G. (2010). Analyzing national health reform strategies with a dynamic simulation model. *American Journal of Public Health, 100*(5), 811–819. https://doi.org/10.2105/AJPH.2009.174490

Morecroft, J. D. W. (1988). System dynamics and microworlds for policymakers. *European Journal of Operational Research, 35*, 301–320.

Morton, A., Reeves, A., Bull, R., & Preston, S. (2020). Empowering and engaging European building users for energy efficiency. *Energy Research and Social Science, 70*. https://doi.org/10.1016/j.erss.2020.101772

Motawa, I., & Oladokun, M. G. (2015). Structural equation modelling of energy consumption in buildings. *International Journal of Energy Sector Management, 9*(4), 435–450. https://doi.org/10.1108/IJESM-11-2014-0004

Nabitz, L., & Hirzel, S. (2019). Transposing the requirements of the energy efficiency directive on mandatory energy audits for large companies: A policy-cycle-based review of the national implementation in the EU-28 member states. *Energy Policy*, 548–561. https://doi.org/10.1016/j.enpol.2017.12.016

Nematchoua, M. K., Marie-Reine Nishimwe, A., & Reiter, S. (2021). Towards nearly zero-energy residential neighbourhoods in the European Union: A case study. *Renewable and Sustainable Energy Reviews*, *135*. https://doi.org/10.1016/j.rser.2020.110198

Nicol, F. (2004). Adaptive thermal comfort standards in the hot-humid tropics. In *Energy and buildings* (Vol. 36, pp. 628–637). https://doi.org/10.1016/j.enbuild.2004.01.016

Nicol, F. (2017). Temperature and adaptive comfort in heated, cooled and free-running dwellings. *Building Research & Information*, *45*(7), 730–744. https://doi.org/10.1080/09613218.2017.1283922

Oktay, D. (2002). The quest for urban identity in the changing context of the city Northern Cyprus. *Cities*, *19*(4), 261–271. https://doi.org/10.1016/S0264-2751(02)00023-9

Oladokun, M. G., & Odesola, I. A. (2015). Household energy consumption and carbon emissions for sustainable cities – A critical review of modelling approaches. *International Journal of Sustainable Built Environment*, *4*(2), 231–247. https://doi.org/10.1016/j.ijsbe.2015.07.005

Owen, S. V., Toepperwein, M. A., Pruski, L. A., Blalock, C. L., Liu, Y., Marshall, C. E., … Lichtenstein, M. J. (2007). Psychometric reevaluation of the Women in Science Scale (WiSS). *Journal of Research in Science Teaching*, *44*(10), 1461–1478. https://doi.org/10.1002/tea.20187

Ozarisoy, B. (2022). Energy effectiveness of passive cooling design strategies to reduce the impact of long-term heatwaves on occupants' thermal comfort in Europe: Climate change and mitigation. *Journal of Cleaner Production*. Advance online publication. https://doi.org/10.1016/j.jclepro.2021.129675

Ozarisoy, B., & Altan, H. (2017a). Energy performance development of non-regulated retrofit mass housing estates in Northern Cyprus. *Design Journal*, *20*(Suppl 1), S1765–S1781. https://doi.org/10.1080/14606925.2017.1352697

Ozarisoy, B., & Altan, H. (2017b). Adoption of energy design strategies for retrofitting mass housing estates in Northern Cyprus. *Sustainability (Switzerland)*, *9*(8), 1477. https://doi.org/10.3390/su9081477

Ozarisoy, B., & Altan, H. (2018). Low-energy design strategies for retrofitting existing residential buildings in Cyprus. *Proceedings of the Institution of Civil Engineers: Engineering Sustainability*, *172*(5), 241–255. https://doi.org/10.1680/jensu.17.00061

Ozay, N. (2005). A comparative study of climatically responsive house design at various periods of Northern Cyprus architecture. *Building and Environment*, *40*(6), 841–852. https://doi.org/10.1016/j.buildenv.2004.08.024

Panayiotou, G., Charalambous, S., Vlochos, S., Kyriacou, O., Theofanous, E. & Flippou, T. (2013). Increase of the energy efficiency of 25 low-income households in Cyprus Increase of the energy efficiency of 25 low-income. https://doi.org/10.13140/2.1.4935.3607

Pelenur, M. (2013). *Retrofitting the domestic built environment: Investigating household perspectives towards energy efficiency technologies.* Unpublished PhD Thesis, University of Cambridge, United Kingdom. Retrieved February 2, 2021, from https://doi.org/10.17863/CAM.14069

Pelenur, M. J., & Cruickshank, H. J. (2012). Closing the energy efficiency gap: A study linking demographics with barriers to adopting energy efficiency measures in the home. *Energy*, *47*(1), 348–357. https://doi.org/10.1016/j.energy.2012.09.058

Pelenur, M. J., & Cruickshank, H. J. (2013). Closing the energy efficiency gap: A study linking demographics with barriers to adopting energy efficiency measures in the home. *Energy*, *47*(1), 348–357. https://doi.org/10.1016/j.energy.2012.09.058

Pulhan, A., Yorucu, V., & Sinan Evcan, N. (2020). Global energy market dynamics and natural gas development in the Eastern Mediterranean region. *Utilities Policy*, *64*, 101040. https://doi.org/10.1016/j.jup.2020.101040

Pulhan, H., & Numan, I (2005). The transitional space in the traditional urban settlement of Cyprus. *Journal of Architectural and Planning Research*, *22*, 160–178.

Pyrgou, A., Hadjinicolaou, P., & Santamouris, M. (2020). Urban-rural moisture contrast: Regulator of the urban heat island and heatwaves' synergy over a mediterranean city. *Environmental Research*, *182*, 109102. https://doi.org/10.1016/j.envres.2019.109102

Ranganath, B. J. and Rodrigues, L. L. R. (2008). *System dynamics: Theory and case studies*. New Delhi: International Publishing House.

Renner, A., & Giampietro, M. (2020). Socio-technical discourses of European electricity decarbonization: Contesting narrative credibility and legitimacy with quantitative storytelling. *Energy Research and Social Science*, *59*, 101279. https://doi.org/10.1016/j.erss.2019.101279

Richardson, G. P. (1996). Problems for the future of system dynamics. *System Dynamics Review*, *12*(2), 141–157. https://doi.org/10.1002/(sici)1099-1727(199622)12:2<141:aid-sdr101>3.3.co;2-f

Roberts, E. B. (1978). System dynamics: An introduction. In E. B. Roberts (Ed.), *Managerial applications of system dynamics*. Waltham: Pegasus Communications Inc.

Roberts, E. B. (1983). System dynamics—An introduction. In E. B. Roberts (Ed.), *Managerial applications of system dynamics*. Waltham: Pegasus Communications Inc.

Rupp, R. F., Parkinson, T., Kim, J., Toftum, J., & de Dear, R. (2021). The impact of occupant's thermal sensitivity on adaptive thermal comfort model. *Building and Environment*. Advance online publication. https://doi.org/10.1016/j.buildenv.2021.108517

Saka, A. B., & Chan, D. W. M. (2020). Knowledge, skills and functionalities requirements for quantity surveyors in building information modelling (BIM) work environment: An international Delphi study. *Architectural Engineering and Design Management*, *16*(3), 227–246. https://doi.org/10.1080/17452007.2019.1651247

Santin, O. G. (2011). Behavioural patterns and user profiles related to energy consumption for heating. *Energy and Buildings*, *43*(10), 2662–2672. https://doi.org/10.1016/j.enbuild.2011.06.024

Schmill, M. D., Gordon, L. M., Magliocca, N. R., Ellis, E. C., & Oates, T. (2014). GLOBE: Analytics for assessing global representativeness. In *Proceedings - 5th international conference on computing for geospatial research and application, COM.Geo 2014* (pp. 25–32). Institute of Electrical and Electronics Engineers Inc. https://doi.org/10.1109/COM.Geo.2014.21

Schouten, B., Cobben, F., & Bethlehem, J. (2009). Indicators for the representativeness of survey response. *Survey Methodology*, *35*(1), 101–113.

Schumacker, R. E. (2017). Chi-square test for categorical data. In *Learning statistics using R* (pp. 207–221). SAGE Publications, Inc. https://doi.org/10.4135/9781506300160.n11

Shaughnessy, J. M. (1977). Research in probability and statistics: Reflections and directions. In D. Grouws (Ed.), *Handbook of research for mathematics education* (pp. 115–147). New York: Macmillan.

Sovacool, B. K., Martiskainen, M., Osborn, J., Anaam, A., & Lipson, M. (2020). From thermal comfort to conflict: The contested control and usage of domestic smart heating in the United Kingdom. *Energy Research and Social Science*, *69*, 101566. https://doi.org/10.1016/j.erss.2020.101566

SPO-State Planning Organization of North Cyprus. (2009). Gross National Product Statistics [Online]. Available at: https://www.devplan.org/index_en.html [Accessed: December 2020].

SPO-State Planning Organization of North Cyprus. (2020). *Gross national product statistics*. Retrieved December 2020, from https://www.devplan.org/index_en.html

Spyridaki, N. A., Stavrakas, V., Dendramis, Y., & Flamos, A. (2020). Understanding technology ownership to reveal adoption trends for energy efficiency measures in the Greek residential sector. *Energy Policy*, *140*, 11413. https://doi.org/10.1016/j.enpol.2020.111413

Thonipara, A., Runst, P., Ochsner, C., & Bizer, K. (2019). Energy efficiency of residential buildings in the European Union – An exploratory analysis of cross-country consumption patterns. *Energy Policy*, *129*, 1156–1167. https://doi.org/10.1016/j.enpol.2019.03.003

Tian, W., Heo, Y., de Wilde, P., Li, Z., Yan, D., Park, C. S., … Augenbroe, G. (2018). A review of uncertainty analysis in building energy assessment. *Renewable and Sustainable Energy Reviews*. Advance online publication. https://doi.org/10.1016/j.rser.2018.05.029

Wang, Z., de Dear, R., Luo, M., Lin, B., He, Y., Ghahramani, A., & Zhu, Y. (2018). Individual difference in thermal comfort: A literature review. *Building and Environment*, *138*, 181–193.https://doi.org/10.1016/j.buildenv.2018.04.040

Weber, L. (1997). Some reflections on barriers to the efficient use of energy. *Energy Policy*, *25*, 833–835. https://doi.org/10.1016/S0301-4215(97)00084-0

Willcoxson, L., & Chatham, R. (2006). Testing the accuracy of the IT stereotype: Profiling IT managers' personality and behavioural characteristics. *Information and Management*, *43*(6), 697–705. https://doi.org/10.1016/j.im.2004.04.009

Wolstenholme, E. F. (1990). *System enquiry: A system dynamics approach*. Chichester: Wiley.

Zachariadis, T., & Hadjinicolaou, P. (2014). The effect of climate change on electricity needs - A case study from Mediterranean Europe. *Energy*, *76*, 899–910. https://doi.org/10.1016/j.energy.2014.09.001

Zittis, G., Bruggeman, A., & Camera, C. (2020). 21st century projections of extreme precipitation indicators for Cyprus. *Atmosphere*, *11*(4). https://doi.org/10.3390/atmos11040343

Zhang, X., Wu, Y., Shen, L., & Skitmore, M. (2014). A prototype system dynamic model for assessing the sustainability of construction projects. *International Journal of Project Management*, *32*(1), 66–76. https://doi.org/10.1016/j.ijproman.2013.01.009

2 A Novel Methodological Framework in Energy Policy

Introduction

This chapter delineated the extent literature review that was conducted to properly identify the knowledge gap related to the integration of a socio-technical systems (STS) conceptual framework in a building-energy simulation (BES) study; to address the energy-efficiency gap related to building overheating risks, the thermal comfort of occupants and the energy use of households; and to explore the novelty of integrating energy-assessment studies with an energy audit and thermal imaging, an area where little research has been undertaken. To fulfil the research aims and objectives, this chapter explained why household socio-demographic characteristics can be implemented and used to reduce energy consumption and optimise household thermal comfort by integrating international assessment criteria into the BES; this research gap has not been addressed in previous similar studies. The literature reviewed in this chapter outlined three key areas relevant to filling the knowledge gap in building-performance evaluations (BPEs): overheating-risk assessment, thermal comfort and occupant behaviour in energy modelling. The Integrated Environmental Solutions (energy-simulation tool) IES software suite was selected for an energy-assessment analysis due to its accuracy.

Several scholars have conducted research to ensure comfortable indoor conditions and to predict the comfort level of a given room in line with the standards set forth in the EU's *CEN BS EN 15251: Indoor Environmental Input Parameters for Design and Assessment of Energy Performance of Buildings*; specifically, these studies sought to address indoor air quality, the thermal environment, lighting and acoustics. A considerable body of literature has been published to evaluate assessment methods for the summer performance of residential buildings that are not air-conditioned. Everything we know about optimising occupant thermal comfort is based on empirical studies that investigated the overheating risks of indoor spaces in light of climate change, which will inevitably result in increased temperatures and more frequent extreme weather events, such as heat waves. Several studies also documented the lack of benchmarks between input parameters and occupant behaviour to measure occupants' thermal comfort and assess building overheating risks.

The literature review demonstrated that integration of the STS into energy-modelling studies is not clearly understood, and that a longitudinal field-study

DOI: 10.4324/9781003393092-3

investigation to calculate and assess the predicted mean vote (PMV) and predicted percentage of dissatisfied (PPD) indices would be worthwhile. Moreover, the Chartered Institution of Building Services Engineers (CIBSE) TM59 Overheating Task Force noted in 2017 that a new design method was needed to define overheating as it relates to occupant thermal comfort, especially in residential buildings without mechanical cooling systems; this approach must follow the methodology and recommendations of BS EN 15251 to determine whether an occupied residential building should be classified as being in danger of becoming overheated, particularly in the summer. The literature review also revealed a lack of data that resulted in a gap between the as-designed and as-built performances of existing housing stock. Consequently, a novel methodology should be developed according to in situ measurements, which include household indoor-air temperature records integrated with thermal-imaging surveys and heat-flux measurements of building-fabric elements, in addition to concurrently monitored environmental conditions and a review of households' energy bills.

This chapter presents the research methodology by explaining the rationale for the present study and the conceptual framework that was developed to address the energy-efficiency gap (EEG) while optimising occupant thermal comfort. The case study residential buildings are described and the research design model that was adopted to conduct field surveys is explained. The present study employed a mixed methodology of qualitative and quantitative data analyses to examine the influence of the socio-technical systems (STS) approach through a building-modelling simulation based on the archetype residential buildings to develop energy policies that are in accordance with the Energy Performance of Buildings Directive (EPBD) objectives. Furthermore, the selection criteria of base-case representative residential tower blocks (RTBs) are explained and the data collection methods that were used, fieldwork procedures and data analysis and interpretation are presented. The mixed-method research approach that was developed through a comprehensive, multidisciplinary research design model is described, and some limitations of the present study are delineated. Finally, issues related to building-energy modelling and validation techniques are discussed.

Building-Energy Performance Gap

The review articles were filtered from a list of journal articles and conference proceedings that were published between 1990 and June of 2019. The source of the selection of articles used for the analysis was the 'Web of Science Core Collection,' which is maintained by Clarivate Analytics. The main procedure involves creating a design for a search of the articles. To retrieve articles for the topic 'Building Performance,' three title (TI) record files were created, as listed in Table 2.1.

Table 2.1 demonstrates a summary of the search data for articles on BPEs conducted in the Web of Science Core Collection database. The set results of the advanced searches were combined using the 'OR' Boolean operator to obtain 784 articles. This chapter discusses the extant literature to address the issues and proposes research trajectories to resolve the major challenges identified in BES

Table 2.1 Search Parameters for Existing Studies

Concepts	*Keyword-SearchSelection Criteria*	*ReviewArticles*	*OriginalResearchPapers*	*ConferenceProceedings*
Overheating risk of buildings	TI = ('building performance*' OR 'overheating risk assessment')	8	171	25
Thermal comfort	TI = (('building performance*' OR 'thermal comfort' OR 'field investigation') AND (('thermal discomfort*' OR 'environmental monitoring')))	12	187	23
Occupant behaviour	TI = (('building performance*' OR 'occupant behaviour' OR 'occupant patterns') AND (('energy use*' OR 'occupant behaviour')))	7	128	12
Energy modelling	TI = (('building performance*' OR 'energy use' OR 'overheating') AND (('building optimisation*')))	9	175	27

studies. Government initiatives at various levels have been made globally, which seek effective solutions to the problems related to household energy consumption and CO_2 emissions, especially for vulnerable households in energy poverty and underlying health conditions in all spheres of the economy (Ozarisoy & Altan, 2017a). Understanding the importance of the energy performance of existing housing stock constitutes a cultural and societal challenge (Ozarisoy & Elsharkawy, 2019).

Zero-carbon targets must be achieved to reduce the detrimental impact of greenhouse emissions and mitigate climate change (Arriazu & Monge-Barrio, 2017). Neither developed nor developing societies will be able to meet the range of targets set by the European Union (EU) and other countries related to the design and procurement of built environments to reduce CO_2 emissions to 80% of 1990 levels by 2030, or the mandates set forth in the 2018 UK *Climate Change Act* to limit CO_2 emissions to 20% by 2050 (Charmpis et al., 2018). In Northern Cyprus (NC) specifically, there are several post-war residential-housing stocks that must attain the EU's 2030 energy-consumption-reduction targets, all of which are worthy of investigation.

Various studies have demonstrated the potential benefits of a greater reduction of energy consumption and the increasing value of the built asset (Domínguez–Amarillo et al., 2019; Fernández–Agüera et al., 2019; Österbring et al., 2019). None have attempted to understand the overheating risks in NC residential buildings and the impacts thereof on occupant thermal comfort, and this issue remains unaddressed. Despite this paucity, it is not important to initially evaluate the energy performance of existing housing stock and assess occupant thermal satisfaction, since these variables can have a significant impact on energy use (Escandón et al., 2017; Fernández–Agüera et al., 2016; Terés-Zubiaga et al., 2015).

By exploring different variations of building-energy performance assessments, the *European Union Statistics on Income and Living Conditions Report* and the 2018 *Household Budget Survey* both indicated that different assessment indicators related to energy use, such as whether or not occupants are in arrears on their utility bills or are unable to keep their homes adequately warm, which homes are uncomfortably hot in the summer, hidden energy performance, energy costs that consume a large proportion of one's income and the presence of a leak, damp or rot, should all be considered.

Alonso et al. (2017) and Sánchez–Guevara (2018) argued that energy-performance-assessment indicators undertaken in EU countries are based on households' self-assessment evaluation of their dwellings. To explain the survey results, it can be seen that the case studies showed slightly low-performing indicators in comparison to the EU overall average. Spain was shown to have better home-energy performance than the EU, which enabled respondents to keep their homes thermally comfortable (San Miguel-Bellod, 2018). While many other countries, particularly those in south-eastern Europe that share the subtropical (i.e., *Csa*) and partly semi-arid (i.e., *Bsh*) climate characteristics of Cyprus, showed significant thermal discomfort, Spain showed a similar approximation to the European overall average with respect to maintaining thermally comfortable indoor environments in the summer. It can therefore be deduced from the above graph that 29% is higher than in the EU average of thermal discomfort (Kyprianou et al., 2019).

More significantly, Bulgaria had the worst overall thermal performance for both of the assessment indicators related to the thermal-comfort aspect of residential buildings, including the criterion related to being in arrears on utility bills; Cyprus also showed a higher percentage of arrears on utility bills than in the EU. Nevertheless, it is evident that Portugal had a slightly better performance than many other countries due to stringent policies that were put into place in 2015 to thoroughly implement energy-performance directives; it should be considered, however, that many Portuguese households rely heavily on biomass burning for space heating and are therefore not properly accounted for in the energy-bills assessment. In terms of assessing the influence of the presence of leaks, damp or rot in residential buildings, Bulgaria has the lowest percentage of its population living in such conditions; this is followed by Spain, which also showed lower indicators than the remainder of the EU.

Lithuania was slightly above average, while households in Cyprus and Portugal have faced thermally uncomfortable indoor environments due to the absence of thermal insulation on building envelopes and ageing residential-building stocks; these findings strongly correlate with the population consensus because distinct deviations between these two Mediterranean countries have been observed. Notably, Lithuania was found to be the only country with an energy-performance indicator that was higher than the EU average; this can be further corroborated by the fact that Lithuania was shown to have one of the highest income coefficients, which indicates unequal income distribution across the total sample size in both surveys from which the results were taken as base-case reference indicators of home-energy performance (Guardigli et al., 2018).

Couched within this emerging energy debate, the EU Framework Programme for Research and Innovation for 2014–2030 includes an action plan that underscores the need to legislate the policy priorities put forth in the EU's 2030 strategy (Fosas et al., 2018). This plan incorporates long-term aims to address major energy-demand concerns that are shared by citizens of Europe and elsewhere (Kalisa et al., 2018). This strategy plan consists of different policy implications related to energy use, including the significance of occupancy patterns and various socio-demographic characteristics that should be considered during the decision-making process for retrofitting efforts of existing housing stock (Page et al., 2008; Santangelo & Tondelli, 2017; Erell et al., 2018).

Review of Current Overheating Drivers and Definitions

To date, studies related to overheating risks in residential buildings can be broadly categorised as endeavours that involved the long-term monitoring of occupied indoor spaces to identify and quantify the risk of overheating (Beizaee et al., 2013; McLeod & Swainson, 2017; Pathan et al., 2017); endeavours that employed dynamic thermal simulation (DTS) modelling to assess current and future overheating risks in existing and newly built residential buildings in the UK (McLeod et al., 2013; Sanchez–Guevara et al., 2019); and endeavours that utilised empirical data to construct predictive models that are capable of assessing overheating risks by employing an STS approach because of a fundamental when interacting with the occupants (Santamouris & Kolokotsa, 2015; Santamouris, 2016). The findings of these studies highlighted the importance of developing a systemic approach when conducting a DTS analysis in conjunction with a primary data source that was obtained from longitudinal field studies to calibrate a building's energy performance. Some researchers have argued that modelling methods that make use of building-fabric in situ measurements and monitor environmental conditions to explain data variations present advantages over other modelling methods employed in BPE studies (Reeves et al., 2010; Serghides et al., 2016); this is because many assumptions that were made via DTS elevate the level of uncertainty in energy-calibration results (Gomes et al., 2018). The study presents an overview of literature studies that considered the impact of climate change on home-energy use, the EPBD implications for the integrity of international assessment criteria on building-thermal performance and occupant thermal comfort and further methodology developed by undertaking a BES analysis for the delivery of effective retrofitting outcomes.

The first pilot study of summertime overheating by Jenkins et al. (2011) reported that despite the relatively mild climate in the UK, there was concern related to increases in the summer air temperatures in airtight low-energy residential buildings due to the effects of high temperatures on occupant thermal comfort. In fact, there is growing evidence of overheating risks in the newly built housing stock (i.e., terraced houses, high-density residential estates) that struggle to achieve the requirements recommended by the EPBD together with energy-performance certificate (EPC) schemes that were put in place to upgrade the energy efficiency of the existing building stock in the UK and across Europe (Attia et al., 2017; Jenkins et al., 2012; Sharifi et al., 2019). Due to the lack of a conceptual framework to assess the thermal performance of buildings and variations in the implementation mechanisms for each EU member state, these energy-efficient building materials and technologies led to increased indoor-air temperatures in the summer (Guerra-Santin et al., 2013; Psomas et al., 2017).

McLeod and Swainson (2017) described overheating that occurred when temperatures made building occupants thermally uncomfortable or heat stressed due to local environmental conditions and low-quality thermal properties of buildings. In a study that set out to define 'overheating,' Ren et al. (2014) found that with consecutive days of hot weather, including warmer-than-average nights, recorded indoor air temperatures in some homes, specifically newly built energy-efficient homes, started to exceed outdoor air temperatures and no longer provided protection from the heat.

Several studies have revealed a correlation between energy use and building-thermal properties (Hens, 2010; Isaacs et al., 2010; Hamilton et al., 2014); several other studies have linked variations in indoor-air temperature fluctuations to occupant health and well-being, particularly during long-term heatwaves (Hatvani-Kovacs et al., 2018; Pathan et al. 2017). Studies have investigated hazardous effects of summer temperatures on occupant thermal-comfort, including indoor air temperature and relative humidity (RH) monitoring studies (Beizaee et al., 2013); building-physics modelling studies (Gupta & Gregg, 2013; Mavrogianni et al., 2012; Oikonomou et al., 2012; Porritt et al., 2012); and epidemiological studies of heat-wave mortalities (Liu et al., 2017). Previous research also determined that overheating is linked to household occupancy and behavioural patterns, which has been corroborated to evaluate the building performance of case study locations, as presented in Table 2.2(a) and (b). Table 2.2(a) and (b) presents a list of previously undertaken pilot research studies for BPEs, which was retrieved from the collection of research articles in the Clarivate Analytics database. A large body of research has been undertaken on the overheating risks of different building variants that could potentially be used to support retrofitting and design decisions (i.e., housing typology, household socio-demographic characteristics). As can be seen, several scholars have conducted building-energy modelling and environmental monitoring to assess the overheating risk of these residential buildings, and an exploratory case study approach was applied to these methodologies to properly understand the building performance of existing housing stock (Beizaee et al., 2013; Ballarini et al., 2014; Dascalaki et al., 2016).

These studies were reviewed to understand the current design methods that are available to assess building overheating risks and the relevance thereof to the development of a new adaptive conceptual framework through an exploratory case study approach undertaken in a post-war social-housing development estate in NC for purposes of comparative analysis. It is therefore important to search for a new conceptual framework that can better explain occupants' real-life energy-use patterns and experiences. For this reason, these studies were limited because they only explored the impact of climate change on building overheating risks, but did not consider human-based factors in their future energy-forecasting scenarios.

Gupta and Gregg (2018) provided an in-depth analysis of the work of Oliveira Panão (2014) and revealed the relevance of Panão's work when identifying the main parameters of overheating risks experienced in the summertime; these parameters can be correlated with heat gain from high external temperatures, direct solar gains on exterior surfaces or penetrating glazing and internal heat gains (IHGs).

Gupta and Gregg's (2018) study also highlighted the developed conceptual framework to increase awareness of issue resolutions related to overheating risks at the local and national levels by promoting a participant-led research design process. This indicates that constraints related to BPEs are not limited to buildings and that studies should consider community awareness when attempting to provide a universal design approach in the implementation of energy-efficient materials and retrofitting technologies.

Overheating Thresholds

Previous studies on overheating risks found that under current and future climates, Natural Ventilation (NV) could potentially reduce indoor-air temperatures, but only to a limited degree (Lomas & Kane, 2013; Moazami et al., 2019). Because

Table 2.2(a) Pilot Studies That Evaluated Building Performance

References	*A. Location and Climate*	*B. Climate-Change Scenarios*	*C. Methodology*	*D. Housing and Occupant Characteristics*
Karimpour et al. (2015)	Adelaide, Australia (BSk): mild temperate climate	Investigated current and future typical meteorological year (TMY) climate TMY for 2070 CC scenario	Energy modelling (AccuRATE); best design based on minimum heating and cooling-energy consumption	• Entire Australian population was targeted • Multi-family houses (MFHs) • Brick-veneer house (typical house design in Australia)
Tong et al. (2010)	Brisbane, Australia (Cfa): subtropical climate (hot and dry in the summer)	Reviewed data for heatwaves in 2004 and data related to air temperatures, air pollutants and health outcomes for a period of 2001 – 2003	Energy modelling (AccuRATE); cooling and heating; base house and modifications with 2.5 – 7 – sta energy rating—utilised regression model to explore correlations between air temperatures and occupant health and well-being	• Detached brick-veneer residential house • Façades ($U = 0.75\,W/m^2K$) • Concrete roof tiles • Simple glazing • Holland blinds • Heating set points (SPs): 20°C in the living room and 18°C in the bedroom • Cooling set points vary from 23 – 26.5°C
Ren et al. (2014)	Brisbane, Australia (Cfa): hot and dry Melbourne, Australia (Cfb): warm summer	Reviewed data for heatwaves in 2004	Energy modelling (AccuRATE); heatwave scenarios for Brisbane (2004) and Melbourne (2009)	Conventional single-family houses (SFHs) without air conditioning (A/C) systems. Steady-state analysis of standardised occupancy profiles

(*Continued*)

Table 2.2(a) (Continued)

References	*A. Location and Climate*	*B. Climate-Change Scenarios*	*C. Methodology*	*D. Housing and Occupant Characteristics*
HatvaniKovacs et al. (2016)	Adelaide, South Australia (BSk)—Subtropical cold and arid	Reviewed data for heatwaves in 2004	Online survey undertaken with representative sample ($N = 393$); Chi-square, Fisher's exact test and Fisher - Freeman - Halton exact test statistical analyses undertaken; Wilcoxon test performed	Vulnerable population living in energy poverty was targeted. • 90% dwellings with cooling systems (entire dwelling or a single room) • 25% rooms without shading • Most were without insulation and with light mass external walls
Brotas and Nicol (2016b)	• Athens, Greece (Csa) • Lisboa, Portugal (Csa) • Rome, Italy (Csa) • Munich, Germany (Cfb) • London, England (Cfb) • Moscow, Russia (Dfb) (see Figure 2.2 in 'Overview' chapter)	Reviewed climate-change projections for 2020, 2050 and 2080 (CCWorldWeatherGen)	Energy modelling; overheating (CIBSE). • Criterion 1: Hours of exceedance (3%) • Criterion 2: Daily weighted exceedance • Criterion 3: Upper-limit temperature	Mid-storey south- and east-facing flats • Uvalue(wall) $= 0.18\,W/m^2K$ • U - value(glass) $= 1.4\,W/m^2K$ • Pattern - of - use $= 24h^{-1}$ • Ventilation rate: $0.3 - 1.0\,h^{-1}$ • Night ventilation • Interior blinds • MFHs

Source: **Adapted from Ana–Sanchez and Monge–Barrio (2018).**

Table 2.2(b) Pilot Studies That Evaluated Building Performances (Continued)

References	*A. Location and Climate*	*B. Climate-Change Scenarios*	*C. Methodology*	*D. Housing and Occupant Characteristics*
Barbosa et al. (2015)	Lisboa, Portugal (Csa)	M1: 2050 – 2080 CCWorldWeatherGen weather file generator was used M2: 2003 heatwave—TMY weather files were used for building-performance simulation	• Energy modelling (EnergyPlus with Design Builder); discomfort hours (STAT or ADAPT15251) • Long-term monitoring for two dwellings; weather station installed to monitor outdoor environmental parameters	Residential building: • Four dwellings per floor; each with eastern or western orientation • Façade: Brick (high mass): $U = 1{,}7\ W/m^2K$ • Double-glazed: $U = 2{,}4\ W / m^2K$ • PVC frame • Concrete slab Vulnerable low-income population was targeted
Santamouris et al. (2010)	Athens, Greece (Csa): Suburban and rural areas in dense urban zones	2009 summer conditions—night-ventilation techniques were used to assess occupant thermal comfort	Monitored secondary-data collection of energy consumption and operational conditions of each building ($N = 210$ dwellings); and TRNSYS was used for building-performance simulations.	Mechanically air-conditioned. Single houses with high thermal mass: • $Uvalue(walls) \approx 0{,}5\ W / m^2K$ • $Uvalue(roof) \approx 0{,}4\ W / m^2K$ Surface ranges from $55 - 480m^2$ high
Santamouris et al. (2015)	Athens, Greece (Csa): Dense urban zones	Very hot summer of 2007 (i.e., $30 - 33°C$ hot spells): Urban Heat Island (UHI) effect	Reviewed article on experimental studies conducted to investigate the impact of UHI effect.	No cooling systems Vulnerable low-income population with underlying health conditions was targeted

(Continued)

Table 2.2(b) (Continued)

References	*A. Location and Climate*	*B. Climate-Change Scenarios*	*C. Methodology*	*D. Housing and Occupant Characteristics*
Pyrgou et al. (2017)	Perugia, Italy (Cfb)	Building-thermal energy-efficiency in 2013 — Heatwaves (i.e., UHI effect)	Energy modelling and environmental monitoring using RStudio software	Four typical single-family detached houses (SFHs) Italian households were targeted
Fahmy (2014)	Alexandria, Cairo and Aswan, Egypt (Bwh)	Examined data for 2020, 2050 and 2080 (CCWorldWeatherGen)	Energy modelling (EnergyPlus with Design Builder)	Two collective buildings: GF and 5F Three typologies or envelopes (GRC)
Saman et al. (2013)	• M1: • Adelaide and Richmond, Australia (Bsk) • Amberley, Melbourne and Hobart, Australia (Cfb) • Brisbane and Sydney, Australia (Cfa) • Perth, Australia (Csa) • Darwin, Australia (Aw)	• M1: Heatwave • M2: 2030, 2050 and 2070 data	Energy modelling (AccuRATE) • M1: Heatwaves, overheating (adapted ASHRAE55:2013); energy model; five case studies • M2: Cooling demand for two dwellings	Different typologies: Mostly single-family and semi-detached houses Vulnerable low-income and ageing population was targeted

Source: Adapted from Ana-Sanchez and Monge-Barrio (2018).

of this and according to climate-change projections, the future increase in external temperatures is expected to diminish the effectiveness of NV as a cooling strategy (Dino & Akgul, 2019; Mata et al., 2019). Various criteria have been developed to assess when occupied rooms in base-case representative flats under investigation in long-term monitoring studies measure summertime overheating in the UK and across Europe (Mavrogianni et al., 2012; McLeod & Swainson, 2017; Escandón et al., 2019); these include the static CIBSE criteria, which suggest that the operative air temperatures (OTs) in living rooms should not exceed 28°C for more than 1% of the occupied hours throughout the year, while the criterion for bedrooms is 1% of hours over 26°C (Chartered Institution of Building Services Engineers, 2006). More recently, a move to use adaptive overheating thresholds that show variations according to outdoor-air temperatures has gained increasing interest for risk assessments in free-running (i.e., naturally ventilated) buildings (CIBSE, 2013).

It is essential to specify information requirements and exchange procedures to devise effective implementation of the EPCs in the decision-making process for energy-use policies (Psomas et al., 2016). This is why, in terms of legislation, the Health and Safety Rating System (HSRS) Operating Guidance stated that there is a significant increase in the risk of strokes and mortality when temperatures exceed 25°C (Gupta & Gregg, 2013). In line with this statement, the HSRS provided the only statutory definition of overheating risks related to morbidity and mortality in UK residential properties to reduce the death toll as a consequence of frequently observed long-term heatwaves in summer across continental Europe (McLeod & Swainson, 2017).

Attention has also been focused on the provision of effective NV and the positive impact that this will have on overheating risks in conjunction with other building-fabric elements, such as thermal insulation, thermal mass and shading, in addition to the potential for temperature stratification in the summer (Guerra-Santin et al., 2017; Porrit et al., 2011, 2012). Some researchers have emphasised that occupants in NV buildings have the benefit of being able to adjust their indoor-air temperatures according to their individual thermal-comfort expectations and that this control facility is also known to make occupants more tolerant of their environment (Baker & Standeven, 1996; Brager & de Dear, 1998).

Several investigations of overheating-risk-assessment criteria have investigated people's adaptive thermal comfort at home (Encinas & de Herde, 2013; Gunawardena & Steemers, 2019). Nicol and Humphreys (2002) argued that the temperature that constitutes overheating in naturally ventilated buildings is higher than in mechanically ventilated structures. To date, longitudinal and transverse survey methods have both been utilised to assess occupant thermal comfort with some degree of integration with the British BS: 15251:2007 standard and ASHRAE 55 standard (van Hoof & Hensen, 2007).

Factors thought to influence overheating-risk issues have been explored in several studies (Peacock et al., 2010; Rodrigues & Gillot, 2013; Pathan et al., 2017); these studies predominantly employed the CIBSE TM52 technical memorandum on building overheating-risk-assessment criteria. In these scholarly investigations and according to the CIBSE Guide A (2006), indoor-comfort temperatures in the summer are 25°C for living rooms and 23°C for bedrooms, and overheating occurs if over the course of one year, 1% of the occupied hours exceeds 28°C in living rooms and 26°C in bedrooms; the CIBSE Guide A (2006) also noted that temperatures that are higher 24°C can impair sleep, which suggests that it is important to differentiate when peak temperatures occur.

Significant research has been conducted to identify different assessment methodologies to evaluate occupant thermal comfort (Schweiker & Wagner, 2015; Singh et al., 2011). Many of these projects primarily adopted the STS design approach in efforts to develop BES models and monitoring campaigns to evaluate long-term general-thermal-comfort conditions in naturally ventilated buildings (Åkerman et al., 2020; Barone et al., 2019; López–González et al., 2016). These pilot-study projects considered different assessment criteria to evaluate the overheating risks in residential buildings and occupant thermal comfort.

One of the most commonly used methodologies is the CIBSE TM52, which was the first set of criteria based on dry-resultant temperature (CIBSE, 2015). As it relates to assessing overheating risks caused by the abovementioned factors, D'Oca et al. (2018) emphasised that the role of occupant behaviour is significant when indoor-air temperatures are assessed by embedding the CIBSE TM52 overheating memorandum into the BES model. Moreover, in separate reviews of vulnerable households in social-housing developments, Pretlove and Kade (2016) and Santangelo and Tondelli (2017) pointed out that existing assessment criteria do not account for the influence of buildings on solar exposure risk and are not reliant on actual representative occupancy patterns in terms of disseminating energy use to vulnerable individuals. To date, no study has employed a dynamic measure to analyse representative housing stock in NC to consider overheating risks and occupant thermal comfort.

Mavrogianni (2012) modelled domestic space-heating demands and heatwave vulnerability within the London urban island heat island (UHI) effect. This case study presented the outcomes of two developed housing-stock models: a heat-demand model that was based on steady-state energy-use calculation techniques and a multiple linear-regression overheating-risk meta-model of an existing dynamic thermal simulation programme. The conceptual framework was developed on input parameters that were collected after monitoring representative flats, which is a well-known, conventional tradition to demonstrate aggregate BES models; the study conducted by Mavrogianni (2012) did not take human-based data into account in the energy-forecasting analysis, because the questionnaire-survey approach was not adopted to obtain household socio-demographic characteristics via semi-structured interviews. Table 2.3 demonstrates the developed thermal-comfort assessment criteria and methodology to assess building overheating risks and occupant thermal comfort.

Regarding different assessment criteria recommended by different regulations and researchers in this field, the international ISO 7730 standard introduced five methods that were developed according to Fanger's comfort model: three of these five indices were repurposed in the EU's EN 15251 standards by extending their scope to also include the adaptive-comfort model (Nicol, 2004). This proposed

Table 2.3 Long-Term Evaluation Indices of General Thermal-Comfort Conditions

Family of Indices	*Based on Comfort Models*				*Based on Reference Temperatures*		
	Year	*IndexName*	*ComfortModel*	*Standard/Author(s)*	*Year*	*IndexName*	*Standard/Author(s)*
Percentage	2005	Percentage outside PMV[a] range	Fanger	ISO7730	2002	CIBSE Guide J Criterion	CIBSE
Cumulative	2005	Percentage outside range	Fanger	ISO7730	2006	CIBSE Guide A Criterion	CIBSE
	2005	Percentage outside range	Adaptive EU	EN15251			
	2005	PPD[b] weighted criterion	Fanger	ISO7730			
	2005	Accumulated PPD	Fanger	ISO7730			
	2005	Degree-hour criterion	Fanger	ISO7730			
	2005	Degree-hour criterion	Adaptive EU	EN15251			
	2010	Exceedance PPD	Fanger	Borgeson-Brager			
	2010	Exceedance Adaptive	Adaptive US	Borgeson-Brager			
Risk	2008	Overheating risk	Adaptive EU	Nicol et al.	2007	Overheating risk	Robinson-Haldi
Averaging	2005	Average PPD	Fanger	ISO7730			

[a]PMV = Predicted mean vote; [b]PPD = Predicted percentage of dissatisfied.
Source: Adapted from Nicol et al. (2008).

methodology enabled researchers to assess thermal comfort while considering different lower- and upper-limit overheating thresholds to develop more accurate information for use in subsequent simulation analyses.

After reporting on analysed data that was measured in free-running buildings during the EU Smart Controls and Thermal Comfort (SCAT) project, Nicol et al. (2009) introduced the overheating-risk-assessment criteria. In their review, Nicol and Humphreys (2002) introduced a novel methodology to estimate the cooling consumption of buildings when seeking to achieve thermally comfortable indoor conditions during hot summer spells by adapting degree-hours[1] to assess the overheating risk of each occupied space, which can be applied to different base-case temperatures as a reference point to assess long-term discomfort indices. Notably, these indices are weighted to consider overheating risks in the 'Exceedance index,'[2] which weighs discomfort hours by the hourly average occupancy in buildings (Liu et al., 2012). As it relates to the previously mentioned overheating risk criteria, this criterion is recommended in the CIBSE TM52 technical memorandum to assess overheating risks in European dwellings and increase understanding of the importance of assigning base-case representative occupancy profiles in building-modelling simulations as an assessment methodology (Lomas & Porritt, 2017). Many scholarly articles mentioned a performance gap between the predicted and actual energy use when adopting the CIBSE TM52 criteria (CIBSE, 2013); for this reason, the design methodology to assess the overheating risk in homes that was put forth in CIBSE TM59 recommended the adoption of representative dominant occupancy patterns as an assessment criterion to calibrate the predicted and actual energy performances of buildings. Several studies concluded that the CIBSE TM59 criteria facilitated more accurate energy-use predictions because of real occupancy patterns that are assigned in the course of building-modelling simulations (Pisello & Asdrubali, 2014; Pignatta et al., 2017; Petrou et al., 2018). To date, no study has analysed multiple factors related to the adoption of CIBSE TM59 assessment criteria while taking dominant representative occupancy profiles obtained from the longitudinal field surveys in the Eastern Mediterranean climate into consideration (Abela et al., 2016; Serghides et al., 2017).

Definition of Thermal Comfort

The notion of 'thermal comfort' identifies the reaction of the human body to the changing indoor environment conditions by means of exploring physiological, psychological and environmental parameters (de Dear & Brager, 2001). The design and physical characteristics of this environment describe the microclimate, which interacts with people's habitual adaptive behaviour to adjust to a thermally comfortable indoor air environment according to their thermal expectations (Nicol & Humphreys, 2010). Many scholars have conducted pilot longitudinal field studies to identify the adaptive thermal comfort threshold levels which are included both in the ASHRAE Global Thermal Comfort Databases I and II. Thus, indicating the variation of these input parameters has shown determinant factors to explore the acceptable PMV range in accordance with these parameters, namely building type; climate;

activity levels, etc. Table 2.4 demonstrates the previous scholars' work on thermal comfort which is available at the ASHRAE Global Thermal Comfort Database II.

Humphreys and Nicol (1998) described thermal comfort as a situation in which the exchange of heat between a person and their environment has a neutral balance. Another conceptual definition of thermal comfort, which was provided by the American Society of Heating, Refrigerating and Air-Conditioning Engineers (ASHRAE), has been globally accepted and frequently used by scholars in this field. In conjunction with the universal thermal comfort criterion, Brager and de Dear (1998) asserted that people's expectations related to thermal comfort led to an undetermined sensation in the investigation of neutral thermal-comfort level.

Table 2.4 Review of ASHRAE Global Database II

References	*Location*	*Benchmarking Criteria*	*Main Findings*
Brager et al. (1993)	San Francisco, US	• ASHRAE 462 - RP data • ASHRAE Standard 55-92 • ASHRAE Standard 55-81	Approximately 12% PPD in occupied space, compared to 5% minimum PPD
Heidari and Sharples (2002)	Western Iran	• ISO 7730 - 1994 • Griffiths Thermal comfort equation	Adaptive thermal comfort temperatures in the summer ranged from 26.7 – 28.4°C
Bouden and Ghrab (2005)	Tunisia, North Africa	• ISO 7730 - 1994 • ASHRAE Standard 55 - 92 • ASHRAE Standard 55 - 81	More than 80% of participants reported comfortable temperatures from 16 – 26.5°C
Han et al. (2009)	Central/ Southern China	Fanger's PMV model	Neutral OT: • Urban residence: 14.0°C • Rural residences: 11.5°C
Cao et al. (2011)	Beijing, China	• Brager and de Dear's adaptive model • Fanger and Toftum's PMV model	Neutral summer OT was 26.8°C ; PMV-predicted temperature was 25.7°C
Djamila et al. (2013)	Malaysia	De Dear's adaptive thermal comfort model based on the ASHRAE RP - 884 database	Predicted adaptive thermal comfort temperature was nearly 30°C
Földváry et al. (2017)	Central Europe, Slovakia	• ISO 16017 - 2 Standard • ISO 16000 - 4 Standard	18% of apartments in unrenovated buildings did not fall in the optimum thermal comfort range (i.e., 20 – 24°C)

Contrarily, Hoes et al. (2009) considered Brager and de Dear's definition of thermal comfort to be more descriptive of a 'psychological approach' to exploring correlations between occupant thermal-sensation votes (TSVs) and thermal-preference votes (TPVs). For this reason, an exploratory approach would be needed to identify the complexity of the physiological, psychological and environmental parameters during an analysis of longitudinal surveys (Kalmár, 2016; Mishra & Ramgopal, 2015).

Nicol et al. (2008) concluded that the subjectivity of population size is underestimated and that a broad range of parameters satisfies individuals, thereby making the term qualitative and introducing behavioural aspects that not only differ among people from different locales but also among people from the same area. Additionally, Yao et al. (2009) explored the influences of different parameters, such as people's expectations and preferences related to environmental conditions, on their thermal comfort; this is considered to be the 'adaptive model' approach to optimise occupant thermal comfort via field surveys and, in turn, allows an understanding of behavioural and subjective assessments of individuals in real settings that reflects more than the physical relationship between people and their environment. Table 2.5(a) and (b) delineates the literature review that was undertaken on field investigations of occupant thermal comfort in various climate zones, including available data on the ASHRAE Global Thermal Comfort Database II.

A significant proportion of the current literature on thermal comfort specifically focuses on the physical environment and physiological conditions to predict comfort levels and quantitatively produce a number of thermal indices to thoroughly assess occupant thermal-comfort levels (Liu et al., 2012; Taleghani et al., 2013; Toe & Kubota, 2013). Nicol et al. (2012) explained that these models, known as 'heat-balanced models,' are predominantly based on physics and physiology and are able to rationally analyse the heat flow between the human body and its surroundings.

Humphreys and Nicol (2000) insisted that occupants' thermal sensations strongly correlate with age, gender, economic and cultural aspects, and location and climatic conditions. In an analysis of the influences of dependent and independent variables on occupant thermal preferences and sensations, Humphreys (2005) identified specific groups of people with more demanding needs—such as children, the elderly, people with disabilities and people who are sick—who are more likely to be vulnerable. This led to a significant contribution toward the assessment of thermal comfort in different climate regions under investigation by many other scholarly articles in this field (Nicol & Humphreys, 2010).

Adaptive Thermal Comfort Theory

Significant research has been conducted to ensure comfortable indoor conditions and to accurately predict the comfort level of a room that is in line with the references provided by the European BS EN 15251 standards (CIBSE, 2016); and a considerable amount of literature evaluated assessment methods of the summer

Table 2.5(a) Field-Investigation Studies on Adaptive Thermal Comfort

References	*A. Study Location*	*B. Primary Aim of Model*	*C. Methodology*	*D. Main Findings*
Tuck et al. (2019)	Kuala Lumpur, Malaysia	To conduct a comparative analysis of OTs recorded with predicted temperature using adaptive thermal-comfort equation in hot and humid climates	Two-storey corner terraced house selected for exploratory case study approach. Field measurements conducted; weather station installed in the front yard of case study house; thermal recorders and hot-wire anemometer installed in each occupied space; CO_2 measurements recorded.	According to ASHRAE Standard 55, recorded air temperature was 1.8°C higher than the same parameter defined by EN15251 and 0.9°C higher than the same parameter defined by ACE hot-humid environment conditions.
Pastore and Andersen (2019)	Switzerland	To analyse the thermal performance of 'Minergie'-labelled buildings	Post-occupancy evaluation (POE) conducted on four Swiss green buildings with 'Minergie' label. POE protocol recruited for winter and summer; long-term environmental monitoring campaign recruited; in situ measurements recorded; extensive online surveys undertaken to collect long-term occupant thermal-comfort options.	According to occupants, indoor conditions never attained commonly used 80% satisfaction threshold.

(*Continued*)

Table 2.5(a) (Continued)

References	*A. Study Location*	*B. Primary Aim of Model*	*C. Methodology*	*D. Main Findings*
Nghana and Tariku (2016)	Burnaby and Vancouver, Canada	To demonstrate the energy effectiveness of implementing PCM onto apartment building envelopes to prove the thermal-comfort effect and energy consumption of mechanical system	Field experimental study conducted: • Two prototype buildings built on-site for experimental study: one had PCMs implemented on building envelopes, the other had no PCMs. • EnergyPlus software used for numeric validation; ASHRAE 62.2 requirements used as international assessment criterion	PCM decreased peak indoor air temperature by as much as 0.6°C and increased trough temperature by 0.8°C.
Zhang et al. (2017)	Guangdong Province, Southern China	To demonstrate climate-design adaption of rural folk houses and the impact thereof on household thermal comfort in a hot and humid climate	Yearlong thermal-comfort survey conducted: 11 traditional folk-house residents selected for sample size. Questionnaire survey conducted concurrently with documentation of in situ measurements; ASHRAE Standard55 adopted to identify neutral thermal-comfort assessment; statistical analysis conducted with SPSS v22.0 software suite, and all differences at 0.05 level were accepted as significant.	Thermally neutral temperature was 0.6 – 1.3°C lower; upper limit of 80% acceptable temperature was decreased by 0.8 – 4.7°C in semi-open spaces.

Table 2.5(b) Field-Investigation Studies on Adaptive Thermal Comfort (Continued)

References	*A. Study Location*	*B. Primary Aim of Model*	*C. Methodology*	*D. Main Findings*
Vellei et al. (2017)	ASHRAE Global Thermal Comfort Database II	To determine a clear explanation for lack of humidity signal or convincing formulation of the effect of humidity on adaptive thermal-comfort development	Global thermal-comfort datasets investigated, including meta-analysis of summary data from 63 field studies and field data from 39 naturally ventilated buildings in eight climate types; experimental study established from ASHRAE RP884 data	The new adaptive thermal-comfort model increased the comfort envelope of naturally ventilated buildings because its overheating prediction was 30% lower than that of the current model
Földváry et al. (2018)	ASHRAE Global Thermal Comfort Database II	To document origins, scope, development, contents and accessibility of ASHRAE Global Thermal Comfort Database II	Dataset created from field studies conducted from 1995 to 2016; 81,846 rows of paired subjective comfort votes and objective instrumental measurements data included in global database development framework; Query Builder used with Javascript to develop visual tool	Web-based interactive thermal-comfort visualisation tool that allows end-users to quickly and interactively explore the data was developed
Jin et al. (2019)	Harbin, Northeast China	To explore gender-related thermal-comfort differences in severely cold regions	Physical measurements conducted; thermal-comfort questionnaire survey distributed to pedestrians; correlations among psychological parameters explored	In transitional seasons, female neutral temperature was 23.2°C, and male neutral temperature was 19.8°C

performances of un-air-conditioned residential buildings has been published (Ferrari & Zanotto, 2009; Haldi & Robinson, 2010; Nicol, 2017).

What is known about optimising occupant thermal comfort is largely based upon empirical studies that investigated the overheating risk in indoor spaces in light of climate change, which anticipates an increase in temperatures and a greater frequency of extreme weather events, such as heatwaves (Kottek et al., 2006; Kovats et al., 2014; Nikolopoulou & Lykoudis, 2006). Furthermore, several studies documented the lack of benchmarking assessment criteria among the input parameters and occupant behaviour intended to measure occupant thermal comfort and assess building overheating risks (Brager & de Dear, 1998; Halawa & Van Hoof, 2012; Guerra-Santin et al., 2013).

Research revealed an increased interest in assessing the calculations of the PMV and PPD indices, in addition to information that is needed to estimate certain localised effects, such as shading and NV (Humphreys & Nicol, 2003). The CIBSE TM52 Overheating Task Force identified a new approach to define overheating that considers occupants' thermal comfort and well-being as essential, especially in residential buildings without mechanical cooling systems (Mann et al., 2012; Olesen, 2012); this follows the methodology and recommendations put forth in the BS EN 15251 guidelines to determine whether an existing occupied residential building can be susceptible to becoming overheated, especially in the summer.

It should be stressed that studies within the Eastern Mediterranean climate revealed both of these effects on high overheating risk of buildings and high proportion of the PPD index. In addition to increasing population and rapid urbanisation, changing climate conditions present a need for cities to adapt to new conditions and develop resilience to provide thermally comfortable buildings (Aydin & Jakubiec, 2018; Gupta & Gregg, 2012; Synenefa et al., 2018).

Many field studies have been conducted in various climates around the world, which demonstrated that comfortable temperatures are closely linked to local climate conditions (Brager & de Dear, 1998; McCartney & Nicol, 2002; Nicol, 2017; Tuck et al., 2019). By following a similar approach, the adaptive thermal-comfort theory explains this phenomenon as it relates to occupants who actively engage with their indoor environments (de Dear & Brager, 1998; Nicol et al., 2012). If an environment causes occupant discomfort, then those residents are likely to take responsive actions to restore their comfort; these responsive actions are said to be rooted in one of three types of adaptation: behavioural, physiological or psychological (Nicol, 2008). Table 2.6 delineates the literature review undertaken on field investigation of occupants' thermal comfort in various climate zones, including the Asia Pacific region to compare the regression analysis results with research studies from other countries with similar climates in Chapter 6.

Several studies have investigated the effects of occupant interactions on energy use (Hitchcock, 1993; Bonte et al., 2014; Buso et al., 2015); and several comfort models have been proposed to address this aspect of assessing optimal indoor conditions as they relate to occupant thermal preferences (Balslev et al., 2015; Evola et al., 2013). Many scholars adopted Fanger's 'static' model, which considers occupant behaviours as containers that passively undertake building management

Table 2.6 Pilot Studies That Adopted EN 15251 Adaptive Thermal Comfort Criteria

References	*A. Study Location*	*B. Climate Zones*	*C. Building Type and Ventilation Strategy*	*D. Methodology*	*E. Main Findings*
de Dear and Brager (2001)	Worldwide	ASHRAE Global Database I	Free-running and NV buildings	ASHRAE RP884 dataset used; field-validation experiments in various climate zones considered; specified laboratory-grade instrumentation used; statistical derivation of adaptive models conducted for 160 buildings in database; statistical analysis conducted	80% (or 90%) acceptability limit equations for the adaptive model were programmed into a hybrid building-management system as critical thresholds to switch the building between passive and active modes.
Yao et al. (2009)	Chongqing, China	Köppen Climate: Cfa (hot in the summer, cold in the winter)	Free-running buildings	Black-box energy model adopted to develop adaptive model of thermal comfort; questionnaire survey and environmental monitoring campaign used; statistical analysis used to determine coefficient for the study area	Adaptive coefficient for warm and cool conditions using data obtained from subject respondents were 0,293 and –0,125, respectively.
Földváry et al. (2018)	U.K. and China	Köppen Climate: • Cfb (temperate oceanic) • Cfa (hot in the summer, cold in the winter)	NV buildings	Group analytic hierarchy process adopted; longitudinal field surveys conducted with 41 UK and 33 Chinese subjects; pair-wise comparison strategy adopted; sensitivity analysis conducted.	Reduction of the current weight of psychological adaptation by 17.54% reversed the rankings between the physiological parameters and personal physical factors for the UK case.

(*Continued*)

Table 2.6 (Continued)

References	*A. Study Location*	*B. Climate Zones*	*C. Building Type and Ventilation Strategy*	*D. Methodology*	*E. Main Findings*
Mishra and Ramgopal (2014)	Chennai, Kolkata and Hyderabad, India	Köppen Climate: tropical (hot and humid)	NV buildings; air conditioning	Five adaptive-comfort equations computed; field-study approach adopted; multiple surveys conducted; ASHRAE TMY2 weather file used.	2°C was able to be added to the upper limit of comfort zone in NV buildings when fans were used during the warm months.
Parkinson et al. (2019)	Worldwide	ASHRAE Global Database II	NV and mix-mode buildings; air conditioning	ASHRAE RP884 database used; RStudio IDE used for statistical analysis; study included historic climatic averages from 27,593 records.	Neutral comfort temperatures in the Asian subset trended 1 – 2°C higher than in Western countries.

(Gagge et al., 1986; Jeong et al., 2016). This is because the adaptive-comfort model offers occupants the ability to adjust their thermal comfort in the outdoor environment according to their preferences and sensations.

According to Fanger et al. (1970), suitable indoor temperatures are commonly defined according to the thermal-comfort theory; this approach bases its definition of thermal comfort on physics and ignores the social and psychological aspects of thermal perception, and its formulation is entirely steady state and determines a narrow range of allowable temperatures throughout the year without regard for outdoor conditions. According to a study by Nicol et al. (2002), an alternative approach to defining comfortable temperatures is the adaptive approach, which stems from the results of a wide range of field studies (McCartney & Nicol, 2002; Nicol, 2017; Nicol & Humphreys, 2002); the study by Nicol et al. (2002) found that occupant thermal expectations are related to the outside climatic conditions on a variable basis.

Despite the fact that adaptation is a fundamental component of the adaptive thermal-comfort theory, little research has addressed the nature of adaptation or the influence of thermal history on current thermal preferences (Pastore & Andersen, 2019). A majority of the studies that have addressed thermal history were conducted. The theory behind adaptive thermal comfort underscores the idea that defining the ideal thermal environment as neutral is based on a deterministic approach, which does not take the psychological and cultural aspects of comfort into account and should therefore be questioned.

Many studies have considered a semantic analysis of experimental questionnaires and detected the influence of underlying culture on the deep meaning of the words used in those surveys (Griffiths, 1990; McCartney & Nicol, 2002; Nicol et al., 2012).

According to Michael et al. (2018), this problem is especially valid when referring to outdoor or hybrid environments, such as environments that can be considered 'warm' in the summer without the actual presence of discomfort. This is why multi-level questionnaires were developed to differentiate between 'sensation,' 'acceptability' and 'preferences' to thoroughly verify the coherence of various answers (Ghahramani et al., 2015; Mishra & Ramgopal, 2013). Investigations by Naylor et al. (2018) and Murtagh et al. (2019) included discussions of previous studies and new experimental data and found that there is a tendency for occupants to adapt to the conditions they normally encounter to measure their discomfort.

It is important to note that little is known about night-time thermal comfort (CIBSE, 2013). Studies have shown that sleep deprivation due to night-time overheating serves as a major motivation to buy domestic-cooling systems (Artmann et al., 2008; Della Valle et al., 2018); this trend is particularly problematic in the urban context, where there is less air movement and the urban heat island (UHI) effects are most noticeable after dark (Santamouris et al., 2007; Oikonomou et al., 2012; Santamouris & Kolokotsa, 2015).

Numerous field studies have found that occupants' thermal comfort varies with local climate (Nikolopoulou & Lykoudis, 2006; Yao et al., 2009; Carlucci et al., 2018). However, there is no generally recommended acceptable comfort range for existing residential buildings, nor are there specific thermal comfort prediction methods, particularly in Eastern Mediterranean countries in Europe. It should be noted that previous scholars work on investigating neutral adaptive thermal comfort in MFHs, which is available on ASHRAE Global Thermal Comfort Database II (Földváry et al., 2018).

This is the first study to undertake a longitudinal analysis of field investigation on the development of adaptive comfort of households in the Eastern Mediterranean climate where the weather is subtropical (*Cfa*) and partly semi-arid (*Bsh*) (Rubel *et al.,* 2017). Consequently, in urban areas of Famagusta, the stringent policy regulations for adopting globalised housing-design standards and the lack of ability to integrate a thermal-comfort assessment when evaluating BPEs for RTBs mean that apartment projects were planned and designed without considering the climatic aspects of the built environment. Overall, evidence indicates an urgent need to examine critical reflections more closely on the integration of the adaptive thermal-comfort theory into the BES to concurrently assess building overheating risks and occupant thermal comfort.

Long-Term Evaluation of General Thermal-Discomfort Indices

Most research on thermal discomfort has emphasised the use of several metrics and methods to assess occupants' thermal perceptions of their environment and their thermal responses to different climate conditions (Castellano et al., 2016; Földváry et al., 2018). Similarly, a new type of discomfort index was developed that aimed to describe the importance of considering long-term thermal indices in residential buildings in the scientific literature and related standards and guidelines (Borgeson & Brager, 2011). While most of these new indices summarise the thermal performance of a building in a single value, existing indices need to be analysed as part of long-term evaluation of the thermal conditions in residential buildings and as part of thermal-risk assessment that considers the environmental conditions of the study areas under investigation.

Surveys, such as those conducted by Kovats et al. (2014), showed that the indoor temperatures of most dwellings range from 17.2°C to 30.5°C and those occupants indicated that they do not feel thermally comfortable outside of this range, with individual tolerance in elderly occupants being on the lower side despite their capacity to adapt their physiological human body to high outdoor temperatures. A strong correlation between the energy consumed for space conditioning and the type of building and services offered to various population groups has also been emphasised (Kwok et al., 2017); this is due to the fact that according to an appropriate standard of annual indoor environment quality, building regulations and assessment criteria for a BPE are inherent in the European Directives on buildings energy-efficiency guidelines that were issued by the EPBD and regulated by the EN 15251 standards.

Notably, Nicol and Humphreys (2002) drew on an extensive range of assessment criteria to investigate occupants' thermal comfort. To be viewed as credible, an evaluation method should be based on sound scientific evidence and a clear understanding of the psychological and physiological aspects of the decisions that occupants are making (Wang et al., 2018). For this reason, different categories of indoor thermal environments that are dependent upon occupant expectations were recommended; these assessment criteria reveal that the highest degree of thermal expectation is applied to buildings inhabited by infants, people with disabilities and ill or elderly occupants—that is, in places where people are the most vulnerable. Table 2.7 describes these categories in line with the recommendation of the EN 15251 assessment criteria.

With this in mind, adopting similar international assessment benchmarking criteria to assess occupant thermal comfort in residential buildings seems like a common-sense decision. This is why the design and evaluation of indoor thermal environments in mechanically cooled and heated buildings were assessed using the following criteria based on the PMV and PPD indices, which were detailed in the EN ISO 7730 standards. Table 2.8 illustrates the summary of cooling and heating temperature ranges according to criteria recommended for mechanically conditioned residential buildings in the EN 15251 standards.

As noted in Table 2.8, the low heating set points in the winter range from 18°C to 21°C, and high cooling set points (SPs) in the summer range from 25.5°C to 27°C; this corresponds with the international thermal-comfort criteria laid out in EN 15251, depending on whether the level of thermal expectation is the degree of association related to vulnerable residents or moderately associated with existing buildings (Haldi & Robinson, 2010); these recommended set points are the maximum and minimum temperatures in the recommended threshold level. The EN 15251 criteria also highlight, however, that with respect to adapting to a neutral thermal-comfort setting, these temperature ranges vary according to building codes, thermal regulations, energy-saving targets and occupant influences on energy use (Wang et al., 2019).

The recommended EN 15251 benchmark criteria serve as an evaluation standard for the thermal environment in naturally ventilated residential buildings, which indicates an expectative adaptation level that is strongly correlated to the outdoor environment. At the same time, the ASHRAE 55 standard (2017), which involves similar conceptual approaches to assess occupant thermal comfort in underlying international norms, can also be incorporated within the adaptive approach. Nicol

Table 2.7 Applicability of Indoor-Environment Categories

ASHRAE 55 Category	*Scope*	*PPD*	*Fanger PMV*	*AdaptiveΔop (°K)*
90%	Utilised when a higher standard of thermal comfort is desired	<10%	$-0.5 < \text{PMV} < +0.5$	±2.5
80%	Utilised for typical applications and when other information is unavailable	<20%	$-0.85 < \text{PMV} < =0.85$	±3.5

Table 2.8 PPD and PMV Indices for Naturally Ventilated Buildings

Criteria	*Description*	*PPD*	*PMV*	*Temp. Range toHeat Clothing(0,5 clo*)*
I	High level of thermal-preference expectation required for vulnerable people with disabilities and underlying health conditions	<6	-0.2 < PMV < +0.2	23.5–25.5°C
II	Neutral thermal-preference expectation recommended for new and existing buildings	<10	-0.5 < PMV < +0.5	23.0–26.0°C
III	Moderate thermal-preference expectation recommended for existing buildings	<15	-0.7 < PMV < +0.7	22.0–27.0°C

clo: Clothing and thermal insulation value.

and Humphreys (2010) pointed out that some parameters lack information, which creates a gap in databases that were developed through different projects, classifications for applicable buildings, derivations of acceptable neutral temperature by respondents and outdoor-air temperatures recorded at the time of longitudinal surveys to assess occupant thermal comfort.

Notably, the proposed thermal-comfort assessment model recommended by the EN 15251 standards is largely based on the EU SCAT pilot-study project, which created a reference database to properly understand occupant thermal preferences and sensations in different climate regions across Europe (Schweiker et al., 2020). It is also important to mention that the ASHRAE 55 criteria (2017) are only applicable to naturally ventilated buildings; while the EN 15251 can be applied to any free-oscillation building type, with or without space-conditioning installations (O'Brien et al., 2020).

On a different note, these standards are applicable for metabolic rates that range from 1.0 to 1.3 MET, because they allow occupants some flexibility to adapt to their clothing. ASHRAE 55 (2017) and EN 15251 benchmark criteria include recommendations for acceptable lower and upper threshold limits for outdoor- and indoor-air temperatures (Hellwig et al., 2019). According to ASHRAE 55 criteria (2017), prevailing mean outdoor-air temperatures can vary from 10°C to 35°C, while the EN 15251 asserts that running mean outdoor-air temperatures can vary between 10°C and 30°C; both indicated that 25°C is the upper limit of acceptable occupant thermal-comfort levels in naturally ventilated buildings and in structures that use mechanical ventilation.

Previous research on thermal-comfort assessments utilised inconsistent and contradictory parameters, which affected the accuracy of the statistical analysis that was conducted on field-survey data (Halawa & Van Hoof, 2012; Haldi & Robinson, 2010). This is partially due to the preliminary experimental tests that took place in climatic chambers to closely control the physical variables involved in the equation (Ascione et al., 2015). Many studies also criticised this evaluation criteria, because tests in climatic chambers cannot produce the conditions of a real environment (Liu et al., 2012; Ascione et al., 2016). Additionally, Barbosa et al. (2015) and Brotas and Nicol (2015) argued that considering occupant interactions and their TPVs and TSVs could bring about more realistic assumptions to validate field-survey findings. The generalisability of the research on this subject is problematic (Indraganti & Rao, 2010; Teitelbaum et al., 2020). Many studies have confirmed the validity of Fanger's long-term discomfort index; in fact, Nicol and Humphreys (2010) suggested that longitudinal field surveys should consider employing the heat-balance model to define comfort.

In summary, none of the reviewed indices have been fully supported by relevant studies, which intended to provide a long-term evaluation of the general thermal-comfort conditions in buildings. This suggests that all boundary conditions that affect respondents' decisions on TPVs and TSVs should be made explicit to produce reliable results that can then be clearly interpreted.

Research Trends on Household Energy Consumption

Occupant behaviour significantly influences building performance and the quality of the indoor environment. To accurately predict occupants' actions, it is of primary importance to understand their decision-making process (Sun & Hong, 2017). Many studies have revolved around this correlation between occupant behaviour and energy use; these include the works of Böhringer and Rutherford (2008), Ozarisoy and Altan (2017b), Swan and Ugursal (2009), Ozarisoy (2022) and Kavgic et al. (2010). It is necessary, however, to update this extant literature review in line with the objective of the present study to establish scholarly precedents that are more relevant to the design methods that are currently available to calibrate building BPEs.

Regarding the matter of energy efficiency in the residential building sector, the EU Commission Delegated Regulation 244/2012 assumed that EPBD mandates would be supplemented by a methodology to calibrate the actual energy use of occupants, while also considering the energy-efficiency directives for residential buildings (Tagliapietra et al., 2019). An evaluation of occupants' energy-use patterns and the manner in which their habitual adaptive behaviours interact with and affect their actual energy use could provide an evidence-based methodological framework for policymaking decisions related to energy use (Stazi et al., 2014). This is why longitudinal surveys or long-term monitoring of buildings are principal determinant factors to establish a guidance framework plan that can be used by EU member states to calibrate the actual energy performance of existing building stocks before they are holistically retrofitted.

According to Cali et al. (2016), another challenge of investigating occupancy patterns on energy use is energy consumption and other effects related to climate change that make it difficult to accurately calibrate the energy performance of MFHs; this is partially due to energy and environmental regulations for these dwellings. Modelling in calibration studies is limited, which is why several studies concluded that a BES does not yield the same results as the actual operational outcomes of occupied dwellings (Barthelmes et al., 2018; Naylor et al., 2018; Santangelo et al., 2018). In a methodological approach, however, several different methodologies can be employed to address this knowledge gap and validate data from a DTS analysis.

Mahdavi and Pröglhöf (2009) determined that occupants of vulnerable neighbourhoods in social-housing developments in the UK and EU member states had a significant impact on energy consumption. This suggests that energy-calibration studies should consider householder occupancy profiles in their BES models to identify building-energy performance gaps in the residential sector. This can be attributed to the exponential importance of upgrading the energy efficiency of the social-housing stock, based on difficult-to-quantify home-energy performances of social-housing occupants. Furthermore, several researchers have attached a great deal of significance to the socio-demographic characteristics and energy-use behaviour of occupants and advocate for the inclusion of this data in BES evaluations conducted in the winter and in the summer (Borgeson & Brager, 2011; Bourgeois et al., 2006). As such, a thorough review of occupants' energy-use behaviour was established, which indicated that there is still much that needs to be done regarding calibrating occupants' actual energy use while continuing to take the thermal properties of buildings, occupants' real-life energy-use experiences and the environmental conditions of the pilot-study projects into consideration.

Regarding the abovementioned determinant energy-use factors, Stevenson and Rijal (2010) argued that uncertain input parameters in the BES model led researchers to establish a new methodology that links the technical aspects of base-case building-energy forecasting to dominant representative occupancy patterns to provide an overview of household energy consumption. The assessment criteria recommended by the CIBSE TM59 design methodology provide a subsequent basis to calibrate occupant energy use while also taking building overheating risks into account (CIBSE, 2017). It was indicated by Rinaldi et al. (2018) that this is an appropriate technical aspect to capture the effect that occupant behaviour has on household energy consumption; as such, limited research was conducted by the previous scholars to prove the validity of integrating the CIBSE TM59 assessment criteria into BPE studies for policymaking decisions related to energy use; these are listed in Table 2.9.

STS Conceptual Framework and Energy-Use Integrity

Research in the area of interaction—between dwellings, occupants and the environment—has primarily focused on occupants' interactions with a given type of heating control system used and the frequency with which these systems were used at home (d'Oca et al., 2018; Serrano–Jimenez et al., 2019). Several empirical studies have focused on occupant behaviour as it relates to the use of windows for

Table 2.9 Longitudinal Field Studies That Explored Occupant Influence on Energy Use

References	*A. Study Location*	*B. Primary Aim of Model*	*C. Methodology*	*D. Main Findings*
Mitra et al. (2019)	USA	To develop typical occupancy schedules for a range of household types and occupants	Twelve years of US 'Time-Use Survey' data used; 'Residential Energy Consumption Survey' data also used; descriptive statistics and correlation analysis conducted; 'Reference Building' and 'Building America' simulation protocols adopted.	Approximately 42 – 44% of occupants under 55 years of age were absent from their homes for 8 – 12 - hour periods.
Rinaldi et al. (2018)	Bari, Italy	To investigate the influence of occupant behaviour on building-energy performance	• Italian residential-building typologies were targeted. • Multivariate RA conducted; occupant behaviour and thermal-comfort preference questionnaire surveys conducted; online questionnaire undertaken with 450 participants; R software used for statistical analysis.	Occupants used heating system for a greater number of hours with higher set-point temperature values.
Erell et al. (2018)	Jerusalem and Nesher, Israel	To investigate the influence of occupant behaviour on the energy use of representative households in coastal Mediterranean and mountain temperate climate	Longitudinal field survey conducted with 120 middle-class urban households; socio-demographic characteristics recorded; BPE undertaken by DTS; multivariate RA conducted; computer simulations incorporating Israeli Standard 5.282 for Energy Labelling of Residential Buildings completed.	There was a weak correlation between simulated energy requirements for heating and cooling based on the floor plan and the thermal properties of the buildings.

thermal comfort, as well as the use of lighting and shading to ensure adequate daylighting in residential buildings (Page et al., 2008; Fabi et al., 2012). Although there is a paucity of evidence of occupant interactions with different types of cooling systems and the number of hours these systems were used in the home, these factors have been discussed in a few scholarly articles (Pesic et al., 2018). Park and Kim (2012) and Roetzel et al. (2010) highlighted the fact that various models are available to calibrate occupant energy-use behaviour based on the quantitative data that are collected and analysed to validate the findings from other research instruments embedded in these processes.

Borgeson and Brager (2011) insisted there are significant correlations between window-opening and occupants' behaviour. There is a colinear relationship between temperature difference and occupants' habitual adaptive behaviour in accordance with changing outdoor air temperatures; this consequently leads to occupant behaviour that follows a non-linear, unpredictable path, which makes modelling difficult. Research conducted by Erell et al. (2018) demonstrated that one of the breakthrough technical solutions proposed by Borgeson and Brager (2011) effectively models occupant behaviour by employing dynamic thermal simulations within the test reference year (TRY) weather files included in the analytical energy model; this methodological approach allows researchers to accurately predict the current energy performance of buildings within the context of climate-change projections. Many scholarly articles in this field have asserted that these energy models are not adequately conceptualised in a sense due to the uncertainty posed by occupant behavioural aspects in the energy models. Table 2.9 presents a two-part list of energy-calibration models developed by previous scholars to investigate correlations between occupant behaviour and energy use.

The importance of assessment methodology was emphasised in the UK and international standards. The UK governmental standard assessment procedure (SAP) for assigning an energy rating to dwellings takes a number of variables related to household size, socio-demographic characteristics, behaviour, etc., into account (Barthelmes et al., 2018). Discrepancies between the predicted and actual energy use have been observed, however, due to failure to include these occupant-related variables (Stazi et al., 2017; Wright & Firth, 2007). As such, there is an urgent need to combine several different approaches into one standardised framework that utilises existing scientific knowledge by establishing a link between occupant behaviour and energy use.

Developing a novel methodological approach that takes occupants' real-life energy-use experiences into consideration to accurately predict residential-building energy consumption is a matter of concern (Csoknyai et al., 2016; Rinaldi et al., 2018; Satre–Meloy, 2019). One reason for this is that in the scientific literature, an analysis of the thermal properties of buildings as it relates to the impact of energy consumption on the BPE studies would fall within the spectrum of a systems-based methodological STS approach (Andersen et al., 2009; Hong et al., 2019). As was previously discussed, interactions between dwellings, occupants and the environment are determinant factors for the calibration of energy models in the housing sector.

Research has revealed strong correlations between technical and social systems that can be used to predict household energy consumption when occupants' habitual adaptive behaviour and occupancy patterns are taken into account (Davies et al., 2011; Park & Kim, 2012; Wright et al., 2013). Moreover, several scholars have concluded that residential buildings relate as a system to outdoor environmental conditions, which directly and indirectly influence the STS design approach (Day & Gunderson, 2015; Gaetani et al., 2016; Jeong et al., 2016). Finally, energy-calibration models significantly correlate with the changes in the STS conceptual framework, which in turn allows researchers to consider modelling energy consumption and CO_2 emissions in a manner that is based on an econometric, statistical and building-physics method within the energy sector (Fitz-Geral et al., 2002; Yu et al., 2011).

These correlations could result in a more comprehensive understanding of household energy consumption and the associated CO_2 emissions (Gaetani et al., 2016). In fact, there are several variables that play a decisive role in the investigation of household occupancy patterns and energy use that are in line with energy- and CO_2-emission-reduction targets (Gatersleben et al., 2002; Gouveia et al., 2017); these factors are interrelated and dependent on one another due to differences in tenure type, building typology, occupants' awareness of energy use and their socio-demographic characteristics, amongst others.

Occupancy patterns have been studied to determine the main input parameters for energy-calibration models in building-modelling simulations to fully understand the significant effects of environmental conditions on home-energy performance (Gill et al., 2010; Kolokotroni et al., 2010); further analysis revealed that climatic variables are unpredictable, and a change in any of these could affect heating, cooling, ventilation and other related factors. Gupta and Gregg (2018) drew on an extensive range of sources to assess the overheating risks in residential buildings, and they concluded that the thermal properties of buildings are complex and there are several interdependencies and multi-causal relationships involved in occupant thermal-comfort optimisation efforts; interestingly, when attempting to assess overheating risks and optimise occupant thermal comfort, especially in vulnerable households, these variables related to changes in occupant behaviour in a nonlinear manner.

Galvin (2013) provided an in-depth analysis of the work by Ozarisoy and Altan (2018), which showed the relevance of occupants' age, health and economic conditions and the significant contribution of these factors when calibrating home-energy performance and taking the geographic domain of the research context into consideration. A possible explanation for this might be found in difficulties in predicting that have been observed and keeping dependent variables in BES models that were the result of current and future climate-change scenarios from being assigned when conducting a DTS analysis concurrently with dominant representative occupancy patterns (Martinez & Richardson, 1963; Santangelo et al., 2018).

In summary, the portion of the literature review involving household home-energy performance draws attention to the integrity of the STS design approach in building-energy calibrations by delving into the issue of using the STS as a new methodology for BPE studies and exploring the complex issue of occupancy patterns as it relates to domestic-energy use with the aim of filling the knowledge gap. This novel approach, which is capable of testing the energy effectiveness of retrofitting strategies to determine a roadmap of principles for policies and regulations in the housing sector, can eventually be proposed to policymakers.

Theoretical Framework Underpinning Household Energy Consumption

There is a plethora of theoretical adaptive frameworks within housing-energy studies that underpin deterministic variables and covariates of the socio-demographic characteristics of households (Hong et al., 2019; Roetzel, 2010; Sorgato et al., 2016; Ringel & Knodt, 2018). Natarajan et al. (2011) highlighted the limitations in disciplinary methods and acknowledged that occupancy patterns and occupants' habitual adaptive behaviour on window-opening patterns had an impact on the development of BES studies, which could result in technical constraints when assigning accurate occupancy profiles in a BES model for purposes of a DTS analysis.

By drawing on the concept of energy-calibration studies, Natarajan et al. (2011) were able to show that the limitations in disciplinary methods are largely dependent on discrepancies between predicted and actual energy consumption that were obtained from the DTS; there appears to be little consensus in the subject of building-energy simulation as to the extent to which limitations in the disciplinary approach to energy-policy conceptualisation could be improved by upgrading the thermal properties of archetype buildings that were identified for an energy-forecasting analysis (Ratti et al., 2005; Pyrgou et al., 2017).

A number of studies in the extant literature have advocated for an integrated framework that would promote a multi-disciplinary approach (Swan & Ugursal, 2009; Serghides et al., 2015; Stazi et al., 2017); since many household socio-demographic characteristics are directly correlated with energy use, an interdisciplinary approach would provide a theoretical framework that could capture the inter-relationships between scientific, technological, societal, economic and cultural factors in the context of an STS design approach.

Numerous studies have attempted to explain the correlations between household energy use and other variables: Ozarisoy and Altan (2017a) delineated a methodological framework to reduce heating-energy consumption based on a heat-transfer method; Ozarisoy (2022) explained the significance of upgrading building envelopes to reduce energy consumption; and Hart and de Dear (2004) provided a framework for weather sensitives that was related to estimating household energy consumption. A study of social-housing tenants in a degraded council estate in Oxfordshire in the UK found that household behavioural responses to technical improvements in building fabrics are behind the scope of the STS framework embodied in decision-making processes when responding to household energy-use requirements (Gupta et al., 2018).

Several studies have investigated various aspects of the effects of occupant behaviour on energy use (Du et al., 2021; Emery & Kippenhan, 2006; Gaetani et al., 2018). Further analyses in this area have highlighted the importance of an economic framework as one of the disciplinary frameworks to conceptualise home-energy performance when a human-based approach is taken into account in energy-calibration studies (Baker, 1991; Swan & Ugursal, 2009). These variables, which cause or explain a social-science-based framework, were delineated by Monyei et al. (2018) in a study on energy use in vulnerable households, which helped to illustrate the general situation before any further action to assess the energy-use habits of households through a field-survey approach was undertaken.

Amasyali and El–Gohary (2018) argued that the STS and the economic approaches were both incomplete when attempting to understand the complex impact of occupant interactions on home-energy performance. In accordance with this statement, Stevenson and Leman (2010) asserted that a combination of these approaches could be adequately provided by engineering and economic theories to form a physical-technical-economic framework, and that longitudinal surveys could be employed to investigate occupancy patterns and the socio-demographic characteristics of households. This would strongly support the manner in which energy policies aimed at upgrading the energy efficiency of building stocks are shaped.

As it relates to the knowledge gap in energy-calibration studies, it is evident that the aforementioned determinant factors are unlikely to capture the kind of complex problems that are plaguing the energy sector; thus, the findings draw attention to the fact that there is an urgent need for a more robust approach that needs to be addressed. Several studies on occupant behaviour, which comprehensively attempted to overcome the limitations of each disciplinary approach, suggested the use of an integrated conceptual framework (Stevenson and Rijal, 2010; Fotopoulou et al., 2018); this is because no modelling technique has been proposed that thoroughly captures the STS design approach to calibrating energy use that takes household socio-demographic characteristics into consideration.

Precedent of Longitudinal Field Studies to Analyse Energy Policy Design

Many field studies have been conducted in various climates across the world, which demonstrated that household energy consumption and occupant thermal comfort are closely linked to the local climate (Stazi et al., 2014; Frederiks et al., 2015; Schweiker et al., 2018). A previous study by Andersen et al. (2009), for example, conducted longitudinal surveys with vulnerable Danish households highlighting that the heat coefficient factor of building envelopes is the main cause for the high level of thermal discomfort. Therefore, this survey was conducted in one case study building only.

It is deemed to indicate that the findings which were intended to demonstrate the national representativeness of Danish housing stock cannot be generalised for the whole region due to the respondent limitation which can generate result bias. According to a study by Schrubsole et al. (2014), an alternative approach to defining representative occupancy profiles is not limited to the integration of standardised assessment criteria for a BES study, which stems from the results of a wide range of steady-state analyses of energy-calibration studies. The present study underscores the importance of identifying the representative housing stock and the manner in which it is integrated into the energy-calibration analysis; Table 2.10 delineates the integration of a BES into the development of an STS approach for policymakers.

Another pilot study conducted by Indraganti and Rao (2010) was the largest housing survey to date due to the quota sampling method that was implemented to conduct the questionnaire survey in a hot and dry climate. The present study identified five underlying determinant factors related to occupant behaviour and energy use: the type of domestic-cooling appliances that are used, the hours when cooling appliances are turned on, window-opening schedules, household size and occupants' socio-demographic characteristics. The appliance factor is related to more use of space conditioning (Wallace et al., 2010). The frequency of cooling appliance uses and window-opening schedules are related to behaviour that leads to even more energy use; household size is related to calculating the internal heat gains of each occupied space; and the socio-demographic factor is related to personal preferences for a warmer indoor environment and understanding the reasons for thermal discomfort.

Based on building-energy performance and to validate the findings of their questionnaire survey, Tink et al. (2018) suggested that monitoring comfort levels on a room-by-room basis would be an effective methodology to investigate biases in the responses of the sampling population. Table 2.11 lists literature that considered the relevance of habitual adaptive energy-use occupant behaviours, while also considering environmental conditions that were observed during longitudinal and transverse surveys of home-energy performance.

Another thought-provoking study by Moore et al. (2019) emphasised challenges in building-energy calibration studies that are derived from the failure of regulatory provisions to capture occupants' real-life energy-use experiences. This research investigated five high-performance state-of-the-art prototype houses in Australia for the purpose of assessing the thermal performance thereof to meet relevant regulatory housing standards and was similar to a research project by Rouleau et al. (2018) that assessed the thermal performance of residential buildings in Canada. Moore et al. (2019) concluded that targeted regulatory concepts have failed to meet expectations due to occupants' behavioural activity, which was not considered during the BPE; another reason for this failure was that generic occupancy profiles that did not consider the climate and other localised effects on energy consumption were assigned in the simulation model.

It should be noted, however, that the standards and regulations in question were unable to predict the comfort levels of occupants and low zero-energy-consumption targets (Symonds et al., 2017; Sempirini et al., 2017; Agliardi et al., 2018). The aforementioned study findings further emphasised the fact that it is essential to have a thorough understanding of the current lifestyles of different socio-demographic groups to develop an effective assessment methodology. The methodological framework developed for the present study and the findings thereof will provide a pathway to better understand current problems with existing post-war social-housing stock and residents' thermal satisfaction with their indoor environmental conditions.

Table 2.10 Previously Developed BES Frameworks

References	*A. Study Location*	*B. Primary Aim of Model*	*C. Methodology*	*D. Selected Software*
Pasichnyi et al. (2019)	Stockholm, Sweden	To develop a novel approach to use rich datasets to improve the energy efficiency of different building archetypes based on specific urban energy challenges	Urban BEM workflow developed to estimate energy savings for 5.532 buildings; aggregated energy models developed for building retrofitting and electric heating	• RStudio IDE • gridExtra Metrics • Tidyverse • UpSetR and VennDiagram • Energy Plus • Design Builder
Yang et al. (2018)	Florida, US	To develop an experimental validation of an early-design 3D dynamic thermal model	Exploratory case study approach at Off-Grid Zero Emissions Building at Florida State University; mathematical equations utilised; BES conducted	• Early-design stage 3D dynamic thermal simulation tool • vemBUILDING • Mathematical modelling tool • Fortan
Rouleau et al. (2019)	Quebec City, Canada (located in ASHRAE Climate Zone 7, a cold climate)	To develop an assessment method to determine energy-consumption robustness and dwelling thermal comfort related to occupant behaviour	High-performance multi-residential building selected for exploratory case study approach	• TRYNSS used to construct thermophysical models • A total of 1,000 annual occupant profiles were stochastically generated
D'Agostino and Parker (2018)	Fourteen locations in the European Union	To develop a simulation-based optimisation framework of cost-effective choices and EEMs for new buildings	Detached SFHs in 14 European locations selected as archetypes; BES conducted	• EnergyPlus and TRNSYS used to run DTS • BEopt energy-simulation software used for the economic evaluation of optimisation

(*Continued*)

Table 2.10 (Continued)

References	*A. Study Location*	*B. Primary Aim of Model*	*C. Methodology*	*D. Selected Software*
Ascione et al. (2019)	Italy	To develop a multi-objective (MO) optimisation approach to address building-envelope energy designs in different climate zones: Palermo (Zone B), Naples (Zone C), Florence (Zone D) and Milan (Zone E)	Genetic algorithm (GA) approach adopted; newly built five-storey residential building chosen for BES	• MATLAB used to build optimisation studies • EnergyPlus used for DTS

Table 2.11 Conceptualisation of Building-Energy Simulation to Develop STS Approach

Oladokun (2015) and Motawa and Oladokun (2015)	*Moustakas et al. (2011)*	*Ozarisoy (2022*	*Zhang et al. (2014)*	*Wei et al. (2018)*	*Walsh et al. (2013)*	*Ozarisoy and Altan (2018)*	*This Study*
Conceptualisation	Problem definition	Diagram construction and analysis	Problem identification and definition	Problem articulation	Problem identification and definition	Problem identification and definition	Problem identification and definition
	System conceptualisation	Simulation procurement	System conceptualisation	Dynamic hypothesis	System conceptualisation	System conceptualisation	System conceptualisation
Formulation	Model representation	—	Model formulation	Formulation	Model formulation	Model formulation	Model formulation
	Energy-performance model	—	Energy-use analysis	—	—	—	Energy-performance analysis
Testing	Model evaluation	Simulation procurement	Model evaluation	Testing	Simulation and validation	Model testing and validation	—
	—	—	Policy analysis	—	Policy analysis and improvement	Model use, implementation and dissemination	Energy-efficient retrofitting interventions
Implementation	Policy analysis and model use	Policy analysis and evaluation	Model use and implementation	Policy formulation and evaluation	Policy implementation	Design of learning strategy, energy efficiency	Policy formulation and analysis

Current Validation Techniques

Several researchers have investigated the development of energy-calibration methods in BES that were employed to determine occupant thermal comfort by optimising indoor-air temperatures on a broad scale and reducing energy consumption with the aim of diminishing the overheating risks in residential buildings (Lomas & Kane, 2012; Tweed et al., 2014; Tardioli et al., 2015). Furthermore, a significant number of steady-state analyses of BES studies have been conducted to assess the thermal performance of existing housing stock (Toftum et al., 2009; Evans et al., 2018). Only a few studies, however, have sought to provide a better understanding of the importance of considering human-based factors in the DTS model and properly calibrate the BES by using primary data sources gathered from longitudinal field studies (Colclough et al., 2018).

Asadi et al. (2014) concluded that the selection criteria of building-simulation input parameters increased the environmental socio-economic value of accurately forecasted energy scenarios. Additional evidence put forth by Emmerich et al. (2008) supported this assertion and demonstrated that incorporating a real-time series of climate files, actual occupancy patterns and household window-opening schedules into the black-box simulation model for the DTS analysis could provide an overview of home-energy performance. With this in mind, it is evident that the potential benefits of a greater reduction in energy consumption and the value of the built asset will increase (Fokaides et al., 2014; Giorgio et al., 2018).

Recognition of the limitations and inherent contradictions of the development of a black-box model for the DTS analysis led a few studies to fully understand overheating and the impact thereof on occupants' thermal comfort, particularly in Eastern Mediterranean EU member states, even though this issue remains unaddressed (Ascione et al., 2019). Despite the decisive role of these factors in demonstrating variations of simulation input parameters and detecting uncertainty in the datasets for energy-calibration analysis, the results reveal a high accuracy for the nearly zero energy building prototype. It was found that the analytical energy model offers a prediction accuracy of 2.2% and 7.03% for energy use and indoor zone temperature, respectively (Hart & de Dear, 2014).

A pilot case study by Kavgic et al. (2010) tested the efficiency of various retrofitting technologies and concluded that it was difficult-to-quantify weather profiles that are concurrently assigned in the black-box model with occupancy patterns gathered through a questionnaire survey. A notable analysis and discussion on this subject by Kylili et al. (2016) mentioned that social-housing RTBs often underperform when compared to design specifications because of discrepancies in building-fabric thermal performance, system efficiency and occupant behaviour.

Even though Agliardi et al. (2018) proposed a building-optimisation study, only a steady-state analysis that embedded future climate scenarios into the black-box model was conducted to assess the validity of the assumptions for the subsequent research phase, as shown in Table 2.12. The results show that an acceptable reduction in cooling-energy consumption in the representative housing typology was achieved during the summer, but additional studies are needed for a more

Table 2.12 Validation Techniques to Assess Overheating Risks and Analyse Model Calibrations

Technique	*Description*	*Application*
Comparison to other models	Various validated simulation-model results compared to results of other valid models	Applied to validate simulation models
Worst-case scenario development	Analytical energy-model structures and outputs for extreme and unlikely factor-level combinations in the system viewed as plausible	Applied as a comparative study of worst-case scenario, such as implementation of CIBSE TM59 overheating-assessment criteria and EN15251 thermal-adaptive theory, to assess overheating risks and occupants' thermal comfort
Face validation	Individuals knowledgeable about system (i.e., practitioners and energy consultants) asked if model and/or behaviour thereof are reasonable	Applied to validate model-input data
Historic data validation	If historic data exist, or if data are collected to build and/ or test system model, some are used to build the model, and remainder are used to determine (i.e., to test) whether model behaved in the same manner as the system.	Applied to validate simulation models
Historic methods (i.e., rationalism, empiricism and positive economics)	Empirical method used to develop study's validation technique, because method requires empirical validation of every assumption and outcome.	Applied to validate simulation models
Multi-stage validation	• Model assumption developed according to theories, observations and general knowledge • Model assumptions validated by empirically testing whenever possible • Model input–output relationship compared (i.e., tested) against real system	Applied to validate simulation model

comprehensive understanding of the implications of considering human-based factors in BES models in retrofitting efforts for residential buildings.

Schneider et al. (2016) conducted an exemplar study that addressed summertime overheating, wherein the authors described overheating risks and delineated methods to assess the likelihood of overheating in a base-case representative-building typology during long-term heatwave peaks in the summer. In addition to this study, Symonds et al. (2017) proposed an index to predict summer overheating risks caused by heat-stress-index factors that were found to influence occupants' thermal comfort.

Roaf et al. (2009) used the 'Percentage Outside Range' index, which facilitated an assessment of cooling-degree days in several building-envelope retrofitting strategies that were implemented in social-housing apartment units throughout Europe. Another pilot study was undertaken by Corrado and Ballarini (2016), in which the significance of adopting the 'Exceedance: PPD' and 'Exceedance: Adaptive' indices were explored, and the aforementioned indices were utilised by employing black-box models for the DTS analysis (Fokaides et al., 2011; Pignatta et al., 2017; Santangelo et al., 2018). One of the main goals of these studies was to investigate the prevalence of summer thermal discomfort in naturally ventilated dwellings located in 16 different climate zones to fully comprehend the impact of climate-related factors on the thermal preferences and sensations of the study participants.

There is a growing recognition that the overheating phenomenon in a variety of field-assessment procedures could be deployed in different experimental studies to corroborate the thermal properties of buildings, occupant behaviour and the physical environment and aid in the development of national adaptive thermal-comfort indices for the European Survey of Thermal Comfort database. In the name of this endeavour, Schweiker and Wagner (2015) adopted the 'Percentage Outside Range' methodological approach, which is based on the European adaptive-comfort model, to reduce the impact of overheating that is created by an increase in thermal mass.

The present study outlines the development of the thermal-comfort indices of previous studies and the outcomes thereof to fully understand overheating risks and household domestic-energy use and accurately assess occupant thermal comfort. It should be emphasised at this point that energy-calibration studies should be considered in relation to the representative in vivo experiences of household energy consumption and the building-fabric thermal performance of buildings, which align with intergenerational occupants, rather than with the state of the buildings.

Review of Available Energy-Simulation Software Packages

There is a growing interest in the use of energy-simulation tools to conduct a BPE, which has led to a wide range of simulation software suites that are accessible to practitioners and designers (Coakley et al., 2014; Harish & Kumar, 2016; Østergård et al., 2016). Analytical tools are classified according to the level of the computational script that was developed and the complexity thereof, including steady-state, computational fluid dynamic (CFD) and dynamic tools (Loga et al., 2016). This classification is limited to the resolution of the digital model, the number of user inputs and the time that is needed to successfully develop BES models. Steady-state tools provide detailed daily or seasonal performances and visualisations of energy flows over a two- or three-dimensional domain that helps to refine the design at later and more advanced design stages (Yang et al., 2018). To properly conceptualise the analytical energy model that was developed for the present study, commonly used BES packages were reviewed globally, as shown in Table 2.13.

Table 2.13 presents a list of BES software suites and plug-in components that were utilised to calculate numeric experiments. This section examines the Integrated Environmental Solutions (IES) software engine, which is used as part of the design process of buildings to predict energy performances of public buildings or high-density residential estates to improve the efficiency of recommended building materials; this software suite is a commercial tool that can be used between designers and their clients.

Several studies employed the IES software to assess the energy performance of archetype buildings and create an overview of household energy use and associated CO_2 emissions for energy-policymaking decisions (Pasichnyi et al., 2019; Stojiljković et al., 2015). In a study conducted by Kristensen et al. (2018), Dutch residential buildings were selected as a sampling strategy for existing housing stock.

The IES software is widely used for commercial purposes, and a few exemplar research case studies utilised the IES software suite as part of their methodologies. Balvedi et al. (2018) insisted that the IES software should be widely used by scholars to demonstrate the universal validity of this BES platform in large-scale residential projects to eliminate research bias and uncertainty related to the results obtained from DTS analyses; this research gap should be addressed.

The IES software offers structural engineers a versatile range of energy-modelling techniques when they are undertaking a calibration analysis to validate available data sources (Choi, 2017). The platform provides effective tools to construct an actual building geometry and assign building-thermal properties, occupancy profiles and ventilation schedules for each room to undertake various numeric experiments targeted for BPE studies (Bateson, 2014). The IES software consists of standardised occupancy profiles and infiltration rates for naturally ventilated buildings, and users are able to adapt an analytical energy model to their own purpose-built design and simulation input parameters, such as occupancy profiles, window-opening schedules, clothing value and metabolic rates to assess household energy performance (Fokaides et al., 2016).

A thorough analysis of previous scholarly work on BPEs revealed that Design Builder software was commonly used as an analytical energy-simulation tool (Hoes et al., 2009). Design Builder, which is an open-source dataset available in EnergyPlus, is interoperable with the EnergyPlus software suite, and it assigns weather files in the simulation platform; this software is limited to using interoperable large-scale weather datasets to assess the overheating risk of buildings.

As can be seen in Table 2.13, the IES software allows large-scale weather files to be uploaded onto the simulation platform and an edit time series is included in

Table 2.13 Summary of Data-Processing Capabilities of BES Software and Plug-Ins

Software Plug-In	*Software Package*	*Open Source*	*Supports Optimisation*	*Supports Calibration*	*BIM[a] Interoper-ability*	*Weather Data Handling*	*Fast Processing Capability*
IESVE	IESVE		✓	✓	✓	✓	High
IDA ICE	IDA ICE		✓		✓		Medium
eQUEST	DOE–2						Low
Design Builder	EnergyPlus		✓		✓		Medium
Open StudioPAT	EnergyPlus	✓	✓	✓	✓	✓	High
Ladybug & Honeybee	EnergyPlus	✓			✓	✓	Medium
jEplus	EnergyPlus	✓	✓				High
Modclkit	EnergyPlus						Low
MLE+	EnergyPlus	✓	✓				Low
EpXL	EnergyPlus	✓	✓				Medium
Eppy	EnergyPlus	✓	✓				High

BIM: Building-information modelling.

Source: Adapted from Ma et al. (2012).

the datasets before the DTS analysis is run (Chen et al., 2016). This is the most advantageous factor in comparison to selecting the Design Builder, EnergyPlus, TRNSYS as a research tool to demonstrate the representativeness of archetype building selection for the development of base-case scenario in energy policy (Aldossary et al., 2014; Ioannou et al., 2018).

The IES computational platform provided the most accurate data related to solar-exposure analyses of buildings (Habibi, 2017); this is because large-scale weather files can demonstrate the solar-diffusion frequency of building-thermal properties for the initial overheating risk analysis. The main advantage of employing the IES software for a solar-exposure analysis is that it incorporates a computational script that was developed to calculate the diffuse parameters of building envelopes. A solar-exposure analysis that was conducted by Kokaraki et al. (2019) led to a better understanding of the solar-irradiance factor and the impact thereof on building envelopes, and the findings of this study were validated by a thermal-imaging survey.

Contrarily, Design Builder does not provide the opportunity to undertake a solar-exposure analysis in conjunction with weather files that are assigned in the simulation model; it only applies industry benchmarks of ASHRAE 55-90.1 standards and CIBSE TM52 for the purpose of an overheating analysis (Jenkins et al., 2013). There is a limited amount of time to develop a new method to implement building EPCs, which do not exist in NC while the IES software applies benchmarking assessments.

The dearth number of studies considered the adoption of industry benchmarks or local standard assessment protocols to report the dynamic thermal simulation findings while assessing the energy performance of buildings (Dodoo et al., 2017). Therefore, most of the studies are neglected to consider human-based approach to energy simulation, which is worthy of investigation. In addition, the IES software allows an assessment of the life cycle cost assessment (LCCA) of buildings and integrates the results into a building regulation-compliant plug-in interface to demonstrate accurate economically viable studies (Mostavi et al., 2017).

The interface of the IES software and Design Builder claim to be able to undertake building-optimisation studies for building retrofitting efforts (Juan et al., 2009; Sierra et al., 2018). The results obtained from Design Builder allows the data to run a parametric analysis by using genetic algorithms (GAs) to demonstrate the energy efficiency of retrofitting design strategies.

An exploratory case study approach was conducted by Kotireddy et al. (2019), which concluded that the GA approach was adopted to develop a new simulation framework based on multi-objective optimisation of Dutch residential buildings; the study results were transferred into the parametric regression models with the use of machine-learning techniques.

In 2020, IES developed a building-optimisation tool for the iSCAN platform for energy-related building renovations. This software implements standardised building-optimisation strategies to test the energy efficiency of different building materials and technologies, which are available in the datasets that are included in the interface; one of the constraints of this tool is that it is unable to design optimisation strategies with embedded human-based data (Atam, 2017; Liu et al., 2019). While it is available to use for commercial purposes, no studies have yet employed this building-optimisation tool to create engineering research. Notably, to date, several scholars have used the Design Builder building-optimisation tool to calculate numeric experiments, including genetic algorithms were undertaken (Andriamamonjy et al., 2019; Schwartz & Raslan, 2013).

In the BPEs, the IES software and Design Builder platform were compatible with each other for a DTS analysis and able to use human-based data in the simulation model and to assign weather files for a building-fabric thermal-performance analysis. Both are able to incorporate the ASHRAE 55-90.1 and CIBSE TM52 industry benchmarks to concurrently assess building overheating risks and occupant thermal comfort (Crawley et al., 2008; Zakula et al., 2019). Even though the CIBSE TM59 guidelines were included in the IES interface in 2020 for overheating-risk assessments by incorporating dominant representative occupancy profiles, this was not included in Design Builder. Figure 2.1 presents a list of energy-simulation software packages that were initially tested to better understand the efficiency of the IES software suite for the present study.

A few studies reported that data obtained from the Energy Plus weather datasets, which are available in the EPW format, were incompatible with the computational script that was developed for the IES software (Hopfe & Hensen, 2011; Tian et al., 2018). To avoid discrepancies, the EPW datasets were corrected using the Weather Analytics software, which is interoperable with the IES simulation platform. Evidence suggests that unlimited data can be obtained from the IES software; any data can be formatted into the gbXML format, which is compatible with the computational script of Design Builder, EDSL Tas, Autodesk® Revit® Green Building Studio® and SketchUp (Abanda & Byers, 2016); this adaptability can be used to develop a new simulation framework that will assess the energy performance of buildings.

One of the constraints of using the gbXML analytical building geometry constructed in the IES platform is that the available and designed thermal properties of a case study building in the thermal-properties-template manager platform are incompatible with the other simulation software engines (Ferrari et al., 2019). As with other energy-simulation engines, the thermal properties of building materials should be manually adjusted in the standardised templates that were previously designed in these software suites to avoid this discrepancy.

The building geometry shown in Figure 2.13 was constructed in the IES platform, and a gbXML file was generated to test the interoperability of the software with Design Builder and Autodesk® Revit® Green Building Studio® by using a steady-state analysis of the thermal performances of buildings. A taxonomy analysis determined that all three software engines provide cooling, heating, energy consumption, overall electricity use, daylight and solar-shading analyses, renewable energy potentialities, a CFD analysis and the LCCA of buildings (Magnier & Haghighat, 2010; Nwodo & Anumba, 2019). After a thorough analysis of all three software platforms, the IES software suite provided detailed time series that were extracted from a DTS analysis through a steady-state BES; it can also be used to conduct a dynamic thermal analysis by including secondary datasets, such as sub-metering data, in the simulation model

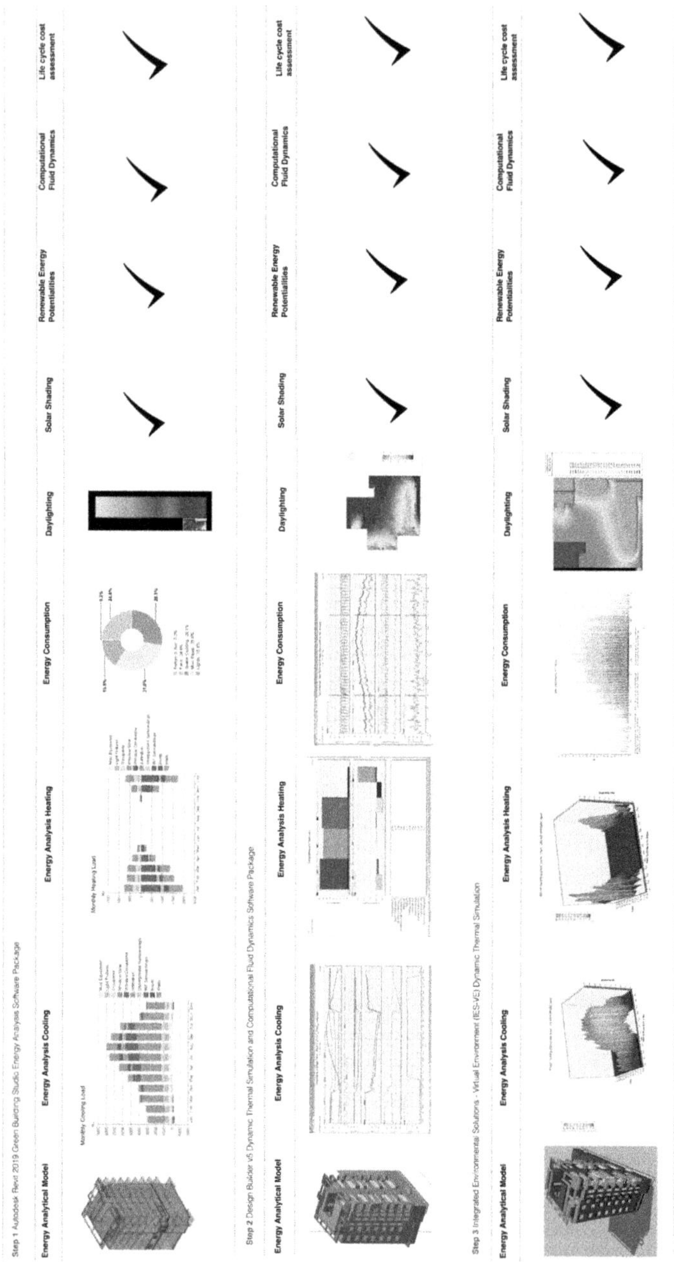

Figure 2.1 Preliminary analysis of energy software tested to explore strengths and weaknesses of IES software.

(Mata et al., 2019). The IES software links to the LCCA plug-in that is available on the IES platform to test the cost-effectiveness of building-optimisation studies.

Design Builder provided simulation targets that were similar to the IES software, except when the obtained data were not detailed; discrepancies were frequently detected due to the lack of available time series for the DTS analysis included in the weather files. Notably, Autodesk® Revit® Green Building Studio® can also be used in BES studies by integrating the gbXML file that is constructed in the IES platform. Revit® is compatible with the Geographic Information System (GIS) software suite when identifying the location of a case study building; unlike Design Builder and IES, however, weather files cannot be assigned in the Revit® energy-analysis plug-in interface to generate an analytical energy model, and the data obtained with this platform for an energy analysis are based on the standardised online dashboard platform in Green Building Studio®, which provides an overview of building-energy performance without actually including human-based data in the model (Machete et al., 2018). This is why Revit® is not preferred for research purposes. The IES simulation interface, the computational script, that was developed to conduct a solar-exposure analysis of buildings and the integration thereof to develop building regulations proved to be determinant factors in the decision to use the IES software suite as the BES tool in the present study.

Rationale for the Present Study

Many post-war European social-housing estates were designed and built in accordance with criteria that typically did not address reduced energy demand due to a lack of regulatory bodies and constraints of construction materials and techniques between the 1950s and the 1980s (Ozarisoy & Altan, 2017a). To date, many of these residential buildings have not yet undergone building-envelope refurbishment or retrofitting; as such, this social-housing stock is characterised by low-quality thermal properties, which led to increased energy consumption; this also resulted in a poor-quality indoor environment, which affects the occupants' health and well-being.

Northern Cyprus (NC) is marked by a lack of construction standards, codes of practice and building regulations associated with a thorough investigation of the building-energy performance of existing housing stock, which does not help to resolve the issue of high energy demand in the residential sector. Moreover, there are no benchmarks for the implementation of the EPBD mandates and the procurement of Energy-Performance Certificates (EPCs) to assess the energy performance of any type of building, nor is there an official plan to regulate any long-term holistic retrofitting schemes and address the knowledge gap in the field of energy efficiency. Due to its standing as a de facto state, EPBD recommendations are not binding in NC, and there is no regulatory framework in place to promote the benefits of energy-efficiency upgrades by integrating STS design models into retrofitting-policy design; a lack of social-housing development proposals and energy-policy implementation were observed in this research context. Because a governmental priority has not been placed on energy-efficiency awareness and understanding the thermal performance of existing housing stock, the present study brought attention to building-fabric thermal performance and the development of a base-case scenario by selecting social households for a sampling size and integrating evidence-based data into building-energy models. Debates on the energy-performance of social housing in EU member states have revealed considerable shortcomings in the integration of current design methods that concurrently assess building overheating risks and optimise occupants' thermal comfort to develop an effective conceptual framework for each member state that considers variations in climate characteristics, building codes and regulations and household types during the decision-making process.

The importance of developing an evidence-based energy-policy framework to assess robust energy-performance evaluation and certification schemes in Eastern Mediterranean EU countries has not yet been addressed. A theoretical investigation of the STS design model and the integrity thereof in a multi-criteria decision-making process have gained momentum in research endeavours related to energy and the social sciences. A thorough empirical analysis of the energy-planning systems and energy-efficiency investments were the result of strategic policies and political issues that arose because of multi-disciplinary research and were developed within the scope of the EPBD mandates. To address the knowledge gap in current energy-efficiency frameworks, the present study adopted the STS design approach to develop a new adaptation of building-energy performance assessment criteria and to identify the neutral thermal-comfort thresholds of households through a longitudinal field survey.

Data obtained from the field investigation provided subsequent information for building-energy simulation (BES) studies to validate the research findings. It should be noted that throughout the development of the STS model, household occupancy patterns and the influence thereof on energy use were corroborated with the BES model to demonstrate the economic viability of retrofitting design strategies that would be developed for policymakers.

Stages of Development of STS Conceptual Framework

This empirical study employed the STS approach to developing a bottom-up energy-policy framework for the residential sector. It adopted a mixed-method research design approach by conducting a questionnaire survey, implementing thermal imaging, monitoring the environment and conducting building-energy simulation studies. The focus of the present study was to statistically determine occupant behavioural patterns that are associated with heating- and cooling-energy consumption and to identify household socio-demographic characteristics that contribute to the development of energy-user profiles.

This study initially adopted a mixed-method research design that primarily utilised a thermal-comfort assessment and questionnaire-based surveys of households to gather information related to home-energy performance and to determine optimum thermal-comfort levels before undertaking a BES study. In an attempt to meet the target research objective and answer the research questions (RQs), a social-science framework was put into place at the start of the present study; this, in turn, provided a rationale for quantitative and qualitative components in the development of an energy-policy framework that is based on this empirical analysis.

The fieldwork for the present study consisted of examining first-hand experiences to fully understand current EPBD implementation schemes and the impact thereof on home-energy performance in the NC (Darby, 2017; Renner & Giampietro, 2020). Before conducting the semi-structured interviews with households, on-site site observations were recorded to analyse the taxonomy of the housing stock (Mould & Baker, 2017; Wolff et al., 2017). The empirical framework is premised on an analysis of the feedback that was collected in 2018 from the households during the hottest summer month of August.

This research consisted of interdisciplinary cooperation in an area where single-discipline studies are typically conducted; in this endeavour, there was communication and collaboration between the research, design and implementation of energy-efficiency retrofitting efforts and challenges that were the result of the EPBD mandates (Cunha et al., 2020). To identify the EEG in the present study, data were primarily collected through feed-forward interviews with households. Additionally, objective data, such as household socio-demographic characteristics and occupancy profiles, were also collected to aid in the interpretation of the study results with the in situ measurements that were concurrently recorded with the interviews. The pragmatist research approach was designed for the present study.

As a mixed-model approach, a convergent parallel-mixed method was considered to be the most appropriate strategy that could be employed in the present study; this is a variation of a mixed-method design in which the researcher converges or merges often-ignored quantitative and qualitative data to provide a comprehensive analysis of the research problem (Flowerdew & Martin, 2002; Ingeborgrud et al., 2020; Wolf et al., 2017). In this research approach, the researcher collects both types of data at approximately the same time, then integrates this information and interprets the overall results; contradictions or incongruent findings are explained or further probed in the survey design. After collecting necessary data via on-site observations, the present study focused on an explanatory case study approach of the prototype base-case post-war social-housing development estates in NC. Semi-structured interviews, which were in the form of a questionnaire survey, were conducted with selected households to provide evidence-based retrofitting design policies and recommendations for energy-efficiency guidelines in the residential sector.

A Bottom-up Energy-Policy Design Approach

The concept of the present study is to integrate a design method into the STS approach to develop a bottom-up energy-policy framework for the implementation of the EPBD objectives through holistic retrofitting schemes across the EU member states. The present study aims to identify gaps in the knowledge related to the challenges of implementing EPCs in buildings to measure the energy-performance gap and properly understand the importance of occupancy patterns on energy use during the decision-making process in the residential sector.

A significant theoretical issue that has dominated the field of energy research and design for many years is related to building-energy modelling approaches that failed to consider the STS conceptual framework for a bottom-up energy-policy design that is worthy of investigation. This is due to a lack of information about household socio-demographic characteristics, occupancy patterns and interactions with the built environment that could be addressed through a BES study. Mahdavi (2020) pointed out that BES tools provide effective retrofitting policy design scenarios, but household energy-use behaviour and thermal-comfort assessments have not been thoroughly investigated to determine the outcomes based on a novel analytical energy-modelling approach; this indicates that energy-demand scenarios from top-down and bottom-up approaches can be aggregated to fill the EEG.

A comprehensive understanding of the manner in which an STS approach contributes to bottom-up energy-policy design is still lacking. To date, several hybrid models of these two approaches have been developed and employed for more-robust building-energy models, but none of these studies considered concurrently optimising occupant thermal comfort as buildings are being retrofitted. According to Geels et al. (2018), a bottom-up approach would be applicable to empirical studies that utilise limited secondary-data sources to develop an analytical framework that will support energy policies at the local and national levels. Alternately, the top-down approach is recommended when data are used to identify the knowledge gap related to energy use and undertake statistical analysis, as shown in Table 2.14.

The comparison revealed that forecasting a household-energy model for the integration of the bottom-up approach would improve nationwide policy subsidisation schemes while considering the EPBD mandates (Balest et al., 2019; Li & Strachan, 2019). A thorough analysis of the STS approach would provide versatile data sources that are compatible with a wide range of BES tools that are available to researchers engaged in steady-state and dynamic thermal analyses. According to Sahakian et al. (2021) and Kunc et al. (2018), integrating a bottom-up approach requires input sources that are based on quantitative data or assessment criteria variables that are measurable on a Likert scale, such as the energy efficiency of hot-water systems and the fabric insulation of dwellings for building-performance evaluations (BPEs).

It should be noted that a similar approach could be applied to energy-policy designs by adopting Forrester's systems dynamic approach that is only based on qualitative data to undertake BES studies (Forrester, 1976); it should be noted that Forrester's tradition in building physics, which was developed in 1946, is widely acknowledged by scholars and is a matter of a conceptual analysis needs a new STS approach design method related to energy use (Forrester, 2007). Notably, the present study contributes to Forrester's systems dynamic approach by exploring correlations between household socio-demographic characteristics and occupancy patterns that influence home-energy use.

A debate has taken place in many energy-modelling studies related to the selection criteria of archetype housing stock and household energy-use behaviour (Bienvenido–Huertas et al., 2021). As a consequence, the STS approach has been challenged by energy-research studies that demonstrated the usefulness of the bottom-up approach, which is widely used for BES studies (Marzouk & Seleem, 2018;

Table 2.14 Benefits and Limitations of Top-Down and Bottom-Up Energy-Modelling Approaches

Characteristics	*Top-Down*	*Bottom-Up Statistical*	*Bottom-UpBuilding Physics*
Benefits	• Focuses on the interaction between the energy sector and the economy at large • Uses aggregated economic data • Does not require detailed technological descriptions • Capable of modelling relationships between different economic variables and energy demand • Able to model the impacts of various social cost–benefit energy-and-emission policies and scenarios	• Includes macro- and socio-economic effects • Able to determine typical end-use energy consumption • Easier to develop and use • Does not require detailed data, only billing data and a simple survey	• Describes current and prospective technologies in detail • Uses physically measurable data • Enables policies to more effectively target consumption • Assesses and quantifies the impact of different combinations of technology related to delivered energy • Estimates the least-cost combination of technological measures to meet given demand
Limitations	• Dependent upon past energy–economy interactions to project future trends • Lacks the necessary level of technological detail • Less suitable to examine technology-specific policies • Typically assumes efficient gaps	• Does not provide much data or flexibility • Limited capacity to assess the impact of energy-conservation measures (ECMs) • Relies on historical consumption data • Requires large samples • Multi-collinearity	• Poorly describes market interactions • Neglects the relationship between energy use and macro-economic activity • Requires a significant amount of technical data • Does not determine human behaviour within the model, but by external assumptions

Source: Adapted from Kavgic et al. (2010).

Shih & Tseng, 2014); these studies concluded that the development of an evidence-based STS conceptual framework would establish a novel design method in line with Forrester's tradition. The present study adopted a mixed-method approach to provide subsequent information for BES studies; in this study, the BES model consisted of human-based data that were collected through a household questionnaire survey and an examination of household energy-bill data to corroborate the dynamic thermal-simulation analysis.

Scholars have long debated integrating Forrester's dynamic approach to developing effective energy-policy designs and subsidisation schemes while delivering an assessment of EPCs that should be addressed. Turning now to the experimental evidence for the STS approach, Forrester (2016) argued that disaggregated quantitative data correlate with the thermal conductivity levels of building materials, household socio-demographic characteristics and climate characteristics of the built environment to provide additional information for BES studies on home-energy performance.

To address the EEG, Lopes et al. (2015) noted that the regression analysis (RA) technique facilitates the development of a quantitative design method that contradicts the theoretical philosophy that undergirds Forrester's systems dynamic approach. As such, the present study implies that the STS approach was developed by undertaking dynamic thermal simulations to evaluate building-fabric thermal performance before designing retrofitting interventions; this study also offers insights into building-energy assessment that are based on real-life occupant data, which were validated to build interval confidence in the analytical energy model for the purpose of a dynamic thermal simulation (DTS) analysis.

Benefits and Constraints of the STS Conceptual Framework

Much of the available literature on home-energy performance surrounds the question of whether the complexity of household socio-demographic characteristics can be corroborated in a building-modelling simulation (Chen et al., 2019; Valentina et al., 2012). Hitchcock (1993) was significantly more concerned, however, with the environmental aspects of a household, consisting of three main dependent variables: the climate, economic and cultural systems. In a review of different environmental parameters, Hitchcock highlighted the importance of a climate system that consists of external temperatures, insulation and wind levels, and he posited that all of these variables work together in a seamless manner to influence household energy consumption. He further found that energy consumption in domestic buildings is correlated with the household level of income. These findings are also visible in other studies of social housing tenants conducted in Europe and the UK (Carpino et al., 2018; Hummel et al., 2021; Willan et al., 2020); these studies indicate that energy consumption is driven by the needs and behaviours of occupants and/or by the thermal properties of dwellings.

Guerra-Santin et al. (2018) emphasised the importance of considering interactions between energy consumption and occupants' socio-demographic characteristics like income and household size; they argued that larger households or households with higher incomes tend to consume more energy, compared to average mean-sized households. Sonetti et al. (2020) examined household consumption by employing a mixed-methods research design with a methodological approach that was based on the concept of occupants' metabolic activity at home. In this present study, to thoroughly investigate the physiological parameters of households, statistical analyses were carried out in accordance with the STS conceptual framework.

A study by Bartiaux and Gram–Hanssen (2005) considered the correlation between socio-political variables and household energy consumption by comparing the EPC datasets of Denmark and Belgium. The findings of that study reveal that the most energy-intensive apartments have a technical constraint in conducting energy-efficiency measures (EEMs) and should anticipate the adoption of cost-effective retrofit design strategies. A study by Abrahamse and Steg (2011), which was proposed as a meaningful, accessible approach that could be adopted by policymakers for upgrading the energy efficiency of post-war social housing stock in Europe, further clarified the importance of the correlation between psychological and socio-demographic variables that influence home-energy performance. That study's findings raise questions as to how long-term retrofit design strategies might be developed such that they will improve indoor-air environment quality and reduce household energy consumption, taking into account interactions between involved householders dependent on local needs.

While several studies have highlighted the potential of the housing sector to contribute to both energy-consumption and CO_2 emission reductions, other studies have investigated different attitudinal and socio-demographic variables and found that an explanatory theory is the most effective approach for identifying income and size of a household as the main dependent variables for energy-saving measures (Mortensen et al., 2014). Additionally, many studies have empirically explored the importance of occupant behaviour as related to socio-demographic characteristics and household size (Gianfrate et al., 2017; Gupta et al., 2018; Kearns et al., 2019). These findings reveal that there is an association between occupancy density and energy consumption, indicating that longer occupancy hours lead to increased energy use.

Some authors have primarily expressed an interest in households that exhibit different behavioural patterns that exemplify adaptive thermal comfort (Hong et al., 2016; Marzouk & Azab, 2017; Murtagh et al., 2019). These studies highlight that the frequency of opening windows, occupancy hours and setting the temperature of wall thermostats or air conditioning (A/C) systems are all associated with influences on household energy use. This is why the STS approach was employed in the present study to investigate these concerns via a questionnaire survey; variables related to the socio-demographic characteristics of households and environmental conditions of the research context were also investigated. This study attempted to fully understand respondents' environmental attitudes toward optimising occupant thermal comfort and thereby provide a basis for subsequent analysis that can be used in building-modelling optimisation efforts.

Lessons to Learn from the STS Approach for Energy-Policy Design

This empirical study set out to investigate the technical issues involved in building a performance evaluation of representative archetype RTBs in a post-war social housing development. This study related two basic principles of building physics to the thermal properties and peculiarities of these archetype buildings. First, the integrated holistic consideration of location, climate, the building and its occupants leads to the subsequent assessment of the risk of overheating and experience of occupants' thermal comfort. Second, building physics helps to determine and diagnose potential problems of high expenditures on energy use in this particular Eastern Mediterranean climate.

Building physics shows that, while heat transmission losses can be precisely predicted from the thermal properties of a building's materials, they are typically derived from quantities of energy consumed, which is highlighted in relation to the theoretical significance of home-energy performance. More recently, other scholarly pilot studies have increased over-calibrating discrepancies between actual- and predicted-energy use by using surrogate energy models (Firth et al., 2010; Kelly et al., 2012).

These studies claim that DTS does not relate well to the actual thermal performances of dwellings either before or after implementing energy-efficient retrofit interventions during the decision-making process for policymaking. This has led to estimates of current energy consumption and savings potentials of retrofitting that do not accurately reflect what happens in actual practice. For this reason, it is deemed appropriate that policymakers review prominent methodological approaches in order to implement effective retrofit solutions by taking into account the location and climate of buildings (Crilly et al., 2012; Wright et al., 2013). Due to the technical challenges of implementing any type of holistic retrofit interventions, emphasis should be given to conducting both longitudinal and transverse surveys with householders to avoid overestimating the impact of retrofit interventions.

It is evident that upgrading the thermal efficiency of existing residential building stock to higher and higher standards has led to basic problems of physics and psychological impacts on occupants' thermal comfort (Wallace et al., 2010; Coleman et al., 2012). A general trend that can be observed is that highly efficient insulation materials or building systems have led to increased indoor-air temperatures for occupied spaces (Firth & Wright, 2008). This can result in thermally uncomfortable temperatures for residents. It therefore appears that retrofitting existing residential buildings requires careful planning using an evidence-based socio-technical systems approach adopted as an inherent methodology for policymaking decisions (Kelly, 2011). Instead, there appears to be an increased uptake in holistic retrofit interventions that are not household orientated. In fact, it is evident that improving the thermal efficiency of building envelopes to higher and higher standards runs up against the basic problems of physics and technical procurements during construction phases (Wright & Firth, 2007). There is a basic law that indicates that economic benefits become greater dependent on the way insulation materials are used in residential buildings. For instance, with thickness, the advantages fall away rapidly when *U*-values are below about 0.4 W/m^2 K, representing a thickness of 8–10 cm of typical insulation material (Wright et al., 2013).

To achieve a significant reduction of heating energy demand, a building's thermal properties and the geometry of attaching thick insulation material(s) to the existing wall–roof configurations, especially to walls alongside balconies and around windows, make for further limitations in what thermal standards that can be achieved economically (Wright, 2008). It is worth mentioning that technical problems also often occur in implementing energy-efficient retrofit interventions during the construction phase. This is partially due to heat loss through construction detail junctions and recesses, or an absence of insulation material on both attic/roof surfaces and external walls with poor orientation to the sun (Gupta & Chandiwala, 2010). Eliminating energy wastage from air leaks by making dwellings fully airtight leads to the need for adequate ventilation due to high indoor-air temperatures; the interviewed householders were found to be markedly unaware of ventilating energy efficiently.

It can be said that, in Cyprus, there has been a lack of policy discourse amongst policymakers and their expert advisers regarding whether it is technically and economically possible to reduce both heating and cooling demands markedly through implementing various types of systemic retrofit interventions. This study provides a stringent standard for improving the thermal efficiency of buildings by taking into account occupants' interactions, building physics and environmental conditions. This STS approach has proven to be related to aspects of household patterns and home-energy use performance, and highlights the importance of indicating clear guidance about the detailed physical features of construction materials in retrofit interventions. Policies need to be based on the better delivery, implementation and procurement of technical aspects, rather than on merely responding to occupants' habitual adaptive behaviours around home-energy use.

Aim and Objectives

The starting point for the present study was the human-based data that enabled triangulation of the findings from the collected data, which were further enriched and verified by a field investigation. To ensure a systematic analysis of the key aims and objectives, this study adopted a mixed-method research design approach by conducting a building-energy performance evaluation with the use of dynamic thermal modelling and simulations, which was then validated by a comprehensive questionnaire survey, thermal imaging and in situ measurements of the base-case prototype RTBs in the post-war social-housing development estate in NC. In general, each phase was carried out in a sequential order to facilitate a discussion of the literature review that was conducted as part of the main research scope. Table 2.15 outlines the development of a novel STS conceptual framework.

The aim of the present study was to fill the research gap in the area of the development of an evidence-based framework for energy-policy decision-making mechanisms related to the integration of the EPBD mandates at the level of conceptual and nationwide implementation schemes. Properties in this particular sector

Table 2.15 Step-by-Step Development of STS Conceptual Framework

STS DevelopmentStructure	*Guidance to Develop a Methodfor Current Design Approach*
Step 1: Literature review	To undertake a literature review based on selected key terms—'overheating risk,' 'thermal comfort,' 'occupant behaviour and energy modelling' and 'building-energy simulations'—to address the knowledge gap in the field of energy efficiency and to develop a new design method for the STS approach.
(a) Step 2: Questionnaire survey	To conduct a questionnaire survey that will assess household energy performance and the energy-use patterns of occupants prior to and following the energy-saving measures implemented in the selected archetype buildings.
(b) Step 3: Thermal-comfort survey	To make recommendations that will support the successful delivery of current and future policy schemes related to retrofitting efforts for existing residential buildings that take occupant thermal comfort into consideration to promote evidence-based retrofitting interventions.
(c) Step 4: Measurements and monitoring	To concurrently conduct in situ measurements and on-site monitoring through semi-structured interviews with households to assess the degree of overheating risk that they experienced and to thoroughly identify their thermal-comfort preferences.
(d) Step 5: Building-energy modelling	To model and simulate the base-case representative RTBs to test the current energy performance of the structures before implementing retrofitting design strategy phases for energy policy. In line with the overheating and thermal-comfort assessments, the CIBSE *TM59 Design Methodology for the Assessment of Overheating Risk in Homes*, which was embedded in the building-modelling simulation phase of the present study.
(e) Step 6: Building performance evaluation	To test the validity of environmental monitoring and modelling outcomes in the IES software suite by using actual meteorological year (AMY) weather files, occupancy patterns and the occupants' habitual adaptive behaviours and window-opening schedules in the summer.
(f) Step 7: Retrofitting policy design	To develop a novel design guideline for retrofitting efforts in post-war housing stock and to demonstrate the feasibility of implementing passive-cooling design systems and energy-consumption-reduction measures during pre- and post-retrofitting phases

account for approximately 38% of the total housing stock and demonstrate some of the worst housing standards in Europe. The present study is the first to integrate and develop comprehensive and multidisciplinary research design approaches to create a roadmap for future BES studies on household-energy consumption and optimal occupant thermal comfort by providing a policy-advice tool to households and government initiatives at the local and national levels.

Socio-demographic Structures

The first census data for Cyprus were recorded in 1901, at which time the island population was 51,309 (Statistical Service of Republic of Cyprus, 2014). The RoC was established on 16 August 1960 with the involvement of two major ethnic communities: the Turkish and Greek Cypriots. After declaring independence from the Great Britain, the first census data were recorded on 11 December 1960, at which time the overall population was 104,942 with an annual growth rate of 1.9% (Moeschberger & Phillips, 2014; SPO, 2020). After NC declared itself a de facto state in 1983, the first census data were recorded in 1996, at which time the overall population was 200,587.[3] A second nationwide census survey was conducted in 2006, and at that time, the population was 256,644 with a 2.6% annual population growth rate.

As a consequence of a property boom and high demand for housing by foreign buyers wishing to take over control of the construction industry, the most-recent nationwide census data were collected by the NC government in 2011; this effort was intended to provide necessary figures on housing-stock data to the Union of Cyprus Turkish Engineers and Architects (UCTCEA). At that time, the overall population was 286,257 with a 2% annual population growth rate[4] (SPO,2011).

Currently, this background information is used every year to estimate population projections; the most recent population and housing-unit census data were updated on 31 December 2019 (SPO, 2020). According to this census data, the NC population was 382,230 in 2019, of which the male population was 207,149 and the female population was 175,081. There were 62,299 individuals in the 20–24 age group, which comprised a large proportion of the overall population; there were 37,972 males and 24,372 females in this age group. The 70–74 age group consisted of 9,465 individuals: 4,551 males and 4,914 females.

The 2019 demographic statistics in the RoC indicate that the estimated population was 888,000, compared to 875,000 at the end of 2018, with an increased annual growth rate of 1.4%[5] (Statistical Office of the RoC, 2019). The census data were distributed according to gender and age in an effort to foresee birth rates and determine the percentage of the ageing population. The data show that the proportion of children who were 0–4 and 10–14 years of age were both estimated to be 16%; the proportion of age groups older than 65 years of age increased to 16.3% in 2019, compared to 22.3% and 11.3%, respectively, in 2000. These results indicate that there was a notable increase in the proportion of age groups 65 years of age and older and a decrease in the proportion of age groups younger than 15 years of age, which suggests that the size of the ageing population will increase in the RoC over the next few decades.[6]

Residential-Building Stock Characteristics

In developing countries where urban growth and rapid urbanisation occurring, urban sprawl, a lack of planning related to land use and the absence of the EPBD mandates has impacted the current state of the housing stock (Bartels, 2007; Fokaides et al., 2017). As it relates to NC, changing the physical layout of the land combined with a lack of regulatory bodies for town planning are two major factors that have resulted in architectural, urban and environmental devastation (Oktay, 2007; Varoglu et al., 2018). It is difficult to compare the urban settlements of NC with other European countries, because they are smaller in size, both in land use and in terms of the overall population (Attia et al., 2017; Yorucu, 2003).

In NC, the rapid urbanisation of cities, rampant construction activity in suburban areas and the structure of the housing sector are connected; within the construction industry, these processes had an impact on land use and the explosive growth in energy use through the lack of control mechanisms in policy design in the urban and suburban systems (Balkiz & Therese, 2014; Savvides, 2017).

Through the adopted explanatory case study approach, the types of buildings in each construction era were analysed and evaluated in relation to a number of environmental factors, including an analysis of the different contextual layers, to ascertain the existing strength of the urban block-development configurations and evaluate the shortcomings thereof under the threat of urban sprawl.

Archetype1 demonstrates the first social-housing scheme developed during the British Colonial administration in the early 1900s with a combination of single-storey row houses (Vehbi & Hoskara, 2010; Yildiz & Manioğlu, 2015). This was the first pilot housing scheme in Cyprus, and it led to an increasing demand to build mass-scale housing schemes, which are illustrated as Archetypes2and3. Gazioglu (1996) stated that 19% of the mass-housing estates were built in the British period (i.e., prior to 1960); 3.8% in the RoC (i.e., 1960–1963); 12.7% in the fenced-off Varosha territory during the outbreak of civil war (i.e., 1963–1974); 8.9% in the Cyprus Turkish Federation (i.e., 1974–1983) and 55.7% when NC declared itself a de facto state[7] (Hoskara et al., 2009). Notably, urbanisation in NC started in the mid-1980s as a result of growth in the population, which prompted a simultaneous increase in demand in the residential-building sector (Ghafoor & Yorucu, 2006). High-density social-housing developments in urban and suburban areas resulted in a surge in the construction of low-, mid- and high-rise apartment blocks across five major cities and urban agglomerations in NC (Safakli, 2011).

According to the 2018 annual report for the Department of Social Housing detailed, from 1984 to 1996, the NC government implemented three different social- and private-housing schemes—row houses, medium-rise RTBs and a combination of the two—which were intended to address the housing shortage that was a consequence of the division of island (SPO, 2011).

A total of 2,712 dwellings were built during the rise of post-war social-housing estate developments under the governmental social-housing scheme (Yorucu & Keles, 2007); an additional 659 dwellings were built in collaboration with local cooperatives in NC.[8] After the completion of mass-scale housing projects, the government did not construct any other social-housing developments (Cogaloglu & Turkan, 2019). It should be noted that during the late-1990s and early 2000s, mass-scale housing projects were largely regulated by the SMEs (Goharddini et al., 2013); according to housing statistics, an additional 3,275 dwellings were built by privately owned construction companies to fill the void in social-housing structures implemented between 2000 and 2005 (SPO, 2011).

Archetypes 4 and 5 demonstrate the government social-housing estates, which were built between 1984 and 1996 to address the housing shortage for young people, as shown in Table 2.16. Notably, within a decade of implementing the same residential-building typology, these types of housing estates were repeated in all five major cities across the country (Günçe et al., 2008; Hoskara et al., 2009). All of these RTBs had the same floor-plan layout (i.e., two flats located on each floor) and the same building-envelope materials, which did not consider local climate conditions and topographical conditions of the project sites.

The housing typology classification reveals that these RTBs were built without informed decision-making related to land use and planning. All of these RTBs lacked planning for a social-housing structure scheme, which led to poor air quality and high thermal conductivity in the summer and caused an overheating risk and thermally uncomfortable indoor environments. Table 2.16 outlines the stages of mass-housing estate construction in Cyprus and reveals that starting with four- to five-storey RTBs (Archetype 5) in the mid-1980s and early 1990s, which ultimately led to changes in construction practices in NC. The development stages had no defined planning schemes for the implementation of EPBD mandates, no governmental policy and no control mechanisms, all to detriment of the environment and the thermal comfort of residents.

Housing Stock

Rapid construction during the 'property boom[9]' led to a revived interest in the property market (Yorucu, 2013). The expectations of the Annan Plan and changing market conditions throughout the world were evidence that people from such countries as Russia, Turkey, Greece, the UK[10] and Germany began to show significant interest in buying a second home in NC (Yorucu et al., 2010). Increasing energy demands from the residential sector were mostly observed in rapid construction activities and a renewed focus on economic improvement (Moutsiou, 2020; Zachariadis, 2010); in NC, the rapid and varied activity throughout the construction sector resulted in economic growth (Aloala, 2019).

The 2008 State Planning Organisation statistics showed that in the pre-construction period of 1997–2001, the average Gross National Product (GNP) rate was 1.8%. During the 2002–2006 accelerated construction activity period, this rate soared to 11% per annum; it should also be noted that during this same period, the construction industry in NC accounted for 8.1% of GNP. The results show the manner in which construction activity stimulated interest in other construction projects. This situation changed after 2010, however, due to the priority that was given to property investors from Russia, Israel, Iran and Turkey wishing to secure their money in NC to only construct medium- or high-rise RTBs on vacant land.

According to the State Planning Organisation, NC is characterised as a market economy that is dominated by the construction sector, which contributes 11% toward the GNP; only 8% was contributed by the private sector and 6% by the transportation sector. The data indicate that the first-time home-buyer rate was 4%

Table 2.16 Government Social-Housing Development Projects in NC

Phase	*Type*	*Nicosia (Urban)*	*Famagusta (Urban)*	*Kyrenia (Urban)*	*Omorphou (Rural)*	*Lefke (Rural)*	*Total*
Phase I (1984–1986)	Duplex	96	80	40	32	10	258
	Apartment	40	—	—	—	—	40
	Total	*136*	*80*	*40*	*32*	*10*	*298*
Phase IIA (1985–1987)	Duplex	60	80	40	32	—	212
	Apartment	48	—	—	—	—	48
	Total	*108*	*80*	*40*	*32*	—	*260*
Phase IIB (1986–1988)	Duplex	128	56	60	—	—	244
	Apartment	56	—	—	—	—	56
	Total	*184*	*56*	*60*	—	—	*300*
Phase IIC (1987–1989)	Duplex	292	116	—	—	—	408
	Apartment	56	8	—	—	—	80
	Total	*348*	*124*	—	—	—	*488*
Phase III (1990–1992)	Duplex	—	—	—	—	—	—
	Apartment	104	88	—	16	16	240
	Total	*104*	*88*	—	*16*	*16*	*240*
Phase IV (1993–1996)	Duplex	—	—	—	—	—	—
	Apartment	608	336	112	64	16	1136
	Total	*608*	*336*	*112*	*64*	*16*	*1136*
Totals for all four phases (1984–1996)	Duplex	576	332	140	64	10	1122
	Apartment	912	432	112	80	32	1568
	Total	***1488***	***764***	***252***	***144***	***42***	***2690***

Source: Data obtained from the Ministry of Housing, Dept. of Rural Affairs and Development.

in 2017 and 5% in 2019.[11] A sharp decrease in the annual growth rate of the construction sector of 4% can be observed in 2019; at this time, a stringent land-use planning policy and town-planning regulations were put in place by the government to discourage invasive construction activities in Famagusta and its agglomerations, especially rural villages with close proximity to the shoreline and Trikomo and its waterfront regions. Nationwide lockdown measures that were sue to the COVID-19 global pandemic and political turmoil in the early months of 2021 negatively impacted the construction sector in NC. To provide a comprehensive overview of the construction sector and highlight the importance of the demand for housing projects and the impact thereof on energy use, statistical data were obtained from the Statistical Office of NC.

The number of construction projects within the distribution of building typology[12] between 2015 and 2019.[13] It can be observed that in all five cities, the majority were residential buildings comprised of one- to five-storey RTBs, followed by apartments (i.e., medium- and high-rise RTBs) comprised of as many as 23 storeys. According to the Annual Report of Housing statistics in 2020, the number of buildings steadily increased; Famagusta is comprised of 568 residential buildings, 336 houses and 232 apartments that were built between 2015 and 2019. Therefore, the graph clearly demonstrates that there was a consistent increase in construction activity due to one-third of the population—approximately 110,201 people—living in the capital city of Nicosia. At the same time, the State Planning Organisation statistics in 2019 indicates that the Famagusta population was estimated at 76,000. The graph demonstrates that the number of construction projects increased steadily in all cities. A gradual increase in construction projects in Trikomo between 2018 and 2019 can be observed.

Housing statistics demonstrate that 214 residential buildings, 139 self-built houses and 75 apartments were constructed between 2018 and 2019, when this area became an attractive location for foreign investors from Israel, Russia and Azerbaijan to construct mass-scale high-density RTBs. The statistical results reveal that the current housing stock in NC exceeds local demand and is predominantly considered to be a foreign-buyer property market; this is because there are no stringent building regulations to control construction activity or to inspect the thermal quality of building stock (Ouria & Sevinc, 2018). Due to the policy gap in residential buildings and in the construction sector, SMEs and large investors relied on internal loans to build these mass-housing estate developments.

Peak completion of construction projects took place in residential buildings in 2018, when approximately 1.3 billion square metres of space was built. Notably, there no data were available for residential structures that were built in 2019 due to stringent town-planning measures that led to the withdrawal of construction-project proposals, and a policy gap in the implementation of those measures affected SMEs and large foreign investors in NC (Alola, 2020).

It can also be observed that approximately 937 million square metres of apartment-type housing stock were built in 2018, with an increase in the total footprint in 2019 of approximately 1 billion square metres. It should be emphasised that these housing types were built by SMEs, which served as the dominant factor for the construction of medium- and high-rise RTBs, compared to self-built housing projects.

According to the 2020 Annual Report of Housing, self-built houses comprised 159 million square metres of space in 2015, and this figure steadily rose to more than 392 million square metres of space in 2019. In observance of this market trend, it appears that priority was given to the construction of purpose-built apartments and residential buildings to obtain a high-profit margin by privately owned construction companies. This underscores the fact that the dominant building characteristics in NC are residential buildings and apartments. This is why the present study focused on investigating high-density medium-rise RTBs as a representative housing typology in NC.

The total number of construction projects in Famagusta that were completed between 2015 and 2019; the highest number of construction projects was recorded in residential buildings. According to the housing data, residential buildings that were completed in 2019 consisted of 154 housing units, followed by 148 condominiums in 2018; the second-most-dominant housing typology was self-built houses, which showed a steady increase between 2015 and 2017. A total of 149 house projects were completed by either building contractors or private construction companies (i.e., single-storey bungalows, two-storey detached or semi-detached houses). Between 2018 and 2019, there was a notable increase in the number of this type of housing projects as a consequence of uncertainty due to the implementation of new town-planning regulations and stringent measures related to the protection of rural villages and shorelines in Famagusta and Trikomo.

According to the Annual Report of the Housing Census, 187 self-built houses were completed between 2018 and 2019. As it relates to apartment construction, 117 apartment buildings were completed between 2015 and 2017, then a slight decrease in the number of built apartments can be observed between 2018 and 2019, during which time 115 projects were completed; these apartment projects were 5- to 23-storey standalone buildings that were built on vacant land or wherever close proximity to the shoreline to attract foreign second home buyers.

The data shows that the dominant housing typology in Famagusta was residential buildings, which comprised 38% of the overall building stock; this was followed by 20% that were self-built houses, 18% were apartments and 6% were commercial properties. Notably, the residential buildings were purpose-built two- to five-storey RTBs with more than two flat units on each floor. The analysis suggests that the RTB archetypes are the national representativeness of the housing stock, which was built in large quantities in all the major cities in NC (Ciftcioglu, 2017). It should be noted that all types of housing classifications reveal that the absence of EPBD mandates led to the construction of residential buildings and apartments that were built without any type of energy-efficient technology or building materials (Ince, 2019). This also relates to the cost of the buildings, except self-built houses for which the house owners implemented energy-efficient materials that were within their budget at the time of construction.

A majority of the housing projects in 2019 were built in the capital city of Nicosia; approximately 1,800 apartment units were completed within that year. This is due to land shortages and high demand from the population of homebuyers who were 20–24 and 25–29 years of age. A significant rise in the number of completed flat units in Famagusta and Trikomo due to demands on the property market from large foreign enterprises can also be observed; approximately 2,500 apartments were constructed between 2015 and 2019. The analysis reveals that the trend of building apartments was always significant in Nicosia because it is the capital city and has a large population; hence, the demand for new housing projects is always on the rise. In comparison, the construction of apartment housing stock in Famagusta only steadily increased between 2018 and 2019, but this is still remarkably high, considering the local population numbers.

To conclude, most of the residential buildings are of the RTB typology with a mean gross floor area of 105 m^2; this corresponds to an average of 75 m^2 per occupant. According to 2018 EU Housing Statistics, the equivalent average numbers are significantly lower than those recorded for Cyprus and are equal to 84.5 m^2 and 33.8 m^2 per occupant, respectively (Eurostat, 2018).

To compare the NC housing stock with that of the RoC and other EU countries, the study examined the 2018 housing statistics available via Eurostat. Recent figures indicate that in 2018, 46% of EU citizens lived in flats, 18.6% lived in semi-detached houses, and 34.7% lived in detached houses. Among the EU member states, the proportion of people living in flats in 2018 was 66.2% in Latvia, 64.9% in Spain, 61.5% in Estonia, 60.6% in Greece, 59.5% in Lithuania and 62.5% in Switzerland. In the RoC, 27% of people lived in flats; the present study found that 56% of people in NC lived in flats between 2015 and 2019, which was significantly higher than in the RoC. The findings prove that political events and demand on the property market by foreign investors led to a notable increase in housing stock in NC. To properly understand the composition of NC housing stock, a sample distribution according to the housing typology classification was presented.

Medium-rise RTBs (i.e., Archetype 5) constructed between 1984 and 1996 were the dominant representative housing typology of the residential-building stock in NC. Currently, the construction projects undertaken by SMEs and large foreigner investors in large quantities utilise similar floor-plan layout designs and scale-of-construction projects, all of which were first introduced under government social-housing schemes. This RTB typology was chosen for the present study to represent a reasonable proportion of the overall housing stock, and the statistical results prove that RTBs comprise a majority (i.e., 56%) of housing stock in NC.

Sample Representativeness Selection Criteria

The present study was intended to identify the most dominant representative housing typology; this was determined to be medium-rise RTBs, which represent 56% of the housing stock in NC. To generalise the findings and create a representative sample for the present study, an archetype-based method was adopted. Residential building-stock in NC is comprised of approximately 6,646 representative buildings, which consist of 2,712 dwellings that were constructed in the 1984–1996 period under the governmental social-housing scheme, and 659 dwellings that were completed in collaboration with local cooperative establishments. An additional 3,275 dwellings were built between 2000 and 2005 by privately owned construction companies due to the absence of a social-housing scheme. After implementing the same residential typology over the course of several decades, these housing estates were repeated in all five major cities across the country. Table 2.17 lists the different building typologies that evolved between 1950 and 2018 in order to justify the selection of the post-war social housing estate: linear block (T1), H-shaped tower (T2) and rectangular-box-shaped tower (T3).

Archetype buildings included statistical composites of the features found within a category of buildings within the housing stock, and the sample buildings represented actual buildings with data that were obtained from field studies and on-site documentation. According to the 2018 *State Planning Organisation, Economic and Social Indicators* statistics, the Follow-Up and Coordination Department in Cyprus is comprised of 1,384 households, of which 1,200 reside in high-density social-housing estates in Famagusta, that were eligible for the sampling criteria. Many social-housing estates were built in urban and suburban city areas in NC. This led to the creation of distinctive neighbourhoods that experienced two significant problems: ongoing building-envelope and urban deterioration and changes in the household socio-demographic characteristics due to the ages and activity levels of the original apartment owners in the social-housing developments.

The most effective starting point of the exploratory case study design for the present study was to fully understand the significant reliance on cooling measures

Table 2.17 Characteristics of the Typologies and Sub-typologies Defined in This Research Context

	Year of Construction	*Height*	*Dwellings per Floor*	*Area of Dwelling (m^2)*	*Orientation*
T1 Linear block					
(g) T1.1 Grouped in quarter	1950–1973	< GF + 4	2	60–118	Double 180°
(h) T1.2 Linear not grouped	1960–1972	< GF + 4	2	54–125	Double 180°
(i) T1.3 Linear with 1 orientation	1950–1971	< GF + 4	4	59–94	Single
T1.4 Linear with minimum courtyard	1962–1973	< GF + 6	2	70–130	Double 180°
T2 H-shaped tower					
(j) T2.1 H-tower with lateral courtyard	1985–1993	< GF + 5	2	55–107	Double 180°
(k) T2.1 Without courtyard	1989–1993	< GF + 5	2	<90	Double 90°
T3 Rectangular box-shaped tower					
(l) T3.1 Block in square	1995–2005	< GF + 8	4	55–107	Triple
(m) T3.2 Block in rectangle	2005–2018	< GF + 15	2–8	25–120	One-Triple

T = Tower block; GF = Gross floor area.

in warmer summer climate conditions. Consequently, the present study was conducted at the neighbourhood level and city level with representative residential building types to determine the contributions thereof to energy demand in accordance with such energy-risk factors as the year of construction, structural features of the thermal envelope, building orientation and the type of heating and cooling devices used, in addition to the socio-demographics of each household (i.e., family structure, occupant ages, income, health conditions, occupations); policymakers have indicated that elements are all useful tools to detect specific energy-related societal vulnerabilities in the Eastern Mediterranean Cypriot climate.

Representative Archetype Post-War Social Housing Estate

Famagusta is an exposed waterfront city that is subject to constant changes in the construction industry due to rapid economic growth and increasing housing demands. This coastal city is an exemplar model for the selection of a high-density social-housing estate development that was built in the heart of the city centre and in close proximity to the old walled Venetian city without considering the value of the historic urban tissue or any bioclimatic environmental design principles at the time of construction.

Medium-rise residential tower blocks are the most common structures in the district; this housing estate contains 288 apartment units in 36 RTBs that have the same floor-plan layout design; the blocks are $15\,m \times 16\,m$ and $4-5$ storeys high (see Data 1). The conditioned gross floor area of the case study multifamily apartment unit is 90 m^2; and the original *U*-values were $3.47\,W/m^2K$ for the external walls, $1.23\,W/m^2K$ for the internal walls, $1.2\,W/m^2K$ for the roof and $2.10\,W/m^2K$ for the doors and windows (see Data 2). There are two types of RTBs in NC: four-storey structures without communal amenities and five-storey structures with commercial premises located beneath the flats.

The key criterion for the representative case study building selection in the present study was that the sample needed to be representative of the post-war social-housing estates that were built in the mid-1980s and early 1990s. A total of 36 RTBs with the same floor-plan layout, construction materials and architectural style were selected to conduct a field study and recruit households according to these criteria.

The definitions of the 36 representative RTB typologies that referenced the year of construction, the urban/suburban morphology of the block, the number of floors in the building and the number of dwellings per floor were derived; sub-typologies were also identified to understand the impact of rapid construction activity on the transformation of the urbanisation and land-use characteristics of the city. The typical physical deterioration of the building envelopes. The buildings that were constructed under the governmental social-housing scheme can be described by three newly defined variables—the energy-consumption patterns of the occupants, the thermal performance of the buildings and the thermal-comfort level of occupants—all of which are worthy of investigation.

In summary, the buildings that were constructed under the governmental social-housing scheme can be described according to the occupants' energy-consumption patterns, the building's thermal performance and the occupants' thermal-comfort levels. The long-term viability of these RTBs will require the incorporation of energy-efficient and energy-saving features within the methodologically planned energy-policy framework.

Building a Stock Model for Energy Policy Design

To fill the energy-efficiency gap, improvements in the physical quality of housing stock that are directly related to human-based factors are needed. This need led to the development of a novel methodological framework for assessing domestic-energy use.

One of the main goals of the present study was to encourage social housing occupants to assess and adopt principles of retrofitting design policies to improve the extant mass-housing stock. This approach will investigate buildings that were built under the governmental social housing scheme, but that have not yet undergone any refurbishments to make the structures more energy efficient and adapted to the local environment. The present study revealed an urgent need for governmental bodies to devise effective policies for the mass-housing sector so that the construction industry applies necessary retrofitting strategies on a rapid and large-scale basis to reduce energy consumption. Table 2.18(a)–(d) delineates previous scholars' work on the development of statistically representative housing archetypes across the world.

Table 2.18(a) identifies representative housing typologies for the development of bottom-up energy policy frameworks in European countries. The study by Mata et al. (2014) investigates the implementation of energy-efficiency strategies by aggregating 593 archetype buildings to represent the entire housing stock, using the national housing databases of France, Germany, Spain and the UK. The sampling population was extracted from the Eurostat database in 2011. This dataset consists of the building characteristics, energy consumption levels and CO_2 emissions of each country and provides a benchmark for the validation of the final energy demand for a reference year. By contrast, the present study only includes data on medium-rise residential tower blocks (RTBs), which represent 56% of the dwellings in Northern Cyprus (NC).[14] The two studies show differences in terms of the development of methodology for building stock aggregation. Mata et al. (2014) primarily investigated the building-thermal properties of both single-family houses (SFHs) and multi-family houses (MFHs), and the energy use of these dwellings was validated through measures of indoor-air temperature, while, in the present study, the nationally representative housing stock data was gathered from the Housing Construction Statistics from 2015 to 2019[15] and applied to the most representative medium-rise RTBs, and the energy simulations were validated by integration of human-based data through a questionnaire survey.

In the present study, 100 households' data was integrated into the building-energy model to develop an evidence-based energy policy framework, and the

Table 2.18(a) The Literature on Building Stock Aggregation through Archetype Buildings

References	*A. Study Location*	*B. Building Type*	*C. Sampling Size*	*D. Primary Aim of Model*	*E. Methodology*	*F. Main Findings*
Mata et al. (2014)	France, Germany, Spain and the UK	Single-family dwellings (SFD); terraced houses (T); multi-family dwellings (MFD)	France—99 archetypes (54 R, 45 NR), Germany—122 R archetypes Spain—120 archetypes (40 R, 80 NR) UK—252 archetypes (168 R, 84 NR)	To assess the possibility of describing the European Union (EU) building stock for the purpose of forming a basis for analysing the effect and costs of applying different energy efficiency intensity (EEI) measures to the entire EU building stock	A dynamic building stock model was used; archetype buildings were selected to represent the building stock of the country; the segmentation was applied to both residential (R) and non-residential (NR) buildings; a total of 593 archetype buildings were investigated; census data and national reports were used; the 3CL-DPE method was used to define building geometry and *U*-values of building-envelope parameters	A final total energy demand that differs by −6% to +2% from statistics for the four countries investigated; the share of space heating of the total energy demand ranges from 59% to 82% in R buildings

(*Continued*)

Table 2.18(a) (Continued)

References	*A. Study Location*	*B. Building Type*	*C. Sampling Size*	*D. Primary Aim of Model*	*E. Methodology*	*F. Main Findings*
Ballarini et al. (2014)	Thirteen EU countries, representation of Italian building typology in three different climatic zones	Single-family houses (SFHs; detached or semi-detached); terraced houses; multi-family houses (MFHs); apartment blocks	Six SFHs; six MFHs; six apartment blocks built between 1901–1920 and 1991–2005	Development of methodology to identify reference buildings for assessing energy-saving potentials; to design a harmonised structure for 'European building typologies' in order to estimate the energy demand; to identify a national 'Building Typology' according to the IEE-TABULA project	The Building Typology Matrix was developed by region/climate area; the Real Example Building (*ReEX*), the Real Average Building (*ReAv*) and the Synthetical Average Building (*SyAv*) approaches were developed; statistical data was used to support the archetype housing stock analysis; the building energy assessment model was developed; a quasi-steady-state monthly model was chosen in order to meet the consistency both with European standards and with national standards; retrofitting interventions applied to the national building stocks were considered	Annual primary energy need for space heating and domestic hot water ranged from 41% (Czech Republic) to 75% (Italy, Middle Climatic Zone); on average, more than 40% of energy savings could be obtained by the whole analysed European residential stock just applying a 'standard' retrofitting scenario
Wang et al. (2015)	Stockholm, Sweden	Swedish low-rise residential buildings	Two- to three-storey low-rise MFHs purpose-built housing estates built between 1965 and 1975	To investigate energy effectiveness of retrofit measures applied onto building envelopes by an exploratory case study analysis	A typical Swedish multi-family archetype was selected; the IDA ICE 4.6 (indoor climate and energy performance simulation programme) was applied for the simulation of thermal performance	Adding insulations on roof and improving air-tightness level achieved a 16% and 18.4% energy consumption reduction, respectively

Table 2.18(b) The Literature on Building Stock Aggregation through Archetype Buildings (Continued)

References	*A. Study Location*	*B. Building Type*	*C. Sampling Size*	*D. Primary Aim of Model*	*E. Methodology*	*F. Main Findings*
Dineen et al. (2015)	Ireland	Two-storey semi-detached houses; one-storey apartments; two-storey detached houses; two-storey terraced buildings; one-storey detached houses (representing 87% of all dwellings)	The National Administration System (NAS) database was used, which contained details of 253,875 dwellings that represent 19% of the total dwelling stock of 1.6 million housing units	To demonstrate a novel bottom-up approach to modelling the energy-saving potential of energy efficiency improvement measures applied through the retrofit of existing dwelling stock	Archetype housing stock analysis was selected; the housing census data of 2011 was used for the calibration analysis; 145 archetypes were used for the model calculations; Global Sensitivity (GA) analysis was conducted; six retrofit measures were examined; energy demand analysis was conducted	There was approximately a 7.5% change in energy consumption for every 1°C internal temperature fluctuation; the energy model underestimated the heat energy demand of the 2011 stock by just 1.2%

(*Continued*)

Table 2.18(b) (Continued)

References	*A. Study Location*	*B. Building Type*	*C. Sampling Size*	*D. Primary Aim of Model*	*E. Methodology*	*F. Main Findings*
Belpoliti and Bizzarri (2015)	Emilia Romagna, Italy	More than two-storey and up to eight-storey standalone apartments	70 buildings that were constructed under the Italian social housing scheme between 1991 and 1995	To develop an effective method of design for the energy performance audit of the social housing stock; to elaborate a parametric calculation protocol to boost effectiveness of the energy audit analysis	A bottom-up energy policy development approach was chosen; national housing census data was used; energy performance analysis was conducted; carbon emission profiles were assessed; three retrofit energy interventions were applied onto the building envelope	Replacing the heating system and single-pane windows with double-pane ones was characterised by a sustainable cost/benefits ratio that ensures a 39.5% reduction in energy consumption
Ozarisoy and Altan (2017a)	Cambridge, Massachusetts, USA	Low-rise residential buildings with one to four dwelling units	A training set of 339 homes was assessed, then a larger test set of 2,263 homes was assessed	To develop a methodology for probabilistic Urban Building Energy Modelling (UBEM) archetype characterisation	Archetype dwellings representing housing data between 1970 and 1990; measured energy data was used; a Bayesian calibration approach was adopted; an hourly weather dataset was created; six high-uncertainty variables were chosen for the calibration analysis	Using a calibration error based on monthly energy resulted in 16.5% of the buildings being compared to 0.03% when using annual error margins

(*Continued*)

Table 2.18(b) (Continued)

References	*A. Study Location*	*B. Building Type*	*C. Sampling Size*	*D. Primary Aim of Model*	*E. Methodology*	*F. Main Findings*
Serrano-Lanzarote et al. (2016)	Valencia, Spain	Terraced buildings; isolated linear buildings; isolated building towers	1,698.470 dwellings were built between 1960 and 1980, representing 12 climatic zones	To quantify the energy-saving potential and the related CO_2 emissions of the housing stock	A top-down approach was used by splitting the actual energy consumption of the regional building stock among the total number of buildings; building energy simulations were conducted	Energy consumption could be reduced up to 2% in 10 years, representing a savings of 247,871 Mwh

Table 2.18(c) The Literature on Building Stock Aggregation through Archetype Buildings (Continued)

References	*A. Study Location*	*B. Building Type*	*C. Sampling Size*	*D. Primary Aim of Model*	*E. Methodology*	*F. Main Findings*
Loga et al. (2016)	20 European countries	SFHs; end-terraced houses; mid-terraced houses; MFHs; apartment blocks; tower buildings	16 EPISCOPE case studies at national, regional and local levels were used; the sample fraction consisted of more than 600 datasets	To develop a common methodological framework with the aim to enable a quantitative comparison of the energy performance of the exemplary buildings; to develop a standardised classification scheme for residential buildings by using an open-access web tool	Cross-country comparisons of building and supply system features were analysed; bottom-up building stock models were used; the energy balance of 'average buildings' was calculated by the use of standard energy rating software; *U*-values of both existing buildings and new-build dwellings were gathered; thermal envelope areas were calculated for improvement of building-energy models; heating supply systems were identified	Supporting national energy advice activities for illustrating the impact of policy instruments; development of strategies for tracking and understanding actual energy performance achievements

(*Continued*)

Table 2.18(c) (Continued)

References	*A. Study Location*	*B. Building Type*	*C. Sampling Size*	*D. Primary Aim of Model*	*E. Methodology*	*F. Main Findings*
Stefanovic and Gordic (2016)	Kragujevac, Serbia	Free-standing tower block; high-rise buildings; apartment blocks; city block; staggered blocks	10,771 multi-family residential buildings were selected in six different construction periods	To improve awareness of energy performance of buildings at the city level	Energy modelling for archetype buildings was constructed; 86 staggered block buildings built between 1981 and 1990 were identified as archetype buildings; a bottom-up design approach was used; a building geodatabase was identified; EnergyPlus software suite was used to undertake building-energy simulations	Implementation of polystyrene thermal insulation achieved 17.91%, 21.20% and 22.70% annual heating energy consumption reductions

(*Continued*)

Table 2.18(c) (Continued)

References	*A. Study Location*	*B. Building Type*	*C. Sampling Size*	*D. Primary Aim of Model*	*E. Methodology*	*F. Main Findings*
Cerezo et al. (2017)	The residential district of AlqQadisyah, Kuwait	Villa-type multi-family residential buildings	336 dwellings built in the 1980s and 1990s under the 1983 Energy Conservation code, representing 42% of the housing stock	To propose a new method for the characterisation of occupant-related parameters in building archetypes using Bayesian calibration with annual energy data	Both deterministic and probabilistic approaches were adopted; urban data gathering; archetype characterisation; UBEM model generation; archetype Bayesian calibration; energy demand simulation; uncertain and probabilistic archetype parameters explored	EUI of archetypes showed a reduction of percentage errors for the 10 and 90 percentiles of 13%–45% against deterministic methods
Pittam and O'Sullivan (2017)	Cork City, Ireland	End-of-terrace (ET) and mid-terrace (MT) MFHs	1551 asset-rating surveys were used	To use the extracted geometrical building information to demonstrate the effects of using default settings	Representative thermal construction properties were identified; 43 variables were identified that were deemed necessary to represent a detailed disaggregated housing stock database	There is a mean 21.5% variation in the predicted annual energy performance of EUI measures

Table 2.18(d) The Literature on Building Stock Aggregation through Archetype Buildings (Continued)

References	*A. Study Location*	*B. Building Type*	*C. Sampling Size*	*D. Primary Aim of Model*	*E. Methodology*	*F. Main Findings*
Streicher et al. (2018)	Sweden	SFHs and MFHs located in urban, suburban and rural regions	10,400 Cantonal Building Energy Certificates; 54 archetypes were identified; SFHs represent 14.4% and 14.1% of the total housing stock; MFHs represent 55% of the total housing stock	To provide the current thermal performance level of the Swiss residential building stock in 2015 based on an analysis of the data available from energy certificates; to estimate a thermal performance level of archetype buildings and their respective building elements	Cantonal Building Energy Performance Certificate data was used; archetype housing stock data was analysed; the statistics of the Federal Register of Buildings and Dwellings were examined; current state of the Swiss residential building stock was assessed; potential improvements in the building stock were proposed	Approximately 75% of all building elements do not yet reach the thermal performance of buildings constructed in the last 15 years; the *U*-values of building elements would have to be reduced by an additional 0.3–0.7 W/m^2K to reach low-energy standards

(*Continued*)

Table 2.18(d) (Continued)

References	*A. Study Location*	*B. Building Type*	*C. Sampling Size*	*D. Primary Aim of Model*	*E. Methodology*	*F. Main Findings*
Yi and Peng (2019)	Seoul, South Korea	High-rise apartment stock, MFHs	The total number of households was 2,830,857, of which about 58% (1,641,383) lived in apartments	To introduce an 'archetype-in-neighbourhood' framework to develop cooling-energy supply planning; to demonstrate estimated increases of the maximal month cooling-energy demand	A bottom-up hybrid approach was adopted; empirical urban data modelling was used; EnergyPlus was used for model calibration; electricity use data of 659 apartment buildings (51,351 households) sampled from 18 city districts; characteristics of residential energy use during the hottest month (August) was examined	The coefficient of determination from the scatter plot between the observed and the predicted was 0.969, representing about 97% variance in observed peak cooling-energy use

(*Continued*)

Table 2.18(d) (Continued)

References	*A. Study Location*	*B. Building Type*	*C. Sampling Size*	*D. Primary Aim of Model*	*E. Methodology*	*F. Main Findings*
Li et al. (2019)	Chongqing, China	Urban residential blocks; MFHs in urban residential districts	Households with one elderly retiree and elderly retired couples accounted for 4.86% and 4.40%, respectively, of all households	To develop a localised residential building stock-space heating and cooling modelling approach to estimate energy consumption and related carbon emissions	A bottom-up engineering approach was used; development of residential archetypes; space heating and cooling-energy consumption simulation and aggregation; stock total floor area calculation and construction age distribution; EnergyPlus was used for model calibration	The total energy consumption for space heating and cooling can be significantly reduced, with estimated reductions of 57.6%–60.70% in 2020 and 55.3%–57.2% in 2050
Pittau et al. (2019)	EU 28	SFHs; MFHs	Post-war buildings built between 1945 and 1969, representing 30% of housing stock	To investigate the effect of massively storing carbon in bio-based construction products	A statistic-based geo-cluster model was developed; a dynamic life-cycle assessment was performed; Eurostat data was used for the archetype housing identification	Up to 3% of the total GHG annually emitted by all sectors in 2015 can be removed by 2050

findings were generalised across eight cities in Cyprus; this method of design provides a universal design approach that could be extrapolated to other Eastern Mediterranean countries. To prove the validity of the methodological framework developed as an output of this field study investigation in Cyprus, the analysis of the archetype presented here also considers the work of Ballarini et al. (2014). In this study, three different archetype housing typologies were selected to represent the entire Italian housing stock and three different climatic zones were considered: (i) the Mediterranean zone up to 2,100 heating degree days; (ii) the middle climatic zone from 2,100 to 3,000 heating degree days and (iii) the Alpine zone, having more than 3,000 heating degree days.

In the present study, the representative archetypes selected from the urban context enable the research findings to be applied to other post-war social housing estates located in other major cities in NC. This chosen method allows identification of both the upper- and lower-neutral adaptive thermal-comfort thresholds of each city across the island; this also contributes to an ability to benchmark to the ASHRAE Global Thermal Comfort Database II.[16] Another study, that of Ballarini et al. (2014), only considers the development of a method of design for the identification of building typology according to the Typology Approach for Building Stock Energy Assessment (TABULA), Intelligent Energy Use (IEE), European Union project.[17] Additionally, the pilot study conducted by Ballarini et al. used secondary data sources for the development of aggregate energy models, and the occupants' thermal comfort was neglected in the project's assessment of the energy-saving potentials of European residential building stocks. This indicates that the study conducted by Ballarini et al. has shortcomings in terms of applying the research outputs to other EU countries' energy policy frameworks. In contrast, this present study provides a universal design approach in terms of integrating a household's in vivo experiences in energy use and validating the findings with the statistical analysis of data collected through a questionnaire survey.

Wang et al. (2015) only considered low-rise residential buildings as nationally representative archetype houses in Stockholm, Sweden. In the present study, by contrast, post-war social housing estates were selected as an archetype housing typology to represent the demand for government social housing schemes in the mid-1980s and early 1990s in NC. The study included 6,646[18] buildings that were constructed during this era and the building typology was extrapolated with the most reliable housing stock data from between 2015 and 2019 to identify a nationally representative housing stock that accounts for 56% of the low-, medium- and high-rise RTBs[19] in NC.

The pilot study conducted by Wang et al. (2015) used building-energy modelling approach by integrating the statistically representative Swedish housing stock for energy policy design. Additionally, this study investigates the building-fabric thermal performance of case study buildings by testing energy efficiency measures (i.e., thermal bridge, air-tightness retrofitting (S1), ventilation retrofitting (S2), window retrofitting (S3), attic/roof retrofitting (S4) and external wall insulation (S5) applied on the existing state of building envelopes, while in the present study, six passive cooling design strategies were developed and applied on the base-case scenario by considering bioclimatic design elements of the Cypriot context and testing energy effectiveness of each strategy with the integration of the questionnaire survey outputs into the building-energy model.

It should also be noted that Wang et al. considered the traditional method of design for testing the energy-effectiveness of state-of-the-art retrofit interventions applied onto building envelopes without the integration of actual data collection or any other research instruments to measure building-fabric thermal performance. The outputs of the Wang et al. study predominantly represent the assumptions of energy consumption profiles. In the present study, however, the data collected through 100 samplings of questionnaire survey outputs and in situ recordings of indoor environmental conditions were integrated into the building-energy model to validate the findings from dynamic thermal simulations (DTSs). The output from the DTS analyses can be extrapolated to assess the building performance of post-war social housing estates in both urban and rural locations across the island. Table 2.18(b) delineates the development of statistical sample criteria for archetype housing stock analyses.

Dineen et al. (2015) adopted bottom-up modelling by integrating the statistical power of housing census data available for Ireland from 2011. Representative datasets were gathered from the national energy balance datasets as part of Energy-Performance Certificate (EPC) calculations. To define the aggregate energy models, 253,875 dwellings were selected from the National Administration System (NAS), representing 19% of the total dwellings in Ireland. In the present study, the nationally representative data obtained from the *Annual Statistical Report* published by the Northern Cyprus Statistical Office in 2019 represents approximately 11,512 dwelling units[20] consisting of residential tower block projects built on mass scale across the island between 2015 and 2019. This statistical data, extrapolated with the total dwellings, shows that these buildings represent 56% of the building stock in NC.[21]

The study conducted by Dineen et al. included a step-by-step development of energy demand calculations and model calibrations by using secondary data sources. In the present study, the building-energy-simulation set-input parameters were developed through a questionnaire survey and in situ physical measurements for environmental conditions were used to validate research findings. There is also of note in the Dineen et al. study, the Global Sensitivity analysis approach was used to determine energy-saving measures and rebound effect calculations for each retrofit measure applied onto the building envelope. Whereas in the present study, the overall energy-efficient implementation measures of six passive cooling design strategies and their life-cycle cost assessments were examined to demonstrate implications for energy policy design.

One study that shows a similar design approach to the present study is that conducted by Belpoliti and Bizzari (2015). That study investigates the existing social housing stock in the Emilia Romagna region of Italy and adopts only the nationally representative standalone RTBs that were built in the 1990s. This type of social housing stock represents 19.5% of the buildings in Italy. For the present study, the post-war social housing stock was identified as a nationally representative building typology and outcomes were extrapolated using the same design approach as that used by Belpoliti and Bizzari. A main difference between these two studies is that where the Belpoliti and Bizzari study only considers a steady-state analysis of energy retrofit strategies tested to calculate energy savings in the residential sector, the present study sets out to demonstrate the DTS of each of six passive cooling design strategies applied onto the existing state of the archetype buildings. The present study also validates the building-energy simulations with the use of household energy bills and the socio-demographic characteristics of households gathered through a questionnaire survey.

The study of Ozarisoy and Altan (2018) develops the Urban Building Energy Modelling (UBEM) design method for exploring energy-efficiency solutions on urban or district scales. In this territorial exploratory case study approach, 339 low-rise residential buildings were selected as an archetype housing typology in Cambridge, Massachusetts, USA. In this pilot study, the Energy Use Intensity (EUI) of the archetype dwellings was assessed to calibrate data with the electricity and gas use of the households. The error margins between the predicted and measured data were calculated to demonstrate annual energy calibration for the region, but the selected sample size does not represent the entire population of this region. To avoid research bias and provide a generalisation of research outputs, the available dataset was multiplied with a larger test set of 2,263 dwellings and applied to measure the accuracy of the validation of the methodology. In the present study, an even larger dataset of 6,646[22] dwellings was used. These dwellings were identified as nationally representative archetype buildings both in an urban district and in rural locations in NC. The urban district of Famagusta was selected as a baseline to extrapolate research findings to other cities. The main methodological difference between the pilot study conducted by Julia et al. and the present study involves the questionnaire survey used in the present study. In the present study, the statistical method of bootstrapping method was used to increase the sample size to test associations between households' actual energy bills and their socio-demographic characteristics gathered through a questionnaire survey. Additionally, DTSs were undertaken to predict the energy use of the identified archetype housing stock by integrating dominant representative occupancy profiles gathered through a questionnaire survey.

A top-down energy policy design approach was utilised by Serrano-Lanzarote et al. (2016) in Valencia, Spain. In this pilot study, four different archetype housing typologies were studied that represented 1,698.470 dwellings built between 1960 and 1980 in 12 climatic zones in Spain. Only steady-state analyses of energy-efficiency measures were calculated through the use of the aggregated data of households' actual energy consumption, the census population and dwellings, national statistics regarding the energy consumption of the residential sector, and 500 surveys about the actual energy consumption for this region referenced to climatic zones.

The traditional method of design used by Serrano-Lanzarote et al. was also used in this present study, after being adopted for the development of a district-scale retrofitting design approach suitable for NC. It should be noted that the study undertaken by Serrano-Lanzarote et al. developed a top-down design approach as these scholars were testing the energy-saving measures of building retrofitting design strategies. In contrast, the present study uses a bottom-up design approach that was developed by integrating the socio-technical-systems (STS) conceptual framework within the extrapolation of field study investigation findings on energy use. The methodological framework developed as an outcome of the present study takes the study conducted by Serrano-Lanzarote et al. one step further by developing an evidence-based energy policy framework to assess robust energy-performance evaluation and certification schemes in Eastern Mediterranean countries. Table 2.18(c) demonstrates the development of statistical methods to aggregate building-energy model studies.

Loga et al. (2016) reviewed the European housing database to develop a common methodological framework for the holistic retrofitting of existing residential buildings. In this statistical analysis method, 600 samples were used for each included EU country across 16 pilot case studies that are available in the TABULA Web Tool.[23] This open-source database offers researchers the ability to extract only those national datasets that were developed under the EPISCOPE-European Union research project[24] to determine the development of EPCs for EU countries. This database consists of the *U*-values of building properties for each nationally representative housing typology identified for each EU country available in the database. In the present study, 36 RTBs that were built under the government's social housing scheme in four major cities across NC were identified as archetype housing stock for conducting the statistical analysis. The Housing Census and Construction Statistics, in conjunction with the most up-to-date statistical data available from 2015 to 2019, were used to extrapolate the representativeness of post-war social housing estates. The data were examined to validate the representativeness of archetype buildings and to provide subsequent background information for the development of a black-box energy model to undertake building-energy simulations.

For this study, 100 households were recruited across 36 RTBs in a post-war social housing estate located in the coastal city of Famagusta where the climate is subtropical (*Csa*) and partly semi-arid (*Bsh*), according to the Köppen-Geiger climate classification data. This densely urban district was selected as a base-case scenario where the statistical findings could be generalised and applied to other cities in Cyprus. To prove that the chosen archetypes were statistically representative, this study first examines statistical data for the construction sector by region, as available in the Eurostat data. The findings demonstrate that 7.9% of the gross domestic product (GDP) of the Republic of Cyprus (RoC) and an average of 5.3% of the GDP of the 27 EU countries was accounted for by investment in housing in 2019. The housing census statistics demonstrate that 38% of residential building stock in NC consists of multi-family residential buildings, SFHs and apartments. These statistical findings further validate the national representativeness of the archetype selected for this study.

The study conducted by Loga et al. (2016) considered a relatively large sample size for statistical analysis. The international database they used includes the building typology and *U*-values of representative archetypes, offering cross-country validation for the development of effective EPC development schemes in EU-27 countries. By comparison, in the present study, the sample size was relatively small. It consists of 100 households' in vivo experiences in energy use that were collected across 36 RTBs in the same region; however, these findings could be applied to other post-war social housing estates in the four different climatic zones in Cyprus because RTBs have similar floor plan layout designs and *U*-values of thermal properties. The dataset that was the output of this empirical case study can therefore contribute to the development of bottom-up energy modelling in the Eastern Mediterranean region.

Stefanovic and Gordic (2016) identified 10,771 multi-family residential buildings, including free-standing RTBs and high-rise apartments, in densely built urban districts in Serbia. In the Stefanovic and Gordic study, 86 RTBs were identified as archetype buildings to develop a method of design for improving energy efficiency in the housing stock. The methodological framework developed by Stefanovic and Gordic shows a similar design approach to the present study by investigating potential thermal improvements in the building envelopes of residential multi-family staggered block buildings constructed between 1981 and 1990. However, Stefanovic and Gordic's study only considered assumptions generated through building-energy modelling and simulations.

In the present study, the building-energy-simulation model was developed by gathering 100 households' socio-demographic characteristics, their habitual adaptive behaviours on home-energy performance, occupancy patterns and thermal-sensation votes on occupants' indoor-air environments, all to feed the black-box model while undertaking DTS. The findings were validated with occupants' actual energy bills. The methodological framework was set to develop simulation set-input parameters and was evidence-based; it predominantly relied on the responses of 100 households across 36 RTBs in a post-war social housing estate.

One another similar methodological framework to that used in this study is that of Cerezo et al. (2017). This study identified 336 villa-type multi-family residential buildings built between 1980 and 1990 in an urban setting in Kuwait as an archetype building. In this pilot study, the authors set out to demonstrate an energy-assessment method with households' actual energy bills to identify discrepancies between metered- and simulated-EUI distributions of the housing stock. In the present study, an evidence-based model analysis was developed to aggregate building-energy simulations by using 36 RTBs as a base-case scenario that could be extrapolated to other post-war social housing estates in four different climatic zones in Cyprus. To prove the validity of the universal design approach for the STS conceptual framework, the study examines the pilot research project conducted by Pittam and O'Sullivan (2017). This pilot study used 1,551 samples gathered from the available EPC database to measure the building-energy performance of residential terraced housing stock (identified as an archetype building typology) for aggregating energy performance of base-case archetype buildings before and after retrofitting.

To validate the energy model, a reasonably large sample size was identified by using *U*-value parameters of building elements to use the power of statistical analysis, with the goal of impacting the research for local policymakers and practitioners. In the present study, Housing Census and Construction Statistics were used to identify the national representativeness of archetype housing stock in four different climatic conditions in Cyprus; the findings were then extrapolated to determine the base-case post-war social housing estate by undertaking a longitudinal field study investigation to create the building-energy simulations. It should be noted that there is no EPC data available for NC, and this study set out to develop an evidence-based energy policy framework to assess robust energy-performance evaluation and certification schemes in Eastern Mediterranean countries. In the present study, 100 households were recruited across 36 RTBs in the same region; this sample was reasonably small compared to the statistical method used by Pittam and O'Sullivan. This is due to the fact that the pilot study conducted by Pittam and O'Sullivan used already available EPC datasets for Ireland, while in the present study, the most up-to-date construction statistics of the RoC were generated to fulfil this technical constraint at the time of identification of archetype building typology for NC, and there is no such available EPC data for NC. To avoid research bias and eliminate the research limitations in the present study, the bootstrapping method was used to increase the sampling size to test associations between households' socio-demographic characteristics and their actual energy bills to provide reliable energy-efficiency implications for the residential sector in NC.

Table 2.18(d) demonstrates the development of a design for an energy policy framework to determine the selection criteria for archetype buildings across world.

Streicher et al. (2018) conducted a pilot study on the assessment of the current thermal performance of the Swiss residential building stock. In this study, a 10,400-household sample of the EPC of buildings was used to determine the *U*-values of building-fabric elements and identify feasible retrofit design scenarios. The representative housing typology was identified through an investigation of the construction periods between 1920 and 2015. This study assessed the thermal performance of housing stock by using available EPC datasets. Findings were examined against the recommended benchmarking criteria for the purpose of developing energy policy for the Swiss context at both regional and national levels.

In the present study, a bottom-up approach was adopted to develop a method of design for the integrity of the STS design approach while conducting a longitudinal field study investigation in the Eastern Mediterranean Island of Cyprus. The archetype buildings were identified from the Housing Census and Construction Statistics of Northern Cyprus in order to represent a general base-case scenario development that could contribute to retrofit energy policy design within the integration of the STS design approach. In the present study, 100 households were recruited from a post-war social housing estate and the findings were applied to other similar post-war social housing estates built between 1984 and 1997 across the island. The large sample size (10,400 available datasets) of the Streicher et al. study allowed the authors to present an accurate energy-policy design. The sample size of the present study was relatively small in comparison; however, the present study utilised the bootstrapping method to increase the sample size while assessing the impact of households' socio-demographic characteristics on home energy performance.

A distinct point of difference between the two studies is that while the study conducted by Streicher et al. considered a technical aspect by using the available EPC datasets, the present study used households' in vivo experiences on energy use and the thermal performance of building elements and retrofit design strategies, all of which were developed thorough an investigative field study. One of the prominent scientific contributions of this longitudinal field study investigation in Cyprus is the step-by-step development of the STS energy-policy design.

Yi and Peng (2019) conducted a comprehensive pilot study by using archetype high-rise multi-family residential buildings in South Korea. To develop the statistical analysis, 659 apartment buildings (51,381 households) were identified as archetype buildings across 18 city districts in Seoul. This study was conducted by using available datasets for the *U*-values of thermal properties of buildings and households' energy bills. All the collected data were calibrated by using the EnergyPlus software suite to develop an archetype-in-neighbourhood framework for modelling the cooling-energy demand of a city's housing stock.

The Yi and Peng's study shows distinct similarities to the present study, as this study collected households' energy bills in the peak cooling period of August and undertook a multiple regression analysis to identify key determinants of cooling-energy use in South Korea. Additionally, Yi and Peng used the EnergyPlus software suite to undertake the energy-assessment analysis, and households' sub-metering data were also used to identify discrepancies between predicted and measured data on home-energy use. In the statistical analysis conducted by Yi and Peng, a k-fold ($k = 4$) validation method was applied to verify the accuracy of the regression model that was integrated for the retrofitting of buildings in South Korea, but in their study, no field investigation was conducted to collect households' in vivo experiences on energy use and thermal comfort was not assessed.

A prominent contribution of the present study is that dominant representative occupancy profiles were integrated into a black-box energy model. This data was gathered through a questionnaire survey, and energy benchmarking of the existing post-war social housing stock was assessed accordingly. While the study conducted by Yi and Peng only considered standardised benchmark criteria to assess the thermal energy performance of its 659 apartment units, the present study set out to develop a reliable black-box energy model to undertake dynamic thermal simulations. In this study, the findings rely on the accuracy of the BES to inform retrofit policy design, while the study conducted by Yi and Peng demonstrates BES findings predominantly based on estimations that predict scenarios of the cooling-energy demand of Seoul's housing stock.

A bottom-up engineering approach for building stock energy modelling was developed by Li et al. (2019). In this pilot study, archetype multi-family residential buildings in urban residential districts were identified as archetype housing stock for an energy-assessment analysis in China. To identify the national representativeness of housing stock, census data was used to conduct a statistical analysis. It was found that households containing one elderly retiree or elderly retiree couples accounted for 4.86% and 4.40%, respectively, of all households in densely built residential urban districts in China. The statistical analysis confirmed that 93%

of all housing-type categories were covered by the selected household structure for the purpose of aggregate energy modelling. In the study, the black-box energy model was verified by using both on-site environmental monitoring and in situ physical measurements of indoor occupied spaces. The study proposed retrofit energy measures as an outcome of the analysis.

The study conducted by Li et al. shows distinct similarities with the present study in terms of the integrity of the field measurements and the building-energy simulations used to assess the energy performance of archetype buildings, but their study did not undertake a questionnaire survey to determine energy use according to households' socio-demographic characteristics. The strength of the Li et al. study is that the sampling size was large enough to represent the entire population in 18 districts in China. To reflect the method of design applied by Li et al. in the present study, findings were applied to four other cities where the post-war social housing estates were also built between 1984 and 1997. The census data supported the nationally representative nature of the post-war social housing estates, and the post-war social housing estate selected for reference enables a generalisation of research findings. To understand the impact of this field study investigation, outcomes were integrated with the Energy Performance Building Directives (EPBD) for the 27 EU countries.

A contrasting study, the pilot study conducted by Pittau et al. (2019), presents the carbon-storage potentials of the EU housing stock; however, this study does have a similar design approach to that developed in the present study. To identify the representativeness of housing stock in the EU, the pilot study conducted by Pittau et al. used the geo-mapping cluster technique to evaluate the thermal performance of buildings in seven climatic zones in the 28 EU countries and develop an effective energy policy design for each country. One of the prominent similarities of this pilot study with the present study is that post-war buildings built between 1945 and 1969 were selected as the archetype building typology. These post-war buildings represent 30% of the overall residential building stock in the EU 28. The Pittau et al.'s study tested the energy effectiveness of bio-based construction products applied onto the building envelopes of post-war social housing estates; their analysis included a life cycle cost assessment that was used to demonstrate the economic viability of these state-of-the-art building materials for retrofitting existing social housing stock. In the present study, modular off-site passive cooling technologies were applied to the archetype housing typology by considering the bio-climatic design elements of evidence-based retrofit energy policy designs, specifically in the Eastern Mediterranean region.

After reviewing the extant worldwide literature on the identification of archetype building typologies and their integration in the development of building-energy models for determining effective energy policy design, it can be concluded that a method of design that undertakes a parametric analysis by integrating collated data gathered through a questionnaire survey and field measurements can play an important role in decision-making criteria regarding domestic-energy use. To reflect the statistical methods used by previous scholars, the present study examined the EU's construction statistics by using the geo-mapping cluster method and the findings were validated with the available housing census data for the EU countries.

There is a high demand for construction projects in the Eastern Mediterranean region. While Portugal, Spain and Italy accounted for the highest number of residential buildings built in 2018, (for these EU countries, it was found that the number of dwellings constructed was between 22,925 and 154,564 annually), these figures were followed by Greece and Cyprus were the number of dwellings built ranged from 9,744 to 13,802 annually (Eurostat, 2018).[25]

The Eurostat data figures present that those Eastern Mediterranean countries offer a wide range of SFHs and MFHs for both locals and foreign buyers. According to the Eurostat data, in 2018, 60% of Spanish households lived in flats, 53% lived in flats in Italy and 47% lived in flats in Portugal. In Greece, while the number of dwellings built in 2018 was slightly less than in these other EU countries, about 57% of Greek households lived in flats. While about 27% of Cypriot[26] households live in flats, the population of the island is relatively smaller than most other EU countries in the Eastern Mediterranean basin, so that 27% of residency in flats is high for the Cypriot context. For the 27 EU countries overall, it was found that 47% of residents live in flats. The obtained average of 27% can be classified as a reasonable fraction to represent the archetype building typology for the RoC. It should be noted that the Housing Census and Construction Report statistics in NC reveal that the low-, medium- and high- rise RTBs account for 56% of the overall residential building stock. This generated statistical data proves that the NC housing stock was slightly above the EU-27 average.

Interestingly, the NC housing stock data is not included in the Eurostat database due to NC being only a de facto[27] state. Northern Cyprus is also underrepresented by the RoC, which does not give a reliable representation of any type of housing stock data for the island of Cyprus. From this statistical analysis, it can be deduced that 56% of high-density residential buildings are nationally representative for NC.[28] This data confirms that high-rise apartments are the representative archetype to be investigated as part of the bottom-up energy policy design. To prove the demand for housing projects, this study investigated housing projects in 2019 by assessing the GNP rate for each of the 27 EU member states.[29] It was found that the island of Cyprus accounted for the highest share rate at 7.2% of GDP spent on housing.[30] These figures were followed by 6.6% in Finland, 6.4% in Germany, 2.3% in both Slovenia and Ireland, 2.2% in Poland, 2.0% in Greece and 0.7% in France.

As the EU-27 average was found to be 5.3% of GNP spent on housing, Cyprus's rate was relatively higher than that of other EU countries. This demonstrates that there is high demand in Cyprus for housing projects. It should be noted that Cyprus's population is smaller than other EU countries, and yet the GDP rate shows that the economy is dominated by the construction sector in Cyprus. This statistical data proves that the selected archetype housing typology is appropriate for developing aggregate energy models to validate the data collection findings integrated into the black-box energy model for this study. In the present study, the representative archetype buildings were selected from four different regions and then one of these post-war social housing estates was chosen to extrapolate data to other dwellings in Cyprus.[31]

To identify the representativeness of each post-war social housing estate, both the census data and Housing and Construction Report statistics were investigated to provide a reliable representation rate for each of the cities where the government's social housing estates were built between 1984 and 1997. An up-to-date statistical analysis was undertaken to comply with the most reliable data available for the housing stock between 2015 and 2019.[32]

It was found that in the coastal city of Famagusta where the base-case post-war social housing estate is located, in urban areas, 62% of dwellings are residential buildings, 28% are apartments and 10% are houses. In suburban areas in Famagusta, 44% of dwellings are residential buildings, 37% are apartments and 19% are houses. It should be noted that according to the Statistical Annual Report in 2019, 38% of the overall buildings represent all housing typologies in NC. In mapping the representativeness of post-war social housing estates, it was found that apartments in suburban areas in Famagusta represent 37% of dwellings, which proves the appropriateness of the representative archetype of RTBs for the study.

In the inland region of Nicosia, apartments comprise the highest share of the overall housing stock at 55% in urban areas, followed by 34% residential buildings and 11% houses. In suburban regions, 44% of housing stock is residential buildings, 34% is apartments and 22% is houses. The vast majority (78%) of housing stock is either residential buildings with two to four storeys, or apartments buildings that are more-than-four-storey high-rise MFHs.

In the coastal city of Kyrenia, 51% of dwellings are residential buildings, 43% are apartments and 6% are houses in the densely built urban region, but recent rapid construction activity has had an impact and in suburban regions 50% are residential buildings, 24% are apartments and 26% are houses. Overall, in Kyrenia, 95% of the housing stock is residential buildings and apartments, which proves the applicability of research findings in the coastal city of Famagusta to this context where the climate is warm and humid in the summer.

Recent figures indicate that, in the mountainous region of Morphou, it was found that the housing stock is 73% residential buildings, 14% apartments and 13% houses in the urban region. Noticeable in this region is a hit record of residential buildings that accounts for 48% of overall housing stock, followed by 44% apartments and 8% houses in the suburban area. It should be noted that this region shows the highest percentage of apartments built amongst the suburban regions of the other cities. It can be deduced that both residential buildings and apartments are nationally representative archetypes, which allows an extrapolation of research findings gathered in the base-case post-war social housing estate in the coastal city of Famagusta to an evidence-based energy policy framework for the Eastern Mediterranean basin.

Methods and Tools

Literature Review

The aim of the present study was to review literature related to building overheating risks, thermal-comfort assessments, occupant behaviour and modelling and design methods developed by previous scholars to undertake a BES. Furthermore, the most commonly used energy-simulation tools related to building-performance evaluation were derived. To fill the EEG and address the RQs outlined for the present study, the bottom-up approach was adopted to analyse the energy performance of the archetype buildings and to validate the field study findings with the in situ measurements and BES study.

A search was conducted using the traditional review method; the Scopus platform was the main engine used for this search. The literature survey resulted in 784 documents, which included review articles, original research papers and conference proceedings that were collated between 1990 and 2019. Abstracts of the documents were reviewed using the meta-analysis method; this was followed by an analysis of the research context, methodology, archetype building selection, research instruments used, sampling size and novelty of each empirical study. Table 2.19 lists the top 11 sources that were included in the literature review for the present study; four additional conference proceedings were included to review extant literature that is within the objective of the present study.

Reviewing these study findings provided an opportunity to identify a new design method for an STS approach that could be developed to address the EEG and assess occupant thermal comfort via a longitudinal field survey, which is outlined in the following section.

Table 2.19 Journal Articles and Conference Proceedings Included in Literature Review

Selected Journals

Top11	*Source*	*Number of Documents*	*Source IF*	*Source SNIP*	*Source SJR*
1	*Energy and Buildings*	154	4,867	2,334	2,061
(n) 2	*Building and Environment*	124	5,20	2,604	1,879
(o) 3	*Energy*	81	6,082	2,012	2,166
(p) 4	*Applied Energy*	38	9,27	2,865	3,455
(q) 5	*Energy Research and Social Sciences*	54	5,45	1,869	2,138
(r) 6	*Energy Policy*	87	4,039	1,931	1,988
(s) 7	*Renewable and Sustainable Energy Reviews*	43	12,110	4,351	3,632
(t) 8	*Solar Energy*	23	4,608	1,651	1,539
(u) 9	*Journal of Building Engineering*	32	2,890	1,777	0,682
(v) 10	*Journal of Building Performance Simulation*	56	3,458	1,764	1,329
(w) 11	*Sustainable Cities and Society*	13	5,268	1,987	1,356

Selected Conference Proceedings: (i) Building Simulation Optimization 2018 (30 papers in total); (ii) Windsor Conference Proceedings 2012–2018 (23 papers in total); (iii) Zero Energy Mass Custom Housing Proceedings 2016–2018 (7 papers in total); (iv) IBPSA Conference Proceedings 2016–2018 (27 papers in total).

Note: Journal metrics updated on 23 March 2021.

Survey Design and Data Acquisition

Survey. A standardised questionnaire survey was developed to collect subjective data from the building occupants related to their domestic-cooling energy use and to evaluate the thermal-comfort levels in specific orientations (Dornyei, 2003); a total of 200 households from 288 flats were randomly selected, which represented the social-housing stock in other municipalities in NC (Black, 2006). A number of research methods were employed in the present study to collect and analyse the research data (Campell & Fiske, 1959; Creswell, 2010; Goodchild et al., 2017). For this reason, a series of quantitative and qualitative research methodologies were considered and designed, as delineated in Table 2.20, and the RQs were devised according to the research methods that were chosen to generate quantitative and qualitative data.

As can be seen in Table 2.20, the questionnaire survey with structured questions and open-ended questions was intended to collect quantitative and qualitative data throughout the standardised means to further probe the details of specific questions. Notably, the data gathered during the qualitative phase of the present study informed the findings of the quantitative phase (Creswell & Clark, 2011). Similarly, the quantitative results demonstrated outcomes related to household energy use and the thermal comfort reported by participants to assist in the findings from the qualitative data (Kieft et al., 2020). A total of 36 RTBs with the same floor-plan layout, construction materials and architectural style were selected to conduct a field study and recruit households.

To conduct an in-depth analysis of the RTB thermal properties that considered household socio-demographic characteristics and environmental conditions of the social-housing project sites, the aforementioned location was selected as a representative application of the described methodology (Ramsden, 2020; Wittmayer et al., 2020). In this way, the most dominant representative urban-built stock was studied, and the results of the present study could be extrapolated to the remainder of the social-housing stock, which was intended to represent post-war social-housing stock in Europe.

Participants. The subject respondents (*P*–set) for the development of an STS conceptual framework were drawn from all 36 RTBs in the post-war social-housing estate in Famagusta, Cyprus. The area boundaries were defined by the demographics and housing-stock datasets associated with the national census of the Office for National Statistics State Planning Organisation. These secondary-data resources were utilised to determine the representativeness of sampling criteria included in the statistical model; 118 households[33] were recruited through a field investigation, which was then extrapolated to represent NC households (see Data 3). All variable differences were calculated to identify the worst-case scenario, and the medium-rise RTB estate with the highest total number of flats was selected; this area represented typical neighbourhoods in Nicosia (i.e., urban), Kyrenia (i.e., urban), Omorphou (i.e., rural) and Lefke (i.e., rural), rather than randomly selected neighbourhoods. The census variables are shown in Table 2.21.

Table 2.20 Data Required to Gather Household Feedback

Research Questions	*Research Methods*	*Data*	*Reason for Methods*
RQ 1: Which household socio-demographic characteristics and home-energy performance factors significantly impact household energy use?	Literature review Questionnaire survey Semi-structured interviews	Qualitative Quantitative Qualitative	To obtain accurate primary data collection, answer research objectives and identify occupant socio-demographic information
RQ 2: Which occupant energy-consumption behaviours might have an impact on the energy performance of the social-housing estate?	Literature review Questionnaire survey Semi-structured interviews	Qualitative Quantitative Qualitative	To obtain accurate primary data to identify dominant representative occupancy profiles and the significance thereof on home-energy use
RQ 3: How can environmental factors affect occupant thermal comfort?	Literature review Environmental monitoring Thermal-comfort survey Semi-structured interviews	Qualitative Quantitative Quantitative Quantitative	To identify the reasons for thermal discomfort and household thermal-sensation votes (TSVs)
RQ 4: How can the present study contribute and inform the design of nearly zero-energy buildings in EU countries?	Questionnaire survey Semi-structuredinterviews	Quantitative Qualitative	Mixed interpretations of research findings in both cases

Source: **Adapted from Creswell and Clark (2011).**

Table 2.21 Household Socio-demographic Characteristics Collected from the Questionnaire Survey

Socio-demographic Variables	
Tenure type	Year of construction
Housing stock with the council tax band	Household occupancy type (i.e., OP1, OP2 and OP3[a])
Housing type	
Space conditioning and different floor-levels	Household energy bills

[a]Occupancy Patterns: Low occupancy (OP1), moderate occupancy (OP2) and high occupancy (OP3)

Source: Restructured in 2018 according to data from the Office for National Statistics.

As can be seen in Table 2.21, all variables were related to household socio-demographic characteristics and the type of housing stock that was chosen. To design standard development models and compare them to the city average, the best approach was to only select one case study location to represent the entire social-housing stock as a base-case scenario (Muresan & Attia, 2017). This deliberate sampling was undertaken to meet the research objective of investigating the effect of household socio-demographic characteristics on home-energy performance in a typical representative neighbourhood (Cross et al., 2017). Each variable was integrated into the statistical model to predict the energy-policy forecasting design scenarios is briefly described below (see Data 4):

(i) Ownership status referred to the overall percentage of social-housing stock who were homeowners or private renters.
(ii) RTB age referred to the five different archetypes that represented a nationwide sampling for a fraction of the overall household population.
(iii) Housing typology classification was based on to council tax band in accordance with the council tax rating indicators obtained from the Famagusta municipality.
(iv) Household occupancy type referred to the number of family members who lived on the same property.
(v) Space conditioning of occupied spaces included natural ventilation, mixed-mode ventilation, mechanical ventilation heat-recovery systems and A/C split units installed in the property.
(vi) Actual household electricity bills obtained from the Cyprus Electricity Authority.

These variables include all available physical built-form and demographic information related to the home at the local level to provide subsequent information for the development of an evidence-based STS conceptual framework (see Data 5). Data collection was guided by a preliminary thematic analysis of key concepts prompted during the interviews with participants. The applied methodology considered the post-war social-housing stock by exploring correlations between the household socio-demographic structure, the actual environmental conditions of the built environment and the thermal-conductivity level of building-thermal properties (see Data 6). It should also be noted that semi-structured interviews were only conducted with occupants in selected building typologies so the findings of the present study could be generalised and applied to other post-war social-housing stock in the Republic of Cyprus and in Europe.

Questionnaire Design and Household Recruitment. This research adopted a methodology that included questionnaire surveys distributed in RTBs with different orientations to assess overheating risks, optimise occupant thermal comfort and determine whether different floor levels have a substantial impact on the energy use of households in a post-war social-housing development estate (see Data 7). A thorough review of the present study was conducted, including several instances of feedback that were obtained during the pilot study. The survey was conducted with members of 118 households between 28 July 2018 and 3 September 2018. The questionnaire included 28 questions and adopted a combination of open-ended, partially closed-ended and mostly closed-ended questions (Creswell, 2012); it was designed to predominantly obtain quantitative feedback from respondents by utilising housing census data obtained from Famagusta Municipality to generate a nationally representative sample of Cypriot households (Darnton, 2008; Doukas, 2020).

The pro forma questionnaire survey was contrived according to the cultural values of the research context, specifically the cultural barriers that prevent a man from entering premises in which only the woman is present; for this reason, the researcher was accompanied by a female throughout the survey processes (see Data 8). The survey was specifically devised to take ethnicity, cultural values, climate characteristics and building codes into account to obtain effective responses from the households. The design structure of this pro forma questionnaire is itself a contribution to the body of knowledge; the pro forma questionnaire survey is an exemplary pilot-survey model that can be applied in other field studies where the climate is shown to be subtropical (*Csa*) and partly semi-arid (*Bsh*).

Importantly, the manner in which the field survey was conducted included going door-to-door with the survey to recruit households. The pro forma questionnaire survey was completed in the form of semi-structured, face-to-face interviews to obtain the most accurate data from the subject respondents; due to the nature of the interviews and discussions, the researcher was able to collect quantitative data to validate the obtained data that included on-site monitoring and in situ measurements of the environmental conditions, which is the contribution; this study presents the human-based data that were extracted from the questionnaire survey for the BES studies.

Data analysis. Semi-structured interviews and participant feedback were transcribed and translated. The Statistical Package for Social Sciences (SPSS) Version 25.0 software (IBM: Armonk, NY, US) was utilised to conduct the quantitative analysis; and tests-of-associations were conducted between the numeric factors and the questionnaire responses to join the questionnaire results with the statistical

Table 2.22 Measures of Association

R	*Interpretation of Linear Relationship*
0.8	Strong positive
0.5	Moderate positive
0.3	Weak positive
0.0	No relationship
−0.2	Weak negative
−0.5	Moderate negative
−0.8	Strong negative
$\|r\| < 0.3 \rightarrow$ Weak relationship	
$0.3 \leq \|r\| \leq 0.5 \rightarrow$ Moderate relationship	
$\|r\| > 0.5 \rightarrow$ Strong relationship	

Source: Khamis (2008).

analysis. Previous studies used analysis-of-variance (ANOVA), Pearson's correlation and ordinal regression and multinominal logistic regression analyses, and these statistical tests effectively explored correlations within a set of variables designed in the dataset (see Data 9). To interpret the statistical analysis, the conventional method was used for the interpretations between two continuous variables. Table 2.22 demonstrates the guidelines are generally in agreement with Cohen's recommended guidelines.[34]

The interview responses were used in the descriptive analysis to determine household socio-demographic characteristics and the occupants' thermal-comfort levels; a correlation analysis of these findings was then conducted to evaluate the correlations amongst the different parameters (i.e., household socio-demographic characteristics and occupant behaviour related to home-energy performance and thermal comfort) (see Data 10).

It should be noted that inferential statistics, which are also referred to as inductive statistics, were employed to make generalisations and inferences about the sample size; the inferential statistical techniques utilised in the present study include Pearson's correlation coefficient and an ordinal RA (see Data 11). Regression forecasting of neutral adaptive thermal-comfort contributes to the ASHRAE Global Thermal Comfort Database II, which is why the descriptive statistics on adaptive thermal comfort were concurrently interpreted with the regression results (see Data 12).

A total of 118 households were successfully recruited, but a 100-sampling size was utilised in the SPSS dataset, because it was determined that 18 households did not provide accurate information when the questionnaire survey was distributed; to avoid a biased interpretation of the field-survey results and to run a parametric-statistical analysis for the present study, these households were disregarded in the dataset (see Data 13).

Table 2.23 Set of Determinant Factors Included in Statistical Model

Questionnaire Variables	*Data Type*	*Test of Association*
Thermal-comfort preference	Likert scale	Spearman's rho
Thermal sensation	Likert scale	Spearman's rho
Energy-saving awareness (yes or no)	Dichotomous nominal	Point-biserial
Gender	Dichotomous nominal	Point-biserial
Age group	Nominal	ANOVA (*F*-test)
Education level	Nominal	ANOVA (*F*-test)
Ethnicity	Nominal	ANOVA (*F*-test)
Household income	Nominal	ANOVA (*F*-test)
Tenure	Nominal	ANOVA (*F*-test)
Length of residency	Nominal	ANOVA (*F*-test)

To run the parametric tests between the dependent and independent variables, the present study adopted the following statistical conventions: the assumed degree-of-confidence interval was 95%, the level of confidence was 0.05, and the significance level (p) was 0.000. Table 2.23 summarises the data types associated with each of the questionnaire variables and the association test or test statistic that was applied to correlate every variable in the questionnaire survey (see Data 14).

Table 2.23 lists all tests-of-association that were employed in the present study. The Benjamin–Hochberg procedure was utilised to adjust the final p-values and control the false-discovery rate (FDR) in the statistical analysis; FDR procedures were implemented in the present study to detect discrepancies in the statistical model (Gimpel et al., 2020). The adjusted p-values helped to correct for errors that were introduced by multiple comparisons and were a more accurate reflection of significant correlations (see Data 15). The number of iterations was determined using a 95% confidence level for each index and following the methods presented in the present study, thereby ensuring that a random sample of 100 inputs for each variable was generated; this sample size strengthened the analysis and improved the overall precision of estimations of the correlation coefficients (Mertens, 2009).

A 95% interval-confidence level was chosen to measure the impact of variables in the statistical analysis, which was designed in accordance with the RQs (see Data 16). This confidence level is a conventional method, and it was selected for the present study because it is a traditional, well-known, established statistical technical information method; moreover, in the event that an insufficient sample is available for statistical analysis, it is compatible with the process whereby a small sample size is extrapolated to larger datasets to provide nationally representative data (see Data 17).

It must be noted that the available sample size for the present study was not transformed into a large dataset by multiplying the data to comply with the recommended sampling size. The 100 questionnaires were correctly identified and deemed to be a reasonable fraction of a sampling size to conduct a statistical analysis (see Data 18). Phi and *Cramer*'s *V* correlation coefficient was used to identify the difficult-to-quantify home-energy performance factors and occupancy profiles gathered through a questionnaire survey and to interpret data within other field instruments that were implemented in the present study; the on-site environmental monitoring and in situ measurements were also included in the dataset, which allowed the researcher to test the determinant factors between household socio-demographic characteristics and the environmental factors of the built environment.

Another important reason to conduct an ordinal—RA analysis was to determine the main dependent factor that influenced the RQs and explore a conventional statistical technique to conduct correlation and regression analyses. The statistical test findings provided additional evidence to identify simulation input parameters for a BES study (see Data 19).

Questionnaire Survey

Design methods. The present study primarily relied on a questionnaire-based survey to investigate household characteristics and the habitual adaptive behaviour of occupants as it relates to home-energy performance. The questionnaire gauged each household's level of knowledge about their heating and cooling systems in an attempt to determine what the respondents considered to be energy when it came to their cooling systems, and how they adapted heating and cooling systems to their personal thermal comfort in changing climate conditions. Table 2.24 presents the questionnaires that included household socio-demographic information in the interviewed RTBs while taking the orientation and floor-level differences thereof into account. A set of questions was developed to inquire about the socio-economic characteristics and tenancy status of each household, including the length of residency at the property.

Another set of questions focused on the household energy-saving awareness and advice received on information on energy-efficient practices that were provided to each household by the Famagusta Municipality or local energy-networking service, because the questionnaire survey was conducted in the summer and the occupants were asked to retrospectively indicate on various multi-factorial home-energy performance indicators from the previous winter (see Data 20). As was already indicated, the pro forma questionnaire survey was designed to consider the cultural assets, values and norms of the research context and ensure an accurate statistical analysis.

Household selection criteria and recruitment. To provide subsequent background information related to household socio-demographic characteristics and the validity of the questionnaire survey in the Eastern Mediterranean climate, the survey participants were selected from among 36 RTBs, all of which had similar floor plans, layout designs and construction characteristics; there were a total of 288 flat units in the social-housing estate, and each had a different orientation and household characteristics (see Data 21).

Table 2.24 Questionnaire Details

Developmental Stages	*Questions*
Step 1: General background information	• Number of interviewed RTBs • Unit orientation • Floor level
Step 2: Socio-demographic information	• Gender • Age • Tenancy status and length of residency • Number of household members, including non-family members • Employment activity • Income • Education • Ethnicity • Health status
Step 3: Energy-saving awareness	• Did respondent receive energy advice from any type of public or private institution? • Availability of electricity meter readings and frequency of checks • Did the respondents consider any type of energy-saving methods in their daily activities?
Step 4: Household energy use and performance	• Types of domestic heating appliances, available heating-system controls and frequency of use • Types of domestic-cooling appliances, available cooling-system controls and frequency of use
Step 5: Occupancy patterns	• Weekday and weekend heating-consumption patterns • Weekday and weekend cooling-consumption patterns • Window-opening patterns in the summer and winter
Step 6: *Energy consumption*	• Average amounts of monthly utility bill

A quota-sampling decision-making criterion was adopted in the present study to demonstrate a nationally representative sample of Northern Cypriot post-war social-housing stock. The extant literature on field-study investigations of social-housing estates in Europe and in the UK recommended that the quota sampling that is needed to investigate correlations between different variables should be gathered through a questionnaire survey, which suggests that issuing a set of quota characteristics (i.e., tenure type, orientation, different floor levels and occupant energy-use patterns) to interviewers and conducting a corresponding number of multi-decision criteria analyses in every category of every household socio-demographic characteristic (see Data 22).

The aim of this technique was to validate the multi-variate statistical analysis that was conducted to demonstrate the representativeness of the sample size and reflect the household socio-demographic overview for which the interviews were sought. To avoid bias when considering the households' responses to the distributed set of questions and minimise the risk of discrepancies in the statistical analysis, the quota sampling approach offered inclusive primary-data output; one reason for this is that it is not possible to determine the exact representatives of a given sample because of potential sampling bias during respondent selection.

Throughout the pro forma questionnaire survey, the present study developed ten interview questions to gather the following binary categories: owners versus renters, length of residency, awareness of energy saving, type of heating and cooling systems used, type of heating– and cooling-control systems utilised, occupancy patterns during the weekdays and on the weekends in the winter and summer, window-opening schedules in the winter and summer and the reasons for thermal discomfort—all of which took into account the different orientations of the RTBs and the different floor levels of each flat. These classifications were selected because the aforementioned factors strongly correlate with the significance of energy-consumption patterns in overall energy use. The sample was based on gathering background information on the overall occupancy of every unit in the RTBs, rather than obtaining individual information of the subject respondents.

To fulfil this research objective and avoid the risk of bias in the household responses related to knowledge of energy use at the household level, the survey method was pilot-tested. A questionnaire-based survey was prepared, partly to hear occupant views on patterns that impacted their home-energy use, and also to collect evidence-based examples of identifying dominant representative occupancy profiles that could be further corroborated in the decision-making process of retrofitting design interventions.

Thermal-Comfort Survey

Design methods. To assess the occupants' degree of thermal discomfort, the pro forma questionnaire was distributed to the subject respondents, the seven-point ASHRAE thermal-sensation band was employed. A thermal-comfort survey was concurrently carried out with on-site monitoring and in situ measurements to understand the significant impact of environmental conditions on the occupants' thermal comfort at the time of the survey administration.

Physical measurements. The outdoor-air temperatures and relative humidity (RH) levels of the environmental conditions were monitored between 28 July 2018 and 3 September 2018 to assess the overheating risk issues of the in situ-measured flats. The outdoor environmental conditions, including the outdoor air temperature, RH and heat-stress index, were monitored with a Wireless Vintage Pro 2 weather station from Davis Instruments Corporation (Hayward, CA, US). Indoor environmental conditions were recorded with a thermometer (resolution 0.1°C); globe temperature was recorded with a 15 cm -diameter globe thermometer with a thin-walled copper sphere that is painted black (resolution 0.1°C); RH was recorded with a 2400 Heat Stress WBGT Meter (resolution 0-1°C) (Extech Instruments: Nashua, NH, US).

To validate the findings from the monitoring campaign, additional in situ measurements of indoor-air environment were carried out using a forward-looking infrared radiometer (FLIR) infrared thermographic camera to assess the occupants' decisions related to their TPVs and TSVs. With regard to the overheating-risk assessment, the indoor air temperature and RH of 100 participant living rooms were concurrently measured with a questionnaire survey to cover the hottest period in summer to assess overheating-risk and occupant thermal comfort.

To identify neutral adaptive thermal comfort and validate the findings from the BPEs, outdoor thermal conditions, including the outdoor-air temperature, RH levels and the HSI, were monitored with a Wireless Vantage Pro weather station. The weather station was installed on the roof of the northwest-facing RTB Block Number 3, which was built in Phase 1, the weather station was mounted on a pole that was approximately 2 metres long. It was equipped with a set of continuously monitored thermocouples that recorded temperature variations throughout the questionnaire survey period.

The temperature measurements were collected at 15-minute intervals over a one-month period. According to the manufacturer specifications, the accuracy of the thermocouples is rated at ±0.05°C to ensure that reliable datasets are recorded and to assess the current thermal performance of the case study building. The environmental monitoring study was concurrently undertaken with the semi-structured household interviews; in addition to the monitored data, meteorological data gathered from the Department of Meteorological Service in NC were collected to compare the accuracy of the monitoring results. The meteorological weather station was located approximately 16 km away from the case study location, which ensured that the outdoor weather observations were representative of the local climate. The details of the instrumentation used in the field studies are summarised in Table 2.25.

As can be seen in Table 2.25, the weather station recorded the abovementioned parameters in 10-minute intervals each day. Data for the relevant days were downloaded, processed and merged using a specific weather-analysis software suite developed for the Vue weather station. It should be mentioned that the outdoor-air temperature was used to calculate the 80% acceptable operative-temperature range in accordance with the ASHRAE Standard 55 specifications (2017); the upper and lower limits of the 80% acceptable range are presented in Equations (2.1) and (2.2). Per the ASHRAE Standard 55 (2017), variable T_{rma} is defined as the prevailing mean outdoor air temperature and is calculated based on the arithmetic average of the mean daily outdoor air temperatures to calibrate the correlations between the outdoor and indoor environmental conditions that were recorded.

Table 2.25 Technical Properties of Weather Station at Case Study Location

ClimateVariables	*Accuracy*	*Resolution*	*MeasurementRange*
Air temperature	±0,5° above −7°C	0.1°C or 1°C	−40°C to +65°C
Relative humidity	±3% for 0–90% and ±4% for 0–90-to -100%	1%	1–100%
Wind speed	1 m/s	0,4 m/s	1–80 m/s

$$\text{Upper 80\% acceptability limit (°C)} = 0.31\,T_{rma} + 21.3°C \qquad \text{(Equation 2.1)}$$

$$\text{Lower 80\% acceptability limit (°C)} = 0.31\,T_{rma} + 14.3°C \qquad \text{(Equation 2.2)}$$

On-Site Measurements

Design methods. While the questionnaire surveys were being conducted, the indoor environmental parameters were also being recorded; this included air temperatures and the RH levels of the measured apartment units. The accuracy of the instrumentation utilised in the field studies met the 2015 *CIBSE-AM11: Building Energy and Environmental Modelling* requirements (Fox et al., 2014). The details of the instrumentation utilised in the field studies are summarised in Table 2.26.

The physical measurements covered the entire period of the questionnaire surveys. The in situ measurements were conducted with the FLIR camera during the field study in August of 2018. In addition to the subjective thermal-sensation responses, these measurements permitted the calculation of comfort temperatures embedded within the Griffiths Method related to adaptive thermal comfort to identify occupant optimum thermal-comfort threshold level.

As it relates to a thermal-comfort analysis, Griffiths suggested that there was a linear relationship between comfort votes and operative temperature (OT) with a constant gradient (Griffiths, 1990). The assessment calculation can thus be interpreted in Equation (2.3):

$$Cv = T_{op} + h \qquad \text{(Equation 2.3)}$$

where Cv is the comfort vote, T_{op} is the OT and h is the constant. This equation model was adopted to assess the results of the building-energy performance studies and gather evidence-based data to develop an STS conceptual framework.

The present study selected a specific methodology—the pass-by thermography method—to speed up the inspection process, so the research consortium could investigate more buildings in each survey period (Theodosiou et al., 2021). The methodology adopted for walk-through surveys in the present study followed the principles established by the American Society for Testing and Materials, the Residential Energy Services Network and British Standard BS EN 13187: 1999 (BR-497:2007, 2007).

Building-Energy Simulation Parameters

Design method. To determine the input parameters for the simulation set, the present study adopted the STS approach, which considers the socio-demographic characteristics of the energy use of each household, the environmental conditions that were monitored and the thermal-conductivity properties of each building as an empirical study. A bottom-up approach was integrated into the comprehensive methodology in the conceptual framework of the present study to achieve the objectives of the building-performance evaluation and the optimisation of existing

Table 2.26 Measurement Range and Accuracy of Instruments Used in Field Studies

Parameter	*InstrumentationModel*	*Range*	*Accuracy*	*AccuracyRequirements**
Air temperature	Fluke TIS20 Thermal Camera	−40°C to +85°C	±1°C for 150°C	±0.5°C
Relative humidity	Fluke TIS20 Thermal Camera	0–100%	±4%	±1%
Air temperature	Fluke 63 Infrared Thermometer	−25°C to 85°C	±0.5°C for0–40°C	Minimum: ±0.5°C Ideal: ±0.2°C
Relative humidity	Fluke 63 Infrared Thermometer	0–95%	±3% at 25°C	±5%

housing stock that was not previously carried out in order to inform policy-making decisions related to energy use.

In the present study, retrofitting design strategies developed as a result of information obtained from the surveyed occupants' semi-structured interview responses associated with each household's energy-use awareness and the main findings of the building-performance evaluation study to design these buildings systems were used in conjunction with the human-based data. This multivariate research approach led to the development of evidence-based design strategies for effective energy-use policy-making decisions. An overview of the step-by-step energy-performance assessment of base-case RTBs.

To feed into the building-performance simulation analysis, target outputs from the data were utilised to describe the overall building construction and technical systems, a broad set of energy-use data and a room-schedule data that described the characteristics of occupied spaces in representative RTB flat units. The data collection method for the present study was designed to maximise the detail and accuracy of the record of the base-case representative RTBs within the time frame and the resources available for data collection.

For each RTB, an initial familiarisation exercise was carried out. This involved a review of building plans, construction materials, construction of room-data schedules and preliminary walk-through and extensive on site photographic documentation. A thorough site walk-round was then performed in each building to diagnose the thermal vulnerability of building envelopes that are susceptible to overheating across the sample of representative flat units. Occupied spaces were also placed in standard space categories according to the floor-plan layout design and the orientation of the units. The present study sought to identify building-envelope thermal performance and to assess the overheating risk of the representative flat units to calibrate domestic-energy use. To ensure a literature analysis of the key aims and objectives, the research adopted a quantitative research design by undertaking a building-performance evaluation based on dynamic thermal modelling and a simulation thereof, and IRT was validated by monitoring indoor and outdoor environmental parameters in the prototype base-case RTBs, including air temperature, RH and household energy bills.

The investigation of the case study RTBs determined that they modelled the cooling-energy demand of the representative medium-rise housing typology and assessed the thermal comfort of occupants during a long-term heat wave while taking the thermal transmittance principles of the *U*-value of the properties into account. The literature review indicated that this step-by-step analysis provided the necessary background information to develop a new design method for the STS approach as a tool for policymakers. To develop an effective energy-design policy and improve the current design methods in building-energy simulation studies, the methodological workflow was conducted in the following manner; all of these are discussed.

(i) Thermal imaging
(ii) In situ measurements

(iii) Household energy-bill analyses
(iv) Building-energy simulations

Household energy bills. To gather reliable data to assess the energy consumption of the occupants and to compare the building-modelling simulation results to the utility-bill analysis, the present study evaluated the occupants' energy consumption in the winter of 2015 – 2016 and the summer of 2016. These data served as the basis for a real-energy-consumption dataset that could be used in the building-modelling simulation. These data also enabled us to evaluate the existing energy performance of the surveyed RTBs to assess the overheating issues experienced in each flat. The household electricity bills were obtained from the Cyprus Electricity Authority database with consent from the householders.

Building-energy modelling. To develop a new STS conceptual framework and analyse the thermal performance of the case study RTBs, it was necessary to use a DTS model. The IES software suite was determined to be the most appropriate application for this purpose, because it used the test reference-year (TRY) weather files for the research context to provide accurate results and simulate actual environmental conditions (Mazzeo et al., 2020); the IES software suite was known to meet a number of international standards, including CIBSE TM52 and CIBSE TM59, and it is accredited according to the BS EN 15251 European standard (IES, 2020). Moreover, IES is a commonly utilised environmental-design software suite that facilitates the design of a simulation set of input parameters in accordance with the findings of the field study (Rhodes et al., 2015); it also enables users to construct the thermal properties of buildings within the local building codes and regulations. Table 2.27 presents the strengths of the IES software suite and its interpolation with industry benchmarks and international assessment criterion to measure overheating risk, thermal comfort and energy consumption of archetype buildings in the analytical building-energy model.

IES 2019.1.0.0 software was utilised throughout the present study to conduct energy-assessment analyses. Specifically, the Thermal Comfort Analytical energy-simulation platform of the IES software suite was determined to be the application that would best be able to measure the adaptive comfort of the prototype RTBs (Hellwig et al., 2019). Utilising this software in combination with the DTS set input parameters such as the thermal-conductivity levels of different building materials, air-infiltration rates, internal heat gains and occupancy profiles assigned in the IES software, was found to be effective.

The model was set up to assess the performance of each dwelling in the south-facing case study RTB under worst-case scenario conditions. The profiles in the present study were set in the IES dynamic thermal-assessment platform as required for each zone to describe the temporal variations of the ventilation flow rates, cooling set-points, lighting usage and occupancy profiles.

The IES software can easily be coupled with the Energy Plus, Design Builder and Revit® Green Building software suites to acquire building geometry and location information from the TRY data available in the Energy Plus databases

Table 2.27 List of Datasets Developed to Undertake DTS for an Empirical Study

Dataset development	Model intent	Early-stage design tool Building optimisation tool Overheating-risk analysis
	Target variable	Total annual energy
	Building archetype	Medium-rise 4- and 5-storey RTBs
	Location and climate	Test Reference Year (TRY), ASHRAE Climate Zone 2A, Larnaca Weather Station, Paralimni, Cyprus
	Energy-Simulation Software	IESVE 2019.1.0
	Statistical analysis andmodelling tool	ApacheSIM–VistaPro software interface
	Base model	Based on the existing calibrated model proposed in 2008 by Swan and Ugursal and updated with BES prototype models recommended in 2020 by Mahdavi
	Features and ranges	*CIBSE TM59: Design methodology to assess the overheating risk in homes* recommended by the CIBSE in 2017 BS EN 15251: 2007: Indoor environmental input parameters to design and assess building-energy performance, which addresses indoor air quality, the thermal environment, lighting and acoustics
	Sampling plan	Latin Hypercube (i.e., the black-box model)
Data Pre-processing	Train/validation/test split	TRY and AMY weather files
	Feature engineering	Input feature standardisation
Building-Energy Simulation Model Development	Feature selection	ApacheSIM: DTS analysis
	Building-performanceevaluation parameters	*U*-values, occupancy profiles, ventilation rates, heating and cooling set-point temperatures, appliances, etc.
	Error metrics	Validated by energy bill

(Brembilla et al., 2020). IES enables users to convert analytical energy models into gbxml. files to provide an interpolation of the analytical model within other energy software suites, such as the EDSL Tas and the Transient System Simulation Tool. IES can also interpret the dynamic thermal simulation results within the recommended CIBSE TM59 benchmarks to assess the risk of overheating and the ASHRAE 55 benchmark criteria (2017) to assess the degree of thermal discomfort (ASHRAE, 2017).

Analytical Energy Simulation Model Development

Black-Box Model Construction

The locations of the base-case RTBs were calculated using the mean postcode grid references for corresponding base-case buildings in the database that were identified by the ArcGIS Pro 2019.1.0 software. The dynamic thermal modelling approach was employed to assess the current energy performance of the specified households. A south-facing RTB was selected as the base-case representative building to reduce the timely process of performing dynamic thermal simulations and numeric calculations in the IES software suite. The scope of the simulations was based on the indoor air temperature in relation to the thermal-comfort temperatures of each selected occupied space in the representative apartment units.

The geometries of the existing RTBs in the present study were constructed in the IES ModelIT module; this was usually done by tracing over the respective computer-aided design survey plans.

For the base-case representative flats, floor heights were determined by on site measurements; glazing heights were also either obtained by on-site measurements or based on external images. The outline geometries of the adjacent buildings were considered to have potential shading effects were included for each building. Table 2.28 summarises the derived geometry parameters for each building form.

The rooms and the openings thereof were located on three differently oriented façades that allowed solar radiation onto building envelopes, through two flats with similar spatial plan layouts per floor of the model. The performance of the three exposures covered the main orientations (i.e., north, south and south-west). The simulation outputs related to the simulated room zones that had the same exposure were also required. Seven rooms were simulated and evaluated in great detail so that all possible performances of the first, intermediate and upper floors of the south-facing representative flats that were based on the boundary condition options were analysed. Before those models can generate recommendations, however, it is important to understand the accuracy of the simulation predictions for actual energy use. The black-box model was developed to calibrate BES to validate the findings from the IRT survey.

The present study sought to determine model accuracy by employing the black-box construction model to calculate the boundary conditions of each space in the analytical energy model. To provide a novel methodological flow for an energy-performance analysis, the development of the black-box model demonstrated the impact of the STS design approach. For this reason, detailed energy models were developed to measure the impact of space volume and the building-envelope thermal properties while documenting occupancy profiles and window-opening schedules in the ApacheSIM interface of the IES model.

Table 2.28 Geometry Parameters for Base-Case Representative Building Form

Parameter	*Urban Form*	
Total building height		17.4 m
Number of floors		5.0 m
Average floor height (slab-to-slab)		3.0 m
Building length		15.0 m
Building width		16.0 m
Average glazing ratio		50.0%
North adjacency	Length	12.0 m
	Height	15.0 m
East adjacency	Length	3.0 m
	Height	17.4 m
South adjacency	Length	6.0 m
	Height	17.4 m
West adjacency	Length	3.0 m
	Height	17.4 m

Heating and Cooling Profiles

Heating profiles were assigned from generic templates because measurements were not recorded in the heating season, but the cooling profiles used data that were measured during the defined cooling-and-monitoring season in August of 2018. For these purposes, only two set-point temperatures for the microclimate control of the active energy systems were defined during operating hours: 20°C during the heating period and 26°C for space-cooling. When possible, the RH control was fixed at a set-point of 50% for the heating and cooling sessions. Moreover, the base-case building was located in the ASHRAE Climate Zone 2A, where a conventional heating period from 16 November to 31 March was established by law. It should be noted that the cooling period was not fixed, but typically began when indoor temperatures exceeded 26°C for 146 consecutive days; this period usually runs from May to September, and cooling hours are sometimes needed on certain days in October.

The natural ventilation settings were based on temperature control, which was determined to be when indoor temperatures were higher than the 25°C set-point of the A/C system and the outdoor temperatures were below this temperature; otherwise, natural ventilation was used. In empty spaces (i.e., corridors, water closets and bathrooms), only the natural ventilation rate was considered. Moreover, a thermal performance of the representative flats was conducted to compare the comfort delivered by natural ventilation when no A/C system was used.

Ventilation Variation Profiles

The comfort requirements in international standards, such as the 2007 EN 15251 specifications, were expressed in terms of the OT, and the representative case study RTB set-point regulation was performed according to this value. Consequently, per the EN 15251 guidelines for normal level-of-comfort expectations, T_{op} values

Table 2.29 Ventilation Variation Profiles Assigned in Simulation Model

Parameter		*Values*	
Maximum daytime ventilation rate when $Q_{op} > 23°C$		$3\ h^{-1}$ from 06:00–23:00	
Maximum overnight ventilation rate when $Q_{op} > 23°C$		$2\ h^{-1}$ from 23:00–06:00	
		$200\ W/m^2$: north, northeast, northwest	
		$300\ W/m^2$: all other directions	
Infiltration	$0.1\ h^{-1}$	**Cooling Set-Point (Comfort Levels)**	
Internal heat gains	$4\ W/m^2$	First floor	24°C
Façade short-wavereflectivity	$0.5\ d_f$	Intermediate floor	25°C
		Upper floor	26°C

of 26°C for cooling were established for the energy-needs analysis of the representative RTB. In this regard, since the CEN adaptive method provided in EN 15251 is valid for outdoor reference temperatures up to 30°C, only the running mean-temperature equation, which can be applied up to 33.5°C and is therefore more applicable in a Mediterranean climate context, was considered for the present study. The parameters for the building simulation are summarised in Table 2.29. From the records of outside air temperature, the running mean outdoor temperatures were calculated using Equations (2.4) and (2.5), which were included in CEN Standard EN 15251:

$$T_{rm} = (1-\infty)\,T_{ed} - 1 + \infty\, T_{rm} - 1 \qquad \text{(Equation 2.4)}$$

$$T_{rm} = (T_{ed} - 1 + 0.8\,T_{ed}\,2 + 0.6\,T_{ed} - 3 + 0.5\,T_{ed} - 4 + 0.4\,T_{ed} - 5 + 0.3\,T_{ed} - 6 + 0.2\,T_{ed} - 6 + 0.2\,T_{ed} - 7)/3.8$$

(Equation 2.5)

where T_{rm} is the running mean temperature for today, $T_{rm} - 1$ is the running mean temperature for the previous day, $T_{ed} - 1$ is the daily mean external temperature for the previous day, $T_{ed} - 2$ is the daily mean external temperature for the day before and so on, and is an $\propto$ constant between 0 and 1 (0.8 is recommended).

In the present study, requirements for standard air-discharge rates in residential buildings were assigned in the DTS interface as follows: the global discharge rate was $1.40\ l/m^2s$ for naturally ventilated buildings; this corresponded to $1.90\ h^{-1}$, which is what should be experienced in the living spaces during peak occupancy hours. At other times, such as when the flat was unoccupied during the weekend, the European Norm (EN) recommended a discharge rate of $0.10–0.20\ l/m^2s$ to provide adequate indoor-air quality during occupancy hours. Importantly, these rates adhered to conventional values for NV through the building envelope. The simulation model adopted a constant infiltration rate of $0.2778\ l/m^2s$, which corresponded to 0.1408 h^{-1}. For indoor environmental input parameters related to the design and assessment of energy performance, which addressed indoor-air quality, the thermal environment and lighting benchmarks, night ventilation was modelled for the period between 23:00 and 07:00 during hot weather, and only when the indoor OT exceeded the cooling SP with a 0.5 h^{-1} increase in the air exchange rate, which is a low-but-consistent recommended ventilation rate that is naturally achievable through single-sided openings.

Limitations

The goal of the present study was to provide effective responses to the RQs with the use of available data and resources, even though this resulted in certain limitations that should be considered. A new STS conceptual framework could provide contributions that would consider real-life occupant energy-use experiences in the decision-making process for future retrofitting interventions. An analytical approach with a high level of abstraction was therefore chosen for energy policy. Table 2.30(a)–(c) demonstrates the summary of research limitations to delineate the

Table 2.30(a) List of Limitations

Key Concepts	*Limitations*
Sampling size	A large sample is required to conduct TSVs and evaluate the collected data, which could affect the generalisation of the results to provide an overall understanding of home-energy performance. A call-back survey was carried out to increase the response rate, but due to time constraints, only five households were successfully recruited; as such, the sampling size was not considered in the statistical analysis.
Statistical analysis	The ranking systems of subject participant responses were estimated from self-reported behaviours and were expected to vary; this lack of integration prevailed, despite evidence that some errors were detected in the parametric (*P*-test) analysis. This is because the respondents did not provide an accurate vote of the thermal-comfort assessment criteria.
Questionnaire survey	The use of a *proforma* questionnaire to conduct semi-structured interviews with certain households meant that other households could not be reached; for example, those who were illiterate, or who did not read or write Turkish, which is the *lingua franca* of the research context; elderly households with disabilities; subjects who were on long-term breaks; and unoccupied sample flats that were not contacted in the door-to-door survey. There is a degree of uncertainty as to whether ethnic minorities were fully represented, because some respondents might not have understood Turkish or English. No direct question was asked about household income, mostly to increase response rates. The researcher identified the respondents' income levels by considering their age and employability.

Table 2.30(b) List of Limitations (Continued)

Key Concepts	*Limitations*
Thermal-comfort assessment	Retrospective questions could be less-accurate than real-time data; moreover, the respondents felt the questions were difficult to follow due to a lack of clarification on how to use the Likert scale to assess thermal comfort. The survey revealed two respondents, an 80-year-old and an 85-year-old, with underlying health issues; they were carefully interviewed by the researcher to answer questions related to thermal comfort. Notably, the subject respondents did not have knowledge about the goals of the research and the rationale behind the comfort measurements; they indicated a desire to provide accurate information on the assessment criteria, however, and as such, technical discrepancies presented limitations when their long-term discomfort indices were assessed in the statistical analysis. The regression value obtained for the TSVs of the subject respondents to room indoor air temperature changes was approximately 0,3 scale–units-per–degree–Celsius, which is in accord with values obtained by Fanger (1976) in the studies that discussed the predicted mean vote (PMV) equation. This assessment criterion could estimate a neutral temperature for a single value of subjective warmth, and for this reason, it presents a limitation toward exploring the significance of regression coefficients between the TSVs of the subject respondents and have understood the indoor environmental conditions that were recorded.
Environmental monitoring	In situ measurements influenced the recruitment of households at different times of the day. To reduce risk impact on error margins arising from technical anomalies, these data were compared with outdoor environmental monitoring results. The in situ measurements were recorded in some flats when the wall-mounted A/C system was in use, while the indoor environmental measurements in other units recorded either portable fans that were in use or open windows. These technical variation profiles presented some limitations related to the identification of variables for the statistical analysis
Thermal imaging	Both the solar-irradiance factor and weather conditions had a significant impact on the researcher's ability to capture accurate data in the day. This could potentially cause discrepancies between building-envelope heat loss and efforts to determine the thermal performance of these buildings according to quantitative data.

(*Continued*)

Table 2.30(b) (Continued)

Key Concepts	*Limitations*
Building performance evaluation	The standardised occupancy profiles recommended by the CIBSE TM52 related to building overheating risks remained unclear when it comes to identifying the necessary benchmark criteria for such activities as occupancy profiles, lighting schedules, miscellaneous equipment, internal loads and other relevant factors. A lack of weather behaviour due to hourly intervals made it difficult to define an appropriate energy-assessment technique to control the physical parameters, especially the solar gains, that were assigned to the energy-simulation model. Discrepancies between actual and predicted energy use were observed in the aggregated models during the energy-model assessment process. The present study identified variations in the outliers, between indoor and outdoor air temperatures and between outdoor and indoor RH levels. This situation could affect the degree of overheating experienced in the building-performance evaluation of base-case RTBs.

Table 2.30(c) List of Limitations (Continued)

Key Concepts	*Limitations*
Energymodelling	The type of weather files assigned to the simulation models to develop base-case scenarios included several variations, because weather data for cooling-degree days (CCDs) were extracted from the TRY files to avoid the inclusion of any missing data in the spreadsheets assigned to the energy models. This lack of integration prevailed despite other factors, such as technical limitations, time constraints for conducting simulation analyses and costs, which were not considered in this approach. The ApacheSim application of the IES software suite used hourly averages for weather information. Occupancy profiles in the model were considered in 15-minute intervals, and the simulation step in ApacheSim was set to 30-minute intervals; this technical aspect allowed us to more accurately simulate the short-term heat accumulation caused by the irradiance factor. The actual energy consumption was only higher than expected when the moderate- and high-occupancy profiles assigned to the building-modelling simulation.
Energy use	Variations in simulation input parameters greatly altered the profile of overall household energy consumption that was estimated by the developed model.

technical constraints that are related to key concepts, which should be addressed by future scholars.

Additional research is required to better understand the possible link between occupant behaviour and energy consumption. Significantly more work still needs to be done to investigate specific climate conditions and different housing typologies, as well as relevant subjective measures, such as the socio-demographic characteristics, backgrounds and social structures of different households. Moreover, other novel methodologies that include advanced modelling features related to occupant behaviour when evaluating the energy performance of buildings (i.e., stochastic and deterministic models) should be developed. Finally, the empirical analysis for this study revealed that the energy-assessment processes still require additional user input.

Validation measures are essential to improve the accuracy of the simulation results. One of the most important technical aspects of the present study was the adoption of robust methods; international benchmark criteria must be assigned to the analytical energy models for further data validation. This could lead researchers and designers to develop better models and improve the comparisons of different variables in energy-simulation models.

Conclusion

This chapter developed an empirical model that demonstrated a new STS conceptual framework integrated with information obtained in the literature review analysis; the analytical building-energy model used data extracted from the questionnaire survey. A total of 100 data inputs were designed with the SPSS statistical tool to measure the impact of household socio-demographic characteristics and occupancy profiles on home-energy use. This dataset also used environmental monitoring and in situ measurements to assess the occupants' thermal comfort and identify the occupants' neutral adaptive thermal-comfort levels. Field measurements were recorded to provide subsequent information to undertake ordinal and multinominal logistic regression analyses. The empirical model developed for the present study is the most applicable design method to corroborate the human-based factors in the BES model. Due to uncertain parameters and technical constraints to measure the differences between actual and predicted home-energy performance of case study RTBs, a methodological workflow was employed in the following manner:

(i) Questionnaire survey
(ii) On-site monitoring
(iii) In situ measurements
(iv) Analysis of household energy bills
(v) Building-energy simulations

This design was established to validate the findings of the questionnaire survey and to integrate evidence-based data into the STS conceptual framework. Any discrepancies detected in the statistical analysis will also appear in the DTS result and the energy-assessment method that was applied to minimise this risk. The IRT survey will also provide good representative indicators to assess the thermal vulnerability of building envelopes. The empirical model was shown to perform well with industry benchmarks adopted to assess building overheating risks, and the adaptive thermal-comfort theory was employed to identify the optimal occupant thermal-comfort levels. Before developing energy-forecasting scenarios, the present study explored the influence of household socio-demographic characteristics on energy use; the households' length of residency, which was considered to understand the adaptability of the human body as it relates to thermal comfort, was also examined. The results obtained from the questionnaire survey will be discussed in Chapters 3 and 4, and the field investigation to conduct a regression forecast of neutral adaptive thermal comfort will be discussed in Chapter 5.

Notes

1 'Degree-hours' represents the overheating risk assessment of each occupied space within the CIBSE TM52 and TM59 criterion. The CIBSE TM59 benchmark criteria were used in the present study to identify the overheating risks of each flat in the RTBs. The IES software suite was selected to provide accurate information on the overheating risk assessment by integrating the Actual Meteorological Year (AMY) weather file into the black-box model developed for the empirical analysis.

2 Exceedance index represents the identification of lower-acceptable-upper limits of benchmarking criterion for the overheating risk assessment.

3 Data represent overall NC population, including settlers sent by the Turkish government after the 1974 civil war to increase the Turkish population in NC. Notably, this data does not include Greek Cypriots living in the RoC.

4 Data obtained from *Annual Statistical Report*, published by the Northern Cyprus Statistical Office: http://www.stat.gov.ct.tr/IST-YIL-2019.aspx (pp. 16–23)

5 RoC data include the following ethnic groups: Greek Cypriots, Armenians, Maronites and Latins. Per the 1960 constitutional agreement, Turkish Cypriots who hold EU citizenships were not included in the census data because their permanent residency was in NC.

6 Data obtained from *Annual Demographic Statistics of Cyprus*, published by the Statistical Service of the Ministry of Finance in the RoC: https://www.mof.gov.cy/mof/cystat/statistics.nsf/All/6C25304C1E70C304C2257833003432B3/$file/Demographic_Statistics_Results-2019-EN-301120.pdf?OpenElement (p.4)

7 Data included housing that was built under governmental social-housing schemes and housing projects built by local cooperatives in NC between 1984–1996.

8 Due to high demand for social-housing construction projects, the government enacted a plan to collaborate with local cooperatives to speed up construction and reduce upfront costs.

9 The 'property boom' resulted from the Annan Plan (i.e., peace talks for the unification of Cyprus) from 2002–2004. During this period, there was a gap in Cyprus's international law as a consequence of the restructuring plan for Cypriot settlements in the northern and southern territories. This led the SMEs to construct an abundance of mass-housing estates without the approval of the Chamber of Architects and Town Planning Department in major cities in NC.

10 Between 2002–2004, British second-home buyers preferred to own a holiday let-house in remote rural locations in NC. This led to construction of mass-scale housing estates in coastal areas and mountainous regions. Unfortunately, this situation led to unsustainable

environmental problems, ecological constraints and energy issues. Notably, the British expatriates preferred to buy property because Cyprus is in the commonwealth countries of Great Britain.

11 Data extracted from the State Planning Organisation: https://www.devplan.org/index_en.html

12 In 'Residential Bu. ildings' represents 2–5 storey RTBs; 'Houses' represents single and two-storey detached or semi-detached houses; 'Apartments' represents 5–23 storey RTBs; 'represents smal. l enterprise buildings; 'represents larg. e enterprise buildings; 'Office' represents privately owned companies; and 'Others' represents industrial buildings, water aquifers, etc.

13 Statistical data cover the period of 2015–2019. Statistical databases were estimated according to the most recent Population and Housing Census data collected in 2011 by the State Planning Organisation. These figures were produced in collaboration with the National Statistics Office in Turkey in 2020.

14 Data obtained from the *Annual Statistical Report*, published by the Northern Cyprus Statistical Office: http://www.stat.gov.ct.tr/IST-YIL-2019.aspx (pp. 16–23).

15 This is the most reliable dataset available. It was selected to identify the nationally representative archetype building typology in NC. The data consists of the Housing Census and Construction Report, and statistics were derived from various resources dated pre-2015. These sources have shown different various indicators in construction projects that were completed, such as high-density measures both in urban and suburban regions of NC.

16 The American Society of Heating, Refrigerating and Air-Conditioning Engineers (ASHRAE) Global Thermal Comfort Database II is the result of a project led by an international team of experts to collate field measurements of thermal comfort for public use. The dataset was processed via a project web tool for quality assurance before being published in the open access ASHRAE Global Thermal Comfort Database II. Available at http://www.comfortdatabase.com

17 During the IEE project, TABULA residential building typologies were developed for 13 EU countries to contribute to the EPBD. Each national typology consists of a classification scheme grouping buildings according to their size, construction age, the *U*-values of the buildings' properties and a set of archetype buildings representing the building types. Available at https://episcope.eu/iee-project/tabula/

18 Data obtained from the Ministry of Housing Department of Rural Affairs and Development in NC. This data consists of government social housing development projects built between 1984 and 1996.

19 The Housing Census and Construction Report statistics were collated to identify the nationally representative housing typology between 2015 and 2019. Due to the limited availability of pre-existing sources on the quantification of housing data in NC, the most-up-to-date statistical data was applied on the verification of the archetype building typology for this empirical study, which was prepared by the Statistical Institute of Northern Cyprus in 2019. Available at http://www.stat.gov.ct.tr/INSAAT-YIL-11.aspx

20 This data only consists of the number of dwelling units that were built in apartment projects across five major cities in NC in 2019. These dwellings account for 38% of the overall building stock that was built between 2015 and 2019. These high-density projects were constructed by small and medium enterprises in NC that are predominantly regulated by family or privately-owned construction companies. The 1998 withdrawal of social housing schemes led to increased demand for construction projects built by the SMEs.

21 According to the Housing Census and Construction Report statistics. The data on the representation of the national building stock is not available on the Eurostat database due to the fact that NC is a *de-facto* state in terms of gaining international recognition and being allowed to implement EU directives for any type of industry, including achieving the net-zero-energy building (nZEB) targets that were recommended for the residential sector in each EU country.

22 Data extracted from the State Planning Organisation, Department of Rural Affairs and Development in NC. Available at https://www.devplan.org/index_en.html
23 The TABULA Web Tool is based on the common DATAMINE data structure and the experiences of typological classification. The TABULA project launched in 2009. This open-source platform set out to make an agreed systematic approach to classifying building stocks according to their energy-related properties. Available at https://webtool.building-typology.eu/#bm
24 This project set out to make the energy refurbishment processes in the European housing sector transparent and effective. Pilot studies were conducted in 16 EU countries to track the implementation of energy saving measures and their effect on consumption in practice. Available at https://episcope.eu/welcome/
25 Geo-cluster mapping of number of dwellings built in EU countries in 2018 extracted from the Eurostat database. Available at https://ec.europa.eu/eurostat/databrowser/view/SBS_R_NUTS06_R2__custom_139216/ bookmark/map?lang=en&bookmarkId=6c9d0532-05e5-46a6-b53d-9ee4b98a73e2 (Accessed on 18/09/2021).
26 Data only represents population and housing stock in the southern territory of the RoC; NC housing stock is not included due to being a *de-facto* state.
27 In law and government, '*de facto*' describes the constitutions that exist in reality, even though they are not officially recognised by law. NC has a parliamentary system that is the result of a unilateral declaration of a republic. Notably, the EU security council condemned the declaration and called on EU member states to respect the independence, sovereignty and territorial integrity of the RoC.
28 Data extracted from the State Planning Organisation: http://www.stat.gov.ct.tr/INSAAT-YIL-11.aspx. The statistical analysis was undertaken to generate the most-up-to-date construction statistics available from 2015 to 2019, and the findings were applied to a cumulative percentage calculation of overall housing stock in NC.
29 Data on the distribution of investment in housing by each EU country in 2019 extracted from the Eurostat data. Available at https://ec.europa.eu/eurostat/databrowser/view/NAMA_10_AN6__custom_138747/bookmark/ map?lang=en&bookmarkId=22dc747f-7535-4c8f-90af-f3264fc51d5b (Accessed on 18/09/2021).
30 This GDP rate demonstrates both the high demand for housing projects in the RoC and that the construction sector accounts for the highest share of the economy in Cyprus. It should be noted that this statistical data does not included NC. To provide reliable background information, the most-up-to-date statistical data was extracted from the Housing and Construction Statistics in NC and applied to the identification of representative archetype buildings in NC.
31 For the identification of representative archetype buildings and the sampling size for the survey, an online calculator was used to aggregate the statistical power of the survey. Available at https://www.calculator.net/sample-size-calculator.html
32 Data extracted from the State Planning Organisation: http://www.stat.gov.ct.tr/INSAAT-YIL-11.aspx
33 The households represent the flats recruited for the present study. Throughout the questionnaire survey, the researcher requested that the households nominate one of their family members who felt confident responding to the questions.
34 For the interpretations of statistical findings, the six possible combinations of variables encountered by researchers are as follows: *(i)* continuous-continuous; *(ii)* continuous-ordinal; *(iii)* continuous-nominal; *(iv)* ordinal-ordinal; *(v)* ordinal-nominal; *(vi)* nominal-nominal. For each of these combinations of variables, one or more measures of association that accurately assess the strength of the relationship between the two variables are discussed in the contribution Chapters where it is necessary to determine the influences of statistical findings for the development of evidence-based energy policy framework.

References

Abanda, F. H., & Byers, L. (2016). An investigation of the impact of building orientation on energy consumption in a domestic building using emerging BIM (Building Information Modelling). *Energy*, *97*, 517–527. https://doi.org/10.1016/j.energy.2015.12.135

Abela, A., Hoxley, M., McGrath, P., & Goodhew, S. (2016). An investigation of the appropriateness of current methodologies for energy certification of Mediterranean housing. *Energy and Buildings*, *130*, 210–218. https://doi.org/10.1016/j.enbuild.2016.07.056

Abrahamse, W., & Steg, L. (2011). Factors related to household energy use and intention to reduce it: The role of psychological and socio-demographic variables. *Human Ecology Review*, *18*(1), 30–40.

Agliardi, E., Cattani, E., & Ferrante, A. (2018). Deep energy renovation strategies: A real option approach for add-ons in a social housing case study. *Energy and Buildings*, *161*, 1–9. https://doi.org/10.1016/j.enbuild.2017.11.044

Åkerman, M., Halonen, M., & Wessberg, N. (2020). Lost in building design practices: The intertwining of energy with the multiple goals of home building in Finland. *Energy Research and Social Science*, *61*. https://doi.org/10.1016/j.erss.2019.101335

Aldossary, N. A., Rezgui, Y., & Kwan, A. (2014). Domestic energy consumption patterns in a hot and humid climate: A multiple-case study analysis. *Applied Energy*, *114*, 353–365. https://doi.org/10.1016/j.apenergy.2013.09.061

Alola, A. A. (2020). Revisiting the housing market dynamics and its fundamentals: New evidence from Cyprus. *Journal of Economic Studies*, *47*(1), 200–216. https://doi.org/10.1108/JES-07-2018-0237

Alola, A. A., & Alola, U. V. (2019). The dynamics of tourism—Refugeeism on house prices in Cyprus and Malta. *Journal of International Migration and Integration*, *20*(2), 521–536. https://doi.org/10.1007/s12134-018-0621-x

Alonso, C., Oteiza, I., Martín-Consuegra, F., & Frutos, B. (2017). Methodological proposal for monitoring energy refurbishment: Indoor environmental quality in two case studies of social housing in Madrid, Spain. *Energy and Buildings*, *155*, 492–502. https://doi.org/10.1016/j.enbuild.2017.09.042

Amasyali, K., & El-Gohary, N. M. (2018). A review of data-driven building energy consumption prediction studies. *Renewable and Sustainable Energy Reviews*, 81, 1192–1205.https://doi.org/10.1016/j.rser.2017.04.095

American Society of Heating, Refrigerating and Air-Conditioning Engineers (ASHRAE). (2017). *Standard 55 thermal environment conditions for human occupancy*. Atlanta, GA: ASHRAE.

Andersen, R. V., Toftum, J., Andersen, K. K., & Olesen, B. W. (2009). Survey of occupant behaviour and control of indoor environment in Danish dwellings. *Energy and Buildings*, *41*(1), 11–16. https://doi.org/10.1016/j.enbuild.2008.07.004

Andriamamonjy, A., Klein, R., & Saelens, D. (2019). Automated grey box model implementation using BIM and Modelica. *Energy and Buildings*, *188–189*, 209–225. https://doi.org/10.1016/j.enbuild.2019.01.046

Arriazu, A., & Monge-Barrio, A. (2017). *Resilience of the built environment to the climate change in the Southern European Region: An initial review.* http://hdl.handle.net/1017/44912.

Artmann, N., Gyalistras, D., Manz, H., & Heiselberg, P. (2008). Impact of climate warming on passive night cooling potential. *Building Research & Information*, *36*(2), 111–128. https://doi.org/10.1080/09613210701621919

Asadi, E., da Silva, M. G., Antunes, C. H., Dias, L., & Glicksman, L. (2014). Multi-objective optimisation for building retrofit: A model using genetic algorithm and artificial neural network and an application. *Energy Building, 81*, 444–456.

Ascione, F., Bianco, N., De Masi, R. F., Mauro, G. M., & Vanoli, G. P. (2015). Design of the building envelope: A novel multi-objective approach for the optimisation of energy performance and thermal comfort. *Sustainability, 7*(8), 10809–10836.

Ascione, F., Bianco, N., De Stasio, C., Mauro, G. M., & Vanoli, G. P. (2016). Simulation-based model predictive control by the multi-objective optimization of building energy performance and thermal comfort. *Energy and Buildings, 111*, 131–144. https://doi.org/10.1016/j.enbuild.2015.11.033

Ascione, F., Bianco, N., Mauro, G. M., & Napolitano, D. F. (2019). Retrofit of villas on Mediterranean coastlines: Pareto optimization with a view to energy-efficiency and cost-effectiveness. *Applied Energy, 254*. https://doi.org/10.1016/j.apenergy.2019.113705

Atam, E. (2017). Current software barriers to advanced model-based control design for energy-efficient buildings. *Renewable and Sustainable Energy Reviews, 73*, 1031–1040. https://doi.org/10.1016/j.rser.2017.02.015

Attia, S., Eleftheriou, P., Xeni, F., Morlot, R., Ménézo, C., Kostopoulos, V., … Hidalgo-Betanzos, J. M. (2017). Overview and future challenges of nearly zero energy buildings (nZEB) design in Southern Europe. *Energy and Buildings, 155*, 439–458. https://doi.org/10.1016/j.enbuild.2017.09.043

Aydin, E. E., & Jakubiec, J. A. (2018). *Sensitivity analysis of sustainable urban design parameters: Thermal comfort, urban heat island, energy, daylight, and ventilation in Singapore Singapore University of Technology and Design, Singapore Abstract.* BSO2018 Papers, (September), pp. 11–12.

Baker, N. V., & Standeven, M. A. (1996). Thermal comfort in free-running buildings. *Energy and Buildings, 23*, 175–182.

Baker, P. (1991). *A model of household gas and electricity expenditures for the UK: The IFS simulation program for energy demand (SPEND)*. London: Institute for Fiscal Studies.

Balest, J., Secco, L., Pisani, E., & Garegnani, G. (2019). Municipal transitions: The social, energy, and spatial dynamics of sociotechnical change in South Tyrol, Italy. *Energy Research and Social Science, 54*, 211–223. https://doi.org/10.1016/j.erss.2019.04.015

Balkiz, Y., & Therese, L.-W. (2014). Small but complex: The construction industry in North Cyprus. *Procedia: Social and Behavioral Sciences, 119*, 466–474. https://doi.org/10.1016/j.sbspro.2014.03.052

Ballarini, I., Corgnati, S. P., & Corrado, V. (2014). Use of reference buildings to assess the energy saving potentials of the residential building stock: The experience of TABULA project. *Energy Policy, 68*, 273–284. https://doi.org/10.1016/j.enpol.2014.01.027

Balslev, Y. J., Potchter, O., & Matzarakis, A. (2015). Climatic and thermal comfort analysis of the Tel-Aviv Geddes Plan: A historical perspective. *Building and Environment, 93*(P2), 302–318. https://doi.org/10.1016/j.buildenv.2015.07.005

Balvedi, B. F., Ghisi, E., & Lamberts, R. (2018). A review of occupant behaviour in residential buildings. *Energy and Buildings*. Advance online publication. https://doi.org/10.1016/j.enbuild.2018.06.049

Barbosa, R., Vicente, R., & Santos, R. (2015). Climate change and thermal comfort in Southern Europe housing: A case study from Lisbon. *Building and Environment, 92*, 440–451. https://doi.org/10.1016/j.buildenv.2015.05.019

Barone, G., Buonomano, A., Calise, F., Forzano, C., & Palombo, A. (2019). Building to vehicle to building concept toward a novel zero energy paradigm: Modelling and case studies. *Renewable and Sustainable Energy Reviews*, *101*, 625–648. https://doi.org/10.1016/j.rser.2018.11.003

Bartels, L. (2007). The trade and development policy of the European Union. *European Journal of International Law*, *18*(4), 715–756. https://doi.org/10.1093/ejil/chm042

Barthelmes, V. M., Li, R., Andersen, R. K., Bahnfleth, W., Corgnati, S. P., & Rode, C. (2018). Profiling occupant behaviour in Danish dwellings using time use survey data. *Energy and Buildings*, *177*, 329–340. https://doi.org/10.1016/j.enbuild.2018.07.044

Bartiaux, F., & Gram-hanssen, K. (2005). Socio-political factors influencing household electricity consumption: A comparison between Denmark and Belgium. *ECEEE Summer Study*, pp. 1313–1325.

Bateson, A. (2014). Comparison of CIBSE thermal comfort assessments and implications for designers. In *CIBSE ASHRAE technical symposium* (p. 11). Dublin.

Beizaee, A., Lomas, K. J., & Firth, S. K. (2013). National survey of summertime temperatures and overheating risk in English homes. *Building and Environment*, *65*, 1–17. https://doi.org/10.1016/j.buildenv.2013.03.011

Belpoliti, V., & Bizzarri, G. (2015). A parametric method to assess the energy performance of the social housing stock and simulate suitable retrofit scenarios: An Italian case study. *Energy and Buildings*, *96*, 261–271. https://doi.org/10.1016/j.enbuild.2015.03.017

Bienvenido-Huertas, D., Sánchez-García, D., & Rubio-Bellido, C. (2021). Adaptive setpoint temperatures to reduce the risk of energy poverty? A local case study in Seville. *Energy and Buildings*, *231*. https://doi.org/10.1016/j.enbuild.2020.110571

Black, I. (2006). The presentation of interpretivist research. *Qualitative Market Research: An International Journal*, *9*, 319–324.

Böhringer, C., & Rutherford, T. F. (2008). Combining bottom-up and top-down. *Energy Economics*, *30*(2), 574–596. https://doi.org/10.1016/j.eneco.2007.03.004

Bonte, M., Thellier, F., & Lartigue, B. (2014). Impact of occupant's actions on energy building performance and thermal sensation. *Energy and Buildings*, *76*, 219–227. https://doi.org/10.1016/j.enbuild.2014.02.068

Borgeson, S., & Brager, G. (2011). Comfort standards and variations in exceedance for mixed-mode buildings. *Building Research and Information*, *39*(2), 118–133. https://doi.org/10.1080/09613218.2011.556345

Bouden, C., & Ghrab, N. (2005). An adaptive thermal comfort model for the Tunisian context: A field study results. *Energy and Buildings*, *37*(9), 952–963. https://doi.org/10.1016/j.enbuild.2004.12.003

Bourgeois, D., Reinhart, C., & Macdonald, I. (2006). Adding advanced behavioral models in whole building energy simulation: A study on the total energy impact of manual and automated lighting control. *Energy and Buildings*, *38*(7), 814–823. https://doi.org/10.1016/j.enbuild.2006.03.002

BR 497:2007. (2007). *Conventions for calculating linear thermal transmittance and temperature factors*. Watford: BRE.

Brager, G., Fountain, M., Benton, C., Arens, E. A., & Bauman, F. (1993). A comparison of methods for assessing thermal sensation and acceptability in the field. *Proceedings of Thermal Comfort: Past, Present and Future*, 0–13.

Brager, G. S., and de Dear, R. J. (1998). Thermal adaptation in the built environment: A literature review. *Energy and Buildings*, *27*, 83–96.

Brembilla, E., Hopfe, C. J., Mardaljevic, J., Mylona, A., & Mantesi, E. (2020). Balancing daylight and overheating in low-energy design using CIBSE improved weather files.

Building Services Engineering Research and Technology, *41*(2), 210–224. https://doi.org/10.1177/0143624419889057

Brotas, L., & Nicol, F. (2015). Adaptive comfort model and overheating in Europe re-thinking the future. In *31th international PLEA conference architecture in (r)evolution proceedings*. Ass. Building Green Futures, Bologna, Italy, 9–11 September.

Buso, T., Fabi, V., Andersen, R. K., & Corgnati, S. P. (2015). Occupant behaviour and robustness of building design. *Building and Environment*, *94*, 694–703. https://doi.org/10.1016/j.buildenv.2015.11.003

Calì, D., Andersen, R. K., Müller, D., & Olesen, B. W. (2016). Analysis of occupants' behavior related to the use of windows in German households. *Building and Environment*, *103*, 54–69. https://doi.org/10.1016/j.buildenv.2016.03.024

Campbell, D., & Fiske, D. (1959). Convergent and discrimination validation by the multi trait: Multimethod matrix. *Psychological Bulletin*, *56*, 81–105.

Cao, B., Zhu, Y., Ouyang, Q., Zhou, X., & Huang, L. (2011). Field study of human thermal comfort and thermal adaptability during the summer and winter in Beijing. *Energy and Buildings*, *43*, 1051–1056. https://doi.org/10.1016/j.enbuild.2010.09.025

Carlucci, S., Bai, L., de Dear, R., & Yang, L. (2018). Review of adaptive thermal comfort models in built environmental regulatory documents. *Building and Environment*. Advance online publication. https://doi.org/10.1016/j.buildenv.2018.03.053

Carpino, C., Bruno, R., & Arcuri, N. (2018). Social housing refurbishment in Mediterranean climate: Cost-optimal analysis towards the n-ZEB target. *Energy and Buildings*, *171*, 642–656. https://doi.org/10.1016/j.enbuild.2018.06.052

Castellano, J., Ribera, A., & Ciurana, J. (2016). Integrated system approach to evaluate social, environmental and economics impacts of buildings for users of housings. *Energy and Buildings*, *123*, 106–118. https://doi.org/10.1016/j.enbuild.2016.04.046

Cerezo, C., Sokol, J., AlKhaled, S., Reinhart, C., Al-Mumin, A., & Hajiah, A. (2017). Comparison of four building archetype characterization methods in urban building energy modeling (UBEM): A residential case study in Kuwait City. *Energy and Buildings*, *154*, 321–334. https://doi.org/10.1016/j.enbuild.2017.08.029

Charmpis, D. C., Kyriakidis, A., Michael, A., Ioannou, I., & Illampas, R. (2018). Thermal performance and embodied energy of standard and retrofitted wall systems encountered in Southern Europe. *Energy*, *161*, 1016–1027. https://doi.org/10.1016/j.energy.2018.07.124

Chartered Institution of Buildings Services Engineers (CIBSE). (2006). *Environmental design, CIBSE guide A*. London: Chartered Institution of Building Services Engineers.

Chen, J., Gao, X., Hu, Y., Zeng, Z., & Liu, Y. (2019). A meta-model-based optimization approach for fast and reliable calibration of building energy models. *Energy*, *188*. https://doi.org/10.1016/j.energy.2019.116046

Chen, L., Basu, B., & McCabe, D. (2016). Fractional order models for system identification of thermal dynamics of buildings. *Energy and Buildings*, *133*, 381–388. https://doi.org/10.1016/j.enbuild.2016.09.006

Choi, J. H. (2017). Investigation of the correlation of building energy use intensity estimated by six building performance simulation tools. *Energy and Buildings*, *147*, 14–26. https://doi.org/10.1016/j.enbuild.2017.04.078

CIBSE. (2013). *TM52: The limits of thermal comfort: Avoiding overheating in European buildings*. London: Chartered Institution of Building Services Engineers.

CIBSE. (2015). *CIBSE TM36: Climate change and the indoor environment: Impacts and adaptation*. London: CIBSE.

CIBSE. (2016). *CIBSE guide A - Environmental design 2015*. London: CIBSE.

CIBSE. (2017). *CIBSE TM59 - Design methodology for the assessment of overheating risk in homes*. London: The Chartered Institution of Building Services Engineers.

Ciftcioglu, G. C. (2017). Social preference-based valuation of the links between home gardens, ecosystem services, and human well-being in Lefke Region of North Cyprus. *Ecosystem Services, 25*, 227–236. https://doi.org/10.1016/j.ecoser.2017.05.002

Coakley, D., Raftery, P., & Keane, M. (2014). A review of methods to match building energy simulation models to measured data. *Renewable and Sustainable Energy Reviews*.Advance online publication. https://doi.org/10.1016/j.rser.2014.05.007

Cogaloglu, M., & Turkan, Z. (2019). Plan organization in XX. Century housing architecture in North Cyprus. *Amazonia Investiga, 8*(22), 381–388. https://www.amazoniainvestiga.info/index.php/amazonia/article/view/738

Colclough, S., Kinnane, O., Hewitt, N., & Griffiths, P. (2018). Investigation of nZEB social housing built to the passive house standard. *Energy and Buildings, 179*, 344–359. https://doi.org/10.1016/j.enbuild.2018.06.069

Coleman, M., Brown, N., Wright, A., & Firth, S. K. (2012). Information, communication and entertainment appliance use - Insights from a UK household study. *Energy and Buildings, 54*, 61–72. https://doi.org/10.1016/j.enbuild.2012.06.008

Corrado, V., & Ballarini, I. (2016). Refurbishment trends of the residential building stock: Analysis of a regional pilot case in Italy. *Energy and Buildings, 132*, 91–106. https://doi.org/10.1016/j.enbuild.2016.06.022

Crawley, D. (2008). Estimating the impacts of climate change and urbanization on building performance. *Journal of Building Performance Simulation, 1*, 91–115. http://dx.doi.org/doi:10.1080/19401490802182079

Creswell, J. W. (2010). Mapping the developing landscape of mixed methods research. In A. Tashakkori & C. Teddlie (Eds.), *SAGE handbook of mixed methods in social and behavioural research* (2nd ed., pp. 45–68). Thousand Oaks, CA: Sage.

Creswell, J. W. (2012). *Educational research: Planning, conducting, and evaluating quantitative and qualitative research* (4th ed.). Upper Saddle River, NJ: Merrill.

Creswell, J. W., & Plano Clark, V. L. (2011). *Designing and conducting mixed methods research* (2nd ed.). Thousand Oaks, CA: Sage.

Crilly, M., Lemon, M., Wright, A., Cook, M., & Shaw, D. (2012). Retrofitting homes for energy efficiency: An integrated approach to innovation in the low-carbon overhaul of UK social housing. *Energy and Environment, 23*(6–7), 1027–1055. https://doi.org/10.1260/0958-305X.23.6-7.1027

Cross, J. E., Shelley, T. O. C., & Mayer, A. P. (2017). Putting the green into corrections: Improving energy conservation, building function, safety and occupant well-being in an American correctional facility. *Energy Research and Social Science, 32*, 149–163. https://doi.org/10.1016/j.erss.2017.06.020

Csoknyai, T., Hrabovszky-Horváth, S., Georgiev, Z., Jovanovic-Popovic, M., Stankovic, B., Villatoro, O., … Szendrő, G. (2016). Building stock characteristics and energy performance of residential buildings in Eastern-European countries. *Energy and Buildings, 132*, 39–52. https://doi.org/10.1016/j.enbuild.2016.06.062

Cunha, P., Neves, S. A., Marques, A. C., & Serrasqueiro, Z. (2020). Adoption of energy efficiency measures in the buildings of micro-, small- and medium-sized Portuguese enterprises. *Energy Policy, 146*. https://doi.org/10.1016/j.enpol.2020.111776

D'Agostino, D., & Parker, D. (2018). A framework for the cost-optimal design of nearly zero energy buildings (NZEBs) in representative climates across Europe. *Energy, 149*, 814–829. https://doi.org/10.1016/j.energy.2018.02.020

Darby, S. J. (2017). Coal fires, steel houses and the man in the moon: Local experiences of energy transition. *Energy Research and Social Science*, *31*, 120–127. https://doi.org/10.1016/j.erss.2017.05.025

Darnton, A. (2008). GSR behaviour change knowledge review. Practical guide: An overview of behaviour change models and their uses. In *Report for government social research unit*. London: Centre for Sustainable Development, University of Westminster.

Dascalaki, E. G., Balaras, C. A., Kontoyiannidis, S., & Droutsa, K. G. (2016). Modeling energy refurbishment scenarios for the Hellenic residential building stock towards the 2020 & 2030 targets. *Energy and Buildings*, *132*, 74–90. https://doi.org/10.1016/j.enbuild.2016.06.003

Davies, M., Biddulph, P., Wilkinson, P., Oikonomou, E., & Mavrogianni, A. (2011). Building characteristics as determinants of propensity to high indoor summer temperatures in London dwellings. *Building and Environment*, *55*, 117–130. https://doi.org/10.1016/j.buildenv.2011.12.003

Day, J. K., & Gunderson, D. E. (2015). Understanding high performance buildings: The link between occupant knowledge of passive design systems, corresponding behaviors, occupant comfort and environmental satisfaction. *Building and Environment*, *84*, 114–124. https://doi.org/10.1016/j.buildenv.2014.11.003

De Dear, R., & Brager, G. S. (2001). The adaptive model of thermal comfort and energy conservation in the built environment. *International Journal of Biometeorology*, *45*(2), 100–108. https://doi.org/10.1007/s004840100093

DellaValle, N., Bisello, A., & Balest, J. (2018). In search of behavioural and social levers for effective social housing retrofit programs. *Energy and Buildings*, *172*, 517–524. https://doi.org/10.1016/j.enbuild.2018.05.002

Dineen, D., Rogan, F., & Ó Gallachóir, B. P. (2015). Improved modelling of thermal energy savings potential in the existing residential stock using a newly available data source. *Energy*, *90*, 759–767. https://doi.org/10.1016/j.energy.2015.07.105

Dino, I. G., & Akgül, C. M. (2019). Impact of climate change on the existing residential building stock in Turkey: An analysis on energy use, greenhouse gas emissions and occupant comfort. *Renewable Energy*. Advance online publication. https://doi.org/10.1016/j.renene.2019.03.150

Djamila, H., Chu, C. M., & Kumaresan, S. (2013). Field study of thermal comfort in residential buildings in the equatorial hot-humid climate of Malaysia. *Building and Environment*, *62*, 133–142. https://doi.org/10.1016/j.buildenv.2013.01.017

D'Oca, S., Hong, T., & Langevin, J. (2018). The human dimensions of energy use in buildings: A review. *Renewable and Sustainable Energy Reviews*. Advance online publication. https://doi.org/10.1016/j.rser.2017.08.019

Dodoo, A., Tettey, U. Y. A., & Gustavsson, L. (2017). Influence of simulation assumptions and input parameters on energy balance calculations of residential buildings. *Energy*, *120*, 718–730. https://doi.org/10.1016/j.energy.2016.11.124

Domínguez-Amarillo, S., Fernández-Agüera, J., Sendra, J. J., & Roaf, S. (2019). The performance of Mediterranean low-income housing in scenarios involving climate change. *Energy and Buildings*, *202*. https://doi.org/10.1016/j.enbuild.2019.109374

Dornyei, Z. (2003). *Questionnaires in second language research: Construction, administration, and processing*. London: Lawrence Erlbaum Associates Publishers.

Doukas, H. (2020). The desirability of transitions in demand: Incorporating behavioural and societal transformations into energy modelling. *Energy Research and Social Science*. Advance online publication. https://doi.org/10.1016/j.erss.2020.101780

Du, C., Yu, W., Ma, Y., Cai, Q., Li, B., Li, N., … Yao, R. (2021). A holistic investigation into the seasonal and temporal variations of window opening behavior in residential buildings in Chongqing, China. *Energy and Buildings, 231.* https://doi.org/10.1016/j.enbuild.2020.110522

Emery, A. F., & Kippenhan, C. J. (2006). A long-term study of residential home heating consumption and the effect of occupant behavior on homes in the Pacific Northwest constructed according to improved thermal standards. *Energy*, *31*(5), 677–693. https://doi.org/10.1016/j.energy.2005.04.006

Emmerich, M. T. M., Hopfe, C., Marijt, R., Hensen, J., Struck, C., & Stoelinga, P. (2008). Evaluating optimization methodologies for future integration in building performance tools. *Proceedings of the 8th international conference on adaptive computing in design and manufacture (ACDM)* (Vol. 1, pp. 1–7). Berlin: Springer.

Encinas, F., & De Herde, A. (2013). Sensitivity analysis in building performance simulation for summer comfort assessment of apartments from the real estate market. *Energy and Buildings*, *65*, 55–65. https://doi.org/10.1016/j.enbuild.2013.05.047

Erell, E., Portnov, B. A., & Assif, M. (2018). Modifying behaviour to save energy at home is harder than we think.… *Energy and Buildings*, *179*, 384–398. https://doi.org/10.1016/j.enbuild.2018.09.010

Escandón, R., Suárez, R., & Sendra, J. J. (2017). On the assessment of the energy performance and environmental behaviour of social housing stock for the adjustment between simulated and measured data: The case of mild winters in the Mediterranean climate of southern Europe. *Energy and Buildings*, *152*, 418–433. https://doi.org/10.1016/j.enbuild.2017.07.063

Escandón, R., Suárez, R., & Sendra, J. J. (2019). Field assessment of thermal comfort conditions and energy performance of social housing: The case of hot summers in the Mediterranean climate. *Energy Policy*, *128*, 377–392. https://doi.org/10.1016/j.enpol.2019.01.009

Eurostat. (2018). *Report on the housing statistics in EU-27*. Retrieved January 2021, from https://ec.europa.eu/eurostat/statistics-explained/index.php/Housing_statistics#Type_of_dwelling

Evans, S., Steadman, P., Godoy-Shimizu, D., & Liddiard, R. (2018). *Building stock modelling and the relationship between density and energy use*. BSO2018 Papers, September, pp. 11–12.

Evola, G., Marletta, L., & Sicurella, F. (2013). A methodology for investigating the effectiveness of PCM wallboards for summer thermal comfort in buildings. *Building and Environment*, *59*, 517–527. https://doi.org/10.1016/j.buildenv.2012.09.021

Fabi, V., Andersen, R. V., Corgnati, S., & Olesen, B. W. (2012). Occupants' window opening behaviour: A literature review of factors influencing occupant behaviour and models. *Building and Environment*, *58*, 188–198. https://doi.org/10.1016/j.buildenv.2012.07.009

Fahmy, M., Mahdy, M. M., & Nikolopoulou, M. (2014). Prediction of future energy consumption reduction using GRC envelope optimization for residential buildings in Egypt. *Energy and Buildings*, *70*, 186–193. https://doi.org/10.1016/j.enbuild.2013.11.057

Fanger, P. O. (1970). *Thermal comfort analysis and applications in environmental engineering*. Copenhagen: Danish Technical Press.

Fanger, P. O., Højbjerre, J., & Thomsen, J. O. B. (1974). Thermal comfort conditions in the morning and in the evening. *International Journal of Biometeorology*, *18*(1), 16–22. https://doi.org/10.1007/BF01450661

Fernández-Agüera, J., Domínguez-Amarillo, S., Sendra, J. J., & Suárez, R. (2016). An approach to modelling envelope airtightness in multi-family social housing in Mediterranean Europe based on the situation in Spain. *Energy and Buildings*, 128, 236–253. https://doi.org/10.1016/j.enbuild.2016.06.074

Fernández-Agüera, J., Domínguez-Amarillo, S., Alonso, C., & Martín-Consuegra, F. (2019). Thermal comfort and indoor air quality in low-income housing in Spain: The influence of airtightness and occupant behaviour. *Energy and Buildings*, *199*, 102–114. https://doi.org/10.1016/j.enbuild.2019.06.052

Ferrari, S., Zagarella, F., Caputo, P., & D'Amico, A. (2019). Results of a literature review on methods for estimating buildings energy demand at district level. *Energy*, *175*, 1130–1137. https://doi.org/10.1016/j.energy.2019.03.172

Ferrari, S., & Zanotto, V. (2009). EPBD and ventilation requirements: Uneven inputs and results in European countries. In *Proceedings of the 30th AIVC conference – Trends in high performance building and the role of ventilation*, Berlin, October 1–2, 2009.

Firth, S. K., Lomas, K. J., & Wright, A. J. (2010). Targeting household energy-efficiency measures using sensitivity analysis. *Building Research and Information*, *38*(1), 24–41. https://doi.org/10.1080/09613210903236706

Firth, S. K., & Wright, A. J. (2008). Investigating the thermal characteristics of English dwellings: Summer temperatures. In *Proceedings of conference: Air conditioning and the low carbon cooling challenge - Windsor 2008 conference.*

FitzGerald, J., Hore, J., & Kearney, I. (2002). *A model for forecasting energy demand and greenhouse gas emissions in Ireland.* Papers (p. 42). https://ideas.repec.org/p/esr/wpaper/wp146.html

Fokaides, P. A., Christoforou, E. A., & Kalogirou, S. A. (2014). Legislation driven scenarios based on recent construction advancements towards the achievement of nearly zero energy dwellings in the southern European country of Cyprus. *Energy*, *66*, 588–597. https://doi.org/10.1016/j.energy.2013.12.073

Fokaides, P. A., Christoforou, E., Ilic, M., & Papadopoulos, A. (2016). Performance of a Passive House under subtropical climatic conditions. *Energy and Buildings*, *133*, 14–31. https://doi.org/10.1016/j.enbuild.2016.09.060

Fokaides, P. A., Maxoulis, C. N., Panayiotou, G. P., Neophytou, M. K. A., & Kalogirou, S. A. (2011). Comparison between measured and calculated energy performance for dwellings in a summer dominant environment. *Energy and Buildings*, *43*(11), 3099–3105. https://doi.org/10.1016/j.enbuild.2011.08.005

Fokaides, P. A., Polycarpou, K., & Kalogirou, S. (2017). The impact of the implementation of the European Energy Performance of Buildings Directive on the European building stock: The case of the Cyprus Land Development Corporation. *Energy Policy*, *111*, 1–8. https://doi.org/10.1016/j.enpol.2017.09.009

Földváry Ličina, V., Cheung, T., Zhang, H., de Dear, R., Parkinson, T., Arens, E., … Zhou, X. (2018). Development of the ASHRAE global thermal comfort database II. *Building and Environment*, *142*, 502–512. https://doi.org/10.1016/j.buildenv.2018.06.022

Forrester, J. W. (2007). System dynamics - A personal view of the first fifty years. *System Dynamics Review*, *23*(2–3), 345–358. https://doi.org/10.1002/sdr.382

Forrester, J. W. (2016). Learning through system dynamics as preparation for the 21st century: System dynamics review. Advance online publication. https://doi.org/10.1002/sdr.1571

Forrester, J. W., Mass, N. J., & Ryan, C. J. (1976). The system dynamics national model: Understanding socio-economic behavior and policy alternatives. *Technological Forecasting and Social Change*, *9*(1–2), 51–68. https://doi.org/10.1016/0040-1625(76)90044-5

Fosas, D., Coley, D. A., Natarajan, S., Herrera, M., Fosas de Pando, M., & Ramallo-Gonzalez, A. (2018). Mitigation versus adaptation: Does insulating dwellings increase overheating risk? *Building and Environment*, *143*, 740–759. https://doi.org/10.1016/j.buildenv.2018.07.033

Fotopoulou, A., Semprini, G., Cattani, E., Schihin, Y., Weyer, J., Gulli, R., & Ferrante, A. (2018). Deep renovation in existing residential buildings through façade additions: A case study in a typical residential building of the 70s. *Energy and Buildings*, *166*, 258–270. https://doi.org/10.1016/j.enbuild.2018.01.056

Fox, M., Coley, D., Goodhew, S., & De Wilde, P. (2014). Thermography methodologies for detecting energy related building defects. *Renewable and Sustainable Energy Reviews*. Advance online publication. https://doi.org/10.1016/j.rser.2014.07.188

Frederiks, E. R., Stenner, K., & Hobman, E. V. (2015). Household energy use: Applying behavioural economics to understand consumer decision-making and behaviour. *Renewable and Sustainable Energy Reviews*. Advance online publication. https://doi.org/10.1016/j.rser.2014.09.026

Gaetani, I., Hoes, P. J., & Hensen, J. L. M. (2016). Occupant behavior in building energy simulation: Towards a fit-for-purpose modeling strategy. *Energy and Buildings*, *121*, 188–204. https://doi.org/10.1016/j.enbuild.2016.03.038

Gaetani, I., Hoes, P. J., & Hensen, J. L. M. (2018). Estimating the influence of occupant behavior on building heating and cooling energy in one simulation run. *Applied Energy*, *223*, 159–171. https://doi.org/10.1016/j.apenergy.2018.03.108

Galvin, R. (2013). Estimating broad-brush rebound effects for household energy consumption in the EU 28 countries and Norway: Some policy implications of Odyssee data. *Energy Policy*, *73*, 323–332. https://doi.org/10.1016/j.enpol.2014.02.033

Gazioglu (1996). *Social housing schemes in Northern Cyprus, Northern Cyprus monthly - Kibris* (Vol. IV, No. 5).

Gagge, A. P., Fobelets, A. P., & Berglund, L. G. (1986). A standard predictive index of human response to the thermal environment. *ASHRAE Transactions*, *92*(2), 709–731.

Gatersleben, B., Steg, L., & Vleck, C. (2002). Measurement and determinants of environmentally significant consumer behaviour. *Envrionmental Behavior*, *34*, 335–362. https://doi.org/10.1177%2F0013916502034003004

Geels, F. W., Schwanen, T., Sorrell, S., Jenkins, K., & Sovacool, B. K. (2018). Reducing energy demand through low carbon innovation: A sociotechnical transitions perspective and thirteen research debates. *Energy Research and Social Science*.Advance online publication. https://doi.org/10.1016/j.erss.2017.11.003

Ghafoor, A., & Yorucu, V. (2006). Public expenditure and productivity puzzle: The case of Northern Cyprus. *METU Studies in Development*, *29*(1), 69–85.

Ghahramani, A., Tang, C., & Becerik-Gerber, B. (2015). An online learning approach for quantifying personalized thermal comfort via adaptive stochastic modeling. *Building and Environment*, *92*, 86–96. https://doi.org/10.1016/j.buildenv.2015.04.017

Gianfrate, V., Piccardo, C., Longo, D., & Giachetta, A. (2017). Rethinking social housing: Behavioural patterns and technological innovations. *Sustainable Cities and Society*, *33*, 102–112. https://doi.org/10.1016/j.scs.2017.05.015

Gill, Z. M., Tierney, M. J., Pegg, I. M., & Allan, N. (2010). Low-energy dwellings: The contribution of behaviours to actual performance. *Building Research Information*, *38*(5), 491–508. https://doi.org/10.1080/09613218.2010.505371

Gimpel, H., Graf, V., & Graf-Drasch, V. (2020). A comprehensive model for individuals' acceptance of smart energy technology – A meta-analysis. *Energy Policy, 138*. https://doi.org/10.1016/j.enpol.2019.111196

Giorgio, L., Manzan, M., & Pezzi, A. (2018). The effect of climatic data on building performance optimization. In *BSO2018 papers* (pp. 11–12).

Gohardani, N., Björk, F., Jensen, P. A., Maslesa, E., Kanarachos, S., & Fokaides, P. A. (2013). Stakeholders and the decision-making process concerning sustainable renovation and refurbishment in Sweden, Denmark and Cyprus. *Architecture & Environment, 1*(2), 21. https://doi.org/10.12966/ae.09.01.2013

Gomes, R., Ferreira, A., Azevedo, L., Costa Neto, R., Aelenei, L., & Silva, C. (2018). Retrofit measures evaluation considering thermal comfort using building energy simulation: Two Lisbon households. *Advances in Building Energy Research*, 1–24. https://doi.org/10.1080/17512549.2018.1520646

Goodchild, B., Ambrose, A., & Maye-Banbury, A. (2017). Storytelling as oral history: Revealing the changing experience of home heating in England. *Energy Research and Social Science, 31*, 137–144. https://doi.org/10.1016/j.erss.2017.06.009

Gouveia, J. P., Seixas, J., & Mestre, A. (2017). Daily electricity consumption profiles from smart meters - Proxies of behavior for space heating and cooling. *Energy, 141*, 108–122. https://doi.org/10.1016/j.energy.2017.09.049

Griffiths, I. D. (1990). Thermal comfort in buildings with passive solar features: Field studies. *Report to the Commission of the European Communities, EN3S–090.*

Guardigli, L., Bragadin, M. A., Della Fornace, F., Mazzoli, C., & Prati, D. (2018). Energy retrofit alternatives and cost-optimal analysis for large public housing stocks. *Energy and Buildings, 166*, 48–59. https://doi.org/10.1016/j.enbuild.2018.02.003

Guerra-Santin, O., Boess, S., Konstantinou, T., Romero Herrera, N., Klein, T., & Silvester, S. (2017). Designing for residents: Building monitoring and co-creation in social housing renovation in the Netherlands. *Energy Research and Social Science, 32*, 164–179. https://doi.org/10.1016/j.erss.2017.03.009

Guerra-Santin, O., Bosch, H., Budde, P., Konstantinou, T., Boess, S., Klein, T., & Silvester, S. (2018). Considering user profiles and occupants' behaviour on a zero-energy renovation strategy for multi-family housing in the Netherlands. *Energy Efficiency, 11*(7), 1847–1870. https://doi.org/10.1007/s12053-018-9626-8

Guerra-Santin, O., Tweed, C., Jenkins, H., & Jiang, S. (2013). Monitoring the performance of low energy dwellings: Two UK case studies. *Energy and Buildings, 64*, 32–40. https://doi.org/10.1016/j.enbuild.2013.04.002

Gunawardena, K., & Steemers, K. (2019). Adaptive comfort assessments in urban neighbourhoods: Simulations of a residential case study from London. *Energy and Buildings, 202*. https://doi.org/10.1016/j.enbuild.2019.07.039

Günçe, K., Ertürk, Z., & Ertürk, S. (2008). Questioning the "prototype dwellings" in the framework of Cyprus traditional architecture. *Building and Environment, 43*(5), 823–833. https://doi.org/10.1016/j.buildenv.2007.01.032

Gupta, R., & Chandiwala, S. (2010). Understanding occupants: Feedback techniques for large-scale low-carbon domestic refurbishments. *Building Research & Information, 38*, 530–548.

Gupta, R., & Gregg, M. (2012). Using UK climate change projections to adapt existing English homes for a warming climate. *Building and Environment, 55*, 20–42. https://doi.org/10.1016/j.buildenv.2012.01.014

Gupta, R., & Gregg, M. (2013). Preventing the overheating of English suburban homes in a warming climate. *Building Research & Information, 41*, 281–300. https://doi:10.1080/09613218.2013.772043.

Gupta, R., Kapsali, M., & Howard, A. (2018). Evaluating the influence of building fabric, services and occupant related factors on the actual performance of low energy social housing dwellings in UK. *Energy and Buildings, 174*, 548–562. https://doi.org/10.1016/j.enbuild.2018.06.057

Habibi, S. (2017). The promise of BIM for improving building performance. *Energy and Buildings, 153*, 525–548. https://doi.org/10.1016/j.enbuild.2017.08.009

Halawa, E., & Van Hoof, J. (2012). The adaptive approach to thermal comfort: A critical overview. *Energy and Buildings*. Advance online publication. https://doi.org/10.1016/j.enbuild.2012.04.011

Haldi, F., & Robinson, D. (2010). On the unification of thermal perception and adaptive actions. *Building and Environment, 45*(11), 2440–2457. https://doi.org/10.1016/j.buildenv.2010.05.010

Hamilton, I. G., Shipworth, D., Summerfield, A. J., Steadman, P., Oreszczyn, T., & Lowe, R. (2014). Uptake of energy efficiency interventions in English dwellings. *Building Research & Information, 42*, 252–275. https://doi.10.1080/09613218.2014.867643

Han, J., Yang, W., Zhou, J., Zhang, G., Zhang, Q., & Moschandreas, D. J. (2009). A comparative analysis of urban and rural residential thermal comfort under natural ventilation environment. *Energy and Buildings, 41*(2), 139–145. https://doi.org/10.1016/j.enbuild.2008.08.005

Harish, V. S. K. V., & Kumar, A. (2016). A review on modeling and simulation of building energy systems. *Renewable and Sustainable Energy Reviews*. Advance online publication. https://doi.org/10.1016/j.rser.2015.12.040

Hart, M., & De Dear, R. (2004). Weather sensitivity in household appliance energy end-use. *Energy and Buildings, 36*(2), 161–174. https://doi.org/10.1016/j.enbuild.2003.10.009

Hatvani-Kovacs, G., Belusko, M., Pockett, J., & Boland, J. (2018). Heat stress-resistant building design in the Australian context. *Energy and Buildings, 158*, 290–299. https://doi.org/10.1016/j.enbuild.2017.10.025

Hatvani-Kovacs, G., Belusko, M., Skinner, N., Pockett, J., & Boland, J. (2016). Heat stress risk and resilience in the urban environment. *Sustainable Cities and Society, 26*, 278–288. https://doi.org/10.1016/j.scs.2016.06.019

Heidari, S., & Sharples, S. (2002). A comparative analysis of short-term and long-term thermal comfort surveys in Iran. *Energy and Buildings, 34*(6), 607–614. https://doi.org/10.1016/S0378-7788(02)00011-7

Hellwig, R. T., Teli, D., Schweiker, M., Choi, J. H., Lee, M. C. J., Mora, R., … Al-Atrash, F. (2019). A framework for adopting adaptive thermal comfort principles in design and operation of buildings. *Energy and Buildings, 205*. https://doi.org/10.1016/j.enbuild.2019.109476

Hens, H. (2010). Energy efficient retrofit of an end of the row house: Confronting predictions with long-term measurements. *Energy and Buildings, 42*(10), 1939–1947. https://doi.org/10.1016/j.enbuild.2010.05.030

Hitchcock, G. (1993). An integrated framework for energy use and behaviour in the domestic sector. *Energy Buildings, 20*, 151–157. https://doi.org/10.1016/0378-7788(93)90006-G

Hoes, P., Hensen, J. L. M., Loomans, M. G. L. C., de Vries, B., & Bourgeois, D. (2009). User behavior in whole building simulation. *Energy and Buildings, 41*(3), 295–302. https://doi.org/10.1016/j.enbuild.2008.09.008

Hong, T., Kim, J., & Lee, M. (2019). A multi-objective optimization model for determining the building design and occupant behaviors based on energy, economic, and environmental performance. *Energy*, *174*, 823–834. https://doi.org/10.1016/j.energy.2019.02.035

Hong, T., Taylor-Lange, S. C., D'Oca, S., Yan, D., & Corgnati, S. P. (2016). Advances in research and applications of energy-related occupant behavior in buildings. *Energy and Buildings*. Advance online publication. https://doi.org/10.1016/j.enbuild.2015.11.052

Hopfe, C. J., & Hensen, J. L. M. (2011). Uncertainty analysis in building performance simulation for design support. *Energy and Buildings*, *43*(10), 2798–2805. https://doi.org/10.1016/j.enbuild.2011.06.034

Hoskara, Ş. Ö., Tevfikler, B. Ç., & Ongul, Z. (2009). Legal frameworks and housing environments in North Cyprus. *Middle East Technical University Journal of the Faculty of Architecture*, *26*(1), 81–100.

Hummel, M., Büchele, R., Müller, A., Aichinger, E., Steinbach, J., Kranzl, L., … Forthuber, S. (2021). The costs and potentials for heat savings in buildings: Refurbishment costs and heat saving cost curves for 6 countries in Europe. *Energy and Buildings*, *231*. https://doi.org/10.1016/j.enbuild.2020.110454

Humphreys, M., and Nicol, J. F. (2003). The validity of ISO-PMV for predicting comfort votes in every-day thermal environments. *Energy and Buildings*, *34*, 667–684.

Humphreys, M. A. (2005). Quantifying occupant comfort: Are combined indices of the indoor environment practicable? *Building Research & Information*, *33*(4), 317–325.

Humphreys, M. A., & Nicol, J. F. (1998). Understanding the adaptive approach to thermal comfort: Field studies of thermal comfort and adaptation. *ASHRAE Technical Data Bulletin*,*14*(1), 1–14.

Humphreys, M. A., & Nicol, J. F. (2000). Outdoor temperature and indoor thermal comfort: Raising the precision of the relationship for 1998 ASHRAE database of field studies. *ASHRAE Transactions*, *206*(2), 485–492.

Ioannou, A., Itard, L., & Agarwal, T. (2018). In-situ real time measurements of thermal comfort and comparison with the adaptive comfort theory in Dutch residential dwellings. *Energy and Buildings*, *170*, 229–241. https://doi.org/10.1016/j.enbuild.2018.04.006

Ince, C. (2019). Reusing gold-mine tailings in cement mortars: Mechanical properties and socio-economic developments for the Lefke-Xeros area of Cyprus. *Journal of Cleaner Production*, *238*. https://doi.org/10.1016/j.jclepro.2019.117871

Indraganti, M., & Rao, K. D. (2010). Effect of age, gender, economic group and tenure on thermal comfort: A field study in residential buildings in hot and dry climate with seasonal variations. *Energy and Buildings*, *42*(3), 273–281. https://doi.org/10.1016/j.enbuild.2009.09.003

Ingeborgrud, L., Heidenreich, S., Ryghaug, M., Skjølsvold, T. M., Foulds, C., Robison, R., … Mourik, R. (2020). Expanding the scope and implications of energy research: A guide to key themes and concepts from the Social Sciences and Humanities. *Energy Research and Social Science*. Advance online publication. https://doi.org/10.1016/j.erss.2019.101398

Integrated environmental solutions (IES) (2020). *IES Software Validation*. Retrieved September 14, 2020, from http://www.iesve.com/software/software-validation

Isaacs, N., Saville-Smith, K., Camilleri, M., & Burroughs, L. (2010). Energy in New Zealand houses: Comfort, physics and consumption. *Building Research Information*, *38*(5), 470–480. https://doi.org/10.1080/09613218.2010.494383

Jenkins, D. P., Gul, M., Patidar, S., Banfill, P. F. G., Gibson, G., & Menzies, G. (2012). Designing a methodology for integrating industry practice into a probabilistic overheating tool for future building performance. *Energy and Buildings*, *54*, 73–80. https://doi.org/10.1016/j.enbuild.2012.07.001

Jenkins, D. P., Ingram, V., Simpson, S. A., & Patidar, S. (2013). Methods for assessing domestic overheating for future building regulation compliance. *Energy Policy*, *56*, 684–692. https://doi.org/10.1016/j.enpol.2013.01.030

Jenkins, D. P., Patidar, S., Banfill, P. F. G., & Gibson, G. J. (2011). Probabilistic climate projections with dynamic building simulation: Predicting overheating in dwellings. *Energy and Buildings*, *43*(7), 1723–1731. https://doi.org/10.1016/j.enbuild.2011.03.016

Jeong, B., Jeong, J. W., & Park, J. S. (2016). Occupant behavior regarding the manual control of windows in residential buildings. *Energy and Buildings*, *127*, 206–216. https://doi.org/10.1016/j.enbuild.2016.05.097

Jin, H., Liu, S., & Kang, J. (2019). Gender differences in thermal comfort on pedestrian streets in cold and transitional seasons in severe cold regions in China. *Building and Environment*, *168*. https://doi.org/10.1016/j.buildenv.2019.106488

Juan, Y. K., Kim, J. H., Roper, K., & Castro-Lacouture, D. (2009). GA-based decision support system for housing condition assessment and refurbishment strategies. *Automation in Construction*, *18*(4), 394–401. https://doi.org/10.1016/j.autcon.2008.10.006

Kalisa, E., Fadlallah, S., Amani, M., Nahayo, L., & Habiyaremye, G. (2018). Temperature and air pollution relationship during heatwaves in Birmingham, UK. *Sustainable Cities and Society*, *43*, 111–120. https://doi.org/10.1016/j.scs.2018.08.033

Kalmár, F. (2016). Investigation of thermal perceptions of subjects with diverse thermal histories in warm indoor environment. *Building and Environment*, *107*, 254–262. https://doi.org/10.1016/j.buildenv.2016.08.010

Karimpour, M., Belusko, M., Xing, K., Boland, J., & Bruno, F. (2015). Impact of climate change on the design of energy efficient residential building envelopes. *Energy and Buildings*, *87*, 142–154. https://doi.org/10.1016/j.enbuild.2014.10.064

Kavgic, M., Mavrogianni, A., Mumovic, D., Summerfield, A., Stevanovic, Z., & Djurovic-Petrovic, M. (2010). A review of bottom-up building stock models for energy consumption in the residential sector. *Building and Environment*, *45*(7), 1683–1697. https://doi.org/10.1016/j.buildenv.2010.01.021

Kearns, A., Whitley, E., & Curl, A. (2019). Occupant behaviour as a fourth driver of fuel poverty (aka warmth & energy deprivation). *Energy Policy*, 1143–1155. https://doi.org/10.1016/j.enpol.2019.03.023

Kelly, S. (2011). Do homes that are more energy efficient consume less energy? A structural equation model of the English residential sector. *Energy*, *36*(9), 5610–5620. https://doi.org/10.1016/j.energy.2011.07.009

Kelly, S., Shipworth, M., Shipworth, D., Gentry, M., Wright, A., Pollitt, M., … Lomas, K. (2012). *A panel model for predicting the diversity of internal temperatures from English dwellings*. Tyndall Centre for Climate Change Research Working Paper 154 (pp. 1–63).

Khamis, H. (2008). Measures of association: How to choose? *Journal of Diagnostic Medical Sonography*. Advance online publication. https://doi.org/10.1177/8756479308317006

Kieft, A., Harmsen, R., & Hekkert, M. P. (2020). Problems, solutions, and institutional logics: Insights from Dutch domestic energy-efficiency retrofits. *Energy Research and Social Science*, *60*. https://doi.org/10.1016/j.erss.2019.101315

Kokaraki, N., Hopfe, C. J., Robinson, E., & Nikolaidou, E. (2019). Testing the reliability of deterministic multi-criteria decision-making methods using building performance simulation. *Renewable and Sustainable Energy Reviews*, *112*, 991–1007. https://doi.org/10.1016/j.rser.2019.06.018

Kolokotroni, M., Davies, M., Croxford, B., Bhuiyan, S., & Mavrogianni, A. (2010). A validated methodology for the prediction of heating and cooling energy demand for buildings within the Urban Heat Island: Case-study of London. *Solar Energy, 84*, 2246–2255.

Kotireddy, R., Hoes, P. J., & Hensen, J. L. M. (2019). Integrating robustness indicators into multi-objective optimization to find robust optimal low-energy building designs. *Journal of Building Performance Simulation, 12*(5), 546–565. https://doi.org/10.1080/19401493.2018.1526971

Kottek, M., Grieser, J., Beck, C., Rudolf, B., & Rubel, F. (2006). World map of the Köppen-Geiger climate classification updated. *Meteorologische Zeitschrift, 15*(3), 259–263. https://doi.org/10.1127/0941-2948/2006/0130

Kovats, S., Valentini, R., Bower, L. M., Georgopoulou, E., E. Jacob, D., Martin, E., … Soussana, J. (2014). Climate change 2014: Impacts, adaptation, and vulnerability. Part B: Regional aspects. Contribution of working group II to the fifth assessment report of the intergovernmental panel on climate change. *Europe*, 1267–1326.

Kristensen, M. H., Hedegaard, R. E., & Petersen, S. (2018). Urban-scale dynamic building energy modeling and prediction using hierarchical archetypes: A case study of two Danish towns. In *Proceedings of BSO 2018: 4th building simulation and optimization conference* (pp. 11–12).

Kunc, M., Morecroft, J. D. W., & Brailsford, S. (2018). Special issue on advances in system dynamics modelling from the perspective of other simulation methods. *Journal of Simulation*. Advance online publication. https://doi.org/10.1080/17477778.2018.1469385

Kwok, Y. T., Lai, A. K. L., Lau, K. K. L., Chan, P. W., Lavafpour, Y., Ho, J. C. K., & Ng, E. Y. Y. (2017). Thermal comfort and energy performance of public rental housing under typical and near-extreme weather conditions in Hong Kong. *Energy and Buildings, 156*, 390–403. https://doi.org/10.1016/j.enbuild.2017.09.067

Kylili, A., Fokaides, P. A., & Lopez Jimenez, P. A. (2016). Key performance indicators (KPIs) approach in buildings renovation for the sustainability of the built environment: A review. *Renewable and Sustainable Energy Reviews*. Advance online publication. https://doi.org/10.1016/j.rser.2015.11.096

Kyprianou, I., Serghides, D. K., Varo, A., Gouveia, J. P., Kopeva, D., & Murauskaite, L. (2019). Energy poverty policies and measures in 5 EU countries: A comparative study. *Energy and Buildings, 196*, 46–60. https://doi.org/10.1016/j.enbuild.2019.05.003210

Li, F. G. N., & Strachan, N. (2019). Take me to your leader: Using socio-technical energy transitions (STET) modelling to explore the role of actors in decarbonisation pathways. *Energy Research and Social Science, 51*, 67–81. https://doi.org/10.1016/j.erss.2018.12.010

Li, Y., Kubicki, S., Guerriero, A., & Rezgui, Y. (2019). Review of building energy performance certification schemes towards future improvement. *Renewable and Sustainable Energy Reviews, 113*. https://doi.org/10.1016/j.rser.2019.109244

Liu, J., Yao, R., & McCloy, R. (2012). A method to weight three categories of adaptive thermal comfort. *Energy and Buildings, 47*, 312–320. https://doi.org/10.1016/j.enbuild.2011.12.007

Liu, J., Yao, R., & McCloy, R. (2017). A method to weight three categories of adaptive thermal comfort. *Energy and Buildings, 47*, 312–320. https://doi.org/10.1016/j.enbuild.2011.12.007

Liu, S., Kwok, Y. T., Lau, K. K. L., Ouyang, W., & Ng, E. (2019). Effectiveness of passive design strategies in responding to future climate change for residential buildings in hot and humid Hong Kong. *Energy and Buildings, 228*. https://doi.org/10.1016/j.enbuild.2020.110469

Loga, T., Stein, B., & Diefenbach, N. (2016). TABULA building typologies in 20 European countries—Making energy-related features of residential building stocks comparable. *Energy and Buildings, 132*, 4–12. https://doi.org/10.1016/j.enbuild.2016.06.094

Lomas, K. J., & Kane, T. (2012). Summertime temperatures in 282 UK homes: Thermal comfort and overheating risk. In *Proceedings of 7th Windsor conference: The changing context of comfort in an unpredictable world.*

Lomas, K. J., & Kane, T. (2013). Summertime temperatures and thermal comfort in UK homes. *Building Research and Information, 41*, 259–280. https://doi.org/10.1080/09613218.2013.757886

Lomas, K. J., & Porritt, S. M. (2017). Overheating in buildings: Lessons from research. *Building Research and Information*. Advance online publication. https://doi.org/10.1080/09613218.2017.1256136

Lopes, M. A. R., Antunes, C. H., & Martins, N. (2015). Towards more effective behavioural energy policy: An integrative modelling approach to residential energy consumption in Europe. *Energy Research and Social Science, 7*, 84–98. https://doi.org/10.1016/j.erss.2015.03.004

López-González, L. M., López-Ochoa, L. M., Las-Heras-Casas, J., & García-Lozano, C. (2016). Energy performance certificates as tools for energy planning in the residential sector. The case of La Rioja (Spain). *Journal of Cleaner Production, 137*, 1280–1292. https://doi.org/10.1016/j.jclepro.2016.08.007

Ma, Z., Cooper, P., Daly, D., & Ledo, L. (2012). Existing building retrofits: Methodology and state-of-the-art. *Energy and Buildings*. Advance online publication. https://doi.org/10.1016/j.enbuild.2012.08.018

Machete, R., Falcão, A. P., Gomes, M. G., & Moret Rodrigues, A. (2018). The use of 3D GIS to analyse the influence of urban context on buildings' solar energy potential. *Energy and Buildings, 177*, 290–302. https://doi.org/10.1016/j.enbuild.2018.07.064

Magnier, L., & Haghighat, F. (2010). Multi-objective optimization of building design using TRNSYS simulations, genetic algorithm, and Artificial Neural Network. *Building and Environment, 45*(3), 739–746. https://doi.org/10.1016/j.buildenv.2009.08.016

Mahdavi, A. (2020). In the matter of simulation and buildings: Some critical reflections. *Journal of Building Performance Simulation, 13*(1), 26–33. https://doi.org/10.1080/19401493.2019.1685598

Mahdavi, A., & Pröglhöf, C. (2009). User behaviour and energy performance in buildings. *Internationalen Energiewirtschaftstagung an Der TU Wien, 6*, 1–13. http://eeg.tuwien.ac.at/eeg.tuwien.ac.at_pages/events/iewt/iewt2009/papers/4E_1_MAHDAVI_A_P.pdf

Mann, B., Passe, U., Rabideau, S., & Takle, E. S. (2012). Future context for thermal comfort: Impact of a changing climate on energy demand and human thermal comfort. In *Proceedings of 7th Windsor conference: The changing context of comfort in an unpredictable world.*

Martinez, I. J., & Richardson, G. P. (1963). Best practices in system dynamics modeling introduction: The importance of best practices. In *The 19th international conference of the System Dinamycs Society*, Atlanta, GA, July 23–27. https://thechangeleader.com/wp-content/uploads/2016/10/Best-practices-in-SD-Modeling-Martinez_1-1.pdf%0Ahttps://thechangeleader.com/wp-content/uploads/2016/10/Best-practices-in-SD-Modeling-Martinez_1-1.pdf%0Ahttp://thechangeleader.com/wp-content/uploads/2

Marzouk, M., & Azab, S. (2017). Analyzing sustainability in low-income housing projects using system dynamics. *Energy and Buildings, 134*, 143–153. https://doi.org/10.1016/j.enbuild.2016.10.034

Marzouk, M., & Seleem, N. (2018). Assessment of existing buildings performance using system dynamics technique. *Applied Energy*, *211*, 1308–1323. https://doi.org/10.1016/j.apenergy.2017.10.111

Mata, É., Sasic Kalagasidis, A., & Johnsson, F. (2014). Building-stock aggregation through archetype buildings: France, Germany, Spain and the UK. *Building and Environment*, *81*, 270–282. https://doi.org/10.1016/j.buildenv.2014.06.013

Mata, É., Wanemark, J., Nik, V. M., & Sasic Kalagasidis, A. (2019). Economic feasibility of building retrofitting mitigation potentials: Climate change uncertainties for Swedish cities. *Applied Energy*, *242*, 1022–1035. https://doi.org/10.1016/j.apenergy.2019.03.042

Mavrogianni, A., Wilkinson, P., Davies, M., Biddulph, P., & Oikonomou, E. (2012). Building characteristics as determinants of propensity to high indoor summer temperatures in London dwellings. *Building and Environment*, *55*, 117–130. https://doi.org/10.1016/j.buildenv.2011.12.003

Mazzeo, D., Matera, N., Cornaro, C., Oliveti, G., Romagnoni, P., & De Santoli, L. (2020). EnergyPlus, IDA ICE and TRNSYS predictive simulation accuracy for building thermal behaviour evaluation by using an experimental campaign in solar test boxes with and without a PCM module. *Energy and Buildings*, *212*. https://doi.org/10.1016/j.enbuild.2020.109812

McCartney, K. J., & Nicol, J. F. (2002). Developing an adaptive control algorithm for Europe: Results of the SCATs project. *Energy and Buildings*, *34*(6), 623–635.

McLeod, R. (2013). *An investigation into the performance of low energy and zero carbon buildings in a changing climate: Applying the Passivhaus standard to the UK context*. PhD Thesis, University of Cardiff. Retrieved April 1, 2019, from http://orca.cf.ac.uk/56966/

McLeod, R. S., & Swainson, M. (2017). Chronic overheating in low carbon urban developments in a temperate climate. *Renewable and Sustainable Energy Reviews*. Advance online publication. https://doi.org/10.1016/j.rser.2016.09.106

Mertens, D. M. (2009). *Transformative research and evaluation*. New York: Guilford.

Michael, A., Gregoriou, S., & Kalogirou, S. A. (2018). Environmental assessment of an integrated adaptive system for the improvement of indoor visual comfort of existing buildings. *Renewable Energy*, *115*, 620–633. https://doi.org/10.1016/j.renene.2017.07.079

Mishra, A. K., & Ramgopal, M. (2015). An adaptive thermal comfort model for the tropical climatic regions of India (Köppen climate type A). *Building and Environment*, *85*, 134–143. https://doi.org/10.1016/j.buildenv.2014.12.006

Moazami, A., Nik, V. M., Carlucci, S., & Geving, S. (2019). Impacts of future weather data typology on building energy performance – Investigating long-term patterns of climate change and extreme weather conditions. *Applied Energy*, 696–720. https://doi.org/10.1016/j.apenergy.2019.01.085

Moeschberger, S. L., & Phillips DeZalia, R. A. (Eds.). (2014). *Symbols that bind, symbols that divide*. Cham: Springer International Publishing. https://doi.org/10.1007/978-3-319-05464-3

Monge-Barrio, A., & Sánchez-Ostiz Gutiérrez, A. (2018). Passive energy strategies for Mediterranean residential buildings: Facing the challenges of climate change and vulnerable populations. *Green Energy and Technology*. Springer International Publishing. https://doi.org/ 10.1007/978-3-319-69883-0

Monyei, C. G., Adewumi, A. O., Akinyele, D., Babatunde, O. M., Obolo, M. O., & Onunwor, J. C. (2018). A biased load manager home energy management system for low-cost residential building low-income occupants. *Energy*, *150*, 822–838. https://doi.org/10.1016/j.energy.2018.03.016

Moore, T., Berry, S., & Ambrose, M. (2019). Aiming for mediocrity: The case of australian housing thermal performance. *Energy Policy*, *132*, 602–610. https://doi.org/10.1016/j.enpol.2019.06.017

Mortensen, A., Heiselberg, P., & Knudstrup, M. (2014). Economy controls energy retrofits of Danish single-family houses. Comfort, indoor environment and architecture increase the budget. *Energy and Buildings*, *72*, 465–475. https://doi.org/10.1016/j.enbuild.2013.12.054

Mostavi, E., Asadi, S., & Boussaa, D. (2017). Development of a new methodology to optimize building life cycle cost, environmental impacts, and occupant satisfaction. *Energy*, *121*, 606–615. https://doi.org/10.1016/j.energy.2017.01.049

Motawa, I., & Oladokun, M. G. (2015). Structural equation modelling of energy consumption in buildings. *International Journal of Energy Sector Management*, *9*(4), 435–450. https://doi.org/10.1108/IJESM-11-2014-0004

Mould, R., & Baker, K. J. (2017). Documenting fuel poverty from the householders' perspective. *Energy Research and Social Science*, *31*, 21–31. https://doi.org/10.1016/j.erss.2017.06.004

Moustakas, K., Loizidou, M., Rehan, M., & Nizami, A. S. (2011). A review of recent developments in renewable and sustainable energy systems: Key challenges and future perspective. *Renewable and Sustainable Energy Reviews*.Advance online publication. https://doi.org/10.1016/j.rser.2019.109418

Moutsiou, T. (2020). Climate, environment and cognition in the colonisation of the Eastern Mediterranean islands during the Pleistocene. *Quaternary International*. Advance online publication. https://doi.org/10.1016/j.quaint.2020.09.012

Muresan, A. A., & Attia, S. (2017). Energy efficiency in the Romanian residential building stock: A literature review. *Renewable and Sustainable Energy Reviews*. Advance online publication. https://doi.org/10.1016/j.rser.2017.02.022

Murtagh, N., Gatersleben, B., & Fife-Schaw, C. (2019). Occupants' motivation to protect residential building stock from climate-related overheating: A study in southern England. *Journal of Cleaner Production*, *226*, 186–194. https://doi.org/10.1016/j.jclepro.2019.04.080

Natarajan, S., Padget, J., & Elliott, L. (2011). Modelling UK domestic energy and carbon emissions: An agent-based approach. *Energy and Buildings*, *43*(10), 2602–2612. https://doi.org/10.1016/j.enbuild.2011.05.013

Naylor, S., Gillott, M., & Lau, T. (2018). A review of occupant-centric building control strategies to reduce building energy use. *Renewable and Sustainable Energy Reviews*. Advance online publication. https://doi.org/10.1016/j.rser.2018.07.019

Nghana, B., & Tariku, F. (2016). Phase change material's (PCM) impacts on the energy performance and thermal comfort of buildings in a mild climate. *Building and Environment*, *99*, 221–238. https://doi.org/10.1016/j.buildenv.2016.01.023

Nicol, F. (2004). Adaptive thermal comfort standards in the hot-humid tropics. *Energy and Buildings*, *36*, 628–637. https://doi.org/10.1016/j.enbuild.2004.01.016

Nicol, F. (2017). Temperature and adaptive comfort in heated, cooled and free-running dwellings. *Building Research & Information*, *45*(7), 730–744. https://doi.org/10.1080/09613218.2017.1283922

Nicol, F., & Humphreys, M. (2010). Derivation of the adaptive equations for thermal comfort in free-running buildings in European standard EN15251. *Building and Environment*, *45*(1), 11–17. https://doi.org/10.1016/j.buildenv.2008.12.013

Nicol, F., Humphreys, M., & Roaf, S. (2012). *Adaptive thermal comfort, principles and practice*. London: Routledge.

Nicol, J. F. (2008). *A handbook of adaptive thermal comfort: Towards a dynamic model. Teaching source*. University of Bath.

Nicol, J. F., Hacker, J., Spires, B., & Davies, H. (2009). Suggestion for new approach to overheating diagnostics. *Building Research and Information, 37*(4), 348–357. https://doi.org/10.1080/09613210902904981

Nicol, J. F., & Humphreys, M. A. (2002). Adaptive thermal comfort and sustainable thermal standards for buildings. *Energy and Buildings, 34*, 563–572.

Nikolopoulou, M., & Lykoudis, S. (2006). Thermal comfort in outdoor urban spaces: Analysis across different European countries. *Building and Environment, 41*(11), 1455–1470. https://doi.org/10.1016/j.buildenv.2005.05.031

Nwodo, M. N., & Anumba, C. J. (2019). A review of life cycle assessment of buildings using a systematic approach. *Building and Environment. Elsevier Ltd.* https://doi.org/10.1016/j.buildenv.2019.106290

O'Brien, W., Wagner, A., Schweiker, M., Mahdavi, A., Day, J., Kjærgaard, M. B., … Berger, C. (2020). Introducing IEA EBC annex 79: Key challenges and opportunities in the field of occupant-centric building design and operation. *Building and Environment, 178*. https://doi.org/10.1016/j.buildenv.2020.106738

Oikonomou, E., Davies, M., Mavrogianni, A., Biddulph, P., Wilkinson, P., & Kolokotroni, M. (2012). Modelling the relative importance of the urban heat island and the thermal quality of dwellings for overheating in London. *Building and Environment, 57*, 223–238. https://doi.org/10.1016/j.buildenv.2012.04.002

Oktay, D. (2007). An analysis and review of the divided city of Nicosia, Cyprus, and new perspectives. *Geography*. Advance online publication. https://doi.org/10.1080/00167487.2007.12094203

Oladokun, M. G., & Odesola, I. A. (2015). Household energy consumption and carbon emissions for sustainable cities – A critical review of modelling approaches. *International Journal of Sustainable Built Environment*. Advance online publication. https://doi.org/10.1016/j.ijsbe.2015.07.005

Olesen, B. W. (2012). Revision of EN15251 standard related to criteria for the indoor environment. In *Proceedings of 7th Windsor conference: The changing context of comfort in an unpredictable world*. Network for Comfort and Energy Use in Buildings.

Oliveira Panão, M. J. N. (2014). Revisiting cooling energy requirements of residential buildings in Portugal in light of climate change. *Energy and Buildings, 76*, 354–362. https://doi.org/10.1016/j.enbuild.2014.02.060

Österbring, M., Camarasa, C., Nägeli, C., Thuvander, L., & Wallbaum, H. (2019). Prioritizing deep renovation for housing portfolios. *Energy and Buildings, 202*. https://doi.org/10.1016/j.enbuild.2019.109361

Østergård, T., Jensen, R. L., & Maagaard, S. E. (2016). Building simulations supporting decision making in early design—A review. *Renewable and Sustainable Energy Reviews*. Advance online publication. https://doi.org/10.1016/j.rser.2016.03.045

Ouria, M., & Sevinc, H. (2018). Evaluation of the potential of solar energy utilization in Famagusta, Cyprus. *Sustainable Cities and Society, 37*, 189–202. https://doi.org/10.1016/j.scs.2017.10.036

Ozarisoy, B. (2022). Energy effectiveness of passive cooling design strategies to reduce the impact of long-term heatwaves on occupants' thermal comfort in Europe: Climate change and mitigation. *Journal of Cleaner Production*. Advance online publication. https://doi.org/10.1016/j.jclepro.2021.129675

Ozarisoy, B., & Altan, H. (2017a). Energy performance development of non-regulated retrofit mass housing estates in Northern Cyprus. *Design Journal*, *20*(Suppl 1), S1765–S1781. https://doi.org/10.1080/14606925.2017.1352697

Ozarisoy, B., & Altan, H. (2017b). Adoption of energy design strategies for retrofitting mass housing estates in Northern Cyprus. *Sustainability (Switzerland)*, *9*(8), 1477. https://doi.org/10.3390/su9081477

Ozarisoy, B., & Altan, H. (2018). Low-energy design strategies for retrofitting existing residential buildings in Cyprus. *Proceedings of the Institution of Civil Engineers: Engineering Sustainability*, *172*(5), 241–255. https://doi.org/10.1680/jensu.17.00061

Ozarisoy, B., & Elsharkawy, H. (2019). Assessing overheating risk and thermal comfort in state-of-the-art prototype houses that combat exacerbated climate change in UK. *Energy and Buildings*, *187*, 201–217. https://doi.org/10.1016/j.enbuild.2019.01.030

Page, J., Robinson, D., Morel, N., & Scartezzini, J. L. (2008). A generalized stochastic model for the simulation of occupant presence. *Energy and Buildings*, *40*(2), 83–98. https://doi.org/10.1016/j.enbuild.2007.01.018

Park, J. S., & Kim, H. J. (2012). A field study of occupant behavior and energy consumption in apartments with mechanical ventilation. *Energy and Buildings*, *50*, 19–25. https://doi.org/10.1016/j.enbuild.2012.03.015

Parkinson, T., & de Dear, R. (2019). Continuous IEQ monitoring system: Context and development. *Building and Environment*, *149*, 15–25. https://doi.org/10.1016/j.buildenv.2018.12.010

Pasichnyi, O., Wallin, J., & Kordas, O. (2019). Data-driven building archetypes for urban building energy modelling. *Energy*, *181*, 360–377. https://doi.org/10.1016/j.energy.2019.04.197

Pastore, L., & Andersen, M. (2019). Building energy certification versus user satisfaction with the indoor environment: Findings from a multi-site post-occupancy evaluation (POE) in Switzerland. *Building and Environment*, *150*, 60–74. https://doi.org/10.1016/j.buildenv.2019.01.001

Pathan, A., Mavrogianni, A., Summerfield, A., Oreszczyn, T., & Davies, M. (2017). Monitoring summer indoor overheating in the London housing stock. *Energy and Buildings*, *141*, 361–378. https://doi.org/10.1016/j.enbuild.2017.02.049

Peacock, A. D., Jenkins, D. P., & Kane, D. (2010). Investigating the potential of overheating in UK dwellings as a consequence of extant climate change. *Energy Policy*, *38*(7), 3277–3288. https://doi.org/10.1016/j.enpol.2010.01.021

Pesic, N., Calzada, J. R., & Alcojor, A. M. (2018). Natural ventilation potential of the Mediterranean coastal region of Catalonia. *Energy and Buildings*, *169*, 236–244. https://doi.org/10.1016/j.enbuild.2018.03.061

Petrou, G., Mavrogianni, A., Symonds, P., Korolija, I., Mylona, A., Raslan, R., … Davies, M. (2018). *What are the implications of building simulation algorithm choice on indoor overheating risk assessment?* London: United Kingdom UCL Institute of Environmental Design and Engineering, United Kingdom Chartered Institution. Bso2018, 11–12.

Pignatta, G., Chatzinikola, C., Artopoulos, G., Papanicolas, C. N., Serghides, D. K., & Santamouris, M. (2017). Analysis of the indoor thermal quality in low-income Cypriot households during winter. *Energy and Buildings*, *152*, 766–775. https://doi.org/10.1016/j.enbuild.2016.11.006

Pisello, A. L., & Asdrubali, F. (2014). Human-based energy retrofits in residential buildings: A cost-effective alternative to traditional physical strategies. *Applied Energy*, *133*, 224–235. https://doi.org/10.1016/j.apenergy.2014.07.049

Pittam, J., & O'Sullivan, P. D. (2017). Improved prediction of deep retrofit strategies for low income housing in Ireland using a more accurate thermal bridging heat loss coefficient. *Energy and Buildings*, *155*, 364–377. https://doi.org/10.1016/j.enbuild.2017.08.088

Pittau, F., Lumia, G., Heeren, N., Iannaccone, G., & Habert, G. (2019). Retrofit as a carbon sink: The carbon storage potentials of the EU housing stock. *Journal of Cleaner Production*, *214*, 365–376. https://doi.org/10.1016/j.jclepro.2018.12.304

Porritt, S., Shao, L., Cropper, P., & Goodier, C. (2011). Adapting dwellings for heat waves. *Sustainable Cities and Society*, *1*(2), 81–90. https://doi.org/10.1016/j.scs.2011.02.004

Porritt, S. M., Cropper, P. C., Shao, L., & Goodier, C. I. (2012). Ranking of interventions to reduce dwelling overheating during heat waves. *Energy and Buildings*, *55*, 16–27. https://doi.org/10.1016/j.enbuild.2012.01.043

Pretlove, S., & Kade, S. (2016). Post occupancy evaluation of social housing designed and built to Code for Sustainable Homes levels 3, 4 and 5. *Energy and Buildings*, *110*, 120–134. https://doi.org/10.1016/j.enbuild.2015.10.014

Psomas, T., Fiorentini, M., Kokogiannakis, G., & Heiselberg, P. (2017). Ventilative cooling through automated window opening control systems to address thermal discomfort risk during the summer period: Framework, simulation and parametric analysis. *Energy and Buildings*, *153*, 18–30. https://doi.org/10.1016/j.enbuild.2017.07.088

Psomas, T., Heiselberg, P., Duer, K., & Bjørn, E. (2016). Overheating risk barriers to energy renovations of single-family houses: Multicriteria analysis and assessment. *Energy and Buildings*, *117*, 138–148. https://doi.org/10.1016/j.enbuild.2016.02.031

Pyrgou, A., Castaldo, V. L., Pisello, A. L., Cotana, F., & Santamouris, M. (2017). On the effect of summer heatwaves and urban overheating on building thermal-energy performance in central Italy. *Sustainable Cities and Society*, *28*, 187–200. https://doi.org/10.1016/j.scs.2016.09.012

Ramsden, S. (2020). Tackling fuel poverty through household advice and support: Exploring the impacts of a charity-led project in a disadvantaged city in the United Kingdom. *Energy Research and Social Science*, *70*. https://doi.org/10.1016/j.erss.2020.101786

Ratti, C., Baker, N., & Steemers, K. (2005). Energy consumption and urban texture. *Energy and Buildings*, *37*(7), 762–776. https://doi.org/10.1016/j.enbuild.2004.10.010

Reeves, A., Taylor, S., & Fleming, P. (2010). Modelling the potential to achieve deep carbon emission cuts in existing UK social housing: The case of Peabody. *Energy Policy*, *38*(8), 4241–4251. https://doi.org/10.1016/j.enpol.2010.03.054

Ren, Z.,Wang, X., & Chen, D. (2014) Heat stress within energy efficient dwellings in Australia. *Architectural Science Review*, *57*(3), 227–236. https://doi.org/10.1080/00038628.2014.903568

Renner, A., & Giampietro, M. (2020). Socio-technical discourses of European electricity decarbonization: Contesting narrative credibility and legitimacy with quantitative storytelling. *Energy Research and Social Science*, *59*. https://doi.org/10.1016/j.erss.2019.101279

Rhodes, J. D., Gorman, W. H., Upshaw, C. R., & Webber, M. E. (2015). Using BEopt (EnergyPlus) with energy audits and surveys to predict actual residential energy usage. *Energy and Buildings*, *86*, 808–816. https://doi.org/10.1016/j.enbuild.2014.10.076

Rinaldi, A., Schweiker, M., & Iannone, F. (2018). On uses of energy in buildings: Extracting influencing factors of occupant behaviour by means of a questionnaire survey. *Energy and Buildings*, *168*, 298–308. https://doi.org/10.1016/j.enbuild.2018.03.045

Ringel, M., & Knodt, M. (2018). The governance of the European Energy Union: Efficiency, effectiveness and acceptance of the Winter Package 2016. *Energy Policy*, *112*, 209–220. https://doi.org/10.1016/j.enpol.2017.09.047

Roaf, S., Crichton, D., & Nicol, F. (2009). *Adapting buildings and cities for climate change: A21st century survival guide second edition*. http://dx.doi.org/10.1016/B978-1-85617-720-7.00001-2

Rodrigues, T. L., & Gillot, M. (2013). Climate resilience of a low energy prototype house. *Proceedings of the Institution of Civil Engineers – Engineering Sustainability*, *166*(6), 337–350. https://doi.org/10.1680/ ensu.12.00009

Roetzel, A., Tsangrassoulis, A., Dietrich, U., & Busching, S. (2010). A review of occupant control on natural ventilation. *Renewable and Sustainable Energy Reviews*. Advance online publication. https://doi.org/10.1016/j.rser.2009.11.005

Rouleau, J., & Gosselin, L. (2018). Probabilistic window opening model considering occupant behavior diversity: A data-driven case study of Canadian residential buildings. *Energy*, *195*. https://doi.org/10.1016/j.energy.2020.116981

Rouleau, J., Gosselin, L., & Blanchet, P. (2019). Understanding energy consumption in high-performance social housing buildings: A case study from Canada. *Energy*, *145*, 677–690. https://doi.org/10.1016/j.energy.2017.12.107

Rubel, F., Brugger, K., Haslinger, K., & Auer, I. (2017). The climate of the European Alps: Shift of very high resolution Köppen-Geiger climate zones 1800–2100. *Meteorologische Zeitschrift*, *26*(2), 115–125. https://doi.org/10.1127/metz/2016/0816

Şafakli, O. (2011). An overview of the construction sector in Northern Cyprus. *African Journal of Business Management*, *5*(35). https://doi.org/10.5897/ajbmx11.015

Sahakian, M., Rau, H., Grealis, E., Godin, L., Wallenborn, G., Backhaus, J., … Fahy, F. (2021). Challenging social norms to recraft practices: A living lab approach to reducing household energy use in eight European countries. *Energy Research & Social Science*, *72*, 101881. https://doi.org/10.1016/j.erss.2020.101881

Saman, W., Boland, J., Pullen, S., Dear, R. D., Soebarto, V., Miller, W., … Zuo, J. (2013). *A framework for adaptation Australian households to heat waves: Final report* (p. 264). Gold Coast: National Climate Change Adaptation Research Facility. http://www.nccarf.edu.au/sites/default/files/attached_files_publications/SI1103-Adapting-Australian-households-to-heat-waves.pdf

San Miguel-Bellod, J., González-Martínez, P., & Sánchez-Ostiz, A. (2018). The relationship between poverty and indoor temperatures in winter: Determinants of cold homes in social housing contexts from the 40s–80s in Northern Spain. *Energy and Buildings*, *173*, 428–442. https://doi.org/10.1016/j.enbuild.2018.05.022

Sanchez-Guevara, C., Núñez Peiró, M., Taylor, J., Mavrogianni, A., & Neila González, J. (2018). Assessing population vulnerability towards summer energy poverty: Case studies of Madrid and London. *Energy and Buildings*, *190*, 132–143. https://doi.org/10.1016/j.enbuild.2019.02.024

Sánchez-Guevara Sánchez, C., Neila González, F. J., & Hernández Aja, A. (2019). Energy poverty methodology based on minimal thermal habitability conditions for low income housing in Spain. *Energy and Buildings*, *169*, 127–140. https://doi.org/10.1016/j.enbuild.2018.03.038

Santamouris, M. (2016). Innovating to zero the building sector in Europe: Minimising the energy consumption, eradication of the energy poverty and mitigation the local climate change. *Solar Energy*, *128*, 61–94. https://doi.org/10.1016/j.solener.2016.01.021.

Santamouris, M., & Kolokotsa, D. (2015). On the impact of urban overheating and extreme climatic conditions on housing, energy, comfort and environmental quality of vulnerable population in Europe. *Energy and Buildings*, *98*, 125–133. https://doi.org/10.1016/j.enbuild.2014.08.050

Santamouris, M., Pavlou, K., Kolokotsa, D., Synnefa, A., & Niachou, K. (2007). Recent progress on passive cooling techniques. *Energy and Buildings*, *39*(7), 859–866. https://doi.org/10.1016/j.enbuild.2007.02.008

Santamouris, M., Sfakianaki, A., & Pavlou, K. (2010). On the efficiency of night ventilation techniques applied to residential buildings. *Energy and Buildings*, *42*(8), 1309–1313. https://doi.org/10.1016/j.enbuild.2010.02.024

Santangelo, A., & Tondelli, S. (2017). Occupant behaviour and building renovation of the social housing stock: Current and future challenges. *Energy and Buildings*, *145*, 276–283. https://doi.org/10.1016/j.enbuild.2017.04.019

Santangelo, A., Yan, D., Feng, X., & Tondelli, S. (2018). Renovation strategies for the Italian public housing stock: Applying building energy simulation and occupant behaviour modelling to support decision-making process. *Energy and Buildings*, *167*, 269–280. https://doi.org/10.1016/j.enbuild.2018.02.028

Satre-Meloy, A. (2019). Investigating structural and occupant drivers of annual residential electricity consumption using regularization in regression models. *Energy*, *174*, 148–168. https://doi.org/10.1016/j.energy.2019.01.157

Savvides, A. L. (2017). The provision of socially minded housing in Cyprus: Examining historical references and addressing recent challenges from an architectural perspective. *Critical Housing Analysis*, *4*(2), 84–98. https://doi.org/10.13060/23362839.2017.4.2.389

Schneider, R., Taylor, J., Davies, M., Mavrogianni, A., & Symonds, P. (2016). Modelling and monitoring tools to evaluate the urban heat island's contribution to the risk of indoor overheating. In *3rd IBPSA-England conference BSO 2016*.

Schrubsole, C., Macmillian, A., Davies, M., & May, N. (2014). 100 Unintended consequences of policies to improve the energy efficiency of the UK housing stock. *Indoor & Built Environment*, *23*, 340–352. https://doi.10.11177//1420326X14524586

Schwartz, Y., & Raslan, R. (2013). Variations in results of building energy simulation tools, and their impact on BREEAM and LEED ratings: A case study. *Energy and Buildings*, *62*, 350–359. https://doi.org/10.1016/j.enbuild.2013.03.022

Schweiker, M., Huebner, G. M., Kingma, B. R. M., Kramer, R., & Pallubinsky, H. (2018). Drivers of diversity in human thermal perception – A review for holistic comfort models. *Temperature*. Routledge. https://doi.org/10.1080/23328940.2018.1534490

Schweiker, M., Rissetto, R., & Wagner, A. (2020). Thermal expectation: Influencing factors and its effect on thermal perception. *Energy and Buildings*, *210*. https://doi.org/10.1016/j.enbuild.2019.109729

Schweiker, M., & Wagner, A. (2015). A framework for an adaptive thermal heat balance model (ATHB). *Building and Environment*, *94*(P1), 252–262. https://doi.org/10.1016/j.buildenv.2015.08.018

Semprini, G., Gulli, R., & Ferrante, A. (2017). Deep regeneration vs shallow renovation to achieve nearly Zero Energy in existing buildings: Energy saving and economic impact of design solutions in the housing stock of Bologna. *Energy and Buildings*, *156*, 327–342. https://doi.org/10.1016/j.enbuild.2017.09.044

Serghides, D. K., Dimitriou, S., & Katafygiotou, M. C. (2016). Towards European targets by monitoring the energy profile of the Cyprus housing stock. *Energy and Buildings*, *132*, 130–140. https://doi.org/10.1016/j.enbuild.2016.06.096

Serghides, D. K., Dimitriou, S., Katafygiotou, M. C., & Michaelidou, M. (2015). Energy efficient refurbishment towards nearly zero energy houses, for the mediterranean region. *Energy Procedia*, *83*, 533–543. https://doi.org/10.1016/j.egypro.2015.12.173

Serghides, D. K., Michaelidou, M., Christofi, M., Dimitriou, S., & Katafygiotou, M. (2017). Energy refurbishment towards nearly zero energy multi-family houses, for Cyprus. *Procedia Environmental Sciences*, *38*, 11–19. https://doi.org/10.1016/j.proenv.2017.03.068

Serrano-Jiménez, A., Lizana, J., Molina-Huelva, M., & Barrios-Padura, Á. (2019). Decision-support method for profitable residential energy retrofitting based on energy-related occupant behaviour. *Journal of Cleaner Production*, *222*, 622–632. https://doi.org/10.1016/j.jclepro.2019.03.089

Serrano-Lanzarote, B., Ortega-Madrigal, L., García-Prieto-Ruiz, A., Soto-Francés, L., & Soto-Francés, V. M. (2016). Strategy for the energy renovation of the housing stock in Comunitat Valenciana (Spain). *Energy and Buildings*, *132*, 117–129. https://doi.org/10.1016/j.enbuild.2016.06.087

Sharifi, S., Saman, W., & Alemu, A. (2019). Identification of overheating in the top floors of energy-efficient multilevel dwellings. *Energy and Buildings*, *204*. https://doi.org/10.1016/j.enbuild.2019.109452

Shih, Y. H., & Tseng, C. H. (2014). Cost-benefit analysis of sustainable energy development using life-cycle co-benefits assessment and the system dynamics approach. *Applied Energy*, *119*, 57–66. https://doi.org/10.1016/j.apenergy.2013.12.031

Sierra, F., Mahdjoubi, L., Gething, B., Alzaatreh, A., Fitton, R., & Marshall, A. (2018). Comparison of prediction tools to determine their reliability on calculating operational heating consumption by monitoring no-fines concrete dwellings. *Energy and Buildings*, *176*, 78–94. https://doi.org/10.1016/j.enbuild.2018.07.012

Singh, M. K., Mahapatra, S., & Atreya, S. K. (2011). Adaptive thermal comfort model for different climatic zones of North-East India. *Applied Energy*, *88*(7), 2420–2428. https://doi.org/10.1016/j.apenergy.2011.01.019

Sonetti, G., Arrobbio, O., Lombardi, P., Lami, I. M., & Monaci, S. (2020). 'Only social scientists laughed': Reflections on social sciences and humanities integration in European energy projects. *Energy Research and Social Science*, *61*. https://doi.org/10.1016/j.erss.2019.101342

Sorgato, M. J., Melo, A. P., & Lamberts, R. (2016). The effect of window opening ventilation control on residential building energy consumption. *Energy and Buildings*, *133*, 1–13. https://doi.org/10.1016/j.enbuild.2016.09.059

SPO-State Planning Organization of North Cyprus. (2011). *Sectoral distribution of GNP, GDP and macroeconomic indicators/2010–2018*. Retrieved December 2020, from https://www.devplan.org/seg-en.html

SPO-State Planning Organization of North Cyprus. (2020). *Gross national product statistics*. Retrieved December 2020, from https://www.devplan.org/index_en.html

Statistical Service of Republic of Cyprus. (2014) *Latest figures: Results of the census of population, 2011*.Retrieved January 21, 2021, from http://www.mof.gov.cy/mof/cystat/statistics.nsf/index_gr/index_gr?OpenDocument

Statistical Service of Republic of Cyprus. (2019) *Latest figures: Results of the census of population, 2011*. Retrieved January 21, 2021, from http://www.mof.gov.cy/mof/cystat/statistics.nsf/index_gr/index_gr?OpenDoc ument

Stazi, F., Marinelli, S., Di Perna, C., & Munafò, P. (2014). Comparison on solar shadings: Monitoring of the thermo-physical behaviour, assessment of the energy saving, thermal comfort, natural lighting and environmental impact. *Solar Energy*, *105*, 512–528. https://doi.org/10.1016/j.solener.2014.04.005

Stazi, F., Naspi, F., & D'Orazio, M. (2017). A literature review on driving factors and contextual events influencing occupants' behaviours in buildings. *Building and Environment.* Advance online publication. https://doi.org/10.1016/j.buildenv.2017.03.021

Stefanović, A., & Gordić, D. (2016). Modeling methodology of the heating energy consumption and the potential reductions due to thermal improvements of staggered block buildings. *Energy and Buildings*, *125*, 244–253. https://doi.org/10.1016/j.enbuild.2016.04.058

Stevenson, F., & Leaman, A. (2010). Evaluating housing performance in relation to human behaviour: New challenges. *Building Research and Information*. Advance online publication. https://doi.org/10.1080/09613218.2010.497282

Stevenson, F., & Rijal, H. B. (2010). Developing occupancy feedback form a prototype to improve housing production. *Building Research Information*, *38*(5), 549–563. https://doi.org/10.1080/09613218.2010.496182

Stojiljković, M. M., Ignjatović, M. G., & Vučković, G. D. (2015). Greenhouse gases emission assessment in residential sector through buildings simulations and operation optimization. *Energy*, *92*, 420–434. https://doi.org/10.1016/j.energy.2015.05.021

Streicher, K. N., Padey, P., Parra, D., Bürer, M. C., & Patel, M. K. (2018). Assessment of the current thermal performance level of the Swiss residential building stock: Statistical analysis of energy performance certificates. *Energy and Buildings*, *178*, 360–378. https://doi.org/10.1016/j.enbuild.2018.08.032

Sun, K., & Hong, T. (2017). A simulation approach to estimate energy savings potential of occupant behavior measures. *Energy and Buildings*, *136*, 43–62. https://doi.org/10.1016/j.enbuild.2016.12.010

Swan, L. G., & Ugursal, V. I. (2009). Modeling of end-use energy consumption in the residential sector: A review of modeling techniques. *Renewable and Sustainable Energy Reviews*. Advance online publication. https://doi.org/10.1016/j.rser.2008.09.033

Symonds, P., Taylor, J., Mavrogianni, A., Davies, M., Shrubsole, C., Hamilton, I., & Chalabi, Z. (2017). Overheating in English dwellings: Comparing modelled and monitored large-scale datasets. *Building Research and Information*, *45*(1–2), 195–208. https://doi.org/10.1080/09613218.2016.1224675

Tagliapietra, S., Zachmann, G., Edenhofer, O., Glachant, J. M., Linares, P., & Loeschel, A. (2019). The European Union energy transition: Key priorities for the next five years. *Energy Policy*, *132*, 950–954. https://doi.org/10.1016/j.enpol.2019.06.060

Taleghani, M., Tenpierik, M., Kurvers, S., & Van Den Dobbelsteen, A. (2013). A review into thermal comfort in buildings. *Renewable and Sustainable Energy Reviews*. Advance online publication.https://doi.org/10.1016/j.rser.2013.05.050

Tardioli, G., Kerrigan, R., Oates, M., O'Donnell, J., & Finn, D. (2015). Data driven approaches for prediction of building energy consumption at urban level. *Energy Procedia*, *78*, 3378–3383. https://doi.org/10.1016/j.egypro.2015.11.754

Teitelbaum, E., Jayathissa, P., Miller, C., & Meggers, F. (2020). Design with Comfort: Expanding the psychrometric chart with radiation and convection dimensions. *Energy and Buildings*, *209*. https://doi.org/10.1016/j.enbuild.2019.109591

Terés-Zubiaga, J., Escudero, C., García-Gafaro, C., & Sala, J. M. (2015). Methodology for evaluating the energy renovation effects on the thermal performance of social housing buildings: Monitoring study and grey box model development. *Energy and Buildings*, *102*, 390–405. https://doi.org/10.1016/j.enbuild.2015.06.010

Theodosiou, T., Tsikaloudaki, K., Kontoleon, K., & Giarma, C. (2021). Assessing the accuracy of predictive thermal bridge heat flow methodologies. *Renewable and Sustainable Energy Reviews*, *136*. https://doi.org/10.1016/j.rser.2020.110437

Tian, W., Heo, Y., de Wilde, P., Li, Z., Yan, D., Park, C. S., … Augenbroe, G. (2018). A review of uncertainty analysis in building energy assessment. *Renewable and Sustainable Energy Reviews*. Advance online publication. https://doi.org/10.1016/j.rser.2018.05.029

Tink, V., Porritt, S., Allinson, D., & Loveday, D. (2018). Measuring and mitigating overheating risk in solid wall dwellings retrofitted with internal wall insulation. *Building and Environment*, *141*, 247–261. https://doi.org/10.1016/j.buildenv.2018.05.062

Toe, D. H. C., & Kubota, T. (2013). Development of an adaptive thermal comfort equation for naturally ventilated buildings in hot-humid climates using ASHRAE RP-884 database. *Frontiers of Architectural Research*, *2*(3), 278–291. https://doi.org/10.1016/j.foar.2013.06.003

Toftum, J., Andersen, R. V., & Jensen, K. L. (2009). Occupant performance and building energy consumption with different philosophies of determining acceptable thermal conditions. *Building and Environment*, *44*(10), 2009–2016. https://doi.org/10.1016/j.buildenv.2009.02.007

Tong, S., Ren, C., & Becker, N. (2010). Excess deaths during the 2004 heatwave in Brisbane, Australia. *International Journal of Biometeorology*, *54*(4), 393–400. https://doi.org/10.1007/s00484-009-0290-8

Tuck, N. W., Zaki, S. A., Hagishima, A., Rijal, H. B., Zakaria, M. A., & Yakub, F. (2019). Effectiveness of free running passive cooling strategies for indoor thermal environments: Example from a two-storey corner terrace house in Malaysia. *Building and Environment*, *160*. https://doi.org/10.1016/j.buildenv.2019.106214

Tweed, C., Dixon, D., Hinton, E., & Bickerstaff, K. (2014). Thermal comfort practices in the home and their impact on energy consumption. *Arch Engineering Design Management*, *10*(1–2), 1–24. https://doi.org/10.1080/17452007.2013.837243

Valentina, F., Andersen, R. V., & Corgnati, S. P. (2012). Window opening behaviour: Simulations of occupant behaviour in residential buildings using models based on a field survey. In *Proceedings of 7th Windsor conference: The changing context of comfort in an unpredictable world.*

van Hoof, J., & Hensen, J. L. M. (2007). Quantifying the relevance of adaptive thermal comfort models in moderate thermal climate zones. *Building and Environment*, *42*(1), 156–170. https://doi.org/10.1016/j.buildenv.2005.08.023

Varoglu, L., Temel, S., & Yilmaz, A. (2018). Knowledge, attitudes and behaviours towards the environmental issues: Case of Northern Cyprus. *Eurasia Journal of Mathematics, Science and Technology Education*, *14*(3), 997–1004. https://doi.org/10.12973/ejmste/81153

Vehbi, B. O., & Hoskara, S. O. (2010). Measuring the sustainability level of Samanbahce residential quarter in Nicosia - Northern Cyprus for its sustainable revitalization. *SB10 conference series*, 1–14.

Vellei, M., Herrera, M., Fosas, D., & Natarajan, S. (2017). The influence of relative humidity on adaptive thermal comfort. *Building and Environment*, *124*, 171–185. https://doi.org/10.1016/j.buildenv.2017.08.005

Wallace, K. N., Irvine, K. N., Wright, A. J., & Fleming, P. D. (2010). Public attitudes to personal carbon allowances: Findings from a mixed-method study. *Climate Policy*, *10*(4), 385–409. https://doi.org/10.3763/cpol.2009.004

Walsh, C. L., Roberts, D., Dawson, R. J., Hall, J. W., Nickson, A., & Hounsome, R. (2013). Experiences of integrated assessment of climate impacts, adaptation and mitigation modelling in London and Durban. *Environment and Urbanization*. Advance online publication. https://doi.org/10.1177/0956247813501121

Wang, J., Wang, Z., de Dear, R., Luo, M., Ghahramani, A., & Lin, B. (2018). The uncertainty of subjective thermal comfort measurement. *Energy and Buildings*, *181*, 38–49. https://doi.org/10.1016/j.enbuild.2018.09.041

Wang, L., Kim, J., Xiong, J., & Yin, H. (2019). Optimal clothing insulation in naturally ventilated buildings. *Building and Environment*, *154*, 200–210. https://doi.org/10.1016/j.buildenv.2019.03.029

Wang, Q., Ploskić, A., & Holmberg, S. (2015). Retrofitting with low-temperature heating to achieve energy-demand savings and thermal comfort. *Energy and Buildings*, *109*, 217–229. https://doi.org/10.1016/j.enbuild.2015.09.047

Wei, Y., Zhang, X., Shi, Y., Xia, L., Pan, S., Wu, J., … Zhao, X. (2018). A review of data-driven approaches for prediction and classification of building energy consumption. *Renewable and Sustainable Energy Reviews*. Advance online publication. https://doi.org/10.1016/j.rser.2017.09.108

Willan, C., Hitchings, R., Ruyssevelt, P., & Shipworth, M. (2020). Talking about targets: How construction discourses of theory and reality represent the energy performance gap in the United Kingdom. *Energy Research and Social Science*, *64*. https://doi.org/10.1016/j.erss.2019.101330

Wittmayer, J. M., de Geus, T., Pel, B., Avelino, F., Hielscher, S., Hoppe, T., … Härtwig, A. (2020). Beyond instrumentalism: Broadening the understanding of social innovation in socio-technical energy systems. *Energy Research and Social Science*. Advance online publication. https://doi.org/10.1016/j.erss.2020.101689

Wolff, A., Weber, I., Gill, B., Schubert, J., & Schneider, M. (2017). Tackling the interplay of occupants' heating practices and building physics: Insights from a German mixed methods study. *Energy Research and Social Science*, *32*, 65–75. https://doi.org/10.1016/j.erss.2017.07.003

Wright, A. (2008). What is the relationship between built form and energy use in dwellings? *Energy Policy*, *36*(12), 4544–4547. https://doi.org/10.1016/j.enpol.2008.09.014

Wright, A., & Firth, S. (2007). The nature of domestic electricity-loads and effects of time averaging on statistics and on-site generation calculations. *Applied Energy*, *84*(4), 389–403. https://doi.org/10.1016/j.apenergy.2006.09.008

Wright, A. J., Korolija, I., & Zhang, Y. (2013). Optimization of dwelling design under current and future climates using parametric simulations in EnergyPlus. *Cibse.Org*, April 11–12. https://www.cibse.org/content/cibsesymposium2013/paper076.pdf

Wright, A. J., Oates, M. R., & Greenough, R. (2013). Concepts for dynamic modelling of energy-related flows in manufacturing. *Applied Energy*, *112*, 1342–1348. https://doi.org/10.1016/j.apenergy.2013.01.056

Yang, S., Pilet, T. J., & Ordonez, J. C. (2018). Volume element model for 3D dynamic building thermal modeling and simulation. *Energy*, *148*, 642–661. https://doi.org/10.1016/j.energy.2018.01.156

Yao, R., Li, B., & Liu, J. (2009). A theoretical adaptive model of thermal comfort—Adaptive predicted mean vote (aPMV). *Building and Environment*, *44*(10), 2089–2096. https://doi.org/10.1016/j.buildenv.2009.02.014

Yi, C. Y., & Peng, C. (2019). An archetype-in-neighbourhood framework for modelling cooling energy demand of a city's housing stock. *Energy and Buildings*, *196*, 30–45. https://doi.org/10.1016/j.enbuild.2019.05.015

Yildiz, D., & Manioğlu, G. (2015). Evaluating sustainability and energy efficiency of a traditional housing: The case of the samanbahçe settlement in Cyprus. *A/Z ITU Journal of the Faculty of Architecture*, *12*(2), 205–220.

Yorucu, V. (2003). The analysis of forecasting performance by using time series data for two mediterranean islands. *Review of Social, Economic & Business Studies*, *2*, 175–196. https://www.researchgate.net/publication/255584205

Yorucu, V. (2013). Construction in an open economy: Autoregressive distributed lag modeling approach and causality analysis—Case of North Cyprus. *Journal of*

Construction Engineering and Management, *139*(9), 1199–1210. https://doi.org/10.1061/(asce)co.1943-7862.0000714

Yorucu, V., & Keles, R. (2007). The construction boom and environmental protection in Northern Cyprus as a consequence of the Annan Plan. *Construction Management and Economics*, *25*(1), 77–86. https://doi.org/10.1080/01446190600902356

Yorucu, V., Mehmet, O., Alpar, R., & Ulucay, P. (2010). Cross-border trade liberalization: The case of Lokmaci/Ledra gate in divided Nicosia, Cyprus. *European Planning Studies*, *18*(10), 1749–1764. https://doi.org/10.1080/09654313.2010.504353

Yu Zhun Jerry, Z. J., Haghighat, F., Fung, B. C. M., Morofsky, E., & Yoshino, H. (2011). A methodology for identifying and improving occupant behavior in residential buildings. *Energy*, *36*(11), 6596–6608. https://doi.org/10.1016/j.energy.2011.09.002

Zachariadis, T. (2010). Forecast of electricity consumption in Cyprus up to the year 2030: The potential impact of climate change. *Energy Policy*, *38*(2), 744–750. https://doi.org/10.1016/j.enpol.2009.10.019

Zakula, T., Bagaric, M., Ferdelji, N., Milovanovic, B., Mudrinic, S., & Ritosa, K. (2019). Comparison of dynamic simulations and the ISO 52016 standard for the assessment of building energy performance. *Applied Energy*, *254*. https://doi.org/10.1016/j.apenergy.2019.113553

Zhang, X., Wu, Y., Shen, L., & Skitmore, M. (2014). A prototype system dynamic model for assessing the sustainability of construction projects. *International Journal of Project Management*, *32*(1), 66–76. https://doi.org/10.1016/j.ijproman.2013.01.009

Zhang, Z., Zhang, Y., & Jin, L. (2017). Thermal comfort in interior and semi-open spaces of rural folk houses in hot-humid areas. *Building and Environment*, *128*, 336–347. https://doi.org/10.1016/j.buildenv.2017.10.028

3 Feed-Forward Household Interviews

Introduction

The objective of this chapter is to focus on the dominant representative occupancy patterns and the underlying determinant factors related to socio-cultural and contextual considerations. An STS approach was employed as a theoretical framework to integrate household socio-demographic characteristics related to energy use, the thermal conductivity level of buildings and various environmental factors, and to determine which energy-policy framework is the most effective and universally applicable to develop the EPBD mandates and improve the energy efficiency of existing housing stock. This chapter also outlines the results as they pertain to the comprehensive information related to the socio-demographic characteristics of each household that was collected via the survey and feedback that was gathered from occupants living in flats with every orientation and floor level; this information is presented.

Sampling-Size Distribution

The results presented in this section were collated using the methodology described to justify sampling size criteria. Figure 3.1(a) presents a summary of the successfully completed interviews across 36 RTB prototypes in the social-housing estate. These findings demonstrate that of 288 flats, only data from 100 households were included in the sampling size dataset, which means that 100% of the questionnaires in the field-survey analysis were valid; this indicates that the sampling size was reasonable to conduct a statistical analysis.

The reasonably high number of completed and returned questionnaires was attributed to the acceptable sample-size criterion of households when the researcher distributed the questionnaire survey in the summer of 2018. It should be noted that the valid questionnaires revealed different percentage variations to identify the most dominant nationally representative sample size and develop a bottom-up energy-policy framework. The medium-rise RTB prototypes in NC represent 56% of the entire post-war social-housing stock that was built in the mid-1980s and early 1990s under a governmental social-housing scheme. Finchman (2008) investigated the viewpoints of other researchers related to the acceptable response rate in a mixed-method design approach and concluded that a reasonable fraction

DOI: 10.4324/9781003393092-4

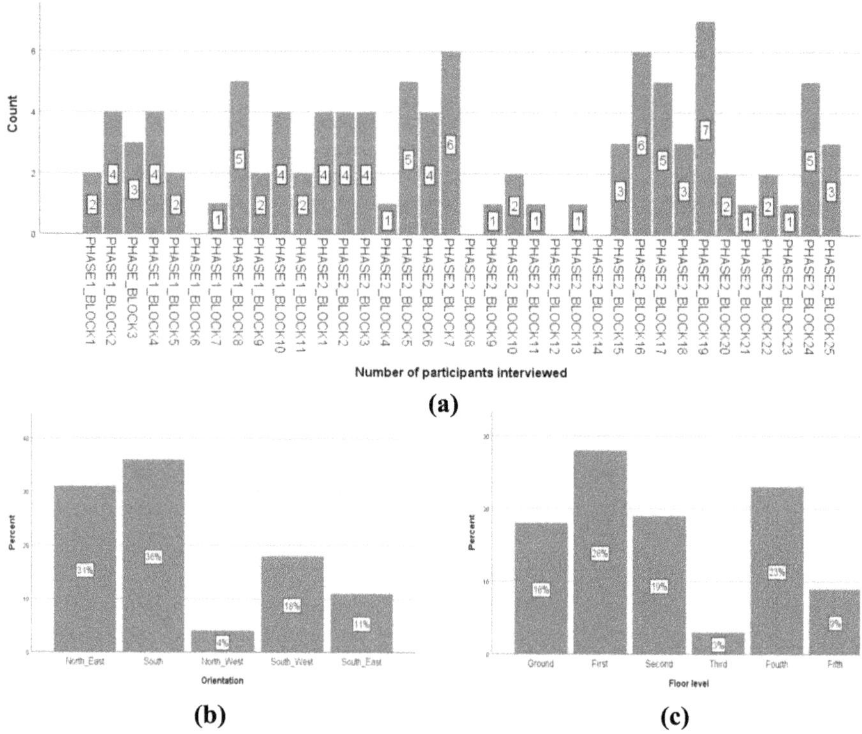

Figure 3.1 (a) Frequency distribution of flats interviewed in survey; percentage distribution of households by (b) orientation and (c) floor level.

rate ranges from 30% to 80%; the conclusions of this study suggested that social researchers should aim to achieve a minimum 30% response rate to select an accurate representative population sample for any integration setting in the STS conceptual framework (i.e., methodology).[1]

In the present exploratory case-study approach, the researcher achieved a 50% response rate from the 200 targeted flats, and a total of 118 questionnaires were completed, which was within the recommended 30–80% threshold limit; this response rate allowed the researcher to assess the participants' responses to develop an evidence-based energy-use policy framework. Figure 3.1(b) and (c) demonstrate the percentage distribution of households recruited when the RTBs' orientations and floor-level differences were taken into account.[2]

Figure 3.1(b) shows that 36% of the recruited households lived in south-facing RTBs, 31% lived in northeast-facing RTBs, 18% lived in southwest-facing RTBs, 11% lived in southeast-facing RTBs and 4% lived in northwest-facing RTBs; in comparison to the other orientations, the lower response rate for the latter orientation is due to the majority of households that did not participate in the survey. Notably, it was observed that most of the occupants in the northwest-facing RTBs were private renters. One other important factor to consider is that only women were present to respond to the questions at the time of the survey, and cultural norms in NC do not allow males to enter a home when men in the household are absent; this cultural barrier contributed to the limitations related to accessing more households in the northwest-facing RTBs.[3]

Figure 3.1(c) presents the summary statistics of the household response rates based on different floor levels: 18% of the respondents lived on the ground floor, 28% lived on the first floor, 19% lived on the second floor, 3% lived on the third floor, 23% lived on the fourth floor and 9% lived on the fifth floor. These findings created a roadmap to gauge the participants' comfort levels, their reasons for thermal discomfort and their thermal-comfort preferences, which are presented in Chapter 5; this information is also highlighted and discussed in Chapter 6 as it related to the development of a conceptual framework to evaluate building-energy performance.

Household Socio-Demographic Characteristics

This section provides basic information about the participants to delineate their demographic characteristics. An analysis of Questions 1–3 and 28–29, which focused on the gender, age, socio-economic position, level of education, tenancy situation, employment status and health conditions of the household members and aimed to establish the participants' ability to provide quality information for this research, is included herein.[4] The survey was developed as a result of a literature review of studies that were undertaken to investigate the influence of household socio-demographic characteristics on energy use, and it was intended to guide the design process of an STS conceptual framework for effective policymaking decisions in the built environment which are presented in Chapter 7.

Gender and Age Distributions

The questionnaires were concurrently administered to the households with the semi-structured interviews. The completed questionnaires revealed that 67% of the responses that were received were from females, and 33% were from males, as shown in Figure 3.2(a). It is important to note that the female occupants were more willing to respond to the survey questions on behalf of their family members, compared to the males; this resulted in nearly two times as many responses from female participants than from males.

According to the survey findings, 26% of the female respondents and 10% of the males lived in the south-facing RTBs, 22% of the females and 9% of the males lived in the northeast-facing RTBs, 7% of the females and 11% of the males lived in the southwest-facing RTBs and 9% of the females and 2% of the males lived in the southeast-facing RTBs; a majority of the northwest-facing RTBs—approximately 88 households—were unoccupied when the survey was undertaken, and only 3% female respondents and 1% of the male respondents lived in these units, as shown in Figure 3.2(b).

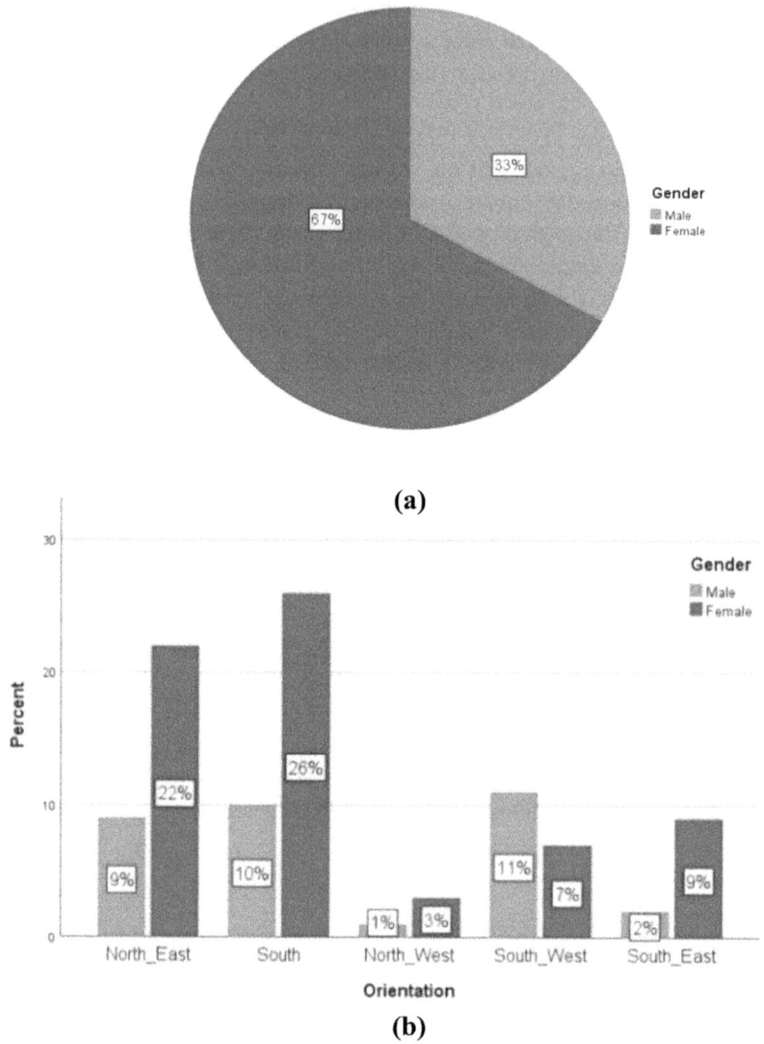

Figure 3.2 Percentage distribution of households by (a) gender and (b) gender, taking RTB orientation into account.

Starting with the youngest common age, the six age groups that were deemed relevant for the present study were 20–25, 25–35, 35–45, 45–55, 55–65 and 65 years of age and older.[5] The percentage distribution of these age groups, which are shown in Figure 3.3(a), shows that across the interviewed RTBs, only 1% of the respondents were in the 20–25 age group,[6] 8% of the females and 7% of the males were 25–35 years of age, 12% of the females and 4% of the males were 35–45 years of age, 13% of the females and 7% of the males were 45–55 years of age,

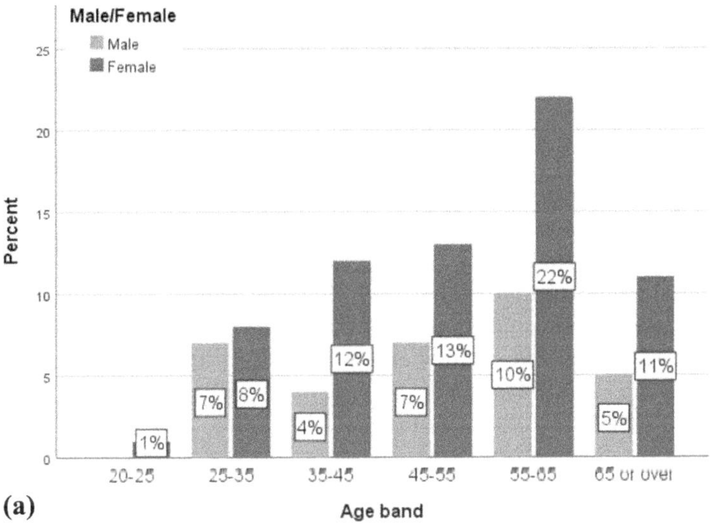

(a)

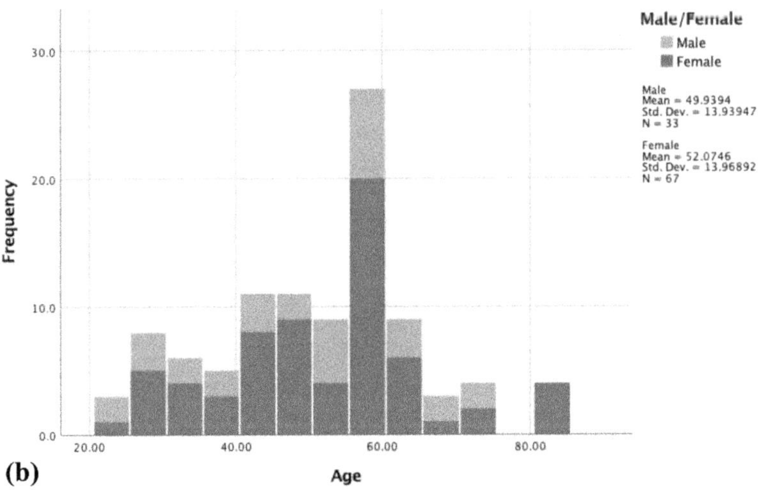

(b)

Figure 3.3 (a) Percentage distribution of age groups by gender and (b) frequency distribution of age by gender. Age was set out as continuous variable for the statistical analysis. The dataset represents age of each household recruited for the study and this data was tabulated into groups for the conceptual-level analysis presented.

22% of the females and 10% of the males were 55–65 years of age and 11% of the females and 5% of the male were 65 years of age and older.

The frequency distribution of the age groups,[7] which is shown in Figure 3.3(b), ranged from 20 to 80 years of age and older; the mean age was 52.07 years

(SD=13.96). The average age group of the respondents ranged from 20 to 65 years of age and older; the mean age was 49.93 years (SD=13.93).

The results highlighted a cluster of participants in the 55–65 and 65-and-older age groups, and a cluster of respondents who were 40–60 years of age was also found. Based on these findings, it was determined that some variations in energy usage according to age group were due to the 22% of respondents who identified as retirees with high pensions and could therefore afford high energy bills; this is why this demographic demonstrated high levels of energy consumption throughout the year.[8]

Research has shown that studies that consider the effects of age on energy consumption discovered significant correlations with income level, but no evidence related to age has been documented (Indraganti & Rao, 2010). This further could be integrated to investigate on forecasting household-energy use in Chapter 5. One of the main reasons to include the gender variable is because gender has been shown to affect an individual's degree of thermal discomfort; according to these data, in fact, gender is a dominant factor to consider when assessing thermal-comfort levels. In the present study, the respondents' ages were also determined to be a significant variable that affected household-energy use.

Socio-Economic Conditions

The employment status of the family members was also explored. Figure 3.4(a) illustrates the employment status of the occupants of the sample households who were 19–85 years of age: 37% of the occupants had family members who were full-time employees, 12% had family members who were part-time employees, 16% had family members who were self-employed, 21% had family members who received a monthly pension and 14% had family members who were unemployed. Some of the respondents' family members were employed to help with daily living expenses; even though this information is not relevant to employment status, it is indicative of the economic vulnerability of households.

The percentage of unemployment was not significantly higher than the national average indicated in the *Social and Economic Indicators Report*,[9] which explains why most of the recruited households were able to pay their electricity bills (Ozarisoy & Altan, 2017a). This is not surprising, given that a majority of households in this research context with occupants who were 25–55 years of age were economically active, and those in the 55–65 age group received pensions; the typical household salary enabled the occupants to pay their monthly energy bills.

Figure 3.4(b) shows the percentage distribution of the employment status of the respondents, taking gender into account. The employment statuses identified in the surveyed flats were 'working outside of the home,' 'working at home,' 'doing household activities,' 'pupil/student,' 'retired,' 'semi-retired' and 'unemployed.' Of the female respondents, 22% worked outside of the home, 11% worked at home, 16% were at home and stayed busy with household activities, 14% were retired and 2% were unemployed. Of the male respondents, 20% worked outside of the home, 2% were students, 7% were retired and 1% were semi-retired. The results

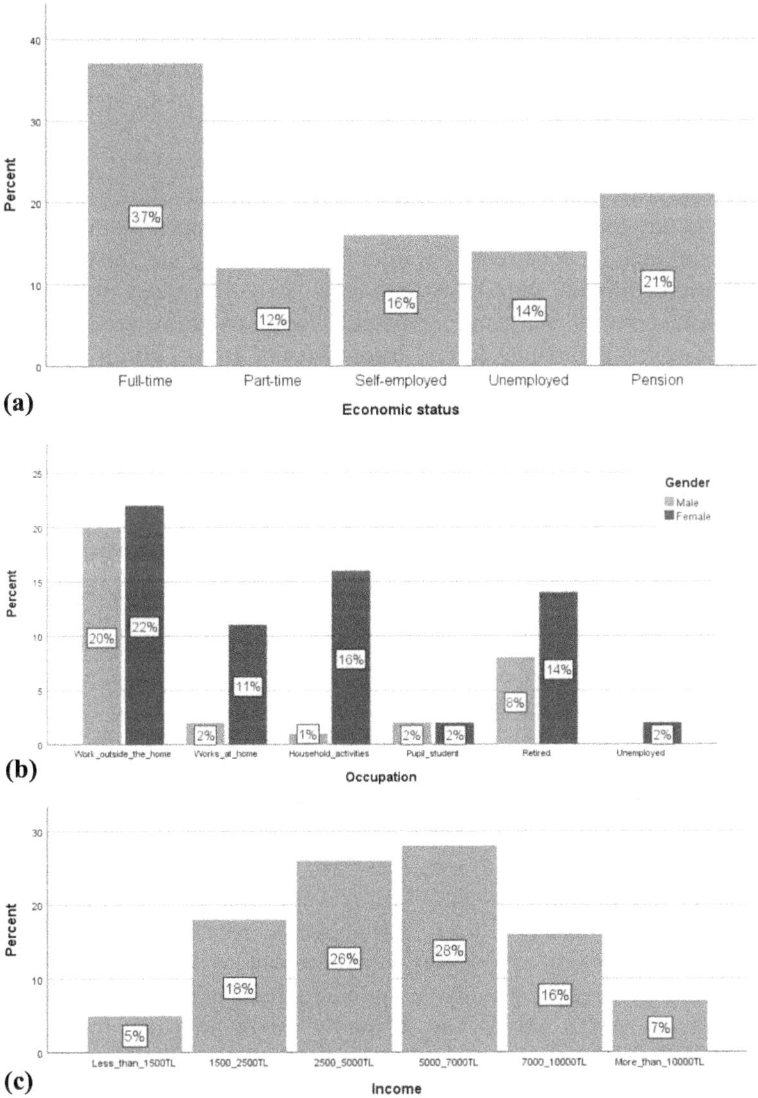

Figure 3.4 (a) Percentage distribution of employment status, (b) percentage distribution of employment status by gender and (c) percentage distribution of total household income. To run the correlation analysis, the household occupation was set out in four groups. The data presents actual information gathered from households (descriptive statistics) without altering the collated original data.

demonstrated that 41% of the female respondents—of whom 11% worked at home, 16% focused on household activities and 14% were retired—spent a majority of their time throughout the year inside their dwellings. These data directly correlate with household-energy use and can also be linked to gender inequality and educational opportunities that are skewed in favour of men, due to religious and cultural beliefs and practices in the NC.

The single most striking finding to emerge from the data showed that 2% of the respondents reported that they had no annual income and were therefore vulnerable to being unable to pay their electricity bills. This can be explained by the unemployment rates and income-generating opportunities in this region; for example, some people living in different states in NC are completely dependent on the government for their income and are therefore classified as a vulnerable group. In the present study, however, the employed (i.e., economically active) group included approximately 55% of the total sample size. Notably, only 2% of the economically inactive group suffered from fuel poverty, particularly in the winter.

A national gross-income survey conducted by the Northern Cyprus State Planning Organisation in 2016 indicated that the dominant group within the Famagusta Municipality is the ‘social-services assistance’ group, which was defined as economically vulnerable families living in social-housing estates, particularly the vulnerable population in the 45–55 age band. In the present study, this group comprised 2% of the total sample size; the total monthly income of these households was less than 1,500 TL,[10] as shown in Figure 3.4(c); this social group largely relied on government benefits and tended to spend their income on basic requirements (e.g., daily living expenses), as presented in Chapter 1.

The bar chart in Figure 3.4(c) illustrates total household income distribution percentages in the different income groups: 5% of the respondents earned less than 1,500 TL every month, 18% earned 1,500–2,500 TL, 26% earned 2,500–5,000 TL, 28% earned 5,000–7,000 TL, 16% earned 7,000–10,000 TL and 7% earned more than 10,000 TL. Referring back to Figure 3.4, 95% of the surveyed households earned more than 1,500 TL each month, which is well above the minimum wage rate in NC for full-time, year-round work; this could foreseeably result in higher household energy consumption rate, because the occupants would be able to pay their electricity bills. In the present study, 5% of the respondent households earned less than 1,500 TL per month, which is below the NC minimum wage.

Furthermore, this study found that this low-income respondent group experience fuel poverty in the winter. One participant admitted that the cold conditions in the winter of 2015–2016 caused their household to heavily rely on a portable electric heating system, and because they were unable to afford the electricity bills from those months, the Cyprus Electricity Authority turned off their electricity from March to May of 2016; this led them to change their energy-consumption patterns to avoid future power cuts.

Education Levels and Ethnic Backgrounds

The levels of education and ethnic backgrounds of the respondent households are examined in this section; assessing the level of education of each household in relation to their awareness of energy-saving measures was an important consideration when effective retrofitting interventions to upgrade building-energy performance were devised in the final phase of the present study. Figure 3.5(a) illustrates the percentage distribution of the household levels of education.

As this figure shows, 6% of the respondents had no diploma or degree, 16% had earned an elementary school diploma, 32% had earned a secondary school diploma, 34% had earned a high school diploma, 11% had earned a bachelor's degree and 1% had earned a master's degree. Because household level of education influences the respondents' knowledge and awareness of energy use and energy-saving measures, the data related to education level were intended to inform the researcher of the appropriate means of disseminating this information to households and social-housing developments similar to those in the present study (Ozarisoy & Altan, 2017b).

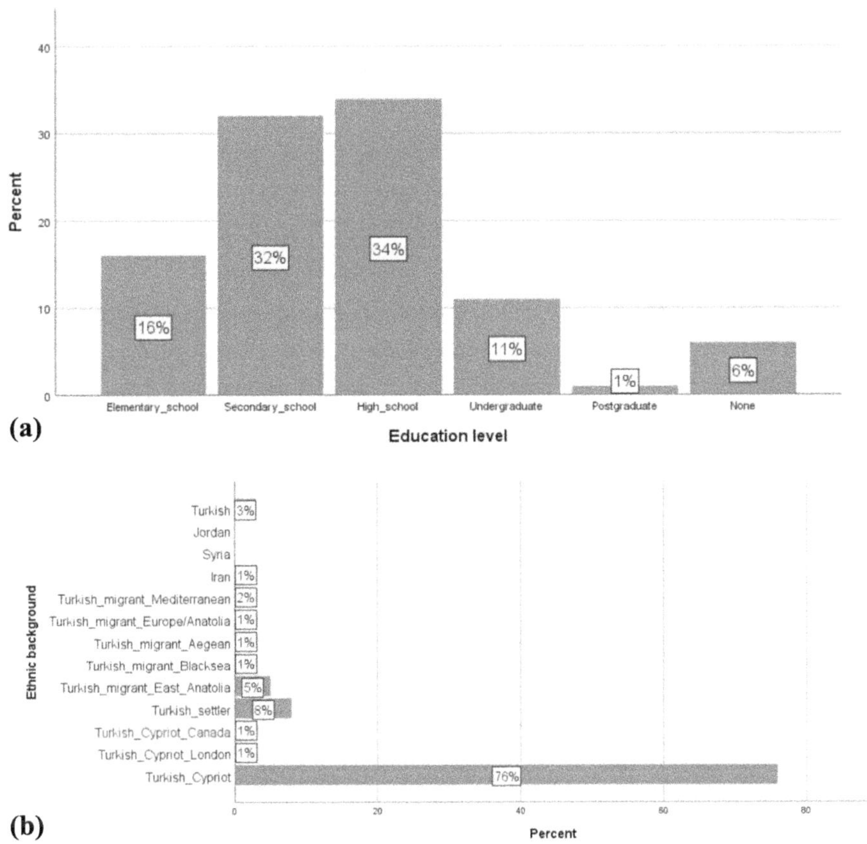

Figure 3.5 (a) Percentage distribution of levels of education and (b) percentage distribution of ethnic backgrounds.

Figure 3.5(b) illustrates the ethnic variations across the interviewed households: 76% were Caucasian Turkish Cypriots; 8% were Turkish settlers; 2% were white Turkish Cypriots who had moved from London and Canada to the social-housing development; 5% were from the Eastern Anatolian region of Turkey; 2% were from the Mediterranean region of Turkey; 1% was from the Black Sea region of Turkey; 1% was from the Aegean region of Turkey; 1% was a Turkish migrant from the Eurasia region of Turkey and 3% were from Iran, Syria and Jordan.

The survey revealed that white Turkish Cypriots and white Turkish migrants were the two most dominant ethnic groups, which were found to directly correlate with the households' tenancy status. A total of 84% of the respondents owned their property and 16% rented their units; the high percentage of the owner-occupied tenure status was due to the central location of the RTB. It should be noted that these flats were predominantly owned by Turkish Cypriots who bought them under the social-housing scheme in the 1980s and 1990s. Many of the original owners had moved out, and most of these flats were rented to migrants or foreign students at affordable prices. Some of the original owners sold their properties to Turkish settlers whose parents emigrated to NC after the physical division of the island in 1974. The owner-occupiers were all approximately the same age when they moved into their flats, when the RTBs were completed in the 1990s. The most dominant age groups in the owner-occupied flats were 55–65 and 65 years of age and older, and the age variable was strongly correlated with tenure type.

Other Indicators

All field-survey analyses in this section are descriptive to observe the general trend of the collected data, which is illustrated in Figure 3.6(a)–(f).

Figure 3.6(a) illustrates that 84% of the sample demographic owned their property, while 16% of the respondents were rental tenants. Of the surveyed households, 73% had lived in their flats for more than ten years, as shown in Figure 3.6(b). It appears as if the respondents' length of residency was correlated with their age group, and a majority of the occupants who owned their property were older than 55 years of age. The number of household members living in these flats also proved to be significant, because it led to a better understanding of the occupants' energy-consumption patterns when their energy bills were analysed, and the amount of heat gain of household members was calculated to validate the survey findings in Chapter 7.

Figure 3.6(c) shows that 42% of the respondents worked outside the home, 13% worked at home, 17% were fully present at home, 4% were students, 20% were retired pensioners and 2% were unemployed; in all, 63% of the respondents in the sample were economically active. These data correlate with household income levels and the occupants' ability to pay high energy bills that were the result of their desire to create thermally comfortable conditions.

The health conditions and genders of the surveyed households are shown in Figure 3.6(d): 57% of the female respondents and 29% of the males reported that their health was between mediocre and very good, and 10% of the females and 4%

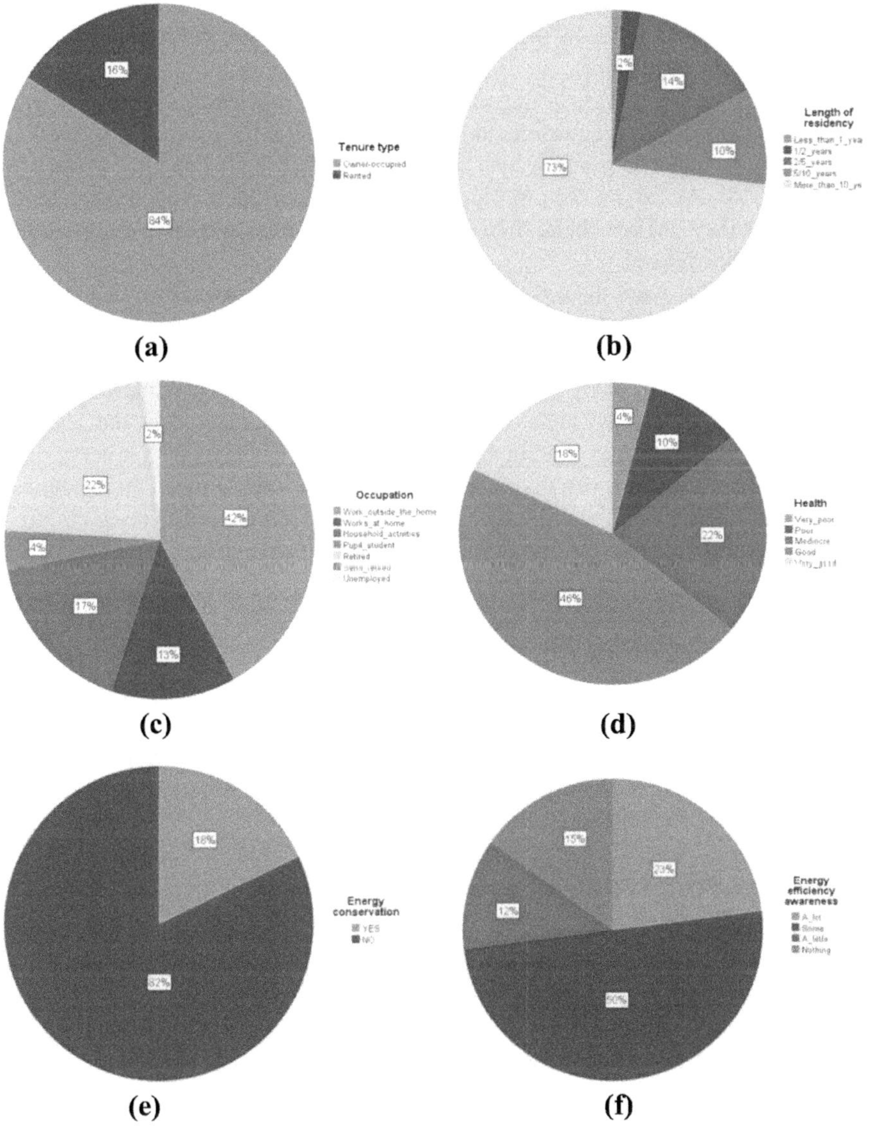

Figure 3.6 Socio-demographic characteristics of respondents: (a) tenancy status, (b) length of residency, (c) employment status, (d) health condition, (e) energy conservation and (f) energy-efficiency awareness. To run the correlation analysis according to the convention, household employment status was recoded as follows. (0 = Work outside the home, 1 = Work at home, 2 = Household activities, 3 = Retired). To run the correlation analysis according to the convention, household health condition was recoded as follows. (1 = Very poor/poor, 2 = Mediocre, 3 = Good, 4 = Very good). Energy conservation was coded to run the statistical analysis accurately (0 = No, 1 = Yes). Energy-efficiency awareness was coded as follows. (0 = Nothing, 1 = A little, 2 = Some, 3 = A lot).

of the males were found to be in poor and very poor health. This was an important statistical finding that correlated with the energy consumption of these households as they attempted to achieve the optimum thermal-comfort conditions for their respective health conditions.

To investigate the energy-saving awareness of each household, the respondents were asked closed-ended questions to determine whether they frequently checked their electricity meter to monitor how much energy they had consumed (Ozarisoy & Altan, 2018). As can be seen in Figure 3.6(e), 82% of the surveyed households reported that they did not check their energy consumption, and 18% reported that they frequently checked.

The households were also asked about their awareness related to energy efficiency; as can be seen in Figure 3.6(f), 20% of the respondents reported that they always took energy-saving methods into consideration, 50% of the respondents infrequently thought of energy-saving methods and 15% never considered energy-saving methods. Based on these results,[11] it can be concluded that the level of awareness related to energy-saving measures not only correlates with level of education, but also income level; many of the households who showed an awareness of energy efficiency were rental tenants and migrant workers with young children who took all possible energy-saving measures into consideration.

Investigating Relationships between Socio-Demographic Characteristics and Other Variables

This section explores the relationships among the household socio-demographic characteristics, energy use and other variables collected from the respondents during the field-study period, and a set of questions developed to undertake statistical tests was utilised to determine the correlations between different socio-demographic characteristics based on the survey findings.

Relationships between RTB Block Numbers and Other Variables

The relationship between orientation and floor level was examined by cross-tabulation using chi-square test.[12] As seen in Table 3.1, no significant relationship was found, $\chi^2(9) = 11.65$,[13] $p = 0.234$, *Cramer*'s $V = 0.197$.[14]

In comparing number of households recruited from each RTB by orientation and by floor level, two separate one-way ANOVAs[15] were used. The results, shown in Table 3.1, indicated that there was a significant difference on block number by orientation, F (3, 96) = 113.90, $p < 0.001$, effect size (*partial* $\eta 2$)= 0.781.[16] Specifically, the block number was significantly different between every two orientations with the largest number in south-east[17] (M= 34,[18] SD= 1[19]), followed by south-west (M = 29, SD = 1) and south (M = 17, SD = 6) orientations, and the smallest number in north-east/north-west (M = 7, SD = 6). No significant difference for block number was found in floor level, $F(3, 96) = 1.56$,[20] p= 0.205,[21] effect size (*partial* $\eta 2$) = 0.046. No relationship was observed between block numbers[22] and floor level, which suggests that building orientation is the most important variable.

Table 3.1 Relationships between Respondents, Orientation and Floor Level.

Variables		*Participants*	*Orientation*	*Floor Level*
Participants	Partial $\eta 2$[a]	1	0.781	0.046
	Significance	—	0.000	0.205
Orientation	Partial $\eta 2$/*Cramer*'s *V*	0.781	1	0.197
	Significance	0.000	—	0.234
Floor Level	Partial $\eta 2$/*Cramer*'s *V*	0.046	0.197	1
	Significance	0.205	0.234	—

RTB scale: 0 (Phase 1, Block 1) to 35 (Phase 2, Block 25)
RTB orientation: 0 (north-east), 1 (south), 2 (north-west), 3 (south-west), 4 (south-east)
Floor levels: 0 (ground); 1 (first); 2 (second); 3 (third); 4 (fourth); 5 (fifth)
Participants–Floor Level,
Orientation–Participants,
Orientation–Floor Level, $\chi^2(9) = 11.65$,[b] $p = 0.234$, *Cramer*'s $V = 0.197$

[a] To calculate the effect size, Cohen's *d* was chosen for differences between two groups when using *t*-tests η p 2 (partial eta squared) for ANOVAs with three or more groups.
[b] For estimating associations between categorical variables, the Pearson chi-squared statistics (χ^2; also developed by Pearson) is often used. A χ^2 estimate (minimum of 0) indicates independence between two nominal variables (chi-squared statistic tends to lose power when estimating ordinal-variable associations).

It was found that a correlation between orientation and floor level would seem intuitive; however, it is noteworthy that orientation was also shown to be a determinant factor with household socio-demographic characteristics. Actual energy consumption was further determined by a statistical analysis of the household socio-demographic characteristics, which are discussed.

Relationships between Occupant Age and Other Variables

The relationships between occupant age, economic status, education level, occupation, income and health conditions were examined using cross-tabulations with chi-square tests,[23] as shown in Table 3.2.

As shown in Table 3.2, age bands were significantly related to health conditions, and this relationship was strong ($\chi^2 = 73.739$,[24] $p < 0.001$, *Cramer*'s $V = 0.496$). Younger age appeared to report better health conditions (good or very good) than older age. Household occupation was significantly related to health conditions, and the relationship was moderate ($\chi^2 = 33.071$,[25] $p < 0.001$, *Cramer*'s $V = 0.342$). A greater proportion of participants with very good health conditions worked outside the home than those with mediocre health conditions, whereas none of the participants who retired had very good health conditions. Household occupations were also significantly associated with age with a moderate–strong relationship ($\chi^2 = 44.810$, $p < 0.001$, *Cramer*'s $V = 0.399$). The results revealed that economic status was significantly related to educational level ($\chi^2 = 48.808$, $p < 0.001$, *Cramer*'s $V =$

Table 3.2 Relationships between Age Band, Economic Status, Education, Occupation, Income and Health Conditions.

Research Questions	*Age Band*	*Economic Status*	*Education Level*	*Occupation*	*Income*	*Health*
Q 1.1: What is your age?	1	0.201	0.114	0.399***	0.213	0.496**
	—	0.447	0.989	0.000	0.324	0.000
Q 1.2: What is your economic status?	0.201	1	0.416**	0.171	0.136	0.178
	0.447	—	0.000	0.763	0.936	0.661
Q 1.3: What is your highest level of education?	0.114	0.416**	1	0.162	0.190	0.288
	0.989	0.000	—	0.648	0.333	0.196
Q 1.4: What is your occupation?	0.399***	0.171	0.162	1	0.275	0.342**
	0.000	0.763	0.648	—	0.092	0.000
Q 29: What is your monthly income?	0.213	0.136	0.190	0.275	1	0.174
	0.324	0.936	0.333	0.092	—	0.480
Q 28: How is your health in general?	0.496**	0.178	0.196	0.342**	0.174	1
	0.000	0.661	0.288	0.000	0.480	—

Age band: 0 (20–25) to 5 (65 and over)
Employment status: 0 (full time) to 4 (pension)
Level of education: 0 (elementary school) to 5 (none)
Occupation: 0 (worked outside home) to 6 (unemployed)
Monthly income: 0 (< 1,500 TL) to 5 (> 10,000 TL)
Health condition: 0 (very poor) to 4 (very good)
Health condition–Age, $\chi^2(12) = 73.74$, $p = 0.000$, *Cramer*'s $V = 0.496$
Health condition–Employment status, $\chi^2(12) = 9.48$, $p = 0.661$, *Cramer*'s $V = 0.178$
Health condition–Education level, $\chi^2(9) = 10.83$, $p = 0.288$, *Cramer*'s $V = 0.196$
Health condition–Occupation, $\chi^2(9) = 33.07$, $p = 0.000$, *Cramer*'s $V = 0.342$
Health condition–Income, $\chi^2(9) = 8.63$, $p = 0.472$, *Cramer*'s $V = 0.170$
Income–Age, $\chi^2(12) = 8.63$, $p = 0.324$, *Cramer*'s $V = 0.213$
Income–Employment status, $\chi^2(12) = 5.58$, $p = 0.936$, *Cramer*'s $V = 0.136$
Income–Education level, $\chi^2(9) = 10.22$, $p = 0.333$, *Cramer*'s $V = 0.190$
Income–Occupation, $\chi^2(9) = 8.55$, $p = 0.480$, *Cramer*'s $V = 0.174$
Occupation–Age, $\chi^2(12) = 44.81$, $p = 0.000$, *Cramer*'s $V = 0.399$
Occupation–Employment status, $\chi^2(12) = 48.81$, $p = 0.000$, *Cramer*'s $V = 0.416$
Occupation–Education, $\chi^2(9) = 6.89$, $p = 0.648$, *Cramer*'s $V = 0.162$
Age–Education, $\chi^2(12) = 3.68$, $p = 0.989$, *Cramer*'s $V = 0.114$
Age–Employment status, $\chi^2(16) = 16.09$, $p = 0.447$, *Cramer*'s $V = 0.201$
Employment status–Education, $\chi^2(12) = 48.81$, $p = 0.000$, *Cramer*'s $V = 0.416$

0.416).[26] A greater proportion of participants with high school level education had full-time jobs than those with only elementary or secondary school, whereas most participants who were pensioners graduated from elementary or secondary school and none of the undergraduates/postgraduates were pensioners. Income was not significantly related to any variables.

Relationships between Occupant Age and Tenancy Status

It was found that 84% of the sample flats were owner occupied, and 16% of the households were tenants; it is important to explore relationships between household age and other variables, because meaningful correlations will facilitate an assessment of occupancy patterns and domestic energy use, which will in turn provide information to assess overheating risk and thermal comfort. Table 3.3 presents the relationships between various household age bands and the tenancy statuses of the respondents; the findings validate the data and provide a better understanding of the relationships between various household socio-demographic characteristics and the respondents' degree of thermal discomfort.

As shown in Table 3.3, age band and tenancy status were significantly and strongly related to each other ($\chi^2 = 24.433$, $p < 0.001$, *Cramer*'s $V = 0.494$). Most participants who rented were 45 years old and younger. Age band and length of residency were also correlated ($\chi^2 = 67.755$, $p < 0.001$, *Cramer*'s $V = 0.582$). It appeared that younger participants had shorter lengths of residency because the rental tenants tended to be younger. Finally, a relationship was discerned between tenancy status and length of residency ($\chi^2 = 35.413$, $p < 0.001$, *Cramer*'s $V = 0.595$). A greater proportion of participants with more than ten years of residency were owner occupied than those who had ten years or less residency.

Table 3.3 Relationships between Household Age Band, Tenancy Status and Length of Residency.

Research Questions	*Age Band*	*Tenancy Status*	*Length of Residency*
Q 1.1: What is your age?	1 —	0.595** 0.000	0.582** 0.000
Q 3: Do you own or rent your dwelling?	0.595** 0.000	1 —	0.494** 0.000
Q 2: How many years have you lived in this flat?	0.582** 0.000	0.494** 0.000	1 —

Age band: 0 (20–25) to 5 (65 and over)
Tenancy type: 0 (owner occupied) or 1 (rented)
Years lived in house: 0 (less than one year) to 1 (more than 10 years)
Age–Length of Residency, $\chi^2(8) = 67.76$, $p = 0.000$, *Cramer*'s $V = 0.582$
Age–Tenure Type, $\chi^2(4) = 24.43$, $p = 0.000$, *Cramer*'s $V = 0.494$
Tenure Type–Length of Residency, $\chi^2(2) = 35.41$, $p = 0.000$, *Cramer*'s $V = 0.595$

Relationships between Energy-Saving Awareness and Income

This section includes an analysis of Questions 4–7, which assessed household energy-use awareness while taking household income levels into account. This portion of the survey investigated whether the occupants obtained sufficient support in energy conservation, and their energy-efficiency awareness was also explored.

The findings revealed that 69% of the respondents paid their monthly energy bills at the higher rate,[27] and 31% paid at the lower rate[28]; this result can be correlated with household income level and the number of family members living in the interviewed flats. When asked about households' awareness of energy-saving methods, 23% of the respondents said they always took into account any type of energy-saving measures; 50% sometimes considered them, 12% considered them quite a few times and 1% never took energy-saving measures into account even though smart meters had already been installed in their dwelling.

The other significant factor derived from the survey was the households' income level as 80% of the households' income was between 2,500 and 5,000 TL and in some cases, more than 10,000 TL. This indicates that the vast majority of respondents were able to afford to pay their annual energy bills while 18% of the respondents earned 1,500–2,500 TL, which resulted in difficulties in paying their energy bills. It should be noted that this lower income group were not homeowners but lived as rental tenants; they were mainly migrant workers predominantly from Turkey. It must also be noted that 5% of the respondents earned less than 1,500 TL, which represents the economically inactive and vulnerable group. Table 3.4 demonstrates the cross-tabulation using chi-square analysis that revealed relationships between household income level and occupant awareness of energy consumption.

As shown in Table 3.4, a moderate relationship was found between energy-efficiency awareness and energy conservation ($\chi^2 = 8.441$, $p = 0.038$, *Cramer*'s $V = 0.291$); 23% of the renting respondents reported that they always checked their electricity meter, and 50% of the renting respondents checked 'sometimes.' A greater proportion of participants with energy conservation had a lot of energy-efficiency awareness while a greater proportion of participants without energy conservation did not have efficiency awareness at all. Income was not significantly associated with energy consumption, energy-efficiency awareness, energy conservation and energy advice. The relationship between household income and whether the occupants had received information from any public or private authorities regarding energy-saving measures was examined. As seen in Table 3.4, no significant relationship was found, $\chi^2(9) = 11.84$,[29] $p = 0.222$,[30] *Cramer*'s $V = 0.199$.

One interviewee reported that they had checked their electricity meter on a weekly basis before their smart meter system was installed; they admitted, however, that due to a lack of knowledge and training on how to read the smart meter system information, they stopped regularly tracking their energy usage, and they commented that they had not checked their energy usage since the smart meter installation. When discussing this issue, another respondent said that their energy bills had slightly increased since the smart meter system was installed, because they never checked the system in their dwelling.

Table 3.4 Relationships between Household Income, Energy Consumption, Energy Advice, Energy Usage and Energy Savings.

Research Questions	*Income*	*Energy Consumption*	*Energy Advice*	*Energy Usage*	*Energy Savings*
Q 29: What is your monthly income?	1 —	0.247 0.107	0.199 0.222	0.176 0.375	0.233 0.061
Q 30: How much electricity (in kWh) did you consume in May through September according to this last overview?	0.247 0.107	1 —	0.116 0.717	0.080 0.424	0.106 0.769
Q 31: Have you received advice on how to reduce your energy bills?	0.199 0.222	0.116 0.717	1 —	0.117 0.713	0.359 0.182
Q 4: Do you check your use of electricity by taking frequent meter readings?	0.176 0.375	0.080 0.424	0.117 0.713	1 —	0.291* 0.038
Q 6: Do you know anything about energy-saving methods?	0.233 0.061	0.106 0.769	0.359 0.182	0.291* 0.038	1 —

Monthly income: 0 (< 1,500 TL) to 5 (> 10,000 TL)
Household-energy cost rates between May and September: 0 (low rate) to 1 (high rate)
Received energy advice and wish to conserve energy: 0 (no) or 1 (yes)
Frequently check electricity meter: 0 (no) or 1 (yes)
Awareness of energy-saving methods: 0 (always) to 3 (never)
Energy Advise–Income, $\chi^2(9) = 11.84$, $p = 0.222$, *Cramer*'s $V = 0.199$
Energy Advise–Energy Savings, $\chi^2(9) = 9.89$, $p = 0.359$, *Cramer*'s $V = 0.182$
Energy Advise–Energy Usage, $\chi^2(3) = 1.37$, $p = 0.713$, *Cramer*'s $V = 0.117$
Energy Advise–Energy Consumption, $\chi^2(3) = 1.35$, $p = 0.717$, *Cramer*'s $V = 0.116$
Energy Savings–Income, $\chi^2(9) = 16.30$, $p = 0.061$, *Cramer*'s $V = 0.233$
Energy Savings–Energy Usage, $\chi^2(3) = 8.44$, $p = 0.038$, *Cramer*'s $V = 0.291$
Energy Savings–Energy Consumption, $\chi^2(3) = 1.13$, $p = 0.769$, *Cramer*'s $V = 0.106$
Income–Energy Usage, $\chi^2(3) = 3.11$, $p = 0.375$, *Cramer*'s $V = 0.176$
Income–Energy Consumption, $\chi^2(3) = 6.09$, $p = 0.107$, *Cramer*'s $V = 0.247$
Energy Consumption–Energy Usage, $\chi^2(1) = 0.64$, $p = 0.424$, *Cramer*'s $V = 0.080$

One occupant claimed an awareness and knowledge of energy conservation due to their expertise in electrical engineering; their family was unable to practice most energy-saving measures in their daily family lives, however, because of the number of people living in their dwelling. This interviewee also expressed their belief that the thermal comfort and health of their grandchildren were more important than their annual energy bill. A common view among the interviewees was that the thermal comfort of their family members was an important factor that led them to want to provide an optimal indoor living environment, which resulted in excessively high energy bills throughout the year. The deeper relationship between household socio-demographic characteristics and associations with survey findings is discussed.

Socio-Demographic Characteristics and Thermal Comfort

The second part of the questionnaire followed up on the questionnaire survey developed for the field study focused on the potential effects of occupant thermal-comfort preferences, while taking household-energy use and the energy performance of the units into account. The survey designed for this portion of the study was intended to map the occupants' real-life energy-use experiences by taking the significance of ingrained habits related to household-energy use and comfort-level preferences into account to help residents manage their home-energy use after their unit is retrofitted (Ozarisoy & Elsharkawy, 2019).

This section includes an analysis of Questions 30, 33 and 34, which concerned the occupants' thermal-comfort preferences (TPVs) and thermal sensation (TSVs)[31] in the winter and summer and were meant to assess their thermal-comfort level and overheating risk. The TSVs were examined using the ASHRAE seven-point thermal preference scale.[32] Figure 3.7(a)–(d) illustrate the determinant factors that were used to analyse the households' thermal comfort in relation to the socio-demographic characteristics of the occupants.

As shown in Figure 3.7(a), the respondents' TPVs[33] were distributed in such a way that 10% of the male respondents and 8% of the females indicated that they

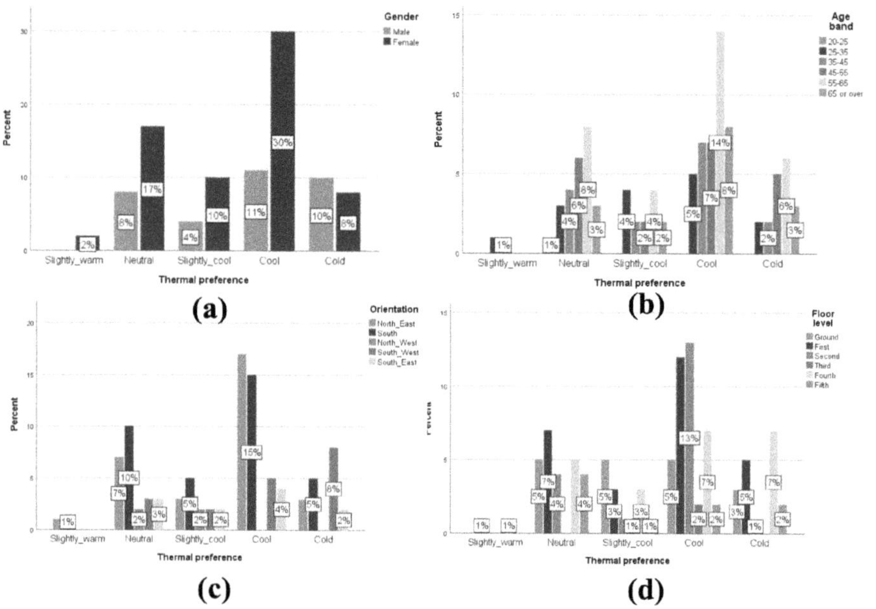

Figure 3.7 (a) Percentage distribution of household thermal-comfort preferences by gender, (b) percentage distribution of household thermal-comfort preferences according to different age bands, (c) percentage distribution of household thermal-comfort preferences by orientation and (d) percentage distribution of household thermal-comfort preferences by floor level.

preferred to feel cold, 11% of the males and 30% of the females preferred to feel cool, 4% of the male and 10% of the female respondents preferred to feel slightly cool, 8% of male and 17% of female respondents preferred to feel neutral and 2% of the female and none of the male respondents preferred to feel slightly warm.

The mean vote was 0.7, which means that on average, the occupants preferred to feel cool in their living rooms in the summer. According to the general survey, 33% of the male participants and 67% of the females who were 25–83 years of age were recruited. It is evident from the results that the female participants' preferences in the TSVs[34] were the dominant factor when assessing the occupants' thermal-comfort levels and understanding the overheating risks in their homes in the summer.

Figure 3.7(b) shows the distribution of the household TPVs who voted on the ASHRAE seven-point thermal-comfort preference scale. It was determined that of the respondents who were 55–65 years of age, 6% preferred to feel cold, 14% preferred to feel cool, 4% preferred to feel slightly cool and 8% preferred to feel neutral; this was because the indoor air temperatures in all the surveyed flats ranged from 25 to 35°C, which did not correlate with the *CIBSE Guide A* benchmarks that assessed temperatures above 25°C as the overheating limit in residential buildings (CIBSE, 2015).

It is worth mentioning here that the households in the upper-floor flats in the south- and southwest-facing RTBs predominantly voted that they preferred to feel cold; notably, the uninsulated roofs and the absence of thermal insulation on external walls, the surfaces of which had major cracks, contributed to thermally uncomfortable indoor environments in the summer.

Of the respondents who were 45–55 years of age, 5% preferred to feel cold, 7% preferred to feel cool, 2% preferred to feel slightly cool and 6% preferred to feel neutral. Of the respondents who were 35–45 years of age, 2% preferred to feel cold, 7% preferred to feel cool, 2% preferred to feel slightly cool and 4% preferred to feel neutral.

Of the respondents who were 25–35 years of age, 2% preferred to feel cold, 5% preferred to feel cool, 3% preferred to feel neutral and 1% preferred to feel slightly warm. Respondents in the upper-floor northeast-facing RTBs commented that their indoor thermal conditions were significantly improved at night by the high-speed prevailing winds that blew through their living rooms; this environmental condition allowed for good-quality natural ventilation (NV) in occupied spaces at night and is why so few of the respondents expressed a preference for feeling slightly warm. There were no TPVs observed in the warm or hot bands of the thermal preference scale, because the questionnaire survey was conducted in the summer (Olesen & Parsons, 2002).

There was a noticeable response related to thermal preferences across the interviewed households in the summer, with a total of 24% of occupants who were 55–65 years of age reporting a preference for feeling slightly cool, cool or cold. There was a noticeable shift in the thermal preferences in the 45–55 age group, however, with a total of 8% of the respondents stating that they preferred to feel neutral or slightly cool.

According to the field-survey observations, a retiree couple, both of whom were 55–65 years of age, were interviewed in their converted balcony space with their windows opened; they commented that they felt thermally comfortable, because they were able to control the level of wind that came into the enclosed balcony area.

Figure 3.7(c) shows the household thermal-comfort preference votes with different RTB orientations to highlight the significant effect of orientation on the energy performance of the total sample. In the northeast-facing RTBs, 3% or the occupants preferred to feel cold, 17% preferred to feel cool, 3% preferred to feel slightly cool and 7% preferred to feel neutral. In the south-facing RTBs, 5% of the respondents preferred to feel cold, 15% preferred to feel cool and 10% preferred to feel neutral; this suggests that the south-facing RTBs were exposed to more hours of sunshine throughout the year, and thermally uncomfortable indoor air temperature fluctuations were observed across these flats due to deficient building envelopes.

In the southwest-facing RTBs, 8% of the respondents preferred to feel cool, 2% preferred to feel slightly cool and 3% preferred to feel neutral; it is worth mentioning that the southwest-facing RTBs experienced direct solar radiation throughout the day, particularly in the late afternoon in the summer.

In Figure 3.7(c), it can be further observed that of the respondents in the southeast-facing RTBs, 2% preferred to feel cold, 2% preferred to feel cool that 3% expressed that they preferred to feel neutral, 2% preferred to feel slightly cool. In the northwest-facing RTBs, 2% of the respondents preferred to feel slightly cool and 2% preferred to feel neutral. The orientation analysis revealed that the occupants' TPVs were correlated with their energy-consumption patterns; this finding underscores the fact that the surveyed and measured flats showed strong indications of overheating risk in the summer which are discussed in detail.

Figure 3.7(d) shows household TPVs according to floor level. Of the interviewees who lived on the ground floor, 3% preferred to feel cold, 5% preferred to feel cool, 5% preferred to feel slightly cool and 5% preferred to feel neutral. Of the respondents living in the first-floor flats, 5% preferred to feel cold, 12% preferred to feel cool, 3% preferred to feel slightly cool and 7% preferred to feel neutral.

Of the residents in the second-floor flats, 1% preferred to feel cold, 13% preferred to feel cool, 1% preferred to feel slightly cool and 4% preferred to feel neutral. Of the occupants in the third-floor flats, 2% of the respondents preferred to feel cool and 1% preferred slightly cool. Notably, only 3% of the respondents lived in the third-floor flats, which was correlated with the time of the day the door-to-door survey was conducted and the high rejection rates of the third-floor households.

Of the respondents living in the fourth-floor flats, 7% preferred to feel cold, 7% preferred to feel cool, 1% preferred to feel slightly cool, 5% preferred to feel neutral and 1% preferred to feel slightly warm. Finally, of the occupants in the fifth-floor flats, 2% preferred to feel cold, 1% preferred to feel slightly cool and 4% preferred to feel neutral.

The findings have an impact on household thermal expectations and lead to a vulnerability that is brought about by needing to adapt to changes in the climate through a combination of behavioural, physiological and psychological mechanisms which are discussed in Chapter 5.

Discussions

Implementation of the EPCs at the household level and building level is the main priority of the EU member states wishing to overcome high household energy consumption related to space conditioning. To address the EEG and implement the EPBD mandates, the stakeholders and government initiatives will play a decisive role in successful energy transitions, albeit one that has thus far not been fully realised (Dell'Anna, 2020). For the adoption of energy-conscious retrofitting technologies to grow from this void, uptake by an evidence-based STS approach will be key (Bolwig et al., 2020). This explanatory case study contributes to a gap in the literature and explores relationships between household socio-demographic characteristics and their degree of thermal discomfort.

Specifically, the feed-forward interviews focused on the households' underlying socio-demographic characteristics and the impact thereof on home-energy performance, and on occupant interactions with local conditions, such as their thermal-comfort preferences. The findings demonstrate that there is an urgent need to implement the EPC schemes and to develop current design methods in energy efficiency (Ozarisoy, 2022). Therefore, these factors should not be limited to only the uptake retrofitting delivery of local regions in the Eastern Mediterranean climate; they should also consider nationwide policy measures that take the socio-cultural factors of each EU member state into account (Levi, 2021; Pappalarado & Reverdy, 2020). The following discussion is structured according to the RQ that guides the findings obtained through feed-forward interviews: (RQ-1) household socio-demographic characteristics and home-energy performance factors to develop nationwide energy policies related to household-energy use and the residents' thermal comfort.

Impact of Socio-Demographic Characteristics on Energy Performance

The first set of questions was intended to explore a number of household socio-demographic characteristics that affect occupant thermal comfort and energy use; the demographic information was presented to give a general view of the character of the respondents from whom the research data were generated.

It was determined that 84% of the sample owned their property and 16% of the respondents were rental tenants. A total of 73% of the households had lived in their flats for more than ten years; the respondents' length of residency correlates with their household age-group distribution, and a majority of households who owned their properties were older than 55 years of age.

It was also important to consider the number of household members living in these flats when analysing energy bills and calculating the amount of heat gain from household members to properly understand and identify the occupants' energy-consumption patterns in the building modelling simulation phase of this study: it was determined that 30% of the flats were occupied by four or five people, then this high-density occupancy profile was followed by three people (30%) and two people (28%), as shown in Figure 3.8(a); this result demonstrated that a majority of the households were multi-family homes, which may help to explain the high rate of energy consumption in the interviewed flats, as shown in Figure 3.8(b).

In addition, the households were asked about their awareness related to energy savings. Even though 20% of the respondents reported that they always took energy-saving methods into consideration, 50% of the respondents admitted that they infrequently thought of energy-saving methods; notably, 15% of respondents never took energy-saving methods into consideration. It can thus be concluded that the degree of awareness related to conserving energy was not only due to education level, but also income level; these households were mostly rental tenants and Turkish migrant workers with young children who needed to take all types of savings into consideration.

The present study showed that age bands were significantly related to health conditions, and this relationship was strong ($\chi^2 = 73.739$, $p < 0.001$, *Cramer*'s $V = 0.496$). Younger age appeared to report better health conditions (good or very good) than older age. Household occupation was significantly related to health conditions, and the relationship was moderate ($\chi^2 = 33.071$, $p < 0.001$, *Cramer*'s $V = 0.342$), which proved the fact that the older age group consumed more energy than the younger households, as shown in Figure 3.8(c) and (d).[35] This underscores the crucial role that age plays when the occupancy patterns and thermal-comfort preferences are taken into account, particularly in the summer.[36]

Figure 3.8(c) and (d) illustrate the actual household energy consumption gathered from annual energy bills. These data cover the winter of 2014–2015 (i.e., December through February) and the summer of 2015 (i.e., June through August). Of the surveyed households, the 17% that were 55–65 years of age consumed 1,250–2,000 kWh, and 7% of the respondents in this age band consumed 750–1,250 kWh in the winter of 2015. A similar energy-consumption pattern was observed in the same age group in the summer of 2015, when 14% consumed 1,250–2,000 kWh, 8% consumed 750–1,250 kWh and 5% consumed 500–750 kWh. A noticeable increase was observed in the 65-and-older age band at this same time: 2% consumed 3,500–4,000 kWh, and 1% consumed more than 4,000 kWh in the summer of 2015.

The findings demonstrate that there is a relationship between occupant age and energy use. It can be deduced from these data that even though age is a determinant factor to quantify home-energy performance, the true cause for high energy consumption is the local environmental conditions and the absence of insulation material on the external walls, which worsened high solar radiation on building envelopes, particularly on the upper-floor flats which are illustrated in Chapter 6. Research has shown that economic status was significantly related to educational level ($\chi^2 = 48.808$, $p < 0.001$, *Cramer*'s $V = 0.416$), which influence households' energy use. Figure 3.8(e) and (f) illustrate household-energy use and consider the respondents' income level in the winter and in the summer.

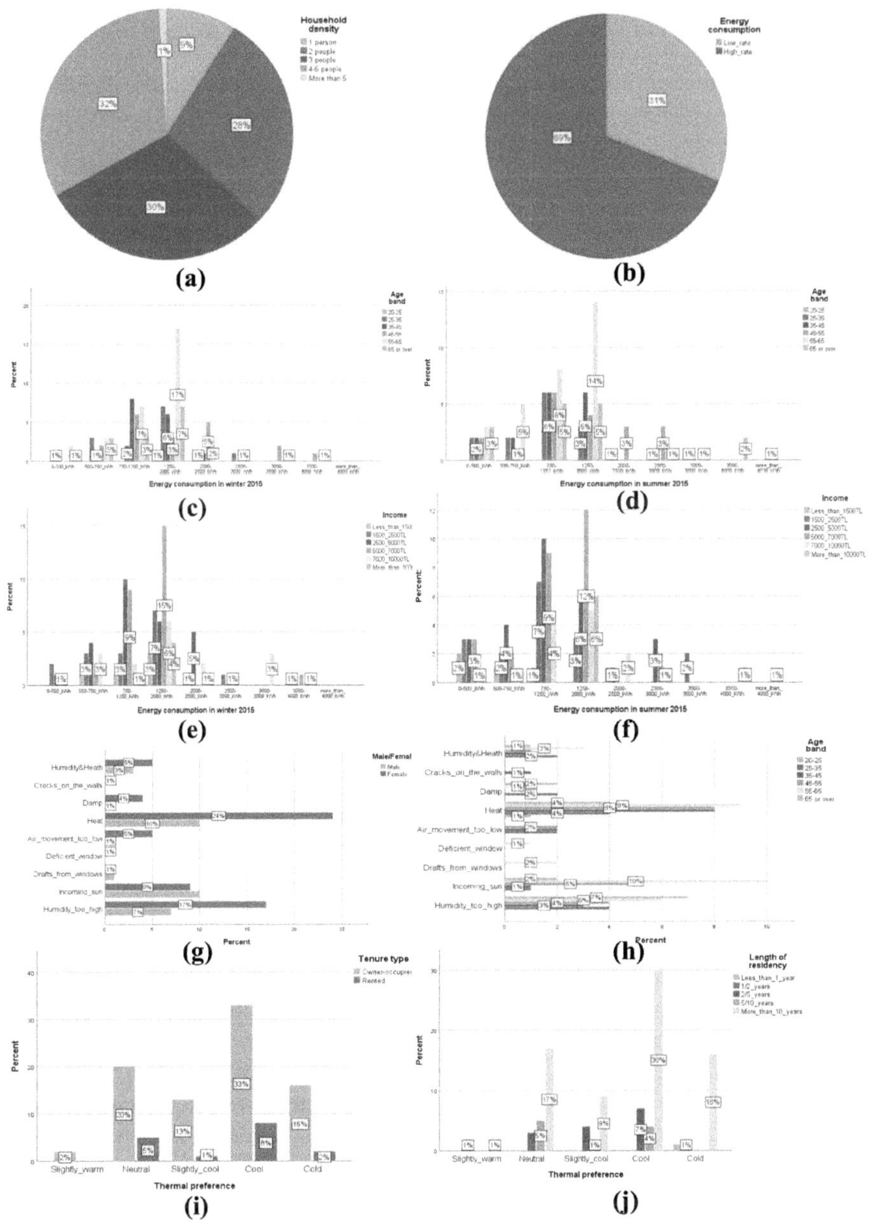

Figure 3.8 (a) Percentage distribution of number of family members in surveyed flats; (b) percentage distribution of household energy-consumption rates; percentage distribution of energy consumption by age group in the (c) winter of 2015 and (d) summer of 2015; percentage distribution of energy consumption by age-group classification in (e) winter of 2015 and (f) summer of 2015; percentage

Figure 3.8 (Continued)

distribution of reasons for thermal discomfort by (g) gender and (h) age band; percentage distribution of thermal preference by (i) tenure type and (j) length of residency. To conduct the correlation analysis accurately, the dataset was recoded and the cooling energy consumption in summer of 2015 was grouped in five values as follows (1 = 0–500 kWh, 1 = 500–750 kWh, 2 = 750–1,250 kWh, 3 = 1,250–2,000 kWh, 4 = more than 2,000 kWh). In the present study, the bar charts show the actual distribution of each households' energy use gathered from the Electricity Authority of Northern Cyprus. However, the households' energy bills were grouped to perform conceptual-level analysis. To undertake the correlation analysis accurately, the reasons for thermal discomfort variable were grouped in four values as follows (0 = Humidity related, 1 = Incoming sun, 2 = Other reasons, 3 = Heat). However, in this present study, the actual data gathered through a questionnaire survey was distributed to avoid research bias while interpreting the findings related to the identification of 'neutral' adaptive thermal comfort in Chapter 6. To undertake the correlation analysis accurately, the thermal preference variable was grouped in four values as follows (0 = Cold, 1 = Cool, 2 = Slightly cool, 3 = Neutral/slightly warm). However, the households' TSVs reported on a Likert scale question were set out to assess occupants' thermal comfort in the questionnaire survey pro forma.

Figure 3.8(e) illustrates household-energy use in the winter of 2015, when 15% of the 5,000–7,000 TL income group consumed 1,250–2,000 kWh, and 9% consumed 750–1,250 kWh. A similar trend was shown in the summer, when 12% consumed 1,250–2,000 kWh and 9% consumed 750–1,250 kWh. Research has shown that household occupations were also significantly associated with age with a moderate–strong relationship ($\chi^2 = 44.810$, $p < 0.001$, *Cramer*'s $V = 0.399$). Households with high incomes consumed more energy than middle-income or economically inactive households.

The survey revealed that a total of 59% of the households consumed 750–1,250 kWh and 1,250–2,000 kWh for cooling during the summer of 2016, and a total of 67% of the households consumed 750–1,250 and 1,250–2,000 kWh for heating during the winter of 2016. This may be an indicator that elderly households in this research consider it more important to heat their homes in the winter than to cool them in the summer.

When it was determined that a majority of household incomes were well above the national average, this variable was removed from the survey findings. A majority of the respondents' energy expenditures were high, because they were economically active and able to pay for optimal thermal comfort; this is primarily due to the cultural habits of the respondents and their economic status, which they used as a means of obtaining optimum thermal comfort. The present study revealed the significant effect that occupancy patterns and household income have on energy use, but the respondents' age, occupation and household size still determined a significant proportion of the energy use in these interviewed flats.

Effect of Socio-Demographic Characteristics on Thermal Comfort

The interviewed households were questioned about their reasons for thermal discomfort to learn the factors that influenced their TPVs during the questionnaire period. This is an important research method intended to examine the predicted people's discomfort and PMV levels and compare the results to the EN 15251 benchmarking criteria. These data enabled the tabulation of the different TSVs of occupants with the *on-site* environmental monitoring and in situ measurements of each occupied space.

Notably, this data triangulation method provided a more reliable dataset to assess the respondents' thermal comfort and the overheating risk of the occupied rooms, which can be incorporated into the building modelling simulation phase of the study in Chapter 6. To identify any relationship between the occupants' decisions related to thermal-comfort preferences, their reasons for thermal discomfort, taking their gender and age-band variations into account, are illustrated in Figure 3.8(g) and (h).

Figure 3.8(g) shows that 10% of the male respondents and 24% of the females reported that the heat was the main issue related to their thermal comfort in the summer. A total of 7% of the male occupants and 17% of the females reported that humidity was too high in the night-time. Notably, 10% of male respondents and 9% of females stated that the incoming sunlight had a direct impact on their relative degree of thermal discomfort; this is because RTB orientation was shown to be the most important factor related to the level of occupant thermal discomfort. It is important to highlight that the different RTB orientations had a significant impact on the occupants' TPVs; these data were correlated with energy consumption, especially during the peak cooling month of August, due to the high solar absorptivity of the thermally vulnerable RTB building envelopes.

Figure 3.8(h) shows that 9% of respondents who were 55–65 years of age reported that heat accumulation led to increased indoor air temperatures, and 10% reported that incoming sunlight (i.e., high solar radiation) was the main determinant factor and source of thermal discomfort; notably, 7% of respondents who were 65 years of age and older reported that the humidity was too high at night. One of the subject participants complained that excessive heat and high humidity led to thermally uncomfortable conditions for the household; they also indicated that they typically used their northwest-facing bedroom early in the morning in the summer, because this space provided a much cooler indoor environment and more effective NV to cool the occupied spaces in their home.

Notably, the health of 29% of the male respondents and 57% of the females were found to be between mediocre and very good, while 4% of the males and 10% of the females reported that their health was poor or very poor. The occupants' health conditions may correlate with their decisions related to their TPVs, and it appears that the age and gender of the households also correlated with their thermal comfort. Because 48% of the households were 55–65 or 65 years of age and older, age bands were significantly related to health conditions, and this relationship was strong ($\chi^2 = 73.739$, $p < 0.001$, *Cramer*'s $V = 0.496$). Younger age appeared to report better health conditions (good or very good) than older age. Household occupation was significantly related to health conditions, and the relationship was moderate ($\chi^2 = 33.071$, $p < 0.001$, *Cramer*'s $V = 0.342$). A greater proportion of participants with very good health conditions worked outside the home than those with mediocre health conditions, whereas none of the participants who retired had very good health conditions.

According to Figure 3.8(i), which illustrates the household thermal-comfort preferences and tenure types, 16% of the owner-occupiers and 2% of the renters preferred to feel cold, 33% of the owner-occupiers and 8% of the renters preferred to feel cool, 13% of the owner-occupiers and 1% of the renters preferred to feel slightly cool, 20% of the owner-occupiers and 5% of the renters preferred to feel neutral and 2% of the owner-occupiers preferred to feel slightly warm.

Notably, 84% of the flats were owner occupied, and 16% were rented. According to Figure 3.8(j), 16% of the occupants who had lived in their units for more than ten years preferred to feel cold, 30% preferred to feel cool, 9% preferred to feel slightly cool and 17% preferred to feel neutral. These results demonstrate a noticeable thermal adaptation to the built environment; this is an important indicator to investigate neutral adaptive thermal comfort in Chapter 6 in 'Thermal-Comfort Assessment Indicators' section. Because a majority of the respondents had lived in their units for more than ten years, it was assumed that they could adapt to the environment and climate in the occupied spaces.

It should be noted that 33% of the male respondents and 67% of the females were 25–84 years of age, age band and tenancy status were significantly and strongly related to each other ($\chi^2 = 24.433$, $p < 0.001$, *Cramer*'s $V = 0.494$). Most participants who rented were 45 years old and younger. Age band and length of residency were also correlated ($\chi^2 = 67.755$, $p < 0.001$, *Cramer*'s $V = 0.582$). It appeared that younger participants had shorter lengths of residency. It should be noted that a strong relationship was found between tenancy status and length of residency ($\chi^2 = 35.413$, $p < 0.001$, *Cramer*'s $V = 0.595$). The survey findings also revealed that four-fifths of the sample owned their property (84%), and renters comprised 16% of the overall tenancy status. Concerning the length of residency, 1% of the households had lived in their current property for less than 12 months, 2% had lived there for 1–2 years, 14% had lived there for 2–5 years and 10% had lived there for 5–10 years. The results show an increasing trend in the number of households having lived there for longer periods, and households living in their current properties for more than ten years made up 73% of all respondents. It was found that 37% of the respondents worked full time, 12% worked part time, 16% were self-employed, 14% were unemployed and 20% were retired pensioners. These results indicate that 63% of the respondents in the sample were economically active. These data provide background information with the households' income level and their ability to pay high energy bills while assessing building-energy performance of the RTBs in Chapter 7. Additionally, in the questionnaire survey, the households were asked if their electricity bills were paid at the lower rate or higher rate in order to understand the degree of energy consumption of that household. Sixty-nine per cent of respondents reported that they paid a higher rate while 31% paid a lower rate. These data indicate that the majority of households had high energy consumption. The survey revealed relationships between household size, income and the age of the respondents and energy consumption in the summer. These parameters also had a significant impact on occupant thermal-comfort sensations which are presented in detail in Chapter 6 in 'Household Energy Bills' section.

Conclusion

This chapter drew conclusions about the determinants of energy consumption to analyse the effects of the occupants' real-life energy-use experiences. This empirical, mixed-method study added to the value of the STS conceptual framework by examining the real-life energy-use experiences of different households to better understand their thermal preferences and diagnose issues that may arise from the thermal properties of a given building. This study adopted the STS design approach in two stages, each of which considered current improvements to the design methods for EPC implementation according to the findings of feed-forward interviews.

An empirical analysis of the household socio-demographic characteristics and a modified Pearson's correlation test were applied in the first stage of the present study to determine the association between these variables, and the ANOVA assessment criteria were applied in the second stage to validate the questionnaire survey findings related to household socio-demographic characteristics to develop an evidence-based STS design approach for energy use.

The relationship between variables was examined by cross-tabulation using the chi-square test. It was found that age bands were significantly related to health conditions, and this relationship was strong ($\chi^2 = 73.739$, $p < 0.001$, *Cramer*'s $V = 0.496$). Younger age appeared to report better health conditions (good or very good) than older age. Household occupation was significantly related to health conditions, and the relationship was moderate ($\chi^2 = 33.071$, $p < 0.001$, *Cramer*'s $V = 0.342$). Age band and tenancy status were significantly and strongly related to each other ($\chi^2 = 24.433$, $p < 0.001$, *Cramer*'s $V = 0.494$). Most participants who rented were 45 years old and younger. Age band and length of residency were also correlated ($\chi^2 = 67.755$, $p < 0.001$, *Cramer*'s $V = 0.582$). The present study also revealed a broad diversity of applicable methods for occupants in the Eastern Mediterranean climate to develop optimum thermal conditions in the summer. It was determined that a total of 48% of the households were 55–65 or 65 years of age and older; for this reason, it is important to consider the impact of age on thermal comfort in these flats. At the time of the survey, the occupants' socio-demographic factors were shown to have an impact on their thermal-comfort preferences, as presented in Chapter 5.

Notes

1 The percentage of missing data has implications for researchers in terms of how the data must be treated to resolve potential biased estimates in the analysis. Complete case analysis is only reliable when the percentage of incomplete values in the data matrix is less than 5%. Beyond the 5% threshold, the data should be treated in some manner (e.g., multiple imputation or maximum-likelihood replacement).

2 The relationship between orientation and floor level was examined by cross-tabulation, comparing block number (over 30 categories considered as a continuous variable) by orientation and by floor level was examined by two separate one-way ANOVAs in the statistical analysis. In order to provide the consistency, the results were presented in crosstab and ANOVA into one table.

3 Notably, the pattern of missing data is a more important factor than the actual amount of missing data. Missing values that are randomly scattered throughout the data matrix (i.e., data is missing completely at random; MCAR) are a less serious problem than are missing values that are not random. If the missing values on a variable are not random but are associated with other variables in the data, this is referred to as missing at random (MAR) and can be alleviated with imputation methods. If the missing values on a variable are associated with the variable itself (i.e., missing not at random; MNAR), this has serious implications for inference regardless of imputation procedures.
4 In the present study, this data was missing completely at random (MCAR). After preparing the data for analysis, it was observed that out of 100 recorded cases, 98 cases contained missing data (98.0%) and out of 53 variables, 2 variables contained missing data (2.8%), which amounted to a total of 0.04% missing information in the dataset. To assess whether the pattern of missing values was missing completely at random (MCAR), Little's MCAR test was conducted (Little, 1988). The null hypothesis of Little's MCAR test is that the pattern of the data is MCAR and follows a $\chi 2$ distribution. Using an expectation–maximisation algorithm, the MCAR test estimates the univariate means and correlations for each of the variables. The results revealed that the pattern of missing values in the data was MCAR, $\chi 2$ (104) = 121.645, $p = 0.114$. The missingness test was conducted and the dataset was recoded to run the statistical analysis in response to the research questions of the present study.
5 Because the proportion of total missing data is less than 5% and this data is MCAR, in the present study, final sample size may still be affected by listwise or pairwise deletion when the analysis is run. Listwise deletion removes a case if a case has any missing values for any of the variables used in an analysis. This is also known as complete case analysis. Pairwise deletion removes a case only if there are missing values for each pair of variables in an analysis. Pairwise deletion better maximises all of the data available in the analysis and is preferred over listwise deletion for increasing the statistical power of the present study.
6 When this was divided according to gender, background information was provided while the degree of thermal discomfort was assessed.
7 Age band was set out as categorical variable to develop conceptual-level analysis.
8 The missing value assessment of the data allows the researcher flexibility when addressing the missing data. First, the proportion of missing data in the sample is less than 5%. Second, the pattern of missing data is MCAR. Based upon these two findings, it should be fine using either pairwise or listwise deletion methods. Listwise deletion and pairwise deletion are unbiased techniques when data is MCAR; however, pairwise deletion increases power.
9 The national average unemployment rate in March 2021 was 11%. *Source*: The State Planning Organisation's Report on *the COVID-19 and its impact on the industry* in 2021.
10 The Turkish Lira (TL) is the currency of Turkey and the self-declared republic of Northern Cyprus. As of April 2021, 1 TLas. equivalent to 11.21 GBPand the. minimum wage in NC was a 4,400 TL monthly stipend.
11 Descriptive statistics were used throughout to quantify and describe the basic characteristics of a dataset. As such, descriptive statistics serve as a starting point for data analysis, allowing researchers to organise, simplify and summarise data. Descriptive analysis was aimed to consider the distribution of the data, as distribution impacts statistical analysis and was considered when deciding which measures were the most appropriate for the analysis.
12 Non-parametric tests were used when the data being analysed were from the nominal or ordinal scale of measurement or when data collected at the interval or ratio level violate assumptions of normality.
13 The chi-square (χ^2) is a non-parametric statistical test used for data analysis when one or more variables are nominal or categorical in nature.

14 *Cramer*'s *V* is a way of calculating correlation in tables which have more than 2×2 rows and columns. It is used as post-test to determine strengths of association after chi-square has determined significance. In statistics, *Cramer*'s *V* (sometimes referred to as Cramer's phi and denoted as φc) is a measure of association between two nominal variables, giving a value between 0 and +1 (inclusive).

15 Analysis of variance (ANOVA) is a collection of inferential statistical tests belonging to the general linear model family that examine whether two or more levels (e.g., conditions) of a categorical independent variable have an influence on a dependent variable. It should be noted that it is possible to utilise ANOVA in quasi-experimental and some correlational designs where random assignment of participants to conditions is too costly or not possible (e.g., gender). Violation of these assumptions can affect the interpretation of the results from these tests; under these conditions non-parametric tests might better serve the appropriate statistical analysis.

16 Eta squared ($\eta 2$) is a common measure of effect size used in ANOVAs. This statistic represents the proportion of the variance in the dependent variable.

17 Mean (*M*) and Standard Deviation (*SD*) were retained as integer because this is block number.

18 The mean is one of the most common statistical measures used to describe a sample population. Commonly referred to as the 'average,' the mean is calculated by finding the sum of all points in a dataset and dividing it by the total number of observations.

19 Standard deviation and variance are types of statistical properties that measure dispersion around a central tendency, most commonly arithmetic mean. They are descriptive statistics that measure variability around a mean for continuous data. In this chosen statistical analysis, it seems to be that using the *SD* was appropriate because the type of measures for the block number variable could be presented within this cross-tabulation analysis.

20 The *F* value in one-way ANOVA is a tool to help answering the research question.

21 The *p* value is the probability of getting a result at least as extreme as the one that was actually observed.

22 RTB block number variable represents number of households which were recruited from each RTB in the social-housing estate. To analyse the questionnaire results, the RTB block number was chosen to guide the method of design which was established while assessing occupants' thermal sensation votes (TSVs) in Chapter 5 to avoid research bias and identify the 'neutral' adaptive thermal comfort thresholds thoroughly in this Eastern Mediterranean climate. It can be deduced that the chosen RTB block number variable provides an indicative analysis selection criteria in conjunction with both *on-site* monitored and in situ recorded environmental parameters investigated with the questionnaire survey findings.

23 The multiple-sample chi-square, sometimes referred to as a contingency analysis or a two-dimensional chi-square, is used when a researcher wishes to test the relationship between the frequencies of two or more nominal variables to determine if they are independent from or dependent on one another. With multiple samples, expected frequencies are calculated through the creation of a contingency table of observed frequencies and each cell in the table generates its own expected frequency.

24 Cramer's statistic facilitates the interpretation of nominal-variable association estimates, given this index ranges from 0 to +1. A higher Cramer value indicates a stronger association. Hence, Cramer value estimates are often reported in addition to χ^2 estimates, as an effect size index.

25 The chi-squared (χ^2) test for independence provides a statistical test of association between two categorical (nominal) variables from a single population. The test is used to determine whether the association between two variables is significant, with the null hypothesis being that the two variables are not dependent on one another.

26 To measure the association between categorical variables that include more than two levels, Cramer recommended the following statistic, commonly referred to as *Cramer*'s

V or Cramer's phi: ΦC = square root of ($\chi 2/N(L-1)$). A modification of the phi coefficient, *Cramer*'s *V*, introduces an adjustment to the denominator, where *L* is the smaller value of either the number of columns or the number of rows. Like the phi coefficient, *Cramer*'s *V* statistic ranges from 0 to 1, with higher values indicating larger strengths of associations or effect sizes.

27 The Cyprus Electricity Authority categorises energy consumption on weekdays in the winter period (1 November through 31 May) as follows: (i) non-peak hours between 22:00 and 07:00t 0.658 TL/kWh. (ii) worki. ng hours between 07:00 and 17:00 at 0.9873 TL/kWh. (iii) peak . hours between 17:00 and 22:00t 1.2908 TL/kWh.

Tariffs a. re implemented on weekdays in the summer period (1 June through 31 October) as follows: (i) non-peak hours 23:00–09:00t 0.6508 TL/kWh. (ii) workin. g hours 18:00–23:00t 0.9873 TL/kWh. nd (iii) pe. ak hours 09:00–18:00t 1.2908 TL/kWh.

28 The ele. ctricity tariff in the winter and in the summer is classified into three categories on weekdays and during holiday periods (including national, religion and bank holidays): (i) non-peak hours 02:00–09:00t 0.6308 TL/kWh. (ii) standa. rd hours 09:00–14:00nd 18:00–02:00. t 0.9873 TL/kWh. (iii) peak . hours 14:00–18:00t 1.2708 TL/kWh. These energ. y tariffs' stipend to average national income of Northern Cyprus was reviewed on 31 March 2021. *Note*: A stipend is offered to cover energy costs in relation to the average national income in Northern Cyprus.

29 χ^2 is derived from Pearson's chi-squared test

30 The *p* value for the significance of *V* is the same one that is calculated using the Pearson's chi-squared test.

31 The households' both TPVs and TSVs were assessed by using the Likert scale conventional method of design. The Likert scale was chosen as a method for measuring attitudes. It is a bipolar approach to scaling that measures responses to statements along a positive-to-negative dimension.

32 Likert and Likert-type scales are scored by assigning numeric values to the response categories, starting with 1 at one end of the scale and assigning consecutively higher numbers to the categories toward the other end of the scale.

33 Depending on how the Likert scale is treated (as either an ordinal or interval measure), the data produced by Likert scales can be analysed with non-parametric or parametric statistics. When the data are considered ordinal, they can be described using frequencies, median, mode and range, and analysed using non-parametric tests such as the chi-square.

34 Rank order data are analysed using non-parametric statistics in Chapter 5. Rank order data can be summarised and described using mean, median, standard deviation, variance and frequency. The significance of rank order data can be tested using a series of non-parametric tests of variance including chi-square.

35 To explore relationships between households' socio-demographic characteristics and their energy use, the households' energy bills were obtained and the data was tabulated to perform conceptual-level analysis while assessing their degree of thermal discomfort in summer.

36 To conduct the correlation analysis accurately, the dataset was recoded and the heating energy consumption in winter of 2015 was grouped in four values as follows (1 = 0–750 kWh, 2 = 750–1,250 kWh, 3 = 1,250–2,000 kWh, 4 = more than 2,000 kWh).

References

Bolwig, S., Bolkesjø, T. F., Klitkou, A., Lund, P. D., Bergaentzlé, C., Borch, K., … Skytte, K. (2020). Climate-friendly but socially rejected energy-transition pathways: The integration of techno-economic and socio-technical approaches in the Nordic-Baltic region. *Energy Research and Social Science*, *67*, 101559. https://doi.org/10.1016/j.erss.2020.101559

CIBSE. (2015). *CIBSE TM36: Climate change and the indoor environment: Impacts and adaptation*. London: CIBSE.

Dell'Anna, F. (2020). Green jobs and energy efficiency as strategies for economic growth and the reduction of environmental impacts. *Energy Policy*, *149*, 112031. https://doi.org/10.1016/j.enpol.2020.112031

Fincham, J. E. (2008). Response rates and responsiveness for surveys, standards, and the journal. *American Journal of Pharmaceutical Education*, *72*(2), 1–3.

Indraganti, M., & Rao, K. D. (2010). Effect of age, gender, economic group and tenure on thermal comfort: A field study in residential buildings in hot and dry climate with seasonal variations. *Energy and Buildings*, *42*(3), 273–281. https://doi.org/10.1016/j.enbuild.2009.09.003

Levi, S. (2021). Why hate carbon taxes? Machine learning evidence on the roles of personal responsibility, trust, revenue recycling, and other factors across 23 European countries. *Energy Research & Social Science*, *73*, 101883. https://doi.org/10.1016/j.erss.2020.101883

Little, R. J. A. (1988). A test of missing completely at random for multivariate data with missing values. *Journal of the American Statistical Association*, (Vol. 83, 1198–1202).

Olesen, B. W., & Parsons, K. C. (2002). Introduction to thermal comfort standards and to the proposed new version of EN ISO 7730. In *Energy and buildings* (Vol. 34, pp. 537–548). https://doi.org/10.1016/S0378-7788(02)00004-X

Ozarisoy, B. (2022). Energy effectiveness of passive cooling design strategies to reduce the impact of long-term heatwaves on occupants' thermal comfort in Europe: Climate change and mitigation. *Journal of Cleaner Production*, *330*, 129675.https://doi.org/10.1016/j.jclepro.2021.129675

Ozarisoy, B., & Altan, H. (2017a). Energy performance development of non-regulated retrofit mass housing estates in Northern Cyprus. *Design Journal*, *20*(Suppl 1), S1765–S1781. https://doi.org/10.1080/14606925.2017.1352697

Ozarisoy, B., & Altan, H. (2017b). Adoption of energy design strategies for retrofitting mass housing estates in Northern Cyprus. *Sustainability (Switzerland)*, *9*(8), 1477. https://doi.org/10.3390/su9081477

Ozarisoy, B., & Altan, H. (2018). Low-energy design strategies for retrofitting existing residential buildings in Cyprus. *Proceedings of the Institution of Civil Engineers: Engineering Sustainability*, *172*(5), 241–255. https://doi.org/10.1680/jensu.17.00061

Ozarisoy, B., & Elsharkawy, H. (2019). Assessing overheating risk and thermal comfort in state-of-the-art prototype houses that combat exacerbated climate change in UK. *Energy and Buildings*, *187*, 201–217. https://doi.org/10.1016/j.enbuild.2019.01.030

Pappalardo, M., & Reverdy, T. (2020). Explaining the performance gap in a French energy efficient building: Persistent misalignment between building design, space occupancy and operation practices. *Energy Research & Social Science*, *70*, 101809. https://doi.org/10.1016/j.erss.2020.101809

4 Home Energy Performance Assessment

Introduction

The aims of this chapter are to statistically determine occupant behavioural patterns associated with heating- and cooling-energy consumption and to identify household socio-demographic characteristics that contribute to the development of energy-user profiles. The collated data are reported, along with an analysis and interpretation thereof. The findings are presented in sequential order based on the order in which the questions were asked to the households, as presented in Chapter 2. This is followed by statistical testing using cross-tabulation within a chi-square test to analyse the relationships of the selected questions for the development of an evidence-based STS conceptual framework for policymakers.

Home-Energy System Information and Habitual Adaptive Behaviour

This section comprises the analyses of Questions 10–11, 14 and 15 concerning the types of heating- and cooling-control systems used in the surveyed flats. It is important to consider the households' heating and cooling appliances to understand the correlation of these with energy consumption.

Heating Systems

This section seeks to learn the types of main and secondary heating systems of the households to ascertain the level of importance they attached to energy consumption. Figure 4.1(a) illustrates the types of heating systems used in the flats in the winter.[1]

In Figure 4.1(a), 34% of the households reported that they used gas heaters as their primary heating system, 8% used wall-mounted air conditioning (A/C) systems as their primary heating system and 14% used both a gas heater and a wall-mounted A/C system as their two main heating systems. At the same time, 23% of the households reported a portable halogen heater (i.e., a home appliance) as their primary heating system, and 2% reported having both a halogen heater and a wall-mounted A/C system as their two main heating systems. The types of heating systems reported in the questionnaires indicated considerable variation in the

DOI: 10.4324/9781003393092-5

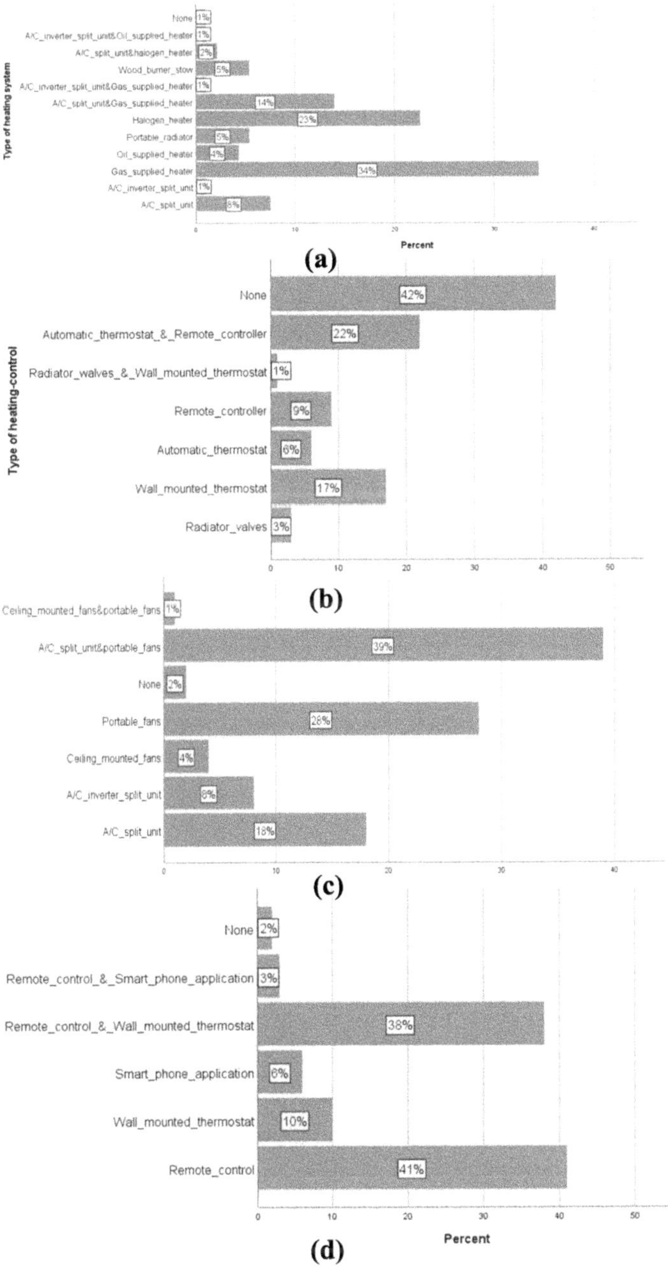

Figure 4.1 (a) Percentage distribution of types of heating systems used in winter, (b) percentage distribution of types of heating control systems used in winter, (c) percentage distribution of types of cooling systems used in summer and (d) percentage distribution of types of cooling control systems used in summer.

information provided by the interviewees. In fact, a whole-gas radiator system with a kombi had never been installed in these flats as the main heating system.

A likely possibility for this variation is that some of the surveyed households believed that using either a halogen heater or a wall-mounted A/C system for heating would be too costly and thus preferred to use their electricity system for heating mainly their living rooms. As for the secondary heating system, the majority of households (70%) reported not having a secondary heating system, 4% used an oil heater, 5% used a portable radiator and 5% of the households had wood-burning stoves as secondary heating systems. Together, these results provide important insights into the importance of the types of heating systems used to relate this to the households' annual energy consumption which are presented in Chapter 6.

One interviewee stated that they preferred to use a wall-mounted A/C system rather than a gas heater because they suffered from asthma. Another interviewee commented that they mostly had to use their portable halogen heater system to protect household members from the cold in the winter due to the absence of insulation material on the external walls. Notably, these surveyed households mainly lived in the upper-floor flats. One household member stated that a gas cylinder and a portable halogen heater were used concurrently to provide a much warmer living environment in their living room on the upper-floor level in the RTB. These findings demonstrate and strongly indicate that these units were too cold in the winter. Also, this study has addressed the overheating risk in the summer with the roofs in the upper-floor flats (Ozarisoy & Altan, 2017a).

One interviewee stated that they preferred to use either a portable radiator or a wall-mounted A/C system as their heating source for 1–2 h to provide a much warmer indoor environment at night. Just over two-thirds of the participants (70%) indicated that they felt cold in their bedrooms at night due to the heat losses from single-glazed windows and the building's orientation, while a minority (5%) mentioned that they felt slightly warmer in the daytime in their bedrooms, and they preferred to use a bedroom as a snug room or reading room in the winter to reduce the demand on the domestic heating appliances at home.

Figure 4.1(a) shows that 5% of the households had wood-burning stoves as a secondary heating system; notably, all of these were used in the top-floor flats. One participant in an upper-floor flat stated that their gas-cylinder heating system was not efficient enough to keep the indoor air temperature of their occupied spaces thermally comfortable for the members of the household in January, the coldest month of winter. Thus, they preferred to use their wood-burning stove as the main heating system in their living room. The interviewee also reported that they did not close all the internal doors because keeping them open would allow warm air to thoroughly penetrate all the indoor spaces in the flat. The interviewee continued by commenting that they have managed to reduce the cost of their energy consumption in the winter; they were concerned, however, about the high levels of CO_2 accumulation that threatened their children's health and well-being when the wood-burning stove was in use in the winter.

Heating Control Systems

The household types of heating control systems used in the winter are examined in this section. With regard to understanding the significance of occupancy patterns in energy use, it is important to map the most commonly used heating control systems, as illustrated in Figure 4.1(b).[2]

Figure 4.1(b) shows the percentage distribution of the type of heating control systems used to regulate the temperature in the flats to create a thermally comfortable indoor air environment in the winter. When the participants were asked how they regulated the indoor air temperature of their living environment, 33% stated they only had one type of heating control system in their flats: 17% had a wall-mounted thermostat, 9% had a remote control, 6% had an automatic thermostat and 3% had radiator valves. Apart from these respondents, 22% of the surveyed households had both an automatic thermostat and a remote control, and 1% had radiator valves and a wall-mounted thermostat. Notably, 42% of the participants reported that they had not previously used any type of heating control system. In response to Question 11, most of the surveyed households indicated that they did not use any type of heating control system more often than another because they mostly used a gas cylinder for heating purposes. Other responses to this question included that the respondents mostly preferred to set up their heating systems between 25 and 27°C to keep the indoor air warm in the winter. However, one interviewee reported that they still felt cold when the automatic wall thermostat in their wall-mounted A/C system was set to 25°C due to the absence of insulation material on the external walls. This can result in using another domestic appliance as a secondary heating system, such as portable heaters or radiator systems. The results indicate that most of the households were reliant on using domestic electric heating appliances in parallel with a gas cylinder to provide thermally comfortable indoor air temperatures. This data directly correlates with their high rate of energy consumption in the winter.

Cooling Systems

To assess the risk of overheating in the surveyed flats and the occupants' thermal comfort, the types of cooling systems used were assessed. Figure 4.1(c) illustrates the types of cooling systems by households and is used here to highlight the significance of energy consumption in the summer.[3]

As shown in Figure 4.1(c), 28% of the surveyed households stated that they used portable fans as their primary cooling system, 18% used wall-mounted A/C systems, 8% used wall-mounted inverter A/C systems and 4% used ceiling-mounted fans. In addition to these respondents, 39% of the households reported that they used both wall-mounted A/C systems and portable fans, and 1% used ceiling-mounted fans and portable fans. Of the remaining respondents, 2% reported that they had no type of cooling systems in their flats.

In summary, 85% of the participants relied on either wall-mounted A/C systems or portable fans to cool their indoor air in the summer. The questionnaire survey revealed that 18% of the respondents used wall-mounted A/C systems, 28% used portable fans and 39% used both types of cooling systems to provide thermally comfortable living environments in the summer. These responses indicate a high potential for overheating risk across the surveyed flats.

A few of the interviewees commented on their reliance on the extended use of cooling systems as being related to the health conditions and thermal preferences of the occupants. In one case, the occupant suffered from chronic heart disease, and one interviewee had a newborn baby and another had a pregnant woman who all felt the need for a cool living environment to optimise their thermal comfort, but they could also afford to pay higher energy bills. On the other hand, another surveyed owner-occupier had a disabled child and mentioned using portable fans for cooling purposes; however, the respondent also pointed out that the family should be using an A/C system for their child's health and thermal comfort, but they could not afford the excessive energy consumption of these A/C systems due to their income level.

Cooling Control Systems

The types of cooling control systems used by the households in the summer are examined in this section.[4] Figure 4.1(d) illustrates the percentage distribution of the types of cooling control systems used in the flats to create a thermally comfortable indoor air environment, particularly in the hottest summer month of August.

As can be seen in Figure 4.1(d), when participants were asked how they regulated the indoor air temperatures of their living environments, 57% reported that they only had one type of cooling control system to control their indoor air temperature: 41% of the households used remote controls, 10% used a wall-mounted thermostat and 6% used a smartphone application. In addition to these respondents, 41% of the surveyed households reported that they had two types of cooling systems in their flats: 38% used a remote control and a wall-mounted thermostat system, and 4% used a remote control and a smartphone application. Of all the participating households, 2% had no type of cooling control systems, because they were unable to afford the use of any type of cooling system in the summer. These results could inform the relationships with the households' level of income, which is discussed.

Occupants' Energy-Use Patterns

To better understand the summer and winter energy-consumption patterns of the surveyed households, questions as to the number of hours each household occupied their flats and the frequency of their window-opening patterns were included in the survey; these will be included in the information related to the incorporation of the occupants' energy-use patterns into the building-modelling simulation phase.[5] This model input is necessary to accurately calculate the real energy-consumption patterns and validate data related to monthly energy bills in Chapter 7.

Recording the actual occupancy patterns required a significant amount of detailed information, however, the respondents could not always remember the details of every room in their flat.[6] To prevent additional missing data in the building-energy performance studies for the building-modelling simulation, occupancy patterns that included heating- and cooling-consumption patterns and the living room window-opening schedules were considered to be the most complete response and were used as representative relevant data in the analysis for the further validation of energy models of the RTBs under investigation in Chapter 7.

Heating-Consumption Patterns

The heating-consumption patterns of the occupants are examined in this section.[7] As it relates to understanding the household energy-use habits, the pattern investigation correlated with the household socio-demographic characteristics, which are discussed in detail in Chapter 3. These patterns provided additional information to assess the thermal-comfort levels of the occupants in conjunction with their energy use in the winter. Figure 4.2(a) illustrates the heating-consumption patterns in the living room of each household on weekdays.

According to Figure 4.2(a), which shows the households' heating-consumption patterns on weekdays, 36% of the respondent households spent 0–4 h in their living room on weekdays, 48% spent 5–9 h in their living room, 12% spent 10–12 h

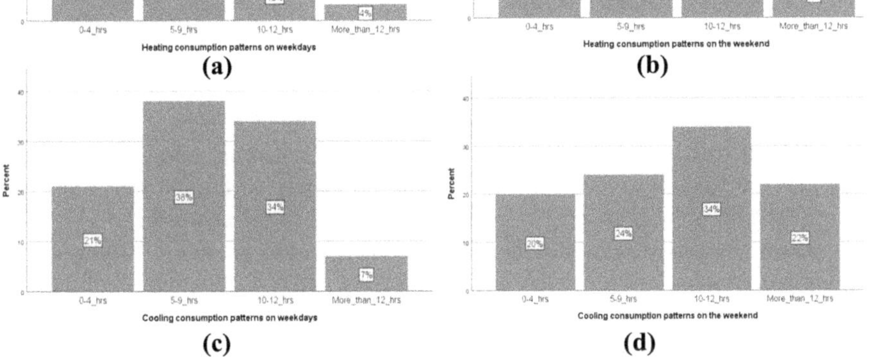

Figure 4.2 (a) Percentage distribution of household heating-consumption patterns on (a) weekdays and (b) the weekend; percentage distribution of household cooling-consumption patterns related to number of hours spent in the living rooms on (c) weekdays and (d) the weekend; percentage distribution of household window-opening patterns in the living room related to number of hours open in (e) winter and (f) summer.

in their living room and 4% spent more than 12 h in their living rooms. The most dominant occupancy pattern was 5–9 h, because most of the family members in 48% of the surveyed households worked full time, and their properties were not occupied on weekdays during working hours, which are between 08:00 and 18:00. Notably, at 36%, the 0–4 h occupancy pattern was found to be the second-most-dominant occupancy schedule.

Figure 4.2(b), which delineates household heating-consumption patterns in terms of the number of hours spent in the living room on the weekend, shows that 32% of the respondents spent 0–4 h in their living room, 40% spent 5–9 h in the living room, 19% spent 10–12 h in the living room and 9% spent more than 12 h in their living room. The 5–9 h occupancy pattern was the most common occupancy schedule on both the weekdays and on the weekend.

Taken together, these results suggest that there was an association between the age group and the employment status of each household. Based on the questionnaire survey, it was determined that the dominant age groups across the recruited households were 35–45 years of age (16%), 45–55 (20%) and 55–65 (33%), while the 65-years-of-age and older age group comprised 16% of the total households. Moreover, 7% of the male respondents were retired, and one male respondent was semi-retired; while for the female respondents—of whom 11% reported that they worked from home, 16% reported that they did household activities, and 14% reported that they were retired—41% spent a majority of their time in their homes throughout the year.

It is important to note that the residents were in their living rooms for slightly longer lengths of time on weekends than on weekdays. No significant differences in heating-consumption patterns were observed between weekdays and weekends, however. Overall, these results indicate that employed occupants spend less time in their homes during the week, but more time on the weekend (Kearns et al., 2019).

Cooling-Consumption Patterns

The primary aim of the present study was to understand the real-life energy-use experiences of occupants during the peak cooling month of August; these data will be used to identify and tabulate different occupancy schedules and to incorporate them into the building-modelling simulation in Chapter 6. Figure 4.2(c) and (d) illustrate the household cooling-consumption patterns in the summer.

As shown in Figure 4.2(c), 21% of the households turned on their living room cooling systems for 0–4 h per day during the week, 38% turned their cooling systems on for 5–9 h per day, 34% turned their cooling systems on for 10–12 h per day and 7% turned their cooling systems on for more than 12 h per day.

Figure 4.2(d), which illustrates cooling-consumption patterns in terms of the number of hours spent in the living rooms on the weekend, shows that 20% of the respondent households kept their living room cooling systems on for 0–4 h per day on the weekend, 24% kept their cooling systems on for 5–9 h per day, 34% kept their cooling systems on for 10–12 h per day and 22% kept their cooling systems on for more than 12 h per day.

There was a noticeable increase in the number of hours of cooling consumption on the weekend (Ozarisoy & Altan, 2017b). It is also worth noting that the most dominant weekend cooling-consumption patterns were observed in the households that cooled their living rooms for 10–12 h and more than 12 h each day; this was due to the high number of households that spent their time at home and preferred to use their cooling systems on the weekend, rather than on weekdays (Galvin, 2010; Hong et al., 2016). This correlates with the fact that employed family members who spend more time at home on the weekend are more likely to use their cooling systems to provide thermally comfortable indoor air temperatures (Galvin, 2012; Nikoofard et al., 2011).

Window-Opening Patterns

The winter and summer window-opening patterns for each subject respondent and the frequency that windows were kept open were also investigated.[8] This section presents the distribution of Questions 18–21, 23 and 24 concerning the households' window-opening patterns and whether windows were opened or closed when the heating or cooling systems were in use.

Figure 4.2(e) illustrates the households' living room window-opening patterns in the winter.[9] Of the surveyed households, 9% reported that they kept their living room windows open for 0–2 h per day during the winter, 38% left their living room windows open for 2–4 h per day, 21% left their living room windows open for 4–6 h per day, 26% left their living room windows open for 6–8 h per day and the remaining 6% kept their living room windows open for more than 8 h each day. The most dominant occupancy pattern was observed in the group in which 38% reported keeping their living room windows open for 2–4 h every day during the winter. This was correlated with the occupant employment patterns, as these households left their windows opened in either the early morning or the late afternoon to facilitate natural ventilation (NV) for the indoor spaces because there were no other ventilation systems (i.e., trickle ventilation) available in these buildings (D'Oca et al., 2018; Fabi et al., 2012; Ortiz et al., 2020). The other two significant window-opening patterns—21% for 4–6 h each winter day and 26% for 6–8 h each winter day—were dependent upon the occupancy hours and orientation of the building; it was observed that 6% of the occupants kept the windows open for more than 8 h a day in the winter.

Similarly, it can be deduced from Figure 4.2(f) that none of the households reported opening their living room windows for 0–2 h per day in the summer, 4% kept their living room windows open for 2–4 h per day, 10% kept their living room windows open for 4–6 h per day, 31% kept their living room windows open for 6–8 h per day and 55% kept their living room windows open for more than 8 h each summer day. The reason for keeping living room windows open was the local climate conditions and the thermal properties of buildings (Murtagh et al., 2019; Sodagar & Starkey, 2016).

It was observed that the occupants who lived on the upper-floor flats and could not afford the high energy-consumption costs of A/C systems kept all their windows open for more than 8 h each day in the summer, and portable fans were used as needed; the other top-floor occupants who could afford to run a wall-mounted A/C system for 24 h a day kept all their windows closed, along with their blinds and curtains. This explains why no occupants were included in the 0–2 h group, as these families ran their A/C systems with their windows closed; most of these occupants were economically active and were able to afford high energy bills, so they tended to frequently use wall-mounted A/C systems.

Household Internal Door- and Window-Opening Habits

This section aims to identify different occupancy patterns in window-opening schedules gathered through feed-forward interviews. This information allows us to explore the households' habitual adaptive behaviour on home-energy performance while undertaking BES studies to validate the survey results in Chapter 6 and 7. Figure 4.3(a) and (b) illustrate the households' internal door-opening patterns in the winter and in the summer.

Figure 4.3(a) illustrates the households' internal door-opening patterns in the winter[10]; 57% of the households reported that they kept the living room door open when the heating was on, while 43% of them kept the living room door closed. This is because of the type of heating system used; to reduce health risks from high CO_2 concentrations with gas heaters, the door was left open to let the polluted air disperse. It is noteworthy that door-opening frequency also relates to the occupants' health condition. One interviewee, who suffered from asthma and heart disease, commented that they need to leave the doors and windows open to allow NV to effectively penetrate the indoor occupied spaces.

Figure 4.3(b) illustrates the households' internal door-opening patterns in the summer[11]; 78% of the respondents reported that they kept the internal doors closed when the A/C system was in use, while 22% revealed that they kept internal doors open. It was observed that three-fourths of the households preferred to close the internal doors when their A/C systems were in use. The reason for this was to keep the internal space cool in the summer. One interviewee with health problems preferred to keep the doors open to dissipate pollutants when the A/C system was in use. On the other hand, the other one-third of the occupants kept the doors open because they used portable fans to cool indoor spaces. The data on these occupancy patterns will be used in the building-modelling simulation to identify accurate infiltration rates to run the dynamic thermal simulation in Chapter 7.

Reasons for Opening and Closing Windows

Questions 20 and 21 were meant to gather data to assess the occupants' thermal comfort, which is discussed in Chapter 6. Question 20 asked the occupants why they kept their windows open in the summer: According to Figure 4.3(c), 25% of the respondent households kept their windows open for fresh air, 67% kept their windows open to cool themselves, 1% kept their windows open to remove condensation and 7% kept their windows open to dissipate dirty air. The most-often

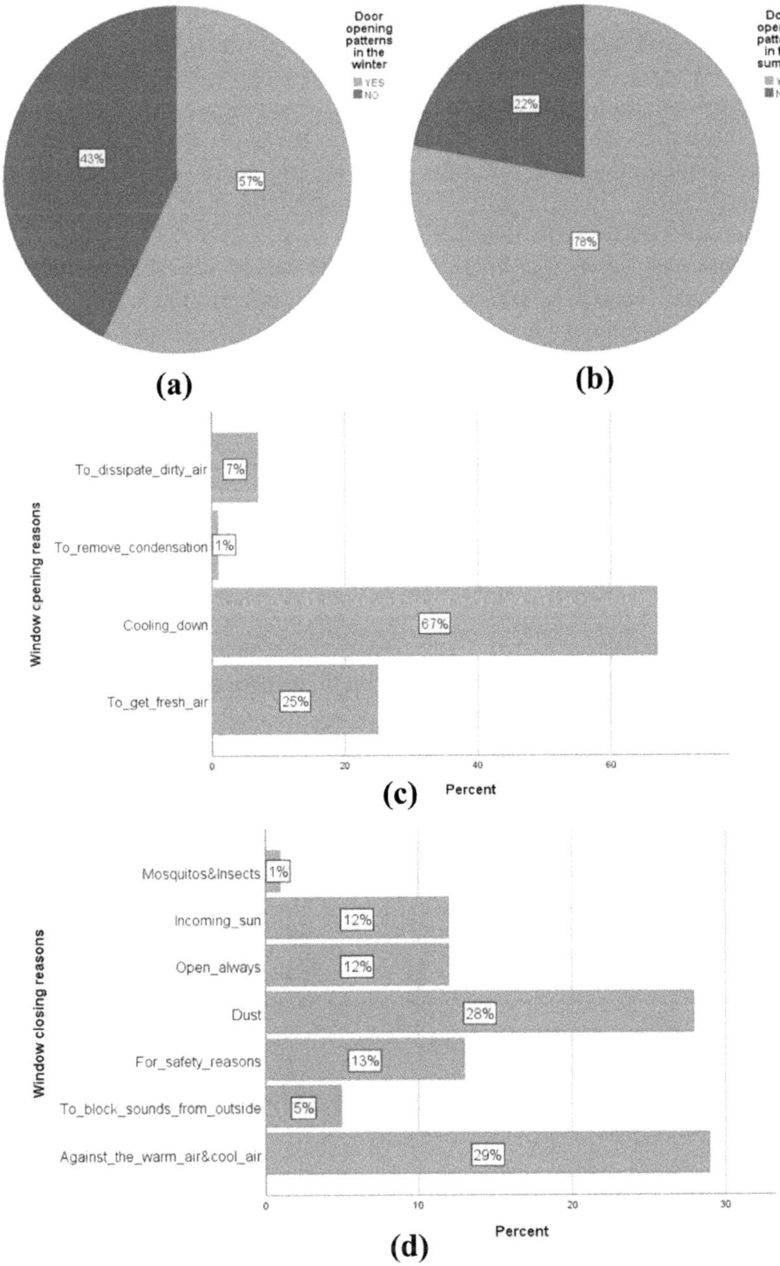

Figure 4.3 Percentage distribution of household internal door-opening patterns in the (a) winter and (b) summer; (c) percentage distribution of reasons for opening windows in summer; (d) percentage distribution of reasons for closing windows in summer.

observed occupant behaviour was opening windows for cooling purposes because of local climate conditions and the poor window design of the RTBs.

As shown in Figure 4.3(c),[12] one-fourth of the respondents kept their windows open to get fresh air, which is significant because of the high level of CO_2 accumulation in those flats. Moreover, one occupant on the upper floor indicated that their flat had condensation issues and the windows and doors were kept open to minimise this problem. This correlates with the data that the majority of occupants kept the windows open for more than 8 h.

Another important factor that emerged from the survey was the presence of children, which was found to be associated with safety concerns that led the households to keep their windows closed due to the lack of safety precautions on the window-opening design that were not taken into consideration during the decision-making process of the development of social-housing estates in NC (Ozarisoy & Altan, 2018); for this reason, the presence of infants or children appeared to be related to the use of heating and cooling systems to provide thermally comfortable indoor air environment throughout the year without the benefit of opened windows (Yohanis, 2012; O'Brien et al., 2020). The survey revealed an association between the presence of people (i.e., the occupancy density) and the use of cooling systems at the lowest setting and portable ventilation devices for longer hours.

Question 21 asked the occupants why they kept their windows closed in the summer: As shown in Figure 4.3(d),[13] 29% reported that they kept their windows closed when their A/C system was in use to keep their indoor air temperature stable; 5% of the respondents lived in flats that faced the main road and kept their windows closed to block traffic sounds; 13% kept their windows closed for safety reasons because their flats were located on the ground floor; 28% of the respondents lived in flats that faced vacant, open land and kept their windows closed to prevent dust from coming in; 12% always kept their windows open due to the local climate conditions; 12% kept their windows closed due to excessive sunlight; the respondents living in flats on southwest-facing blocks (i.e., Blocks 17–21 in Phase II) complained of excessive sunlight coming into their living rooms in the afternoon, while the occupants in Blocks 22–25 in Phase II complained of excessive sun rays coming into their living rooms in the morning. This correlates with data related to windows and blinds being closed when cooling systems were in use.

Relationships of Exploring Household Habitual Adaptive Behaviour on Energy Use

To follow up the research questions (RQs), the types of relationships that were investigated are explained.

Relationships between Household Occupation and Cooling and Heating Energy-Consumption Patterns

Based on the general survey findings, 52% of the respondents stated that they preferred to use electric domestic heating appliances in the winter, and 75% preferred to use either portable fans or wall-mounted A/C systems in the summer to create thermally comfortable indoor air temperatures. This was shown to be related to a number of multi-domain deterministic factors of households' energy-use patterns and their home-energy performance, as shown in Table 4.1.

In this questionnaire survey, the occupants were asked an open-ended question regarding their weekday and weekend heating-consumption patterns. Forty-eight per cent of the occupants reported that they turn on heating systems for 5–9 h on weekdays while 4% of the respondents reported turning on their heating systems for more than 12 h. For weekends, 40% of the respondents stated that they turn on their heating systems for 5–9 h while 9% said they preferred to turn on their heating systems for more than 12 h at weekends. These results indicate that there is an increase in the number of hours the heating systems are turned on at weekends, but this gap is very narrow, which is due to the fact that many of the occupants (mostly female) are at home on weekdays.

It can be observed that there is no significant difference in the overall percentage distribution of the households' weekday and weekend cooling-consumption patterns, except the 7% range (more than 12 h) during the week went up to 22% at weekends. This is due to the increase in the occupancy hours of the surveyed flats at weekends. The most significant finding among the heating- and cooling-consumption patterns was the increase in the need to use cooling systems for more hours during summer. Table 4.1 demonstrates the relationships between household occupation[14] and their heating- and cooling-consumption patterns both on weekdays and on the weekend.[15]

In this analysis, the correlation between the respondents' occupation patterns and their heating and cooling patterns was investigated.[16] As shown in Table 4.1,[17] weekday cooling-consumption patterns were significantly and strongly related to weekend heating-consumption patterns on weekend ($\chi^2 = 54.590$, $p < 0.001$, *Cramer*'s $V = 0.522$). This was because 58% of the respondents spent most of their time at home because they were retired; worked from home; or were housewives, students or unemployed (Frederiks et al., 2015; Freire et al., 2008). This resulted in a majority of the households consuming more energy.

Specifically, a longer duration of heating consumption was related to a longer duration of cooling consumption. A similar result was also found between weekend cooling-consumption patterns and weekend heating-consumption patterns ($\chi^2 = 99.687$, $p < 0.001$, *Cramer*'s $V = 0.706$), between weekday cooling-consumption patterns and weekday heating-consumption patterns ($\chi^2 = 74.565$, $p < 0.001$, *Cramer*'s $V = 0.611$) and weekend cooling-consumption patterns and weekday heating-consumption patterns ($\chi^2 = 50.767$, $p < 0.001$, *Cramer*'s $V = 0.504$). This was due to the occupants' need to achieve optimum thermal comfort due to the local climate conditions and the buildings' thermal properties. Notably, the cultural habits of these households were such that they believed their main priority is overall thermal comfort, without taking into consideration high energy bills or alternative solutions to improve energy efficiency of their flats (Lindén et al., 2006; Santamouris et al., 2007). This suggests that cooling- and heating-consumption patterns are directly related to the thermal conductivity of building materials, because

Table 4.1 Relationships between Unit Occupation, Weekday Heating-Consumption Patterns, Weekend Heating-Consumption Patterns, Weekday Cooling-Consumption Patterns and Weekend Cooling-Consumption Patterns.

Research Questions	*Occupation*	*Weekday Heating-Consumption Patterns*	*Weekend Heating-Consumption Patterns*	*Weekday Cooling-Consumption Patterns*	*Weekend Cooling-Consumption Patterns*
Q 1.4: What is your occupation?	1	0.253	0.109	0.098	0.167
	—	0.060	0.895	0.938	0.552
Q 16: When do you turn on heating device(s) on	0.253	1	0.373**	0.611**	0.504**
weekdays?	0.060	—	0.000	0.000	0.000
Q 17: When do you turn on heating device(s) on the	0.109	0.373**	1	0.522**	0.706**
weekend?	0.895	0.000	—	0.000	0.000
Q 12: When do you turn on cooling device(s) on	0.098	0.611**	0.522**	1	0.774**
weekdays?	0.938	0.000	0.000	—	0.000
Q 13: When do you turn on cooling device(s) on the	0.167	0.504**	0.706***	0.774**	—
weekend?	0.552	0.000	0.000	0.000	1

Occupation: 0 (work outside the home) to 6 (unemployed)
Weekday heating consumption: 0 (0–4 h) to 4 (more than 12 h)
Weekend heating consumption: 0 (0–4 h) to 4 (more than 12 h)
Weekday cooling consumption: 0 (0–4 h) to 4 (more than 12 h)
Weekend cooling consumption: 0 (0–4 h) to 4 (more than 12 h)
Occupation–Weekend heating consumption, $\chi^2(8) = 2.25$, $p = 0.895$, *Cramer*'s $V = 0.109$
Occupation–Weekday heating consumption, $\chi^2(8) = 12.07$, $p = 0.060$, *Cramer*'s $V = 0.253$
Occupation–Weekend cooling consumption, $\chi^2(9) = 7.82$, $p = 0.552$, *Cramer*'s $V = 0.167$
Occupation–Weekday cooling consumption, $\chi^2(6) = 1.79$, $p = 0.938$, *Cramer*'s $V = 0.098$
Weekday cooling consumption–Weekend heating consumption, $\chi^2(4) = 54.59$, $p = 0.000$, *Cramer*'s $V = 0.522$
Weekday cooling consumption–Weekday heating consumption, $\chi^2(4) = 74.57$, $p = 0.000$, *Cramer*'s $V = 0.611$
Weekday cooling consumption–Weekend cooling consumption, $\chi^2(6) = 119.77$, $p = 0.000$, *Cramer*'s $V = 0.774$
Weekend cooling consumption–Weekend heating consumption, $\chi^2(6) = 99.69$, $p = 0.000$, *Cramer*'s $V = 0.706$
Weekend cooling consumption–Weekday heating consumption, $\chi^2(6) = 50.77$, $p = 0.000$, *Cramer*'s $V = 0.504$
Weekday heating consumption–Weekend heating consumption, $\chi^2(4) = 27.89$, $p = 0.000$, *Cramer*'s $V = 0.373$
*p>0.05 moderate; **p>0.001 strong

they have led to an increase in household space-conditioning energy expenditures for the summer and the winter (Sunikka-Blank & Galvin, 2012).

For heating patterns, weekday consumption was moderately associated with weekend consumption ($\chi^2 = 27.890$, $p < 0.001$, *Cramer*'s $V = 0.373$). For cooling patterns, weekday consumption was strongly associated with weekend consumption ($\chi^2 = 119.765$, $p < 0.001$, *Cramer*'s $V = 0.774$); this highlights the fact that the households' main concern was their optimum thermal comfort (Schweiker et al., 2018). However, household occupation was not significantly related to any cooling- or heating-consumption patterns. It is also evident from the correlation analysis that the number of family members living in a particular household was an important factor in the amount of energy that was consumed (Majcen et al., 2013; Ozarisoy & Altan, 2019).

Relationships between Household Occupation and Window-Opening Patterns

The relationships between occupation and window-opening patterns in the winter and summer were analysed, and the results are shown in Table 4.2.

As seen in Table 4.2, window-opening patterns in winter were significantly associated with that in summer ($\chi^2 = 42.177$, $p < 0.001$, *Cramer*'s $V = 0.459$), and this relationship was moderate–strong. It appears that a longer opening duration in winter was related to a longer opening duration in summer. Regarding the heating control type at home, it was only significantly related to window-opening patterns in summer ($\chi^2 = 16.031$, $p = 0.042$, *Cramer*'s $V = 0.283$). A greater proportion of participants with more than 8 h window-opening time had none of the heating controls at home than participants with 6–8 h windows opening. However, occupation was not significantly associated with any opening patterns or opening reasons.

Cross-tabulation Tables

The data provided subsequent information on the multi-domain factors for a statistical analysis that took the significance of summer and winter occupancy patterns into account. As such, the correlation analysis was able to identify relationships among two separate nominal variables, which followed ordered series or ranking sequences among different categories to tabulate the data within the scope of the RQs, as discussed in this study.

Relationships between Occupation and Household Heating- and Cooling-Consumption Patterns

In the questionnaire survey, households were asked 'Where and when do you turn on your heating device(s) on weekdays?' and 'Where and when do you turn on your heating device(s) on weekends?', and household occupation were categorical variables, cross-tabulations using chi-square test were adopted to help interpret significant correlations and detect discrepancies from among the multi-domain factors related to occupancy patterns for the purpose of exploring household energy performance for heating purposes in line with considerations related to different

Table 4.2 Relationships between Household Occupation, Window-Opening Patterns in the Winter, Window-Opening Patterns in the Summer and Heating Control.

Research Questions	*Occupation*	*Winter*	*Summer*	*Heating Control*
Q 1.4: What is your occupation?	1 —	0.164 0.578	0.167 0.153	0.170 0.773
Q 23: When do you open your windows in the winter?	0.164 0.578	1 —	0.459** 0.000	0.283* 0.042
Q 18: When do you open your windows in the summer?	0.167 0.153	0.459** 0.000	1 —	0.139 0.926
Q 24: Do you keep room doors open when you do not have heating on?	0.114 0.747	0.246 0.109	0.030 0.956	1 —
Q 19: Do you keep room doors open when you do not have cooling on?	0.114 0.746	0.262 0.077	0.168 0.245	0.229 0.262
Q 20: Why do you open the windows?	0.201 0.291	0.124 0.676	0.185 0.182	0.200 0.410
Q 21: Why do you close the windows?	0.260 0.087	0.230 0.195	0.234 0.205	0.118 0.992

Window-opening patterns in winter–Door-opening preference in summer, $\chi^2(3) = 6.85$, $p = 0.077$, *Cramer*'s $V = 0.262$
Window-opening patterns in winter–Window-opening pattern in summer, $\chi^2(6) = 42.18$, $p = 0.000$, *Cramer*'s $V = 0.459$
Window-opening patterns in winter–Door-opening preference in winter, $\chi^2(3) = 6.05$, $p = 0.109$, *Cramer*'s $V = 0.246$
Window-opening patterns in winter–Window-opening reason, $\chi^2(3) = 1.53$, $p = 0.676$, *Cramer*'s $V = 0.124$
Window-opening patterns in winter–Window-closing reason, $\chi^2(12) = 15.92$, $p = 0.195$, *Cramer*'s $V = 0.230$
Window-opening patterns in summer–Door-opening preference in summer, $\chi^2(2) = 2.81$, $p = 0.245$, *Cramer*'s $V = 0.168$
Window-opening patterns in summer–Door-closing preference in winter, $\chi^2(2) = 0.09$, $p = 0.956$, *Cramer*'s $V = 0.030$
Window-opening patterns in summer–Window-opening reason, $\chi^2(2) = 3.41$, $p = 0.182$, *Cramer*'s $V = 0.185$
Window-opening patterns in summer–Window-closing reason, $\chi^2(8) = 10.94$, $p = 0.205$, *Cramer*'s $V = 0.234$
Occupation–Window-opening pattern in summer, $\chi^2(6) = 5.24$, $p = 0.513$, *Cramer*'s $V = 0.167$
Occupation–Window-opening pattern in winter, $\chi^2(9) = 7.57$, $p = 0.578$, *Cramer*'s $V = 0.164$
Occupation–Window-opening reasons, $\chi^2(3) = 3.74$, $p = 0.291$, *Cramer*'s $V = 0.201$
Occupation–Window-closing reasons, $\chi^2(12) = 19.07$, $p = 0.087$, *Cramer*'s $V = 0.260$
Occupation–Heating control, $\chi^2(12) = 8.16$, $p = 0.773$, *Cramer*'s $V = 0.170$
Heating control–Window-opening pattern in summer, $\chi^2(8) = 5.79$, $p = 0.926$, *Cramer*'s $V = 0.139$
Heating control–Window-opening pattern in winter, $\chi^2(8) = 16.03$, $p = 0.042$, *Cramer*'s $V = 0.283$
Heating control–Window-opening reason, $\chi^2(4) = 3.93$, $p = 0.410$, *Cramer*'s $V = 0.200$
Heating control–Window-closing reason, $\chi^2(16) = 5.55$, $p = 0.992$, *Cramer*'s $V = 0.118$

occupations (Blight & Coley, 2013). The survey findings revealed similar weekday and weekend occupancy patterns: According to the survey, 48% of the respondent households preferred to turn their heating systems on for 5–9 h on weekdays, and 12% kept their heating systems on for 10–12 h. Alternately, 40% of the households kept their heating systems on for 5–9 h on the weekend, and 19% kept their heating systems on for 10–12 h each day of the weekend.[18] Another important aspect emerged from the general survey findings: The statistical figures presented below demonstrate that household occupation is an important consideration when seeking to identify occupancy patterns in the surveyed flats. According to the survey, 13% of the respondents worked at home, 16% were housewives, 22% were retired and 2% were unemployed. Tables 4.3[19] (a)–(c) delineate the relationships between household occupation, heating-consumption patterns on weekdays and heating-consumption patterns on the weekend.

Table 4.3(c) presents the relationships between household occupation and heating-consumption patterns. Unfortunately, neither heating-consumption patterns on weekdays nor at weekends were significantly related to household occupations.

To prove that there was no relationship between household occupation and heating-consumption patterns, the study explored the relationships with the values, which were set to run the cross-tabulation method of design. This is one of the reasons why it is difficult to determine households' habitual adaptive behaviour on home energy performance and also to predict their occupancy patterns. The study chose to explore the variations rather than undertake statistical analysis and interpret results according to the convention. In this section, the primary aim was to demonstrate the variations in occupancy patterns in order to provide background information to identify dominant representative occupancy patterns for building-energy simulations in Chapter 7.

The survey results revealed that the lowest peak, $f < 1.40$, was for 0–4 occupancy hours; the first-highest peak, $f > 2.40$, was for more than 12 h and the second-highest peak, $f > 1.80$, was for 10–12 h. Research has shown that the highest peak, $f = 2.20$, was for 0–4 h, due to a majority of the surveyed occupants who preferred to turn on their heating systems at high temperatures for a few hours, then switch them off to reduce heating costs; and the lowest peak of $f = 1.0$ was for 10–12 h.

It should be noted that the flats where some household members were present at home during the day were found to be those of retirees with high pensions, which resulted in more energy consumption than in the flats where no one was at home during the day or in the households where the presence of family members during the day varied considerably (Andersen et al., 2009); this also held true for the weekend in all the surveyed flats. Tables 4.4(a)–(c) demonstrate the relationships between household occupation, cooling-consumption patterns on weekdays and on the weekend.

In the questionnaire survey, households were asked 'Where and when do you turn on the cooling device(s) on weekdays?' and 'Where and when do you turn on the cooling device(s) at weekends? and occupation were all categorical variables, cross-tabulations using chi-square tests were then used to help interpret significant correlations. Table 4.4(c) shows the relationships between occupants' weekday cooling-consumption patterns and occupation. However, household occupation was not significantly associated with weekday or weekend cooling consumptions, $ps > 0.05$.[20]

The survey revealed that 38% of the households kept their cooling systems on for 5–9 h each weekday, and 34% kept their systems on for 10–12 h; on weekends,

Table 4.3(a) Relationships between Household Occupation and Heating-Consumption Patterns on Weekdays.

			Occupation				
			Work Outside the Home	*Works at Home*	*Household Activities*	*Retired*	*Total*
Heating-consumption patterns on weekdays	**0–4 h**	Count	15_a	4_a	9_a	7_a	35
		%	35.7	30.8	52.9	31.8	37.2
	5–9 h	Count	18_a	$7_{a,b}$	2_b	12_a	44
		%	54.8	53.8	11.8	54.5	46.8
	More than 10 h	Count	4_a	2_a	6_a	3_a	15
		%	9.5	15.4	35.3	13.6	16
Total		Count	42	13	17	22	94
		%	100	100	100	100	100

Each subscript letter denotes a subset of occupation categories whose column proportions do not differ significantly from each other at the 0.05 level.

Table 4.3(b) Relationships between Household Occupation and Heating-Consumption Patterns on the Weekend.

			Occupation				
			Work Outside the Home	*Works at Home*	*Household Activities*	*Retired*	*Total*
Heating-consumption patterns on the weekend	**0–4 h**	Count	14$_{a}$	3$_{a}$	4$_{a}$	9$_{a}$	30
		%	33.3	23.1	23.5	40.9	31.9
	5–9 h	Count	18$_{a}$	6$_{a}$	8$_{a}$	7$_{a}$	39
		%	42.9	46.2	47.1	31.8	41.5
	More than 10 h	Count	10$_{a}$	4$_{a}$	5$_{a}$	6$_{a}$	25
		%	23.8	30.8	29.4	27.3	26.6
Total		Count	42	13	17	22	94
		%	100	100	100	100	100

Each subscript letter denotes a subset of occupation categories whose column proportions do not differ significantly from each other at the 0.05 level.

Table 4.3(c) Relationships between Household Occupation and Heating-Consumption Patterns.

Variables		*Weekday Heating Consumption*	*Weekend Heating Consumption*
Household occupation	*Cramer's V*	12.068	2.249
	Significance	0.060	0.895

Occupation–Weekday, $\chi^2(6) = 12.07$, $p = 0.060$, *Cramer's* $V = 0.253$
Occupation–Weekend, $\chi^2(6) = 2.25$, $p = 0.895$, *Cramer's* $V = 0.109$

24% kept their cooling systems on for 5–9 h each day, and 34% kept their systems on for 10–12 h. After a thorough analysis of the occupants' weekday cooling-consumption patterns, it was found that the highest peak, $f > 2.50$,[21] was for more than 12 h; and the lowest peak, $f = 1.25$, was for 10–12 h. This is due to the fact that a majority of the households were retired pensioners who mostly stayed at home on weekdays. The study also examined the households' weekend cooling consumption.

The results revealed that the first-highest peak, $f > 2.0$, was for 5–9 h; the second-highest, $f > 1.75$, was for 10–12 h; the third-highest, $f > 1.75$, was for 0–4 h and the lowest peak, $f < 0.75$, was for more than 12 h. The reason for the inverse peaks between weekdays and the weekend was that the households cleaned their flats on the weekend with all their windows and doors left open; notably, residents also spent more time outside of their homes on the weekend (Nair et al., 2010).

Relationships between Occupation and Window-Opening Patterns

In the questionnaire survey, households were asked 'Where and when do you open your windows in the winter?' and 'Where and when do you open your windows in the summer?', and household occupation were all categorical variables; cross-tabulations using chi-square tests were implemented to interpret significant correlations. Because the households' ingrained lifestyles and the impact thereof on their home-energy performance were difficult to quantify, a cross-tabulation test between household occupation and window-opening patterns was conducted to avoid discrepancies in the sample dataset. It should be noted that the survey revealed that during the winter, a majority of the households only opened their windows for a few hours each day.

A cross-tabulation test was conducted to determine the variance of the window-opening patterns on energy use in line with considerations related to household occupation variations and to provide information for the building-modelling simulation phase. These data enabled the assignment of different window-opening

Table 4.4(a) Relationships between Household Occupation and Heating-Consumption Patterns on Weekdays.

			Occupation				
			Work Outside the Home	*Works at Home*	*Household Activities*	*Retired*	*Total*
Cooling-consumption patterns on weekdays	**0–4 h**	Count	11_a	2_a	3_a	4_a	20
		%	26.2	15.4	17.6	18.2	21.3
	5–9 h	Count	15_a	6_a	6_a	10_a	37
		%	35.7	46.2	35.3	45.5	39.4
	More than 10 h	Count	16_a	5_a	8_a	8_a	37
		%	38.1	38.5	47.1	36.4	39.4
Total		Count	42	13	17	22	94
		%	100	100	100	100	100

Each subscript letter denotes a subset of occupation categories whose column proportions do not differ significantly from each other at the 0.05 level.

Table 4.4(b) Relationships between Household Occupation and Heating-Consumption Patterns on the Weekend.

			Occupation				
			Work Outside the Home	*Works at Home*	*Household Activities*	*Retired*	*Total*
Cooling-consumption patterns on the weekend	**0–4 h**	Count	11_a	2_a	3_a	9_a	30
		%	26.2	15.4	17.6	40.9	31.9
	5–9 h	Count	11_a	3_a	4_a	7_a	39
		%	26.2	23.1	23.5	31.8	41.5
	More than 10 h	Count	10_a	4_a	6_a	6_a	25
		%	23.8	30.8	35.3	27.3	26.6
Total		Count	42	13	17	22	94
		%	100	100	100	100	100

Each subscript letter denotes a subset of occupation categories whose column proportions do not differ significantly from each other at the 0.05 level.

Table 4.4(c) Relationships between Household Occupation and Cooling-Consumption Patterns.

Variables		*Weekday Cooling Consumption*	*Weekend Cooling Consumption*
Household occupation	*Cramer's V*	1.792	7.824
	Significance	0.938	0.552

Occupation–Weekday, $\chi^2(6) = 1.79$ $p = 0.938$, *Cramer's* $V = 0.098$
Occupation–Weekend, $\chi^2(9) = 7.82$, $p = 0.552$, *Cramer's* $V = 0.167$

schedules to test the significance of occupancy patterns. As it relates to assessing overheating risks and occupants' thermal comfort, window-opening schedules were important to consider when tabulating different infiltration rates into the macro-flow simulations (Ozarisoy, 2022).

Notably, the survey found that 38% of the households preferred to keep their windows open for 2–4 h every day in the winter, 21% kept their windows open for 4–6 h, 26% kept their windows open for 6–8 h, 55% kept their windows open for more than 8 h and 31% kept their windows open for 6–8 h every day. Tables 4.5(a)–(c) present the relationship between household occupation and window-opening patterns.

Table 4.5(c) reveals a non-significant relationship between household occupation and window-opening patterns. Taken together in this section, household occupations appear nothing to do with heating-consumption patterns, cooling-consumption patterns and window-opening patterns. To understand the occupancy patterns and their influences on occupants' thermal comfort, the study examined the value of variables whether exploring the variants of patterns integration while assessing occupants' thermal comfort in Chapter 6 and evaluating building-energy performance in Chapter 6 before developing evidence-based passive-cooling design strategies for retrofitting base-case RTBs in Chapter 7.

Research has shown that the highest peak of window opening, $f > 1.80$, was for 4–6 h; the second-highest, $f = 1.60$, was for 6–8 h; the third-highest, $f < 1.80$, was for 0–2 h and the lowest peak, $f = 1.0$, was for more than 8 h. The varied results were due to variations in the occupant profiles which are tabulated in Chapter 7. Occupants who worked outside were correlated with windows that were kept open for 6–8 h; occupants with young children who mostly stayed at home were correlated with windows that were kept open for 0–2 h and occupants who closed their windows for more than 8 h were in the slightly older age group and reported that their health was between poor and very poor, which was why they kept their windows closed during the winter.

It was also found that the highest peak, $f > 2.0$, was for 4–6 h; the second-highest peak, $f > 1.80$, was for 6–8 h; the third-highest peak, $f < 1.40$, was for more than 8 h and the lowest peak, $f < 0.80$, was for 2–4 h. The reversal in the analysis was because wall-mounted A/C systems were used during the night to achieve the required thermal comfort due to local climate conditions and the thermal properties of the buildings.

Table 4.5(a) Relationships between Household Occupation and Window-Opening Patterns in Winter.

			Occupation				
			Work Outside the Home	*Works at Home*	*Household Activities*	*Retired*	*Total*
Window-opening patterns in winter	**0–2 h**	Count	3_a	1_a	3_a	0_a	7
		%	7.1	7.7	17.6	0.0	7.4
	2–4 h	Count	19_a	5_a	4_a	8_a	36
		%	45.2	38.5	23.5	36.4	38.3
	4–6 h	Count	7_a	2_a	4_a	7_a	20
		%	16.7	15.4	23.5	31.8	21.3
	More than 6 h	Count	13_a	5_a	6_a	7_a	31
		%	31.0	38.5	35.3	31.8	33.0
Total		Count	42	13	17	22	94
		%	100	100	100	100	100

Each subscript letter denotes a subset of occupation categories whose column proportions do not differ significantly from each other at the 0.05 level.

Table 4.5(b) Relationships between Household Occupation and Window-Opening Patterns in Summer.

			Occupation				
			Work Outside the Home	*Works at Home*	*Household Activities*	*Retired*	*Total*
Window-opening patterns in summer	**2–6 h**	Count	6_a	1_a	3_a	2_a	12
		%	14.3	7.7	17.6	9.1	12.8
	6–8 h	Count	10_a	3_a	8_a	7_a	28
		%	23.8	23.1	47.1	31.8	29.8
	More than 8 h	Count	26_a	9_a	6_a	13_a	54
		%	61.9	69.2	35.3	59.1	57.4
Total		Count	42	13	17	22	94
		%	100	100	100	100	100

Each subscript letter denotes a subset of occupation categories whose column proportions do not differ significantly from each other at the 0.05 level.

Table 4.5(c) Relationships between Household Occupation and Window-Opening Patterns.

Variables		*Window-Opening Patterns in Winter*	*Window-Opening Patterns in Summer*
Household occupation	*Cramer*'s *V*	7.566	5.244
	Significance	0.578	0.513

Occupation–Winter, $\chi^2(9) = 7.56$, $p = 0.578$, *Cramer*'s $V = 0.164$
Occupation–Weekend, $\chi^2(6) = 5.24$, $p = 0.513$, *Cramer*'s $V = 0.167$

Discussions

In this chapter, different statistical methods were applied according to the types of RQs that were distributed to respondent households that were in line with the research aim and objectives of the present study. The following discussion is structured according to the RQs that guided the findings obtained through feed-forward interviews—(RQ–2) Which occupant energy-consumption behaviours may have an impact on energy performance?—in order to outline the dominant representative energy-user profiles for the BES, which is presented in Chapter 7.

The results demonstrated that as a respondent's age increased, their energy consumption also increased; weekday cooling-consumption patterns were significantly and strongly related to weekend heating-consumption patterns on weekend ($\chi^2 = 54.590$, $p < 0.001$, *Cramer*'s $V = 0.522$), which indicated that the older age group consumed more energy than younger residents. This underscores the fact that household age was an important consideration when identifying the occupancy patterns and taking different thermal-comfort preferences—particularly in the summer—into account. Furthermore, strong correlations were found between weekend cooling-consumption patterns and weekend heating-consumption patterns ($\chi^2 = 99.687$, $p < 0.001$, *Cramer*'s $V = 0.706$), between weekday cooling-consumption patterns and weekday heating-consumption patterns ($\chi^2 = 74.565$, $p < 0.001$, *Cramer*'s $V = 0.611$) and weekend cooling-consumption patterns and weekday heating-consumption patterns ($\chi^2 = 50.767$, $p < 0.001$, *Cramer*'s $V = 0.504$). Figure 4.4(a) and (b) demonstrate the relationships between household density, heating-consumption patterns on weekdays and on the weekend.

Figure 4.4(a) demonstrates that 7% of the 4–5 people occupancy type used their heating appliances for 10–12 h on weekdays, and 17% used their appliances for 5–9 h. Of the three-people occupancy type, 18% used their heating appliances for 5–9 h on weekdays, and 11% used their appliances for 0–4 h. According to Figure 4.4(b), 6% of the 4–5 people occupancy type used their heating appliances for more than 12 h on the weekend, 8% used their appliances for 10–12 h, 12% used their appliances for 5–9 h and 6% used their appliances for 0–4 h. A total of 6% of the respondent households were continuously at home on the weekend, and 20% of households preferred to stay at home for longer hours on weekends.

These results reveal a correlation between heating-consumption patterns and occupancy density, which is associated with high energy consumption in the winter.

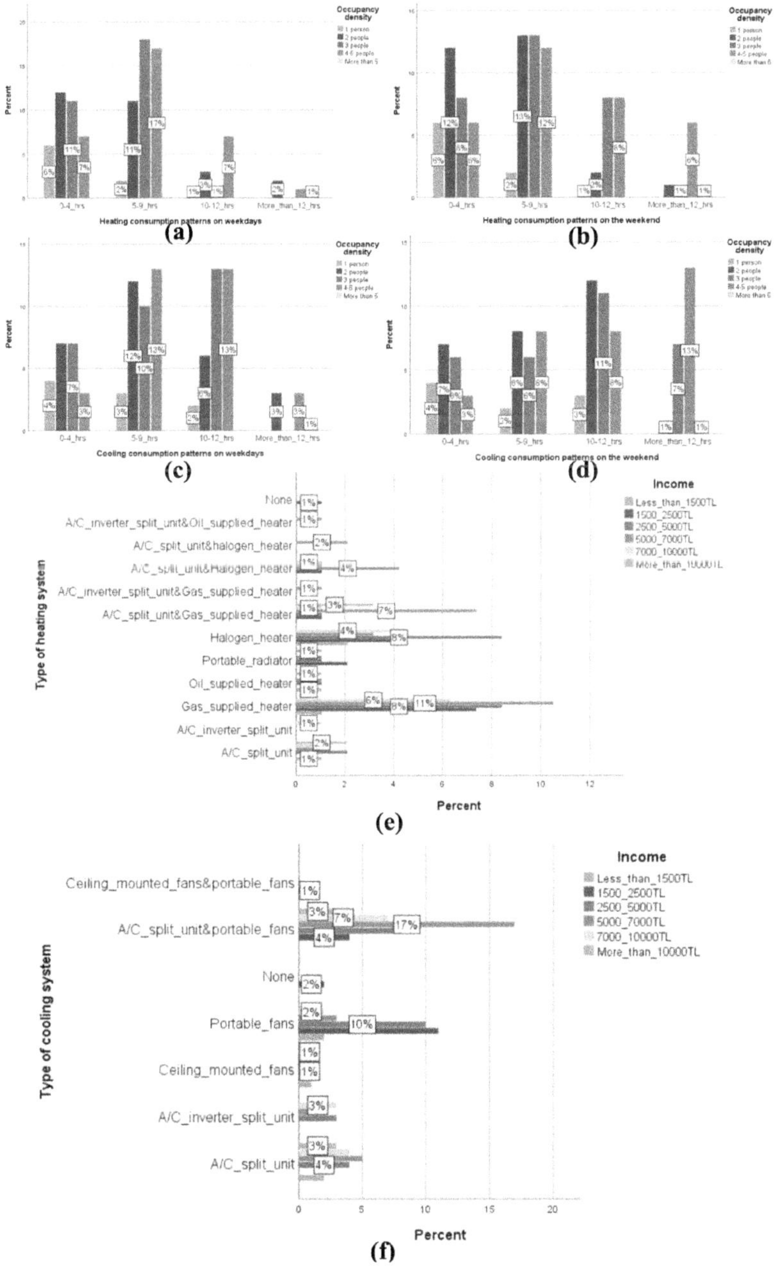

Figure 4.4 Percentage distribution of heating-consumption patterns by taking occupancy density type into account on (a) weekdays and (b) the weekend; percentage distribution of cooling-consumption patterns taking occupancy density type into account on (c) weekdays and (d) the weekend; percentage distribution of the household's types of (e) heating systems and (f) cooling systems, taking income level into account.

Conversely, for heating patterns, weekday consumption was moderately associated with weekend consumption ($\chi^2 = 27.890$, $p < 0.001$, *Cramer*'s $V = 0.373$); the occupants' weekday and weekend energy usage revealed their deterministic characteristics, which further highlights the strong impact of household size on energy consumption (Costa–Carrapiço et al., 2020; Haddad et al., 2020). This finding correlates with an assessment of overheating risks that was incorporated into the building-modelling simulation phase of the current study which is discussed in Chapter 6.

As shown in Figure 4.4(c), 3% of the 4–5 people occupancy type used cooling appliances for more than 12 h every weekday, 13% used their appliances for 10–12 h, 13% used their appliances for 5–9 h each day and 3% used their appliances for 0–4 h. On the weekend, 13% of the 4–5 people occupancy type used their cooling appliances for more than 12 h each day, 3% used their appliances for 10–12 h, 8% used their appliances for 5–9 h and 3% used their appliances for 0–4 h; the slight variation was due to the cooling appliances that were used during the night.

According to Figure 4.4(d), 7% of the three-people occupancy type used their cooling appliances for more than 12 h each weekend day; this cooling-consumption pattern suggests that household size directly affects the number of hours that cooling appliances are utilised. Notably, cooling-energy consumption patterns were not limited to occupancy density; they were also linked to the household level of income.

For cooling patterns, weekday consumption was strongly associated with weekend consumption ($\chi^2 = 119.765$, $p < 0.001$, *Cramer*'s $V = 0.774$), which indicates that households with high-income levels consumed more energy than middle-income or economically inactive households.

Figure 4.4(e) depicts the associations between types of heating systems and household income: households that earned 5,000–7,000 TL per month preferred to use a gas cylinder for heating purposes; 7% of the same group used both A/C and gas cylinders in the winter. Overall, 34% of all households used gas cylinders, 23% used portable halogen heaters and 14% used both an A/C system and a gas cylinder. It was difficult to predict the households' habitual adaptive behaviour on the selection of the type of heating systems when household income was considered to identify heating-consumption patterns.

The results revealed a limitation when considering the household heating systems and the influence thereof on the residents' habitual adaptive behaviour related to home-energy performance in the winter. This research approach has been neglected by the previous scholars which was discussed in Chapter 2. Hence, in this study the focus was to explore variations in household energy use in the hottest summer month of August.

Figure 4.4(f) demonstrates that 17% of the 5,000–7,000 TL income group used their A/C and portable fans for cooling purposes, 7% of the 7,000–10,000 TL income group used both of these cooling appliances, 12% of the 1,500–2,000 TL income group used portable fans. It should be noted that the 2019 State Planning Organisation statistics indicated that 2% of NC households live in energy poverty, and these results confirm the validity of this vulnerable population in social-housing estates, as presented in Chapter 1.

Perhaps the most striking result to emerge from the data was that a majority of the surveyed households used electric home appliances for heating and cooling purposes because there were no central gas systems installed in their properties. Taken together, these results suggest an association between household income level, occupancy patterns and energy usage. As has been noted that the larger the household, the more the occupants thereof tend to use heating or cooling systems (Ascione et al., 2020); this is related to the occupants' tendency to pay more in energy costs to provide a thermally comfortable indoor air environment for the members of their households in the winter and in the summer due to the low quality of construction materials used in the RTBs and the absence of insulation materials on the external walls.

One of the striking findings emerging from the cross-tabulation analysis was that window-opening patterns in winter were significantly associated with that in summer ($\chi^2 = 42.177$, $p < 0.001$, *Cramer*'s $V = 0.459$), and this relationship was moderate–strong. It appears that a longer opening duration in winter was related to a longer opening duration in summer. Regarding the heating control type at home, it was only significantly related to window-opening patterns in summer ($\chi^2 = 16.031$, $p = 0.042$, *Cramer*'s $V = 0.283$). Because the type of heating- and cooling-control system used in the model seemed to not have a correlation with the household income level that was introduced in the deterministic model (Park & Kim, 2012; Papadopoulos et al., 2018).

Conclusion

The aim of the present research was to draw conclusions related to multi-domain factors related to households' socio-demographic characteristics, occupancy patterns and home-energy performance. A field-study approach was adopted to gauge household information related to energy use.

The survey revealed that for heating patterns, weekday consumption was moderately associated with weekend consumption ($\chi^2 = 27.890$, $p < 0.001$, *Cramer*'s $V = 0.373$). For cooling patterns, weekday consumption was strongly associated with weekend consumption ($\chi^2 = 119.765$, $p < 0.001$, *Cramer*'s $V = 0.774$), because this was when occupants spent the greatest amount of time at home and desired optimum thermal comfort. The most compelling finding in this chapter was that the presence of heating and cooling appliances seemed to have a significant effect on energy consumption. Correlations were found between energy consumption and the type of heating and cooling systems that the occupants used in their homes. However, household occupation was not significantly related to any cooling- or heating-consumption patterns.

This chapter presented two outcomes: it identifies the significance of occupant behaviour on energy use in conjunction with analysing the correlation between occupation and household heating- and cooling-consumption patterns. By exploring correlations between occupation and the socio-demographic characteristics of individual households, behavioural variables related to the use of domestic appliances were considered to develop behavioural profiles that can be applied in simulation programmes or when making energy-saving calculations according to households with specific behaviours; this then facilitated the identification of dominant representative occupancy profiles to undertake dynamic thermal simulations that will thoroughly assess the energy performance of different buildings in Chapters 6 and 7.

As was explained in the description of the methodology and validation measures, occupancy profiles can be used to formulate targeted energy-saving policies for the social-housing sector. The findings presented thus far suggest that the methodological approach plays a decisive role in the validation of building-energy performance. As such, this debate predominantly lies within the STS approach, which emphasises the importance of upgrading the energy efficiency of buildings within an appropriate methodology and effective retrofit interventions that are influenced by human actions.

Notes

1 To undertake the correlation analysis accurately, the types of heating systems variable were coded as follows: 1 = A/C split units only, 2 = Gas heater types, 3 = Halogen heater types, 4 = Other (Oil, Wood and Portable radiator). However, in Figure 5.1, the actual data gathered through a questionnaire survey was presented without altering households' in vivo experience in energy use which directly effects on their home-energy performance.

2 To undertake the correlation analysis accurately, the types of heating control systems variable were coded as follows: 1 = Wall-mounted thermostat, 2 = Other types, 3 = Remote controller, 4 = Automatic thermostat and remote controller, 5 = None. However, in Figure 5.2, the actual data gathered through a questionnaire survey was presented without altering households' in vivo experience in energy use which directly effects on their home-energy performance.

3 To undertake the correlation analysis accurately, the types of cooling systems variable were coded as follows. 0 = A/C split unit, 1 = A/C inverter split unit and ceiling-mounted fans, 2 = Portable fans, 3 = A/C split unit and portable fans. However, in Figure 5.3, the actual data gathered through a questionnaire survey was presented without altering households' in vivo experience in energy use which directly effects on their home-energy performance.

4 To undertake the correlation analysis accurately, the types of cooling control systems variable were coded as follows: 0 = Remote control, 1 = Wall-mounted thermostat, 2 = Smartphone application, 3 = Remote control and wall-mounted thermostat, 4 = Remote control and smartphone application, 5 = None. However, in Figure 5.4, the actual data gathered through a questionnaire survey was presented without altering households' in vivo experience in energy use which directly effects on their home-energy performance.

5 For the statistical analyses, frequencies were conducted to present the survey findings. Frequency distributions are descriptive statistics that provide information and summarised datasets. A frequency distribution provides categorical information on number of occurrences.

6 Frequency and relative frequency distribution provide succinct, descriptive data for quick evaluation. In the present study, a frequency distribution describes a population (households) by summarising the information into meaningful intervals. In the present

study, a frequency distribution bar chart presents the categories, number of occurrences and percentage of total.

7 To undertake the correlation analysis, the households' heating-consumption patterns variable was grouped for the conceptual-level analysis to feed the data while conducting the building-energy simulations in Chapter 7.

8 Window-opening patterns were set out as categorical variables to perform correlation analysis accurately.

9 Categorical variables are sets of variables with values assigned to distinct and limited groups or categories. Categorical variables take on values in a set of categories, different from a continuous variable, which takes on a range of values. Categorical variables are also called discrete or nominal variables.

10 Categorical variables are common in social sciences for measuring attitudes, opinions and behaviours and have two primary types of scales: nominal and ordinal levels of measurement. When variables have categories without a natural ordering, the variable is nominal.

11 Categorical variables can be used in statistical analyses as either explanatory (independent) or response (dependent) variables. At the nominal level, mode (frequency of the variable) is the only measure of central tendency appropriate for categorical variables. Chi-square is an appropriate test for categorical data at the nominal level.

12 To undertake the correlation analysis accurately, the reasons for opening windows in summer variable were coded/grouped as follows: 0 = Fresh air/dissipate dirty air, 1 = Cooling down. However, the actual data gathered through a questionnaire survey was presented without altering households' in vivo experience in energy use which directly effects on their home-energy performance.

13 To undertake the correlation analysis accurately, the reasons for closing windows in summer variable were coded/grouped as follows: 0 = Against the warm air, 1 = To block outside disturbances/annoyances, 2 = For safety reasons, 3 = Dust, 4 = Open always. However, in Figure 5.10, the actual data gathered through a questionnaire survey was presented without altering households' in vivo experience in energy use which directly effects on their home-energy performance.

14 To undertake the correlation analysis accurately, the household occupation variable was coded/grouped as follows: 0 = Work outside the home, 1 = Work at home, 2 = Household activities, 3 = Retired.

15 Cross-tabulation method was used. The traditional way to identify a relationship, or association, between two categorical variables is to calculate percentages within categories of the independent variable and to compare these percentages across the categories of the independent variable.

16 To assess the association between two nominal variables, *Cramer*'s *V* coefficient is preferred over the x2 statistic or contingency coefficient, *C*. To appreciate its advantages, however, a discussion of the x2 statistic and the contingency coefficient *C* is also needed.

17 To interpret the statistical findings according to the convention, Little (1988) suggested interpretation of Phi (φ) and *Cramer*'s *V* Coefficients—Value of φ or *Cramer*'s *V* (i) 0.00 through 0.10—weak/small effect, (ii) 0.11 through 0.30—moderate/medium effect, (iii) 0.31+—strong/large effect.

18 These survey findings were set out to interpret the findings by using the frequency. ***f*** represents the frequency of the values indicated in the statistical dataset to determine the findings of variables related to households' socio-demographic characteristics in order to provide subsequent background information while developing evidence-based energy-policy design in the Eastern Mediterranean basin.

19 Tables present the cross-tabulation analysis of variables selected to analyse the *Phi* and *Cramer*'s *V* test to provide accurate subsequent background information while validating the survey results by employing building-energy simulations in Chapters 6 and 7.

20 *Ps – significance value* was used to report the results of a one-way ANOVA, begin by reporting the significance test results.

21 *f* represents the frequency of the values indicated in the statistical dataset to determine the findings of variables related to households' socio-demographic characteristics in order to provide subsequent background information while developing evidence-based energy-policy design in the Eastern Mediterranean basin.

References

Andersen, R. V., Toftum, J., Andersen, K. K., & Olesen, B. W. (2009). Survey of occupant behaviour and control of indoor environment in Danish dwellings. *Energy and Buildings*, *41*(1), 11–16. https://doi.org/10.1016/j.enbuild.2008.07.004

Ascione, F., Bianco, N., Iovane, T., Mastellone, M., & Mauro, G. M. (2020). Is it fundamental to model the inter-building effect for reliable building energy simulations? Interaction with shading systems. *Building and Environment*, *183*. https://doi.org/10.1016/j.buildenv.2020.107161

Blight, T. S., & Coley, D. A. (2013). Sensitivity analysis of the effect of occupant behaviour on the energy consumption of passive house dwellings. *Energy and Buildings*, *66*, 183–192. https://doi.org/10.1016/j.enbuild.2013.06.030

Costa-Carrapiço, I., Raslan, R., & González, J. N. (2020). A systematic review of genetic algorithm-based multi-objective optimisation for building retrofitting strategies towards energy efficiency. *Energy and Buildings*. Advance online publication. https://doi.org/10.1016/j.enbuild.2019.109690

D'Oca, S., Hong, T., & Langevin, J. (2018). The human dimensions of energy use in buildings: A review. *Renewable and Sustainable Energy Reviews*. Advance online publication. https://doi.org/10.1016/j.rser.2017.08.019

Fabi, V., Andersen, R. V., Corgnati, S., & Olesen, B. W. (2012). Occupants' window opening behaviour: A literature review of factors influencing occupant behaviour and models. *Building and Environment*, *58*, 188–198. https://doi.org/10.1016/j.buildenv.2012.07.009

Frederiks, E. R., Stenner, K., & Hobman, E. V. (2015). Household energy use: Applying behavioural economics to understand consumer decision-making and behaviour. *Renewable and Sustainable Energy Reviews*. Advance online publication.https://doi.org/10.1016/j.rser.2014.09.026

Freire, R. Z., Oliveira, G. H. C., & Mendes, N. (2008). Development of regression equations for predicting energy and hygrothermal performance of buildings. *Energy and Buildings*, *40*(5), 810–820. https://doi.org/10.1016/j.enbuild.2007.05.014

Galvin, R. (2010). Thermal upgrades of existing homes in Germany: The building code, subsidies, and economic efficiency. *Energy and Buildings*, *42*(6), 834–844. https://doi.org/10.1016/j.enbuild.2009.12.004

Galvin, R. (2012). German federal policy on thermal renovation of existing homes: A policy evaluation. *Sustainable Cities and Society*, *4*(1), 58–66. https://doi.org/10.1016/j.scs.2012.05.003

Haddad, S., Barker, A., Yang, J., Kumar, D. I. M., Garshasbi, S., Paolini, R., … Santamouris, M. (2020). On the potential of building adaptation measures to counterbalance the impact of climatic change in the tropics. *Energy and Buildings*, *229*. https://doi.org/10.1016/j.enbuild.2020.110494

Hong, T., Taylor-Lange, S. C., D'Oca, S., Yan, D., & Corgnati, S. P. (2016). Advances in research and applications of energy-related occupant behavior in buildings. *Energy and Buildings*. Advance online publication. https://doi.org/10.1016/j.enbuild.2015.11.052

Kearns, A., Whitley, E., & Curl, A. (2019). Occupant behaviour as a fourth driver of fuel poverty (aka warmth & energy deprivation). *Energy Policy*, 1143–1155. https://doi.org/10.1016/j.enpol.2019.03.023

Lindén, A. L., Carlsson-Kanyama, A., & Eriksson, B. (2006). Efficient and inefficient aspects of residential energy behaviour: What are the policy instruments for change? *Energy Policy*, *34*(14), 1918–1927. https://doi.org/10.1016/j.enpol.2005.01.015

Little, R. J. A. (1988). A test of missing completely at random for multivariate data with missing values. *Journal of the American Statistical Association*, *83*, 1198–1202.

Majcen, D., Itard, L. C. M., & Visscher, H. (2013). Theoretical vs. actual energy consumption of labelled dwellings in the Netherlands: Discrepancies and policy implications. *Energy Policy*, *54*, 125–136. https://doi.org/10.1016/j.enpol.2012.11.008

Murtagh, N., Gatersleben, B., & Fife-Schaw, C. (2019). Occupants' motivation to protect residential building stock from climate-related overheating: A study in southern England. *Journal of Cleaner Production*, *226*, 186–194. https://doi.org/10.1016/j.jclepro.2019.04.080

Nair, G., Gustavsson, L., & Mahapatra, K. (2010). Factors influencing energy efficiency investments in existing Swedish residential buildings. *Energy Policy*, *38*(6), 2956–2963. https://doi.org/10.1016/j.enpol.2010.01.033

Nikoofard, S., Ugursal, V. I., & Beausoleil-Morrison, I. (2011). Effect of external shading on household energy requirement for heating and cooling in Canada. *Energy and Buildings*, *43*(7), 1627–1635. https://doi.org/10.1016/j.enbuild.2011.03.003

O'Brien, W., Wagner, A., Schweiker, M., Mahdavi, A., Day, J., Kjærgaard, M. B., … Berger, C. (2020). Introducing IEA EBC annex 79: Key challenges and opportunities in the field of occupant-centric building design and operation. *Building and Environment*, *178*. https://doi.org/10.1016/j.buildenv.2020.106738

Ortiz, M., Itard, L., & Bluyssen, P. M. (2020). Indoor environmental quality related risk factors with energy-efficient retrofitting of housing: A literature review. *Energy and Buildings*, *221*. https://doi.org/10.1016/j.enbuild.2020.110102

Ozarisoy, B. (2022). Energy effectiveness of passive cooling design strategies to reduce the impact of long-term heatwaves on occupants' thermal comfort in Europe: Climate change and mitigation. *Journal of Cleaner Production*.Advance online publication. https://doi.org/10.1016/j.jclepro.2021.129675

Ozarisoy, B., & Altan, H. (2017a). Energy performance development of non-regulated retrofit mass housing estates in Northern Cyprus. *Design Journal*, *20*(Suppl 1), S1765–S1781. https://doi.org/10.1080/14606925.2017.1352697

Ozarisoy, B., & Altan, H. (2017b). Adoption of energy design strategies for retrofitting mass housing estates in Northern Cyprus. *Sustainability (Switzerland)*, *9*(8), 1477. https://doi.org/10.3390/su9081477

Ozarisoy, B., & Altan, H. (2018). Low-energy design strategies for retrofitting existing residential buildings in Cyprus. *Proceedings of the Institution of Civil Engineers: Engineering Sustainability*, *172*(5), 241–255. https://doi.org/10.1680/jensu.17.00061

Ozarisoy, B., & Elsharkawy, H. (2019). Assessing overheating risk and thermal comfort in state-of-the-art prototype houses that combat exacerbated climate change in UK. *Energy and Buildings*, *187*, 201–217. https://doi.org/10.1016/j.enbuild.2019.01.030

Papadopoulos, S., Bonczak, B., & Kontokosta, C. E. (2018). Pattern recognition in building energy performance over time using energy benchmarking data. *Applied Energy*, *221*, 576–586. https://doi.org/10.1016/j.apenergy.2018.03.079

Park, J. S., & Kim, H. J. (2012). A field study of occupant behavior and energy consumption in apartments with mechanical ventilation. *Energy and Buildings*, *50*, 19–25. https://doi.org/10.1016/j.enbuild.2012.03.015

Santamouris, M., Pavlou, K., Kolokotsa, D., Synnefa, A., & Niachou, K. (2007). Recent progress on passive cooling techniques. *Energy and Buildings*, *39*(7), 859–866. https://doi.org/10.1016/j.enbuild.2007.02.008

Schweiker, M., Huebner, G. M., Kingma, B. R. M., Kramer, R., & Pallubinsky, H. (2018). *Drivers of diversity in human thermal perception–A review for holistic comfort models temperature*. Routledge. https://doi.org/10.1080/23328940.2018.1534490

Sodagar, B., & Starkey, D. (2016). The monitored performance of four social houses certified to the code for sustainable homes level 5. *Energy and Buildings*, *110*, 245–256. https://doi.org/10.1016/j.enbuild.2015.11.016

Sunikka-Blank, M., & Galvin, R. (2012). Introducing the prebound effect: The gap between performance and actual energy consumption. *Building Research and Information*, *40*(3), 260–273. https://doi.org/10.1080/09613218.2012.690952

Yohanis, Y. G. (2012). Domestic energy use and householders' energy behaviour. *Energy Policy*, *41*, 654–665. https://doi.org/10.1016/j.enpol.2011.11.028

5 Adaptive Thermal Comfort

Introduction

The findings of the environmental monitoring that concurrently assessed overheating risks and the occupants' thermal comfort with a one-point time survey are presented. The occupants' TSVs, which were ascertained during the questionnaire survey, are discussed to understand and convey the environmental conditions of measured flats. The findings of the subject participants' TSVs were used to measure the indoor air temperature and relative humidity (RH) to undertake a regression forecasting analysis for the purpose of determining what constitutes neutral adaptive thermal comfort. Bar charts depicting relationships between indoor- and outdoor-environmental conditions and the occupants' TSVs are considered, and the overall results are presented.[1]

Physical Measurements

The field instruments were recruited to investigate absolute accuracy measures related to the degree of thermal discomfort experienced in the summer in this Eastern Mediterranean climate. In this study, physical measurements were carried out in the summer, and the measured indoor occupied spaces were analysed.

On-Site Monitoring

A Vantage Vue weather station was installed on the roof of the RTB, and the monitoring console of the weather station was plugged into the specialist weather software suite. Temperature measurements were collected at 15-minute intervals over a period of one month.

External weather data were collected from the ASHRAE Climate Zone 2A weather station at Larnaca Airport, Cyprus, to compare the outdoor environmental readings with the actual meteorological year (AMY) weather file. In the study context, the period of monitoring occurred during the field-survey period in August 2018. A hot spell was observed from 9 to 12 August, during which outdoor temperatures reached a maximum of 38.7°C at the Larnaca Airport weather station and averaged 28.7°C during the daytime and 25.4°C at night. The monitoring results of the weather data that were extracted from the weather station in August 2018 can be seen in Figure 5.1(a).

DOI: 10.4324/9781003393092-6

Figure 5.1(a) demonstrates fluctuations in the outdoor air temperature, RH, heat-stress index (HSI) factor, maximum and minimum outdoor air temperatures and dew point temperatures for the duration of a hot summer at the case-study location. As the graph depicts, the outdoor air temperature ranged from 27 to 36°C on 1–4 August, fluctuated from 26 to 36°C on 5–11 August and reached its final peak of 38°C on 11 August. Outdoor air temperatures fluctuated between 25 and 34°C on 17–23 August, then slightly increased to 37°C on 24 August. It

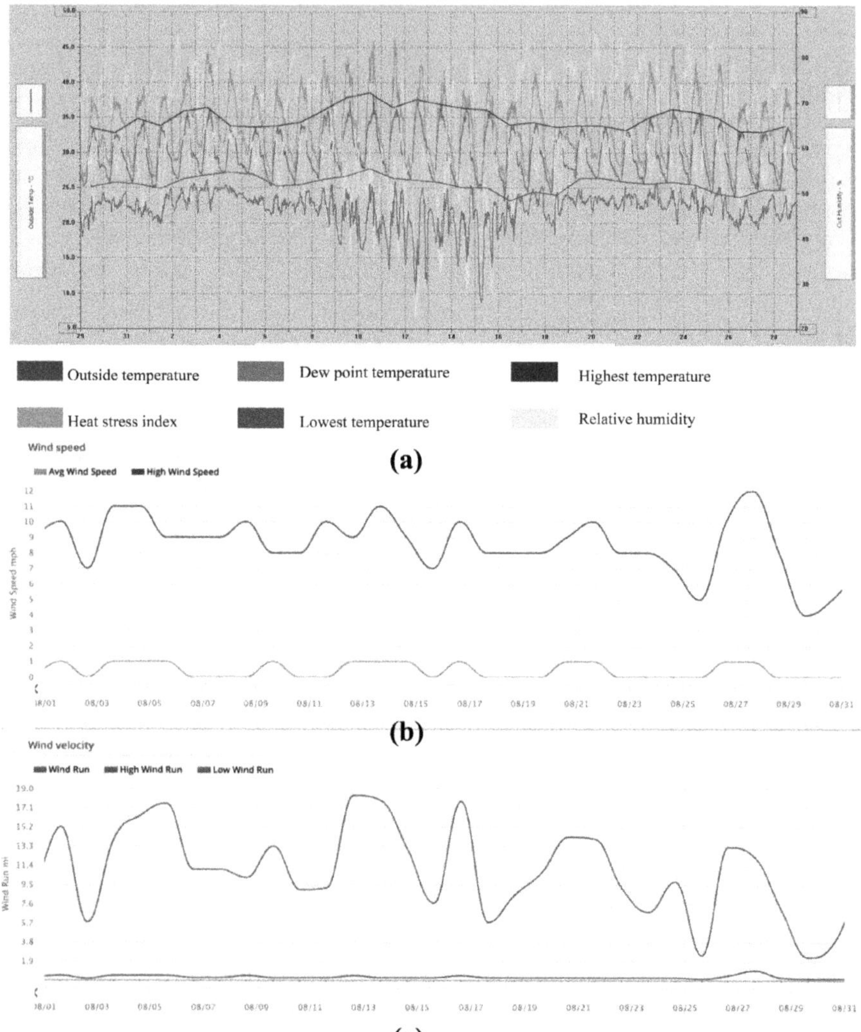

Figure 5.1 (a) *On-site* environmental monitoring readings between 29 July and 29 August 2018, (b) air movement with average- and high-speed recordings and (c) wind velocity–frequency recordings.

should be noted that along with the findings from epidemiology, which considered an external temperature of greater than 23°C to constitute a critical threshold, these data represent increased health risks for occupants in their homes (Nicol et al., 2012).

The findings demonstrate that the average daily temperature for the remaining days of the monitoring period was above 23°C, which is the lower limit of acceptable thermal-comfort levels (CIBSE, 2016). As can be seen in Figure 5.1(a), outdoor air temperatures fluctuated between 24 and 35°C on 25–30 August; this resulted in a high heat-stress index factor for the occupants at the time the survey was conducted. Furthermore, the external temperature during the final two days of the monitoring period, 29 and 30 August, rose above 25°C; temperatures were over 25°C for 21 h each day.

It must be stressed that the running mean temperature of the measured external temperature, T_{rm} 23°C,[2] as defined in BS EN 15251 (BSI, 2005), reached the 23°C benchmark for the entire month. The results suggest that the overall monitored period was significantly warmer than the recommended lower thermal-comfort threshold level described in the *CIBSE Guide A* (CIBSE, 2016). Notably, the Meteorological Office of Cyprus reported that August temperatures in previous years were lower than the average monthly temperature of 27.1°C that was recorded in 2018 at the Larnaca Airport weather station (Ozarisoy & Altan, 2018).

It can therefore be deduced that in the first week of August 2018, which was the peak of the heatwave, heat stress temperatures fluctuated between 29 and 44°C before peaking at 46°C on 11 August. Notably, the highest outdoor air temperatures were recorded between 9 and 13 August and reached 38°C on 11 August. As such, it can be observed that the heat-stress index and the outdoor air temperatures both had similar fluctuation patterns, even though a 44°C heat-stress index temperature is considered to be a highly unacceptable outdoor air temperature when considering the occupants' thermal comfort.

Figure 5.1 (a) further shows that from 14 to 17 August, the heat-stress index temperature ranged between 36 and 44°C before slightly rising to 45°C on 23 August, then decreased to 36°C on 26 August. Between 27 and 30 August, the heat-stress index temperature ranged between 36 and 40°C; this reveals a pattern that is similar to outdoor air temperature fluctuations, even though the outdoor temperatures were much higher due to the long-lasting heatwave period across continental Europe in 2018. The highest outdoor air temperature of 37°C was recorded on 11 August, and the highest heat-stress index temperature of 46°C was also recorded on that day; the lowest outdoor air temperature of 24°C was recorded on 16 August.

Figure 5.1 (a) shows the manner in which the fluctuation patterns in outdoor air temperatures affected the outdoor RH fluctuations during the heatwave of August 2018: In the first week, the outdoor RH reached a 48% relative humidity index (RHI) level, and the RH fluctuated between 65% and 87%; the RH fluctuated between 60% and 80% through the second and third weeks, then dropped to 25% on 12 August.

It should be highlighted that the final week of August included a heatwave, and the RH fluctuated between 60% and 80% in this period. RH plummeted to 35% on

24 August and then remained stable—between 60% and 80%—for the remainder of the month, notwithstanding external air temperature fluctuations. The findings demonstrate that the RHI recorded throughout the monitoring period was above the range of acceptable limits of RHI recommended by the *CIBSE Guide A* criteria for occupants' thermal comfort (CIBSE, 2016). The results reveal that thermally uncomfortable indoor air environmental conditions were observed due to the high outdoor RH recorded at the case-study location.

Figure 5.1(a) shows that on 1–12 August, the dew point temperature fluctuated between 20 and 25°C, then it plummeted to 10°C on 12 August and to 8°C on 15 August, before significantly increasing to 24°C on 18 August. It was observed that from 13 to 30 August, the dew point temperature fluctuated between 21 and 25°C; this shows that hot and humid outdoor weather conditions affect the indoor comfort level of occupants. The overall monitoring results indicated that indoor space temperatures increased during the peak time of the heatwave to levels that created a high degree of thermal discomfort for the occupants.

Air velocities were also considered because they are important to restore the occupants' thermal comfort; as such, the airspeed frequency was recorded. The occupants were not asked to record their thermal perceptions while considering the impact of air movement on their adaptive thermal comfort at that time. The readings that were obtained were taken into consideration to avoid bias in the subject participants' responses related to their TPVs and TSVs. Figure 5.1(b) and (c) illustrate the ventilation rate readings for outdoor environmental conditions that were concurrently monitored as the questionnaire survey was being conducted.

As can be seen in Figure 5.1(b) and (c), the average recorded wind speed throughout the field-survey period was 0.2 m/s. The Cyprus Meteorological Service data indicate that the minimum and maximum wind speeds in Cyprus in December are 2.98 and 6.16 m/s, respectively; while they tend to be 3.75 and 7.0 m/.s, respectively, in August (Cyprus Meteorological Service, 2020). The environmental monitoring studies revealed that the airspeed fluctuations that were noted within the other environmental parameters that were recorded at the time of the survey affected the occupants' habitual adaptive behaviour that led them to adjust their thermal-comfort levels due to the acclimatisation of high indoor air temperatures, which directly impacted the participants' TSVs and TPVs.

In Situ Measurements

The field investigation in the present study was carried out in the summer, and the measured indoor occupied spaces were analysed; indoor environmental conditions were recorded with a Model HT200 Heat Stress WBGT Meter from Extech Instruments (resolution 0.1°C); to validate these findings, in situ measurements were performed using a forward-looking infrared radiometer (FLIR) infrared thermographic camera to assess the occupants' TSVs.[3] Table 5.1 presents a descriptive analysis of the monitored and measured environmental parameters during the summer period surveyed.[4]

Table 5.1 Outdoor and Indoor Climate Parameter Data in Representative Interviewed/Measured Flats

Environmental Parameters	*Minimum (°C)*	*Maximum (°C)*	*Mean (°C)*	*Standard Deviation*
Indoor air temperature	25.40	34.10	30.595	1.76860
Indoor RH	31.10	75.00	57.838	8.75611
Outdoor air temperature	23.70	36.00	32.118	2.17015
Outdoor RH	19.60	78.00	59.166	11.76264
Outdoor HSI	33.00	43.00	36.700	2.33766

The results of environmental monitoring findings showed the typically warm conditions of the environment during the survey period in the summer. Maximum indoor and outdoor air temperatures peaked at 34.1°C ($SD = 1.76$) and 36°C ($SD = 2.17$), respectively. It was further observed that the RH levels of the indoor environment were not excessively high on hot summer days, with a mean of 57.83%, a maximum of 75% and a minimum of 31.10% ($SD = 8.75$). However, the outdoor environment had a mean humidity level of 59.16% ($SD = 11.76$), and it was found that outdoor temperatures during these six weeks were above 23°C for 95% of the time.

The mean indoor air temperature was recorded for 100 flats in the present study, and it was found that the indoor air temperatures ranged from 25.4 to 34.1°C, which was significantly higher than the 28°C acceptable thermal-comfort upper threshold cited in the *CIBSE Guide A* (CIBSE, 2016). The results revealed that all 36 RTB households suffered from uncomfortable indoor environmental conditions that should be further investigated to predict neutral adaptive thermal comfort by way of an ordinal regression analysis (RA). Notably, the low quality of building materials and significant heat losses through building envelopes were found to increase indoor air temperatures, particularly intense solar radiation on the top floor flats.

Table 5.2[5] delineates the indoor air temperature recordings that were obtained by using infrared radiometer thermography (IRT) to explore correlations between the impact of solar radiation on building envelopes and the occupants' thermal comfort, while concurrently taking both the wet- and dry-bulb temperature readings into account.[6]

As can be seen in Table 5.2, when the occupants responded to the questionnaire survey, a limited range of thermal conditions that could be considered slightly warm or very warm according to the thermal-sensation scale is recommended by the BS EN ISO 7730:2005 standard. The mean indoor air temperature for the 100 living room spaces that was recorded at the time that the participants responded to the questions ranged from 25.4 to 34.1°C, which is significantly higher than the acceptable upper thermal-comfort threshold of 28°C indicated by the *CIBSE Guide A* (CIBSE, 2016); this implies that local climate conditions are the determinant factor that influences adaptive thermal-comfort levels. It was therefore necessary

Table 5.2 In Situ Measurements of Building Envelopes and Indoor Air Temperature Parameter Recordings

Frequencies			*In Situ Measurements*	*Indoor WET*	*Indoor DEW*
N (normality)	**Valid**		100	100	100
Mean (°C)			33.64	24.35	21.48
Standard error of mean			0.23545	0.32722	0.33602
Median (°C)			32.90	24.60	21.90
Standard deviation (*SD*)			2.35445	3.27217	3.36021
Skewness			0.840	3.844	−0.0567
Standard error of skewness			0.241	0.241	0.241
Kurtosis			−0.036	29.640	3.067
Standard error of kurtosis			0.478	0.478	0.478
Minimum (°C)			29.10	18.70	11.40
Maximum (°C)			39.80	48.50	32.40
Percentiles (°C)		25th	32.10	23.00	20.20
		50th	32.90	24.60	21.90
		75th	34.80	25.57	23.40

to pair the humidity value to the occupants' thermal sensations, especially neutral sensations that were associated with 28.5°C. The neutral temperature was explored in the present study to better understand the relationship between the occupants' TSVs and indoor operative air temperatures (OTs). Figure 5.2(a)–(d) depicts the indoor air temperatures, RH, outdoor air temperatures and RH fluctuations during the heatwave of August 2018.[7]

According to Figure 5.2(a)–(d), the recorded temperatures were above the acceptable benchmark of 25°C that was determined to maintain the occupants' thermal comfort (BSI, 2005; CIBSE, 2017; CEN, 2007).[8] Additionally, the average mean temperatures that were recorded across the indoor measurement results and the outdoor monitoring results ranged from 30.59 to 32.12°C, which is above the recommended thermal-comfort level of 23–25°C indicated by the CIBSE TM52 Overheating Task Force. It is worth noting that recorded daily running mean outdoor temperatures reflected the thermal experiences of the occupants more accurately than the monthly mean temperatures, because the outdoor mean temperatures sometimes changed in significantly shorter intervals (Nicol et al., 2012).[9] Even though the monthly mean temperature was taken as an average temperature of the month as a whole in the present study, the occupants' TSVs were found to be correlated with their thermal experiences and their ability to adapt their physiological body temperatures to changing summer climate conditions (Ozarisoy & Altan, 2017a).

On-site Observations

To investigate how the occupants' thermal perceptions of their indoor occupied spaces can be explained by a physiological approach, subjective thermal sensations

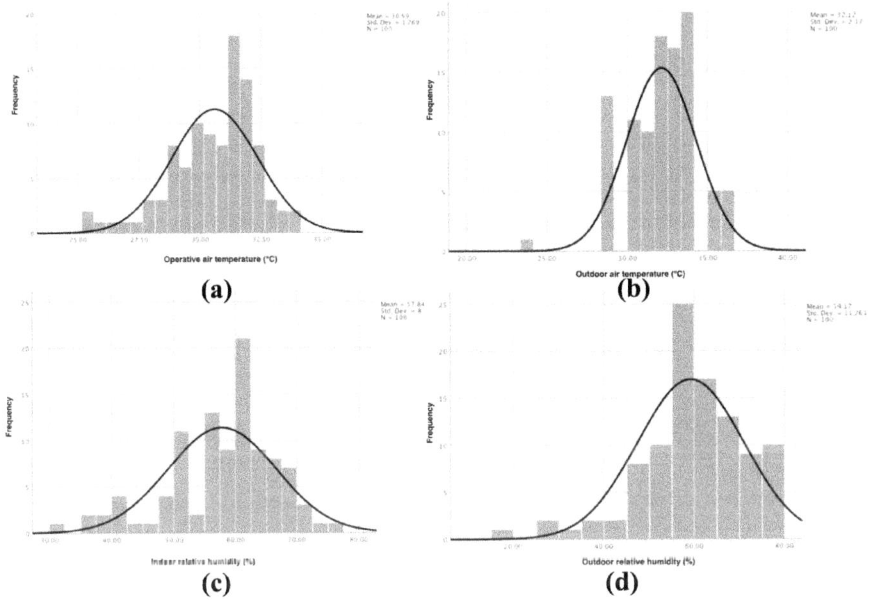

Figure 5.2 Distribution of environmental conditions: (a) operative air temperature, (b) outdoor air temperature, (c) indoor RH and (d) outdoor RH.

need to be compared with the heat balance model. Brager and de Dear (1998) indicate that the thermal comfort of each occupied space is perceived using the physical factors of the space as well as the occupants' impressions of thermal sensation.

To identify adaptive thermal-comfort thresholds for the case-study location, the research instruments were used to investigate the significance of the physical factors and their influence on thermal comfort. This section illustrates the field equipment that were used to measure subjective sensations of thermal comfort. Figure 5.3(a)–(f) demonstrates the field survey diaries and archival photographic documentation of the surveyed flats, taking into consideration the different orientations of the RTBs in the social-housing estate.

In Question 33, occupants were asked how satisfied they were with the temperature in their living rooms; the reason for this question was so that the answers could be correlated with the building orientation to identify the overheating risk of the occupied spaces, as illustrated in Figure 5.4(a).

According to Figure 5.4(a),[10] 2% of the occupants in the northeast-facing RTBs stated that they felt cold, 11% felt cool, 8% felt slightly cool, 4% felt neutral and 5% felt slightly warm. In the south-facing RTBs, 5% of the respondents stated that they felt cold, 8% felt cool, 10% felt neutral, 2% felt slightly warm, 4% felt warm and 1% felt hot; this is due to the south-facing RTBs absorbing a high level of solar radiation throughout the day in the summer, which resulted in high indoor air

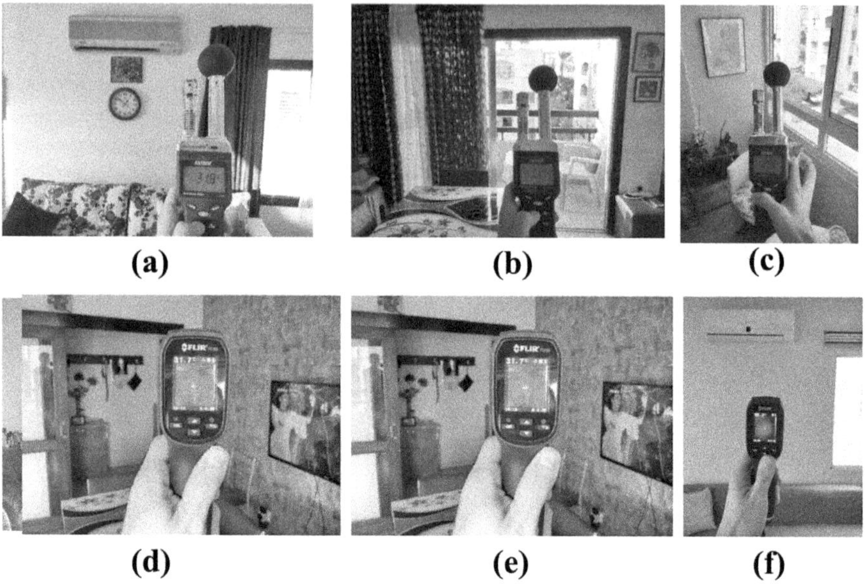

Figure 5.3 In situ measurements recorded while (a) wall-mounted A/C system was in use in late afternoon; (b) single-glazed aluminium-framed window was open in late afternoon; (c) double-glazed window was open in early morning (participant was interviewed in balcony); (d) internal doors were open in early morning (participant was interviewed in balcony, and portable fan was in use during survey); (e) windows were open and (f) inverter A/C system was in use.

temperature fluctuations that prompted these households to rely on domestic cooling systems to adjust their indoor air temperatures.

In the northwest-facing RTBs, 2% of the respondents reported that they felt neutral, 1% felt slightly warm and 1% felt warm. In the southwest-facing RTBs, 6% of the respondents felt cool due to the fact that most of these participants lived in ground-floor flats, and the shading factor from adjacent buildings had a significant impact on their TSVs; in addition to these respondents, 5% of the participants in these RTBs felt cold, 1% felt slightly cool and 1% felt slightly warm. In the southeast-facing RTBs, 2% of the respondents expressed that they felt cold, 2% felt cool, 1% felt slightly cool, 5% felt neutral and 1% felt slightly warm.

The findings reveal that the households in the south-facing RTBs experienced high levels of discomfort in the summer: Overall, 23% of the total participants asserted that they felt between slightly cool and slightly warm, which emphasises the fact that the risk of overheating is most likely to occur in the south-facing RTBs. One interviewee who suffered from asthma reported that the high indoor air temperatures lead to thermally uncomfortable conditions for their family members. The interviewee also commented that due to his health issues, he preferred to open windows and use a portable fan to cool down the indoor air temperature.

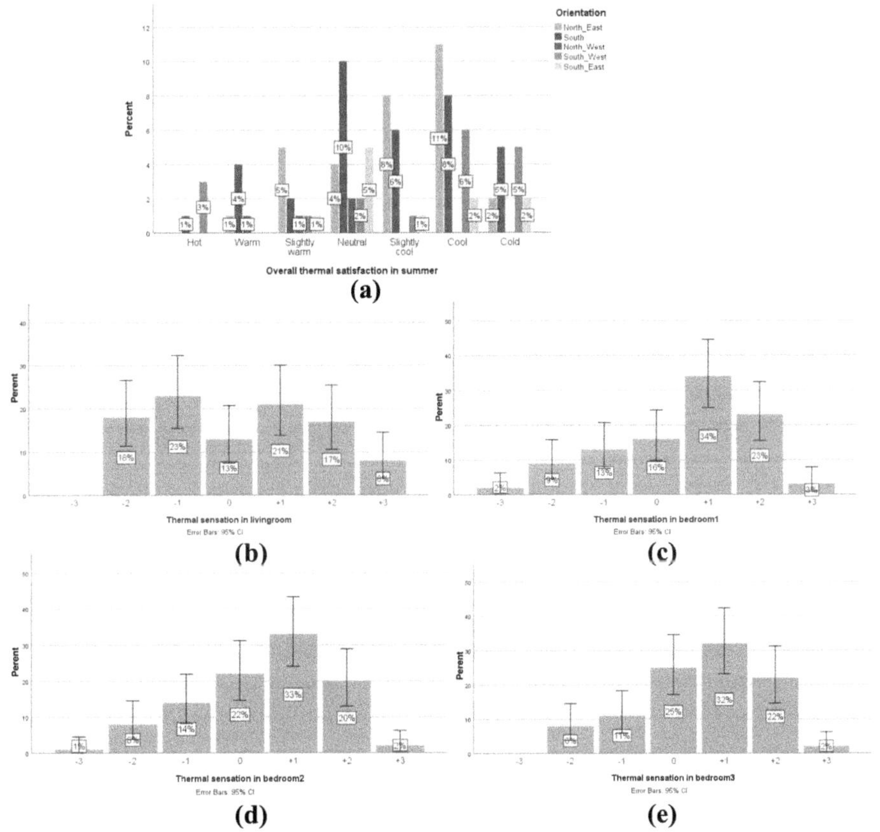

Figure 5.4 (a) Percentage distribution of household thermal-comfort satisfaction votes in the summer according to different building orientations; percentage distribution of occupants' TSVs in (b) living room and (c) Bedroom 1; percentage distribution of occupants' TSVs in (d) Bedroom 2 and (e) Bedroom 3.

It is important to note that during the field survey, it was observed that some households had enclosed their balcony spaces and installed large, double-glazed aluminium frames that worked as window systems to allow natural ventilation (NV) into their living rooms more effectively (Ozarisoy & Altan, 2017b). Additionally, some respondents were interviewed in their converted balcony spaces, where they expressed feeling thermally comfortable, and they indicated spending most of their time in the converted balcony and adjusting the windows according to their thermal-comfort preferences throughout the day. From the field-survey observations, a retiree couple who were in the 55–65 age band were interviewed while sitting in their converted balcony space with only the windows opened; they stated that they felt thermally comfortable because they were able to control the prevailing winds coming into the enclosed balcony area.

The results indicate that RTB orientation plays a crucial role in the occupants' TPVs. Therefore, the household size, occupancy patterns and window-opening behaviour must be taken into account to assess the degree of thermal discomfort and identify adaptive thermal-comfort thresholds. The following section examines the occupants' TSVs for each occupied space in their properties to assess the risk of overheating and provide subsequent background information on building-performance evaluation of base-case RTBs in Chapter 6.

Investigation of Occupants' TSVs

Statistical analyses were therefore used to determine the factors that influence the occupants' TSVs in order to investigate the degree of overheating experienced in the summer. The analyses carried out in this research were explanatory in nature, and the objective was to determine the relationships among different variables (i.e., respondents' age, RTB orientation, different floor levels of the flats and indoor OT and outdoor air temperatures). This section presents the findings of the relative influence and interaction among the variables and paves the way for an assessment of the occupants' thermal-comfort level for certain groups.

Descriptive Statistics

To fulfil the research objective, the study investigated the occupants' TSVs in accordance with their socio-demographic characteristics, including gender and age, and the physical structure of the RTBs was also taken into consideration in terms of the orientation and different floor levels of the flats. The TSVs were rated using the ASHRAE seven-point thermal-sensation scale[11]: cold (−3), cool (−2), slightly cool (−1), neutral (0), slightly warm (+1), warm (+2) and hot (+3). The TSVs of very dissatisfied, slightly dissatisfied, neutral, slightly satisfied, satisfied and very satisfied with the indoor environment were also assessed using a seven-point scale from −3 to +3 (Parkinson et al., 2020). Figure 5.4(b)–(e) illustrates the findings of the occupants' TSVs in each occupied space across the surveyed sample size.[12]

As shown in Figure 5.4(b), 8% of the respondents reported that they felt too warm in their living room in the summer, 17% felt too warm, 21% felt comfortably warm, 13% felt comfortable, 23% felt comfortably cool and 18% felt too cool. A further 41% of the respondents reported that they felt comfortably cool and too cool in their living rooms. However, 46% expressed feeling comfortably warm and much too warm in the summer due to the RTB orientations.

Figure 5.4(c) shows that 3% of the respondents felt too warm in their Bedroom 1 space in the summer, 23% felt too warm, 34% felt comfortably warm, 16% felt comfortable, 13% felt comfortably cool, 9% felt too cool and 2% felt much too cool. Thus, approximately two-thirds (60%) of the participants voted that the space felt comfortably warm and much too warm.

According to Figure 5.4(d), 2% of the surveyed households reported that they felt much too warm in their Bedroom 2 space in the summer, 20% felt too warm, 33% felt comfortably warm, 22% felt comfortable, 14% felt comfortably cool, 8%

felt too cool and 1% felt much too cool. On the other hand, 22% of the respondents indicated that they were comfortable in their Bedroom 2 spaces. Over half (56%) of the participants reported that they preferred to feel comfortably warm or much too warm. However, 22% of the participants expressed feeling thermally comfortable. This may be directly related to the different RTB orientations and floor levels.

The TSV results for the Bedroom 3 spaces more or less reflected the same patterns as the Bedroom 1 and Bedroom 2 spaces. According to Figure 5.4(e), 2% felt much too warm in their Bedroom 3 space, 22% felt too cool, 32% felt comfortably warm, 25% felt comfortable, 11% felt comfortably cool and 8% felt too cool. As was previously mentioned, this could have been due to the RTB orientations and the different floor levels of the measured flats. The findings revealed that there were signs of thermal discomfort in all of these indoor spaces, which were probably caused by the RTBs' low-quality construction materials and high solar absorptivity, based on their orientation. It also emerged from the findings that most of the occupants experienced slightly high indoor air temperatures in their living room spaces due to the poor window design and the absence of shading strategies to provide protection from the direct sun. This highlights the fact that the occupants' TSV ranking scale distribution included a lot of variation, thus indicating relatively thermally uncomfortable conditions in the summer.

Relationships for the Identification of Thermal Comfort

Cross-tabulations[13] using chi-square[14] analysis explored the reasons for thermal discomfort with respect to the household age, the orientation of the RTBs and the different floor levels in each occupied space based on the collected data from the respondents. This analysis was conducted because socio-demographic characteristics have been shown to be a significant factor in people's behaviour in any setting. Considering the age band in this cross-tabulation analysis was necessary because nearly half (48%) of the households were in the 55–65 and 65-years-of-age and older age groups, it is important to consider the impact of age on thermal comfort in these measured flats.

In conjunction with households' socio-demographic analysis, the different RTB orientations and floor levels were taken into consideration. The results of feed-forward interviews highlight that 24% of the occupants complained about high humidity in the southwest-facing RTBs in the summer, and 17% complained about incoming sun. This indicated that the occupants may have experienced thermally uncomfortable conditions due to the high outdoor air temperatures and humid conditions in this Eastern Mediterranean climate. This became clear when the study determined that there were negative relationships between the occupants' reasons for thermal discomfort and the different floor levels for their respective flats, as shown in Table 5.3.

As shown in Table 5.3, the results indicate a moderate–strong relationship between orientation and reasons for thermal discomfort ($\chi^2 = 49.327$, $p < 0.001$, *Cramer*'s $V = 0.405$). A greater proportion of participants living in south-facing

Table 5.3 Relationships between Reasons for Thermal Discomfort and Household Age Band, RTB Orientation and Floor Level

Research Question and Variables		*Discomfort*	*Age Band*	*Orientation*	*Floor Level*
Q 35: How would you best describe the source of this discomfort?	*Cramer's V*	1	0.203	0.405**	0.233
	Significance	—	0.416	0.000	0.062
Age band	*Cramer's V*	0.203	1	0.229	0.211
	Significance	0.416	—	0.202	0.347
Orientation	*Cramer's V*	0.405**	0.229	1	0.197
	Significance	0.000	0.202	—	0.234
Floor level	*Cramer's V*	0.233	0.211	0.197	1
	Significance	0.062	0.347	0.234	—

Household age band scale ran from 0 (20–25) to 5 (65 and over)
RTB orientation: 0 (north-east), 1 (south), 2 (north-west), 3 (south-west) and 4 (south-east)
Different floor levels: 0 (ground), 1 (first), 2 (second), 3 (third), 4 (fourth) and 5 (fifth)
Age band scale ran from 0 (20–25) to 5 (65 and over)
Reasons for thermal discomfort–Floor level, $\chi^2(9) = 16.26$, $p = 0.062$, *Cramer's* $V = 0.233$
Reasons for thermal discomfort–Orientation, $\chi^2(9) = 49.33$, $p = 0.000$, *Cramer's* $V = 0.405$
Reasons for thermal discomfort–Age bands, $\chi^2(12) = 12.38$, $p = 0.416$, *Cramer's* $V = 0.203$
Age bands–Floor level, $\chi^2(12) = 13.31$, $p = 0.347$, *Cramer's* $V = 0.211$
Age bands–Orientation, $\chi^2(12) = 15.77$, $p = 0.202$, *Cramer's* $V = 0.229$
Orientation–Floor level, $\chi^2(9) = 11.65$, $p = 0.234$, *Cramer's* $V = 0.197$

*p > 0.05; **p > 0.001

RTBs felt thermal discomfort due to humidity than participants living in the south-west. A greater proportion of participants living in the south-west selected incoming sun as thermal discomfort reason than participants living in the other areas; this was due to the poor window design in the RTBs, which prevented NV into the indoor occupied spaces. This led to a difference of 2–3°C between the ground and upper floor level flats due to a lack of NV and as a result of the upper floor receiving the intense horizontal radiation on the roof surfaces. Thus, it appeared that the occupants' habitual adaptive behaviour in window-opening patterns also played a crucial role in their TSV decisions. Nevertheless, reasons for thermal discomfort were not significantly related to age and floor levels.

According to the survey findings, 55% of the respondents reported opening windows for more than 8 h in the summer, which highlighted the fact that most of the respondents preferred to open their windows to acclimatise their indoor air temperatures. This possibly reflected a relationship between household socio-demographic characteristics and the RTBs' physical positions, partly because the occupants had experienced relatively uncomfortable indoor air temperatures in their occupied spaces in the summer. From this analysis, it was determined that the different floor levels played a crucial role in the households' habitual adaptive behaviours with respect to thermal comfort.

Table 5.4(a) Relationships between Occupants' TSVs for Each Occupied Space in the Summer: Living Room, Kitchen, Bedroom 1, Bedroom 2, Bedroom 3, RTB Orientation and Floor Level

Variables		*Living Room*	*Kitchen*	*Bedroom 1*	*Bedroom 2*	*Bedroom 3*	*Orientation*	*Floor Level*
Living Room	*Cramer*'s *V*/Pearson's correlation	1	0.462**	0.302**	0.146	0.200*	0.226	0.236
	Significance	—	0.000	0.002	0.147	0.046	0.432	0.376
Kitchen	*Cramer*'s *V*/Pearson's correlation	0.462**	1	0.133	0.205*	0.220*	0.279	0.222
	Significance	0.000	—	0.187	0.041	0.028	0.077	0.467
Bedroom 1	*Cramer*'s *V*/Pearson's correlation	0.302**	0.133	1	0.763**	0.724**	0.274	0.177
	Significance	0.002	0.187	—	0.000	0.000	0.210	0.949
Bedroom 2	*Cramer*'s *V*/Pearson's correlation	0.146	0.205*	0.763**	1	0.829**	0.272	0.194
	Significance	0.147	0.041	0.000	—	0.000	0.222	0.884
Bedroom 3	*Cramer*'s *V*/Pearson's correlation	0.200*	0.220*	0.724**	0.829**	1	0.263	0.221
	Significance	0.046	0.028	0.000	0.000	—	0.143	0.478
Orientation	*Cramer*'s *V*	0.226	0.279	0.274	0.272	0.263	1	0.197
	Significance	0.432	0.077	0.210	0.222	0.143	—	0.234
Floor Level	*Cramer*'s *V*	0.236	0.222	0.177	0.194	0.221	0.197	1
	Significance	0.376	0.467	0.949	0.884	0.478	0.234	—

Occupants' TSVs for living room, kitchen and bedrooms 1, 2 and 3 in the summer: (−3) to (+3)
RTB orientation: 0 (north-east), 1 (south), 2 (north-west), 3 (south-west) and 4 (south-east)
Different floor levels: 0 (ground), 1 (first), 2 (second), 3 (third), 4 (fourth) and 5 (fifth)
***p > 0.05; **p > 0.001**

Table 5.4(b) (Continued)

Living room TSV–Floor level, $\chi^2(15) = 16.09$, $p = 0.376$, *Cramer's V* = 0.236
Kitchen TSV–Floor level, $\chi^2(15) = 14.79$, $p = 0.467$, *Cramer's V* = 0.222
Bedroom 1 TSV–Floor level, $\chi^2(18) = 9.42$, $p = 0.949$, *Cramer's V* = 0.177
Bedroom 2 TSV–Floor level, $\chi^2(18) = 11.24$, $p = 0.884$, *Cramer's V* = 0.194
Bedroom 3 TSV–Floor level, $\chi^2(15) = 14.63$, $p = 0.478$, *Cramer's V* = 0.221
Orientation–Floor level, $\chi^2(9) = 14.63$, $p = 0.234$, *Cramer's V* = 0.197
Living room TSV–Orientation, $\chi^2(15) = 5.27$, $p = 0.432$, *Cramer's V* = 0.226
Kitchen TSV–Orientation, $\chi^2(15) = 23.37$, $p = 0.077$, *Cramer's V* = 0.279
Bedroom 1 TSV–Orientation, $\chi^2(18) =22.53$, $p = 0.210$, *Cramer's V* = 0.274
Bedroom 2 TSV–Orientation, $\chi^2(18) = 22.22$, $p = 0.222$, *Cramer's V* = 0.272
Bedroom 3 TSV–Orientation, $\chi^2(15) = 20.80$, $p = 0.143$, *Cramer's V* = 0.263

In Questions 22–25, the occupants were asked to evaluate the overall quality of the indoor air temperature in an open-ended question form. The question concerning the respondents' rating of the quality of their indoor air environment was intended to assess the degree of thermal discomfort in the summer. Tables 5.4(a) and (b) present the cross-tabulations using chi-square tests comparing thermal sensations with orientation and floor, and Pearson's correlations[15] comparing thermal sensations between the households' TSVs in the summer and the physical position of the RTBs, which also take different RTB orientations into account.

As shown in Tables 5.4(a) and (b), several strong and moderate positive correlations related to the occupants' decisions on TSVs in the summer were detected. TSVs in Bedroom 1, Bedroom 2 and Bedroom 3 were strongly and positively correlated with each other (rs = 0.724–0.829,[16] ps < 0.001[17]). A moderate positive correlation was noted between the TSVs in the living room and kitchen spaces ($r = 0.462$, $p < 0.001$). TSVs in the living room were significantly but weakly correlated with TSVs in Bedroom 1 ($r = 0.302$, $p = 0.002$) and Bedroom 3 ($r = 0.200$, $p = 0.046$). TSVs in the kitchen were significantly but weakly related to TSVs in Bedroom 2 ($r = 0.205$, $p = 0.041$) and Bedroom 3 ($r = 0.220$, $p = 0.028$), which indicates that the position of the rooms in the flats should be taken into account to assess the occupants' thermal comfort and provide a basis for an ordinal logistic regression analysis; this is discussed in the following section.

The results revealed that orientation and floor level were not significantly related to any TSVs. This was probably due to the small floor area of these spaces, which means the physical condition of the RTBs can lead to thermally uncomfortable indoor air temperatures due to the poor window design in the interviewed flats. This also seemed to be consistent in spite of the energy consumption, and in particular, the problems of overheating strongly related to high electricity bills, where the houses gained heat at high rates due to the high transmittance U-values of the building properties across all 36 RTBs.

Regression Forecasting Analysis

This section includes an analysis of Question 34, which concerned the occupants' overall thermal sensation for each occupied space in the summer. Furthermore, the results of household TSVs for each occupied space against indoor air temperature recorded by undertaking in situ measurements are also presented herein.

An ordinal logistic regression was conducted by calculating numerical values of the predicted mean vote (PMV) results to identify the neutral thermal-comfort benchmark level. When comparing the subject respondents' TSVs with the PMV predictor model, it must be emphasised that nearly all of the statistical tests revealed slightly warm conditions that ranged 10% outside the acceptable thermal environment for comfort (−0.5 < PMV < 0.5) (Földváry et al., 2018). However, when the occupants' PMVs were normalised into a seven-point scale of TSVs (i.e., −0.5 < PMV < 0.5 set as 0 [neutral], 0.5 < PMV < 1.5 set as +1 [slightly warm], etc.), 80% of the results produced by the heat balance model were in the 'warmer-than-neutral' region (i.e., > +1) (BSI, 2005). Figure 5.5(a) and (b) demonstrates the development of an adaptive model to identify world global thermal-comfort benchmark criteria for multi-family houses (MFHs).

Figure 5.5(a) shows that the PMV index ranged from 16 to 29°C in naturally ventilated buildings, which are included in the ASHRAE Global Thermal Comfort Database II. The PMV index ranged from 12 to 28°C when the outdoor environmental conditions were considered to identify the adaptive model, as depicted in Figure 5.5(b). The satisfaction metric was selected to develop a baseline for a regression forecasting analysis. The occupants' TSVs were paired with indoor

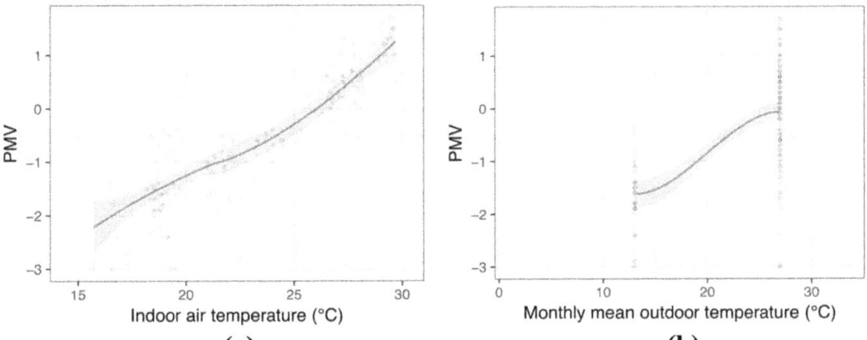

Figure 5.5 Scatter-plot distribution of adaptive model of MFHs: (a) indoor air temperature and (b) outdoor air temperature. Graphs extracted from the thermal-comfort visualisation tool PMV-index interface, an open-access source: https://cbe-berkeley.shinyapps.io/comfortdatabase *Source*: ASHRAE Global Thermal Comfort Database II (graphs extracted from the thermal-comfort visualisation tool PMV-index interface, an open-access source: https://cbe-berkeley.shinyapps.io/comfortdatabase).

RH to explore the impact thereof on neutral sensation thresholds, and a regression coefficient analysis of the relationship between the respondents' TSVs for each occupied space and outdoor air temperatures that were recorded by the weather station at the time the semi-structured interviews were conducted was undertaken at the same time (see Data 23).

The participants were asked, 'How would you rate the overall thermal satisfaction of indoor air temperature for living room spaces?', and their responses were evaluated according to the thermal-sensation scale to identify optimum indoor air temperatures in the summer. An ordinal logistic regression[18] was performed, and the result revealed no significant relationship between occupants' TSVs and living room OTs, *OR*= 0.993[19] (95% *CI* [0.816, 1.209]),[20] $p = 0.947$, *Nagelkerke* $R^2 <$ 0.001,[21] as shown in Table 5.5.[22] Figure 5.6(a) shows the respondents' TSVs plotted against OTs recorded during the field-survey period.

The occupants' preferred temperatures for their living room spaces are shown in Figure 5.6(a). Research has shown that the occupants were slightly uncomfortable when indoor air temperatures in their living room spaces ranged from 25 to 35°C. Of the respondents, 18% felt too warm (T_a 28–34°C, ±3°C and ±9°C); 23% felt comfortably warm (T_a 26–33°C, ±1°C and ±8°C); 13% felt comfortable (T_a 28.0–32.5°C, ±3°C and ±7.5°C); 21% felt comfortably cool (T_a 26–33°C, ±1°C and ±8°C); 17% felt too cool (T_a 27–33°C, ±2°C and ±8°C) and 8% felt much too cool (i.e., a similar pattern to that of the 'much too cool' thermal sensation). These results suggest that different thermal sensations significantly influence thermal comfort and also indicate that occupants feel uncomfortable at 32.5°C and very uncomfortable at 35°C (CIBSE, 2015).

The participants were asked, 'How would you rate the overall thermal satisfaction of the indoor air temperature for the Bedroom 1 spaces in the summer?', and their responses were evaluated according to the thermal-sensation scale to assess their degree of thermal discomfort and predict acceptably comfortable summer temperatures. An ordinal logistic regression was performed, and the result revealed no significant relationship between occupants' TSVs and Bedroom 1 OTs, *OR* =

Table 5.5 Summary of Ordinal Logistic Regression Predicting Living Room OTs from Occupants' TSVs

						95% CI of OR	
Predictor	*β*[a]	*SE*[b]	*Wald*[c]	*OR*	*p*	*Lower*	*Upper*
Occupants' TSVs	−0.007	0.100	0.000	0.993	0.947	0.816	1.209

[a]The beta regression weights *β* (standardised coefficient) were used in ordinal linear regression to assess which predictor variables were the most important and contributed to the prediction of *Y*.
[b]Like the multiple linear regression, this is how much the unstandardised regression weight can vary by. It is similar to a standard deviation to a mean.
[c]The Wald chi-square test is computed as the logistic regression coefficient squared and divided by the square of the standard error (variance).

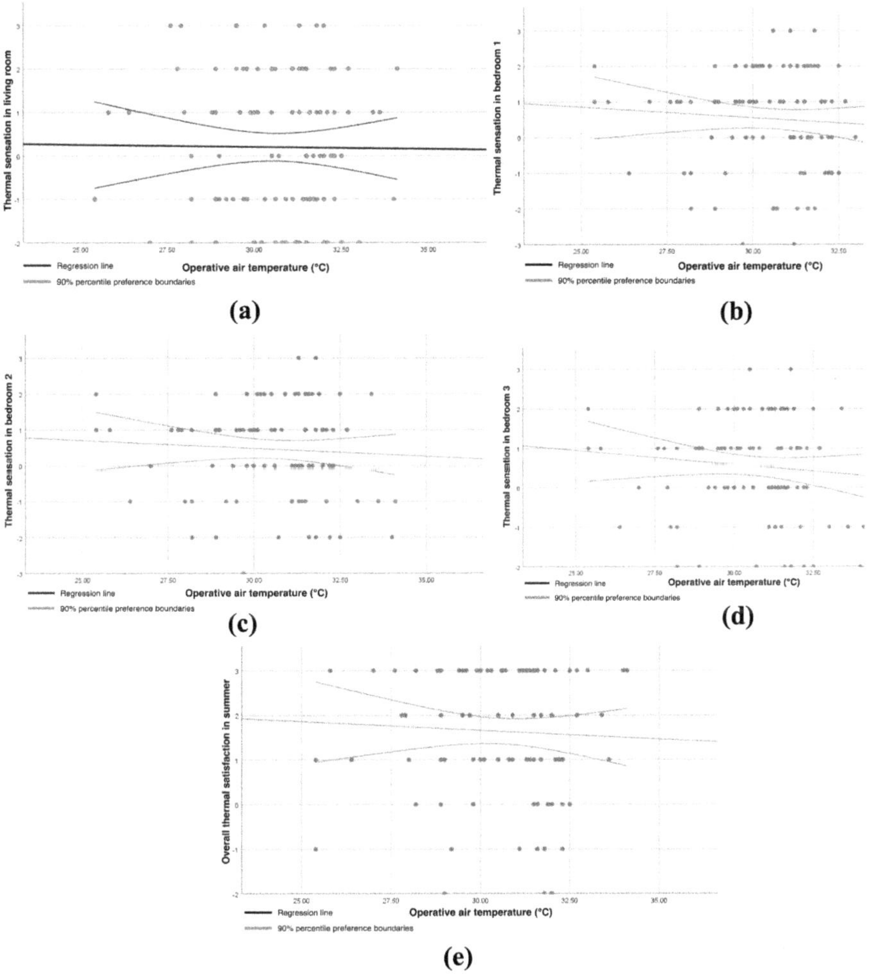

Figure 5.6 (a) Relationship between occupants' TSVs and living room OTs (a linear line was added at total), (b) relationship between occupants' TSVs and Bedroom 1 OTs (a linear line was added at total), (c) relationship between occupants' TSVs and Bedroom 2 OTs (a linear line was added at total), (d) relationship between occupants' TSVs and Bedroom 3 OTs (a linear line was added at total) and (e) relationship between occupants' TSVs and operative air temperature (a linear line was added at total).

0.933 (95% *CI* [0.764, 1.139]), $p = 0.493$, *Nagelkerke* $R^2 = 0.005$, as shown in Table 5.6. Figure 6.10 shows the TSVs plotted against OTs; to avoid discrepancies in the statistical data, the dataset was computed within each half-degree bin (see Data 24).

Research has shown that of the respondents, 3% felt much too warm (*Ta* 31–32°C, ±6°C and ±7°C); 9% felt too warm (*Ta* 26–33°C, ±1°C and ±8°C); 13%

Table 5.6 Summary of Ordinal Logistic Regression Predicting Bedroom 1 OTs from Occupants' TSVs

						95% CI of OR	
Predictor	β	*SE*	*Wald*	*OR*	*p*	*Lower*	*Upper*
Occupants' TSVs	−0.070	0.100	0.470	0.933	0.493	0.764	1.139

felt comfortably warm (*Ta* 25.5–33°C, ±0.5°C and ±8°C); 16% felt comfortable (*Ta* 28–33°C, ±3°C and ±8°C); 23% felt too cool (*Ta* 28–34°C, ±3°C and ±9°C) and 3% felt much too cool (*Ta* 29–32°C, ±4°C and ±7°C); this indicates that the 90% percentile preference boundaries ranged from comfortable to comfortably warm. Thermally acceptable indoor air temperatures ranged from 26 to 28°C, which was 1–3°C higher than the upper thermal-comfort threshold recommended in the *CIBSE Guide A* (CIBSE, 2013).

A quantitative scale ranking of data related to the occupants' TSVs was gathered to further explore the influences of the environmental parameters that were concurrently recorded as the questionnaire survey was being conducted when the participants were asked, 'How would you rate the overall thermal satisfaction of indoor air temperature for the Bedroom 2 spaces in the summer?'

An ordinal logistic regression was performed, and the result revealed no significant relationship between occupants' TSVs and Bedroom 2 OTs, $OR = 0.939$ (95% *CI* [0.769, 1.146]), $p = 0.536$, *Nagelkerke* $R^2 = 0.004$, as shown in Table 5.7. Figure 5.6(c) shows the participants' TSVs plotted against OTs.

The results revealed that of the respondents, 2% felt much too warm (*Ta* 31–32°C, ±6°C and ±7°C); 8% felt too warm (*Ta* 26–33°C, ±1°C and ±8°C); 14% felt comfortably warm (*Ta* 26–32.5°C, ±1°C and ±7.5°C); 22% felt comfortable (*Ta* 27–32°C, ±2°C and ±7°C); 32% felt comfortably cool (*Ta* 26–34°C, ±1°C and ±9°C); 20% felt too cool (*Ta* 28–33°C, ±3°C and ±8°C) and 1% felt much too cool (*Ta* 29°C, ±4°C). Based on the findings of ordinal logistic regression, it was concluded that in the summer, the thermally comfortable indoor air temperatures showed patterns similar to those for the Bedroom 1 spaces. However, the scattered

Table 5.7 Summary of Ordinal Logistic Regression Predicting Bedroom 2 OTs from Occupants' TSVs

						95% CI of OR	
Predictor	β	*SE*	*Wald*	*OR*	*p*	*Lower*	*Upper*
Occupants' TSVs	−0.063	0.100	0.380	0.939	0.536	0.769	1.146

regression plot demonstrated that the thermally acceptable outdoor air temperatures were from 33°C to above 35°C (CIBSE, 2015).

To determine the optimum thermal-comfort level in relation to a range of thermal sensations predicted by the PMVs, participants were asked, 'How would you rate the overall thermal satisfaction of indoor air environment for the Bedroom 3 spaces in the summer?' An ordinal logistic regression was performed, and the result revealed no significant relationship between occupants' TSVs and Bedroom 3 OTs, $OR = 0.908$ (95% *CI* [0.743, 1.109]), $p = 0.344$, *Nagelkerke* $R^2 = 0.009$, as shown in Table 5.8. Figure 5.6(d) shows the participants' TSVs plotted against OT. The thermal-sensation graphs were obtained by plotting the participants' TSVs against the environmental parameters.

As shown in Figure 5.6(d), 8% of respondents felt too warm (*Ta* 28–32.5°C, ±3°C and ±7.5°C); 11% felt comfortably warm (*Ta* 26–34°C, ±1°C and ±9°C); 25% felt comfortable (*Ta* 26–32°C, ±1°C and ±7°C); 32% felt comfortably cool (*Ta* 26–33°C, ±1°C and ±8°C); 22% felt too cool and 2% felt much too cool (*Ta* 31–32°C, ±6°C and ±7°C).

According to the findings of ordinal regression analysis, thermally comfortable temperatures in the respondents' living room spaces ranged from 26 to 28°C during the summer (CIBSE, 2017). Considering that the influence of outdoor air temperature on the occupants' thermal sensations in their living room spaces ranged from 23 to 35°C, these results indicate that even higher adaptation ranges occurred across the measured flats in the summer (Jeong et al., 2016). Notably, the living room measurements that were concurrently gathered when the questionnaire survey was conducted also suggested that comfortable temperatures were well above the recommended international benchmark criteria for the spaces, with high values that indicated a strong relationship.

According to the respondents' TSVs related to their Bedroom 1 spaces, the indoor air temperatures at which they stated that they felt thermally comfortable ranged from 26 to 28°C when outdoor air temperatures were not in the 90% percentile range; this was partially due to the occupants' higher thermal-comfort preferences and the positions of the bedroom spaces in their flats (Ozarisoy, 2022). These results suggest that the occupants were better able to adapt to a thermal environment that was within a wide range of thermally comfortable threshold levels than to slightly warmer indoor air temperatures.

Table 5.8 Summary of Ordinal Logistic Regression Predicting Bedroom 3 OTs from Occupants' TSVs

						95% CI of OR	
Predictor	β	*SE*	*Wald*	*OR*	*p*	*Lower*	*Upper*
Occupants' TSVs	−0.097	0.100	0.890	0.908	0.344	0.743	1.109

Similar patterns were found among the occupants' thermal sensations associated with their Bedroom 2 spaces. On the ordinal regression plot, thermally comfortable TSVs were not scattered within the 90% percentile preference boundaries, which suggests that the occupants experienced overheating in their Bedroom 2 spaces. Thermally comfortable outdoor air temperatures ranged from 33°C to above 35°C, however, when the outdoor temperatures peaked at 36°C, which suggests that the occupants preferred higher indoor air temperature in their Bedroom 2 spaces in the summer (Teitelbaum et al., 2020).

As it relates to the influence of indoor air temperatures on the occupants' TSVs for their Bedroom 3 spaces, it was determined that thermally comfortable temperatures ranged from 26 to 28°C when outdoor air temperatures ranged from 28 to 30°C (Ryu et al., 2020). The analysis indicated that occupants preferred temperatures in the Bedroom 2 and Bedroom 3 spaces that were 2°C higher than in the Bedroom 1 spaces; the findings also revealed a significant difference of 5°C between preferred indoor and outdoor air temperatures in all the bedroom spaces. Table 5.9 demonstrates the summary of ordinal logistic regression predicting summer temperature satisfaction from operative air temperature in order to understand the impact of RH on occupants' thermal comfort. Figure 5.6(e) shows the relationship between the occupants' overall TSVs in summer and the operative air temperature of the interviewed flat units.

As shown in Table 5.9, an ordinal logistic regression was performed, and the result revealed a significant relationship between in situ recorded operative air temperature and summer temperature satisfaction, $OR = 0.958$ (95% CI [0.918, 1.000]), $p = 0.050$, *Nagelkerke* $R^2 = 0.042$. Research has shown that 18% of respondents felt 'too warm' (*Ta* from 28 to 34 ± 3°C and ± 9°C), 23% felt 'comfortably warm' (*Ta* from 28 to 35 ± 3°C and ± 10°C) and 13% felt 'comfortable' (*Ta* showed patterns similar to 'comfortable'), while 21% voted for feeling 'comfortably cool' (*Ta* fell from 23 to 35 ± 10°C), 17% felt 'too cool' (*Ta* fell from 28°C to above 35 ± 3°C and > ± 10°C) and 8% felt 'much too cool' (*Ta* from 28 to 35 ± 3°C and ± 10°C). Further analysis revealed that, in summer, the relationship between thermal sensation in the living room spaces and the outdoor air temperature was considered 'comfortable' when the outdoor air temperature reaches 28°C. The analysis indicates 'comfortable' for the indoor air temperature at 26°C with a possibility for feeling 'comfortably cool' with an outdoor air temperature of 23°C in summer, suggesting optimum comfortable temperatures with ±3°C differences.

Table 5.9 Summary of Ordinal Logistic Regression Predicting Summer Temperature Satisfaction from Operative Air Temperature

						95% CI of OR	
Predictor	β	*SE*	*Wald*	*OR*	*p*	*Lower*	*Upper*
Indoor RH	−0.043	0.020	3.860	0.958	0.050	0.918	1.000

It was also noted that on average, the temperatures of the proposed model were 2°C higher than the temperatures that were recommended in the EN 15251 standards for naturally ventilated buildings (Ozarisoy & Elsharkawy, 2019). Notably, the TSVs that fell within the recommended benchmark parameters of the EN 15251 adaptive model were plotted against the 80% and 90% upper- and lower-acceptability limits; Figure 5.7(a) and (b) depict the acceptability of the thermal sensations that were available in the ASHRAE Global Thermal Comfort Database II.

Figure 5.7(a) shows that the participants' TSVs in naturally ventilated multi-family residential buildings ranged from 20% to 30% acceptability when the monthly mean outdoor temperatures were 25–30°C. To identify a baseline model and determine neutral adaptive thermal-comfort levels for the present study, acceptable thermal-comfort levels in the hot summer Mediterranean climate included in the ASHRAE Global Thermal Comfort Database II were examined; as is shown in Figure 5.7(b), acceptable thermal sensations were felt between 19 and 33°C in subtropical (*Csa*) and partly semi-arid (*Bsh*) climates.

Importantly, significant proportions of the occupants' TSVs fell outside the upper and lower limits, which suggests that the occupants found a wider range of thermal-sensation conditions to be comfortable than was delineated in the adaptive model. It can therefore be concluded that the difference between the preferred temperatures and the neutral temperatures that were recorded from two different environmental conditions demonstrates the occurrence of thermal adaptation against the hot and dry climate of Cyprus; when validating the questionnaire variables, comparing the neutral temperatures and the preferred temperatures served to highlight which group was better adapted to its thermal environment. According to these findings, the differences between neutral temperatures and preferred temperatures

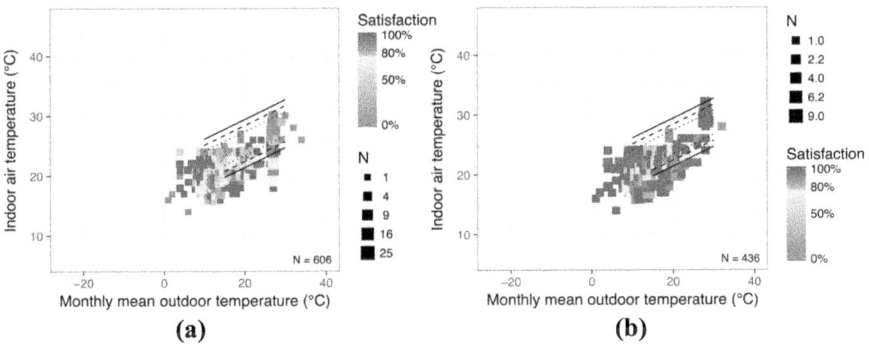

Figure 5.7 Scatter-plot distribution of thermal sensation by (a) building typology (naturally ventilated multi-family residential buildings were selected by using the Query Builder on the ASHRAE Global Comfort Database II) and (b) climate type (the hot summer Mediterranean climate was selected to extract the graph). *Source*: ASHRAE Global Thermal Comfort Database II (graphs were extracted from an open-access thermal-comfort visualisation tool that utilised the satisfaction metric (i.e., Acceptability [TSV±2]), which is available at https://cbe-berkeley.shinyapps.io/comfortdatabase/).

in the summer are ±0.4°C and ±9°C, respectively; this confirms that the study participants who reported the greatest differences between neutral temperatures and preferred temperatures had the best ability to adapt to their indoor thermal environments in the summer.

Discussions

Adaptive comfort is a subject worthy of investigation with the purpose of reducing heating- and cooling-energy consumption. Because of the differences between the populations in their climate, culture, behaviour, acclimatisation and other factorial variables, standard ranges of thermal comfort must be abolished. As the majority of the residents/participants have been living in the social-housing estate for more than ten years, it is expected that occupants can adapt to the environment and climate in the living spaces.

Brager and de Dear (1998) identified three thermal-adaptation types: physiological, which is related to bodily reactions due to temperature change; psychological, which is related to the state of mind based on previous experience; and behaviour-related adaptation. Nicol and Roaf (2015) asserted that comfort can be reached if there are sufficient opportunities for people to adapt. Comfortable temperatures are changeable, rather than fixed. To capture the wider types of occupants and not create direct generalisations that have the potential to introduce a higher bias, a cluster analysis was conducted to validate the field investigation findings in thermal comfort.

The cluster analysis will result in better mapping of the thermal comfort and the occupants' habits related to their energy spending. With these cluster groups, analysis can be one within clusters to form more uniform data. If needed, the general conclusion can be drawn using the comparison against the cluster. With this approach, the study presents that the result will have less bias if the case is generalised for the whole region. The following discussion is structured according to the research question that guides the findings obtained through feed-forward interviews: (RQ-3) how environmental factors affect occupants' thermal comfort to identify neutral adaptive thermal-comfort thresholds in this Eastern Mediterranean climate.

Physiological Thermal Adaptation

Because the aim of this chapter is to test the factors that affected the occupants' thermal sensations, a statistical test was performed to determine the relationship between occupants' TSVs and environmental parameters. An ordinal logistic regression was performed, and the result revealed no significant relationship between occupants' TSVs and living room OTs, $OR = 0.993$ (95% CI [0.816, 1.209]), $p = 0.947$, $Nagelkerke\ R^2 < 0.001$. On the contrary, a significant relationship between operative air temperature and households' overall summer temperature satisfaction, $OR = 0.958$ (95% CI [0.918, 1.000]), $p = 0.050$, $Nagelkerke\ R^2 = 0.042$ (see Data 25).

It was found that the TSVs indicated that the minimum threshold for adaptive indoor air temperature was 28.5°C, and the upper threshold was 31.5°C. The statistical value of *r*-squared ($R^2 = 0.042$) was extrapolated by the slightly weak regression coefficient factor to optimise indoor air temperature, which was strongly correlated with the TSVs.

A multinominal logistic regression was conducted[23] predicting space conditioning/length of residency from operative air temperature, outdoor air temperature, overall thermal satisfaction in winter, thermal preference and type of cooling system. The results revealed that both of these two overall models were not significant, $\chi2(18) = 46.162$, $p = 0.120$,[24] *Nagelkerke* $R^2 = 0.393$, as shown in Tables 5.10(a) and (b).

An ordinal regression using the logit link[25] function was conducted on perception of length of residency from operative air temperature, outdoor air temperature, overall thermal satisfaction in winter, thermal preference and type of cooling system. The results revealed that overall models were not significant, $\chi2(9) = 14.523$, $p = 0.105$, *Nagelkerke* $R^2 = 0.178$, as shown in Table 5.11.

In this study, in situ indoor air temperature measurements were recorded because indoor air movement will significantly influence neutral thermal sensations and can make occupants feel comfortable despite relatively high indoor temperatures. In Question 19, the occupants were asked to report their door-opening habits when their air conditioning (A/C) system was not in use, as illustrated in Figure 5.8(a). Additionally, in the pro forma questionnaire, the physical conditions and respondent locations within their living rooms were recorded to assess the occupants' thermal discomfort and identify neutral adaptive thermal comfort. The respondents' locations are illustrated in Figure 5.8(b).

Figure 5.8(a) shows that 78% of the respondents kept internal doors closed when using their A/C system, while 22% kept internal doors open. The reason that more than three-fourths of the respondents kept their internal doors closed was to keep the internal space cool in the summer. One interviewee with health problems preferred to keep the doors open to dissipate pollutants when the A/C was in use. On the other hand, less than one-third (33%) of the occupants kept the doors open because they used portable fans to cool indoor spaces. Figure 5.8(b) shows that 57% of respondents were surveyed near an open window and 43% near a closed window, across 36 RTBs in the social-housing estate.

To accurately assess the occupants' thermal-comfort votes concurrently with the in situ measurements, it is important to consider the respondents' locations. This research method implies that the occupants' TSVs directly correlate with the environmental conditions and the thermal properties of their flats. Figure 5.8(c) illustrates the percentage distribution of the respondents' room conditions to show the effect of this information on the occupants' in vivo experiences associated with their thermal comfort.

One significant factor in evaluating thermal comfort was whether sitting near an open or a closed window had an effect on questionnaire responses. During the survey, 39% of the female and 17% of the male respondents were surveyed near an open window, while 27% of the female and 16% of the male respondents were surveyed near a closed window. These results show that the occupants either received NV or used portable fans when the windows were open (57%), or they used an A/C

Table 5.10(a) Summary of Multinominal Regression Predicting Space Conditioning

	Predictors	*B*	*SE*	*Wald*	*OR*	*p*	*95% CI*	
							Lower	*Upper*
Natural ventilation[a]	Operative air temperature (°C)	−0.015	0.292	0.003	0.985	0.959	0.555	1.747
	Outdoor air temperature (°C)	−0.646	0.247	6.867	0.524	0.009	0.323	0.850
	Overall thermal satisfaction in winter	−0.515	0.307	2.823	0.597	0.093	0.327	1.090
	Thermal preference: cold[b]	3.268	1.458	5.023	26.259	0.025	1.507	457.599
	Thermal preference: cool[b]	1.246	1.067	1.363	3.477	0.243	0.429	28.156
	Thermal preference: slightly cool[b]	−20.555	0.000	0.000	0.000	1.000	0.000	0.000
	Type of cooling system: A/C split unit[c]	0.848	1.258	0.454	2.334	0.500	0.198	27.461
	Type of cooling system: A/C inverter split unit and ceiling-mounted fan[c]	0.207	1.424	0.021	1.230	0.885	0.075	20.049
	Type of cooling system: portable fan[c]	0.741	1.128	0.431	2.097	0.512	0.230	19.150
Mixed mode[a]	Operative air temperature (°C)	−0.353	0.233	2.300	0.703	0.129	0.445	1.109
	Outdoor air temperature (°C)	−0.349	0.223	2.446	0.705	0.118	0.456	1.092
	Overall thermal satisfaction in winter	−0.189	0.289	0.427	0.828	0.513	0.470	1.458
	Thermal preference: cold[b]	3.286	1.461	5.055	26.728	0.025	1.524	468.766
	Thermal preference: cool[b]	2.301	1.071	4.612	9.981	0.032	1.223	81.481
	Thermal preference: slightly cool[b]	0.673	1.182	0.324	1.961	0.569	0.193	19.887
	Type of cooling system: A/C split unit[c]	0.221	1.238	0.032	1.247	0.859	0.110	14.117
	Type of cooling system: A/C inverter split unit and ceiling-mounted fan[c]	1.340	1.203	1.241	3.819	0.265	0.361	40.367
	Type of cooling system: portable fan[c]	0.961	1.046	0.845	2.616	0.358	0.337	20.321
Air Conditioning (A/C)[a]	Operative air temperature (°C)	−0.397	0.228	3.029	0.673	0.082	0.430	1.051
	Outdoor air temperature (°C)	−0.431	0.218	3.913	0.650	0.048	0.424	0.996
	Overall thermal satisfaction in winter	−0.352	0.273	1.656	0.704	0.198	0.412	1.202
	Thermal preference: cold[b]	2.812	1.392	4.081	16.637	0.043	1.087	254.537

Table 5.10(b) (Continued)

	Predictors	B	SE	Wald	OR	p	95% CI	
							Lower	Upper
Air Conditioning (A/C)[a]	Thermal preference: Slightly cool[b]	0.011	1.075	0.000	1.011	0.992	0.123	8.319
	Type of cooling system: A/C split unit[c]	1.143	1.082	1.117	3.136	0.291	0.377	26.125
	Type of cooling system: A/C inverter split unit and ceiling-mounted fan[c]	0.494	1.227	0.162	1.639	0.687	0.148	18.148
	Type of cooling system: Portable fan[c]	1.163	0.991	1.375	3.198	0.241	0.458	22.326
Portable fan/Air Conditioning[a]	Operative air temperature (°C)	−0.100	0.264	0.143	0.905	0.705	0.540	1.517
	Outdoor air temperature (°C)	−0.422	0.236	3.193	0.656	0.074	0.413	1.042
	Overall thermal satisfaction in winter	−0.518	0.287	3.263	0.596	0.071	0.340	1.045
	Thermal preference: Cold[b]	0.835	1.653	0.255	2.304	0.614	0.090	58.777
	Thermal preference: Cool[b]	1.144	0.975	1.377	3.139	0.241	0.465	21.203
	Thermal preference: Slightly cool[b]	−0.451	1.110	0.165	0.637	0.685	0.072	5.609
	Type of cooling system: A/C split unit[c]	0.822	1.127	0.532	2.275	0.466	0.250	20.717
	Type of cooling system: A/C inverter split unit and ceiling-mounted fan[c]	0.044	1.260	0.001	1.045	0.972	0.088	12.342
	Type of cooling system: Portable fan[c]	−0.279	1.081	0.066	0.757	0.797	0.091	6.301

Note: $\chi 2$ (36) = 46.162, $p = 0.120$, *Nagelkerke* $R^2 = 0.393$, [a]Compared to Portable fan. [b]Compared to Neutral/slightly warm. [c]Compared to A/C split unit and portable fans.

Table 5.11 Summary of Ordinal Regression Predicting Length of Residency

Predictor	β	*SE*	*Wald*	*OR*	*p*	95% CI of OR	
						Lower	*Upper*
Operative air temperature (°C)	−0.010	0.137	0.005	0.990	0.944	0.757	1.296
Outdoor air temperature (°C)	−0.055	0.118	0.215	0.946	0.643	0.751	1.194
Overall thermal satisfaction in winter	−0.012	0.167	0.006	0.988	0.940	0.712	1.369
Thermal preference: cold[a]	1.309	0.888	2.174	3.702	0.140	0.650	21.115
Thermal preference: cool[a]	0.156	0.612	0.065	1.169	0.798	0.352	3.881
Thermal preference: slightly cool[a]	−0.490	0.753	0.423	0.613	0.515	0.140	2.680
Type of cooling system: A/C split unit[b]	0.012	0.698	0.000	1.012	0.986	0.258	3.971
Type of cooling system: A/C inverter split unit and ceiling-mounted fan[b]	−1.373	0.703	3.821	0.253	0.051	0.064	1.004
Type of cooling system: portable fan[b]	1.105	0.757	2.127	3.019	0.145	0.684	13.316

Note: $\chi2\ (9) = 14.523$, $p = 0.105$, *Nagelkerke* $R^2 = 0.178$. [a]Compared to Neutral/slightly warm. [b]Compared to A/C split unit and portable fans.

system when the windows were closed (34%). It is important to consider the effect of RTB orientation and the different floor levels of the flats. In this study, these variables were found to significantly affect the occupants' TSVs, which is helpful to identify the neutral adaptive thermal comfort.

Question 36 examined different room conditions and took the different RTB orientations into account. The analysis reveals potential challenges that arose with the RH and outdoor HSI factor that can cause thermally uncomfortable summer indoor air environments. When the effects of OTs and RH are considered, their impact on indoor thermal-comfort conditions is notable and can potentially affect the occupants' TSVs. Figure 5.8(d) illustrates household living room conditions and takes the different RTB orientations into account.

According to Figure 5.8(d),[26] 16% of the northeast-facing flats only opened their windows, 9% opened their windows and used a portable fan, 3% only used a portable fan and 2% used an A/C system. In the south-facing flats, 15% only opened their windows, 8% opened their windows and used a portable fan, 5% only used a portable fan and 5% used wall-mounted A/C systems. In the northwest-facing flats, 2% only opened their windows, 1% opened their windows and used a portable fan and 1% used A/C systems. In the southwest-facing flats, 3% only opened their windows, 5% opened their windows and used a portable fan and 8% used A/C systems. In the southeast-facing flats, 4% only opened their windows, 3% opened their windows and used a portable fan and 3% used an A/C system.

It can therefore be concluded that the observed dominant factor in the surveyed rooms was found in the south-facing flats, where 26% majority of respondents had the windows open and portable fans in use, as shown in Figure 5.8(e). Additionally, it was observed that a greater percentage (44%) of the south-facing flats only had their windows open. This is because the interviews were conducted in the afternoon, when outdoor air temperatures peak; this is also why 5% of the respondents had their A/C systems in use. Furthermore, the dominant factor was observed in the southwest-facing flats, where 8% of respondents used A/C systems and 5% used portable fans with their windows open; this indicates the importance of solar angulation on the building, which causes a high degree of thermal discomfort. Question 36 examined the households' room conditions and took the different floor levels of the flats into account. It was found that RTB orientation plays a crucial role in assessing the occupants' thermal comfort in the summer. However, it is also important to examine the effect of the different floor levels to provide more reliable information in determining the neutral adaptive thermal-comfort level. It seems that both the physical position and thermal properties of the RTBs had a significant influence on the occupants' TSVs.

Psychological Thermal Adaptation

According to the findings of the present study, when the indoor air temperatures ranged from 25 to 27.5°C, the participants' TSVs all fell within an acceptable comfort zone, and the occupants indicated that they were mostly satisfied with

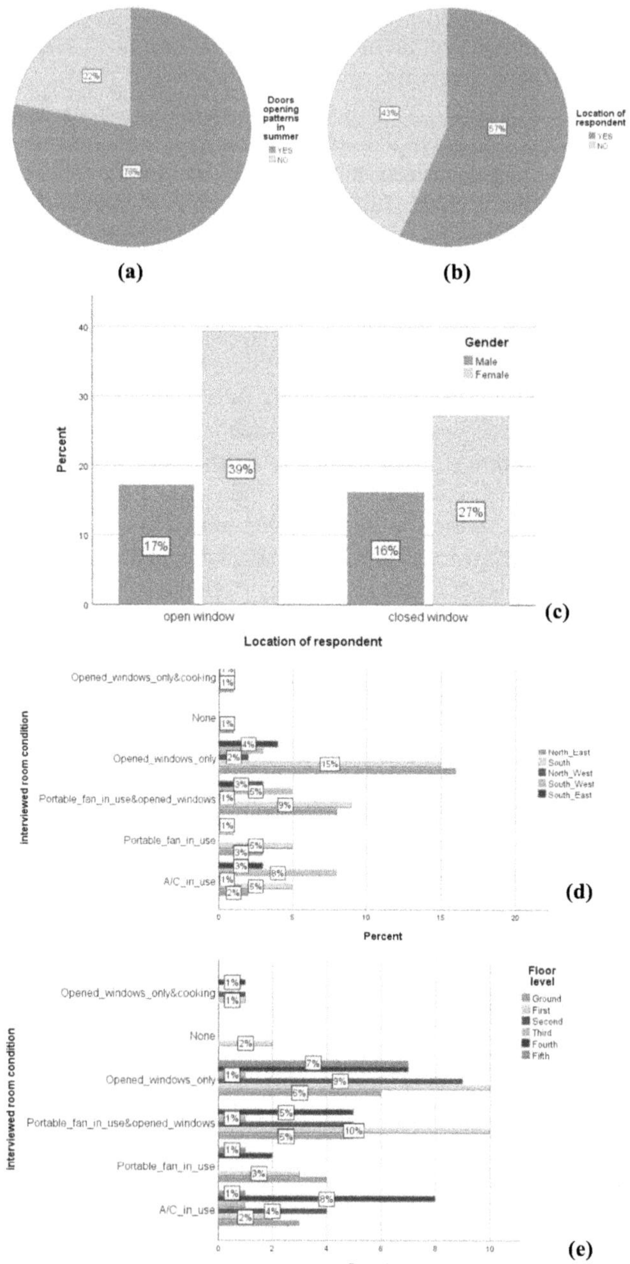

Figure 5.8 (a) Distribution of household internal door-opening patterns in summer; (b) participant location in living rooms during survey; (c) distribution of living room conditions; (d) room condition and RTB orientation and (e) household room conditions, taking different floor levels into account.

their indoor air temperatures. Notably, 6% of participants reported feeling thermally uncomfortable and 94% of participants reported feeling thermally comfortable in the 27.5–30°C temperature range. When indoor operative air temperatures increased by 2.5°C to slightly above the neutral temperature range of 30–32.5°C, the respondents' predicted percentage of dissatisfied (PPD) with their indoor air temperatures rose to 23%; the occupants' PMVs increased to 41% when temperatures ranged from 32.5 to 35°C, and no participants felt thermally comfortable when outdoor air temperatures exceeded 35°C.

Figure 5.9(a)[27] depicts the analysis of patterns that was conducted between the use of space conditioning and the environmental conditions at the time of the survey, when the indoor air temperature was recorded at 32°C, which is considered to be a thermally uncomfortable indoor air temperature. The participants reported that they used both their A/C systems and mixed-mode (MM) ventilation when temperatures ranged from 28 to 36°C; A/C systems were utilised when temperatures ranged from 34 to 36°C; one participant used a portable fan when the outdoor temperature was 24°C, which is 1°C below the thermally acceptable comfort level; and MM ventilation was used to optimise indoor air temperatures between 32 and 34°C, which was the most notable pattern. These findings demonstrate that the buildings' thermal properties and poor window design were the reason that high indoor air temperatures were reported when outdoor air temperatures were thermally acceptable.

Figure 5.9(b) illustrates the test of subjects between the space conditioning and the influences of the indoor and the outdoor RH conditions. It was determined that a majority of the participants used their A/C systems when outdoor RH levels were between 50% and 60%, which suggests that the participants' bodies were not thermally adaptable to slightly humid environmental conditions. These results indicate that the thermal discomfort of these types of social-housing residents was not within the recommended lower thermal-comfort threshold level of 40% or the upper comfort threshold level of 60% (Santangelo & Tondelli, 2017); this is why most of the households relied on their A/C systems for optimal thermal comfort. The present study also determined that the respondent households utilised their A/C systems and mixed-mode cooling strategies when outdoor RH levels were between 60% and 80%, which suggests that the outdoor RH was a determining factor in the occupants' thermal comfort.

Figure 5.9(c) delineates the relationships between the use of space conditioning, the in situ measurements of the building envelopes and the *on-site* environmental-condition measurements. It was found that a majority of the respondents relied on their A/C systems when indoor air temperatures ranged from 32 to 34°C and outdoor heat stress factors ranged from 34 to 38°C; this suggests that the solar mask is determined by the outdoor heat-stress index. Due to the poor quality of construction materials used in all 36 of the RTBs and the hot Cypriot summer climate, solar irradiance on the building envelopes caused high indoor air temperatures. The respondents used portable fans to optimise their thermal comfort when indoor air temperatures were between 36 and 40°C; this is because of the participants'

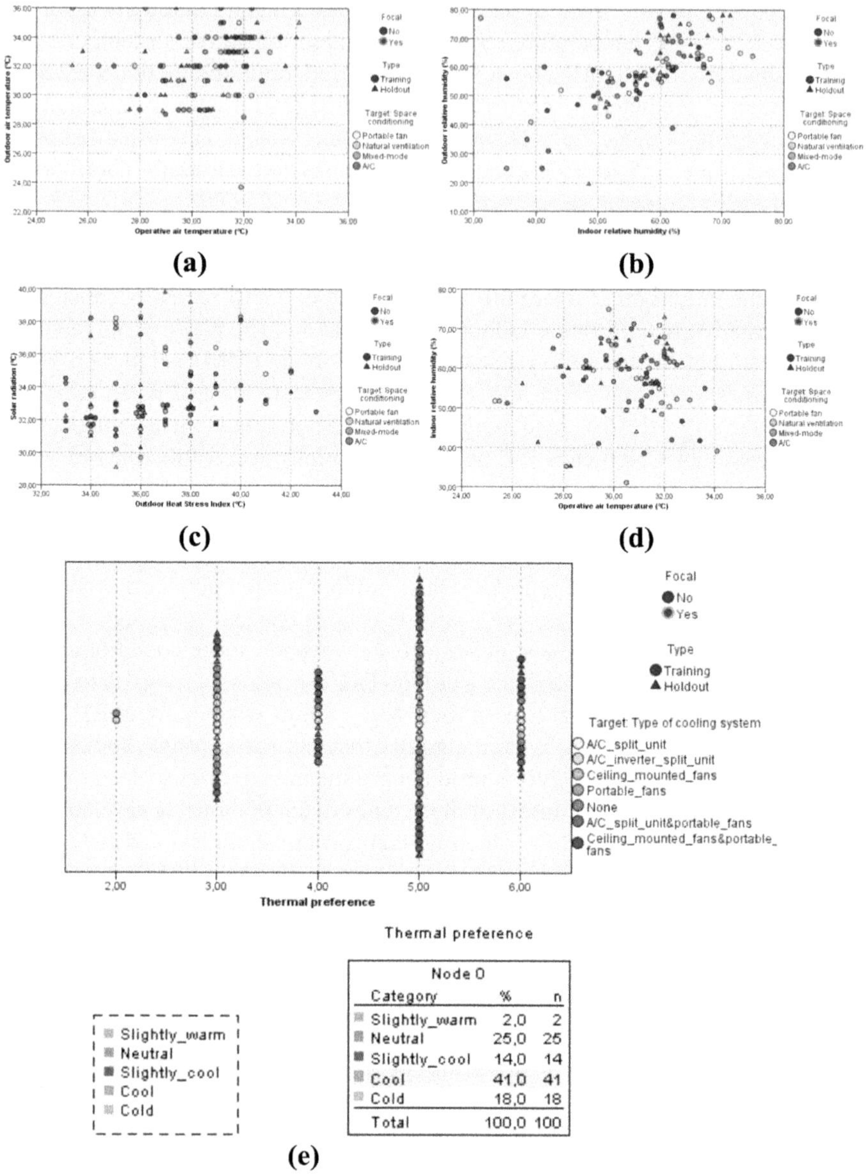

Figure 5.9 (a) Cluster analysis of outdoor air temperature and OTs for different types of space conditioning; (b) cluster analysis of outdoor and indoor RH for different types of space conditioning; (c) cluster analysis of solar radiation and outdoor HSI for different types of space conditioning; (d) cluster analysis of indoor RH and OTs for different types of space conditioning and (e) cluster analysis of household TSVs, taking different types of space conditioning into account.

income levels. Notably, it was observed that the participants who were 55–65 and 65 years of age and older also utilised NV when their portable fans were in use.

Figure 5.9(d) depicts the relationships between the use of space conditioning and indoor environmental conditions. A majority of participants used every type of available space-conditioning system to create thermally comfortable indoor air environments when the indoor RH was 50–70% and the OT was between 28 and 33°C. The results indicate that a neutral adaptive thermal-comfort level was identified, despite variations between space conditioning and environmental conditions (Bateson, 2014).

The above graph reveals that the type of space-conditioning systems directly affected the occupants' TSVs. To reduce the risk of bias in the TSVs, this graph shows that the social-housing residents preferred to use all available sources for space conditioning in the summer (Balvedi et al., 2018). The RA found that the neutral adaptive thermal-comfort temperature was 28.5–31.5°C when space conditioning was maintained between 28 and 33°C; it can therefore be concluded that the identification of the adaptive thermal-comfort threshold level is not limited by environmental conditions, but the thermal properties of buildings and household space-conditioning preferences should be considered as the determinant factors to reduce research bias on thermal-comfort studies.

The strong correlations that were found between the optimum thermal-comfort threshold levels and OTs were clearly shown in the RA. Of the respondents, 80% were slightly comfortable in the 28.5–31.5°C temperature range; notably, the acceptable comfort range that was identified was considerably higher than both Fanger's adaptive thermal-comfort level and the industrial benchmark of the EN 15251 recommendations for naturally ventilated buildings. It was determined that when indoor air temperatures were 5°C higher than the temperatures cited in the recommended benchmark criterion, a majority of the respondents in the surveyed flats reported that they felt thermally comfortable.

Furthermore, the thermally comfortable indoor air temperature range could have been extrapolated by 2–3°C if the respondents had used either portable fans or A/C systems (Barthelmes et al., 2018); this can be explained by the decrease in the number of TSVs when any type of cooling system was utilised. In this case, when acceptable thermal-comfort levels are observed when temperatures fell to 30.0–32.5°C, the PPD index of participants could rise to 90%. Additionally, 23% of the respondents reported that they were using a portable fan or their A/C system at the time of the survey; this could be explained by a combination of behavioural adjustments and physiological adaptations (Brager & de Dear, 1998). The results of the field survey in conjunction with the linear RA determined that the neutral temperature was 28.5°C, and the upper acceptable limit was 31.5°C.

Figure 5.9(e) illustrates the relationship between the use of space conditioning and the occupants' thermal preferences. It was found that 25% of the occupants felt thermally comfortable; it was further observed that these participants were using every type of space-conditioning system at the time of the survey. The graph in Figure 5.9(e) shows that these participants predominantly used ceiling-mounted and portable fans to optimise their thermal comfort. The most notable finding was that 41% of the participants reported that they felt cool in their environment; the aforementioned graph reveals that this group used every type of space cooling system to lower indoor air temperatures.

These results are consistent with data related to the optimisation of occupants' thermal comfort that were obtained by considering the *on-site* monitoring and in situ measurements for the present study. According to the survey analysis, 73% of the total sample who reported that they felt slightly cool to cold were more likely to experience thermally comfortable indoor air environments at 26°C (M=25.7°C, SD=12°C). Regression forecasting revealed that the lowest (i.e., 23.6°C) and highest (i.e., 27.1°C) operative air temperatures were achieved, which resulted in PMV values of –0.64°C—which was closer to the 'slightly cool' sensation—and –1.64°C, respectively; this suggests that achieving desired indoor air environment temperatures improves the occupants' thermal-comfort levels and possibly reduces cooling energy consumption in the summer (Day & Gunderson, 2015).

The in situ measurements and *on-site* environmental monitoring findings from the field study depicted in the graph were recorded from the in vivo experiences of the households' TSVs, and a determination of the influence thereof on the identification of neutral adaptive thermal-comfort levels took the participants' habitual adaptive behaviours into account. Of the respondents, 41% preferred to use all types of domestic cooling appliances, and 25% of the surveyed households also used all types of space-conditioning systems to acclimatise their indoor air environments; this indicates that the household TSVs are strongly correlated with observed indoor environmental conditions (i.e., type of space conditioning used, in situ measurements and *on-site* environmental monitoring). Figure 5.10(a)–(h) illustrates the climate characteristics of the cities in Cyprus to represent the generalisation of applied thermal-comfort threshold levels as identified through regression forecasting analysis.

The present study investigates the effects of local climate conditions on the psychological adaptation of human thermal comfort. The pilot case study was conducted in the coastal city of Famagusta; this city was selected as a baseline model to represent all major cities in the same climate conditions. One of the primary reasons this study was not conducted in the laboratory environment of a climatic chamber was so the experiment parameters could be properly identified and consequently be widely applied to the climate zone of the Eastern Mediterranean basin.

To test the validity of the field-study investigation in post-war social-housing estates in Cyprus, the climate datasets of eight Cypriot cities were extracted from EnergyPlus as an EPW weather file; this information was then assigned to the IES software weather datasets. Dynamic thermal simulations were conducted to generate the climate patterns of each city, with the intention of assessing the results derived from the building energy-simulation platform to validate the field-study findings.

The results revealed a discrepancy between the in situ physical measurements and the building energy-simulation predictions. The field-study findings demonstrate that the neutral adaptive thermal-comfort threshold was found to be

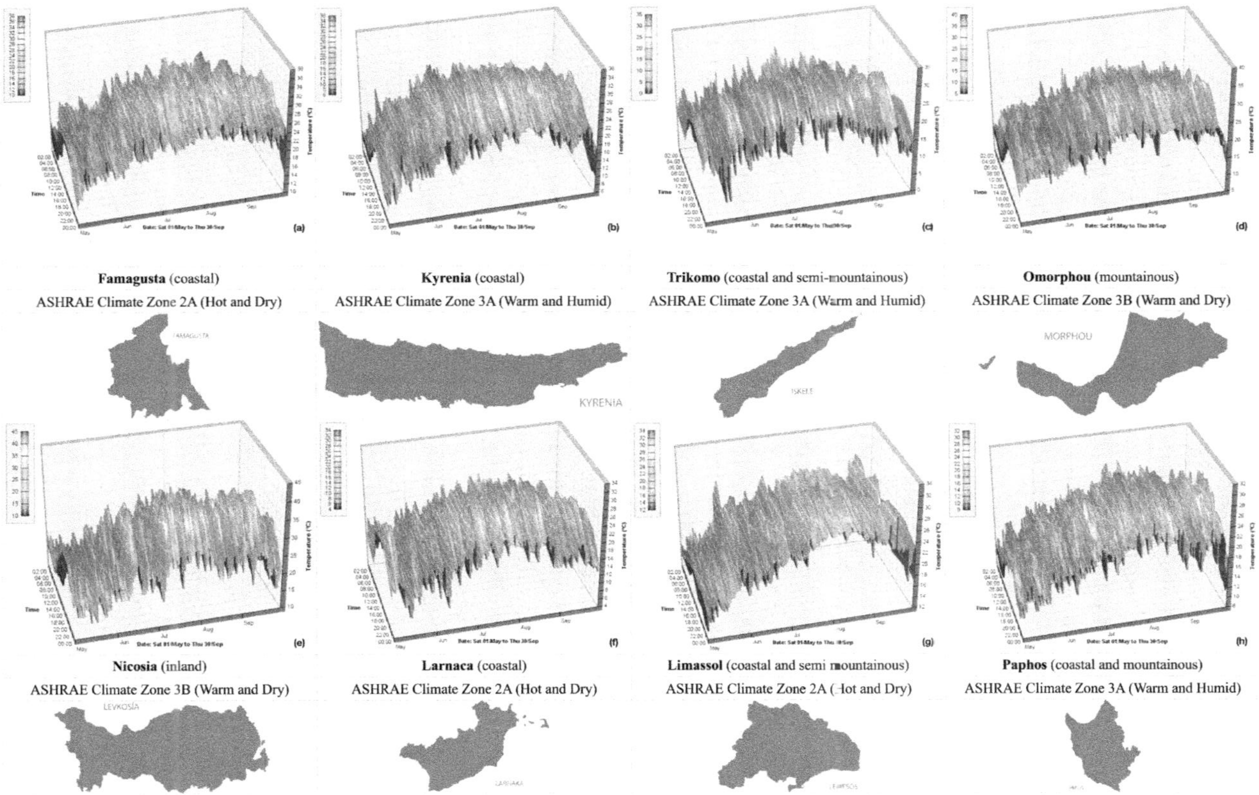

Figure 5.10 (a)–(h) Mapping of climate variations of eight cities in Cyprus.

28.5–31.5°C in the case-study location. On the contrary, the building-energy simulation results indicate that the climate shows variations around 10–15°C among the eight representative cities in Cyprus.

According to Figure 5.10(a), the air temperature in Famagusta from May to September, which is the cooling period for this Eastern Mediterranean island, fluctuated between 28 and 38°C. Air temperatures peaked at 36°C in the second week of June, then oscillated between 26 and 32°C until the third week of August, at which time temperatures peaked at 38°C, then decreased and hovered between 28 and 32°C until the end of September. The climate-pattern variations were within the acceptable neutral adaptive thermal-comfort thresholds developed through this empirical study investigation in the baseline scenario; the benchmark criteria for thermally comfortable MFHs in Cyprus range between 28.5 and 31.5°C, and slightly warmer temperature fluctuations between 32 and 38°C were observed.

To understand the representativeness of the neutral adaptive thermal-comfort threshold level, the climate characteristics of seven other cities were then examined to prove the general applicability of the benchmarking criterion and determine whether it can be applied to the whole of Cyprus.

Figure 5.10(b) illustrates the air temperature in Kyrenia, which showed temperature variations between 24 and 28°C, which peaked at 36°C in the middle of June, then steadily decreased to 25°C throughout the month. Air temperatures rose to 35°C at the end of the first week of July and fluctuated between 28 and 32°C until the end of August; thermally comfortable temperatures between 22 and 28°C were predicted throughout the month of September. The neutral adaptive thermal-comfort threshold level fell within the benchmark threshold, and climate patterns observed in the simulation prediction also fell within 30% of the recommended upper thermal-comfort limit in the ASHRAE Global Thermal Comfort Database II.

Figure 5.10(c) illustrates the air temperature patterns in Trikomo, fluctuated between during the peak cooling period between July and August 30–35°C; a difference of ±3.5°C was identified when the neutral adaptive thermal-comfort threshold was selected as a benchmark criterion. As shown in the graph, steady, continuous warm air temperature was observed through most of the summer months; notably, the air temperature in the third week of September peaked at 30°C, which is the upper thermal-comfort limit according to the ASHRAE Global Thermal Comfort Database II criteria.

Figure 5.10(d) depicts pleasant air temperature patterns in Omorphou, which steadily fluctuated between 20 and 25°C from the beginning of May to the first week of June, at which time temperatures increased to 32°C, fluctuated between 25 and 28°C until the first week of August, then peaked at 40°C; temperature variations between 28 and 32°C were then observed until the end of September. Air temperatures exhibited a ±8.5°C difference from the upper neutral adaptive thermal-comfort threshold for the Cypriot climate.

Figure 5.10(e) demonstrates the slightly cool environmental conditions of Nicosia: air temperatures varied between 10 and 25°C from the beginning of May to the end of the first week of June, rose to 35°C early in the second week of June and remained consistent through the third week, then steadily decreased to 30°C from the last week of June through the second week of July. Air temperatures peaked at 45°C in the second week of July and stayed in this range until the middle of August, at which time air temperatures slightly decreased to 36°C and fluctuated between 36 and 42°C until the third week of September, then steadily decreased to 34°C through the end of September.

The results revealed that there was a significant ±15°C variation difference between day and night temperatures due to the inland geographical location of Nicosia and the city's location between two high altitude mountains that block effective summer breezes from the coastline regions; this also caused the urban heat island (UHI) effect, which led to thermally uncomfortable indoor air environments. In the graph, the upper thermal-comfort limit was above 35°C from the first week of July through the third week of September; the simulation prediction was ±3.5°C higher than the 31.5°C upper neutral adaptive thermal-comfort threshold, which suggests that a higher adaptive thermal-comfort limit is needed for MFHs in Nicosia.

Figure 5.10(f) delineates the thermally acceptable (i.e., neutral) temperatures in Larnaca, which hovered between 22 and 24°C in the first week of May, then fluctuated between 10 and 16°C until the third week of May; air temperatures oscillated between 24 and 34°C from the third week of June through the first week of September. Pleasant air temperatures were predicted between 20 and 26°C until the end of September; notably, the peak air temperatures were observed on several occasions. From the middle of July through the first week of September, the upper thermal-comfort limit was found to be in the range of 30–32°C; this threshold fell within the 28.5–31.5°C neutral adaptive thermal-comfort benchmark criterion developed in the course of the field study.

Continuous warm air fluctuations that were above the upper thermal-comfort limit recommended in the ASHRAE Global Thermal Comfort Database II were observed for a prolonged period of time; these climate patterns fell within the thermally acceptable air temperature range of 30–33°C that is recommended for Mediterranean countries with hot, dry summer climate characteristics.

Figure 5.10(g) details the pleasant weather fluctuations in Limassol, which ranged between 8 and 23°C from the beginning of May to the first week of June; at this time, air temperatures peaked at 32°C, then decreased to 30°C in the second week of the same month. The curvilinear weather patterns depicted in the graph fluctuated between 25 and 32°C from the middle of June through the end of August, then peaked at 34°C in the second week of September and steadily decreased to 22°C by the end of September; peak air temperature ranged between 26 and 30°C, which fell within the neutral adaptive thermal-comfort threshold developed for the present study.

Figure 5.10(h) shows the reasonably comfortable air temperatures in Paphos, which fluctuated between 12 and 22°C from the beginning of May through the final week of June. Temperatures peaked at 29°C in the first week of July, fluctuated between 30 and 32°C from mid-July through mid-September, peaked again at 32°C in the second week of August; notable variations in air temperatures that ranged between 18 and 30°C were observed until the end of September.

Predicted air temperatures fell within the neutral adaptive thermal-comfort threshold developed for the baseline coastal city of Famagusta. Notably, the significant difference in air temperatures between Paphos and the baseline city is due to its geographical location on the south-western corner of the island, which benefits from effective summer breezes from the Eastern Mediterranean Sea; this demonstrates that the high frequency of outdoor air movement is a determinant environmental factor that ensures pleasant thermal conditions, even during the peak cooling period. The results suggest that the lower neutral adaptive thermal-comfort threshold is needed for this part of the island.

It should be noted that the neutral adaptive thermal-comfort threshold developed through the longitudinal field study represents 80% of the Cypriot climate zones, which encompass 56% of the low-, medium- and high-rise RTBs in the country. The matrix presented in Figure 5.10(a)–(g) demonstrates the natural representativeness of housing stock by exploring the neutral adaptive thermal comfort in the designated areas, and the results can be extrapolated to other Eastern Mediterranean cities with similar climate characteristics to those of Cyprus. This figure can be applied to different climate zones in Cyprus and provide a roadmap of the methodological workflow developed as an outcome of this empirical study; this workflow is not limited to exploring the thermal comfort of MFHs in social-housing estates, but can also be generalised to other housing typologies in areas in the Mediterranean basin that experience hot, dry summer climate characteristics.

Conclusion

The present study sought to draw conclusions related to the optimisation of occupants' thermal-comfort levels to fully explore the influences of various environmental parameters that were monitored and/or measured in a post-war social-housing development in Famagusta, Cyprus, where the climate is subtropical (*Csa*) and partly semi-arid (*Bsh*) (i.e., hot and dry in the summer). Numerous field studies have determined that occupants' thermal-comfort levels vary according to the climate conditions; as such, there is no generally recommended acceptable comfort range for MFHs, nor are there specific adaptive thermal-comfort prediction methods.

The findings of this study enhanced the overall understanding of the complex interrelationships between household socio-demographic characteristics, buildings' thermal properties and occupants' habitual adaptive behaviour related to thermal comfort in heat-vulnerable MFHs. It was found that TSVs in living rooms were significantly but weakly correlated with TSVs in Bedroom 1 ($r = 0.302$, $p = 0.002$) and Bedroom 3 ($r = 0.200$, $p = 0.046$). TSVs in kitchens were significantly but weakly related to TSVs in Bedroom 2 ($r = 0.205$, $p = 0.041$) and Bedroom 3 ($r = 0.220$, $p = 0.028$). An ordinal logistic regression was performed, and the result revealed no significant relationship between occupants' TSVs and living room OTs, $OR = 0.993$ (95% CI [0.816, 1.209]), $p = 0.947$, *Nagelkerke* $R^2 < 0.001$. On the contrary, a significant relationship between operative air temperature and overall summer temperature satisfaction, $OR = 0.958$ (95% CI [0.918, 1.000]), $p = 0.050$, *Nagelkerke* $R^2 = 0.042$. The occupants' TSVs indicated that the neutral temperature was 28.5°C, and the upper limit of the comfort range in warm indoor air temperature conditions was 31.5°C; this suggests that occupants in hot and dry climates where thermally uncomfortable indoor environments occur are able to tolerate warmer conditions than residents of other high and medium altitudes.

Data related to the occupants' adaptation to slightly warmer indoor environmental conditions and outdoor air temperatures could be seen as a significant contribution to the ASHRAE Global Thermal Comfort Database II in terms of the delineation of a specific method to conduct a longitudinal field survey in this particular Eastern Mediterranean climate and the prediction of neutral adaptive thermal-comfort levels with the use of an ordinal logistic regression analysis. The present study also provides a roadmap to the EN 15251 thermal-comfort assessment criteria in the event that industry-based temperature design criteria are unable to comply with the ASHRAE Global Thermal Comfort Database II because they conflict with the occupants' adaptive comfort temperatures.

Notes

1 A general rule for sample sizes might be that group sizes are approximately equal if the *n* of the largest group is no more than about twice the *n* of the smallest group. Another general rule for sample sizes is at least 10% of the sample in each group. Categorical variables with very uneven splits between categories present problems to several of the multivariate analyses.

Additionally, all categorical variables were coded in ordinal sequence where possible (e.g., metabolic rate) All variables were coded from cold to hot All variables were coded from smallest values to largest values All dichotomous variables were coded to 1 = yes, 0 = no

2 Running mean temperature) is described as 'an exponentially weighted running mean of the daily average external air temperature' and is computed using the following formula:

3 To assess normality, skewness and kurtosis statistics were assessed. Skewness refers to the symmetry of the distribution and kurtosis refers to the peakedness. Variables that have distributions that are very asymmetrical, flat or peaked could bias any test that assumes a normal (i.e., bell-shaped) distribution. Generally, skewness and kurtosis values (converted as z-scores) that fall outside ± 4 should be further inspected for potential outlier removal, non-parametric testing or transformation. However, the researchers may have flexibility in larger samples.

4 Environmental parameters were set out as continuous variables to undertake the descriptive analysis. Continuous variables are variables that can take on any value within a range. Continuous variables are also considered metric or quantitative variables, where the variable can have an infinite number or value between two given points.

5 Outliers are a primary consideration, and it is important to remember that both the median and the mode are not affected by extreme values. In the present study, the outliers test was conducted to detect any issues related to the continuous variables (environmental parameters) before conducting the statistical analysis.

6 Some normality tests are done for sample sizes smaller than 100 (i.e., Shapiro–Wilk and Kolmogorov–Smirnov tests). If these tests are significant beyond $p < 0.001$, these variables should be further inspected. Graphical methods are also employed for assessing normality. These graphs include inspecting histograms, normal quantile–quantile (Q–Q) plots and box plots.

7 Histograms should look fairly bell shaped. Q–Q plots should follow a straight line when plotting the expected values against the observed values. Box plots show the overall interquartile range and whether extreme values exist in the variable.

8 If the data contains outliers, the researchers looked at the graphical displays both with and without the outliers to see how the graphs changed. If a continuous variable has serious deviations from normality, it must be addressed through transformation (log, inverse, Box-Cox, etc.), recoding into an ordinal variable or assessed for whether non-parametric analysis needed to be conducted. Regardless, the researchers should run the analysis both with and without outliers to see whether the pattern of results changes.

9 Sample of Validation Results for the Statistical Analyses. All continuous variables are presented horizontally in the sheet with the following information: statistics summary table, histogram, normal quantile–quantile plot (also known as Q–Q plot), box plot and relevant notes of outliers (if applicable). The statistics summary, histogram, Q–Q plot and box plots were reviewed together to determine if variables were significantly skewed, flat or peaked. A variable that violates normality will present as being non-normal across most, if not all, of the graphs and summary information. Please see an information titled 'Test of Normality', which displays the results from the Kolmogorov–Smirnov and Shapiro–Wilk tests. There are three remedies for violations of normality: mathematical transformation, categorisation and non-parametric testing. Because the eventual analysis will be fairly simple bivariate test, we are recommending non-parametric testing as an alternative.

10 To undertake the correlation analysis, the overall thermal satisfaction in summer variable was coded as follows: −1 = Cool or Slightly cold, 0 = Comfortable, 1 = Slightly warm, 2 = Warm, 3 = Hot. However, the actual data gathered through a questionnaire survey presented without altering households' in vivo experiences on their thermal-comfort assessment.

11 The Likert scale is a measure of a person's attitudes, beliefs or opinions about some object or event. Traditional Likert scales include the following features: declarative statements that express clearly positive or negative attitudes, seven ordered response options, particularly for the thermal-comfort assessment (known as the response set), an equal number of positive and negative response options and numeric values assigned to each response option for analysis purposes.

12 Univariate and multivariate outliers are also known as extreme values and can significantly bias any parametric test. In the present study, univariate outliers were tested. After thorough analysis, SPSS identifies these values as being three times the interquartile range beyond the 25th and 75th percentile values. Multivariate outliers were also tested before primary analyses were conducted if they were appropriate to the analysis. If outliers are detected, the box plots represent these values as stars in the box plot.

13 Cross-tabulation was chosen to assess occupants' TSVs. The traditional way to identify a relationship or association, between two categorical variables, is to calculate percentages within categories of the independent variable and to compare these percentages across the categories of the independent variable.

14 Chi-square analysis was conducted to examine how a statistical association is detected when the two variables are measured on a nominal scale.

15 The Pearson's correlation coefficient (also known as Pearson's product-moment correlation coefficient) ***r*** is a measure to determine the relationship (instead of difference) between two quantitative variables (interval/ratio) and degree to which the two variables coincide with one another—that is, extent to which two variables are linearly related: changes in one variable correspond to changes in another variable. Pearson's correlation coefficient (also referred to Pearson's *r*) is the most common measure of correlation and has been widely used in the sciences as a measure of the degree of linear dependence between two paired data.

16 Spearman's rank-order correlation coefficient (***ρ*** or ***rs***) is a statistical measure of the strength of a relationship between two variables. Spearman's correlation is a non-parametric variation of Pearson's product-moment correlation, used most commonly for a relatively short series of measurements that do not follow a normal distribution pattern.

17 Pearson's correlation coefficient is traditionally used in a referred to as the *ps* correlation that partials out the subject effect.
18 Logistic regression provides an equation for circumstances in which the dependent variable is categorical, usually dichotomous (although there is a form of logistic regression for ordinal variables).
19 The odds ratio can be interpreted as follows. (i) OR = 1: the variable does not affect the odds of the outcome; (ii) OR > 1: the variable is associated with higher odds of the outcome; (iii) OR < 1: the variable is associated with lower odds of the outcome.
20 A confidence interval (***CI***) around the logistic regression coefficient *bj* provides important information for interpreting the coefficient. The confidence interval is formed using the regression coefficient plus or minus the product of a tabled critical value and standard error.
21 *Nagelkerke* R^2 is an adjusted version of the Cox and Snell *R*-square that adjusts the scale of the statistic to cover the full range from 0 to 1.
22 The *R*-squared analogue tests are considered pseudo-*R*-squared values or analogues to the *R*-squared value in ordinal logistic regression.
23 Multinominal logistic regression is a statistical analysis procedure that expands linear regression by including more than one independent variable in an equation to understand their association with a dependent variable. Typically, the data used for multiple regression are made up of continuous variables (e.g., interval-level measurements such as Likert scales or amounts of observable behaviour), but it is also possible to use categorical data (e.g., demographic information such as gender or ethnicity). To use categorical data in multiple regression, one must employ a technique called dummy coding. Unlike correlation, which shows the co-occurrence of variables (e.g., perceptions of liking), regression can be used for prediction and casual inference.
24 The ***p*** value refers to the probability for the observed empirical result or more extreme results to occur under the assumption that the null hypothesis is true.
25 The process of logistic regression provides the generation of an equation in order to provide an improved means of prediction that extends beyond an individual variable.
26 To undertake the correlation analysis correctly, the interviewed room condition variable was coded as follows: 0 = A/C in use, 1 = Portable fan in use, 2 = Portable fan in use and opened windows, 3 = Opened windows only. However, the actual data gathered through a questionnaire survey was presented without altering households' in vivo experience on their thermal-comfort assessment.
27 Cluster analysis intends to provide groupings of set of items, objects or behaviours that are similar to each other. The outcome of a cluster analysis provides the set of associations that exist among and between various groupings that are provided by the analysis. The actual technique depends on the application of multivariate statistics and the generation of association from available inputs. The choice of input variables becomes important in both providing the basis for similarity within a grouping and differentiating the differences between groupings. The method can apply to any form of data (categorical, ordinal, interval, ratio) and permits combinations of forms of data in the analysis.

References

Balvedi, B. F., Ghisi, E., & Lamberts, R. (2018). A review of occupant behaviour in residential buildings. *Energy and Buildings*. Advance online publication. https://doi.org/10.1016/j.enbuild.2018.06.049

Barthelmes, V. M., Li, R., Andersen, R. K., Bahnfleth, W., Corgnati, S. P., & Rode, C. (2018). Profiling occupant behaviour in Danish dwellings using time use survey data. *Energy and Buildings*, *177*, 329–340. https://doi.org/10.1016/j.enbuild.2018.07.044

Bateson, A. (2014). Comparison of CIBSE thermal comfort assessments and implications for designers. In *CIBSE ASHRAE technical symposium* (p. 11). Dublin.

Brager, G. S., & de Dear, R. J. (1998). Thermal adaptation in the built environment: A literature review. *Energy and Buildings*, *27*, 83–96.

BSI. (2005). *BS EN ISO 7730: 2005: Ergonomics of the thermal environment: analytical determination and interpretation of thermal comfort using calculation of the PMV and PPD indices and local thermal comfort criteria*. Geneva: International Standards Organization.

CEN. (2007). *Indoor environmental input parameters for design and assessment of energy performance of buildings addressing indoor air quality, thermal environment, lighting and acoustics*. EN 15251. Technical report, European Committee for Standardization, Bruxelles. Retrieved November 5, 2018.

CIBSE. (2013). *TM52: The limits of thermal comfort: Avoiding overheating in European buildings*. London: Chartered Institution of Building Services Engineers.

CIBSE. (2015). *CIBSE TM36: Climate change and the indoor environment: Impacts and adaptation*. London: CIBSE.

CIBSE. (2016). *CIBSE guide A – Environmental design 2015*. CIBSE.

CIBSE. (2017). *CIBSE TM59 – Design methodology for the assessment of overheating risk in homes*. London: The Chartered Institution of Building Services Engineers.

Cyprus Meteorological Service. (2020). Meteorological statistical data for Cyprus; The Annual Report, Department of Meteorology: Nicosia, Cyprus. [accessed on 03/10/2020

Day, J. K., & Gunderson, D. E. (2015). Understanding high performance buildings: The link between occupant knowledge of passive design systems, corresponding behaviors, occupant comfort and environmental satisfaction. *Building and Environment*, *84*, 114–124. https://doi.org/10.1016/j.buildenv.2014.11.003

Földváry Ličina, V., Cheung, T., Zhang, H., de Dear, R., Parkinson, T., Arens, E., … Zhou, X. (2018). Development of the ASHRAE global thermal comfort database II. *Building and Environment*, *142*, 502–512. https://doi.org/10.1016/j.buildenv.2018.06.022

Jeong, B., Jeong, J. W., & Park, J. S. (2016). Occupant behavior regarding the manual control of windows in residential buildings. *Energy and Buildings*, *127*, 206–216. https://doi.org/10.1016/j.enbuild.2016.05.097

Nicol F., Humphreys, M., & Roaf, S. (2012). *Adaptive thermal comfort, principles and practice*. London: Routledge.

Nicol, F., Humphreys, M. and Roaf, S. (2015). *Adaptive Thermal Comfort, Principles and practice*. London: Routledge.

Ozarisoy, B. (2022). Energy effectiveness of passive cooling design strategies to reduce the impact of long-term heatwaves on occupants' thermal comfort in Europe: Climate change and mitigation. *Journal of Cleaner Production*. Advance online publication. https://doi.org/10.1016/j.jclepro.2021.129675

Ozarisoy, B., & Altan, H. (2017a). Energy performance development of non-regulated retrofit mass housing estates in Northern Cyprus. *Design Journal*, *20*(Suppl 1), S1765–S1781. https://doi.org/10.1080/14606925.2017.1352697

Ozarisoy, B., & Altan, H. (2017b). Adoption of energy design strategies for retrofitting mass housing estates in Northern Cyprus. *Sustainability (Switzerland)*, *9*(8), 1477. https://doi.org/10.3390/su9081477

Ozarisoy, B., & Altan, H. (2018). Low-energy design strategies for retrofitting existing residential buildings in Cyprus. *Proceedings of the Institution of Civil Engineers: Engineering Sustainability*, *172*(5), 241–255. https://doi.org/10.1680/jensu.17.00061

Ozarisoy, B., & Elsharkawy, H. (2019). Assessing overheating risk and thermal comfort in state-of-the-art prototype houses that combat exacerbated climate change in UK. *Energy and Buildings*, *187*, 201–217. https://doi.org/10.1016/j.enbuild.2019.01.030

Parkinson, T., de Dear, R., & Brager, G. (2020). Nudging the adaptive thermal comfort model. Energy and Buildings, 206. https://doi.org/10.1016/j.enbuild.2019.109559

Ryu, J., Kim, J., Hong, W., & de Dear, R. (2020). Defining the thermal sensitivity (Griffith's constant) of building occupants in the Korean residential context. *Energy and Buildings, 208,* 210–219. https://doi.org/10.1016/j.enbuild.2019.109648

Santangelo, A., & Tondelli, S. (2017). Occupant behaviour and building renovation of the social housing stock: Current and future challenges. *Energy and Buildings*, 145, 276–283. https://doi.org/10.1016/j.enbuild.2017.04.019

Teitelbaum, E., Jayathissa, P., Miller, C., & Meggers, F. (2020). Design with comfort: Expanding the psychrometric chart with radiation and convection dimensions. *Energy and Buildings*, *209,* 305–317. https://doi.org/10.1016/j.enbuild.2019.109591

6 Heat Vulnerability of Residential Buildings

Introduction

This chapter examines the significance of the orientation factor of the 36 base-case representative RTBs and the impact thereof on the building-fabric thermal performance of the surveyed flats, while also taking different floor levels into consideration. The aim of this chapter is to investigate the overheating risk experienced in each occupied space in the representative flats against the acceptable adaptive thermal-comfort limits and industry benchmark of the *CIBSE TM59: Design Methodology for the Assessment of Overheating Risk in Homes*. The thermal performance of the archetype buildings is then validated by conducting a solar-exposure analysis in an energy-simulation platform to develop a reliable energy-use assessment for space conditioning and optimise occupants' thermal comfort.

In the following sections, the results of the IRT survey and analysis of data collected from *on-site* monitoring, in situ physical measurements, household energy bills and building-energy modelling (BEM) are detailed to implement an evidence-based framework in domestic energy use policy. Finally, the energy-model procedure is delineated to provide subsequent information related to the BEM and retrofitting design strategies that are presented in Chapter 7.

Thermal Imaging: Walk-Through Survey

This section presents the findings of a walk-through thermal-imaging survey that was conducted in the winter prior to the *on-site* questionnaire survey, in situ physical indoor environment measurements and *on-site* environmental monitoring that were performed in August 2018. These results were also validated by the SunCast application of the IES software suite, which sought to analyse the importance of the solar irradiance factor in building envelopes. A total of 36 case-study RTBs were surveyed, and IRT imaging was conducted with a Fluke TiS20 thermal camera twice each day during the winter period—in the early morning and late evening—to avoid possible errors caused by direct solar radiation. A thermal-imaging survey was carried out beforehand to diagnose the building, and after these data were taken into account, they were used to determine feasible retrofitting strategies for policymakers (Ozarisoy & Altan, 2017a).

DOI: 10.4324/9781003393092-7

Table 6.1 demonstrates the timeline for the thermal-imaging investigations related to heat loss and overheating-risk assessment that was conducted between 26 December 2017 and 12 January 2018, and Figure 6.1 illustrates the mapping of the thermal vulnerability of the archetype buildings in the social-housing estate.

Figure 6.1 presents overall observations to demonstrate the heat vulnerability of the base-case RTBs. Temperature readings from approximately 2,830 images were analysed using the forward-looking infrared radiometer (FLIR) analysis tool to diagnose the thermal performance of all 36 prototype RTBs for the worst-case scenario development that is presented in Chapter 7. These assessments were performed during the 2017–2018 winter months, and all of the survey data were used to model the base-case building and validate the building-energy-simulation findings (Bayomi et al., 2021); the field-observation *on-site* thermal images and photographic documentation and the quantitative temperature recordings of the building-fabric systems also validated the findings related to the development of adaptive thermal-comfort thresholds, which are presented in Chapter 5. This documentation indicates that the identification of 'neutral' adaptive thermal comfort is not only limited by local climate conditions; building-fabric thermal performance should also be taken into consideration when developing a robust thermal-adaptive threshold benchmark for the Mediterranean region (Ozarisoy & Altan, 2017b). Figure 6.2(a) and (b) illustrate the built-environment parameters that had a direct impact on the thermal-imaging results.

Figure 6.2(a) shows the location of the archetype buildings, which represent 38% of the housing stock in Northern Cyprus (NC). The social-housing estate is located 900 m away from the fortifications of the Old Walled city, which is surrounded by 18-metre walls and several historic towers with heights up to 32.5 m; this urban-fabric feature provides constraints in terms of minimising the penetration of prevailing winds and direct summer breezes from the Mediterranean Sea. It should be emphasised that the built-environment features also impact occupants' thermal comfort, which has previously been explored by scholars (Dartevelle et al., 2021; Gao et al., 2021; Yang et al., 2021).

Anecdotally, in the questionnaire survey, one interviewee who lived in a first-floor northeast-facing RTB commented that there was insufficient natural ventilation due to the close proximity of these urban blocks and that the height of the city walls caused an overheating risk. Another interviewee in a fourth-floor northeast-facing RTB indicated that they were very satisfied with the effectiveness of the natural ventilation to acclimatise their indoor air environment in the summer, because they received good-quality summer breezes from the sea; this participant reported that they relied on their wall-mounted air conditioning (A/C) system and a gas cylinder to heat their rooms in the winter. Figure 6.2(b) presents a map of the social-housing estate to aid in the discussion of the thermal-imaging survey findings in which the different RTB orientations were taken into account.

The walk-through thermal-imaging analysis examined temperature differences and variations across each RTB building envelope and potential thermal anomalies.

Table 6.1 Timeline of Base-Case Representative RTBs Surveyed in December 2017 and January 2018

Date	*Time*	*Weather Conditions Observed at Time of Walk-Through Survey*	*Outdoor Temperature Mean (°C) (In situ)*	*Outdoor Temperature Min (°C) (In situ)*	*Outdoor Temperature Max (°C) (Ercan Airport)*
26 December 2017	06:30–07:45	Sunny/clear cloudy; slightly cold	13.4	9.0	19.1
26 December 2017	16:00–16:45	Sunny/clear cloudy; slightly cold	13.4	9.0	19.1
28 December 2017	06:30–07:45	Sunny/clear cloudy; warm	17.4	11.6	20.5
28 December 2017	16:00–17:00	Sunny/clear cloudy; warm	17.4	11.6	20.5
29 December 2017	06:30–07:45	Sunny/clear cloudy; warm	15.0	9.3	18.8
29 December 2017	16:00–17:00	Sunny/clear cloudy; warm	15.0	9.3	18.8
2 January 2018	16:00–17:00	Sunny/clear cloudy; slightly cold	15.6	11.9	19.6
3 January 2018	06:30–08:15	Cloudy/scattered rain; no wind; warm	15.6	11.6	19.1
3 January 2018	16:00–17:15	Cloudy; torrential rain; slightly windy; warm	15.6	11.6	19.1
4 January 2018	16:00–17:15	Rainfall AM; cloudy; mild weather	14.8	13.2	17.1
6 January 2018	06:30–07:45	Cloudy; no wind	15.0	10.1	17.2
6 January 2018	16:00–17:30	Cloudy/sunny; slightly cold	15.0	10.1	17.2
8 January 2018	06:30–08:15	Clear sky; cold	13.7	9.4	18.9
8 January 2018	16:00–17:30	Sunny/clear sky; warm	13.7	9.4	18.9
9 January 2018	06:30–08:15	Sunny/clear sky; warm	14.1	10.0	18.2
11 January 2018	15:35–17:30	Sunny/cloudy; warm	16.9	11.9	19.6
12 January 2018	16:00–17:30	Sunny/cloudy; warm	14.6	9.9	19.5

Note: Max outdoor temperature collected by Meteorological Office of Northern Cyprus in September 2018; data retrieved from Ercan Airport in Nicosia, which is approximately 50 km away from case-study location.

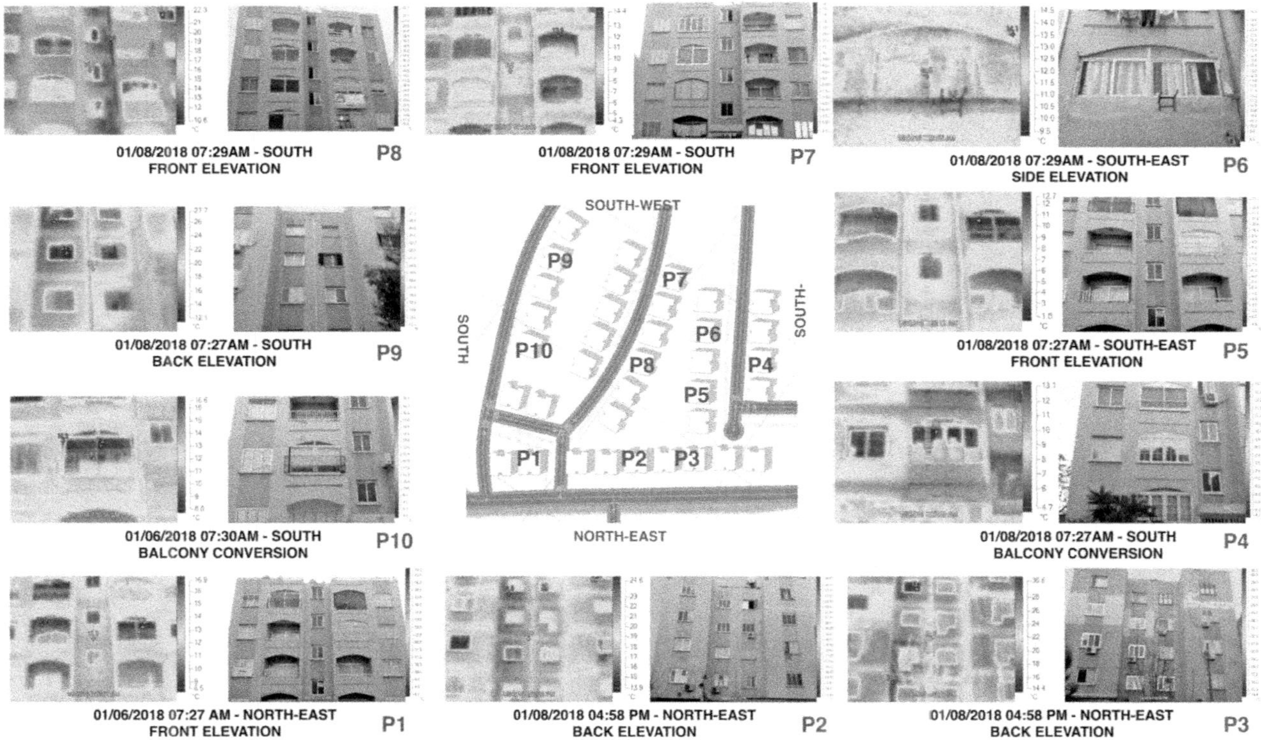

Figure 6.1 Point-by-point mapping of walk-through thermal-imaging survey conducted in winter 2017–2018, taking RTB orientations and impact of different time of day on overheating-risk assessment into account.

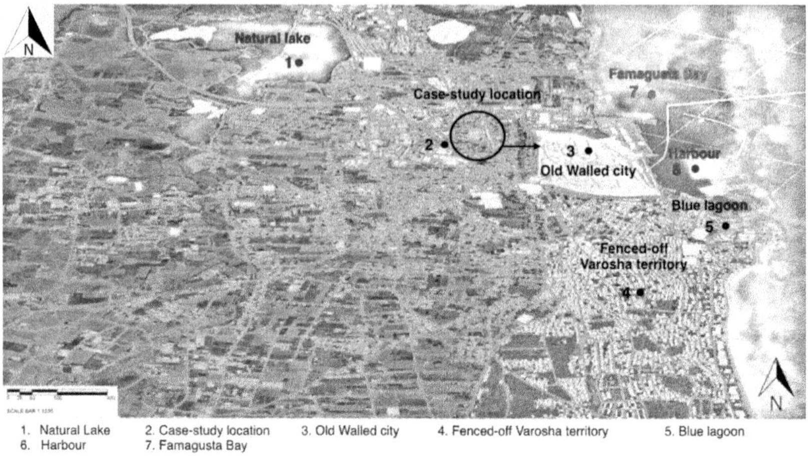

(a)

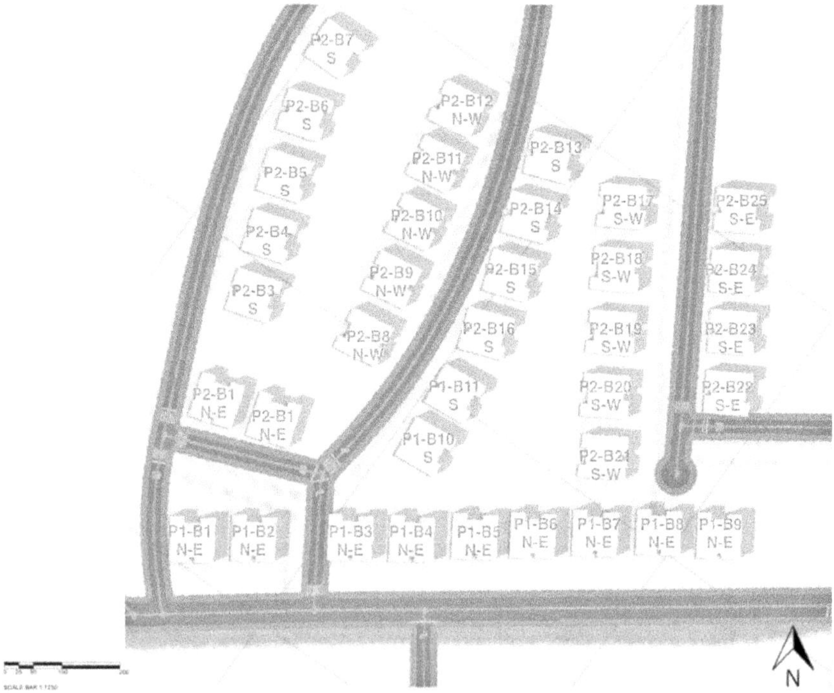

(b)

Figure 6.2 (a) Location of urban-built social-housing estate and proximity to Old Walled city and (b) locations of participating RTBs for street-by-street thermal-imaging survey to diagnose thermal anomalies in building-fabric elements.

This process validated the thermal performance of the buildings, overheating-risk assessment and domestic energy use by triangulating the research methods with the energy bills of each household and the BES analysis that was previously recommended by scholars who researched energy and thermal comfort (Defruyt et al., 2013; Mahmoud et al., 2019). To examine the building-energy performance gap caused by household modifications to the building envelope, a series of images from the living room and kitchen balcony were recorded to document the various refurbishment activities. Figure 6.3(a)–(j) provides details of thermographs of the base-case representative buildings that were conducted.

Building-envelope surface temperatures of the southeast-oriented RTB shown in Figure 6.3(a) ranged between 7.1 and 14.5°C, and these units experienced heat loss through the external wall, possibly due to the absence of insulation material; the thermograph image was taken on 29 December 2017 between 06:30 and 07:30, when the outdoor temperature was recorded at 10°C. Occupants in these units installed large glazed windows and an aluminium external shutter system to avoid incoming solar radiation; a photograph of these modifications is shown in Figure 6.3(b). Throughout the *on-site* observations, it was noted that this was the most common refurbishment effort that occupants implemented to avoid incoming sun, acclimatise indoor air temperatures and lessen noise pollution.

Building-envelope surface temperatures of the northeast-oriented RTB shown in Figure 6.3(c) ranged from 14.5 to 26.3°C, and this building exhibited significant heat loss through the windows, wall junction details and cracks on the building surface; the thermograph image was taken on 29 December 2017 between 16:30 and 17:00, when the outdoor air temperature was recorded at 10°C. Figure 6.3(d) is a photograph of the wood-burning stove and heating system installed by occupants, because these units did not have a central heating system due to the absence of a natural gas system infrastructure in Cyprus; this led to significant heat loss, which suggests that this type of housing stock is susceptible to overheating in the summer. In addition, these households installed mechanical ventilation shafts for their wood-burning stoves, but failed to consider the health implications, and the close proximity of these shafts to the A/C compressor damaged the building envelope and resulted in significant heat loss.

Building-envelope surface temperatures of the southwest-oriented RTB shown in Figure 6.3(e) ranged between 7.7 and 15.4°C, and this structure demonstrated heat loss through the external wall and the windows; the thermographic image was taken on 6 January 2018 between 06:30 and 07:45, when the outdoor air temperature was recorded at 10°C. Most of these households installed operable double-glazed window systems that covered the balcony areas to adjust the frequency and effectiveness of natural ventilation and increase the living room floor area. The photograph in Figure 6.3(f) shows this refurbishment, and that these occupants also utilised internal roller blinds in the summer to minimise sun exposure.

Building-envelope surface temperatures in the southwest-oriented RTB shown in Figure 6.3(g) ranged between 5.4 and 13.9°C, and this structure exhibited heat loss through the external wall; the thermographic image was taken on 8 January 2018 between 06:30 and 07:54, when the air temperature was recorded at 9.4°C.

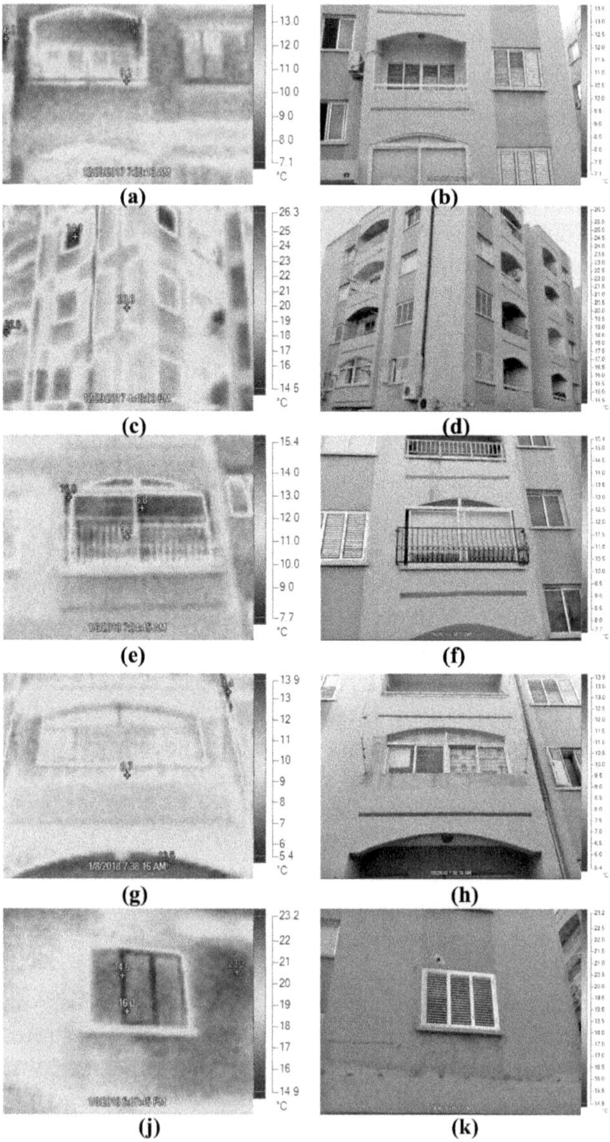

Figure 6.3 (a) Heat acclimatisation on southeast-facing RTB balcony area (P2-B23), (b) photograph of large glazed windows of converted balcony area with closed internal blind, (c) heat loss of concrete-made southeast-facing RTBs due to absence of insulation materials and various structural issues (P1-B6), (d) photograph of wood-burning stove service shaft installed by first-floor occupants, (e) heat loss through large glazed windows of converted balcony space in southwest-facing RTB (P2-B20), (f) photograph of refurbishment articulated by second-floor occupants, (g) heat loss of southwest-facing RTB kitchen extension (P2-B18), (h) photograph of refurbishment activity articulated by third-floor occupants, (i) heat absorptivity of south-facing corner block (P2-B13) and (j) aluminium-framed shutters installed on first-floor flat.

The detected thermal anomalies were possibly due to the small kitchens in these units; motivated by limited floor area and inadequate meal preparation, most of the surveyed households had refurbished balcony areas of their kitchen spaces, and these modifications led to significant heat loss through the wall surfaces. The photograph in Figure 6.3(h) shows occupant refurbishments to the kitchen space at the balcony enclosure with large glazed window openings.

Building-envelope surface temperatures of the south-facing RTBs shown in Figure 6.3(i) ranged between 14.9 and 23.2°C, and these units experienced heat loss through external walls; the thermographic image was taken on 28 December 2017 between 17:00 and 17:34, when the outdoor air temperature was recorded at 10°C. The recorded heat loss was possibly due to a crack in the wall surface. The photograph in Figure 6.3(k) shows aluminium-framed window shutters that were installed in the southeast-facing buildings. This was a popular refurbishment which has caused high absorptivity of solar radiation both in winter and summer.

The survey results for the base-case RTB buildings demonstrated that most heat loss resulted from air infiltration, primarily through uninsulated exterior walls and windows, which necessitated a high annual energy demand for heating and cooling purposes across the surveyed RTBs. Notably, this section only discussed a small selection of the experiment images; the full findings were tabulated into spreadsheets to assess the overheating risk of each RTB while evaluating building-energy performance.

In Situ Measurements: Walk-In Survey

To validate the BES findings, which revealed the overheating risk of different indoor occupied spaces, thermography measurements were taken with a FLIR thermographic camera to assess the thermal behaviour of the construction materials for the base-case RTBs. This method validated the IRT survey that was conducted between 28 July 2018 and 3 September 2018, which concurrently investigated the degree of thermal discomfort when the *on-site* questionnaire survey was administered; a total of 118 flats were inspected with this technology. Figure 6.4(a)–(f) illustrates the recorded temperature readings and demonstrates the detected thermal anomalies of the different building envelopes.

Figure 6.4(a) shows the thermal performance of the living room ceiling surface of a top-floor southwest-facing flat, which was measured at 40.2°C; this image was taken on 10 August 2018 at 17:35, when the outdoor air temperature was recorded at 36°C, and confirms that these roof surfaces absorbed a high level of solar radiation due to a lack of insulation on the building envelopes. Figure 6.4(b), which was taken at the same time as the thermal image reading in the previous figure, illustrates the thermal performance of the kitchen side-wall surface of the same flat, which was measured at 35.1°C. These images reveal the overheating risk for the living room and kitchen due to high transmittance of building properties and local climate conditions; notably, the windows in the living room and kitchen spaces were kept open 6–8 h every day in the summer.

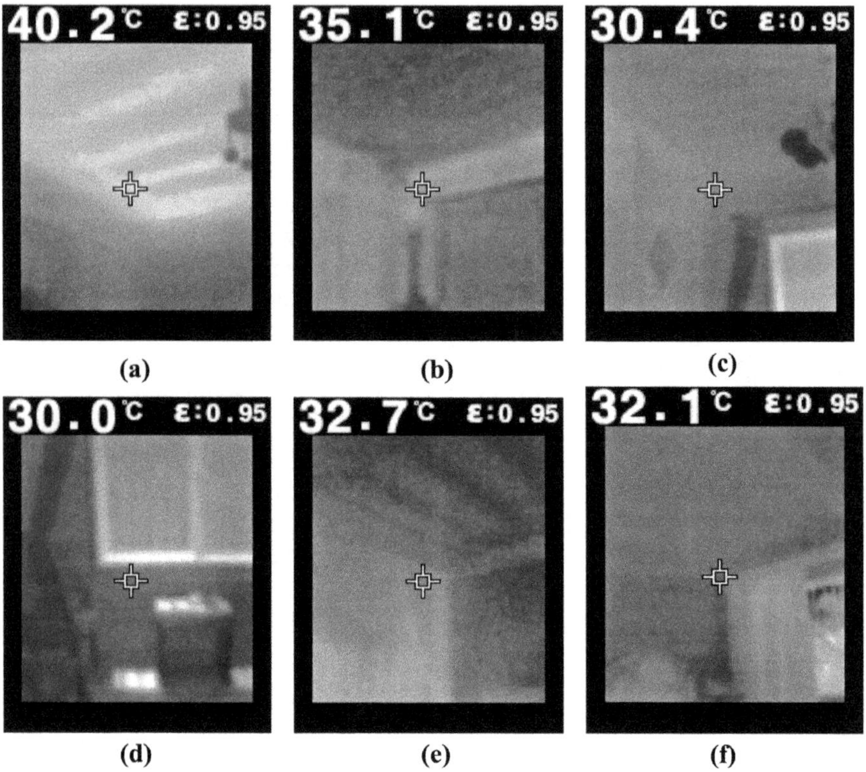

Figure 6.4 (a) High solar transmittance of ceiling surface of top-floor flat (measurement recorded when all windows were closed), (b) heat acclimatisation of third-floor living room space (measurement recorded when balcony door and two side windows were open), (c) heat acclimatisation of living room air environment when wall-mounted A/C system was in use, (d) high transmittance of aluminium single-glazed windows, (e) heat acclimatisation of living room space in first-floor flat and (f) heat absorptivity of corner junction details of ground-floor flat.

Figure 6.4(c) depicts the thermal performance of the living room ceiling surface of the southeast-oriented intermediate-floor flat, which was measured at 30.4°C; this image was taken on 1 August 2018 at 10:05, when the recorded outdoor temperature was 29°C. At the time of the thermography survey, the wall-mounted A/C system was set at 19°C and had been in use for approximately 2 h. Thermal anomalies of regular shapes and clearly identified boundaries were associated with the underlying structure, and temperature distribution within this pattern was demonstrated; this image reveals an area of the ceiling from the flat that was located above this unit, which had high *U*-values. Figure 6.4(d), which was taken at the same time as the thermal image reading in the previous figure, reveals the thermal performance of the living room side wall of the same flat, which was measured at 30°C. Significant heat gains through the aluminium-framed single-glazed windows were recorded. Furthermore, air leakage caused thermal anomalies with irregular shapes, and large temperature variations that formed characteristic 'streaks' or 'ray' patterns were detected.

Figure 6.4(e) illustrates the thermal performance of the living room ceiling surface of a south-facing first-floor flat, which was measured at 32.7°C; this image was taken on 16 August 2018 at 09:25, when the outdoor air temperature was recorded at 29.7°C. The living room windows were open for natural ventilation at the time of the thermography survey. Similar anomalies to those in Figure 6.4(c) that were caused by construction flaws were detected on the ceiling surfaces, and the thermography survey also captured heat gains through the large glazed opaque window surfaces in the enclosed balcony space; it was concluded that this structural modification led to a 2–3°C increase in indoor air temperatures. Figure 6.4(f) shows the thermal performance of the living room ceiling surface of a southeast-oriented ground-floor flat, which was recorded at 32.1°C; this image was taken on 1 August 2018 at 11:25, when the outdoor air temperature was recorded at 30.1°C. At the time of the thermography survey, a portable fan was in use and the windows were open; a significant thermal anomaly was detected on the aluminium-framed single-glazed window structure.

The indoor walk-through thermography surveys determined that all 36 participating RTBs and 118 flats exhibited signs of thermal anomalies, which were characterised as either air leakages or heat conductivity. Figure 6.5 illustrates the overheating-risk mapping of the selected flats to provide an overall understanding of the thermal vulnerability of social-housing stock.

In situ measurements of the indoor air environments were conducted to understand the impact of the building's thermal properties on overheating risks and the occupants' thermal comfort; the results are shown in Figure 6.5. It should be noted that the use of a solar-mask form of adaptation to the physical environment, which directly influenced the occupants' psychology when their thermal-sensation votes (TSVs), were assessed with the *on-site* environmental monitoring through the questionnaire survey (Lassen et al., 2021). The solar radiation readings of the building envelopes and the time-of-day factor were also examined to avoid research bias related to the generated results that are presented in Chapter 6, and the results are shown in Figure 6.6(a).

The building-envelope temperatures shown in Figure 6.6(a) ranged between 29.1 and 39.8°C; these were recorded on 27 July 2018 and 3 September 2018 between 10:00 and 21:00, when the *on-site* questionnaire survey was conducted. Most of the scatter dot lines are positioned between 17:00 and 20:00, because 73% of the households were recruited in the afternoon; this was intentionally done to increase the sample size. Even though the ASHRAE 55 standards (2017) recommend an optimum thermal-comfort temperature of 25°C, according to the in situ measurements findings, indoor air temperatures during the survey period were never below 29.1°C; it should be noted that 27% of the flats were surveyed late in the morning, when indoor air temperatures fluctuated between 29.1 and 34.1°C. These results revealed that the building-envelope *U*-values were a determinant factor of the heat vulnerability of the recruited RTBs.

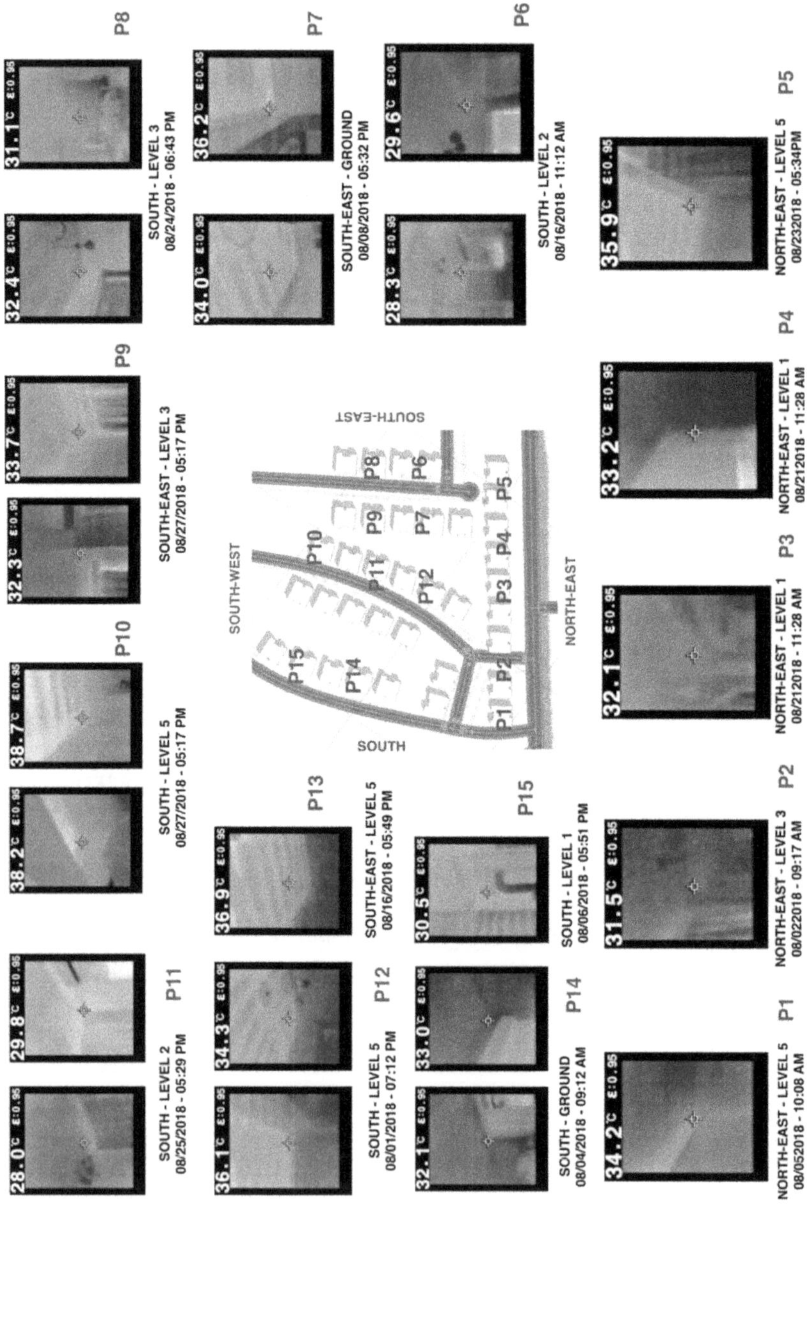

Figure 6.5 Point-by-point mapping of indoor walk-through thermal-imaging survey conducted while questionnaire survey was administered, taking different floor levels and impact of different time of day on overheating-risk assessment into account.

Indoor walk-through surveys of the base-case representative flats were conducted to identify potential defects and provide a basis for information that would be needed for the BES studies; when the survey results were compared, few differences that were recorded in the walk-through inspections were attributable to the orientations or floor levels of the flats. Notably, no moisture-related anomalies or service faults were detected. Further observations revealed that only a few of the surveyed flats experienced structural draughts and that a majority of ventilation defects were because of windows; this could be due to the thermal conductivity of the aluminium-framed single-glazed windows, compared to that of the doors, and flawed seals between windows and window frames that were documented. Similarly, conductivity heat loss was the most common building defect observed across the sample; significant heat loss was likely due to uninsulated roof surfaces, and additional heat loss was recorded through the walls, windows and doors.

Household Energy Bills

An evidence-based factor that was used to validate the thermal anomalies that were detected throughout the IRT survey was the monthly utility bills for each household.[1] The residents' monthly electricity bills were collected for the energy assessment analysis to assess the thermal performance of their RTBs, especially during the hottest period in August. To determine the overheating risk of the investigated flats, the orientation of each unit was taken into consideration; based on these data, the orientation of each block was found to be an important factor in the energy-consumption patterns of each household. These data covered the winter of 2014–2015[2] (i.e., December through February) and the summer of 2015 (i.e., June through August). Figure 6.6(b) and (c) illustrate the energy-bill analysis for each household, taking the orientation factor into account.

Figure 6.6(b) illustrates the energy consumption of the occupants in the winter of 2014–2015: of the households living in south-facing RTBs, 5% consumed 500–750 kWh; 8% consumed 750–1,250 kWh; 15% consumed 1,250–2,000 kWh; 3% consumed 2,000–2,500 kWh; another 3% consumed 2,500–3,000 kWh and 3% consumed 3,500–4,000 kWh. The energy-consumption patterns in the southwest-facing RTBs were as follows: 4% of the households consumed 750–1,250 kWh, 6% consumed 1,250–2,000 kWh, 5% consumed 2,500–3,000 kWh and 5% consumed 3,500–4,000 kWh. In the south- and southwest-facing RTBs, 3% consumed 500–750 kWh, 11% consumed 750–1,250 kWh, 12% consumed 1,250–2,000 kWh, 4% consumed 2,000–2,500 kWh and 4% consumed 3,500–4,000 kWh. Contrary to expectations, the northeast-facing RTBs revealed higher levels of household energy consumption than the average of the entire sample, and the south-facing RTBs exhibited the highest levels of energy consumption of the entire sample.

Figure 6.6(c) illustrates the household energy-consumption patterns in the summer of 2015. It was determined that the south-facing flats consumed the most energy: 7% of the households consumed 0–500 kWh, 4% consumed 500–750 kWh, 8% consumed 750–1,250 kWh, 11% consumed 1,250–2,000 kWh, 3% consumed 2,000–2,500 kWh and 3% consumed more than 4,000 kWh. In the

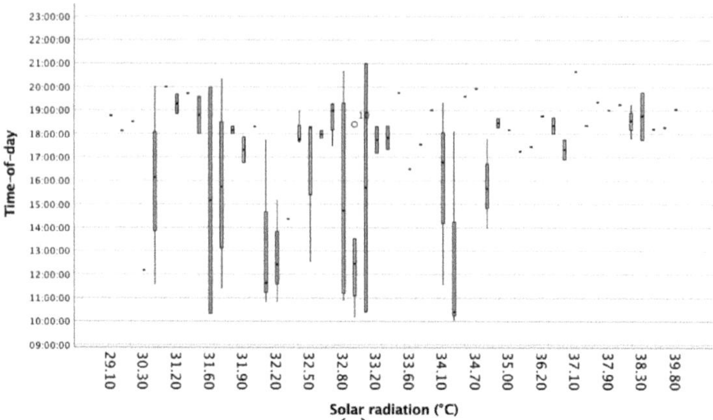

(a)

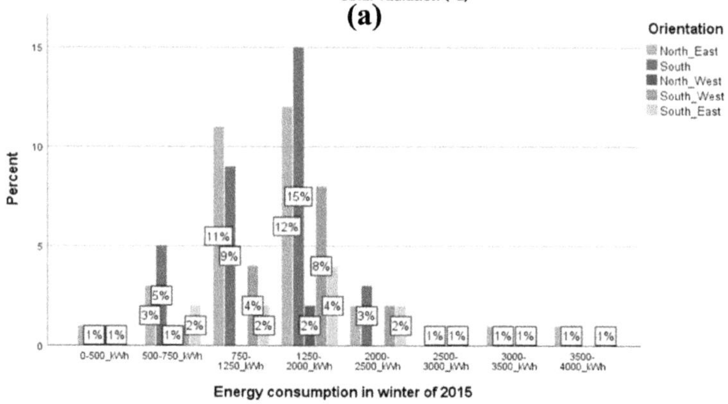

(b)

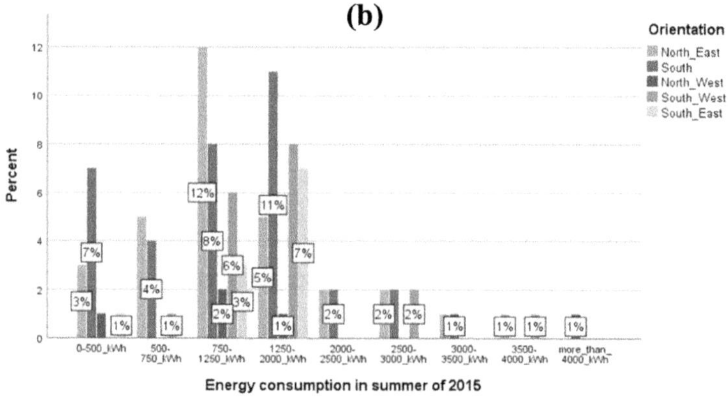

(c)

Figure 6.6 (a) Distribution of associations between solar radiation and time of day; (b) percentage distribution of winter energy consumption of households, taking different orientations into account and (c) percentage distribution of summer energy consumption of households, taking different orientations into account.

southwest-facing blocks, 6% of the households consumed 750–1,250 kWh, 8% consumed 1,250–2,000 kWh, 2% consumed 2,500–3,000 kWh and 1% consumed 3,500–4,000 kWh. The highest level of energy use was observed in the south-facing RTBs: 3% of the households consumed 0–500 kWh, 5% consumed 500–750 kWh, 12% consumed 750–1,250 kWh, 5% consumed 1,250–2,000 kWh, 3% consumed 2,000–2,500 kWh and 3% consumed 3,500–4,000 kWh.

These findings demonstrate that households that were situated on the southwest-facing blocks consumed more energy because of the absorption of strong solar radiation through the building envelopes of these RTBs, and northeast-facing flats consumed the same amount of energy as those on south-facing blocks. It can be deduced from these data that even though orientation is an important factor related to energy consumption, the actual cause of high energy consumption was heat loss through the building envelopes and the absence of insulation material on external walls.

The effect of different floor levels on the energy consumption of each representative flat was investigated. The results revealed that the fifth-floor flats were cold due to heat loss through the uninsulated roof surfaces and thus consumed more energy; the first-floor flats were cold because of their floor position, which led to inadequate sun exposure. It was determined that the energy consumption of the ground and first floors was similar to that of the top floor due to the high number of occupancy patterns that were observed in the first-floor flats. Table 6.2 delineates the minimum, maximum, mean and standard deviation (*SD*) of actual household-energy consumption in the summer of 2015 and winter of 2015–2016.

Table 6.2 reveals that the households expended approximately the same amount of energy to keep their respective indoor air environments warm in the winter and cool in the summer. These results also confirmed that the occupants experienced highly uncomfortable indoor conditions due to the RTB building envelopes. The energy consumption of each household provided information that validated the *on-site* questionnaire survey, in situ measurements and the building-modelling simulation results that are described.

Building-Energy Model Development

In this section, the set-up of the energy simulation studies that were derived from the recommended international benchmarks and criteria to assess overheating risks

Table 6.2 Descriptive Analysis of Actual Household Energy Bills.

Energy Consumption	*Minimum kWh*	*Maximum kWh*	*Mean kWh*	*SD kWh*
2015 Winter	355	3,961	1,454.99	734.28062
2015 Summer	171	4,639	1,366.40	824.53727
2016 Winter	355	3,961	1,454.99	734.28062
2016 Summer	291	4,798	1,583.82	986.62216
2015 August	27	1,658	465.56	317.6126
2016 August	63	1,223	374.58	262.5003

and occupants' thermal comfort, taking occupants' real-life experiences on energy use into consideration, are described. The energy-performance assessment analysis was developed in conjunction with data that were gathered through the questionnaire survey.

Weather Files Assigned in Simulation Model

Using the Integrated Environmental Solutions (IES) energy-simulation tool, building-energy modelling and a dynamic thermal simulation (DTS) were conducted to validate the field-survey findings and determine the energy-use reliability of the surveyed households. The aim of this section is to develop a viable model that can be adopted for the building-performance evaluation and for future retrofitting design strategies.

The IES software suite is an advanced building simulation tool that has been approved for the dynamic thermal modelling of large and complex buildings (IES, 2020). The base-case model in the present study was simulated by using a weather file that was defined with data obtained between May and September of 2018 from the closest weather station[3]; this was located in Paralimni[4] in the Famagusta district[5] (i.e., *Ammochostos* in Greek), which is in the ASHRAE Climate Zone 2A. The dynamic thermal-simulation output was then compared to the actual household energy bills collected in 2015–2016 to accurately assess the cooling demand of each occupied space by determining the deviations and the relevant uncertainty parameters in the simulation model (Carnieletto et al., 2021).

Test reference year (TRY) weather files for the one-year period of January through December of 2018 were utilised to conduct the DTS. Several modifications were made during the energy assessment phase to minimise data loss when the actual meteorological weather files were generated (Hosseini et al., 2021; Liu et al., 2021); these modifications were primarily related to the inner load and occupancy schedules, which were updated with information provided in the questionnaire survey. The TRY and actual meteorological year (AMY) weather files were comprehensively analysed to avoid discrepancies; in addition to the customised weather files utilised in the simulation programme, the present study also used weather files constructed according to meteorological data gathered from EnergyPlus weather datasets (Sakiyama et al., 2021). To adjust these weather files, constructed weather profiles, which included heating-degree days (HDDs) and cooling-degree days (CDDs), were compared with weather files assigned to weather profiles in the IES building-energy modelling platform.

An energy-performance assessment model was developed to provide subsequent information that would be utilised to establish the simulation input parameters for the DTS analysis (Ozarisoy & Elsharkawy, 2019); the base model was simulated with weather file input that was created from available data from the closest station for the same year or with weather files of a typical reference year that were recorded according to the recommended building-thermal-performance algorithm put forth in the EN ISO 15927-4: 2005 standards (Prataviera et al., 2021). Available datasets were then generated into IES weather file extensions by the

Weather Analytics software suite to analyse the overheating period that extended from May to September of 2018; the benchmarking criteria for each configuration deviated from the threshold value, and the calibrated model needed to be evaluated (Ozarisoy, 2022).

Occupancy-Pattern Variations

A DTS was devised for occupancy and schedules for occupying rooms to determine the likelihood of overheating in the summer; the data for this were obtained from a questionnaire-based survey that was conducted in August 2018 to gain insight into the occupants' patterns related to the manner in which they operated their homes to provide evidence-based data for the building-performance evaluation that was conducted for the present study. The occupancy and energy-use patterns of the surveyed flats were separately incorporated into the simulation model as three dominant scenarios—low, moderate and high—to properly assess energy use.

An energy-consumption assessment that utilised representative occupancy profiles was compared to the standard assessment protocols recommended by the EN 15251 and CIBSE TM59 standards to evaluate overheating risk and investigate each household's degree of thermal discomfort (Sun et al., 2020; Uddin et al., 2021). The primary focus of the BES studies was to use the dominant occupancy and energy-use patterns to determine the impact of different occupancy schedules on the building-energy-performance evaluation. Table 6.3 delineates the cooling-energy-use schedules and occupancy patterns for the representative flats according to three different occupancy profiles, which were later implemented in the IES simulation tool.

According to Table 6.3, Flat A was located on the first floor and was occupied by a retired couple who used a portable fan in the living room between 13:00 and 18:00 and in the bedroom between 22:00 and 07:00. The respondents also indicated that their living room and bedroom windows were open during occupancy hours every day of the week; the window and door in their kitchen space were opened during meal preparation between 11:30 and 14:00.

Flat B, which was located on the intermediate floor, was occupied by an elderly couple and their two grandchildren, who typically used their wall-mounted A/C system in the living room and Bedroom 1 between 11:30 and 18:00. All windows were kept closed when their grandchildren were present in the home, but the respondents stated that they kept their windows open from 18:00 to 07:00 to dissipate stale air. The occupants reported that they used their A/C system between 22:00 and 03:00 with all of their windows closed, and they used a portable fan in Bedroom 2 from 03:00 to 06:00 with all their windows open; the kitchen window and door were open 24 h a day. The A/C system in the living room and bedroom spaces was set to 21°C.

Flat C was located on the upper floor and was occupied by a family of two adults and three children who turned their A/C system on in the living room between 09:00 and 19:00. Two adults predominantly used a portable fan in Bedroom 1 between 23:00 and 06:00. The A/C system was used in Bedroom 2, which was

Table 6.3 Low, Moderate and High Occupancy Patterns Assigned to Representative Flats A, B and C in BES Model

Spaces		*OP1**	*OP2***	*OP3****
Living Room	Cooling	13:00–18:00	11:30–18:00	09:00–19:00
	Occupancy	Two people: 07:00–22:00 every day	Four people: 07:30–18:00 weekdays Two people: 18:00–22:00 every day	Two people: 09:00–16:00 every day Three people: 16:00–17:00 weekdays Four people: 17:00–23:00 weekdays
Bedroom 1	Cooling	22:00–07:00	11:30–18:00 22:00–03:00 03:00–06:00	23:00–06:00
	Occupancy	Two people: 22:00–07:00 every day	Four people: 07:30–18:00 weekdays Two people: 22:00–06:00 every day	Two people: 23:00–06:00 every day
Bedroom 2	Cooling	Off	Off	23:00–06:00
	Occupancy	None	None	Two people: 23:00–06:00 every day
Bedroom 3	Cooling	Off	Off	17:30–07:00
	Occupancy	None	None	One person: 17:30–07:00 weekdays
Kitchen	Cooling	Off	Off	17:30–19:30
	Occupancy	Usually one person: 07:00–08:00, 11:30–13:00 and 17:00–19:30 weekdays	Usually four people: 07:00–08:00 and 11:30–13:00 weekdays Usually two people: 19:00–20:00 every day	Three people: 06:00–06:45 weekdays Five people: 18:00–19:00 weekdays Five people: 10:00–11:30 weekends Five people: 17:00–18:00 weekends

*OP1: Occupancy pattern 1 (low).
**OP2: Occupancy pattern 2 (moderate).
***OP3: Occupancy pattern 3 (high).

occupied by two children who were 8 and 14 years of age, from 23:00 to 08:00, and their windows were closed. The A/C system was used in Bedroom 3, which was occupied by one 16-year-old youth, between 17:00 and 08:00, and their windows were closed. The A/C system was set to 18°C in the living room, 21°C in Bedroom 2 and 16°C in Bedroom 3. The kitchen space was occupied between 17:30 and 19:00, and the A/C system was used during those hours; the window and door in the kitchen were only open between 06:00 and 17:30.

It should be emphasised that the dominant representative occupancy profiles that were recommended by the CIBSE TM59 industry benchmark criteria were adapted in the simulation model (CIBSE, 2017). It should also be noted that the starting point in this study was the human-based data, which facilitated the triangulation of the findings from the primary data sources that are discussed in Chapter 8.

Thermal-Comfort Assessment Indicators

In this section, determinant factors gathered through the questionnaire survey that were found to affect the occupants' thermal comfort are explained, and an adaptive thermal-comfort assessment is delineated. Adaptation of the occupants' physiological body temperature to their indoor environmental conditions is also discussed, and the manner in which an adaptation analysis using the simulation tool was conducted is also explained. This section discusses how and why thermal-comfort results were validated in the simulation outputs according to the occupants' metabolic rates and clothing-insulation levels and included in the building-performance evaluation.

Metabolic Activity. During the questionnaire survey, participants were asked to record their activity level for the previous 20 min, and their metabolic rates were calculated to validate the findings discussed in Chapter 6. The mean average metabolic rate of the participants was 3.22 *met* (SD = 1.931), as shown in Figure 6.7(a).

These results were compiled using the metabolic-rate range included in the ASHRAE 55 adaptive thermal-comfort standards (2017). Notably, the ASHRAE adaptive-comfort model is applicable to spaces in which occupants are engaged in near-sedentary physical activities with metabolic rates that range from 0.8 to 2.10 *met* (ASHRAE, 2017).[6] According to the frequency statistics for this survey, the overall average metabolic rate was 1.93 *met*, and the most frequent metabolic rate was 0.3 *met*; it was determined that the activities in which the residents had engaged during the 20-min period prior to the survey were largely sedentary in nature. Figure 6.7(b) illustrates the variations in participant metabolic rates, taking gender into account.

Prior to being surveyed, 10% of the males were involved in high-intensity activity, 2% were reclining, 6% were standing (relaxed), 7% were engaged in medium-intensity activity, 3% were seated, 5% were involved in light activity (standing) and 10% were engaged in high-intensity activity. Before the female respondents were surveyed, 4% were reclining, 12% were standing (relaxed), 8% engaged in light activity, 18% were seated, 4% engaged in light activity (standing), 1% engaged in high-intensity activity and 20% were involved in medium-intensity activity.

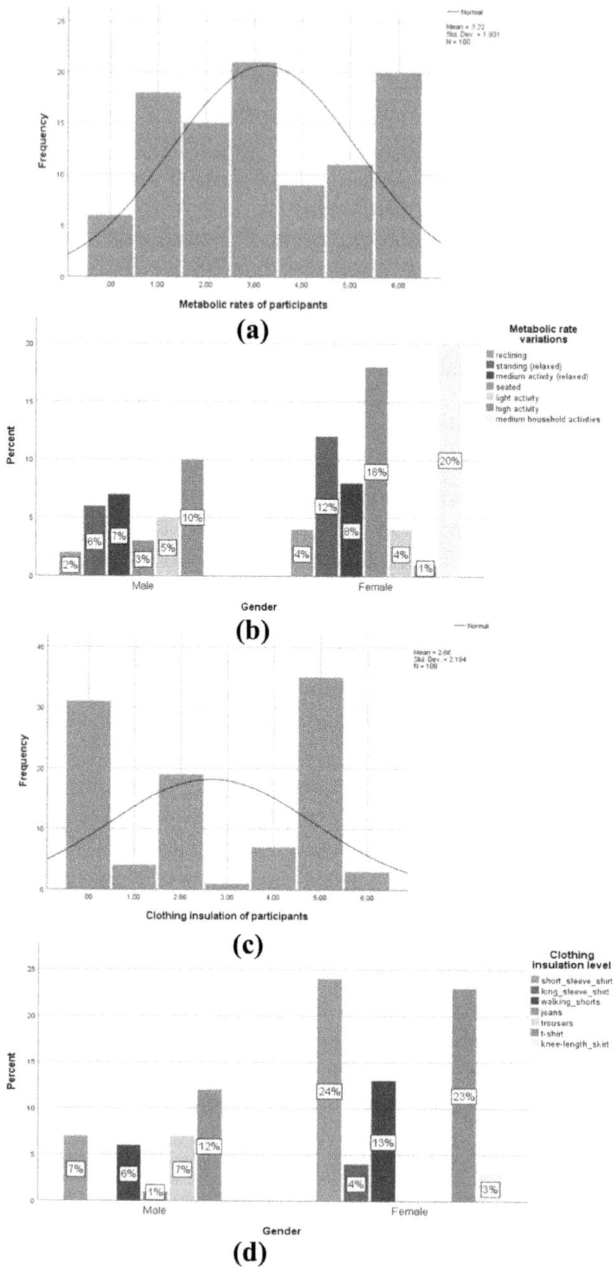

Figure 6.7 (a) Average participant metabolic rates; (b) percentage distribution of participant metabolic rates, taking gender into account; (c) distribution of household clothing-insulation values and (d) percentage distribution of participant clothing levels, taking gender into account.

The male participants who reported high-intensity activities were repairing indoor wall surfaces or damaged building components in their properties to avoid heat losses through the building envelopes, and the male participants who reported medium-intensity activity were either standing up and were involved in household activities. Of the female respondents who were engaged in medium-intensity household activities, 20% were busy with meal preparation in the kitchen; in this regard, it is important to consider the additional internal heat-gain factor from domestic kitchen appliances, which was found to have a significant impact on the TSVs.

One of the main reasons to ask a question related to the household metabolic activity was to ensure that all metabolic rate activities could be tabulated and examined in line with the benchmark scale of the ASHRAE 55 standards (2017) so a reliable dataset could be created for the BES. All input parameters were entered into the thermal-comfort assessment application in the IES software platform.

Clothing Insulation. This section is comprised of an analysis of Question 31, which concerned the participants' clothing. The level of insulation of the clothing that the respondents were wearing at the time of the questionnaire survey was observed and recorded in the questionnaire checklist, and the impact of the respective clothing-insulation levels on the occupants' thermal-preference votes (TPVs) was evaluated; this was then converted into a numerical clothing value (*clo*), according to the ASHRAE 55 standards (2017) to assess the occupants' thermal comfort in naturally ventilated residential buildings.

Clothing-level adjustment is an important adaptation process that maintains comfort at different temperatures (Verbruggen et al., 2019). The occupants estimated the statistical summaries of their clothing-insulation values from the clothing-insulation list. Due to the chair-insulation effect, the insulation of a chair in the present study was assumed to be 0.35 *clo*, because the participants were all sitting on fabric sofas during the survey (de Dear & Brager, 1998). Figure 6.7(c) shows the clothing-insulation value frequencies; the occupants' mean clothing insulation in the cooling season was 2.66 *clo* ($SD = 2.19$).

Previous scholarly work related to the identification of adaptive thermal comfort determined that there are three types of thermal adaptation: physiological, which is related to the body reaction due to the temperature change; psychological, which is derived from the state of mind of previous experiences; and adaptations related to behaviour (Brager & de Dear, 1998). According to Nicol et al. (2008), comfort can be achieved if there are sufficient opportunities for people to adapt. Comfortable temperatures are changeable, rather than fixed; as such, clothing is a behavioural adjustment that directly affects heat balance, and it is a key thermal-adaptive response (de Dear & Brager, 1998). Figure 6.7(d) illustrates the various garments worn by respondents, taking gender into account.

Figure 6.7(d) demonstrates the summer period classification of clothing types worn by the participants: Of the male respondents, 7% wore a short-sleeve shirt, 12% wore a T-shirt, 6% wore walking shorts, 1% wore jeans and 7% wore trousers; this correlates with the NC cultural domain, where most men prefer to wear long trousers when they have guests in their home out of respect for the cultural and religious norms of the research context. Of the female respondents, 24% wore a short-sleeve shirt, 23% wore a T-shirt, 13% wore walking shorts and 3% wore a knee-length skirt; in the cool season, 4% of the elderly women wore long-sleeve shirts and straight, thin trousers, because of the cultural domain of these female respondents, most of whom were religious.

Notably, it is important to consider the occupants' physiological characteristics to optimise their thermal comfort, which correlated with the occupants' real-life energy-use experiences (Yan et al., 2021). When the BES study was conducted, the households' in vivo experiences related through their TPVs and TSVs were shown to be significant determinant factors (Ozarisoy & Altan, 2018). The base-case representative flats were selected for this reason, and the predicted percentage of dissatisfied (PPD) was retrieved from the simulation results that are presented in Chapter 7.

Equation Formula. To calculate the impact of occupancy patterns on the occupants' thermal comfort, the household metabolic activity and clothing-insulation levels were used to adjust the equation formula for the energy-performance analysis. Table 6.4 demonstrates the summary of household metabolic rates and clothing-insulation levels used in the energy analysis.

A key criterion to validate 'neutral' adaptive thermal-comfort levels is an evaluation of the subject participants' metabolic rates and clothing-insulation levels, in situ measurements of their indoor environmental conditions and *on-site* environmental monitoring (Ahmed et al., 2021; Földváry et al., 2018). When undertaking a DTS analysis, the IES simulation platform allows an automation of the equation formula within a standard spreadsheet in the thermal-comfort plug-in.

According to Fanger (1976), a given environment could be considered comfortable ±1°C corresponding to a PPD of 20%; when it is above ±2°C, however, the

Table 6.4 Evidence-Based Input Parameters Gathered through Questionnaire Survey

Statistical Features		*Participants' Metabolic Rates (met)*	*Participants' Clothing Insulation (clo)*
N (Sampling Size)	Valid	100	100
	Missing	0	0
Mean		3.2200	2.6600
Std. Error of Mean		0.1931	0.21937
Median		3.0333[a]	2.5500[a]
Mode		3.00	5.00
Std. Deviation		1.93103	2.19375
Variance		3.729	4.813
Skewness		0.102	−0.029
Std. Error of Skewness		0.241	0.241
Kurtosis		−1.222	−1.688
Std. Error of Kurtosis		0.478	0.478
Percentiles	25th	1.6061[b]	0.5429[b]
	50th	3.0333	2.5500
	75th	5.0323	4.7857

[a]Median total calculated from grouped data.
[b]Percentiles calculated from grouped data.

environment is considered to be too hot or too cold. To develop a set-up for the identification of adaptive thermal thresholds, Fanger's equation model was utilised to calibrate simulation data collected from the survey findings; PPD is computed with the predicted mean vote (PMV) as follows:

$$\mathrm{PPD} = 100 - 95 \times e - (0.03353\ \mathrm{PMV} + 0.2179)$$

This equation is notable because it has a minimum PPD of 5% for thermally acceptable (i.e., neutral) votes; it provides an evidence-based method to calculate the manner in which the occupants' TPVs and TSVs will be utilised in the BES study. The step-by-step development of an evidence-based analysis demonstrates how thermal comfort can be concurrently improved while the retrofitting design strategies delineated in Chapter 7 are implemented.

Table 6.5 demonstrates the thermal-comfort parameters that were assigned in the IES simulation platform. Notably, the representative room-design settings widened due to the adjustability of comfort parameters in the ApacheSim module. After the DTS analyses were completed according to the defined occupancy patterns, thermal comfort was evaluated in the IES software as a post-simulation process; post-simulation processing occurred within the VistaPro application of the IES software suite. The ASHRAE 55 (2017) adaptive-comfort criteria were chosen to evaluate the occupants' thermal comfort; this ensured constant metabolic activity rates and clothing-insulation levels in the black-box model that was developed for the BES.

Building-Performance Evaluation

To achieve the objective of the present empirical study, a socio-technical-systems (STS) conceptual framework was implemented to assess the influence of retrofitting design interventions that are proposed in Chapter 7.

South-facing RTBs were chosen as the base-case representative buildings in the present study to investigate the building-fabric thermal performance of the representative flats for future energy simulations. The worst-performing representative flats were considered to be free running (i.e., naturally ventilated buildings), and

Table 6.5 Simulation Input Parameters for Thermal-Comfort Assessment

Representative Room-Design Settings	*Comfort Parameters*
Nominal design airspeed	0.15 m/s
Activity level	1.93
Clothing level	2.19
Summer elevated airspeed	0.80 m/s

Category I for existing buildings was selected in line with CIBSE TM59 overheating-risk assessment criteria.

Note: Indicator parameters identified through questionnaire survey.

an emphasis was placed on the peak cooling period in August 2018 for purposes of conducting the BES analysis.

To validate the simulation model that will be applied to the suggested archetype social-housing typology, the present study compared the operative air temperature values and the households' electricity data that were obtained during the experimental study with those that were simulated in the high-density social-housing estate. It should be noted that this was the first exemplar simulation model developed in the existing social-housing stock, which can be applied in similar social-housing typology because building-energy simulations have not yet been built in the Eastern Mediterranean Cypriot climate that specifically targets the post-war social-housing stock.

Overheating Risk-Assessment Criteria

The building-performance evaluation considered in the present study can be calculated in the following manner:

$$T_{max} = 0.33\ T_{rm} + 18.8°\text{C} + \text{SAR}$$

where T_{rm} is the exponentially weighted running mean of the daily mean outdoor air temperature, and the suggested acceptable range (SAR) is 4°C; notably, the maximum benchmark range suggested by the CIBSE as a performance expectation is lower for the context of this study (CIBSE, 2017).

An additional method was suggested in *CIBSE Guide A: BS EN 13779* (CIBSE, 2017), which asserts that building ventilation is an applicable performance requirement for ventilation and A/C systems. The chosen criteria for the thermal-comfort analyses in the present study were as follows:

- Criterion 1: Percentage of hours above 33°C
- Criterion 2: Percentage of hours above 35°C
- Criterion 3: Percentage of hours below 18°C

To properly take the contextual features and simulation benchmarks of the representative RTBs into account, all three criteria use indoor dry-resultant temperatures. Percentages of hours were calculated as the percentage of hours out of the total hours in a year (CIBSE, 2017). It is important to note that these assessment criteria do not only refer to the occupied hours in each building, since exact information related to occupancy patterns was difficult to find (Cuerda et al., 2020; Deb & Schlueter, 2021); this knowledge gap initiated the development of certain building-energy-simulation models within the dominant representative occupancy patterns in the RTBs that were gathered from the findings of the questionnaire survey (Salata et al., 2020; Ahmed & Asif, 2020). This resulted in the inclusion of the most accurate data in the simulation model and minimised discrepancies between predicted household energy use and actual energy consumption (Ding et al., 2021; Zhang et al., 2020).

Notably, baseline experimental data in several pilot studies concurrently validated the simulation model while the black-box model energy assessment was being set up (Ahmed et al., 2021; Miszczuk & Heim, 2020; Wills et al., 2021); as such, the inclusion of human-based data for a thermal-comfort assessment was neglected while the BES study was being undertaken (Carpino et al., 2020; Dong et al., 2020).

Solar-Exposure Analysis

The SunCast software interface tool was implemented in the building-modelling simulation to assess the amount of solar radiation that was absorbed by any given external surface of the prototype RTB, based on the orientation thereof and the effects from adjacent buildings. The SunCast simulation module was used to validate the qualitative and quantitative analyses of the survey findings that were obtained from the thermal-imaging survey. *On-site* observations and in situ physical measurements before the DTS studies were conducted for the purpose of black-box model development.

The solar-exposure analyses were divided into three stages to fully understand the impact of the building envelope on the overall energy performance of the social-housing stock. The first stage was carried out for the entire building simulation between January and December of 2018; the second phase was undertaken between May and September of 2018, which is the cooling period that was recommended by the CIBSE TM59 standards to assess the overheating risks in residential buildings and the final phase focused on the peak cooling month of August 2018 to provide a basis to compare the simulation results with the survey findings. Figure 6.8(a)–(f) show the maximum solar radiation and mean values of the three analyses that were adopted for the worst-case scenario of the south-facing RTB.

The SunCast simulation analysis in Figure 6.8(a), which shows the positions of Bedroom 2 and Bedroom 3 in the southeast-oriented RTBs, revealed that between January and December of 2018, annual maximum-conduction gains due to higher absorptivity were characterised by a high-transmittance roof construction with a *U*-value of 1.20 W/m^{2}K, and the deficient building surfaces absorbed 1,818.09 kWh/m^{2}K. The southeast- and southwest-oriented façades shown in Figure 6.8(b) experienced 3,905.03 h of solar-radiation exposure between January and December of 2018, and the mutual shading factor from the adjacent building significantly affected the southwest-oriented building façade.

According to Figure 6.8(c)—which shows where the living room spaces are positioned in RTBs with a south-oriented front façade, and where the living room, kitchen, Bedroom 1 and Bedroom 2 spaces were positioned in southeast-oriented flats—annual maximum conduction gains due to higher absorptivity were characterised by high-transmittance external wall construction with a *U*-value of 3.47 W/m^{2}K, and the high transmittance *U*-values of the building surfaces absorbed 1,818.09 kWh/m^{2}K between January and December of 2018. The southeast-oriented façades shown in Figure 6.8(d) experienced 3,905.03 h of solar-radiation exposure between January and December of 2018; it is evident from these figures that the upper floor of the southeast-oriented unit absorbed a particularly high level of solar radiation throughout the year.

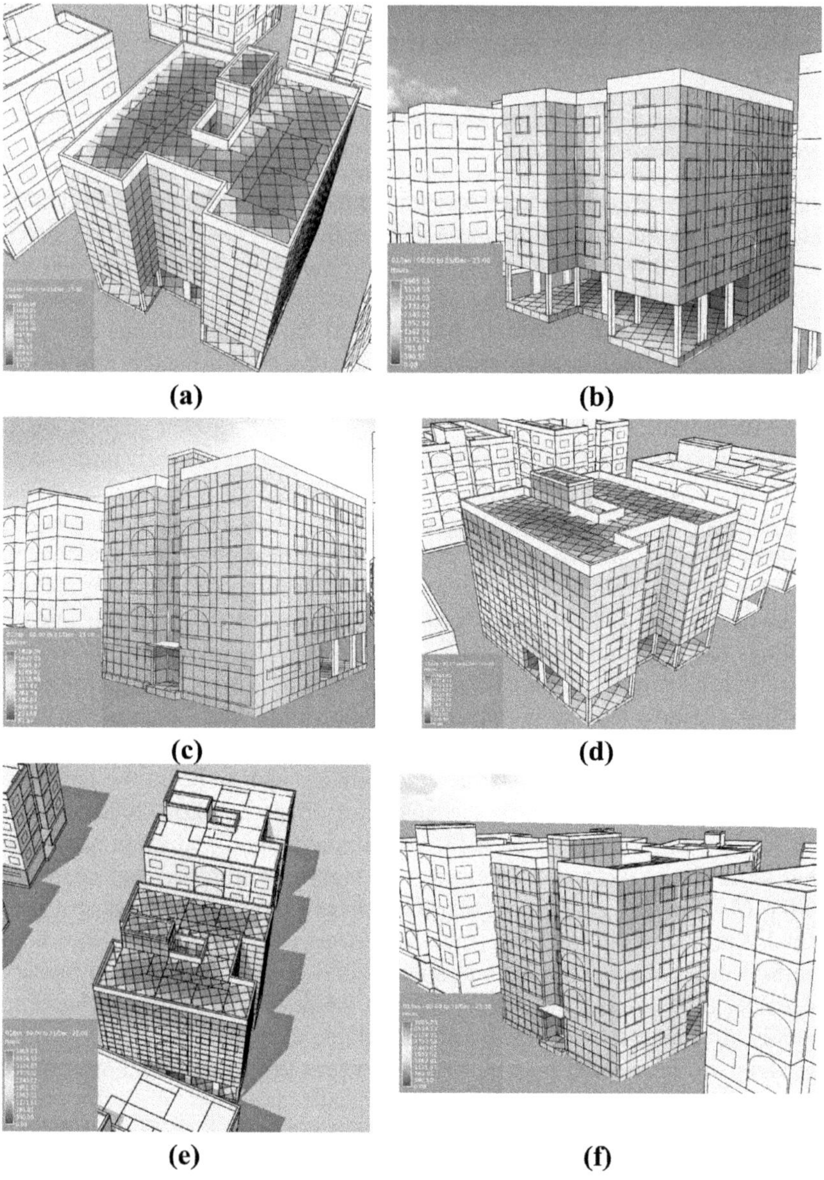

Figure 6.8 Step-by-step solar-exposure analysis of south-facing prototype RTB for worst-case scenario: (a) High solar radiation absorbed on uninsulated roof surface; (b) mutual-shading-impact factor from adjacent RTBs that minimised direct sunlight on building; (c) mutual-shading-impact factor of adjacent RTBs; (d) high absorption of solar radiation, due to RTB orientation and lack of insulation materials and water-proofing system; (e) high solar transmittance of roof surfaces and southeast-facing building envelopes and (f) graphic showing susceptibility of upper-floor flats to high risk of overheating in the summer.

Between January and December of 2018, the south- and southeast-facing exposed surfaces shown in Figure 6.8(e) absorbed high levels of solar radiation due to the high transmittance of the building *U*-values, and occupants in the upper-floor flats of these RTBs experienced thermally uncomfortable indoor environmental conditions; the SunCast simulation for the building analysis validated the results of the thermography walk-through survey in the winter and the in situ measurements that were recorded in the summer to prove overheating risk of RTBs' building envelopes. The southeast-facing façade depicted in Figure 6.8(f) experienced 3,905.02 h of solar-radiation exposure between January and December of 2018; this figure reveals the significant effect of orientation and distance from adjacent buildings on home-energy performance.

Only three external surfaces were exposed in Figure 6.8(a)–(f), and all three exhibited different heat gains throughout the year due to poor insulation in the exposed wall, with noted exacerbations in the summer, which created overheating risks. Upper-floor flats demonstrated the greatest risk of overheating due to the impact of the *U*-values of the building envelopes and the solar panels for the hot water tanks that were placed on top of the original surface; for this reason, all bedroom spaces in the upper- and intermediate-floor flats experienced a greater likelihood to overheat, compared to the CIBSE TM59 overheating criteria (CIBSE, 2017). It was determined that the living rooms of these flats were also susceptible to overheating, but this was because of different factors: the rooms had significant window-opening ratios with no shading, and the spaces all faced either south or south-east and were therefore exposed to high-intensity sunlight throughout most of the day; the external walls, which were constructed from brick and exterior rendering without insulation, were also exposed to high solar-heat gains. A combination of these factors led to overheating issues and significant occupant discomfort, especially in the summer.

The field-survey findings revealed that most of the south-facing RTBs and upper-floor flats experienced high indoor air temperature ranges that were above the 28°C upper threshold comfort limit (CIBSE, 2017); notably, participants were recruited at different times of the day, which directly influenced their TSVs and thermal-preference votes (TPVs). This determinant factor was taken into consideration to identify the most accurate findings for the building-performance evaluation that was conducted in the present study (Weinberger & Mosfegh, 2021). The findings of the building-energy simulations were developed based on this technical detail, which was neglected by previous scholarly work related to thermal comfort (Lei et al., 2021; Pungercar et al., 2021). A statistical analysis was undertaken between the time of day and the *on-site* environmental monitoring conditions to concurrently validate the overheating risk and the occupants' TSVs that were gathered through the questionnaire survey that is described in Chapter 5. The impact of outdoor environmental conditions on the overheating risk of buildings is shown in Figure 6.9(a).

Figure 6.9(a) illustrates the monitoring period for the case-study location, where thermal comfort should be between 23 and 25°C; on the first day that data were recorded, the outdoor heat-stress index reached 30°C, which demonstrates that

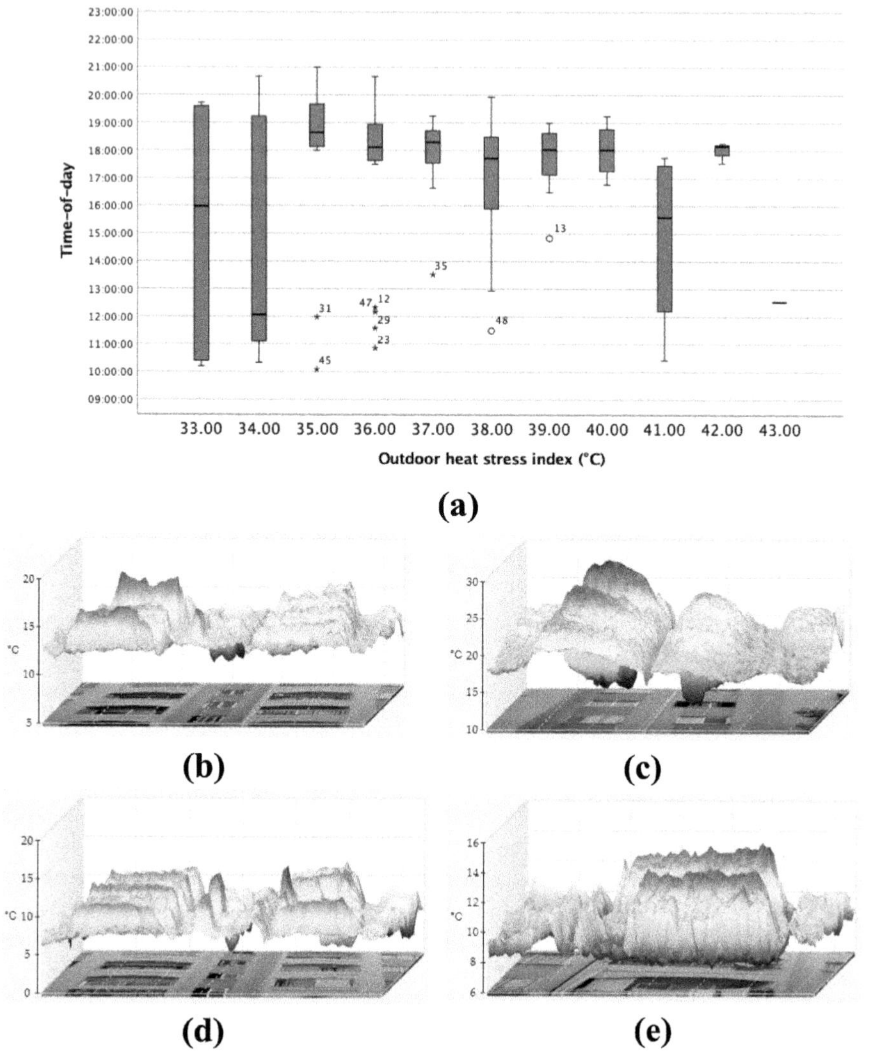

Figure 6.9 (a) Associations between HIS factor and time of day and (b)–(e) sample of winter thermal-imaging analysis.

local climate conditions are determinant factors for the indoor air environment (Maggiotto et al., 2021). This high temperature trend fluctuated with high and low peaks, but it was always above Criterion 1 (i.e., percentage of hours above 33°C) (CIBSE, 2017). This reveals a pattern that is similar to outdoor air temperature fluctuations, even though the outdoor temperatures were much higher; this is due to the long-lasting heatwave period that enveloped the European continent in the summer of 2018 (Khan et al., 2021). The highest thermally uncomfortable heat-stress factor of 39°C was recorded between 16:45 and 18:45, while the highest overall heat-stress index temperature of 42°C was recorded between 17:45 and 18:15. The lowest heat-stress temperature of 33°C, which showed no sign of overheating risk, was recorded between 10:15 and 19:45. Notably, the occupants' TSVs indicated that the 'neutral' temperature was 28.5°C, and the upper limit of the comfort range for warm indoor air temperature conditions was 31.5°C. These results suggest that the subject participants were able to tolerate high-temperature environmental conditions (Abokersh et al., 2021).

Discussions

This section provides a discussion of the findings of the present study to identify the knowledge gap related to the implementation of EPBD directives; to address climate change and the detrimental impact thereof on the overheating risk of buildings, the occupants' thermal comfort and the energy use of households; and to explore the novelty of a BES study that is integrated with an energy audit and thermal imaging, which is an area in which little research has been undertaken. The following discussion is structured according to the research question that guided the findings obtained through the field survey—specifically, (RQ–4) 'How this empirical study will contribute to and inform the design of net-zero buildings in the EU countries?'—to develop a universally acceptable energy-policy framework for the Eastern Mediterranean Cypriot climate.

The overheating risk within the living room spaces was evaluated using the static CIBSE TM59 overheating risk criterion and Fanger's dynamic adaptive thermal-comfort equation. Alterations were made to the base models to simulate the current building-fabric thermal performance and overheating that was experienced, and the corresponding changes that can be utilised to develop accurate black-box energy model set-up are discussed.

Impact of Building-Fabric Thermal Properties on Overheating Risk

This section presents the in situ measurements of the building-fabric elements to validate the overheating risk of buildings and the degree of the occupants' thermal discomfort. To demonstrate the thermal performance of the RTBs, Figure 6.9(b)–(e) illustrates the heat loss of the different building envelopes.

Figure 6.9(b) reveals that the living room balcony spaces of the southwest-facing RTBs accumulated heat with a maximum recorded temperature of 18°C at 06:45 on 29 December 2017; a maximum temperature of 32°C was recorded on the upper-level flat at 16:45 on the same day, as presented in Figure 6.9(c). Notably, warm winter weather conditions were observed at the time the thermal-imaging survey was conducted, which is why relatively high temperature readings were recorded, compared to typical Cypriot winter conditions.

According to Figure 6.9(d), heat accumulation in the living room balcony areas resulted in a maximum recorded temperature of 16°C at 06:55 on 6 January 2018. Figure 6.9(e) illustrates the side view of the southwest-facing RTB; the enclosed balcony spaces caused accumulated heat throughout the structure, which is why the enclosed balcony areas were susceptible to overheating in the summer. Furthermore, significant heat loss was observed through the external walls, which lacked any type of insulation material.

Results from the thermal-imaging analysis indicated three types of anomalies in the RTBs that were examined: thermal bridges, degradation of the building-envelope material and structural failure of the concrete-and-steel skeleton system. In the present study, the areas with the greatest heat loss were located at the connections between the junction details, especially the penetrations that were formed when doors and windows interrupted the façade. Damaged structural connections were observed at the corners of the RTBs where the walls met the floor, especially on the ground-floor flats and on the roof surfaces of the upper-floor flats.

Notably, significant heat loss was detected where the front façades (i.e., the living room spaces) of the south-, southeast- and southwest-facing RTBs met the corner of the construction junction. Most of the south-oriented flats showed signs of significant thermal loss in the winter, and it appeared as if these RTBs also demonstrated a greater risk of overheating in the summer. The *on-site* measurement method allowed the worst-performing RTB to be identified so further energy-performance studies could be conducted in the building-modelling phase of the present study, which is described and discussed in Chapter 7.

The thermal transmittance of building-fabric elements, such as external walls, doors and windows and roofs, was considered in the present study to confirm that the local climate characteristics and the types of construction materials of buildings are vital components of energy consumption. These findings are supported by information related to the occupants' energy-use variations, which provided useful insights that will aid in the development of evidence-based retrofitting design interventions and increase the life-cycle span of buildings.

Impact of Local Climate Conditions on Overheating Risk

This section presents the OTs of the living room spaces in the measured flats, which highlighted the significance of the different RTB orientations and floor levels on the occupants' TPVs and TSVs. Figure 6.10(a) and (b) illustrate the in situ measurements of the surveyed flats, taking these factors into consideration.

According to Figure 6.10(a), indoor air temperatures during the summertime survey in the northeast-facing RTBs ranged between 26 and 33°C, temperatures in the south-facing RTBs ranged from 28 to 34°C, temperatures in the northwest-facing RTBs ranged between 31 and 32.5°C, temperatures in the southwest-facing RTBs ranged from 25 to 33°C and temperatures in the southeast-facing RTBs ranged between 28 and 34°C.

The static method criteria outlined in *CIBSE Guide A* (2006) state that overheating is likely when the temperature in a room exceeds a threshold temperature for more than 1% of the occupied hours (i.e., bedroom threshold temperature is 26°C and living room threshold temperature is 28°C). The occupied hours of the inspected living room spaces were based on the questionnaire-survey findings to ensure that the accuracy of overheating risk measures was in line with the *on-site* monitoring

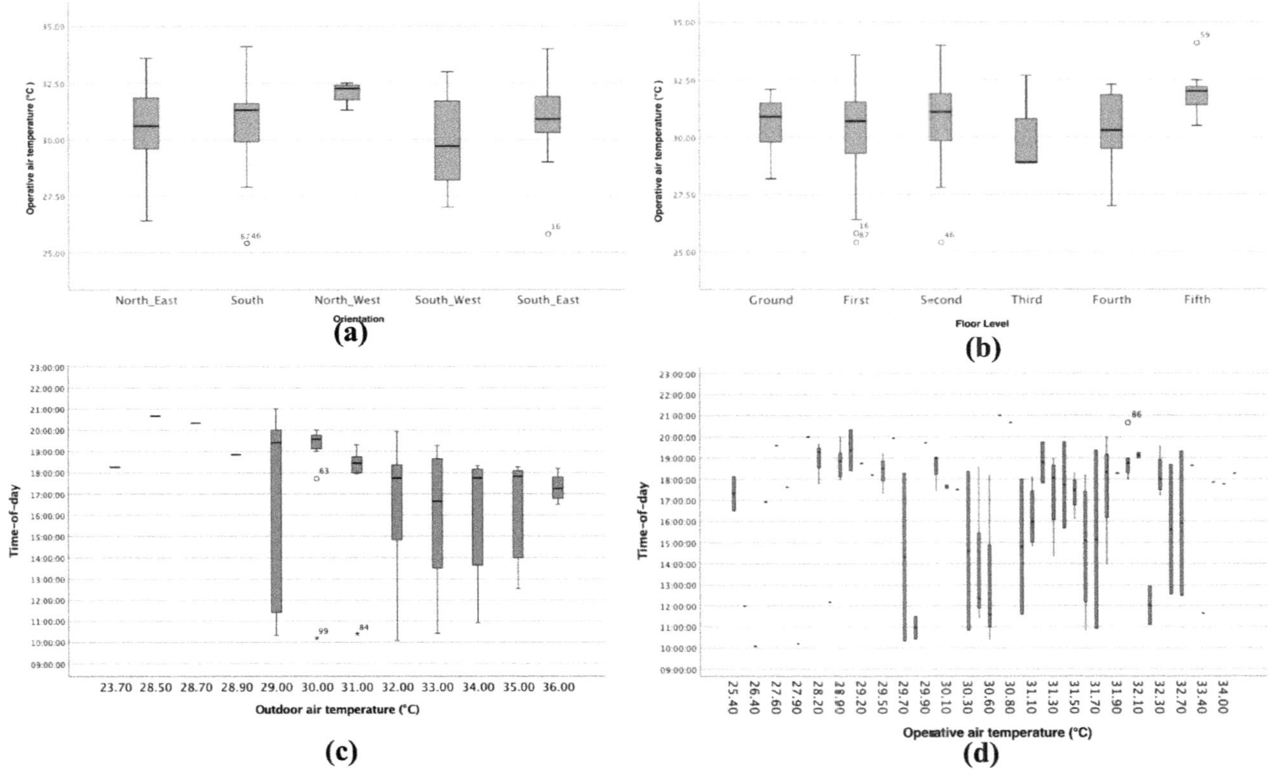

Figure 6.10 (a) Distributions of measured OTs, taking different RTB orientations into account; (b) distributions of measured indoor air temperatures, taking different floor levels into account; (c) associations between outdoor air temperature and time of day and (d) associations between OT and time of day.

Table 6.6 In Situ Recordings of Indoor Environmental Conditions of Representative RTBs

	Orientation	*Percentiles*		
		25th	*50th*	*75th*
Weighted Average Operative Air Temperature (°C)	North-east	29.50	30.60	31.90
	South	29.85	31.30	31.60
	North-west	31.52	32.25	32.45
	South-west	28.20	29.70	31.72
	South-east	30.10	30.90	32.30

of actual weather conditions (Mukhopadhyay et al., 2021). Table 6.6 delineates the recorded operative air temperature according to the different RTB orientations.

According to Table 6.6, the northwest- and northeast-facing RTBs experienced the highest levels of overheating within the 75th percentile cluster group; this is likely due to the position of the RTBs and the properties of the buildings during the summer months. These findings were not limited to the local climate conditions; the occupants' habitual adaptive behaviour related to window opening and their occupancy patterns were also considered (Beckmann et al., 2021; Etxebarria-Mallea et al., 2021).

In the present study, 26% of the respondents used wall-mounted A/C systems, 28% used portable fans and 39% used a combination of the above cooling systems. Furthermore, 78% of the respondents closed their internal doors and windows when their wall-mounted A/C system was in use, and 20% kept their internal doors open and their windows closed when their A/C systems were in use. These variations provided a wide range of acceptable thermal sensations that influence an assessment of the impact of building-fabric thermal performance on overheating risk (Verbruggen et al., 2019). Notably, occupants in the south-facing RTBs comprised the highest percentage (36%) of the total sample size; these prototype buildings were chosen to represent the overall thermal performance of the prototype RTBs and provide accurate information while assessing the overheating risk against the industry CIBSE TM59 industry benchmarks.

An adaptive approach is currently implemented in the EN 15251 international standard concerning thermal comfort, but it is usually considered to be an assessment method for the summer performances of naturally ventilated multi-family residential buildings (Dracou et al., 2017; Piselli et al., 2020). As such, inclusion of human-based approach has been neglected by previous thermal-comfort studies (Castaño-Rosa et al., 2021). The findings of the present study will contribute to the development of adaptive thermal-comfort models on hot summer days in the Mediterranean region. To provide subsequent background information for the BES studies, the associations between operative air temperatures and the different floor levels were also explored and are shown in Figure 6.10(b).

According to Figure 6.10(b), indoor air temperatures in the ground-floor flats ranged from 28 to 32°C, temperatures in the first-floor flats ranged between 26 and 33°C, temperatures in the second-floor flats ranged from 28 to 34°C, temperatures in the third-floor flats ranged between 28 and 33°C, temperatures in the fourth-floor flats ranged from 26 to 32°C and temperatures in the fifth-floor flats ranged between 31 and 32.5°C. Indoor air temperatures recorded in the living room spaces of these units during the *on-site* environmental monitoring period exceeded the 28°C overheating threshold; and according to the in situ physical measurements, the 25°C upper thermal-comfort threshold was regularly exceeded. It should be noted that similar indoor environmental conditions were also observed at a later time, when cooling systems were likely to have been switched on.

According to the questionnaire survey, 21% of the respondents turned on their cooling systems for 0–4 h, 38% for 5–9 h, 34% for 10–12 h and 7% for more than 12 h on weekdays. On the weekends, 20% of the respondents used their cooling systems for 0–4 h, 24% for 5–9 h, 34% for 10–12 h and 22% for more than 12 h. Table 6.7 presents the OTs that were recorded for each floor level.

According to Table 6.7 the indoor air temperature of 75th percentile cluster group was well above the CIBSE TM59 Criterion I overheating threshold for the entire field-survey period. The results presented above indicate that the interviewed flats are prone to overheating during a period of hot weather under the current climate if the static threshold approach is adopted, which does not factor in heat acclimatisation and other adaptation actions the residents may take (de la Flor et al., 2021; Gupta & Gregg, 2018).

Considering that the adaptive capacity of most vulnerable individuals residing in social-housing units is likely to be fairly limited, this finding indicates that attention should be paid to the thermal properties of the buildings and occupancy patterns to thoroughly assess the overheating risk of archetype RTBs that were selected (Abbas et al., 2021; Ahmed & Asif, 2021). However, when the EN 15251 adaptive approach was used, the risk of overheating appears significantly lower than under the environmental conditions measured at the time of survey. This could relate to a wide range of acceptable thermal-adaptive thresholds limits that were found to influence the occupants' TPVs and TSVs, taking the physiological thermal-comfort approach into account (Liao & Laverge, 2019; Shin et al., 2021).

Table 6.7 In Situ Recordings of Indoor Environmental Conditions of Representative RTBs

	Floor Level	*Percentiles*		
		25th	*50th*	*75th*
Weighted Average Operative Air Temperature (°C)	Ground	30.00	32.00	33.00
	First	30.25	32.00	33.00
	Second	30.00	33.00	34.00
	Third	28.90	32.00	—
	Fourth	30.00	32.00	34.00
	Fifth	31.00	33.00	34.00

During the data processing, it was observed that the PPD in all of the flats was observed to be above the maximum limit of 15% set by ISO 7730 for a Category C thermal environment, which is the least-strict category indicated for naturally ventilated residential buildings (Ozarisoy & Altan, 2018). It is worth mentioning that the manner in which the PPD assessment criterion defines adaptive comfort according to votes outside of the indicated benchmark categories is questionable; earlier research determined that some participants may find the thermal environment acceptable, even if the occupants voted outside of these categories (Laverge et al., 2013; Tsang et al., 2021). To capture a wider variety of occupants and not create a direct generalisation, the time-of-day factor was also considered; this is shown in Figure 6.10(c) and (d).

Outdoor air temperatures were recorded between 10:05 and 17:35 on 28 July 2018 and at the end of September of the same year and are shown in Figure 6.10(c); acceptable temperature-fluctuation levels ranged between 30 and 31°C. Most of the flats were recruited between 10:05 and 20:00, when the recorded temperature was 29°C; this is why a wide range of acceptable thermal sensations were observed. The *on-site* monitoring results indicated that the highest peak outdoor air temperature of 36°C was recorded on 16 August 2018; this was +5°C higher than the 28°C upper thermal-comfort limit recommended by the CIBSE TM59 overheating risk-assessment guidelines. These findings confirm that in addition to the *U*-values of the RTB thermal properties, the time-of-day factor had a direct impact on the participants' TSVs.

Only the outdoor air movement was recorded in the present study, because indoor air movement has been shown to affect the likelihood of achieving neutral thermal sensations by causing occupants to feel comfortable in relatively high indoor air temperatures (Lu & Warsinger, 2020). To properly consider behaviour-related adaption that was developed in 1998 by Brager and de Dear, tests of associations between the time of day and OTs were conducted; the results are presented in Figure 6.10(d).

According to Figure 6.10(d), the indoor air temperature of the occupied spaces between 16:30 and 18:00 was 25.4°C. Relatively high indoor air temperatures were observed late in the morning: the recorded temperature at 10:05 was 29.7°C. The subject participants were interviewed between 17:45 and 20:45, and scattered patterns were detected in the range of 28.2–34.0°C. In situ measurements that were collected during the field survey showed that the indoor air temperature in all the flats was above 25°C, which confirms the risk of overheating during the summer. Notably, the maximum outdoor air temperature recorded during this period was 36°C, and the highest and lowest temperatures in the living room spaces were 34.10 and 25.40°C, respectively; these variations require further investigation to better understand adaptive household behaviours and attitudes that could improve the existing energy performance of the worst-performing base-case prototype RTB, which is described and discussed in Chapter 7.

Conclusion

A quantitative research methodology based on in situ measurements was employed. These measurements included recorded household indoor air temperatures that were integrated with thermal-imaging surveys and *on-site* heat-flux measurements of the building-fabric elements, in addition to concurrently monitored environmental conditions and a review of household energy bills to accurately determine actual energy use.

The thermal-imaging readings demonstrated that the primary reasons for thermal anomalies were air infiltration through the building fabric, a lack of NV through living spaces and excessive heat gains through sizable glazed windows. The findings suggest that the percentage of hours that fell into Category 1 of the CIBSE TM59 overheating criterion directly influenced the solar irradiance factor and the thermal absorptivity levels of the building envelopes. During the field-survey period, outdoor air temperatures ranged from 25.3 to 38.7°C with a mean temperature of 28.7°C, which indicates hot-and-dry weather conditions at the time. Moreover, the recorded indoor air temperatures ranged between 25.0 and 35.0°C with an average temperature of 27.8°C and an *SD* of 1.8°C; global temperatures at this same time ranged between 24.5 and 37.0°C with an average temperature of 28°C and an *SD* of 1.9°C. It was determined that occupants felt thermally comfortable indoors when the mean temperature was 29°C with an *SD* of 1.1 and maximum and minimum mean temperatures of 31.5 and 28.5°C, respectively; the recruited sample size was thermally comfortable at higher indoor air temperatures than those recommended by such international standards as ISO EN 7730:2005.

The IRT survey, which integrated the in situ measurements, led to a better understanding of the thermal behaviour of building *U*-values and facilitated the development of an assessment methodology for the implementation of the energy-performance certificates. The findings suggest that the building's thermal characteristics included in the overheating-risk assessment for the base-case representative RTBs clarified the difference between the expected and actual energy-consumption rates, and the longitudinal survey for the present study revealed a strong correlation between building fabric and local climate conditions in the summer and winter. This conclusion highlights the need for future energy-performance development studies to conduct BES analyses; the thermal lag of the building envelopes, which had a significant impact on energy consumption, should also be further studied.

Notes

1 Sampling size consisted of recruited households' energy bills; consent was given when questionnaire survey was distributed. Household energy-bill data was collected in 2018 from the Electricity Authority of Northern Cyprus.

2 Sampling size consisted of recruited households' energy bills data between December 2014 and December 2016; field survey was conducted in August 2018. Due to the security concerns, the Electricity Authority of Northern Cyprus does not share the most-up-to-date annual energy-consumption data with researchers, so permission was obtained for the sampling size between 2015 and 2016.

3 Weather data obtained from Larnaca Airport, which is approximately 60 km away from case-study location.

4 Paralimni is located on the Famagusta Bay shoreline, which is approximately 20 km away from case-study location; this area has typical Eastern Mediterranean coastal climate characteristics.

5 Due to the geopolitical situation of Cyprus, the Famagusta district is divided into two entities, the RoC and NC; data was collected from Larnaca Airport, which is located in the RoC, and Ercan Airport, which is located in the NC. A mobile weather station was installed at the case-study location at the time of the survey to monitor the *on-site* environmental conditions. The weather datasets were extrapolated together to avoid discrepancies in weather files assigned to the building-energy-simulation model. Open-source *.epw* files were generated from the EnergyPlus databases to identify accurate information for DTS analysis.

6 The ASHRAE 55 standards (2017) recommend the following thermal-comfort assessment criterion for subject participants: 1 *met* = 58.2 W/m^2.

References

Abbas, K., Xu, D., Li, S., & Baz, K. (2021). Health implications of household multidimensional energy poverty for women: A structural equation modeling technique. *Energy and Buildings*, *234*, 110661. https://doi.org/10.1016/j.enbuild.2020.110661

Abokersh, M. H., Spiekman, M., Vijlbrief, O., Goch, T. A. J., Vallès, M., & Boer, D. (2021). A real-time diagnostic tool for evaluating the thermal performance of nearly zero energy buildings. *Applied Energy*, *281*, 116091. https://doi.org/10.1016/j.apenergy.2020.116091

Ahmed, A. I., McLeod, R. S., & Gustin, M. (2021). Forecasting underheating in dwellings to detect excess winter mortality risks using time series models. *Applied Energy*, *286*, 116517. https://doi.org/10.1016/j.apenergy.2021.116517

Ahmed, W., & Asif, M. (2020). BIM-based techno-economic assessment of energy retrofitting residential buildings in hot humid climate. *Energy and Buildings*, *227*. https://doi.org/10.1016/j.enbuild.2020.110406

ASHRAE. (2017). *ASHRAE Standard 55-2017. Thermal environmental conditions for human occupancy*. Atlanta: American Society of Heating, Refrigerating and Air-Conditioning Engineers.

Bayomi, N., Nagpal, S., Rakha, T., & Fernandez, J. E. (2021). Building envelope modeling calibration using aerial thermography. *Energy and Buildings*, 110648. https://doi.org/10.1016/j.enbuild.2020.110648

Beckmann, S. K., Hiete, M., & Beck, C. (2021). Threshold temperatures for subjective heat stress in urban apartments—Analysing nocturnal bedroom temperatures during a heat wave in Germany. *Climate Risk Management*, *32*. https://doi.org/10.1016/j.crm.2021.100286

Carnieletto, L., Ferrando, M., Teso, L., Sun, K., Zhang, W., Causone, F., … Hong, T. (2021). Italian prototype building models for urban scale building performance simulation. *Building and Environment*, *192*. https://doi.org/10.1016/j.buildenv.2021.107590

Carpino, C., Loukou, E., Heiselberg, P., & Arcuri, N. (2020). Energy performance gap of a nearly zero energy building (nZEB) in Denmark: The influence of occupancy modelling. *Building Research and Information*, *48*(8), 899–921. https://doi.org/10.1080/09613218.2019.1707639

Castaño-Rosa, R., Barrella, R., Sánchez-Guevara, C., Barbosa, R., Kyprianou, I., Paschalidou, E., … Palma, P. (2021). Cooling degree models and future energy demand in the residential sector. A seven-country case study. *Sustainability (Switzerland)*, *13*(5). https://doi.org/10.3390/su13052987

CIBSE. (2006). *CIBSE guide A – Environmental design 2006*. CIBSE.

CIBSE. (2017). *CIBSE TM59 – Design methodology for the assessment of overheating risk in homes*. London: The Chartered Institution of Building Services Engineers.

Cuerda, E., Guerra-Santin, O., Sendra, J. J., & Neila, F. J. (2020). Understanding the performance gap in energy retrofitting: Measured input data for adjusting building simulation models. *Energy and Buildings*, *209*. https://doi.org/10.1016/j.enbuild.2019.109688

Dartevelle, O., van Moeseke, G., Mlecnik, E., & Altomonte, S. (2021). Long-term evaluation of residential summer thermal comfort: Measured vs. perceived thermal conditions in nZEB houses in Wallonia. *Building and Environment*, *190*. https://doi.org/10.1016/j.buildenv.2020.107531

De Dear, R. J., & Brager, G. S. (1998). Developing an adaptive model of thermal comfort and preference. In *ASHRAE transactions* (Vol. 104, pp. 145–167). ASHRAE.

De la Flor, F. J. S., Jara, E. Á. R., Pardo, Á. R., Lissén, J. M. S., & Kolokotroni, M. (2021). Energy-efficient envelope design for apartment blocks: Case study of a residential building in Spain. *Applied Sciences (Switzerland)*, *11*(1), 1–16. https://doi.org/10.3390/app11010433

Deb, C., & Schlueter, A. (2021). Review of data-driven energy modelling techniques for building retrofit. *Renewable and Sustainable Energy Reviews*. https://doi.org/10.1016/j.rser.2021.110990

Defruyt, T., Delghust, M., Laverge, J., Janssens, A., & Roelens, W. (2013). Evolution of energy performance of houses and the interaction with energy performance regulation: An analysis of the Flemish EPBD-database. In *11th REHVA World Congress & 8th international conference on IAQVEC*. https://biblio.ugent.be/publication/3823882/file/6797855

Ding, Z., Chen, W., Hu, T., & Xu, X. (2021). Evolutionary double attention-based long short-term memory model for building energy prediction: Case study of a green building. *Applied Energy*, *288*. https://doi.org/10.1016/j.apenergy.2021.116660

Dong, J., Lan, H., Liu, Y., Wang, X., & Yu, C. (2020). Indoor environment of nearly zero energy residential buildings with conventional air conditioning in hot-summer and cold-winter zone. *Energy and Built Environment*. Advance online publication. https://doi.org/10.1016/j.enbenv.2020.12.001

Dracou, M. K., Santamouris, M., & Papanicolas, C. N. (2017). Achieving nearly zero energy buildings in Cyprus, through building performance simulations, based on the use of innovative energy technologies. *Energy Procedia*, *134*, 636–644. https://doi.org/10.1016/j.egypro.2017.09.578

Etxebarria-Mallea, M., Oregi, X., Grijalba, O., & Hernández-Minguillón, R. (2021). The impact of energy refurbishment interventions on annual energy demand, indoor thermal behaviour and temperature-related health risk. *Energy Policy*, *153*. https://doi.org/10.1016/j.enpol.2021.112276

Fanger, P. O. (1976). Assessment of man's thermal comfort in practice. https://doi.org/10.1016/0003-6870(74)90044-1

Földváry Ličina, V., Cheung, T., Zhang, H., de Dear, R., Parkinson, T., Arens, E., … Zhou, X. (2018). Development of the ASHRAE global thermal comfort database II. *Building and Environment*, *142*, 502–512. https://doi.org/10.1016/j.buildenv.2018.06.022

Gao, N., Shao, W., Rahaman, M. S., Zhai, J., David, K., & Salim, F. D. (2021). Transfer learning for thermal comfort prediction in multiple cities. *Building and Environment*, *195*. https://doi.org/10.1016/j.buildenv.2021.107725

Gupta, R., & Gregg, M. (2018). Assessing energy use and overheating risk in net zero energy dwellings in UK. *Energy and Buildings*, *158*, 897–905. https://doi.org/10.1016/j.enbuild.2017.10.061

Hosseini, M., Bigtashi, A., & Lee, B. (2021). Generating future weather files under climate change scenarios to support building energy simulation – A machine learning approach. *Energy and Buildings, 230*. https://doi.org/10.1016/j.enbuild.2020.110543

Integrated Environmental Solutions (IES). (2020). *IES software validation*. Retrieved September 14, 2020, from http://www.iesve.com/software/software-validation

Khan, H. S., Santamouris, M., Paolini, R., Caccetta, P., & Kassomenos, P. (2021). Analyzing the local and climatic conditions affecting the urban overheating magnitude during the Heatwaves (HWs) in a coastal city: A case study of the greater Sydney region. *Science of the Total Environment, 755*. https://doi.org/10.1016/j.scitotenv.2020.142515

Lassen, N., Josefsen, T., & Goia, F. (2021). Design and in-field testing of a multi-level system for continuous subjective occupant feedback on indoor climate. *Building and Environment, 189*. https://doi.org/10.1016/j.buildenv.2020.107535

Laverge, J., & Janssens, A. (2013). Optimization of design flow rates and component sizing for residential ventilation. *Building and Environment, 65*, 81–89. https://doi.org/10.1016/j.buildenv.2013.03.019

Lei, L., Chen, W., Wu, B., Chen, C., & Liu, W. (2021). A building energy consumption prediction model based on rough set theory and deep learning algorithms. *Energy and Buildings, 240*. https://doi.org/10.1016/j.enbuild.2021.110886

Liao, C., & Laverge, J. (2019). Association between indoor air quality and sleep quality. *Sleep, 42*(Suppl 1), A74–A74. https://doi.org/10.1093/sleep/zsz067.180

Liu, S., Kwok, Y. T., Lau, K., & Ng, E. (2021). Applicability of different extreme weather datasets for assessing indoor overheating risks of residential buildings in a subtropical high-density city. *Building and Environment, 194*. https://doi.org/10.1016/j.buildenv.2021.107711

Lu, D. B., & Warsinger, D. M. (2020). Energy savings of retrofitting residential buildings with variable air volume systems across different climates. *Journal of Building Engineering, 30*. https://doi.org/10.1016/j.jobe.2020.101223

Maggiotto, G., Miani, A., Rizzo, E., Castellone, M. D., & Piscitelli, P. (2021). Heat waves and adaptation strategies in a mediterranean urban context. *Environmental Research, 197*. https://doi.org/10.1016/j.envres.2021.111066

Mahmoud, R. M., Sharifi, M., Himpe, E., Delghust, M., & Laverge, J. (2019). Estimation of load duration curves from general building data in the building stock using dynamic BES-models. In *E3S web of conferences* (Vol. *111*). EDP Sciences. https://doi.org/10.1051/e3sconf/201911101078

Miszczuk, A., & Heim, D. (2020). Parametric study of air infiltration in residential buildings—The effect of local conditions on energy demand. *Energies, 14*(1), 127. https://doi.org/10.3390/en14010127

Mukhopadhyay, B., Weitz, C. A., & Das, K. (2021). Indoor heat conditions measured in urban slum and rural village housing in West Bengal, India. *Building and Environment, 191*. https://doi.org/10.1016/j.buildenv.2020.107567

Nicol, J. F. (2008). *A handbook of adaptive thermal comfort: Towards a dynamic model. Teaching source*, University of Bath.

Ozarisoy, B. (2022). Energy effectiveness of passive cooling design strategies to reduce the impact of long-term heatwaves on occupants' thermal comfort in Europe: Climate change and mitigation. *Journal of Cleaner Production*. Advance online publication. https://doi.org/10.1016/j.jclepro.2021.129675

Ozarisoy, B., & Altan, H. (2017a). Energy performance development of non-regulated retrofit mass housing estates in Northern Cyprus. *Design Journal, 20*(Suppl 1), S1765–S1781. https://doi.org/10.1080/14606925.2017.1352697

Ozarisoy, B., & Altan, H. (2017b). Adoption of energy design strategies for retrofitting mass housing estates in Northern Cyprus. *Sustainability (Switzerland)*, *9*(8), 1477. https://doi.org/10.3390/su9081477

Ozarisoy, B., & Altan, H. (2018). Low-energy design strategies for retrofitting existing residential buildings in Cyprus. *Proceedings of the Institution of Civil Engineers: Engineering Sustainability*, *172*(5), 241–255. https://doi.org/10.1680/jensu.17.00061

Ozarisoy, B., & Elsharkawy, H. (2019). Assessing overheating risk and thermal comfort in state-of-the-art prototype houses that combat exacerbated climate change in UK. *Energy and Buildings*, *187*, 201–217. https://doi.org/10.1016/j.enbuild.2019.01.030

Piselli, C., Di Grazia, M., & Pisello, A. L. (2020). Combined effect of outdoor microclimate boundary conditions on air conditioning system's efficiency and building energy demand in net zero energy settlements. *Sustainability (Switzerland)*, *12*(15). https://doi.org/10.3390/su12156056

Prataviera, E., Romano, P., Carnieletto, L., Pirotti, F., Vivian, J., & Zarrella, A. (2021). EUReCA: An open-source urban building energy modelling tool for the efficient evaluation of cities energy demand. *Renewable Energy*, *173*, 544–560. https://doi.org/10.1016/j.renene.2021.03.144

Pungercar, V., Zhan, Q., Xiao, Y., Musso, F., Dinkel, A., & Pflug, T. (2021). A new retrofitting strategy for the improvement of indoor environment quality and energy efficiency in residential buildings in temperate climate using prefabricated elements. *Energy and Buildings*, *241*. https://doi.org/10.1016/j.enbuild.2021.110951

Sakiyama, N. R. M., Mazzaferro, L., Carlo, J. C., Bejat, T., & Garrecht, H. (2021). Natural ventilation potential from weather analyses and building simulation. *Energy and Buildings*, *231*. https://doi.org/10.1016/j.enbuild.2020.110596

Salata, F., Ciancio, V., Dell'Olmo, J., Golasi, I., Palusci, O., & Coppi, M. (2020). Effects of local conditions on the multi-variable and multi-objective energy optimization of residential buildings using genetic algorithms. *Applied Energy*, *260*. https://doi.org/10.1016/j.apenergy.2019.114289

Shin, H., Kang, M., Mun, S. H., Kwak, Y., & Huh, J. H. (2021). A study on changes in occupants' thermal sensation owing to CO_2 concentration using PMV and TSV. *Building and Environment*, *187*. https://doi.org/10.1016/j.buildenv.2020.107413

Sun, Y., Hao, W., Chen, Y., & Liu, B. (2020). Data-driven occupant-behavior analytics for residential buildings. *Energy*, *206*. https://doi.org/10.1016/j.energy.2020.118100

Tsang, T. W., Mui, K. W., & Wong, L. T. (2021). Investigation of thermal comfort in sleeping environment and its association with sleep quality. *Building and Environment*, *187*. https://doi.org/10.1016/j.buildenv.2020.107406

Uddin, M. N., Wei, H. H., Chi, H. L., & Ni, M. (2021). Influence of occupant behavior for building energy conservation: A systematic review study of diverse modeling and simulation approach. *Buildings*. MDPI AG. https://doi.org/10.3390/buildings11020041

Verbruggen, S., Delghust, M., Laverge, J., & Janssens, A. (2019). Inclusion of window opening habits in a window model based on activity and occupancy patterns. In *E3S web of conferences* (Vol. *111*). EDP Sciences. https://doi.org/10.1051/e3sconf/201911104058

Weinberger, G., & Moshfegh, B. (2021). Techno-economic investigation of the potential for energy efficiency measures of multi-story apartment buildings at cluster level using different district heating tariffs. *Energy and Buildings*, *236*. https://doi.org/10.1016/j.enbuild.2021.110758

Wills, A. D., Beausoleil-Morrison, I., & Ugursal, V. I. (2021). A modelling approach and a case study to answer the question: What does it take to retrofit a community to net-zero energy? *Journal of Building Engineering, 40*. https://doi.org/10.1016/j.jobe.2021.102296

Yan, S., Liu, N., Wang, W., Han, S., & Zhang, J. (2021). An adaptive predicted percentage dissatisfied model based on the air-conditioner turning-on behaviors in the residential buildings of China. *Building and Environment, 191*. https://doi.org/10.1016/j.buildenv.2020.107571

Yang, J., Wang, L., Yin, H., & Wang, P. (2021). Thermal responses of young males of three thermal preference groups in summer indoor environments. *Building and Environment, 194*. https://doi.org/10.1016/j.buildenv.2021.107705

Zhang, Y., Bai, X., & Mills, F. P. (2020). Characterizing energy-related occupant behavior in residential buildings: Evidence from a survey in Beijing, China. *Energy and Buildings, 214*. https://doi.org/10.1016/j.enbuild.2020.109823

7 Forecasting of Domestic Energy Use

Introduction

The present study elucidated the potential applicability of passive-cooling design strategies (PCDS) in various retrofitting interventions to improve the energy efficiency of existing residential buildings. Based on this study, passive-cooling design principles resulted in significant reductions in energy consumption and optimised thermally comfortable indoor air for occupants. This important finding needs to be further explored by robust energy performance certification schemes, which will provide a wider domain to assess and optimise the risk of overheating and better understand occupants' thermal comfort when seeking to enhance 'night cooling' effects in RTBs in the Eastern Mediterranean climate.

Implementation of the EPCs at the household level and building level is seen by stakeholders and government initiatives as a decisive factor for the successful transition of the EPBD objectives, yet one that has thus far not been fully realised (Dell'Anna, 2020). Uptake by an evidence-based STS approach will be key for the adoption of energy-conscious retrofitting technologies that will grow from this void (Bolwig et al., 2020). The following discussion is structured according to the main research question that guided this study: What is the most effective and universally applicable energy-policy framework to implement the EPBD mandates recommended by the EU and improve the energy efficiency of housing stock in NC?

In the dynamic thermal simulation (DTS) analysis, the energy consumption of the base-case representative flats was assessed by conducting a full one-year simulation between January and December 2018 (Ozarisoy & Elsharkawy, 2019). The aim of this research strategy was to predict the energy consumption of these flats, and the conclusions are presented.

Overall Electricity-Consumption Assessment

This section examines the overall electricity consumption for the base-case representative flats for the purpose of a building-performance evaluation that will take the different floor levels of the flats into consideration. Three occupancy patterns were identified from the field-survey findings to represent the interviewed sample: low (i.e., OP1), moderate (i.e., OP2) and high (i.e., OP3) occupancy. Once these

DOI: 10.4324/9781003393092-8

were established, they were compared to the occupants' actual energy bills to validate the data. Figure 7.1(a)–(c) delineates the overall energy consumption of the first-, intermediate- and upper-level base-case representative flats.

The results of the energy-consumption simulation for the south- and southwest-facing first-floor flats are shown in Figure 7.1(a). The dashed line at 780 kWh indicates the recommended upper limit for average energy consumption, and the margin line at 310 kWh delineates the lower limit of acceptable energy consumption range; energy-consumption fluctuations throughout the year fell between these two levels, and excessive energy demand was generally greater than 780 kWh.

Energy consumption for Flat A fluctuated between 350 and 450 kWh in January and February and peaked at 650 kWh in the first week of February; after this spike, energy consumption decreased to 350 kWh, peaked above 740 kWh in the first week of March, then dropped to 400 kWh in the second week of March. From the second week of March to mid-July, consumption fluctuated between 520 and 800 kWh; from mid-July until September, usage wavered between 740 and 950 kWh, which is above the upper limit, and peaked at 999.4 kWh in the first week of August. Energy consumption then steadily decreased from 740 to 550 kWh throughout September and October, and usage hovered around 500 kWh from the first week of October until November. Consumption continued to follow this trend until reaching the lowest-recorded level of 310 kWh in the first week of December, after which usage increased and peaked at 580 kWh in the final week of the month.

It should be noted that the upper recommended limit for energy consumption in this case-study flat was 780 kWh, which was significantly surpassed in the first week of August. According to the energy-bill analysis, however, actual mean energy consumption was calculated to be 540.7 kWh, which means that at its peak, the energy consumption of this flat was just below the level delineated in the relevant criterion.

According to the simulation predictions, overall energy consumption between January and December was predicted to be 27,405 kWh. Notably, the occupants' actual energy consumption between January and December of 2016 was calculated to be 3,079 kWh. It can therefore be concluded that in the peak cooling summer month of August, the average energy-consumption level for this flat was above the benchmark level for what the occupants needed for cooling purposes; this was also validated by an analysis of the actual energy bills, which concluded that peak energy consumption in the first week of August was actually 910 kWh.

The energy-consumption fluctuations of the south- and southeast-oriented intermediate-floor Flat B in August 2016 are shown in Figure 7.1(b). The lower energy-consumption margin was 300 kWh, and the upper margin was 2,200 kWh, which was higher than that of the first-floor flats due to internal heat gains from appliances and different floor levels and building-envelope orientations. Energy consumption in January was 780 kWh, and this fluctuated between 520 and 910 kWh until the second week of February, when it peaked at 1,500 kWh. These variations continued through the end of February, when usage reached 1,400 kWh; at this time, usage dropped to 700 kWh and hovered around this level until the end of March, then steadily increased from 800 to 2,200 kWh between April and mid-June.

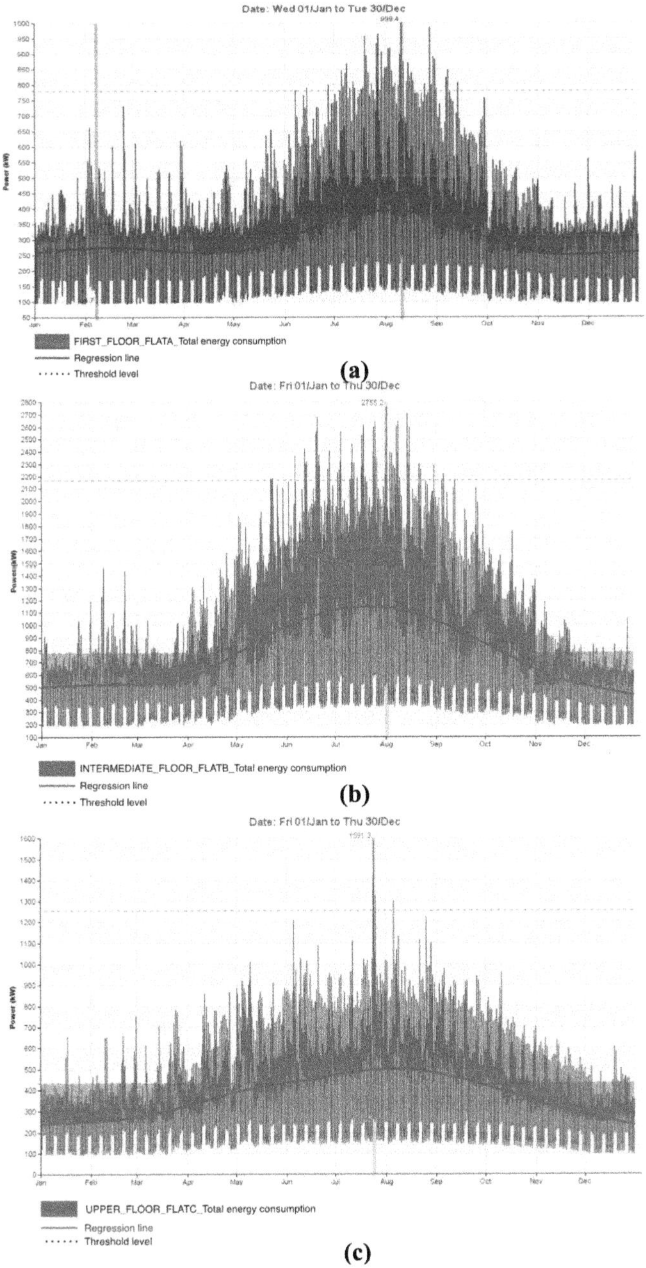

Figure 7.1 (a) Maximum monthly energy consumption of worst-performing south- and southwest-facing first-floor flats in August was 999.4 kWh, (b) maximum monthly energy consumption of worst-performing south- and southeast-facing intermediate-floor flat in August was 2,755.2 kWh and (c) maximum monthly energy consumption of worst-performing south- and southwest-facing upper-floor flat in August was 1,591.3 kWh.

Energy consumption remained near or above the upper margin from mid-July through September and peaked at 2,755.2 kWh in the beginning of August. From September through November, energy usage decreased to 1,100 kWh and fluctuated around this level, then continued to decrease until December; energy consumption peaked at 1,000 kWh in the final week of December.

The regression line stayed well above the lower 300 kWh recommended limit for average energy consumption throughout the year and peaked above the lower margin at 1,100 kWh in August. It can be concluded that although there was a potential risk for overheating, overall consumption was well above the recommended energy-consumption benchmark because of the occupants' heavy reliance on cooling systems in the summer (Ozarisoy & Altan, 2017a).

It should be noted that the heating temperature for the energy simulations was set to 21.0°C in the ApacheSIM module construction profiles (Salvati et al., 2020); this was because the occupants predominantly used gas-cylinder heating systems in the winter, which was why energy consumption fluctuated around 780 kWh between December and February. It is also notable that energy consumption increased in February and March and varied from 780 to 1,450 kWh, which strongly indicates that portable domestic heating systems were used in the winter when children were present in the flat.

According to the simulation predictions, overall energy consumption between January and December was predicted to be 4,440.5 kWh; actual energy consumption for the year, however, was 5,259 kWh. It can therefore be concluded that in the peak cooling summer month of August, the average energy consumption of the case-study flat was above the benchmark level for what the occupants needed for cooling purposes (Gulotta et al., 2020). This was validated by an analysis of the actual energy bills, which revealed that peak energy consumption in the first week of August was recorded at 2,453 kWh, even though the energy-consumption benchmark for Flat B was 2,200 kWh; this is because the Type 2 occupancy pattern was assigned to represent the continuous day- and night-time presence of retiree couples who engaged in high energy consumption. These results can be extrapolated to represent the energy-use intensity of the surveyed households.

Interestingly, based on these simulation measurements, it can be concluded that the energy consumption of this base-case unit consistently remained above the recommended benchmark (Ozarisoy & Altan, 2018). The energy-bill analysis determined, however, average energy consumption for Flat B was 1,999.7 kWh, and energy consumption in the peak cooling month of August was 2,755.2 kWh. According to these data, there was a contradictory finding related to actual energy consumption, because the CIBSE TM59 guidelines were intended to assess the overheating risk of existing residential buildings in the UK, yet the research context of the present study was in a different geographic domain (i.e., the Eastern Mediterranean area).

The energy-consumption simulation for the south- and southwest-facing upper-floor Flat C is delineated in Figure 7.1(c). The line at 1,250 kWh indicates the recommended upper limit for average energy consumption, and the margin line at 410 kWh is the lower limit for average energy consumption; the acceptable range for energy consumption is between these margins, and usage above the 1,250 kWh margin indicates high energy consumption. Energy consumption for this flat remained below the recommended 1,250 kWh usage benchmark throughout most of the year and only surpassed the upper limit at the end of July, when 1,591.3 kWh of energy was utilised. Energy consumption for Flat C was 420 kWh in the beginning of January, and usage fluctuated between 450 and 800 kWh until the first week of May, then increased to 1,000 kWh in the second week of May. Consumption then decreased to 800 kWh and hovered around this level until the final week of July, at which time usage peaked at 1,591.3 kWh, then plummeted to 750 kWh. From August until mid-October, energy consumption continued to decrease from 750 to 600 kWh, then sharply decreased from 600 to 400 kWh between mid-October and December and fluctuated at this level until the end of December.

The regression line was initially well below the lower margin for average energy consumption. From January to April, it fluctuated around 220 kWh, then steadily increased to 500 kWh; peak energy consumption peaked at 1,591.3 kWh in the final week of July, then decreased and fluctuated around 210 kWh, which was below the lower margin. Notably, the generated benchmark for Flat C was 1,250 kWh. Overall electricity consumption decreased below the lower limit for average energy consumption in the final week of July, but usage was still well above the upper limit; moreover, even though relatively high energy consumption that was in line with both the simulation predictions and actual energy consumption was observed, overall energy consumption was well below the upper limit for the recommended average usage. The findings related to energy consumption during the peak cooling period were therefore validated.

Validation Study Results Based on Occupants' Energy Bills

Validation for the simulation model was performed using the occupants' annual energy bills. To fulfil the aim and objectives of the present study, a cooling-energy consumption assessment between the predicted and actual energy consumption with a target error of 10% was conducted (Ozarisoy & Altan, 2017b; Pasichnyi et al., 2019). It is worth noting at this point those internal temperatures were iteratively adjusted during the model development process until the simulated annual energy-consumption totals converged with the actual energy-usage totals with values that were less than the target error. Table 7.1 summarises the validation study results.

Validation of the simulation predictions with the actual household energy bills is delineated in Table 7.1. The first-floor flat, which had a Type 1 (i.e., low) occupancy pattern, was predicted to consume 2,740.5 kWh of energy during the summer, and actual energy consumption was 3,079.0 kWh; the position of the RTB in the social-housing estate and local climate conditions caused variations in the predicted model, which suggests that the TRY weather files that were assigned in the black-box model require further modification to accurately represent the actual conditions of the built environment. Flats on the intermediate-level floors were predicted to consume 4,450.5 kWh of energy, but their actual bills data revealed

Table 7.1 Comparative Results of Overall Occupant Energy Consumption between DTS and Analysis of Actual Energy Bills

Flat Information	*Occupancy-Pattern Type*	*Simulation Prediction (kWh)*	*Actual Consumption (kWh)*	*Difference (%)*
FIRST_FLOOR_FLATA	OP1	2,740.5	3,079.0	−4
INTERMEDIATE_FLOOR_FLATB	OP2	4,440.5	5,259.0	−7.2
UPPER_FLOOR_FLATC	OP3	9,689.6	10,004.0	−2.4

OP1: Low occupancy
OP2: Moderate occupancy
OP3: High occupancy

5,259.0 kWh of energy use. The upper-floor flats were predicted to consume 9,689.6 kWh of energy, but actual energy use for these units was 10,004.0 kWh. In the present study, it was found that actual energy consumption was higher than predicted energy use in all the base-case representative flats.

The present study validates the actual energy-consumption data for most of the base-case representative flats. With the exception of Flat C on the upper floor, all results fell within the acceptable percentage difference; longer occupancy hours led to increased energy consumption, which is why there was a −2.4% difference between the simulation prediction and actual consumption for Flat C. For this reason, the simulation prediction required a 5% deduction from the initial prediction to align with the actual occupancy patterns; after this deduction rate was taken into consideration, the simulation prediction was 10,468.8 kWh, and the simulation prediction was 3%, a difference that was within the acceptable range. As such, the Flat C simulation model can also be confirmed as a valid model.

Forecasting Household Energy Use

To validate the simulation findings and address building energy-performance gaps, the present study examined household energy bills and developed a prediction for a large sampling size through the main determinant factors that were discerned and recorded from the feed-forward interviews; the sampling size was limited to a 100-representative population. This statistical method was intended to provide evidence-based data and confirm the BES model. Figure 7.2(a)–(g) details household energy consumption in the summer and winter, taking the household sociodemographic characteristics presented in Chapters 4 and 5 into consideration.

The household energy-consumption patterns in the southeast-facing RTBs, which are shown in Figure 7.2(a), were predominantly between 900 and 1,200 kWh; the southwest-facing RTBs was within the range of 1,000–1,800 kWh and the south-facing RTBs consumed between 2,000 and 2,800 kWh. Of the participants, 36% were recruited from south-oriented RTBs, and 31% lived in northeast-facing

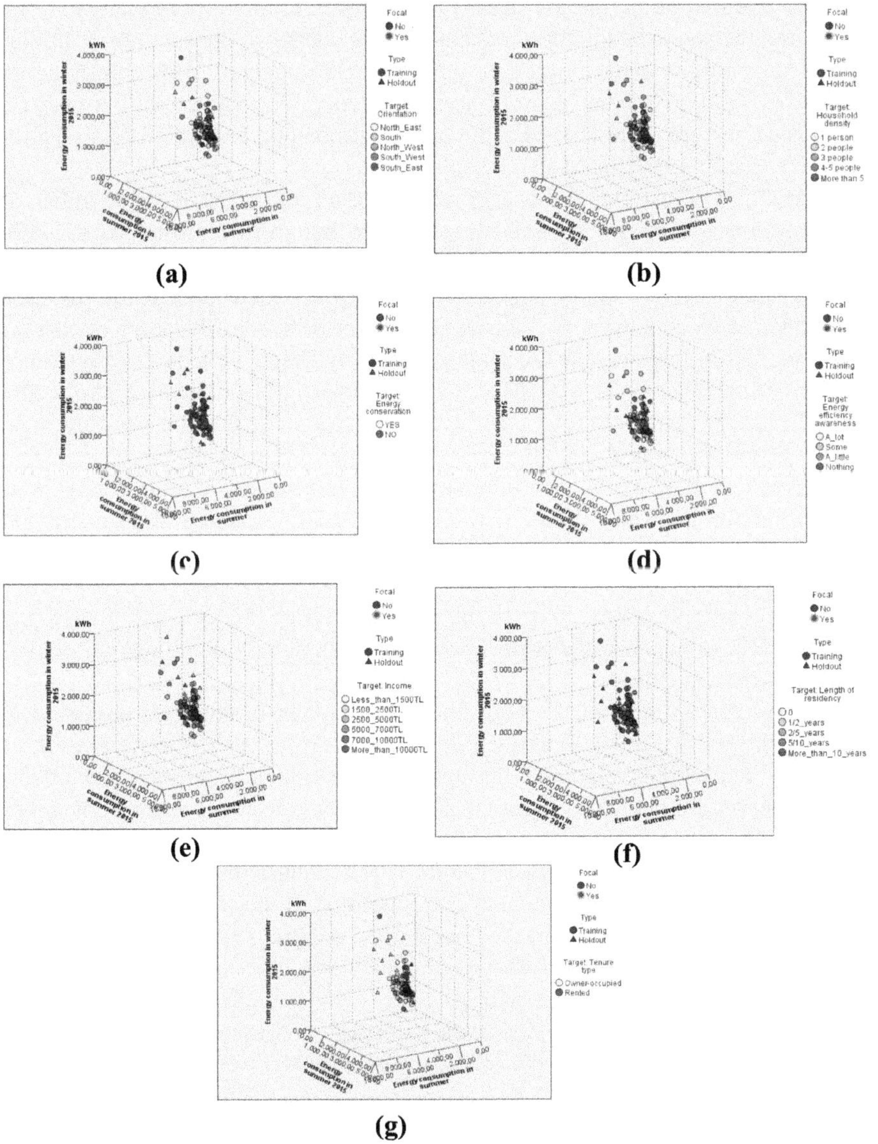

Figure 7.2 (a) Distribution of energy consumption by RTB orientation, (b) distribution of energy consumption by household density, (c) distribution of energy consumption by energy conservation, (d) distribution of energy consumption by energy-efficiency awareness, (e) distribution of energy consumption by income, (f) distribution of energy consumption by length of residency and (g) distribution of energy consumption by tenure type.

RTBs. As it relates to the portion of the sampling size that lived in the south- and northeast-oriented units, the northeast-facing flats consumed more energy in the winter, and the south-facing flats consumed more energy in the summer; a similar energy-consumption pattern was detected in the BES analysis. This confirms that orientation is a determinant factor of household energy consumption, but because this physical feature is not limited to the built environment, household socio-demographic characteristics should also be considered.

Figure 7.2(b) illustrates the energy consumption according to the number of occupants in each household. For units with more than five occupants, which were designated as the OP3 (i.e., high) occupancy type in the BES model, energy usage was 900–1,200 kWh. Flats occupied by 4–5 people, which represented the OP2 (i.e., moderate) occupancy type, consumed between 900 and 2,800 kWh of energy. Flats occupied by three people consumed as much as 2,800.0 kWh of energy; these were owner-occupiers who were 65 years of age and older and in the high-income group (i.e., more than 10,000 TL), and they represented 16% of the sampling size. The occupants who reported high energy consumption were in the 55–65 age band and represented 32% of the sampling size, and these residents looked after their grandchildren in their homes on the weekends; the BES analysis also determined that this group represented the OP2 (i.e., moderate) occupancy type. These findings confirm that occupancy patterns are a determinant factor to consider when calibrating building-energy performance for the development of energy-performance certificates (EPCs) in accordance with Energy Performance of Buildings Directives (EPBD) recommendations.

To prove the validity of the high energy consumption that was predicted in the BES, the present study examined data related to the energy conservation of respondent households obtained through the questionnaire survey; the results of this analysis are shown in Figure 7.2(c). Overall household energy consumption ranged between 900 and 3,800 kWh, with a majority of households in the 500–1,700 kWh range; this suggests that most of the households consumed greater amounts of energy than the national average, because of the socio-economic status of the occupants and the effect of the households' cultural assets (i.e., high-quality lifestyle, continuous presence at home) on their behaviour and their expectations for comfortable indoor air temperatures.

According to Figure 7.2(d), which shows energy consumption in light of each household's awareness of energy-efficiency measures, 15% of the households reported that they had no knowledge of energy efficiency and consumed between 900 and 1,800 kWh of energy, 12% claimed to have 'a little' awareness of this topic and utilised between 2,000 and 2,800 kWh, 50% stated that they had 'some' knowledge of energy efficiency and consumed between 900 and 2,100 kWh, and 23% asserted that they knew 'a lot' and used 500 kWh or less. After evaluating these results, it can be concluded that household energy consumption could potentially decrease when the occupants' knowledge of EEMs is increased.

Energy-consumption patterns according to income are shown in Figure 7.2(e): energy usage for high-income households (i.e., more than 10,000 TL) ranged between 900 and 1,600 kWh, energy consumption for those in the 7,000–10,000

TL income group ranged between 1,000 and 2,800 kWh and households in the 2,500–5,000 TL income group utilised between 900 and 2,800 kWh of energy. The wide range of usage for the latter group was due to different floor levels; the simulation study predicted that energy consumption in the upper-floor flats would be 9,869.0 kWh, but actual energy consumption was 10,004.0 kWh, which suggests that these flats experienced significant overheating risks that were exacerbated when the households used every type of cooling appliance.

According to Figure 7.2(f), which shows the effect of length of residency on energy use, energy consumption of households who had lived in their flats for more than ten years ranged between 400 and 3,800 kWh; this wide variance was due to the number of household members in each flat and the age bands of the participants. Of the sampling population, 47% were 55–65 and 65 years of age and older; this age group was primarily retirees in the high-income group (i.e., more than 10,000 TL) who spent most of their time at home. Notably, the energy consumption of residents who had lived in their units for 5–10 years, who comprised 10% of the sampling size, ranged between 900 and 1,600 kWh; even though these flat owners were younger, they had children living in their home, and their high energy consumption was due to attempts to acclimatise their indoor air environments. These results suggest that when EPCs are being developed, length of residency should be considered in addition to other socio-demographic factors to properly understand and address the building energy-performance gap and to foresee and avoid discrepancies between predicted and actual energy use.

Previous scholars have indicated that their BES predictions always provided higher energy-intensity rates at the time they conducted an archetype analysis for energy policy (Ascione et al., 2019; D'Agostino & Parker, 2018). The present study did, in fact, determine that predicted energy consumption is relatively higher than the actual energy consumption to investigate the influences of determinants' effect on household energy consumption.

To avoid research bias and reduce discrepancies in predicted energy use, the present study examined associations between household energy consumption and type of tenancy; the findings of this analysis are presented in Figure 7.2(g). With the exception of one unit that used 3,800 kWh of energy, most renters consumed between 100 and 800 kWh of energy, and the energy consumption of owner-occupiers ranged between 200 and 2,800 kWh; these results indicate that a household's socio-economic status is a more important factor for energy consumption than their type of tenancy. This contradicts the traditional manner in which EU member states have verified energy consumption according to tenancy type, and confirms that other factors, such as socio-economic status, the physical properties of the building elements, local climate conditions and most importantly, cultural assets of the case-study locations.

Retrofitting Design Strategies

This study presents an analysis of the PCDS development framework to demonstrate an evidence-based integrated design approach for energy use. The multiple objectives of the building assessment provided information related to the energy effectiveness of retrofitting interventions by determining the life-cycle cost assessment (LCCA) for policymakers in the residential sector.

Implications for Energy Use

This section examines the impact and applicability of passive-cooling design strategies to retrofit base-case buildings, optimise the thermal comfort of occupants and reduce overheating risks in the summer.

This analysis was divided into six strategies, each of which consisted of a set of dynamic building-energy simulations that were intended to assess the current energy performance of the representative flat units. The first strategy was considered the balcony space addition on the front elevation. The second strategy considered the energy performance of a combination of passive-cooling design measures, which included appropriate shading systems, external wall insulation on the roof and the more exposed walls and natural ventilation. The third strategy was a newly proposed architectural intervention for RTBs that included a new fenestration design and the addition of an operable external shading system. The fourth, fifth and sixth strategies utilised adaptable passive cooling designs to evaluate an improvement in energy use according to the percentage of hours of thermal discomfort. These strategies, including the analysis methods and descriptions thereof, are detailed in Table 7.2.

The six retrofitting design strategies, which are illustrated in Figure 7.3, were initially applied separately, then the obtained results were applied together to test the effectiveness of these design strategies as a whole. Table 7.3 delineates the construction properties of the base-case RTBs and the six strategies that were applied in the simulation.

Strategy 1 was a volumetric space addition with a sunscreen blade affixed to the southeast-facing building envelope in the living room area. This modification was in the form of a room extension with a slanted overhanging roof that measured 1.8 m (length) × 2.1 m (height); the external walls were made of operable double-glazed windows with 50% opening ratios. The living room was chosen because, according to various findings, this was the worst-performing room that was under the greatest threat of overheating in the summer; the aim of this strategy was to determine to what extent this passive cooling application could diminish the overheating risk in this room. The simulation resulted in a significant decrease in the living room energy-consumption patterns, while at the same time, indoor air temperature was decreased due to an optimised, effective infiltration rate on the building envelope.

In Strategy 1 retrofitting design, the primary aim of which was to provide solar protection to the living room. The solar exposure analysis demonstrated that prior to the retrofitting, annual solar radiation for this room peaked at 8,908.92 h; solar radiation was reduced to a maximum of 1,818.09 h as a result of this endeavour, which means that implementing these passive shading elements led to a 50% improvement in energy effectiveness. To reduce the thermal vulnerability of the building envelopes, S1 was implemented to predict the effect of these retrofitting design interventions.

Table 7.2 Structure of Step-by-Step Applicable Retrofitting Strategies and Those of Existing Base Case

Strategy: Base Case	*Description: Base-Case Design*	*Analysis Method: Thermal Performance*	*Dynamic Thermal Simulations: Currently Assigned Construction Materials for Building-Performance Evaluation*
Strategy 1 (S1)	Proposed design	Thermal performance of living room	Base-case design + volumetric sunspace Addition Base-case design + operable pinewood external shutters
Strategy 2 (S2)	Natural-ventilation analysis	Thermal performance of living room and kitchen	Base-case design + volumetric sunspace Addition Base-case design + operable external venetian blinds
Strategy 3 (S3)	Natural-ventilation analysis	Thermal performance of Bedrooms 1 and 2 and kitchen	Base-case design + window opening Projections Base-case design + overhanging window Canopy Base-case design + horizontal external pinewood louvres
Strategy 4 (S4)	Natural-ventilation analysis	Thermal performance of Bedroom 1	Base-case design + volumetric window opening projection Base-case design + folded window system Base-case design + overhanging window Canopy Base-case design + operable pinewood external shutters
Strategy 5 (S5)	Natural-ventilation analysis	Thermal performance of Bedroom 2	Base-case design + fixed overhanging solar-shading systems
Strategy 6 (S6)	All-proposed designs	Thermal performance	Base-case design + S1 + S2 + S3 + S4 + S5 in combination

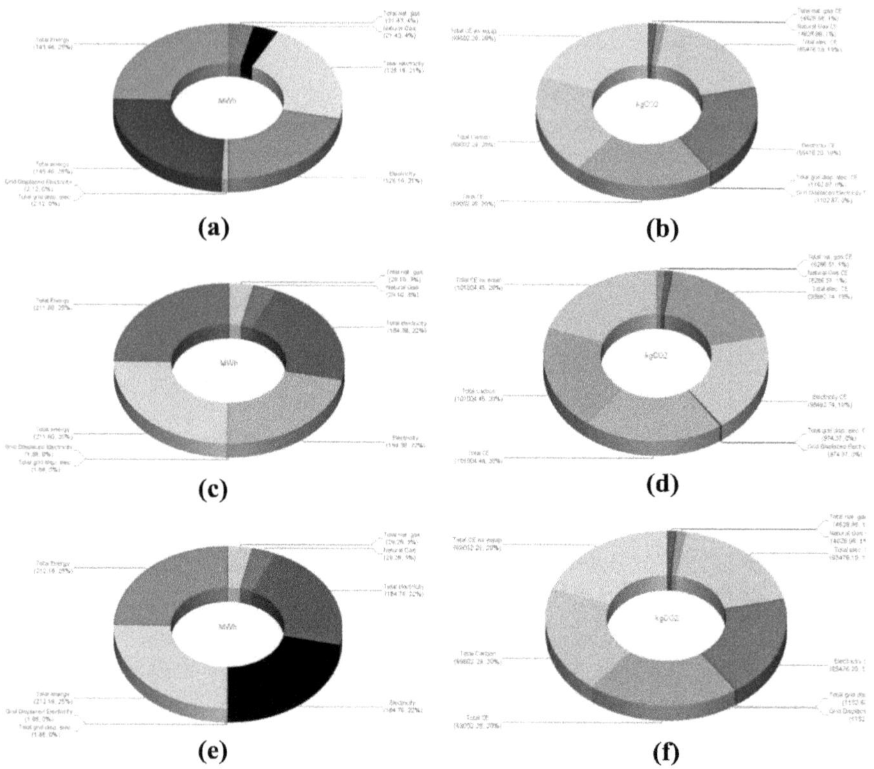

Figure 7.3 (a) Monthly electricity consumption of representative flat with low-occupancy profile (i.e., OP1); (b) overall first-floor CO_2 emissions; (c) monthly electricity use of intermediate-floor flat with medium-occupancy profile (i.e., OP2); (d) overall intermediate-floor CO_2 emissions; (e) monthly electricity use of upper-floor flat with high-occupancy profile (i.e., OP3); and (f) overall upper-floor CO_2 emissions.

The monthly cooling-energy consumption during the cooling period extends from May to October after the implementation of the first two strategies. It should be noted that the energy-consumption data representing the actual energy use of 100 households was included in the statistical data. As such, the BES demonstrated data obtained from three representative flats (i.e., first-, intermediate- and upper-level floors) to provide representative sampling criteria and test the energy effectiveness of the PCDS implemented into building envelopes (Kotireddy et al., 2019).

Following the implementation of Strategy 1, peak cooling-energy consumption was reduced to 83.6 kWh; the upper threshold was determined to be 66.0 kWh, and the lower threshold was 16.0 kWh. Notably, household energy bills revealed that energy consumption between June and September of 2016 was 291.0 kWh, and energy consumption in August specifically was 33.0 kWh. After Strategy 2 was

Table 7.3 Specifications of State-of-the-Art Retrofitting Strategies and Those of Existing Base-Case

Strategy	*Element Details*	*U-value (W/m²K)*	*R-value (m²K/W)*	*Thickness (mm)*	*Mass (kg/m²)*	*Thermal mass (kJ/m²K)*
Base-Case	Common brick: HF-C4 + brickwork (inner leaf) + clear-float 4 mm	4.05	0.076	28.0	56.17	11.16
S1	Clay tile: HF-C1 + vermiculite insulating brick + thermalite-high strength + thermo-clear 8 mm polycarbonate cliffing + clear-float 4 mm	0.95	0.88	110.5	83.32	34.6
S2	Asphalt mastic roofing + particleboard: High density + roof insulation + thermo-clear 8 mm polycarbonate cliffing + clear-float 4 mm + insulation board—HF-B2 + timber solar shield with adjustable blinds (500 mm)	0.80	1.10	285.5	511.65	240.0
S3	Combination of S1 + S2 envelope rehabilitation with shading and 0.63 h^{-1} ventilation rate	0.80	1.10	285.5	511.65	240.0
S4	Combination of S1 + S2 envelope rehabilitation with shading and 0.4 h^{-1} ventilation rate	0.80	1.10	285.5	511.65	240.0
S5	Combination of S1 + S2 envelope rehabilitation with shading without passive night-time ventilation in summer and 0.4 h^{-1} ventilation rate	0.80	1.10	285.5	511.65	240.0
S6	Common brick: HF-C4 + brickwork (inner leaf) + clear-float 4 mm + combination of S1 +S2 envelope rehabilitation with shading and 0.4 h^{-1} ventilation rate	1.30	0.5	61.5	38.75	21.39

implemented, energy consumption was reduced to 75.3 kWh; the upper threshold was 60.0 kWh, and the lower threshold was 55 kWh. The results confirm that Strategy 2 increased natural ventilation and acclimatised the indoor air environment and thereby significantly reduced cooling-energy consumption. Unfortunately, the strategy was ineffective against solar radiation, which caused overheating risk, so Strategies 3 and 4 were developed to provide a solution that will affect climate conditions.

In Strategy 2, a volumetric space addition was installed on the southwest- and southeast-facing kitchen spaces within the area of the existing balcony areas; this addition created more liveable space and provided additional NV for every kitchen in the RTB. Three operable vertical windows and three top-window openings were installed on this modular system to provide effective NV. Implementing the horizontal louvre window openings proposed in Strategy 2 led to a 20% decrease in cooling-energy consumption, because the Venetian louvres offered a simple, cost-effective method to improve indoor air quality and regulated indoor air temperatures to enhance the occupants' thermal comfort and decrease their energy costs (Ozarisoy, 2022).

Strategy 3 was implemented to address the overheating risk for all occupied spaces in the worst-performing prototype RTB and to test the efficiency of the passive ventilation system in the building. In this strategy, a traditional overhanging volumetric space addition was applied to the building envelope; this was in the form of a rectangular wedge that projected 2.2 m (length) × 0.6 m (width) × 2.8 m (height) from the external wall surface. The three exposed wall surfaces of this volumetric space-addition design were constructed out of double-glazed glass with 50% opening ratios, and horizontal pinewood louvres were affixed to the exterior of these windows for the purpose of shading.

The aim of Strategy 3 and Strategy 4 was to provide sufficient natural ventilation to indoor spaces, which would then create an 'air-buoyancy-driven' natural ventilation effect whereby the accumulated indoor heat would be circulated into the outside environment, resulting in lower indoor air temperatures. This was tested on the representative base-case RTB and led to reduced overheating risks and decreased electricity consumption during high cooling-demand periods, and the occupants' thermal comfort was optimised.

It should be noted that peak energy consumption after Strategy 3 was implemented was reduced to 43.4 kWh; the upper energy-consumption threshold was 34 kWh, and the lower threshold was 8 kWh. Notably, actual household energy use in August 2016 was 63.0 kWh, and there was a 68% reduction in overall energy consumption. It is important to highlight that the thermal comfort of all treated indoor spaces after this intervention was within the acceptable limits defined by the CIBSE TM59 standards, even though the indoor air temperatures in the living room and Bedroom 2 remained slightly higher than the acceptable thermal-comfort threshold.

A 57% reduction in energy consumption was achieved after Strategy 1, Strategy 2 and Strategy 3 were implemented, but a significant overheating risk remained for the upper-floor flats due to the absence of rooftop insulation material. To reduce high solar radiation on the flat roof surfaces, the volumetric overhanging roof in Strategy 4 was designed to provide solar protection to the occupied spaces in the upper-floor flats; ventilation openings were positioned on the overhang to improve natural air flow and avoid heat accumulation in the summer. Peak energy consumption was reduced to 26.8 kWh; the upper energy-consumption threshold was 21 kWh, and the lower threshold was 5 kWh. It can be concluded that implementation of Strategy 4 had a significant overall impact on the thermal performance of the base-case RTBs.

In Strategy 5, angular pinewood vertical louvres were affixed midway down the length of the windows. This type of shading system absorbs the wind from different angles and promotes NV in indoor spaces. Moreover, this strategy reduces excessive incoming solar radiation.

In Strategy 6, the living room was retrofitted with balcony projections within a fenestration design that was fitted onto the building envelope to allow NV to penetrate into the occupied spaces. This solution was constructed by removing the two existing glazed windows, opening up the space between them and lowering the opening to the floor. The new window openings were then covered with double-glazed glass and folding window panels, which were divided into upper and lower sections; the top portion had small windows that opened to the outside, and the lower portion had long windows that also opened. The aim of this strategy was to improve NV at night, and the extended window opening yielded a large surface area that provided NV that cooled the room and lowered the indoor air temperature a noticeable amount. Unfortunately, this solution also allowed direct solar radiation into the main southeast-oriented living room area, which already received direct sunlight throughout the day, thereby leading to an overheating risk for this space in the summer; the use of vertical sunscreen-building systems only resulted in a 32% reduction.

Overall, an 81% reduction in cooling-energy consumption was achieved after the implementation of all six strategies. To fully understand the effect of PCDS on home-energy performance—specifically, to determine the impact of PCDS on heating-consumption patterns and demonstrate that these strategies would not lead to increased heating-energy consumption in the winter—a one-year DTS analysis was conducted (Rouleau et al., 2019). It should be emphasised that even though this study investigated the energy effectiveness of all the proposed PCDS to assess cooling-energy consumption, the effect of Strategy 5 and Strategy 6 on household heating needs was also considered.

It must be stressed that peak cooling consumption after Strategy 5 was implemented was 30.5 kWh; the upper energy-consumption threshold was 24 kWh, and the lower threshold was 6 kWh. It demonstrates that after Strategy 6 was implemented, peak cooling consumption was reduced to 23.4 kWh, the upper threshold was 18 kWh and the lower threshold was 4 kWh. Notably, these strategies did not have a negative effect on heating-energy consumption, and a significant reduction in cooling-energy consumption was observed.

Table 7.4 delineates the overheating risks for each criterion using the adaptive-comfort method. Based on the recorded design and construction parameters,

Table 7.4 Effects of Six Strategies on Summer Overheating

Room Name and Location	*Occupied Days (%)*	*Criterion 1 (% of Hrs Top T_{max} ≥ 1 K*	*Criterion 2 (Max. Daily Deg. Hrs)*	*Criterion 3 (Max. ΔT)*	*Failing Criteria*
FIRST_Livingroom	100	0.8	4.5	2	—
FIRST_Bedroom1	100	1.4	4.5	2	—
FIRST_Bedroom2	100	0.7	5.5	3	—
FIRST_Bedroom3	100	1.4	4.5	2	—
INTERMEDIATE_Livingroom	100	1.8	5.5	3	—
INTERMEDIATE_Bedroom1	100	0.7	4.5	2	—
INTERMEDIATE_Bedroom2	100	0.5	4.0	3	—
INTERMEDIATE_Bedroom3	100	1.4	4.5	2	—
UPPER_Livingroom	100	1.5	4.5	3	—
UPPER_Bedroom1	100	1.4	4.5	3	—
UPPER_Bedroom2	100	0.5	5.5	3	—
UPPER_Bedroom3	100	0.8	5.5	2	—

overheating was not a problem after the proposed passive-cooling design systems were implemented, even though the living room in the upper-floor flat still demonstrated an overheating risk.

It should be noted that all living rooms in the development had large, double-glazed windows that absorbed direct solar radiation, instead of the aluminium-framed single-glazed window with 50% window-opening ratios in Bedroom 1 and Bedroom 2. It should also be noted that Bedroom 1 faced south-west and overheated to a slightly greater degree than Bedroom 2. Importantly, no signs of overheating were observed when the above-tested strategies were input into the building-model simulation, but the living room and Bedroom 1 still displayed overheating, albeit to a lesser degree.

The efficiency of the analysed and tested passive-cooling design measures was evaluated for the south-facing RTB prototype. According to the results, the Venetian (i.e., a brise-soleil) louvre system proposed in Strategy 1 was the most efficient in the summer when the blind apparatus was completely controlled by the occupants; specifically, tilting the blinds to a 60° angle was shown to be the most effective. To ensure these benefits, combining this shading strategy with an automated system that manages the window opening in a dynamic manner might prove to be very useful.

The addition of the shading system proposed in Strategy 3 to an existing balcony or the addition of a volumetric space onto the existing building structure also yielded noteworthy results, especially when these strategies were combined with horizontal blinds that were tilted to a 30° angle; notably, the depth of the balcony in this passive-cooling design strategy was 0.8–1.2 m, which affected the results to a limited extent.

The shading system proposed in Strategy 4 and the opaque horizontal overhang exhibit proposed in Strategy 5 both resulted in a 50% decrease in solar-radiation exposure. Furthermore, the effectiveness of the analysed sunscreens for the RTBs with south-west orientations was confirmed; specifically, the external Venetian blind systems proposed in Strategy 1 that included the balcony and integrated shield, the sunshade proposed in Strategy 4 that was constructed perpendicular to the façade with horizontal blinds and the horizontal overhang proposed in Strategy 5 were all shown to be highly efficient.

After running the simulations to determine the overheating risks and thermal comfort for each strategy, several conclusions can be drawn. Even though all six strategies reduced overheating risk and optimised the occupants' thermal comfort in the summer, Strategy 5 and Strategy 6 addressed the three criteria related to overheating most effectively. Another important factor that emerged from the analyses was associated with the indoor air temperature in occupied spaces: Combining Strategy 5 and Strategy 6 was shown to improve indoor thermal comfort by reducing the indoor air temperature in the living room of the upper-floor flat from 36.4 to 28.1°C. Furthermore, these results demonstrated the impact of all six implemented strategies on the PPD, which the CIBSE TM59 standards determined should not exceed 15%; PPD was reduced from 100% in the base-case scenario to 30.5% with the combination of Strategy 5 and Strategy 6, but this is still considered unacceptable and underscores the need for additional building-performance optimisation interventions (Rinaldi et al., 2018).

The neutral adaptive thermal-comfort thresholds of the households involved in this portion of the present study ranged between 28.5 and 31.5°C, which demonstrates that the occupants' thermal acceptability was within the range that was obtained from the longitudinal field survey. This suggests that a significant proportion of respondents wanted drier air and decreased humidity; implementing the six strategies led to a decrease in RHI, which in turn increased the occupants' thermal acceptability.

Table 7.5 presents the implementation of all retrofitting design interventions that were undertaken after the local climate characteristics, locally available building materials and passive-cooling design strategies that evolved during the construction of vernacular buildings in Cyprus were all taken into consideration.

Table 7.5 Synthesis of Achievable Results of Each Strategy and Those of Base Case

Strategy 1 (S1): Fixed-blade sunscreen façade implementation			
Description: *Outdoor solar shading; most effective for RTBs with south and west orientations; more frequently applied to residential buildings. Pre-oriented blades affixed to the façade; can also be applied to balconies. Blades can be vertical.*			
Energy-performance total	*1,146.5 kWh/m²*	**Savings**	*43%*
Strengths	*Lower cost; single interventions are allowed; reduced construction time*		
Weaknesses	*Less effective; thermal bridges are not avoided*		
Strategy 2 (S2): Venetian blinds or brise-soleil louvres volumetric addition			
Description: Outdoor solar shield with adjustable, packable blinds; can also be applied to screen balconies. Blinds can be rolled up and compact when not in use			
Energy performance total	1,084.5 kWh/m²	**Savings**	52%
Strengths	Effective		
Weaknesses	Longer construction time; greater cost; comprehensive intervention is required		
Strategy 3 (S3): Overhanging fenestration design			
Description: Fixed opaque overhang made of different materials; consists of horizontal and vertical elements in a grate pattern			
Energy performance total	902.8 kWh/m²	**Savings**	57%
Strengths	Effective; single interventions are allowed; reduced construction time		
Weaknesses	Complex design		

Table 7.5 (Continued)

Strategy 4 (S4): Venetian or roller blinds volumetric roof addition			
Description: *Double-glazed, integrated into interior chamber; stored in a sealed package with desiccants to ensure humidity and condensation control.*			
Energy performance total	*836.7 kWh/m²*	*Savings*	*68%*
Strengths	*Effective; single interventions are allowed; reduced construction time; increases usable floor area*		
Weaknesses	*Complex design; higher construction costs*		
Strategy 5 (S5): Fixed overhang			
Description: Fixed vertical, opaque overhang made of different materials; structurally integrated or anchored to the wall; most effective for RTBs with east and west orientations. Shields may also have a vertical arrangement perpendicular to the façade			
Energy performance total	735.4 kWh/m²	**Savings**	72%
Strengths	Reduced cooling-energy consumption; optimised thermal comfort; effective; flexible interventions are allowed		
Weaknesses	Longer construction time and higher costs; comprehensive intervention is required		

[a]Base-case energy consumption in the peak cooling month of August was 2,081.35 kWh/m².

Implications for Energy-Policy Design

An LCCA, which referred to the net usable area, was required and a reference optimisation criterion needed to be defined to compare the energy investment with the energy demand that is needed to operate each passive-cooling design system after implementation. The amount of embodied energy was therefore spread throughout the net floor area, and the obtained value was converted from MJ/m² to kWh/m². The presented scenarios were studied globally, and sustainable energy-efficiency implementation measures, local construction practices and models of improvement that were suitable for the present research context were created. Table 7.6 shows the typical assumptions related to energy consumption and CO_2 emissions of the building that formed energy-optimisation measures during the pre- and post-retrofitting phases.

The LCCA, the aim of which was to assess the overall effect of applying all six retrofitting strategies to devise effective energy policies, was developed in the following manner: the LCCA study period had a 30-year lifespan, and the hours of operation were input in the life-cycle cost application on the IES platform as a 1.00 stipend. The Turkish Lira was not an available currency in the application, so the U.S. dollar was chosen for the LCCA analysis to ensure a globally recognised

Table 7.6 Energy-Consumption Reduction Measures Pre- and Post-Retrofitting

Base-Case Energy, Carbon and Cost Summary			*Retrofitting Interventions Estimated Energy and Cost Summary*	
Annual Energy Cost	\$4,254		**Annual Energy Cost**	\$2,643
Life-Cycle Cost	\$60,937		**Life-Cycle Cost**	\$44,456
		Annual Energy		
EUI	1.218 MJ/m²/year		**EUI**	1.214 MJ/m²/year
Electricity	30.674 kWh		**Electricity**	22.349 kWh
Fuel	10.309 MJ		**Fuel**	8.966 MJ
Annual Peak Demand	103 kW		**Annual Peak Demand**	2.4 kW
		Life-Cycle Energy		
Electricity		913.423 kW	**Electricity**	640.437 kW
Fuel		218.054 MJ	**Fuel**	128.870 MJ

EUI: Energy-use intensity

calculation rate. The present study demonstrates energy consumption before and after the retrofitting solutions were implemented.

Annual household energy expenditures were $4,254 prior to the retrofitting, and this rate decreased to $2,643 after implementation of the PCDS. The LCCA for each RTB prototype was $60,937 in the pre-retrofitting phase; this was reduced to $44,456 post-retrofitting, which is still relatively high. The proposed PCDS will initially be introduced to the construction industry as retrofitting solutions that will require high-quality workmanship, and trained, qualified energy assessors will monitor the long-term impact of these modifications.

Implementing these passive-cooling design strategies resulted in 43–81% energy savings. Annual peak demand was reduced from 103.0 to 2.4 kWh; this confirms that the households became independent of their reliance on domestic cooling appliances in the summer, which is a good indicator of energy effectiveness. Even though energy consumption was reduced from 30.674 to 22.349 kWh, the energy-consumption threshold was still relatively high due to discrepancies between the actual and predicted energy use of the three occupancy patterns in the black-box energy model developed for this empirical study; extrapolating three different weather profiles to minimise discrepancies did not resolve the DTS constraints in the IES software platform.

Extensive ventilation is crucial in the summer to prevent shaded terraces from generating additional heat due to unregulated natural ventilation systems and under-ventilated apartments. The discounted rate is a key variable for the LCCA; the energy-use intensity and the life-cycle energy use and costs of the retrofitting strategies are presented in Table 7.7. It should be noted that these costs were independently calculated in the life-cycle assessment module of the IES software suite, which can be used to determine benchmarks in retrofitting efforts (Mostavi et al., 2017).

Implementation of all six strategies decreased the amount of electricity that was required to maintain the occupants' thermal comfort for a full year; while the baseline model of energy was 2,081.35 kWh/m^2, annual energy-use intensity with these strategies was 240.0 kWh/m^2, which is a significant reduction in energy consumption. Due to the condition of the thermal conductivity parameters, the energy-use intensity of heating- and cooling-energy demand in relation to optimum cost was

Table 7.7 Energy-Use Intensity and Life-Cycle Energy Use of Base-Case RTB Costs

Energy-Use Intensity		*Life-Cycle Energy Use and Cost*	
Electricity EUI	240 kWh/m^2/year	**Life-Cycle Electricity Use**	630.570 kWh
Fuel EUI	406 MJ/m^2/year	**Life-Cycle Fuel Use**	812.600 MJ
Total EUI	1.444 MJ/m^2/year	**Life-Cycle Energy Cost**	$46,396

EUI: Energy-use efficiency

approximately 630,570.0 kWh/m^2 per year. Figure 7.3(a)–(f) details the energy use and carbon footprint of the PCDS that were implemented.

The total energy consumption for the representative first-floor flat, which is shown in Figure 7.3(a), was 145.46 kWh; total electricity usage was 126.16 kWh; actual household energy consumption peaked at 1,223 kWh; mean energy consumption was 374.58 kWh and the standard deviation (*SD*) was 262,500.0 kWh. The BES analysis determined that energy consumption in August peaked at 999.4 kWh before the retrofittings, and energy consumption after the retrofittings was below the mean energy-consumption levels; the significant reduction in energy use also had a direct impact on the CO_2 emissions, which is shown in Figure 7.3(b).

Total energy consumption in the intermediate-floor flat after implementation of all six PCDS, which is shown in Figure 7.3(c), was 211.6 kWh; total electricity usage was 184.38 kWh; actual household energy consumption peaked at 1,233.0 kWh; mean energy consumption was 374.58 kWh and the *SD* was 262.5 kWh; the simulation prediction demonstrated that total energy consumption on a hot summer day peaked at 2,755.2 kWh. The intermediate-floor flats consumed relatively high levels of energy due to additional heat gains from the flats located above and below these units. Notably, flats with the Type 2 occupancy pattern (i.e., moderate) also had this effect. These were mostly occupied by retired couples who were 65 years of age and older and looked after their grandchildren from 08:00 to 17:00 while they were on school holiday[1]; these residents kept their windows open for natural ventilation and to dissipate dirty air. Moreover, CO_2 emissions, which are shown in Figure 7.3(d), were reduced to 101,004.45 ppm.

Total energy consumption of the upper-floor flat, which is shown in Figure 7.3(e), was 212.6 kWh; actual household energy peaked at 1,223.0 kWh and peak electricity consumption was 1,591.3 kWh; the simulation predictions were slightly higher than actual energy consumption because of the dominant representative occupancy type (i.e., OP3) that was assigned in the black-box model for this study (Bamdad et al., 2020). Energy consumption post-retrofitting was reduced from 1,591.3 to 212.6 kWh; this significant reduction confirms the energy effectiveness of the PCDS, which also reduced CO_2 emissions, as shown in Figure 7.3(f).

These findings demonstrate that input parameters (i.e., benchmarks), such as life-cycle data and the discount rate of the price of energy, should be carefully planned for. Furthermore, energy-efficiency measures can improve indoor air quality and reduce overheating risks throughout the building (Harputlugil & de Wilde, 2021). In addition to directly impacting energy consumption, household energy bills will also be significantly reduced (Gupta & Gregg, 2018).

When the PCDS were applied to the other prototype RTBs, economic and energy-performance analyses were performed to determine the feasibility of these retrofitting scenarios. These assessments confirmed that based on the significant energy-cost savings, decreased energy usage and lower CO_2 emissions, the proposed retrofitting interventions should be considered so the existing housing stock in Cyprus can be renovated in a systematic manner to achieve significant energy savings.

Energy Performance

The simulation results were analysed to better understand existing energy-use conditions and to calibrate energy-consumption patterns, especially those related to the cooling demands of the representative first-, intermediate- and upper-floor flats. When examining energy consumption as it relates to specific heat loss, the prototype flats consumed 237.1 kW of energy during the pre-retrofitting phase and 140.2 kW during the post-retrofitting phase due to implementation of PCRDS onto the existing building envelope.

Energy consumption prior to the retrofittings was 174.4 kWh, mean energy consumption fluctuated within the range of 20–25 kWh with an upper energy-consumption limit of 150 kWh and mean actual energy consumption was 374.58 kWh. Actual household energy consumption, which was higher than the simulation prediction, was determined by the energy-bill data for 100 flats; as was previously explained, discrepancies between predicted and actual energy use were due to the three different occupancy patterns (i.e., OP1, OP2 and OP3) that were assigned in the black-box model for the DTS analysis.

According to peak cooling-energy consumption post-retrofitting was 17.1 kWh, mean energy consumption fluctuated between 0.8 and 1.5 kWh with an upper energy-consumption limit of 13.0 kWh and peak energy consumption between June and September of 2016 fluctuated between 2.5 and 11.5 kWh. Implementing these passive-cooling design strategies resulted in an 81% reduction in energy consumption during peak summer-cooling demand, which confirms that the differences in energy use before and after the retrofittings can be correlated with energy management; this suggests that the energy-usage ranges obtained from the BES analysis can be applied as a benchmark to confirm the energy effectiveness of PCDS for future energy policy decisions.

The adaptive comfort temperatures in the present study represented an acclimatisation system set point of 21°C, which was autonomously managed by the occupants according to external climate conditions. During the peak cooling summer season, the occupied spaces displayed significant differences from the adaptive temperature set point for heavy construction materials, especially for the base-case model, according to the occupants' energy-use patterns and comfort levels in different seasons (Hellwig et al., 2020). It depicts the mean cooling-energy sensible load of the representative flats in the pre- and post-retrofitting phases between May and September, taking the time-of-day factor into account.

The mean peak cooling sensible load decreased from 50 to 28 kWh during the cooling period; these results revealed that a 43% cooling-energy consumption reduction was achieved after the retrofitting interventions were applied. These graphs depict the time-of-day factor as it relates to cooling sensible load fluctuations to demonstrate the highest peak of mean energy consumption in the summer; prior to retrofitting, peak cooling was required in the middle of August between 11:05 and 13:25, when the peak reached 50 kWh, but this decreased to a median peak of 28 kWh post-retrofitting.

It demonstrates the mean cooling-energy sensible load of the representative flats between January and December in the pre- and post-retrofitting phases. According to these results, when all six strategies were implemented onto the building envelope, the cooling-sensible load between May and September decreased from 4.0 to 2.4 kWh.

Notably, the cooling-consumption pattern that is depicted in the study reveals that there were variations after all six strategies were implemented; starting at the beginning of April 2018, cooling-energy consumption was 0.5 kWh, and it was 1.8 kWh in the first week of November. The results suggest that even though substantial overall energy-consumption reduction was achieved, occupants will still need to use some type of domestic cooling appliances to optimise their thermal comfort; this is due to the occupants' socio-demographic characteristics and occupancy patterns, which directly influence thermal adaptability, in addition to physical conditions that are determinant factors on cooling-energy use. Notably, the occupants' cultural assets that were gathered through the regression forecasting analysis, such as their neutral adaptive thermal-comfort threshold of 28.5–31.5°C, are among the important factors that affect their adaptability in any physical environment.

It should be highlighted that the small proportion of cooling-energy use still needed after the six strategies were implemented suggests that PCDS would not make the prototype RTB completely independent of mechanical cooling. Further research is required to assess the energy effectiveness of PCDS in the Eastern Mediterranean climate.

One of the significant findings of this study was that cooling-energy consumption decreased by 81% after all six passive-cooling design strategies were implemented. These conclusions will create the prerequisites and the background information that are needed for the development of a novel methodological framework and a ground-breaking epistemological design approach in the area of development and design, energy-related policymaking, the drafting of subsidisation schemes and targeted actions to improve the energy efficiency of existing housing stock.

The novelty of this study could mean, however, that the retrofitting interventions developed herein may not be economically feasible with current energy-efficiency policy targets, even though the applicability of the research context and the recommended EPBD objectives from the EU may lead to an increased demand for domestic cooling options. As such, it can be asserted that the economic and environmental benefits of these strategies are mutually supportive of one another and addressing current methods of design related to thermal comfort, overheating risk and building optimisation will eventually lead to a win–win situation.

Roadmap to EU Energy-Policy Framework

Importantly, the present study reveals typical household awareness of energy use and provides a cultural assessment to develop a methodological framework for building optimisation at the policy level. This novel benchmark criterion could radically change the manner in which energy development studies evaluate and optimise the energy efficiency of residential buildings in post-war social-housing developments and would significantly increase the likelihood of implementing different strategies, which would in turn encourage early stage designs and policy decision-making related to domestic energy use.

These findings suggest that EPCs do not correlate with the actual thermal performance of dwellings when energy-efficient retrofitting interventions are implemented during the decision-making process (Arcipowska et al., 2016; Niskanen & Rohracher, 2020). This has led to current energy-consumption estimates and savings potentials that do not accurately reflect what actually happens in practice during retrofitting efforts (Dascalaki et al., 2016; Levi, 2021). For this reason, policymakers will need to review prominent methodological approach to implement effective retrofitting solutions that will take local contextual factors, including a socio-technical evaluation of a given society, into account (Galvin & Sunikka-Blank, 2014; Nematchoua et al., 2021). The present study recommends that an emphasis should be placed on conducting longitudinal and transverse surveys with households to avoid underestimating the impact of retrofitting interventions due to the technical challenges of implementing any type of holistic retrofitting intervention.

The scope to conduct a building-energy simulation in this study was limited to input parameters that were obtained from longitudinal field surveys, the archetype building analysis and the results that demonstrated that the differences in energy use between the existing state of a building and one that has been retrofitted were correlated with the degree of energy management after cost-effective energy-efficient systems were implemented; this study limitation will, however, provide future opportunities for additional research.

Conclusion

In the present empirical study, the thermal performance of building elements in a base-case post-war social-housing estate in Famagusta, Cyprus, was analysed, and different retrofitting efforts were undertaken to optimise the energy performance of each structure. The objective of this study was to develop evidence-based passive-cooling retrofitting design strategies to improve the occupants' thermal comfort and reduce the overheating risks in the base-case RTBs. This study employed a socio-technical-systems (STS) approach to develop a bottom-up energy-policy framework for the residential sector.

The results indicate that indoor air temperatures in Famagusta, Cyprus, follow a consistent pattern throughout the month of August. Indoor air temperatures in the sample units range from 28.5 to 36.5°C throughout the day and night; this lack of diurnal temperature variation suggests that internal operative air temperatures (OTs) remain relatively high and do not induce cooling at night. Furthermore, the external building fabric, uninsulated roof and three exposed wall surfaces were found to be key determinant factors due to the high *U*-value of the building's properties, the surface area and the amount of solar gain exposure, all of which resulted in high heat transmittance into and out of the upper-floor flats and had a significant effect on the OTs of all the flats.

In the non-retrofitted buildings, 73% of the total energy consumption was for cooling and heating. Six different passive-cooling design strategies were analysed, and after the LCCA of each was considered, off-site modular building applications were developed and implemented. After the buildings were retrofitted, cooling consumption was reduced by approximately 81%; this confirms that considering design, ventilation and servicing strategies and implementing passive shading systems, which was previously recommended by the EPBD objectives, will improve the energy efficiency and indoor air quality of residential buildings. Furthermore, energy models that were calibrated via temperature monitoring resulted in less-extreme energy-performance gaps than model validation that simply replaced the design values with the simulation results.

Insights from this study will enhance the national energy network for Cyprus and improve subsidisation schemes throughout Europe. Moreover, energy policies and regulations will benefit from a conceptual-level analysis of the climate characteristics of each EU member state, as this will allow more accurate planning.

Note

1 It is a cultural tradition for Cypriot grandparents to look after their grandchildren during school holidays while their parents are at work.

References

Arcipowska, A., Cosmina, M., Šijanec Zavrl, M., Rakuščček, A., Stegnar, G. S., Wittchen, K. B., … Popović, M. J. (2016). *Monitor progress towards climate targets in European housing stocks* (p. 36). http://episcope.eu/fileadmin/episcope/public/docs/reports/EPISCOPE_FinalReport.pdf

Ascione, F., Bianco, N., Mauro, G. M., & Vanoli, G. P. (2019). A new comprehensive framework for the multi-objective optimization of building energy design: Harlequin. *Applied Energy*, *241*, 331–361. https://doi.org/10.1016/j.apenergy.2019.03.028

Bamdad, K., Cholette, M. E., & Bell, J. (2020). Building energy optimization using surrogate model and active sampling. *Journal of Building Performance Simulation*, *13*(6), 760–776. https://doi.org/10.1080/19401493.2020.1821094

Bolwig, S., Bolkesjø, T. F., Klitkou, A., Lund, P. D., Bergaentzlé, C., Borch, K., … Skytte, K. (2020). Climate-friendly but socially rejected energy-transition pathways: The integration of techno-economic and socio-technical approaches in the Nordic-Baltic region. *Energy Research and Social Science*, *67*. https://doi.org/10.1016/j.erss.2020.101559

D'Agostino, D., & Parker, D. (2018). A framework for the cost-optimal design of nearly zero energy buildings (NZEBs) in representative climates across Europe. *Energy*, *149*, 814–829. https://doi.org/10.1016/j.energy.2018.02.020

Dascalaki, E. G., Balaras, C. A., Kontoyiannidis, S., & Droutsa, K. G. (2016). Modeling energy refurbishment scenarios for the Hellenic residential building stock towards the 2020 & 2030 targets. *Energy and Buildings*, *132*, 74–90. https://doi.org/10.1016/j.enbuild.2016.06.003

Dell'Anna, F. (2020). Green jobs and energy efficiency as strategies for economic growth and the reduction of environmental impacts. *Energy Policy*. Advance online publication. https://doi.org/10.1016/j.enpol.2020.112031

Galvin, R., & Sunikka-Blank, M. (2014). The UK homeowner-retrofitter as an innovator in a socio-technical system. *Energy Policy*, *74*(C), 655–662. https://doi.org/10.1016/j.enpol.2014.08.013
Gulotta, T. M., Cellura, M., Guarino, F., & Longo, S. (2020). A bottom-up harmonized energy-environmental models for Europe (BOHEEME): A case study on the thermal insulation of the EU-28 building stock. *Energy and Buildings*, *231*. https://doi.org/10.1016/j.enbuild.2020.110584
Gupta, R., & Gregg, M. (2018). Assessing energy use and overheating risk in net zero energy dwellings in UK. *Energy and Buildings*, *158*, 897–905. https://doi.org/10.1016/j.enbuild.2017.10.061
Harputlugil, T., & de Wilde, P. (2021). *The interaction between humans and buildings for energy efficiency: A critical review*. Energy Research and Social Science. Elsevier Ltd. https://doi.org/10.1016/j.erss.2020.101828
Hellwig, R. T., Schweiker, M., & Boerstra, A. (2020). The ambivalence of personal control over indoor climate – How much personal control is adequate? In *E3S web of conferences* (Vol. 172). EDP Sciences. https://doi.org/10.1051/e3sconf/202017206010
Kotireddy, R., Hoes, P. J., & Hensen, J. L. M. (2019). Integrating robustness indicators into multi-objective optimization to find robust optimal low-energy building designs. *Journal of Building Performance Simulation*, *12*(5), 546–565. https://doi.org/10.1080/19401493.2018.1526971
Levi, S. (2021). Why hate carbon taxes? Machine learning evidence on the roles of personal responsibility, trust, revenue recycling, and other factors across 23 European countries. *Energy Research & Social Science*, *73*, 101883. https://doi.org/10.1016/j.erss.2020.101883
Mostavi, E., Asadi, S., & Boussaa, D. (2017). Development of a new methodology to optimize building life cycle cost, environmental impacts, and occupant satisfaction. *Energy*, *121*, 606–615. https://doi.org/10.1016/j.energy.2017.01.049
Nematchoua, M. K., Marie-Reine Nishimwe, A., & Reiter, S. (2021). Towards nearly zero-energy residential neighbourhoods in the European Union: A case study. *Renewable and Sustainable Energy Reviews*, *135*. https://doi.org/10.1016/j.rser.2020.110198
Niskanen, J., & Rohracher, H. (2020). Passive houses as affiliative objects: Investment calculations, energy modelling, and collaboration strategies of Swedish housing companies. *Energy Research and Social Science*, *70*. https://doi.org/10.1016/j.erss.2020.101643
Ozarisoy, B. (2022). Energy effectiveness of passive cooling design strategies to reduce the impact of long-term heatwaves on occupants' thermal comfort in Europe: Climate change and mitigation. *Journal of Cleaner Production*. Advance online publication. https://doi.org/10.1016/j.jclepro.2021.129675
Ozarisoy, B., & Altan, H. (2017a). Energy performance development of non-regulated retrofit mass housing estates in Northern Cyprus. *Design Journal*, *20*(Suppl 1), S1765–S1781. https://doi.org/10.1080/14606925.2017.1352697
Ozarisoy, B., & Altan, H. (2017b). Adoption of energy design strategies for retrofitting mass housing estates in Northern Cyprus. *Sustainability (Switzerland)*, *9*(8), 1477. https://doi.org/10.3390/su9081477
Ozarisoy, B., & Altan, H. (2018). Low-energy design strategies for retrofitting existing residential buildings in Cyprus. *Proceedings of the Institution of Civil Engineers: Engineering Sustainability*, *172*(5), 241–255. https://doi.org/10.1680/jensu.17.00061
Ozarisoy, B., & Elsharkawy, H. (2019). Assessing overheating risk and thermal comfort in state-of-the-art prototype houses that combat exacerbated climate change in UK. *Energy and Buildings*, *187*, 201–217. https://doi.org/10.1016/j.enbuild.2019.01.030

Pasichnyi, O., Wallin, J., & Kordas, O. (2019). Data-driven building archetypes for urban building energy modelling. *Energy*, *181*, 360–377. https://doi.org/10.1016/j.energy.2019.04.197

Rinaldi, A., Schweiker, M., & Iannone, F. (2018). On uses of energy in buildings: Extracting influencing factors of occupant behaviour by means of a questionnaire survey. *Energy and Buildings*, *168*, 298–308. https://doi.org/10.1016/j.enbuild.2018.03.045

Rouleau, J., & Gosselin, L. (2019). Probabilistic window opening model considering occupant behavior diversity: A data-driven case study of Canadian residential buildings. *Energy*, *195*. https://doi.org/10.1016/j.energy.2020.116981

Salvati, A., Palme, M., Chiesa, G., & Kolokotroni, M. (2020). Built form, urban climate and building energy modelling: Case-studies in Rome and Antofagasta. *Journal of Building Performance Simulation*, *13*(2), 209–225. https://doi.org/10.1080/19401493.2019.1707876

Conclusion

A number of significant advances were made in the present study to provide a comprehensive understanding of the thermal performance of archetype residential buildings and occupants' thermal-comfort levels; the findings allow direct comparison, where applicable, against the objectives of this book.

A literature review was undertaken to fill the existing knowledge gap in four key areas: building overheating risks, thermal comfort, occupant behaviour and energy modelling. Occupancy patterns and habitual household adaptive behaviours were already known to be significant determinant factors related to home-energy performance, but occupants' thermal comfort in relation to the development of a socio-technical systems (STS) conceptual framework had not been addressed, and existing available data on the neutral adaptive thermal comfort of social-housing residents were not found in the American Society of Heating, Refrigeration and Air-Conditioning Engineers (ASHRAE) Global Thermal Comfort Database II. It was therefore determined that a quantitative assessment of the thermal performance of the building fabric of representative residential tower blocks (RTBs) in a post-war social-housing estate in the subtropical (*Csa*) and partly semi-arid (*Bsh*) Eastern Mediterranean climate, along with a quantitative assessment of social-housing occupants' thermal-preference votes (TPVs) and thermal-satisfaction votes (TSVs), would provide valuable input for the global database.

Accordingly, the present empirical study introduced selection criteria for housing stock and developed evidence-based retrofitting design interventions by conducting an *on-site* questionnaire survey and recording in situ physical measurements for a variety of building envelopes to assess the overheating-risk assessment of the base-case RTBs. This study utilised an exemplar energy-policy design strategy whereby data was collected through a comprehensive methodology that was then applied to the RTB prototypes; this will contribute to the limited number of published reviews related to retrofitting efforts for high-density residential buildings in Europe. The present study explored the reason the building-energy-performance evaluation method was chosen, utilised a standardised assessment procedure to investigate actual energy use and assessed the study findings against existing international thermal-comfort benchmark criteria.

A comprehensive methodological framework to develop energy-performance certificate (EPC) schemes in Northern Cyprus (NC) was presented in this book. The primary research question (RQ) that was addressed was: What is the most

DOI: 10.4324/9781003393092-9

effective and universally applicable energy-policy framework to implement the EPBD mandates recommended by the EU and improve the energy efficiency of existing housing stock in NC? This research question set out to contribute to the body of knowledge an integration of the human-based approach in modelling; it emphasises the importance of an STS conceptual framework to investigate housing-energy use and CO_2 emission reductions with the aim of improving the overall understanding of the complex issue of occupancy patterns as they relate to energy use. Even though scholars have previously conducted building-energy modelling and *on-site* environmental monitoring to assess the overheating risk of residential buildings, the present study applied these methodologies to fully explore the existing building performance of the case-study RTBs by understanding the in vivo experiences of social-housing residents related to their home-energy performance and occupancy patterns. This is a novel approach for testing the effectiveness of different retrofitted design strategies as part of the development and integration of EPBD mandates in the housing sector.

The following research outcome is structured according to the RQ that guides the findings obtained through the feed-forward interviews, specifically RQ-1. The finding is that household socio-demographic characteristics and home-energy performance factors should be used to develop nationwide energy policies related to household-energy use and residents' thermal comfort.

Feed-forward interviews of the residents of 100 flats revealed that age bands were significantly related to health conditions, and this relationship was strong ($\chi^2 = 73.739$, $p < 0.001$, *Cramer*'s $V = 0.496$). Younger age appeared to report better health conditions (good or very good) than older age. Household occupations were also significantly associated with age with a moderate–strong relationship ($\chi^2 = 44.810$, $p < 0.001$, *Cramer*'s $V = 0.399$). Of the surveyed flats, 73% had owner-occupiers whose ages ranged between 55 and 65 or were 65 and older; these age bands were in the high-income group, and the energy consumption of these households was higher than the national average, all of which demonstrates an association between age and level-of-income factors, which suggests that household socio-demographic characteristics should be evaluated before any type of building retrofitting is developed.

The results of the present study confirm that the design method that has traditionally been implemented by EU countries to develop EPCs would not be effectively applied and integrated into an STS conceptual framework. At the time the energy-policy design presented in this book was developed, there were no EPBD recommendations that considered the thermal comfort of occupants in relation to local climate conditions, specifically in the context of the Eastern Mediterranean climate; as such, occupant behaviour was not considered when implementing energy-efficiency standards. These concerns led to RQ-2: Which occupant energy-consumption behaviours may have an impact on energy performance?

The following research outcome is structured according to the RQs that guided the findings obtained through the feed-forward interviews: in order to outline the dominant representative energy-user profiles for the BES benchmarking, criteria must be developed to fulfil EEG in the residential sector.

The present study revealed that weekday cooling-consumption patterns were significantly and strongly related to weekend heating-consumption patterns (χ^2 = 54.590, p < 0.001, *Cramer*'s V = 0.522). Specifically, longer duration of heating consumption was related to longer duration of cooling consumption. Similar result was also found between weekend cooling-consumption patterns and weekend heating-consumption patterns (χ^2 = 99.687, p < 0.001, *Cramer*'s V = 0.706), between weekday cooling-consumption patterns and weekday heating-consumption patterns (χ^2 = 74.565, p < 0.001, *Cramer*'s V = 0.611) and weekend cooling-consumption patterns and weekday heating-consumption patterns (χ^2 = 50.767, p < 0.001, *Cramer*'s V = 0.504); these findings indicate that the cultural assets of the research context directly influence household behaviour related to home-energy use on weekdays and throughout the weekend. The cultural–behavioural factors of NC residents, who prefer to spend weekends at home with their families, are distinct from typical European households, who seek recreation outside of their homes on the weekend; this is likely the cause of the high weekend energy bills in the archetype buildings.

The study findings revealed that a thorough analysis of the significance of occupancy patterns and habitual household behaviour on home-energy performance was useful background information for the development of evidence-based retrofit design policy. Even more relevant here are the decision-making processes, as these reflect the main knowledge gap both in the literature and practice. Consideration should, where possible, be given to the investigation of energy-efficiency measures (EEMs) and their effects on occupant behaviour. The most obvious finding to emerge from this analysis was that occupants' decisions on how they use domestic cooling appliances have an important effect on the efficiency of their buildings. Nevertheless, no conclusions can be generalised without consideration of occupants' actual behaviour on energy use. This is the reason that further studies should take into account the influence of occupant behaviour and take a broader vision of comfort requirements for optimised energy models and the development of policy mechanisms to improve the energy efficiency of the archetype buildings.

The following research outcome is structured according to the RQs that guided the findings obtained through subject respondents' thermal-sensation votes and the findings of both *on-site* environmental monitoring and in situ physical measurements of households' indoor occupied spaces. These methods were adopted in response to RQ-3: How do environmental factors affect occupants' thermal comfort and how can neutral adaptive thermal-comfort thresholds be identified in this Eastern Mediterranean climate?

Other variants that were considered in the present study included the physical features of the built environment (i.e., site layout plans and different building orientations and floor levels). When the occupants' reasons for thermal comfort were included as a dependent variable, a moderate–strong relationship was found between orientation and reasons for thermal discomfort (χ^2 = 49.327, p < 0.001, *Cramer*'s V = 0.405). Individual levels of thermal comfort were not limited to household socio-demographic characteristics; however, environmental factors were also determinants in the development of adaptive thermal-comfort theory. An ordinal logistic regression was performed, and the result revealed a significant relationship between operative air temperature and households' overall summer temperature satisfaction, $OR = 0.958$ (95% *CI* [0.918, 1.000]), $p = 0.050$, *Nagelkerke* $R^2 = 0.042$; the occupants' TSVs indicated that in a Eastern Mediterranean climate, 28.5°C is considered a neutral temperature, and the upper limit of the indoor air thermal-comfort range is 31.5°C.

According to the ASHRAE Global Thermal Comfort Database II, occupants' thermal acceptability in the Eastern Mediterranean climate ranges from 25 to 30°C on hot summer days; the thermal acceptability of households in multi-family social-housing RTBs was +1.5°C higher than that of the sampling size included in the ASHRAE database. The comparable sample in the database was developed in 2005 by Bouden and Ghrab and represents a small sample population in Tunisia. Notably, there was not a sampling population available in the ASHRAE Global Thermal Comfort Database II that represented the Eastern Mediterranean climate in Europe; due to the limited sampling size, the 28.5–31.5°C neutral adaptive thermal-comfort threshold proposed in the present study could not be effectively compared with Fanger's predicted mean vote method for thermal comfort. This is an important outcome of the methodological framework developed in this study—it contributes to current adaptive thermal-comfort studies. The ASHRAE Global Thermal Comfort Database II is the result of a project led by an international team of experts to collate field measurements of thermal comfort for public use. The output of this research is a valuable contribution to the ASHRAE Global Thermal Comfort Database II. The field study in the Eastern Mediterranean climate of Cyprus is a unique context and a noteworthy addition to this public source.

This is the first study to undertake a longitudinal analysis of a field investigation on the development of the adaptive thermal comfort of households in the Eastern Mediterranean climate. The present study provided an important opportunity to advance the current knowledge of adaptive thermal-comfort theory in the Cypriot context in the following ways: (i) it questioned existing adaptive thermal-comfort models for naturally ventilated residential buildings, (ii) it developed a novel framework that combined an assessment methodology with existing benchmark criteria for thermal comfort and (iii) it demonstrated in vivo experiences of subject respondents' thermal-sensation votes to analyse individual aspects of adaptive thermal comfort and influences on the validity of feed-forward interviews gathered through a questionnaire survey.

The present study makes a major contribution to research on the development of a thermal-comfort assessment benchmark criteria as the present study was used to systematically evaluate the results obtained from the questionnaire survey and environmental monitoring. The primary data demonstrates the actual numeric experimentation of a statistical analysis to identify adaptive thermal-comfort indices for this research context. The methodological framework developed for the present study was novel in that it adopted industry benchmarks from the *Comité Européen de Normalisation* (*CEN*) Standard EN 15251, which is based on adaptive thermal-comfort conventions developed by Bedford in 1946 and Fanger in

1970 and a scientific conceptual framework developed by Nicol and Humphreys in 2002.

The following research outcome is structured according to the RQs that guided the findings through the thermal-imaging survey and building-performance evaluation of representative archetype buildings by developing a universally acceptable energy-policy framework for the Eastern Mediterranean Cypriot climate. Specifically, this outcome addresses RQ-4: 'How will this empirical study contribute to and inform the design of net-zero buildings in EU countries?'

The empirical model that was created for this study addressed the development of an evidence-based STS conceptual framework that could explore the influence of building thermal properties on occupants' thermal comfort; the results revealed relatively warm global temperatures ranging from 24.5 to 37.0°C. According to the CIBSE TM59 Criterion 1, the upper thermal-comfort limit for this region is 33°C, yet the *on-site* monitoring in this study recorded a maximum outdoor temperature of 38.7°C, and the in situ measurements revealed indoor air temperatures that ranged from 25 to 35°C, which is well above the acceptable threshold limits.

The building-performance evaluation studies revealed that there were significant signs of overheating risks, and these indoor air temperatures negatively affected the occupants' physiological thermal adaptation to their environments; elevated temperatures fluctuated with high and low peaks, but always rose above the recommended 25°C upper thermal-comfort threshold. Notably, the highest indoor air temperatures were predicted 14–16 August, and they reached 37.3°C on 28 August; a peak outside temperature of 43.2°C was recorded on 16 August at 14:55 by the weather station that was installed on the site.

Even though the recommended overheating threshold is 28°C, the indoor and outdoor air temperatures followed a pattern of overheating. Peak indoor air temperatures were recorded +5.3°C above the comfort-level zone, and the regression line fluctuated between 25 and 27°C, which is near or above the upper comfort-threshold margin. These fluctuating temperatures could be perceived as acceptable thermal-comfort levels, however, due to the psychological adaptation of the occupants to their local climate. Taken together, these results suggest an association between the *U*-values of building properties and the occupants' thermal comfort. The daily variation ΔT exceeded a 6.2°C increase per hour on several occasions over the simulation period in August, which highlights the importance of considering *on-site* environmental monitoring data when assessing overheating risks and developing neutral adaptive thermal-comfort thresholds.

Owner-occupier residents reported that they felt thermally comfortable in warmer indoor air temperatures than those recommended by international standards such as ISO EN 7730:2005 and EN 15251:2007. Previous scholarly work that focused on the Eastern Mediterranean climate found that occupants felt thermally comfortable within the 19–33°C range; these different threshold limits were because the associated studies were conducted in a climatic chamber with control variables to represent optimal thermal-comfort conditions. However, the empirical model for the present study was based on a case study and application of a longitudinal field survey; as such, the findings of this study represent actual scenarios for the development of accurate neutral adaptive thermal-comfort measures in Cyprus.

The following research outcome is structured according to the RQs that guided the findings of a novel methodological framework for the optimisation of post-war social-housing developments in the Eastern Mediterranean climate. RQ-5: What are the main determinants of energy use in archetype RTBs, and to what extent do retrofitting options have the potential to achieve optimum indoor comfort conditions?

Building-energy simulations were conducted to confirm the validity of the neutral adaptive thermal-comfort thresholds. The results indicated a lack of diurnal temperature variations within the sample flats, which suggests that internal operative temperatures remained relatively high throughout the day and night; indoor air temperatures ranged from 28.5 to 36.5°C, and there was a difference of +5°C between the actual and the simulated-and-predicted operative air temperatures. The 36.5°C upper thermal-comfort threshold identified in the building-energy-simulation analysis was +3.5°C higher than the recommended thermally acceptable threshold for hot Mediterranean climates in the summer.

The present study detailed a model that can be employed to investigate a range of potential retrofitting interventions related to housing-energy consumption and to address issues associated with overheating risks experienced during the summer; as such, the research design and methodology of the present study aims to enhance policymakers' understandings of the complex nature of energy consumption and occupants' thermal comfort. The developed framework provides a scientific background that can be included in the BES platform to serve as a set of guidelines for the EPBD scientific committee for energy-policy design and retrofitting strategies.

The study findings can be extrapolated by current industry benchmarks or assessment criteria as a new European Norm (EN) that can be adopted by other EU countries. The present study is the first to follow the recommended methodology laid out in EN 15251. To date, no other studies have focused on the development of this particular EN 15251 standard; as such, the present study developed an STS conceptual framework to provide a significant contribution to the body of knowledge related to a novel methodological framework for BPEs.

The present study concluded that the proportion of people who wanted a drier indoor air environment was expected to decrease with diminishing sensations of humidity, which indicates that relative humidity is a significant source of thermal discomfort in the summer. According to the Köppen climate classification system, the weather in Cyprus is subtropical (*Csa*) and partly semi-arid (*Bsh*), but the field study findings contradicted these world climate data due to the geological and topographical characteristics of the Eastern Mediterranean peninsula of Cyprus that served as the research context for this study. The local climate characteristics necessitated the use of cooling devices at night to optimise thermal comfort in the summer.

The conclusions of the present study provide evidence that a methodological approach can play a decisive role in the assessment of building-energy performance.

As such, this study predominantly lies within the STS approach, which highlights the importance of utilising an innovative methodology to upgrade the energy efficiency of buildings and implementing effective retrofitting interventions that are influenced by human actions. The energy-consumption reduction measures for social-housing estates developed in the course of this study will further benefit from a conceptual-level analysis and prioritisation in accordance with the climate characteristics of the regional context.

The implications of the present study are two-fold: the knowledge and practices developed throughout the research process will benefit Cyprus and the Cypriot community, including the Republic of Cyprus (RoC), and the capacity-building process will directly benefit the everyday lives of social-housing residents as well as help researchers with limited resources who are engaged in thermal-comfort studies for the Eastern Mediterranean climate to achieve neutral adaptive thermal-comfort benchmark criteria. Moreover, the level of awareness and understanding of EEMs, both in the current construction process and as it relates to demands on the property market, and the impact of energy usage on the environment are all addressed in the present study.

As of the writing of this book, there are no existing energy efficiency, retrofitting and energy-consumption awareness policies in the Eastern Mediterranean region, the study outcomes therefore present a roadmap for improving and enhancing the building performance of existing post-war social-housing development estates and demonstrate how the NC and RoC governments can use these findings to accelerate policymaking decisions. Furthermore, this study contributes to the EU's energy-policy framework, because public agencies and institutions (i.e., non-profit organisations) will be able to use the findings to determine and prioritise the types of dwellings for which greater energy savings can be obtained and invest in effective measures that will provide energy-efficiency awareness information to households through economic viability studies.

Insights from this study will enhance the national energy network for Cyprus and improve subsidisation schemes throughout Europe. Moreover, energy policies and regulations will benefit from a conceptual-level analysis of the climate characteristics of each EU member state, as this will allow for more accurate planning. The application of passive-cooling design strategies from an archetype post-war social-housing estate to the regional scale retrofitting of high-density residential buildings will result in the effective development of EPC schemes for occupants and policymakers alike. In addition to this, the present study attempts to fulfil EEG to contribute to the EU Horizon 2030 framework and retrofitting initiatives among the EU member states that currently implement similar energy policies, most specifically the other southern EU member states that have similar building regulations. The impact of implementing evidence-based retrofitting strategies will be beneficial for society, as these strategies will result in the development of effective and engaged local communities for whom energy-efficiency awareness improvement involves the social, economic and natural ecologies of their contextual sites.

Appendix A: Guidance for the Development Stage of a Statistically Representative Sample Size

Box A.1 Step-by-Step Development of the Study Sample

Introduction

This appendix details the problems with invalid data and how invalid data can be assessed based upon research. This appendix provides a summary of the data preparation stages, as well as explaining the concept of developing a statistically representative sample size.

Stage 1: Checking for Invalid Data

Checking a dataset for invalid cases or values is a critical part of data preparation. Invalid datapoints are observations that reflect inaccurate, inattentive or careless response values. Cases that exhibit these types of responses can seriously bias a study. The appropriate procedure for handling invalid data is typically removal of the data in the invalid case, which often results in a reduction of sample size. This appendix is a tool to help future scholars write an appropriate discussion about case removal in their own methodological framework.

Reasons for Removal of Data

Cases and/or observations are flagged as invalid if they meet any of several criteria:

Duplicate cases: Duplicate cases can occur when respondents take a survey more than once. Avoiding this requires the use of unique identifiers (e.g., participant ID, IP address or email address) in order to isolate whether respondents may have been duplicated in the data. Duplicated cases bias results and should be removed (Johnson, 2005). In the present study, no unique identifier was used.

Participant did not consent: Respondents who did not consent are excluded from the study for ethical reasons. In the present study, no data was excluded on this basis.

Met exclusion criteria: Cases that do not meet the inclusion criteria, outlined in the sampling strategy, need to be excluded in order to meet the objectives of the study. No data was removed based on this criterion.

Dropped out without responding: Cases that may have begun but dropped off with no response on some/all of the items of interest. These cases should not be counted as part of the final sample and should be excluded from the rest of the analysis to avoid any research bias in the interpretation of the results. In the present study, cases with only two responses entered were removed during the dataset preparation stage.

Impossible values: Impossible values refer to values in a variable that lies outside the theoretical range for that particular variable, for example: a case with a negative value for body mass index (BMI) would be impossible. Unless the convention recommends that the researcher go back to the original source (e.g., the questionnaire survey) and confirm the correct value, it is recommended that these values be set as missing values. In the present study, an impossible *In_WET* temperature of 48.50°C was corrected to 25.60°C.

Summary of the Identification of Invalid Data

Table A.1 shows each of the reasons for removal due to duplicate, non-consent, cases that did not meet the inclusion criteria, and cases that dropped off at onset of the questionnaire survey. These categories are considered critical removal reasons. The column titled 'Met Removal Criteria' presents the frequencies and percentages of each individual case removal reason found in the sample population. The frequencies do not reflect the total number of invalid cases that were removed because some cases had more than one

Table A.1 Invalid Data Summary for Critical Removal and Removal with Two or More Removal Reasons

Valid categorisation	*N*	*%*
Critical invalid cases	0	0.0
Potential invalid cases with two or more removal reasons	0	0.0
Valid cases	100	100.0
Total	100	100.0

Note: This table presents the data included into the dataset after the completion of necessary data-mining process.

removal reason (e.g., an observation/case may not have met the inclusion criteria and was a duplicate). In the present study, there were zero duplicate cases and there were zero impossible values.

Box A.2 Step-by-Step Development of the Study Sample. (Continued)

Introduction

This section details the problem of missing data and how it is assessed. In this study, the researcher also prepared a summary of the missing data to avoid any research bias while interpreting the statistical analysis, and here presents a list of options for this process to guide future readers of the study.

Stage 2: Missing Data Report

Missing data can have a profound effect on a study's validity depending on how severe the missing data is within a dataset (Little & Rubin, 2002). Therefore, missing data should not be ignored and best practices should be followed to handle it appropriately. Fortunately, within the last few decades, there have been advances in statistical methodology to properly identify and correct missing data issues. The impact of missing data on an analysis depends on three factors: sample size, the proportion of missing values in the data and the pattern of missing values in the data.

Sample size

Sample size matters in missing data for two reasons: (1) small to moderate samples with missing data are prone to a higher likelihood of biased estimates and larger standard errors, and (2) as sample size increases the standard errors for the estimates decrease, leading to more efficient estimates regardless of the presence of missing data (Cheema, 2014; Dong & Peng, 2013; Little & Rubin, 2002). In other words, the larger the sample size, the less of an effect missing data will have on a study.

Proportion of Missing Data

The percentage of missing data present in the data matrix has implications for researchers in terms of how the missing data must be treated to resolve potential biased estimates in the analysis. Complete case analysis is only reliable when the percentage of incomplete values in the data matrix is less than 5% (Little & Rubin, 2002; Schafer, 1999). Beyond the 5% threshold, the data should be treated in some manner (e.g., multiple imputation or maximum-likelihood replacement).

Pattern of Missing Data

Little and Rubin (2002) suggest that the pattern of missing data is a more important factor than the actual amount of missing data. Missing values that are randomly scattered throughout the data matrix (i.e., data is missing completely at random; MCAR) are a less serious problem than missing values that are not random. If the missing values on a variable are not random but are associated with other variables in the data, this is referred to as missing at random (MAR) and can be alleviated with imputation methods. If the missing values on a variable are associated with the variable itself (i.e., missing not at random; MNAR), this has serious implications for inferences, regardless of imputation procedures (Dong & Peng, 2013). Recently, Schouten et al. (2009) proposed two definitions of representativeness with respect to survey response: strong (given in Definition 1.1) and weak (given in Definition 1.2).

Definition 1.1 (strong). A response subset is representative with respect to the sample if response propensities are the same for all units in the population:

$$\forall_i E(R_i) = \rho_i = P(R_i = 1 \mid I_i = 1) = \rho \qquad (1)$$

The response of a unit is independent of the response of all other units, where the constant variable denotes the response of unit *i* and is an indicator showing whether a unit took part in the survey. Schouten et al. (2009) note that strong representativeness corresponds to the Missing Completely at Random (MCAR) pattern for every target variable *y*. This means that non-response does not cause estimators to be biased. Although this definition is appealing, its validity can never be tested in practice. To solve this problem, a weaker definition of representativeness was introduced by Schouten et al. (2009).

$$\bar{\rho}_h = \frac{1}{N_h}\sum_{i=1}^{N_h} \rho_{ih} = \rho, \textit{for } h = 1, 2, \cdots, H, \qquad (2)$$

Definition 1.2 (weak). A response subset is representative of categorical variable *x* with *H* categories if the average response propensity over the categories is constant, where the constant variable is the population size of independent category *h*, is the response propensity of unit *i* in category *h* and summation is over all units in this category.

Box A.3 Step-by-Step Development of the Study Sample. (Continued)

Summary of the Proportion of Missing Data

An extensive analysis of missing data was conducted for the present study. The results and recommendations are presented below.

The three pie charts below summarise the frequency and percentage of missing data in the dataset by variable, case/observation and individual values. The third pie chart represents the full data matrix and was used to evaluate the 5% threshold of the proportion of missing values in the data matrix that was discussed above.

Figure 1: Overall summary of missing data values.

Note: There is a distinction being drawn between missing data removed for critical reasons and data was not removed. This graph presents the detection of missing data prior to the data-mining process of the dataset before conducting the statistical analysis.

Summary of the Pattern of Missing Data

It was found that the data were missing completely at random (MCAR). After preparing the data for analysis, it was observed that out of 100 recorded cases, 98 cases contained missing data (98.0%) and out of 53 variables, 2 variables contained missing data (2.8%), which amounted to a total of 0.04% missing information in the dataset. To assess whether the pattern of missing values was MCAR, Little's MCAR test (Little, 1988) was conducted. The null hypothesis of Little's MCAR test is that the pattern of the data is MCAR and follows a chi-square distribution. Using an expectation-maximisation algorithm, the MCAR test estimates the univariate means and correlations for each of the variables. The results revealed that the pattern of missing values in the data was MCAR: χ^2 (104) = 121.645, p = 0.114. Even though the proportion of the total missing data is less than 5% and the data is MCAR, the final sample size may still be affected by listwise or pairwise deletion when the analysis is run. Listwise deletion removes a case if a case has any missing value for any of the variables used in an analysis. This is also known as complete case analysis. Pairwise deletion better maximises all the data available in the data analysis and is preferred over listwise deletion for increasing the statistical power of the study (Newman, 2014).

Table A.2 Comparison of Minimum Pairwise and Listwise N for the Final 53 Variables of Interest

Deletion Method	*Minimum N*
Listwise	98
Pairwise	98

Note: Pairwise and listwise *Ns* are the same because the same two participants had the same missing values. The final *N* may be higher upon analysis. This table presents the data at the time of detecting the missingness data in the data-mining process.

Recommendations

The missing values of data allow flexibility when addressing missing data because the proportion of missing data in the sample is less than 5% and the pattern of missing data is MCAR. Based upon these two findings, the data should be fine using either pairwise or listwise deletion methods. Listwise deletion and pairwise deletion are unbiased techniques when data are MCAR; however, pairwise deletion increases power (Newman, 2014). Given the sufficient sample size for the present study, the proportion of missing data and the pattern of missing data, listwise or pairwise deletion, is recommended.

Box A.4 Step-by-Step Development of Study Sample. (Continued)

Stage 3: Basic Assumption Testing Report

Introduction

This section details the importance of basic assumption testing in inferential analyses, as well as how basic assumptions were assessed, the summary of the data preparation process and options for coding data prior to conducting analysis.

Basic Assumptions and Inferential Analyses

Before any inferential analyses are conducted, basic assumptions must be met to avoid bias in a study's findings. The validity of conclusions drawn from a statistical analysis depends on the validity of any assumptions made. Where data is lacking, assumption testing may have to be restricted to simply making a judgement about whether an assumption is reasonable. In addition, scholars may have to judge what effect the violation of an assumption might have on the findings. The effect of violating any of the assumptions is a change in the probability of making a Type I or a Type II error, and the researchers won't usually know whether the change has made it more or less likely to commit an inferential error. Basic assumptions are also accompanied by analysis-specific assumptions. Analysis-specific assumptions are tested during the analysis phase of the project.

How Are Basic Assumptions Tested?

In the present study, the researcher used available descriptive statistics in order to fully understand the data. When it comes to making inferences, both parametric and non-parametric analysis can be applied. Non-parametric analyses are considered when there is reason to worry about parametric assumptions, or when the measurements being considered demand them.

Below are the assumptions tested and the recommended guidelines for how to handle assumption violations. Keep in mind that for some assumptions there are no hard and fast rules on cut-offs. It is up to the researcher to account for them and report any biases that may result from not addressing assumption violations.

Sample Sizes of Comparison Groups

A general rule for sample sizes is that group sizes are approximately equal if *n* of the largest group is no more than about twice *n* of the smallest group. Another general rule for sample sizes is at least 10% of the sample should be in each group. Categorical variables with very uneven splits between categories present problems for several multivariate analyses (Tabachnick & Fidell, 2007). The following variables were recoded to reflect the conceptualisation of statistically representative findings in accordance with the research hypotheses.

Table A.3 Coded Variables during the Data Preparation Stage

Age band	*Cooling-energy consumption in August 2015*	*Floor level*
Cooling consumption on weekdays	Cooling-energy consumption in summer 2015	Health condition
Clothing insulation levels of participants	Heating-energy consumption in winter 2015	Occupation
Type of cooling control in home	Cooling-energy consumption in August 2016	Heating consumption on the weekend
Ethnicity	Cooling-energy consumption in summer 2016	Household density
Thermal preference	Heating-energy consumption in winter 2016	Income
Interviewed room condition	Metabolic rates of participants	Length of residency
Orientation	Reasons for thermal discomfort	Space conditioning
Overall thermal satisfaction in summer	Thermal sensation in Bedrooms 1, 2, 3 and living room	Type of cooling system
Window-closing reasons	Window-opening patterns in winter	Type of heating system

Note: Additionally, all categorical variables were recoded in ordinal sequence where possible (e.g., metabolic rate).
Variables related to occupants' thermal preferences were recoded from very cold to very hot.
All variables were recoded from smallest value to largest value.
All dichotomous variables were recoded to 1 = yes, 0 = no.

Box A.5 Step-by-Step Development of Study Sample. (Continued)

Stage 3: Basic Assumption Testing Report (Continued)

Normality

Virtually all parametric statistics have an assumption that the data comes from a population that follows a known distribution. This assumption of normality is often erroneously applied, however, because many populations are not normally distributed. Therefore, researchers need to understand what their samples consist of. It is standard practice to assume that the sample mean from a random sample is normal because of the central-limit theorem. However, almost all variables have a slight departure from normality. If researchers have a large enough sample, then any statistical test will reject the null hypothesis. In other words, the data will never be normally distributed if the sample size is large enough.

To assess normality, skewness and kurtosis statistics are assessed. Skewness refers to the symmetry of the distribution and kurtosis refers to the peakedness. Variables that have distributions that are very asymmetrical, flat or peaked could bias any test that assumes a normal (i.e., bell-shaped) distribution. Generally, skewness and kurtosis values (converted as z-scores) that fall outside ±4 should be further inspected for potential outlier removal, non-parametric testing or transformation. However, researchers may have flexibility in larger samples (Field, 2013). Some normality tests are done for sample sizes smaller than 100 (i.e., Shapiro–Wilk and Kolmogorov–Smirnov tests). If these tests are significant beyond $p < 0.001$, these variables should be further inspected (Gamst et al., 2008). Graphing methods are also employed for assessing normality. These graphs include histograms, normal quantile–quantile (Q–Q) plots and box plots.

Histograms should look fairly bell-shaped. Q–Q plots should follow a straight line when plotting the expected values against the observed values. Box plots show the overall interquartile range and whether extreme values exist in the variable (see 'Outliers' section). If the data contains outliers, graphic displays both with and without the outliers should be examined to see how the graphs changed. If a continuous variable has serious deviations from normality, it must be addressed through transformation (log, inverse, Box-Cox, etc.), recoding into an ordinal variable or assessment for whether non-parametric analysis needs to be conducted. Regardless, researchers should run analysis both with and without outliers to see whether the pattern of results changes.

Outliers

Univariate and multivariate outliers are also known as extreme values and can significantly bias any parametric test. We have checked our variables for univariate outliers. SPSS identifies these values as being three times the interquartile range beyond the 25th and 75th percentile values. In the present study, multivariate outliers were tested before the primary analyses were conducted where appropriate.

Summary of Basic Assumptions—Normality

All continuous variables were constructed horizontally in the dataset with the following information: statistics summary table, histogram, normal Q–Q plot, box plot and relevant notes about outliers (if applicable). The statistics summary, histogram, Q–Q plot and box plots were reviewed together to determine if variables were significantly skewed, flat or peaked. A variable that violates normality will present as being non-normal across most, if not all, of the graphs and summary information.

In this appendix, the representative findings titled 'Test of Normality' can be found: this displays the results from the Kolmogorov–Smirnov and Shapiro–Wilk tests. If the sample size is smaller than 100, we highlight the variables that violated one or both of these tests. If the sample size is larger than 100, this tab can be reviewed, but reviewing these tests is not necessary. Note that if data contains variables with outliers then the 'outliers removed' variables were tested as well. Skewness, time-of-day/kurtosis issues, indoor DEW and data-mining methods were used to resolve the issues detected in these variables before undertaking the relevant statistical analyses.

There are three remedies for violations of normality: mathematical transformation, categorisation and non-parametric testing. Because the eventual analysis will be a fairly simple bivariate test, in the present study we are recommending non-parametric testing as an alternative.

Appendix B: Descriptive Analysis

Information on the Convention Applied to Designing the Concept of the Thermal-Comfort Assessment

In this study, a dataset related to occupants' thermal-sensation votes (TSVs) was designed in accordance with the thermal-comfort assessment convention recommended by Wang et al. (2018). In accordance with Wang et al. (2018), the thermal-sensation scale was set out in two conceptual assessment criteria in order to undertake the statistical analysis accurately.

First, Wang et al. (2018) recommend a seven-point discrete thermal-sensation scale that can be applied to assess occupants' TSVs. In this case, the TSV is set as an ordinal variable, thus enabling researchers to undertake *Cramer*'s *V* test for the statistical analysis and apply the statistical findings whenever it is appropriate at the time of developing an evidence-based energy-policy design. In the present study, the dataset was coded as follows: 0 = −3, 1 = −2, 2 = −1, 3 = 0, 4 = +1, 5 =+2, 6 = +3. Notably, the [−3, +3] scale band represents the outcome of occupants' thermal sensation as an ordinal measure used to accurately conduct the *Cramer*'s *V* test. This type of coding was applied to determine households' TSVs gathered through a questionnaire survey. In the questionnaire survey, questions related to households' thermal sensation were ranked on seven-point Likert scale that could be used as an ordinal measure. In this dataset, to provide consistency of the interpretation of households' TSVs [0 to 6], a coding range representation of thermal-sensation scale band at [−3, +3] was used, which was developed by Fanger in the 1970s and was commonly used by thermal-comfort scholars between 1990 and 2000.

Second, Wang et al. (2018) recommend a seven-point continuous thermal-sensation scale that can be applied to assess occupants' TSVs. With the TSV set as a continuous variable, researchers are able to undertake Pearson's correlation analysis. This method of design is commonly applied by thermal-comfort researchers to identify 'neutral' adaptive thermal-comfort thresholds. Using occupants' TSVs as continuous variables is the most well-known method for reporting field-survey findings concurrently with in situ measurements or *on-site* environmental monitoring findings. This is an essential method of design that was developed by a team of experts at the University of California at Berkeley to contribute to the ASHRAE Global Thermal Comfort Database II. Further to this ongoing method of analysis in thermal-comfort studies, in the present study, the dataset was coded as follows: −3 = Cold, −2

= Cool, −1 = Slightly cool, 0 = Comfortable, +1 = Slightly warm, +2 = Warm, +3 = Hot. Notably, the [−3, +3] scale band enables thermal-comfort researchers to identify ‘neutral’ adaptive thermal-comfort thresholds for benchmarking. In this dataset, to provide consistency in the interpretation of households’ TSVs, the [−3, +3] coding range represents the [Cold to Hot] thermal-sensation scale, which was recommended by Fanger in the 1970s and further developed by de Dear in 1998 and 2001.

Table B.1 Descriptive Analysis of the Variables Related to Identification of 'Neutral' Adaptive Thermal-Comfort Thresholds for Benchmarking

Variable Name	*Mean*	*Median*	*Mode*	*Std. Deviation*	*Minimum*	*Maximum*	*Percentiles* 25	50	75
Overall thermal satisfaction in summer [0 to 6]—Discrete	1.64	2.00	3	1.453	−2	3	1.00	2.00	3.00
Overall thermal satisfaction in summer [−3, +3]—Continuous	1.68	2.00	3.00	1.36241	−1.00	3.00	1.00	2.00	3.00
Thermal sensation in Bedroom 1 [0 to 6]—Discrete	0.52	1.00	1	1.396	−3	3	0.00	1.00	2.00
Thermal sensation in Bedroom 2 [0 to 6]—Discrete	0.46	1.00	1	1.290	−3	3	0.00	1.00	1.00
Thermal sensation in Bedroom 3 [0 to 6]—Discrete	0.55	1.00	1	1.234	−2	3	0.00	1.00	1.00
Thermal sensation in kitchen [0 to 6]—Discrete	−0.35	−1.00	−2[a]	1.533	−2	3	−2.00	−1.00	1.00
Thermal sensation in living room [0 to 6]—Discrete	0.20	0.00	−1	1.595	−2	3	−1.00	0.00	1.75
Thermal sensation in Bedroom 1 [−3, +3]—Continuous	0.51	1.00	1.00	1.30651	−2.00	2.00	0.00	1.00	2.00
Thermal sensation in Bedroom 2 [−3, +3]—Continuous	0.45	1.00	1.00	1.23399	−2.00	2.00	0.00	1.00	1.00
Thermal sensation in Bedroom 3 [−3, +3]—Continuous	0.53	1.00	1.00	1.20147	−2.00	2.00	0.00	1.00	1.00
Thermal sensation in kitchen [−3, +3]—Continuous	−0.42	−1.00	−2.00[a]	1.39393	−2.00	2.00	−2.00	−1.00	1.00
Thermal preference	1.50	1.00	1.00	1.07778	0.00	3.00	1.00	1.00	3.00

[a]*Multiple mode exists. The smallest value is shown.*

All these variables had scales with smaller scores indicating colder whereas larger scores indicating warmer.

Table B.2 Descriptive Analysis of the Variables Related to Households' Socio-demographic Characteristics

Variable Name	*Mean*	*Median*	*Mode*	*Std. Deviation*	*Minimum*	*Maximum*	*Percentiles*		
							25th	*50th*	*75th*
Age	51.37	53.50	60.00	13.92524	23.00	84.00	42.00	53.50	60.00
Energy-efficiency awareness	1.81	2.00	2	0.961	0	3	1.00	2.00	2.00
Health condition	2.68	3.00	3.00	0.93073	1.00	4.00	2.00	3.00	3.00
Metabolic rates of participants (*met*)	4.10	4.00	2.00	1.87757	1.00	7.00	2.00	4.00	6.00
Household density	1.88	2.00	3.00	0.99778	0.00	4.00	1.00	2.00	3.00

[a]*Multiple mode exists. The smallest value is shown.*

Table B.3 Descriptive Analysis of the Variables Related to Households' Habitual Adaptive Behaviour on Home-Energy Use

Variable Name	*Mean*	*Median*	*Mode*	*Std. Deviation*	*Minimum*	*Maximum*	*Percentiles*		
							25th	*50th*	*75th*
Cooling-consumption patterns on weekdays	1.20	1.00	2.00	0.76541	0.00	2.00	1.00	1.00	2.00
Cooling-consumption patterns on the weekend	1.58	2.00	2.00	1.04621	0.00	3.00	1.00	2.00	2.00
Cooling-energy consumption in summer of August 2015	1.25	1.00	1.00	1.02863	0.00	3.00	0.00	1.00	2.00
Cooling-energy consumption in summer of 2015	2.33	2.00	3.00	1.28751	0.00	5.00	2.00	2.00	3.00
Cooling-energy consumption in summer of August 2016	1.33	1.00	1.00	1.02548	0.00	3.00	1.00	1.00	2.00
Cooling-energy consumption in summer of 2016	1.79	2.00	1.00	1.28153	0.00	4.00	1.00	2.00	3.00
Heating-consumption patterns on weekdays	0.80	1.00	1.00	0.69531	0.00	2.00	0.00	1.00	1.00
Heating-consumption patterns on the weekend	0.96	1.00	1.00	0.77746	0.00	2.00	0.00	1.00	2.00
Heating-energy consumption in winter of 2015	3.00	4.00	4.00	1.47710	1.00	4.00	1.00	4.00	4.00
Heating-energy consumption in winter of 2016	3.00	4.00	4.00	1.47710	1.00	4.00	1.00	4.00	4.00

[a] *Multiple mode exists. The smallest value is shown.*

Table B.4 Descriptive Analysis of the Variables Related to Both *On-site* Monitored and In Situ Recorded Environmental Parameters

Variable Name	*Mean*	*Median*	*Mode*	*Std. Deviation*	*Minimum*	*Maximum*	*Percentiles*		
							25th	*50th*	*75th*
Indoor DEW (°C)	21.48	21.90	20.20[a]	3.36021	11.40	32.40	20.20	21.90	23.40
Indoor relative humidity (%)	57.83	59.95	56.10	8.75611	31.10	75.00	52.15	59.95	63.27
Operative air temperature (°C)	30.59	31.10	31.50	1.76860	25.40	34.10	29.52	31.10	31.80
Solar radiation (°C)	33.64	32.90	32.90	2.35445	29.10	39.80	32.10	32.90	34.80
Indoor WET (°C)	24.12	24.60	18.70[a]	2.18689	18.70	31.00	23.00	24.60	25.57
Indoor wet bulb ground temperature (°C)	26.12	26.60	26.80	2.03956	21.00	30.70	25.02	26.60	27.40
Outdoor heat-stress index (°C)	36.70	36.00	36.00	2.33766	33.00	43.00	35.00	36.00	38.00
Outdoor relative humidity (%)	59.16	59.00	57.00[a]	11.76264	19.60	78.00	54.00	59.00	67.00
Outdoor air temperature (°C)	32.11	32.00	34.00	2.17015	23.70	36.00	30.25	32.00	34.00
Outdoor DEW (°C)	22.82	23.00	23.00	2.21538	13.00	26.00	22.00	23.00	24.00
Indoor temperature ground (°C)	31.23	31.35	31.80	3.42791	24.70	60.20	29.80	31.35	32.20

[a] *Multiple mode exists. The smallest value is shown.*

Appendix C: Type of Measures for Each Variable

Table C.1 List of the Type of Measures for Each Variable

Variable Name	*Measures*
Residential tower block (RTB) number	Nominal
Age	Scale
Age bands	Ordinal
Energy-efficiency awareness	Ordinal
Energy conservation	Nominal
Location of subject respondent	Nominal
Thermal preference	Nominal
Door-opening patterns in summer	Nominal
Door-opening patterns in winter	Nominal
Overall thermal satisfaction in summer (Discrete thermal sensation scale)	Ordinal
Overall thermal satisfaction in summer (Continuous thermal sensation scale)	Scale
Thermal sensation in Bedroom 1 (Discrete thermal sensation scale)	Ordinal
Thermal sensation in Bedroom 2 (Discrete thermal sensation scale)	Ordinal
Type of heating control at home	Nominal
Thermal sensation in Bedroom 3 (Discrete thermal sensation scale)	Ordinal
Thermal sensation in kitchen (Discrete thermal sensation scale)	Ordinal
Thermal sensation in living room (Discrete thermal sensation scale)	Ordinal
Thermal sensation in living room (Continuous thermal sensation scale)	Scale
Thermal sensation in Bedroom 1 (Continuous thermal sensation scale)	Scale
Thermal sensation in Bedroom 2 (Continuous thermal sensation scale)	Scale
Thermal sensation in Bedroom 3 (Continuous thermal sensation scale)	Scale
Thermal sensation in kitchen (Continuous thermal sensation scale)	Scale
Type of cooling control at home	Nominal
Clothing insulation level of participants	Nominal
Reasons for thermal discomfort	Nominal
Length of residency	Nominal
Floor level	Nominal
Ethnicity	Nominal
Orientation	Nominal
Interviewed room condition	Nominal
Cooling-consumption patterns on weekdays	Ordinal
Cooling-consumption patterns on the weekend	Ordinal
Cooling-energy consumption in summer of August 2015	Ordinal
Cooling-energy consumption in summer of 2015	Ordinal
Cooling-energy consumption in summer of August 2016	Ordinal
Cooling-energy consumption in summer of 2016	Ordinal

Table C.2 List of the Type of Measures for Each Variable. (Continued)

Variable Name	*Measures*
Energy consumption in April 2015	Scale
Energy consumption in August 2015	Scale
Energy consumption in December 2015	Scale
Energy consumption in February 2015	Scale
Energy consumption in January 2015	Scale
Energy consumption in July 2015	Scale
Energy consumption in June 2015	Scale
Energy consumption in March 2015	Scale
Energy consumption in May 2015	Scale
Energy consumption in November 2015	Scale
Energy consumption in October 2015	Scale
Energy consumption in September 2015	Scale
Energy consumption in April 2016	Scale
Energy consumption in August 2016	Scale
Energy consumption in December 2016	Scale
Energy consumption in February 2016	Scale
Energy consumption in January 2016	Scale
Energy consumption in July 2016	Scale
Energy consumption in June 2016	Scale
Energy consumption in March 2016	Scale
Energy consumption in May 2016	Scale
Energy consumption in November 2016	Scale
Energy consumption in October 2016	Scale
Energy consumption in September 2016	Scale
Energy consumption in January 2017	Scale
Indoor temperature ground (°C)	Scale
Overall cooling-energy consumption in summer of 2015	Scale
Overall heating-energy consumption in winter of 2015	Scale
Overall cooling-energy consumption in summer of 2016	Scale
Overall heating-energy consumption in winter of 2016	Scale

Appendix D: Contingency Tables

Information on the Presentation of Contingency Tables

In this study, while correlations are indicative of association, there is scope with the data to perform hypothesis testing of significant differences between variables that would add weight to the results. To provide a clear representation of the study findings and report research outcomes in accordance with the research questions, which were set out to develop a novel methodological framework for the universal applicability of the Energy Performance of Buildings Directives (EPBD) in the residential sector, the relevant concepts of statistical convention were presented as follows: (i) The Concept of Statistical Representativeness, (ii) References to the Works of Other Scholars on Representativeness and (iii) Sample Size Calculation Criteria.

This appendix presents the contingency tables that support the findings of the statistical analysis presented. These findings are presented in the appendix to provide guidance on the applied statistical method in order to comply with the convention of supporting research outcomes. It should be noted that Chapter 5 presents the identification of a 'neutral' adaptive thermal comfort threshold by conducting statistical analysis with in situ measurements, *on-site* environmental monitoring and a thermal comfort assessment questionnaire survey to develop benchmarking criteria for the Eastern Mediterranean climate of Cyprus. These contingency tables are presented in the appendix because, according to the conventions of thermal comfort studies, representation of households' thermal sensation by using descriptive statistics, frequencies, *Cramer*'s *V* test, Pearson's correlations and further ordinal logistic regression analysis methods could provide a valid background for the development of reliable thermal comfort thresholds. In Chapter 5, the convention of the thermal comfort assessment method was applied in accordance with the concept of a statistically representative sampling size, which was achieved by undertaking a longitudinal field survey. This field study enables researchers to present households' in vivo experiences on thermal satisfaction.

It must be stressed that the contingency tables were also produced at the time of conducting *Cramer*'s *V* test to understand households' socio-demographic characteristics and their habitual adaptive behaviour on energy use. The relevant *Cramer*'s *V* tests are presented, but, in order to avoid lengthy documentation, only the *Cramer*'s *V* tests of the contingency tables are presented. In this appendix, the researcher decided to demonstrate the below-listed contingency tables because they are noteworthy contributions to the building and environment field where researchers could apply and adopt the statistical conventions presented in Chapter 4. At the same time, in Chapter 2, scholars in the literature review recommend that reliable representativeness of sampling size within the variables identified to develop the concept of statistical convention plays an important role at the time of developing an evidence-based energy-policy design. This is the reason that contingency tables for thermal comfort studies are not the primary factor used for identifying 'neutral' adaptive thermal comfort thresholds, but the contingency tables are still presented. In this present study, Chapter 5 aims to demonstrate the longitudinal field-survey findings with occupants' TSVs and, because of this, contingency tables are not presented in Chapter 4 but instead in the appendix to provide useful guidance for future scholars.

These are the contingency tables that support the statistical analysis in Table 5.3(b) in Chapter 5. In this statistical analysis, occupants' TSVs were identified as ordinal variables to conduct the *Cramer*'s *V* test accurately. In the contingency tables presented in this appendix, it can be seen that household thermal sensation is represented by the terminology of 'thermal feeling' indicators to provide a clear understanding to readers about household thermal sensation. It must be stressed that, in the dataset, the TSV code was set to [0 to 6] which represents the [−3, +3] thermal sensation band according to thermal comfort convention. Hence, the researcher decided to report the findings by using the terminology of each thermal feeling at the time of undertaking the statistical analysis for the contingency tables.

Table D.1 Relationships between Occupation, Age Bands, Economic Status and Education

Occupation	*Work Outside the Home*		*Work at Home*		*Household Activities*		*Retired*				
	n	*%*	*n*	*%*	*n*	*%*	*n*	*%*	*Fisher's Exact*	*p*	*Cramer's V*
Age bands									44.81	<0.001	0.399
Less than 35	10	23.8[a]	2	15.4[a]	0	0.0[a]	0	0.0[a]			
35–45	10	23.8[a]	2	15.4[a]	4	23.5[a]	0	0.0[a]			
45–55	11	26.2[a]	4	30.8[a]	3	17.6[a]	2	9.1[a]			
55–65	9	21.4[a]	4	30.8[a]	9	52.9[a]	8	36.4[a]			
65 or over	2	4.8[a]	1	7.7[a]	1	5.9[a]	12	54.5[b]			
Economic status									8.69	0.743	0.171
Full time	18	42.9[a]	4	30.8[a]	7	41.2[a]	6	27.3[a]			
Part time	6	14.3[a]	2	15.4[a]	2	11.8[a]	2	9.1[a]			
Self employed	3	7.1[a]	2	15.4[a]	4	23.5[a]	6	27.3[a]			
Unemployed	5	11.9[a]	1	7.7[a]	2	11.8[a]	4	18.2[a]			
Pensioner	10	23.8[a]	4	30.8[a]	2	11.8[a]	4	18.2[a]			
Education									7.49	0.591	0.162
Elementary school	9	24.3[a]	2	16.7[a]	0	0.0[a]	4	18.2[a]			
Secondary school	12	32.4[a]	4	33.3[a]	6	35.3[a]	8	36.4[a]			
High school	13	35.1[a]	5	41.7[a]	7	41.2[a]	7	31.8[a]			
Undergraduate/Postgraduate	3	8.1[a]	1	8.3[a]	4	23.5[a]	3	13.6[a]			

Note: For each row category, pairs of column proportions with different superscripts differed significantly, $p < 0.05$.

Table D.2 Relationships between Household Age Bands, Tenure Type and Length of Residency

Education	*Elementary School*		*Secondary School*		*High School*		*Undergraduate/ Postgraduate*		*Fisher's Exact*	*p*	*Cramer's V*
	n	*%*	*n*	*%*	*n*	*%*	*n*	*%*			
Age bands									4.08	0.991	0.114
Less than 35	1	6.3 ^{a}	5	15.6 ^{a}	6	17.6 ^{a}	2	16.7 ^{a}			
35–45	2	12.5 ^{a}	5	15.6 ^{a}	6	17.6 ^{a}	3	25.0 ^{a}			
45–55	4	25.0 ^{a}	6	18.8 ^{a}	4	11.8 ^{a}	2	16.7 ^{a}			
55–65	6	37.5 ^{a}	10	31.3 ^{a}	12	35.3 ^{a}	4	33.3 ^{a}			
65 or over	3	18.8 ^{a}	6	18.8 ^{a}	6	17.6 ^{a}	1	8.3 ^{a}			
Economic status									48.81	<0.001	0.416
Full time	2	12.5 ^{a}	7	21.9 ^{a}	23	67.6 ^{b}	5	41.7 $^{a, b}$			
Part time	4	25.0 ^{a}	7	21.9 ^{a}	1	2.9 ^{a}	0	0.0 ^{a}			
Self employed	0	0.0 ^{a}	4	12.5 ^{a}	9	26.5 ^{a}	3	25.0 ^{a}			
Unemployed	3	18.8 $^{a, b}$	5	15.6 $^{a, b}$	0	0.0 ^{b}	4	33.3 ^{a}			
Pensioner	7	43.8 ^{a}	9	28.1 $^{a, b}$	1	2.9 ^{c}	0	0.0 $^{b, c}$			

Note: For each row category, pairs of column proportions with different superscripts differed significantly, $p < 0.05$.ss

Table D.3 Relationships between Household Income, Energy Advice and Energy Savings

Income	*Less than 2,500 TL*		*2,500–5,000 TL*		*5,000–7,000 TL*		*More than 7,000 TL*				
	n	*%*	*n*	*%*	*n*	*%*	*n*	*%*	*Fisher's Exact*	*p*	*Cramer's V*
Energy advice									11.55	0.194	0.199
Famagusta Municipality	2	8.7 [a]	3	11.5 [a]	5	17.9 [a]	2	8.7 [a]			
The Electricity Authority	1	4.3 [a]	6	23.1 [a]	1	3.6 [a]	7	30.4 [a]			
None	18	78.3 [a]	16	61.5 [a]	20	71.4 [a]	13	56.5 [a]			
Other	2	8.7 [a]	1	3.8 [a]	2	7.1 [a]	1	4.3 [a]			
Energy savings									16.24	0.049	0.233
Nothing	4	17.4 [a, b]	8	30.8 [b]	1	3.6 [a]	2	8.7 [a, b]			
A little	3	13.0 [a]	5	19.2 [a]	4	14.3 [a]	0	0.0 [a]			
Some	9	39.1 [a]	9	34.6 [a]	17	60.7 [a]	15	65.2 [a]			
A lot	7	30.4 [a]	4	15.4 [a]	6	21.4 [a]	6	26.1 [a]			

Note: For each row category, pairs of column proportions with different superscripts differed significantly, $p < 0.05$.

Table D.4 Relationships between Household Occupation and Cooling- and Heating Energy-Consumption Patterns

Heating-Consumption Patterns on the Weekend	*0–4 h*		*5–9 h*		*More than 10 h*				
	n	*%*	*n*	*%*	*n*	*%*	*Fisher's Exact*	*p*	*Cramer's V*
Occupation							2.41	0.896	0.109
Work outside the home	14	46.7 [a]	18	46.2 [a]	10	40.0 [a]			
Work at home	3	10.0 [a]	6	15.4 [a]	4	16.0 [a]			
Household activities	4	13.3 [a]	8	20.5 [a]	5	20.0 [a]			
Retired	9	30.0 [a]	7	17.9 [a]	6	24.0 [a]			
Cooling-consumption patterns on weekdays							54.59*	<0.001	0.522
0–4 h	19	59.4 [a]	1	2.5 [b]	1	3.6 [b]			
5–9 h	8	25.0 [a]	24	60.0 [b]	6	21.4 [a]			
More than 10 h	5	15.6 [a]	15	37.5 [a]	21	75.0 [b]			
Cooling-consumption patterns on the weekend							99.69*	<0.001	0.706
0–4 h	19	59.4 [a]	1	2.5 [b]	0	0.0 [b]			
5–9 h	9	28.1 [a]	15	37.5 [a]	0	0.0 [b]			
10–12 h	4	12.5 [a]	22	55.0 [b]	8	28.6 [a,b]			
More than 12 h	0	0.0 [a]	2	5.0 [a]	20	71.4 [b]			
Heating-consumption patterns on weekdays							27.89*	<0.001	0.373
0–4 h	21	65.6 [a]	13	32.5 [b]	2	7.1 [c]			
5–9 h	9	28.1 [a]	23	57.5 [b]	16	57.1 [a,b]			
More than 10 h	2	6.3 [a]	4	10.0 [a]	10	35.7 [b]			

Note: For each row category, pairs of column proportions with different superscripts differed significantly, $p < 0.05$. * indicates the chi-square test.

Table D.5 Relationships between Household Occupation, Window-Opening Patterns in the Winter, Window-Opening Patterns in the Summer and Heating Control

Heating-Consumption Patterns on the Weekdays	*0–4 h*		*5–9 h*		*More than 10 h*				
	n	*%*	*ssn*	*%*	*n*	*%*	*Fisher's Exact*	*p*	*Cramer's V*
Occupation							12.49	0.042	0.253
Work outside the home	15	42.9 [a]	23	52.3 [a]	4	26.7 [a]			
Work at home	4	11.4 [a]	7	15.9 [a]	2	13.3 [a]			
Household activities	9	25.7 [a]	2	4.5 [b]	6	40.0 [a]			
Retired	7	20.0 [a]	12	27.3 [a]	3	20.0 [a]			
Cooling-consumption patterns on weekdays							74.57*	<0.001	0.611
0–4 h	21	58.3 [a]	0	0.0 [b]	0	0.0 [b]			
5–9 h	15	41.7 [a]	23	47.9 [a]	0	0.0 [b]			
More than 10 h	0	0.0 [a]	25	52.1 [b]	16	100.0 [c]			
Cooling-consumption patterns on the weekend							49.70	<0.001	0.504
0–4 h	20	55.6 [a]	0	0.0 [b]	0	0.0 [b]			
5–9 h	6	16.7 [a]	15	31.3 [a]	3	18.8 [a]			
10–12 h	8	22.2 [a]	21	43.8 [a]	5	31.3 [a]			
More than 12 h	2	5.6 [a]	12	25.0 [a, b]	8	50.0 [b]			

Note: For each row category, pairs of column proportions with different superscripts differed significantly, * $p < 0.05$.

Table D.6 Relationships between Reasons for Thermal Discomfort and Household Age Band, RTB Orientation and Floor Level—Floor Level Variable

Floor	*Ground*		*First*		*Second*		*Third–Fourth*				
	n	*%*	*n*	*%*	*n*	*%*	*n*	*%*	*Fisher's Exact*	*p*	*Cramer's V*
Age bands									12.72	0.380	0.211
Less than 35	1	5.6 [a]	3	10.7 [a]	4	21.1 [a]	8	22.9 [a]			
35–45	2	11.1 [a]	3	10.7 [a]	5	26.3 [a]	6	17.1 [a]			
45–55	2	11.1 [a]	7	25.0 [a]	3	15.8 [a]	8	22.9 [a]			
55–65	10	55.6 [a]	9	32.1 [a]	3	15.8 [a]	10	28.6 [a]			
65 or over	3	16.7	6	21.4	4	21.1	3	8.6			
Orientation									12.11	0.188	0.197
South	6	33.3 [a]	9	32.1 [a]	7	36.8 [a]	14	40.0 [a]			
North East or North West	3	16.7 [a]	13	46.4 [a]	7	36.8 [a]	12	34.3 [a]			
South West	6	33.3 [a]	2	7.1 [a]	2	10.5 [a]	8	22.9 [a]			
South East	3	16.7 [a]	4	14.3 [a]	3	15.8 [a]	1	2.9 [a]			
Reasons for thermal discomfort									17.16	0.037	0.233
Humidity related	10	55.6 [a]	11	39.3 [a, b]	7	36.8 [a, b]	4	11.4 [b]			
Incoming sun	4	22.2 [a]	3	10.7 [a]	4	21.1 [a]	8	22.9 [a]			
Other reasons	2	11.1 [a]	4	14.3 [a]	1	5.3 [a]	8	22.9 [a]			
Heat	2	11.1 [a]	10	35.7 [a]	7	36.8 [a]	15	42.9 [a]			

Note: For each row category, pairs of column proportions with different superscripts differed significantly, [a] $p < 0.05$.

Table D.7 Relationships between Reasons for Thermal Discomfort and Household Age Band, RTB Orientation and Floor Level—Orientation Variable

Orientation	*South*		*North East or North West*		*South West*		*South East*				
	n	*%*	*n*	*%*	*n*	*%*	*n*	*%*	*Fisher's Exact*	*p*	*Cramer's V*
Age bands									15.84	0.165	0.229
Less than 35	6	16.7 [a]	9	25.7 [a]	0	0.0 [a]	1	9.1 [a]			
35–45	8	22.2 [a]	4	11.4 [a]	2	11.1 [a]	2	18.2 [a]			
45–55	9	25.0 [a]	4	11.4 [a]	4	22.2 [a]	3	27.3 [a]			
55–65	6	16.7 [a]	12	34.3 [a, b]	10	55.6 [b]	4	36.4 [a, b]			
65 or over	7	19.4 [a]	6	17.1 [a]	2	11.1 [a]	1	9.1 [a]			
Reasons for thermal discomfort									39.52	<0.001	0.405
Humidity related	15	41.7 [a]	13	37.1 [a, b]	1	5.6 [b]	3	27.3 [a, b]			
Incoming sun	2	5.6 [a]	4	11.4 [a]	13	72.2 [b]	0	0.0 [a]			
Other reasons	3	8.3 [a]	9	25.7 [a]	0	0.0 [a]	3	27.3 [a]			
Heat	16	44.4 [a]	9	25.7 [a]	4	22.2 [a]	5	45.5 [a]			

Note: For each row category, pairs of column proportions with different superscripts differed significantly, * $p < 0.05$.

Table D.8 Relationships between Reasons for Thermal Discomfort and Household Age Band, RTB Orientation and Floor Level—Age Band Variable

Age bands	*Less than 35*		*35–45*		*45–55*		*55–65*		*55–65*				
	n	*%*	*n*	*%*	*n*	*%*	*n*	*%*	*n*	*%*	*Fisher's Exact*	*p*	*Cramer's V*
Reasons for thermal discomfort											11.53	0.479	0.203
Humidity related	6	37.5 [a]	4	25.0 [a]	5	25.0 [a]	9	28.1 [a]	8	50.0 [a]			
Incoming sun	1	6.3 [a]	1	6.3 [a]	5	25.0 [a]	10	31.3 [a]	2	12.5 [a]			
Other reasons	4	25.0 [a]	3	18.8 [a]	2	10.0 [a]	4	12.5 [a]	2	12.5 [a]			
Heat	5	31.3 [a]	8	50.0 [a]	8	40.0 [a]	9	28.1 [a]	4	25.0 [a]			

Note: For each row category, pairs of column proportions with different superscripts differed significantly, * $p < 0.05$.

Table D.9 Relationships between Occupants' TSVs for Each Occupied Space in the Summer: Living room, Kitchen, Bedroom 1, Bedroom 2, Bedroom 3, RTB Orientation and Floor Level—RTB Orientation

Orientation	*South*		*North East or North West*		*South West*		*South East*				
	n	*%*	*n*	*%*	*n*	*%*	*n*	*%*	*Fisher's Exact*	*p*	*Cramer's V*
Thermal sensation in living room									15.40	0.379	0.226
Cool	6	16.7 [a]	4	11.4 [a]	6	33.3 [a]	2	18.2 [a]			
Slightly cool	8	22.2 [a]	5	14.3 [a]	8	44.4 [a]	2	18.2 [a]			
Comfortable	5	13.9 [a]	5	14.3 [a]	1	5.6 [a]	2	18.2 [a]			
Slightly warm	8	22.2 [a]	9	25.7 [a]	2	11.1 [a]	2	18.2 [a]			
Warm	7	19.4 [a]	8	22.9 [a]	0	0.0 [a]	2	18.2 [a]			
Hot	2	5.6 [a]	4	11.4 [a]	1	5.6 [a]	1	9.1 [a]			
Thermal sensation in kitchen									19.72	0.118	0.279
Cool	11	30.6 [a, b]	5	14.3 [b]	10	55.6 [a]	2	18.2 [a, b]			
Slightly cool	12	33.3 [a]	9	25.7 [a]	4	22.2 [a]	3	27.3 [a]			
Comfortable	7	19.4 [a]	7	20.0 [a]	1	5.6 [a]	1	9.1 [a]			
Slightly warm	4	11.1 [a]	5	14.3 [a]	2	11.1 [a]	3	27.3 [a]			
Warm	1	2.8 [a]	3	8.6 [a]	1	5.6 [a]	2	18.2 [a]			
Hot	1	2.8 [a]	6	17.1 [a]	0	0.0 [a]	0	0.0 [a]			

Note: For each row category, pairs of column proportions with different superscripts differed significantly, * $p < 0.05$.

Table D.10 Relationships between Occupants' TSVs for Each Occupied Space in the Summer: Living room, Kitchen, Bedroom 1, Bedroom 2, Bedroom 3, RTB Orientation and Floor Level—RTB Orientation (Continued)

Orientation	*South*		*North East or North West*		*South West*		*South East*				
	n	*%*	*n*	*%*	*n*	*%*	*n*	*%*	*Fisher's Exact*	*p*	*Cramer's V*
Thermal sensation in Bedroom 1									20.81	0.176	0.274
Cold	2	5.6 ^{a,b}	0	0.0 ^{a}	0	0.0 ^{a}	0	0.0 ^{a}			
Cool	3	8.3 ^{a}	2	5.7 ^{a}	2	11.1 ^{a}	2	18.2 ^{a}			
Slightly cool	5	13.9 ^{a}	4	11.4 ^{a}	3	16.7 ^{a}	1	9.1 ^{a}			
Comfortable	7	19.4 ^{a}	3	8.6 ^{a}	5	27.8 ^{a}	1	9.1 ^{a}			
Slightly warm	15	41.7 ^{a}	9	25.7 ^{a}	6	33.3 ^{a}	4	36.4 ^{a}			
Warm	3	8.3 ^{a}	15	42.9 ^{b}	2	11.1 ^{a,b}	3	27.3 ^{a,b}			
Hot	1	2.8	2	5.7 ^{a}	0	0.0 ^{a}	0	0.0 ^{a}			
Thermal sensation in Bedroom 2									22.54	0.121	0.272
Cold	1	2.8 ^{a}	0	0.0 ^{a}	0	0.0 ^{a}	0	0.0 ^{a}			
Cool	2	5.6 ^{a}	3	8.6 ^{a}	2	11.1 ^{a}	1	9.1 ^{a}			
Slightly cool	6	16.7 ^{a}	4	11.4 ^{a}	4	22.2 ^{a}	0	0.0 ^{a}			
Comfortable	10	27.8 ^{a}	4	11.4 ^{a}	5	27.8 ^{a}	3	27.3 ^{a}			
Slightly warm	14	38.9 ^{a}	10	28.6 ^{a}	6	33.3 ^{a}	3	27.3 ^{a}			
Warm	3	8.3 ^{a}	13	37.1 ^{b}	1	5.6 ^{a,b}	3	27.3 ^{a,b}			
Hot	0	0.0 ^{a}	1	2.9 ^{a}	0	0.0 ^{a}	1	9.1 ^{a}			
Thermal sensation in Bedroom 3									20.19	0.094	0.263
Cool	2	5.6 ^{a,b}	3	8.6 ^{a}	2	11.1 ^{a}	1	9.1 ^{a}			
Slightly cool	4	11.1 ^{a}	2	5.7 ^{a}	4	22.2 ^{a}	1	9.1 ^{a}			
Comfortable	14	38.9 ^{a}	3	8.6 ^{b}	5	27.8 ^{a,b}	3	27.3 ^{a,b}			
Slightly warm	12	33.3 ^{a}	12	34.3 ^{a}	5	27.8 ^{a}	3	27.3 ^{a}			
Warm	4	11.1 ^{a}	13	37.1 ^{a}	2	11.1 ^{a}	3	27.3 ^{a}			
Hot	0	0.0 ^{a}	2	5.7 ^{a}	0	0.0 ^{a}	0	0.0 ^{a}			

Note: For each row category, pairs of column proportions with different superscripts differed significantly, * $p < 0.05$.

Table D.11 Relationships between Occupants' TSVs for Each Occupied Space in the Summer: Living room, Kitchen, Bedroom 1, Bedroom 2, Bedroom 3, RTB Orientation and Floor Level—Floor Level

Floor	*Ground*		*First*		*Second*		*Third–Fourth*				
	n	*%*	*n*	*%*	*n*	*%*	*n*	*%*	*Fisher's Exact*	*p*	*Cramer's V*
Thermal sensation in Bedroom 1									10.23	0.952	0.177
Cold	0	0.0[a]	0	0.0[a]	1	5.3[a]	1	2.9[a]			
Cool	2	11.1[a]	3	10.7[a]	2	10.5[a]	2	5.7[a]			
Slightly cool	2	11.1[a]	4	14.3[a]	1	5.3[a]	6	17.1[a]			
Comfortable	2	11.1[a]	2	7.1[a]	5	26.3[a]	7	20.0[a]			
Slightly warm	7	38.9[a]	11	39.3[a]	5	26.3[a]	11	31.4[a]			
Warm	4	22.2[a]	7	25.0[a]	5	26.3[a]	7	20.0[a]			
Hot	1	5.6[a]	1	3.6[a]	0	0.0[a]	1	2.9[a]			
Thermal sensation in Bedroom 2									12.09	0.891	0.194
Cold	0	0.0[a]	0	0.0[a]	0	0.0[a]	1	2.9[a]			
Cool	2	11.1[a]	1	3.6[a]	2	10.5[a]	3	8.6[a]			
Slightly cool	2	11.1[a]	5	17.9[a]	2	10.5[a]	5	14.3[a]			
Comfortable	3	16.7[a]	4	14.3[a]	5	26.3[a]	10	28.6[a]			
Slightly warm	7	38.9[a]	11	39.3[a]	4	21.1[a]	11	31.4[a]			
Warm	3	16.7[a]	6	21.4[a]	6	31.6[a]	5	14.3[a]			
Hot	1	5.6[a]	1	3.6[a]	0	0.0[a]	0	0.0[a]			
Thermal sensation in Bedroom 3									13.86	0.489	0.221
Cool	2	11.1[a]	1	3.6[a]	2	10.5[a]	3	8.6[a]			
Slightly cool	2	11.1[a]	6	21.4[a]	1	5.3[a]	2	5.7[a]			
Comfortable	3	16.7[a]	5	17.9[a]	4	21.1[a]	13	37.1[a]			
Slightly warm	6	33.3[a]	11	39.3[a]	5	26.3[a]	10	28.6[a]			
Warm	4	22.2[a]	4	14.3[a]	7	36.8[a]	7	20.0[a]			
Hot	1	5.6[a]	1	3.6[a]	0	0.0[a]	0	0.0[a]			

Note: For each row category, pairs of column proportions with different superscripts differed significantly, * $p < 0.05$.

Table D.12 Relationships between Occupants' Window-Opening Patterns and the Outdoor Environmental Conditions

Window-Opening Reasons	*Fresh Air/Dissipate Dirty Air*		*Cooling Down*				
	n	%	*n*	%	*Chi-Square*	*p*	*Cramer's V*
Occupation					3.74*	0.291	0.201
Work outside the home	14	46.7^{a}	28	44.4^{a}			
Work at home	3	10.0^{a}	10	15.9^{a}			
Household activities	8	26.7^{a}	8	12.7^{a}			
Retired	5	16.7^{a}	17	27.0^{a}			
Window-opening patterns in winter					1.53*	0.676	0.124
0–2 h	2	6.3^{a}	6	9.0^{a}			
2–4 h	12	37.5^{a}	26	38.8^{a}			
4–6 h	9	28.1^{a}	12	17.9^{a}			
More than 6 h	9	28.1^{a}	23	34.3^{a}			
Window-opening patterns in summer					3.41*	0.182	0.185
2–6 h	7	21.9^{a}	6	9.0^{a}			
6–8 h	8	25.0^{a}	23	34.3^{a}			
More than 8 h	17	53.1^{a}	38	56.7^{a}			
Type of heating control at home					3.97*	0.410	0.200
Wall-mounted thermostat	6	18.8^{a}	11	16.4^{a}			
Other types	1	3.1^{a}	8	11.9^{a}			
Remote controller	4	12.5^{a}	5	7.5^{a}			
Automatic thermostat and remote controller	9	28.1^{a}	12	17.9^{a}			
None	12	37.5^{a}	31	46.3^{a}			

Note: For each row category, pairs of column proportions with different superscripts differed significantly, * $p < 0.05$.

Table D.13 Relationships between Occupants' Habitual Adaptive Behaviour and the Reasons of Environmental Factors

Window-Closing Reasons	*Against the Warm Air*		*To Block Outside Disturbances/ Annoyances*		*For Safety Reasons*		*Dust*		*Open Always*				
	n	*%*	*n*	*%*	*n*	*%*	*n*	*%*	*n*	*%*	*Fisher's Exact*	*p*	*Cramer's V*
Occupation											16.23	0.142	0.260
Work outside the home	16	59.3 [a]	7	41.2 [a]	4	36.4 [a]	11	39.3 [a]	4	36.4 [a]			
Work at home	4	14.8 [a]	4	23.5 [a]	1	9.1 [a]	4	14.3 [a]	0	0.0 [a]			
Household activities	4	14.8 [a]	1	5.9 [a]	5	45.5 [a]	6	21.4 [a]	1	9.1 [a]			
Retired	3	11.1 [a]	5	29.4 [a, b]	1	9.1 [a, b]	7	25.0 [a, b]	6	54.5 [b]			
Window-opening patterns in winter											15.02	0.197	0.230
0–2 h	3	10.3 [a]	0	0.0 [a]	3	23.1 [a]	3	10.7 [a]	0	0.0 [a]			
2–4 h	6	20.7 [a]	6	33.3 [a]	7	53.8 [a]	13	46.4 [a]	6	50.0 [a]			
4–6 h	7	24.1 [a]	4	22.2 [a]	1	7.7 [a]	6	21.4 [a]	3	25.0 [a]			
More than 6 h	13	44.8 [a]	8	44.4 [a]	2	15.4 [a]	6	21.4 [a]	3	25.0 [a]			
Window-opening patterns in summer											11.44	0.153	0.234
2–6 h	6	20.7 [a]	0	0.0 [a]	3	23.1 [a]	4	14.3 [a]	1	8.3 [a]			
6–8 h	5	17.2 [a]	5	27.8 [a]	6	46.2 [a]	11	39.3 [a]	4	33.3 [a]			
More than 8 h	18	62.1 [a]	13	72.2 [a]	4	30.8 [a]	13	46.4 [a]	7	58.3 [a]			
Type of heating control at home											6.22	0.994	0.118

(*Continued*)

Table D.13 (Continued)

Window-Closing Reasons	*Against the Warm Air*		*To Block Outside Disturbances/ Annoyances*		*For Safety Reasons*		*Dust*		*Open Always*		*Fisher's p Exact*	*Cramer's V*
	n	%	*n*	%	*n*	%	*n*	%	*n*	%		
Wall-mounted thermostat	4	13.8 ^{a}	3	16.7 ^{a}	2	15.4 ^{a}	5	17.9 ^{a}	3	25.0 ^{a}		
Other types	1	3.4 ^{a}	3	16.7 ^{a}	1	7.7 ^{a}	2	7.1 ^{a}	2	16.7 ^{a}		
Remote controller	4	13.8 ^{a}	1	5.6 ^{a}	1	7.7 ^{a}	2	7.1 ^{a}	1	8.3 ^{a}		
Automatic thermostat and remote controller	7	24.1 ^{a}	4	22.2 ^{a}	3	23.1 ^{a}	6	21.4 ^{a}	2	16.7 ^{a}		
None	13	44.8 ^{a}	7	38.9 ^{a}	6	46.2 ^{a}	13	46.4 ^{a}	4	33.3 ^{a}		

Note: For each row category, pairs of column proportions with different superscripts differed significantly, * $p < 0.05$.

Appendix E: *Cramer*'s *V* Tests

Table E.1 Relationship between Respondents, Orientation and Floor Level

Variables		*Participants*	*Orientation*	*Floor Level*
Participants	Partial η^2	1	0.781	0.046
	Significance	—	<0.001	0.205
Orientation	Partial η^2/*Cramer*'s *V*	0.781	1	0.197
	Significance	<0.001	—	0.234
Floor Level	Partial η^2/*Cramer*'s *V*	0.046	0.197	1
	Significance	0.205	0.188	—

Participants–Floor Level, $F(3, 96) = 1.56, p = 0.205$, *Partial* $\eta^2 = 0.046$
Orientation–Participants, $F(3, 96) = 113.90, p < 0.001$, *Partial* $\eta^2 = 0.781$
Orientation–Floor Level, *Fisher's exact* = 12.11, $p = 0.188$, *Cramer*'s $V = 0.197$

Outcome: The relationship between orientation and floor level was examined by cross-tabulation using chi-square test. As seen in Table E.1, no significant relationship was found, *Fisher's exact* = 12.11, $p = 0.188$, *Cramer*'s $V = 0.197$.

Table E.2 Relationship between Age Band, Occupation, Income and Health Conditions

Research Questions	*Age Band*	*Economic Status*	*Education Level*	*Occupation*	*Income*	*Health*
Q 1.1: What is your age?	1	0.201	0.114	0.399*	0.213	0.496*
	—	0.447	0.991	<0.001	0.245	0.001
Q 1.2: What is your economic status?	0.201	1	0.416*	0.171	0.136	0.178
	0.447	—	<0.001	0.743	0.950	0.708
Q 1.3: What is your highest level of education?	0.114	0.416*	1	0.162	0.190	0.196
	0.991	<0.001	—	0.591	0.386	0.315
Q 1.4: What is your occupation?	0.399*	0.171	0.162	1	0.174	0.342*
	<0.001	0.743	0.591	—	0.488	<0.001
Q 29: What is your monthly income?	0.213	0.136	0.190	0.174	1	0.174
	0.245	0.950	0.386	0.488	—	0.480
Q 28: How is your health in general?	0.496*	0.178	0.196	0.342*	0.174	1
	0.001	0.708	0.315	<0.001	0.480	—

Health condition–Age, *Fisher's exact* = 73.74, $p < 0.001$, *Cramer's* $V = 0.496$
Health condition–Employment status, *Fisher's exact* = 9.06, $p = 0.708$, *Cramer's* $V = 0.178$
Health condition–Education level, *Fisher's exact* = 10.20, $p = 0.315$, *Cramer's* $V = 0.196$
Health condition–Occupation, *Fisher's exact* = 33.81, $p < 0.001$, *Cramer's* $V = 0.342$
Health condition–Income, *Fisher's exact* = 8.63, $p = 0.472$, *Cramer's* $V = 0.170$
Income–Age, *Fisher's exact* = 14.71, $p = 0.245$, *Cramer's* $V = 0.213$
Income–Employment status, *Fisher's exact* = 5.64, $p = 0.950$, *Cramer's* $V = 0.136$
Income–Education level, *Fisher's exact* = 9.53, $p = 0.386$, *Cramer's* $V = 0.190$
Income–Occupation, *Fisher's exact* = 8.49, $p = 0.488$, *Cramer's* $V = 0.174$
Occupation–Age, *Fisher's exact* = 44.81, $p < 0.001$, *Cramer's* $V = 0.399$
Occupation–Employment status, *Fisher's exact* = 8.69, $p = 0.743$, *Cramer's* $V = 0.171$
Occupation–Education, *Fisher's exact* = 7.49, $p = 0.591$, *Cramer's* $V = 0.162$
Age–Education, *Fisher's exact* = 4.08, $p = 0.991$, *Cramer's* $V = 0.114$
Age–Employment status, *Fisher's exact* = 16.09, $p = 0.447$, *Cramer's* $V = 0.201$
Employment status–Education, *Fisher's exact* = 48.81, $p < 0.001$, *Cramer's* $V = 0.416$

$*p < 0.5$; $**p < 0.001$

Outcome: Age bands were significantly related to health conditions, and this relationship was strong (*Fisher's exact* = 73.74, $p < 0.001$, *Cramer*'s $V = 0.496$). Younger age appeared to report better health conditions (good or very good) than older age. Household occupation was significantly related to health conditions, and the relationship was moderate (*Fisher's exact* = 33.81, $p < 0.001$, *Cramer*'s $V = 0.342$). A greater proportion of participants with very good health conditions worked outside the home than those with mediocre health conditions, whereas none of the participants who retired had very good health conditions. Household occupations were also significantly associated with age with a moderate–strong relationship (*Fisher's exact* = 44.81, $p < 0.001$, *Cramer*'s $V = 0.399$). Economic status was significantly related to educational level (*Fisher's exact* = 48.81, $p < 0.001$, *Cramer*'s $V = 0.416$).

Note: The relationships between occupant age, economic status, education level, occupation, income and health conditions were examined using cross-tabulations with chi-square tests or Fisher's exact tests if over 25% of cells had less than five expected counts, as shown in Table E.2.

Table E.3 Relationships between Household Age Band, Tenancy Status and Length of Residency

Research Questions	*Age Band*	*Tenancy Status*	*Length of Residency*
Q 1.1: What is your age?	1 —	0.595* <0.001	0.582* <0.001
Q 3: Do you own or rent your dwelling?	0.595* <0.001	1 —	0.494* <0.001
Q 2: How many years have you lived in this flat?	0.582* <0.001	0.494* <0.001	1 —

Age–Length of Residency, *Fisher's exact* = 56.03, $p < 0.001$, *Cramer*'s $V = 0.582$
Age–Tenure Type, *Fisher's exact* = 21.28, $p < 0.001$, *Cramer*'s $V = 0.494$
Tenure Type–Length of Residency, *Fisher's exact* = 32.00, $p < 0.001$, *Cramer*'s $V = 0.595$
Outcome: Age band and tenancy status were significantly and strongly related to each other (*Fisher's exact* = 21.28, $p < 0.001$, *Cramer*'s $V = 0.494$). Most participants who rented were 45 years old and younger. Age band and length of residency were also correlated (*Fisher's exact* = 56.03, $p < 0.001$, *Cramer*'s $V = 0.582$). It appeared that younger participants had shorter lengths of residency. A strong relationship was discerned between tenancy status and length of residency (*Fisher's exact* = 32.00, $p < 0.001$, *Cramer*'s $V = 0.595$). A greater proportion of participants with more than ten years of residency were owner occupied than those who had ten years or less residency.
*p < 0.5; ** p < 0.001

Table E.4 Relationships between Household Income, Energy Consumption, Energy Advice, Energy Usage and Energy Savings

Research Questions	*Income*	*Energy Consumption*	*Energy Advice*	*Energy Usage*	*Energy Savings*
Q 29: What is your monthly income?	1 —	0.247 0.108	0.199 0.194	0.176 0.340	0.233* 0.049
Q 30: How much electricity (in kWh) did you consume in May through September according to this last overview?	0.247 0.108	1 —	0.116 0.702	0.080 0.416	0.106 0.754
Q 31: Have you received advice on how to reduce your energy bills?	0.199 0.194	0.116 0.702	1 —	0.117 0.826	0.182 0.364
Q 4: Do you check your use of electricity by taking frequent meter readings?	0.176 0.340	0.080 0.416	0.117 0.826	1 —	0.291* 0.040
Q 6: Do you know anything about energy-saving methods?	0.233* 0.049	0.106 0.754	0.182 0.364	0.291* 0.040	1 —

Energy Advise–Income, *Fisher's exact* = 11.55, $p = 0.194$, *Cramer*'s $V = 0.199$
Energy Advise–Energy Savings, *Fisher's exact* = 9.07, $p = 0.364$, *Cramer*'s $V = 0.182$
Energy Advise–Energy Usage, *Fisher's exact* = 1.09, $p = 0.826$, *Cramer*'s $V = 0.117$
Energy Advise–Energy Consumption, *Fisher's exact* = 1.42, $p = 0.702$, *Cramer*'s $V = 0.116$
Energy Savings–Income, *Fisher's exact* = 16.24, $p = 0.049$, *Cramer*'s $V = 0.233$
Energy Savings–Energy Usage, *Fisher's exact* = 7.87, $p = 0.040$, *Cramer*'s $V = 0.291$
Energy Savings–Energy Consumption, *Fisher's exact* = 1.27, $p = 0.754$, *Cramer*'s $V = 0.106$
Income–Energy Usage, *Fisher's exact* = 3.26, $p = 0.340$, *Cramer*'s $V = 0.176$
Income–Energy Consumption, $\chi^2(3) = 6.09$, $p = 0.107$, *Cramer*'s $V = 0.247$
Energy Consumption–Energy Usage, $\chi^2(1) = 0.64$, $p = 0.424$, *Cramer*'s $V = 0.080$

*p > 0.5; **p > 0.001

Outcome: A moderate relationship was found between energy-efficiency awareness and energy conservation (*Fisher's exact* = 7.87, p = 0.040, *Cramer*'s V = 0.291). A greater proportion of participants with energy conservation had a lot of energy-efficiency awareness while a greater proportion of participants without energy conservation did not have efficiency awareness at all. Income was moderately associated with energy savings (*Fisher's exact* = 16.24, $p = 0.049$, *Cramer*'s $V = 0.233$), but income was not significantly associated with energy consumption, energy-efficiency awareness and energy advice.

Note: Table E.4 demonstrates the cross-tabulation using chi-square analysis or Fisher's exact tests if over 25% of cells had less than five expected counts that revealed relationships between household income level and occupant awareness of energy consumption.

Table E.5(a) Relationships between Household Occupation and Cooling- and Heating Energy-Consumption Patterns

Research Questions	*Occupation*	*Weekday Heating-Consumption Patterns*	*Weekend Heating-Consumption Patterns*	*Weekday Cooling-Consumption Patterns*	*Weekend Cooling-Consumption Patterns*
Q 1.4: What is your occupation?	1	0,253*	0,109	0,098	0,167
	—	0,042	0,896	0,955	0,579
Q 16: When do you turn on heating device(s) on weekdays?	0,253*	1	0,373*	0,611*	0,504*
	0,042	—	<0,001	<0,001	<0,001
Q 17: When do you turn on heating device(s) on the weekend?	0,109	0,373*	1	0,522*	0,706*
	0,896	<0,001	—	<0,001	<0,001
Q 12: When do you turn on cooling device(s) on weekdays?	0,098	0,611*	0,522*	1	0,774*
	0,955	<0,001	<0,001	—	<0,001
Q 13: When do you turn on cooling device(s) on the weekend?	0,167	0,504*	0,706*	0,774*	—
	0,579	<0,001	<0,001	<0,001	1

Occupation–Weekend heating consumption, *Fisher's exact* = 2.41, $p = 0.896$, *Cramer*'s $V = 0.109$
Occupation–Weekday heating consumption, *Fisher's exact* = 12.49, $p = 0.042$, *Cramer*'s $V = 0.253$
Occupation–Weekend cooling consumption, *Fisher's exact* = 7.63, $p = 0.579$, *Cramer*'s $V = 0.167$
Occupation–Weekday cooling consumption, *Fisher's exact* = 1.76, $p = 0.955$, *Cramer*'s $V = 0.098$
Weekday cooling consumption–Weekend heating consumption, $\chi^2(4) = 54.59$, $p < 0.001$, *Cramer*'s $V = 0.522$
Weekday cooling consumption–Weekday heating consumption, $\chi^2(4) = 74.57$, $p < 0.001$, *Cramer*'s $V = 0.611$
Weekday cooling consumption–Weekend cooling consumption, $\chi^2(6) = 119.77$, $p < 0.001$, *Cramer*'s $V = 0.774$
Weekend cooling consumption–Weekend heating consumption, $\chi^2(6) = 99.69$, $p < 0.001$, *Cramer*'s $V = 0.706$
Weekend cooling consumption– Weekday heating consumption, *Fisher's exact* = 49.70, $p < 0.001$, *Cramer*'s $V = 0.504$
Weekday heating consumption–Weekend heating consumption, $\chi^2(4) = 27.89$, $p < 0.001$, *Cramer*'s $V = 0.373$

Table E.5(b) Relationships between Household Occupation, and Cooling- and Heating Energy-Consumption Patterns. (Continued)

Outcome: Weekday cooling-consumption patterns were significantly and strongly related to weekend heating-consumption patterns on weekend ($\chi^2 = 54.59$, $p < 0.001$, *Cramer*'s $V = 0.522$). Specifically, longer duration of heating consumption was related to longer duration of cooling consumption. Similar result was also found between weekend cooling- consumption patterns and weekend heating-consumption patterns ($\chi^2 = 99.69$, $p < 0.001$, *Cramer*'s $V = 0.706$), between weekday cooling-consumption patterns and weekday heating -consumption patterns ($\chi^2 = 74.57$, $p < 0.001$, *Cramer*'s $V = 0.611$) and weekend cooling-consumption patterns and weekday heating-consumption patterns (*Fisher's exact* = 49.70, $p < 0.001$, *Cramer*'s $V = 0.504$). For heating patterns, weekday consumption was moderately associated with weekend consumption ($\chi^2 = 27.89$, $p < 0.001$, *Cramer*'s $V = 0.373$). For cooling patterns, weekday consumption was strongly associated with weekend consumption ($\chi^2 = 119.77$, $p < 0.001$, *Cramer*'s $V = 0.774$). Occupation was only significantly and moderately related to weekly heating consumption (*Fisher's exact* = 12.49, $p = 0.042$, *Cramer*'s $V = 0.253$), but it was not significantly related to any other cooling- or heating- consumption patterns.

Note: The relationships between household occupation and cooling- and heating energy-consumption patterns were examined using cross-tabulations with chi-square tests or Fisher's exact tests if over 25% of cells had less than five expected counts, as shown in Table E.6(a).

*p > 0.5; **p > 0.001

Table E.6(a) Relationships between Household Occupation, Window-Opening Patterns in the Winter, Window-Opening Patterns in the Summer and Heating Control

Research Questions	*Occupation*	*Winter*	*Summer*	*Heating Control*
Q 1.4: What is your occupation?	1	0.164	0.167	0.170
	—	0.594	0.525	0.709
Q 23: When do you open your windows	0.164	1	0.459*	0.139
in the winter?	0.594	—	<0.001	0.961
Q 18: When do you open your windows	0.167	0.459*	1	0.283
in the summer?	0.525	<0.001	—	0.053
Q 24: Do you keep room doors open	0.114	0.246	0.030	1
when you do not have heating on?	0.747	0.109	0.956	—
Q 19: Do you keep room doors open	0.114	0.262	0.168	0.229
when you do not have cooling on?	0.746	0.113	0.245	0.262
Q 20: Why do you open the windows?	0.201	0.124	0.185	0.200
	0.291	0.676	0.182	0.410
Q 21: Why do you close the windows?	0.260	0.230	0.234	0.118
	0.142	0.197	0.153	0.994

Table E.6(b) Relationships between Household Occupation, Window-Opening Patterns in the Winter, Window-Opening Patterns in the Summer and Heating Control (Continued)

Window-opening patterns in winter–Door-opening preference in summer, *Fisher's exact* = 5.82, $p = 0.113$, *Cramer*'s $V = 0.262$
Window-opening patterns in winter–Window-opening pattern in summer, *Fisher's exact* = 36.80, $p < 0.001$, *Cramer*'s $V = 0.459$
Window-opening patterns in winter–Door-opening preference in winter, $\chi^2(3) = 6.05$, $p = 0.109$, *Cramer*'s $V = 0.246$
Window-opening patterns in winter–Window-opening reason, $\chi^2(3) = 1.53$, $p = 0.676$, *Cramer*'s $V = 0.124$
Window-opening patterns in winter–Window-closing reason, *Fisher's exact* = 15.02, $p = 0.197$, *Cramer*'s $V = 0.230$
Window-opening patterns in summer–Door-opening preference in summer, $\chi^2(2) = 2.81$, $p = 0.245$, *Cramer*'s $V = 0.168$
Window-opening patterns in summer–Door-opening preference in winter, $\chi^2(2) = 0.09$, $p = 0.956$, *Cramer*'s $V = 0.030$
Window-opening patterns in summer–Window-opening reason, $\chi^2(2) = 3.41$, $p = 0.182$, *Cramer*'s $V = 0.185$
Window-opening patterns in summer–Window-closing reason, *Fisher's exact* = 11.44, $p = 0.153$, *Cramer*'s $V = 0.234$
Occupation–Window-opening patterns in summer, *Fisher's exact* = 5.18, $p = 0.525$, *Cramer*'s $V = 0.167$
Occupation–Window-opening patterns in winter, *Fisher's exact* = 7.35, $p = 0.594$, *Cramer*'s $V = 0.164$
Occupation–Window-opening reasons, $\chi^2(3) = 3.74$, $p = 0.291$, *Cramer*'s $V = 0.201$
Occupation–Window-closing reasons, *Fisher's exact* = 16.23, $p = 0.142$, *Cramer*'s $V = 0.260$
Occupation–Heating control, *Fisher's exact* = 8.94, $p = 0.709$, *Cramer*'s $V = 0.170$
Heating control–Window-opening patterns in winter, *Fisher's exact* = 5.41, $p = 0.961$, *Cramer*'s $V = 0.139$
Heating control–Window-opening patterns in summer, *Fisher's exact* = 14.14, $p = 0.053$, *Cramer*'s $V = 0.283$
Heating control–Window-opening reason, $\chi^2(4) = 3.93$, $p = 0.410$, *Cramer*'s $V = 0.200$
Heating control–Window-closing reason, *Fisher's exact* = 6.22, $p = 0.994$, *Cramer*'s $V = 0.118$
*p > 0.5; **p > 0.001

Outcome: As seen in Table E.6(b), window-opening patterns in winter were significantly associated with that in summer (*Fisher's exact* = 36.80, $p < 0.001$, *Cramer*'s $V = 0.459$), and this relationship was moderate–strong. It appears that longer opening duration in winter was related to longer opening duration in summer. Heating control type at home and occupation was not significantly associated with any opening patterns or opening reasons.

Note: The relationships between household occupation, window-opening patterns in the winter, window-opening patterns in the summer and heating control were examined using cross-tabulations with chi-square tests or Fisher's exact tests if over 25% of cells had less than five expected counts, as shown in Table E.6(a).

Appendix F: Worldwide Statistically Representative Archetypes

Table F.1 The Literature on Building Stock Aggregation through Archetype Buildings—Energy Modelling

References	*A. Study Location*	*B. Building Type*	*C. Sampling Size*	*D. Primary Aim of Model*	*E. Methodology*	*F. Main Findings*
Streicher et al. (2018)	Sweden	SFHs and MFHs located in urban, suburban and rural regions	10,400 Cantonal Building Energy Certificates; 54 archetypes were identified; SFHs represent 14.4% and 14.1% of the total housing stock; MFHs represent 55% of the total housing stock	To provide the current thermal performance level of the Swiss residential building stock in 2015 based on an analysis of the data available from energy certificates; to estimate a thermal performance level of archetype buildings and their respective building elements	Cantonal Building Energy Performance Certificate data was used; archetype housing stock data was analysed; the statistics of the Federal Register of Buildings and Dwellings were examined; current state of the Swiss residential building stock was assessed; potential improvements in the building stock were proposed	Approximately 75% of all building elements do not yet reach the thermal performance of buildings constructed in the last 15 years; the *U*-values of building elements would have to be reduced by an additional 0.3–0.7 W/m^2K to reach low-energy standards

(*Continued*)

Table F.1 (Continued)

References	*A. Study Location*	*B. Building Type*	*C. Sampling Size*	*D. Primary Aim of Model*	*E. Methodology*	*F. Main Findings*
Yi and Peng (2019)	Seoul, South Korea	High-rise apartment stock, MFHs	The total number of households was 2,830,857, of which about 58% (1,641,383) lived in apartments	To introduce an 'archetype-in-neighbourhood' framework to develop cooling energy supply planning; to demonstrate estimated increases of the maximal month cooling energy demand	A bottom-up hybrid approach was adopted; empirical urban data modelling was used; EnergyPlus was used for model calibration; electricity use data of 659 apartment buildings (51,351 households) sampled from 18 city districts; characteristics of residential energy use during the hottest month (August) was examined	The coefficient of determination from the scatter plot between the observed and the predicted was 0.969, representing about 97% variance in observed peak cooling energy use

(Continued)

Table F.1 (Continued)

References	*A. Study Location*	*B. Building Type*	*C. Sampling Size*	*D. Primary Aim of Model*	*E. Methodology*	*F. Main Findings*
Li et al. (2019)	Chongqing, China	Urban residential blocks; MFHs in urban residential districts	Households with one elderly retiree and elderly retired couples accounted for 4.86% and 4.40%, respectively, of all households	To develop a localised residential building stock-space heating and cooling modelling approach to estimate energy consumption and related carbon emissions	A bottom-up engineering approach was used; development of residential archetypes; space heating- and cooling-energy consumption simulation and aggregation; stock total floor area calculation and construction age distribution; EnergyPlus was used for model calibration	The total energy consumption for space heating and cooling can be significantly reduced, with estimated reductions of 57.6–60.70% in 2020 and 55.3–57.2% in 2050
Pittau et al. (2019)	EU 28	SFHs; MFHs	Post-war buildings built between 1945 and 1969, representing 30% of housing stock	To investigate the effect of massively storing carbon in bio-based construction products	A statistic-based geo-cluster model was developed; a dynamic life-cycle assessment was performed; Eurostat data was used for the archetype housing identification	Up to 3% of the total GHG annually emitted by all sectors in 2015 can be removed by 2050

Table F.2 The Literature on Building Stock Aggregation through Archetype Buildings—Energy Modelling. (Continued)

References	*A. Study Location*	*B. Building Type*	*C. Sampling Size*	*D. Primary Aim of Model*	*E. Methodology*	*F. Main Findings*
Wang et al. (2020)	Netherlands, Amsterdam	Residential buildings	- 2,178 buildings were included then this data was aggregated at the post code level rather than an individual building - 84 residential postcodes fulfil simulation data requirements	To present a data-driven urban scale energy modelling framework from open-source data harmonisation, sensitivity analysis, heating demand simulation at the postcode level to develop energy modelling phase	- City Sim energy modelling software was used to undertake dynamic thermal simulations - Data inputs; weather data, building geometry, construction data, system data, operation data, energy consumption data - Energy model was validated with six years of measured consumption data	- Generalisability of the methodology was developed - Data availability and levels of detail integrated into the BEM - Accelerating building stock retrofit was presented in urban scale

(*Continued*)

Table F.2 (Continued)

References	*A. Study Location*	*B. Building Type*	*C. Sampling Size*	*D. Primary Aim of Model*	*E. Methodology*	*F. Main Findings*
Molina et al. (2018)	South America, Chile	Residential buildings	- 83,887 households and 266,968 people living in 15 regions of the country is considered nationally representative - 15,312 dwellings were selected for a representative and randomly sampled group - 496 archetypes were used to classify the housing stock	- To develop archetypal Chilean houses with statistically significant representative values for design optimisation parameters related to energy use and indoor air quality - To analyse data and develop housing archetypes can be applied to other building stocks in comparable economically developed countries	- National census data was gathered - Building permit's dataset was gathered -National socioeconomic characterisation survey was used - The Use of Time National Survey database was used to demonstrate a nationwide cross-sectional study - National housing monitoring network data was used - Dwelling quantity, year of construction, occupancy, cooking and heating, construction and finishing materials were used	- Models of the archetypes require calibration after the simulation process to minimise the predictive error - A stochastic approach is required to capture both stock variability and parametric uncertainty - Categorical descriptors and occupant behaviours and poor granularity of physical data were identified as knowledge gap

(*Continued*)

Table F.2 (Continued)

References	*A. Study Location*	*B. Building Type*	*C. Sampling Size*	*D. Primary Aim of Model*	*E. Methodology*	*F. Main Findings*
Molina et al. (2020)	Santiago, Chile	Residential buildings	- In their database set, 7, 19 and 46 archetypes were found to represent 32%, 58% and 83% of the national stock - A detached single storey house was identified as nationally representative archetype	To demonstrate the simulation of indoor environmental conditions using representative models of a housing stock, is a more common method of investigation for policymaking decisions	-A single multi-zone archetype is modelled in CONTAM where model inputs are randomly selected - The archetypes were identified by geometry, building size, dwelling type and construction period, values for the floor area and the number of storeys and number of occupants assigned into a simulation model	The outputs can be used to inform future standards and guidelines for Chilean houses that simultaneously focus on energy demand reduction

Table F.3 The Literature on Building Stock Aggregation through Archetype Buildings—Energy Modelling. (Continued)

References	*A. Study Location*	*B. Building Type*	*C. Sampling Size*	*D. Primary Aim of Model*	*E. Methodology*	*F. Main Findings*
Molina et al. (2021)	Santiago, Chile	Residential buildings	- 496 common Chilean archetypes were used - A detached single storey house was identified as nationally representative archetype - eight probabilistic inputs were used	- To demonstrate the Chilean Housing Archetypes Air quality model and a stochastic framework for predicting uncertainties in indoor pollutant concentrations - To predict uncertainties in indoor pollutant concentrations, ventilation and infiltration rates and their associated energy demand	- CONTAM—open-source freely available multi-zone indoor ventilation and pollutant transport tool was used - Dwelling parameters—airflow paths and envelope air permeability were used - Both indoor and outdoor environment parameters were used -Pollutants—emission rates from cooking, emission rates from heating were used - Occupancy and activity data were assigned - Sensitivity analysis and statistical tests were conducted	- 34% of Chilean dwellings are predicted to have unacceptable daily $PM_{2.5}$ concentrations if their windows are closed at all times - Many houses require remediation measures to improve airtightness and to reduce their annual space heating demand

(*Continued*)

Table F.3 (Continued)

References	*A. Study Location*	*B. Building Type*	*C. Sampling Size*	*D. Primary Aim of Model*	*E. Methodology*	*F. Main Findings*
Li et al. (2018)	Yuzhong District, Chongqing (China)	Residential buildings	- A population of around 649,500 was identified in the district - 334 of residential buildings accounting for 60% of the total as a sampling size	- To test and demonstrate a regional district retrofitting scheme by comparing the Energy Use Intensity (EUI) of the nationally representative archetypes	- Building shape, the glazing ratio, building envelope properties, occupancy pattern and heating/cooling equipment were used in the BES model - Correlation analysis for cluster variable selection was conducted - Energy consumption simulations—building-by-building approach was undertaken	A very small variation was found in the estimated stock (+0.03% in heating-energy consumption and +2.97% in cooling-energy consumption)
Martins et al. (2019)	Toulouse, France	Residential buildings	Three representative urban blocks were identified	- To identify the statistical sensitivity of multi-scale urban design factors regarding buildings' energy demand	- Urban archetypes characterisation and parametrisation - Sensitivity analysis was conducted - Statistical sensitivity analysis with a variance-based method was applied	The courtyard aspect ratio and the standard deviation of the built height account for almost 50% of the overall impact on heating demand

(*Continued*)

Table F.3 (Continued)

References	*A. Study Location*	*B. Building Type*	*C. Sampling Size*	*D. Primary Aim of Model*	*E. Methodology*	*F. Main Findings*
Tardioli et al. (2018)	Geneva, Switzerland	Residential buildings	A total of 67 representative buildings were identified in the urban dataset	- To present a novel methodology for identifying building groups and associated representative buildings in urban datasets	- Clustering algorithms are applied to the datasets - Data cleaning, skew distributions and the presence of outliers were conducted - Datasets are classified using building typology information	Clustering techniques achieved an average accuracy of 89.6% across many building typologies and up to 97% in some instances

Table F.4 The Literature on Building Stock Aggregation through Archetype Buildings—Energy Modelling. (Continued)

References	*A. Study Location*	*B. Building Type*	*C. Sampling Size*	*D. Primary Aim of Model*	*E. Methodology*	*F. Main Findings*
Bianco and Marmori (2022)	Italy	Single and multi-family houses	Typology 6 was selected as an archetype to represent housing stock built after 2005—represents 8,000 new buildings per year	- To estimate the energy savings obtained when specific energy efficiency measures are applied - To bridge the identified gap and introduce a novel calculation tool	- Geometric and thermal features of buildings were used - I-REM energy modelling framework was used - Energy consumption data was extracted from the Eurostat and Odyssee databases for the validation study	- A saving of 76.8 kWh is fixed for 2030, the double with respect to EU Policy scenario, and 100 kWh for 2040

(*Continued*)

Table F.4 (Continued)

References	*A. Study Location*	*B. Building Type*	*C. Sampling Size*	*D. Primary Aim of Model*	*E. Methodology*	*F. Main Findings*
McKenna et al. (2013)	Germany	- Single- and two-family houses - Multi-family houses	-10,000 objects related to energy use was used - 4,575 single- and two-family houses - 5,491 multi-family houses were selected as an archetype	-To analyse the role of refurbishment measures on the reaching, or not of these energy political goals by developing an aggregated building-stock model	- Building stock projections data 2011–2050 was gathered - Micro-census survey data was used - Age categorisation of housing stock was applied - Renovation measures were predicted by using statistical analysis methods - Sensitivity analysis was conducted to identify effective renovation measures	-The renovation probability of the SFH is increased by 2020 from 1% to 4% -The model results regarding total final energy demand are significantly higher than in other studies

(*Continued*)

Table F.4 (Continued)

References	*A. Study Location*	*B. Building Type*	*C. Sampling Size*	*D. Primary Aim of Model*	*E. Methodology*	*F. Main Findings*
Famuyibo et al. (2012)	Ireland	Residential buildings	13 representative archetypes were identified for the statistical analysis	-To present a methodology for the development of archetypes based on information from literature and a sample of detailed energy-related housing data	- Multilinear regression analysis, clustering and descriptive statistics were used - A housing database was used - The Energy Performance Survey of Irish Housing and the Irish National Survey of Housing Quality databases were used	The linear regression indicates a coefficient of determination R^2 0.391, indicating that 39.1% of the variance in household total energy use
Ahern and Norton (2020)	Ireland	Residential buildings	35 reference dwellings were selected to appropriately characterise 406,918 dwellings	-To present a methodology for the derivation of simplified default-free inputs to a bottom-up energy modelling	- Energy Use Intensity of housing stock was calculated - Housing typology was identified - Analysis of single field empirical data was applied -Heat loss throughout the building fabric was investigated -Orientation factor was considered	The recommended default U-values for walls and roofs for a different dwelling typology correlate with those recommended for the building typology examined

Table F.5 The Literature on Building Stock Aggregation through Archetype Buildings—Energy Modelling. (Continued)

References	*A. Study Location*	*B. Building Type*	*C. Sampling Size*	*D. Primary Aim of Model*	*E. Methodology*	*F. Main Findings*
Pittam et al. (2014)	Cork City, Ireland	Residential buildings	- 20 house typologies represent a total of 10,449 housing units - 4 representative archetypes were selected	-To develop representative archetypes using a bottom-up approach for stock modelling	-The GIS web-based mapping application was used -Geometric properties and thermal characteristics for each typology were used -Statistical analysis was used to aggregate bottom-up housing model	-A 6% variation is recorded when compared to an averaged 121 archetypes

(Continued)

Table F.5 (Continued)

References	*A. Study Location*	*B. Building Type*	*C. Sampling Size*	*D. Primary Aim of Model*	*E. Methodology*	*F. Main Findings*
Kazas et al. (2017)	Turin, Italy	Residential buildings	-Representative urban district was selected to develop energy model -300 scenarios were developed and simulated in a parametric analysis	-To generate detailed thermal energy profiles, an urban district scale has been developed -To developed engineering bottom-up housing model for policymaking decisions in energy use	-A parametric analysis of the variables of building energy performance was carried at an urban scale -Thermal energy demand profile database was developed -The application of the aggregation method to generate the average thermal energy demand profile was developed -Parametric analysis was conducted to develop cost-effective and energy-efficient design scenarios	The development of an aggregation method, which could cover the uncertainties of a parametric analysis and would be sufficiently precise and general to be suitable for the existing housing stock

(*Continued*)

Table F.5 (Continued)

References	*A. Study Location*	*B. Building Type*	*C. Sampling Size*	*D. Primary Aim of Model*	*E. Methodology*	*F. Main Findings*
Allacker et al. (2019)	EU-27 Member states	Residential buildings	-24 representative residential buildings were selected as an archetype within the EU	- To develop a methodological framework that bridges a gap by using the outcomes from the BES and LCCA studies - To evaluate both energy and cost-effectiveness of optimisation scenarios	- Dynamic thermal simulations were undertaken - Life-cycle cost assessment method was applied - Archetypes were selected from the Typology Approach for Building Stock Energy Assessment database	The use of archetypes is useful for analysing the effects of scenarios acting at the European level but implies also a certain degree of approximation at the building level
Ortiz and Bluyssen (2018)	Netherlands, Amsterdam	Residential buildings	-316 emails were sent out inviting participants to complete the questionnaire -Six groups were represented with the 25 final predicting variables	-To demonstrate the effectiveness of the Two-Step cluster analysis and the development -To present the results of a new questionnaire survey for measuring comfort, health and energy habits	-The questionnaire survey was developed -The questionnaire was developed with the Qualtrics online platform -SPSS software suite was used to conduct the relevant statistical analysis	The archetype analysis represents the greatest social challenge and thus should be considered a 'high priority' method of design to explore subject respondents' behaviour on energy use

Table F.6 The Literature on Building Stock Aggregation through Archetype Buildings—Energy Modelling. (Continued)

References	*A. Study Location*	*B. Building Type*	*C. Sampling Size*	*D. Primary Aim of Model*	*E. Methodology*	*F. Main Findings*
Zhang et al. (2019)	Singapore	High-rise residential buildings	30 urban blocks in six typologies that represent a diverse range of urban forms were examined	- To identify correlations between solar harvesting potential and energy consumption - To develop optimisation scenarios for planning of appropriate building geometry	- Building-energy modelling approach was adopted - EnergyPlus software suite was used - Urban planning layout and geometric parameters were constructed - Sky Exposure Factor and Sky View Factor were calculated concurrently - Solar energy harvesting potential was calculated - Regression analysis was conducted for the energy optimisation scenarios	- The building cooling load intensity of the proposed hybrid urban block design was 4.7% lower than that of the current linear slab building typology, which can be attributed to the combined effects of the reduction of solar gain (13.2%)

(*Continued*)

Table F.6 (Continued)

References	*A. Study Location*	*B. Building Type*	*C. Sampling Size*	*D. Primary Aim of Model*	*E. Methodology*	*F. Main Findings*
Guevara-Sanchez et al. (2016)	Spain	Linear-type medium-rise residential blocks	ASHRAE RP-884 database	- To develop a methodological framework to identify acceptable temperature thresholds	- Spanish climate data was used for Avila, Seville and Madrid - Vulnerable household population was selected by using census data - EnergyPlus software suite was used - Spanish Technical Code criteria were used for the BPE studies - Adaptive temperature thresholds for selected climates were investigated	-This study can set the basis for fuel poverty definitions for all Mediterranean and Southern European countries developing their own methodologies

(Continued)

Table F.6 (Continued)

References	*A. Study Location*	*B. Building Type*	*C. Sampling Size*	*D. Primary Aim of Model*	*E. Methodology*	*F. Main Findings*
Calama-Gonzalez et al. (2022)	Spain	H-typology of social housing estates	H-typology represents around 13,890 social housing dwellings, in contrast to approximately 10,715 linear-typology buildings	- To assess the current performance of representative building typologies in social-housing stock	- Open-access energy simulation tool was used - Statistical analysis was conducted - The Andalusian Agency for Housing and Retrofitting dataset was used - *On-site* environmental monitoring was conducted - Sensitivity analysis was conducted - Statistical analysis was undertaken by using R v.3.5.3 software suite	An average annual discomfort hours of around 68% with higher percentage of annual undercooling discomfort hours

Table F.7 The Literature on Building Stock Aggregation through Archetype Buildings—Energy Modelling. (Continued)

References	*A. Study Location*	*B. Building Type*	*C. Sampling Size*	*D. Primary Aim of Model*	*E. Methodology*	*F. Main Findings*
Pasichnyi et al. (2019)	Stockholm, Sweden	Residential buildings	5,532 buildings from seven retrofitting packages were selected	- To present a methodological framework by using rich datasets to develop different building archetype for bottom-up energy modelling approach	- Urban building energy modelling approach was adopted by using archetyping approaches - The case-study method was applied - Energy performance certificates data were used - Climate data and reference data on standardised use and building envelope were used - Mean Absolute Scaled Error was applied for the statistical analysis	Archetype subsets would be not only sufficiently large, but also sufficiently homogenous to ensure feasibility of the proposed retrofitting measures

(*Continued*)

Table F.7 (Continued)

References	*A. Study Location*	*B. Building Type*	*C. Sampling Size*	*D. Primary Aim of Model*	*E. Methodology*	*F. Main Findings*
Wang and Holmberg (2014)	Sweden, Switzerland	Residential buildings	1,400 existing Swedish building stock statistics from derived field studies were employed to validate the baseline scenario	-To present a methodological framework that combines energy demand modelling and retrofit option rankings with life-cycle cost analysis	- The archetypes and the representative housing stock were developed - The ranking of implementing different retrofit alternatives to the energy-saving potential is identified - Sensitivity analysis was conducted - Cost-effectiveness model was conducted - Life-cycle cost assessment method was applied	- Energy-saving potential of retrofitting is 36–54% in the archetypes - Slightly larger sample size to identify representative housing stock should be identified for retrofitting on a municipal level, it would contribute to energy-policy design

(*Continued*)

Table F.7 (Continued)

References	*A. Study Location*	*B. Building Type*	*C. Sampling Size*	*D. Primary Aim of Model*	*E. Methodology*	*F. Main Findings*
Nageli et al. (2018)	Sweden, Switzerland	Residential buildings	The building stock size is limited to a representative sample stock of 10,000 synthetic buildings	-To present a new method of building stock modelling based on the generation of synthetic building stocks	- Data available from national statistics was used - Building typology analysis was conducted through Monte Carlo sampling from a distribution - Building characteristics, age, structural type were used for the statistical analysis	-The variation within common classifications of building type and construction period can be much larger than the average differences between construction periods and building types

Table F.8 The Literature on Building Stock Aggregation through Archetype Buildings—Energy Modelling. (Continued)

References	*A. Study Location*	*B. Building Type*	*C. Sampling Size*	*D. Primary Aim of Model*	*E. Methodology*	*F. Main Findings*
Dodoo and Gustavsson (2016)	Sweden, Switzerland	Residential buildings	T.1—a prefab concrete-frame T.2—a massive timber frame T.3—a light timber frame	-To determine the impacts of climate change on the performance of different building configurations	-Dynamic hour-by-hour energy balance modelling and systems analysis were conducted -Climate datasets were used -Hourly downscaling of future climate dataset was applied -Overheating-risk assessment was conducted	- Overheating risk was found to be slightly higher for the massive-frame building and slightly lower for the light-frame building

(*Continued*)

Table F.8 (Continued)

References	*A. Study Location*	*B. Building Type*	*C. Sampling Size*	*D. Primary Aim of Model*	*E. Methodology*	*F. Main Findings*
Froemelt et al. (2018)	Zurich, Switzerland	Residential buildings	Detailed information on the characteristics and consumption behaviour of 9,734 households were identified	-To provide an appropriate basis in support of effective environmental policymaking decisions	- Two-tiered clustering method was applied - Wald-clustering method was applied for the statistical analysis - Swiss Household Budget Survey was used - Swiss energy consumption data was used - Pattern recognition and clustering of households were explored - Individual archetypes and their interrelations were explored	- Delivering tailor-made insights into households' consumption behaviour for policymakers to derive and prioritise targeted measures

(Continued)

Table F.8 (Continued)

References	*A. Study Location*	*B. Building Type*	*C. Sampling Size*	*D. Primary Aim of Model*	*E. Methodology*	*F. Main Findings*
Heeren et al. (2013)	Zurich, Switzerland	Residential buildings	The building stock is clustered into 13 construction periods according to their year of construction	- To demonstrate an innovative assessment methodology in the form of a life-cycle-based building stock model - To investigate the feasibility of a sustainable energy vision	- Bottom-up energy framework was adopted - Archetype analysis was applied for retrofitting of building envelope - LCCA analysis was applied - Swiss building stock was analysed - Algorithms were developed for the statistical analysis	- Developed model will be enhanced by means of GIS integration of Zurich, the city will be clustered in supply and demand regions in order to increase the model's resolution
Lopez-Moreno et al. (2021)	Madrid, Spain	Residential buildings	Eight residential urban classes selected for an archetype analysis	-To present a systematic methodology to identify and classify residential urban areas according to representative homogenous urban zones	-Data detailing urban classifications and indicators were collected from previous studies -Cluster analysis was conducted to define and validate archetypes -Statistical Institute of the Community of Madrid dataset was used	The correlation is higher for the open mid-rise, with values greater than 55% for both low- and mid-rise urban blocks

Table F.9 The Literature on Building Stock Aggregation through Archetype Buildings—Energy Modelling (Continued)

References	*A. Study Location*	*B. Building Type*	*C. Sampling Size*	*D. Primary Aim of Model*	*E. Methodology*	*F. Main Findings*
Brogger and Wittchen (2017)	Denmark	Residential buildings	Using data from the Danish Energy Performance Certificate (EPC) scheme—27 archetypes were identified as nationally representative sample size	-To identify characteristics of building stock models that are essential for determining the energy-saving potential in national building stocks accurately	-Example building approach was adopted -Statistical approach was adopted to determine bottom-up energy-policy design -Heat and electricity supply models were investigated to provide a valid background for the BES analysis -Building energy simulation models were built at a disaggregated level	It was found that the most cost-effective retrofitting strategy is to reduce the energy demand in buildings by only 12–17%, even though an energy-saving potential of around 40% was identified

(*Continued*)

Table F.9 (Continued)

References	*A. Study Location*	*B. Building Type*	*C. Sampling Size*	*D. Primary Aim of Model*	*E. Methodology*	*F. Main Findings*
Perera et al. (2018)	Nablus, Palestine	Residential buildings	The study is limited in the scope to a single urban archetype focusing more on the urban density	-To quantify the impact of urban climate on energy system design and assessing the consequences of neglecting this specific aspect on energy system performance	-Urban microclimatic conditions, urban design, energy demand and optimisation of energy system modelling were conducted -BES analysis method was applied -CitySim—open-source software suite was used - Pareto optimisation of selected urban blocks parameters was conducted	-Energy use increase by 5–8% while grid dependency increases by up to 57% -More fluctuations in demand profile are observed when moving from stand-alone buildings to dense urban areas

(*Continued*)

Table F.9 (Continued)

References	*A. Study Location*	*B. Building Type*	*C. Sampling Size*	*D. Primary Aim of Model*	*E. Methodology*	*F. Main Findings*
Ben and Steemers (2018)	Cambridge, United Kingdom	Residential buildings	A total 78 households participated in the surveys, including 55 usable cases (response rate 28%) from face-to-face surveys and 23 usable cases (response rate 12%) from postal surveys	-To identify household archetypes and behavioural patterns in order to allow a targeted approach in energy-saving policy and retrofit improvement	- A statistical approach to cluster households based on empirical data collected from a household survey - Non-parametric correlation analysis was carried out in order to determine the relationship between behavioural factors and the households or dwellings characteristics - The questionnaire was paired with data on building characteristics obtained from the Domestic Energy Performance Certificates dataset - Factor analysis method was applied by using SPSS software suite	-The research has identified five different household archetypes to serve as a basis for targeted policy interventions tailored to specific socio-demographic groups regarding domestic energy demand reduction

Table F.10 The Literature on Building Stock Aggregation through Archetype Buildings—Energy Modelling. (Continued)

References	*A. Study Location*	*B. Building Type*	*C. Sampling Size*	*D. Primary Aim of Model*	*E. Methodology*	*F. Main Findings*
Taylor et al. (2014)	London, United Kingdom	Residential buildings	3,456 dwelling variants identified for an archetype analysis, identified through six different Design Summer Year (DSY) climate files from locations within the UK	- To examine the overheating risk in London dwelling archetypes when simulated under different UK climates, both in the present and under 'hot future' conditions	- Dynamic thermal simulations were undertaken - EnergyPlus—open-source energy simulation tool was used - 15 dwelling archetypes (27 variants including ground-, mid- and top-floor flats) - Risk of overheating risk in UK cities was predicted - Regression analysis was conducted - The Kendall's computation criterion was applied to determine statistically representative findings	- The weather files can influence the ranking of relative overheating risk between dwelling types, with significant variations in the relative ranking criterion - The calculated overheating metrics of dwelling archetypes could be found within a central range 2–3°C

(*Continued*)

Table F.10 (Continued)

References	*A. Study Location*	*B. Building Type*	*C. Sampling Size*	*D. Primary Aim of Model*	*E. Methodology*	*F. Main Findings*
Oikonomou et al. (2012)	London, United Kingdom	Residential buildings	Among 92 different built form and dwelling age combinations identified, the 15 most common were selected for simulation	-To assess variations in indoor temperatures in London dwellings during periods of hot weather, and the degree to which those dwelling-to-dwelling variations influences the BEM	- EnergyPlus—open-source energy simulation tool was used - Geometry and structure of analytical energy model were constructed - English House Condition Survey data was used - Occupancy schedules were assigned into the BEM - Weather files were assigned into the BEM - Housing typology analysis was conducted	- The effects of built form and other dwelling characteristics appear to be more important determinants of variation in high indoor temperatures than the location of a dwelling within London's urban heat island effect

(*Continued*)

Table F.10 (Continued)

References	*A. Study Location*	*B. Building Type*	*C. Sampling Size*	*D. Primary Aim of Model*	*E. Methodology*	*F. Main Findings*
Nishimwe and Reiter (2021)	Wallonia Region, Belgium	Building stock in general	- Using cadastral data of more than 1,700,000 Walloon buildings - 9,876 statistical sectors were identified as an archetype for the statistical analysis	- To assess the Energy Performance Certificates of the whole building stock and test to what extent different types of variables (building factors and socio-demographics) explain annual domestic energy use	- Cadastral map data was used - GIS software suite was used to develop building geometry into the model - Data-mining process was conducted - Ordinal logistic regression analysis method was used to test the parameters for an archetype analysis - Lasso regression method was applied - Descriptive statistics of predictors were conducted	- Considering residential buildings, the building usages explained 66.46% of EPCs, whereas tertiary building usages explained 50.53%

Table F.11 Pilot Studies That Evaluated on the Literature on Infrared Thermography for the Energy Audit of Buildings.

References	*A. Study Location*	*B. Building Type*	*C. Primary Aim of Model*	*C. Methodology*	*D. Main Findings*
Tejedor et al. (2021)	Italy, all the regions including the Mediterranean island of Sicily	Buildings (i.e., residential, offices)	- To propose a critical review on the employment of the quantitative IRT survey for the assessment of the *U*-value of the building envelope - To demonstrate a novel methodological framework for the IRT technique and its impact on building performance evaluation studies - To highlight the necessity for specialised thermographers who deal with an evolving methodology	- A systematic literature review was conducted - Laboratory test, in situ measurements and infrared radiometer thermography approaches were selected as main keyword for the bibliographic analysis - Common approaches to the *U*-value assessment were discussed as follows: (i) analogies with coeval buildings, (ii) calculation method, (iii) heat flow meter measurements, (iv) laboratory testing, (v) IRT survey	- The *U*-value can be calculated by using IRT - Further research is required between simulation and experimental data in order to provide reliable results for the development of new techniques based on IRT - Experimental field-testing studies demonstrate more reliable findings than steady-state analysis of *U*-values of building envelopes - Sensitivity analysis is required to validate discrepancies between the effects of radiations and boundary conditions

(*Continued*)

Table F.11 (Continued)

References	*A. Study Location*	*B. Building Type*	*C. Primary Aim of Model*	*C. Methodology*	*D. Main Findings*
Cardani et al. (2021)	Worldwide	Buildings (i.e., residential, offices)	- To provide an analytical framework for energy auditors and thermographers - To present a critical review of the use of the IRT survey in the building energy audit	- Bibliographic analysis was conducted - Current energy audit approaches in energy audit were conducted - Both passive and active thermography measures and its implications on building performance evaluation were conducted	- Passive approach was found to be the most common driver to detect thermally significant defects - Significance of integration of different non-destructive testing of building envelopes could contribute to the IRT survey development framework - Further research is required to represent archetype housing stock analysis for the development of benchmarking criterion in residential sector
Habaibeh et al. (2021)	San Siro—Milan, Italy	Social-housing stock	To identify an innovative and up-to-date methodological didactic approach for defining the most appropriate solutions for the refurbishment of a social-housing stock	Exploratory case-study approach was conducted. Design-driven approach was adopted by employing the historical research and survey, on-site visit, hands-on-training and on-site exposition	To improve the awareness of the students on the possibilities of building renovation and design applications for social-housing stock

Table F.12 Pilot Studies That Evaluated on the Literature on Infrared Thermography for the Energy Audit of Buildings. (Continued)

References	*A. Study Location*	*B. Building Type*	*C. Primary Aim of Model*	*C. Methodology*	*D. Main Findings*
Sbrogio et al. (2021)	Worldwide	Buildings (i.e., residential, offices)	To present a methodological framework for evaluating energy and environmental performance of building stock by the use of non-invasive techniques	A review of instrumental analysis was conducted as follows: (i) visual testing, (ii) thermographic inspection, (iii) thermal comfort, (iv) post-occupancy evaluation	Only the use of coring showed the presence of moisture and water percolation on thermal insulation Sonic trial proved the presence of some mechanical anomalies revealed by different velocities of the sound propagation in the masonry
Gupta and Gregg (2021)	Victoria, Canada	*On-site* experimental structure	To develop an external IRT method to determine clear wall *U*-values To determine the viability of an external thermographic survey technique for use in energy audits	The IRT measures were conducted on a conditioned at-scale insulated wood-frame wall structure. FLIR A65 IR camera was used A 3D thermal modelling of the Nx software package was used to validate IRT-survey findings	*U*-value measurement with IRT in the best-case scenario deviated between 6.25% and 25.00% The *U*-value results with IRT were validated and ranged between 11.53% and 10.00% in the best-case scenario

(*Continued*)

Table F.12 (Continued)

References	*A. Study Location*	*B. Building Type*	*C. Primary Aim of Model*	*C. Methodology*	*D. Main Findings*
Abrahao et al. (2021)	Porto, Portugal	*On-site* experimental structure	To develop a thermographic 2D *U*-value map for the characterisation of heavy walls in stationary regime To assess the temperature distribution of each transition phase between each defect and its undisturbed surroundings	Measurements were conducted in a walk-in climatic chamber—FITOCLIMA 1000. 2D *U*-value map is created. 2D colour map was developed to identify the distribution of the thermal transmittance of the walls In situ QIRT test was conducted	Optimisation of a TWALL mesh comprised of 1,600 elements of 8 × 6 pixels Image quality losses were estimated at 6.65% 2D correlation coefficient, *R* was equal to 0.287 which means that only 8.23% of the processed thermal image can be attributed to the original thermogram
Bartesaghi-Koc et al. (2021)	Brescia, Italy	Residential Tower Block	To verify the applicability of the energy rating system which was newly drawn up by the Green Building Council in Italy To design a methodological framework for low-energy design and retrofitting	On-site building diagnostic method was used. EnergyPlus software suite was used to undertake dynamic thermal simulations IRT survey was carried out. The PAN software was used to process the IRT-survey findings	The rock wool insulation under the ventilated façade with a density of 70 kg/m^3 and a thickness of 12 cm which is highly breathable allows surface temperatures of over 18°C to be reached and guarantees good hygrometric behaviour

Table F.13 Pilot Studies That Evaluated on the Literature on Infrared Thermography for the Energy Audit of Buildings. (Continued)

References	*A. Study Location*	*B. Building Type*	*C. Primary Aim of Model*	*C. Methodology*	*D. Main Findings*
De Angelis et al. (2020)	Nottingham, United Kingdom	19th century detached house (renovated cottage house)	To develop a novel methodological framework where infrared thermography of a deep retrofitted building is combined with deep learning neural networks To predict the future effectiveness and economic viability of wall insulation in terms of energy savings	Exploratory case-study approach was adopted A mathematical model was developed to predict the accuracy of lifelong monitoring of buildings Infrared thermography and temperature sensors were used to assess building-fabric thermal performance. FLIR E25 thermal camera was used as building diagnostic tool. The Matlab was used to validate temperature recordings	High accuracy of predicting the actual energy savings with success rate of about 82% when compared with the calculated values The Artificial Neural Networks (ANN) predicted heat losses are slightly higher than the calculated ones in 14 out of 21 cases for each wall type The range of error for the insulated wall is −13% to +15% and for the uninsulated wall is −14% to +17.5%

(*Continued*)

Table F.13 (Continued)

References	*A. Study Location*	*B. Building Type*	*C. Primary Aim of Model*	*C. Methodology*	*D. Main Findings*
Lei et al. (2021)	Mestre-Venice, Northern Italy	20th century multi-family medium-rise apartment building	To assess the current condition and propose cost-effective and energy-efficient retrofit design interventions To develop a methodological workflow to provide a guidance on the development of retrofit interventions in order to improve structural resistance of existing housing stock	The housing typology classification was conducted to identify nationally representative housing type for archetype analysis IRT survey was conducted 3D analytical model was developed to perform structural seismic analysis. The 3Muri software suite was used to perform overall seismic behaviour of building	In respect to out-of-plane mechanisms, the weakest panel was n. 1 in wall 15 in the north wing and n. 1 in the west wing Building-fabric thermal performance analysis confirmed low temperatures on internal surfaces (10–14°C) close to the dew point temperatures, especially in the junctions between floor slabs and walls and between the roof and the walls
Santos-Herrero et al. (2021)	The city of York—England, United Kingdom	Low-energy dwellings which were built according to Passivhaus standard	To present the methodology and results of in situ testing of building-fabric thermal performance to calibrate as-built energy models	Integrated Environmental Solutions (IES) software suite was used The in situ tests included repeat testing of air permeability integrated with thermal-imaging survey and heat flux measurements of the building-fabric elements	Validation of the model by altering the wall *U*-value to 0.26 W/m^2K made sense as this brought the external wall *U*-values closer to the BRUKL limiting parameter of 0.30 W/m^2K

Appendix G: Benchmarking Indicators—Part 1 (Measured/Collected)

Table G.1 Conceptualisation of the Variables in the Dataset.

Contribution to Key Research Area(s)	*In Situ Measurements (Measured)*	*On-site Environmental Monitoring (Recorded)*	*Secondary Data (Collected from the Authorities)*	*Primary Data I—Questionnaire Survey (Gathered)*	*Primary Data II—Thermal Comfort Survey (Gathered)*
Thermal Comfort + Overheating Risk	Indoor DEW (°C)	Outdoor heat-stress index (°C)	Cooling-energy consumption in summer of August 2015	Age	Location of subject respondent
Thermal Comfort + Overheating Risk	Indoor relative humidity (%)	Outdoor relative humidity (%)	Cooling-energy consumption in summer of 2015	Age bands	Thermal preference [0 to 6]
Thermal Comfort + Energy Modelling	Operative air temperature (°C)	Outdoor air temperature (°C)	Cooling-energy consumption in summer of August 2016	Energy-efficiency awareness	Overall thermal satisfaction [−3, +3]
Overheating Risk + Energy Modelling	Solar radiation (°C)	Outdoor DEW (°C)	Cooling-energy consumption in summer of 2016	Energy conservation	Thermal sensation in living room [−3, +3]
Thermal Comfort + Energy Modelling	Indoor WET (°C)	—	Heating-energy consumption in winter of 2015	Doors opening patterns in summer	Thermal sensation in kitchen [−3, +3]
Energy Modelling	Time of day	—	Heating-energy consumption in winter of 2016	Doors opening patterns in winter	Thermal sensation in Bedroom 1 [−3, +3]
Thermal Comfort + Energy Modelling	Indoor temperature ground (°C)	—	Energy consumption in April 2015	Type of heating control at home	Thermal sensation in Bedroom 2 [−3, +3]

(*Continued*)

Table G.1 (Continued)

Contribution to Key Research Area(s)	*In Situ Measurements (Measured)*	*On-site Environmental Monitoring (Recorded)*	*Secondary Data (Collected from the Authorities)*	*Primary Data I—Questionnaire Survey (Gathered)*	*Primary Data II—Thermal Comfort Survey (Gathered)*
Thermal Comfort + Energy Modelling	—	—	Energy consumption in August 2015	Type of cooling control at home	Thermal sensation in Bedroom 3 [−3, +3]
Thermal Comfort + Energy Modelling	—	—	Energy consumption in December 2015	Length of residency	Clothing insulation level of participants
Thermal Comfort	—	—	Energy consumption in February 2015	Floor level	Reasons for thermal discomfort
Thermal Comfort	—	—	Energy consumption in January 2015	Orientation	Interviewed room condition
Thermal Comfort	—	—	Energy consumption in July 2015	Cooling-consumption patterns on weekdays	Metabolic rates of participants
Energy Modelling	—	—	Energy consumption in June 2015	Cooling-consumption patterns on the weekend	—
Energy Policy	—	—	—	Health condition	—
Energy Modelling	—	—	—	Household density	—
Energy Policy	—	—	—	Income	—
Energy Policy	—	—	—	Energy advice	—
Energy Policy	—	—	—	Energy consumption	—
Abbreviations:	TC: Thermal Comfort; OR: Overheating Risk; EM: Energy Modelling; EP: Energy Policy				

Table G.2 Conceptualisation of the Variables in the Dataset. (Continued)

Contribution to Key Research Area(s)	*In Situ Measurements (Measured)*	*On-site Environmental Monitoring (Recorded)*	*Secondary data (Collected from the Authorities)*	*Primary Data I—Questionnaire Survey (Gathered)*	*Primary Data II—Thermal Comfort Survey (Gathered)*
Thermal Comfort + Energy Modelling	—	—	Energy consumption in March 2015	Heating-consumption patterns on weekdays	Overall thermal satisfaction [0 to 6]
Thermal Comfort + Energy Modelling	—	—	Energy consumption in May 2015	Heating-consumption patterns on the weekend	Thermal sensation in living room [0 to 6]
Thermal Comfort + Energy Modelling	—	—	Energy consumption in November 2015	Window-opening reasons	Thermal sensation in kitchen [0 to 6]
Thermal Comfort + Energy Modelling	—	—	Energy consumption in October 2015	Economic statues	Thermal sensation in Bedroom 1 [0 to 6]
Thermal Comfort + Energy Modelling	—	—	Energy consumption in September 2015	Occupation	Thermal sensation in Bedroom 2 [0 to 6]
Thermal Comfort + Energy Modelling	—	—	Energy consumption in April 2016	Space conditioning	Thermal sensation in Bedroom 3 [0 to 6]
Thermal Comfort + Energy Policy	—	—	Energy consumption in August 2016	Tenure type	—
Overheating Risk + Thermal Comfort	—	—	Energy consumption in December 2016	Type of heating system	—
Overheating Risk + Thermal Comfort	—	—	Energy consumption in February 2016	Type of cooling system	—
Thermal Comfort + Energy Modelling	—	—	Energy consumption in January 2016	Window-closing reasons	—
Thermal Comfort + Energy Modelling	—	—	Energy consumption in July 2016	Window-opening patterns in winter	—
Thermal Comfort + Energy Modelling	—	—	Energy consumption in June 2016	Window-opening patterns in summer	—

(*Continued*)

Table G.2 (Continued)

Contribution to Key Research Area(s)	*In Situ Measurements (Measured)*	*On-site Environmental Monitoring (Recorded)*	*Secondary data (Collected from the Authorities)*	*Primary Data I—Questionnaire Survey (Gathered)*	*Primary Data II—Thermal Comfort Survey (Gathered)*
Energy Modelling	—	—	Energy consumption in March 2016	—	—
Energy Modelling	—	—	Energy consumption in May 2016	—	—
Energy Modelling	—	—	Energy consumption in October 2016	—	—
Energy Modelling	—	—	Energy consumption in September 2016	—	—
Abbreviations:	TC: Thermal Comfort; OR: Overheating Risk; EM: Energy Modelling				

References

Abrahão, A. C., Fábio, G., Teixeira, L., Denise, D., & Silva, H. (2021). The recent residential apartment buildings' thermal performance under the combined effect of the global and the local warming. *Energy and Buildings*, 110828. https://doi.org/10.1016/j.enbuild.2021.110828

Ahern, C., & Norton, B. (2020). A generalisable bottom-up methodology for deriving a residential stock model from large empirical databases. *Energy and Buildings*, *215*. https://doi.org/10.1016/j.enbuild.2020.109886

Allacker, K., Castellani, V., Baldinelli, G., Bianchi, F., Baldassarri, C., & Sala, S. (2019). Energy simulation and LCA for macro-scale analysis of eco-innovations in the housing stock. *International Journal of Life Cycle Assessment*, *24*(6), 989–1008. https://doi.org/10.1007/s11367-018-1548-3

Bartesaghi-Koc, C., Haddad, S., Pignatta, G., Paolini, R., Prasad, D., & Santamouris, M. (2021). Can urban heat be mitigated in a single urban street? Monitoring, strategies, and performance results from a real scale redevelopment project. *Solar Energy*, *216*, 564–588. https://doi.org/10.1016/j.solener.2020.12.043

Ben, H., & Steemers, K. (2018). Household archetypes and behavioural patterns in UK domestic energy use. *Energy Efficiency*, *11*(3), 761–771. https://doi.org/10.1007/s12053-017-9609-1

Bianco, V., & Marmori, C. (2022). Modelling the deployment of energy efficiency measures for the residential sector. The case of Italy. *Sustainable Energy Technologies and Assessments*, *49*. https://doi.org/10.1016/j.seta.2021.101777

Calama-González, C. M., Suárez, R., & León-Rodríguez, Á. L. (2022). Thermal comfort prediction of the existing housing stock in southern Spain through calibrated and validated parameterized simulation models. *Energy and Buildings*, *254*. https://doi.org/10.1016/j.enbuild.2021.111562

Cardani, G., Massetti, G. E., & Riva, D. (2021). Multipurpose retrofitting of a tower building in Brescia. *Sustainability*, *13*(16), 8877. https://doi.org/10.3390/su13168877

Cheema, J. R. (2014). Some general guidelines for choosing missing data handling methods in educational research. *Journal of Modern Applied Statistical Methods*, *13*(2), 53–75.

De Angelis, A., Ascione, F., De Masi, R. F., Pecce, M. R., & Vanoli, G. P. (2020). A novel contribution for resilient buildings. Theoretical fragility curves: Interaction between energy and structural behavior for reinforced concrete buildings. *Buildings*, *10*(11), 1–28. https://doi.org/10.3390/buildings10110194

Dodoo, A., & Gustavsson, L. (2016). Energy use and overheating risk of Swedish multi-storey residential buildings under different climate scenarios. *Energy*, *97*, 534–548. https://doi.org/10.1016/j.energy.2015.12.086

Dong, Y., & Peng, C.-Y. J. (2013). Principled missing data methods for researchers. *SpringerPlus*, *2*(222), 1–17.

Famuyibo, A. A., Duffy, A., & Strachan, P. (2012). Developing archetypes for domestic dwellings – An Irish case study. *Energy and Buildings*, *50*, 150–157. https://doi.org/10.1016/j.enbuild.2012.03.033

Field, A. (2013). *Discovering statistics using IBM SPSS statistics* (fourth edn.). Los Angeles, CA: Sage.

Froemelt, A., Dürrenmatt, D. J., & Hellweg, S. (2018). Using data mining to assess environmental impacts of household consumption behaviors. *Environmental Science and Technology*, *52*(15), 8467–8478. https://doi.org/10.1021/acs.est.8b01452

Gamst, G., Meyers, L. S., & Guarino, A. J. (2008). *Analysis of variance designs: A conceptual and computational approach with SPSS and SAS*. New York: Cambridge University Press.

Gupta, R., & Gregg, M. (2021). Integrated testing of building fabric thermal performance for calibration of energy models of three low-energy dwellings in the UK. *Sustainability (Switzerland)*, *13*(5), 1–24. https://doi.org/10.3390/su13052784

Habaibeh, A., Sen, A., & Chilton, J. (2021). Evaluation tool for the thermal performance of retrofitted buildings using an integrated approach of deep learning artificial neural networks and infrared thermography. *Energy and Built Environment*, *2*(4), 345–365. https://doi.org/10.1016/j.enbenv.2020.06.004

Heeren, N., Jakob, M., Martius, G., Gross, N., & Wallbaum, H. (2013). A component based bottom-up building stock model for comprehensive environmental impact assessment and target control. *Renewable and Sustainable Energy Reviews*. https://doi.org/10.1016/j.rser.2012.11.064

Johnson, J. A. (2005). Ascertaining the validity of individual protocols from web-based personality inventories. *Journal of Research in Personality*, *39*(1), 103–129. https://doi.org/10.1016/j.jrp.2004.09.009

Kazas, G., Fabrizio, E., & Perino, M. (2017). Energy demand profile generation with detailed time resolution at an urban district scale: A reference building approach and case study. *Applied Energy*, *193*, 243–262. https://doi.org/10.1016/j.apenergy.2017.01.095

Lei, L., Chen, W., Wu, B., Chen, C., & Liu, W. (2021). A building energy consumption prediction model based on rough set theory and deep learning algorithms. *Energy and Buildings*, *240*. https://doi.org/10.1016/j.enbuild.2021.110886

Li, F. G. N., & Strachan, N. (2019). Take me to your leader: Using socio-technical energy transitions (STET) modelling to explore the role of actors in decarbonisation pathways. *Energy Research and Social Science*, *51*, 67–81. https://doi.org/10.1016/j.erss.2018.12.010

Li, X., Yao, R., Liu, M., Costanzo, V., Yu, W., Wang, W., … Li, B. (2018). Developing urban residential reference buildings using clustering analysis of satellite images. *Energy and Buildings*, *169*, 417–429. https://doi.org/10.1016/j.enbuild.2018.03.064

Little, R. J. A. (1988). A test of missing completely at random for multivariate data with missing values. *Journal of the American Statistical Association*, *83*(404), 1198–1202.

Little, R. J. A., & Rubin, D. B. (2002). *Statistical analysis with missing data* (2nd ed.). New York: Wiley.

Martins, T. A. de L., Faraut, S., & Adolphe, L. (2019). Influence of context-sensitive urban and architectural design factors on the energy demand of buildings in Toulouse, France. *Energy and Buildings*, *190*, 262–278. https://doi.org/10.1016/j.enbuild.2019.02.019

McKenna, R., Merkel, E., Fehrenbach, D., Mehne, S., & Fichtner, W. (2013). Energy efficiency in the German residential sector: A bottom-up building-stock-model-based analysis in the context of energy-political targets. *Building and Environment*, *62*, 77–88. https://doi.org/10.1016/j.buildenv.2013.01.002

Molina, C., Jones, B., Hall, I. P., & Sherman, M. H. (2021). CHAARM: A model to predict uncertainties in indoor pollutant concentrations, ventilation and infiltration rates, and associated energy demand in Chilean houses. *Energy and Buildings*, *230*. https://doi.org/10.1016/j.enbuild.2020.110539

Molina, C., Jones, B., Kent, M., & Hall, I. P. (2018, September). *A stochastic approach to estimate uncertainty in pollutant concentrations in an archetypal Chilean house*.

Molina, C., Kent, M., Hall, I., & Jones, B. (2020). A data analysis of the Chilean housing stock and the development of modelling archetypes. *Energy and Buildings*, *206*. https://doi.org/10.1016/j.enbuild.2019.109568

Newman, D. A. (2014). Missing data: Five practical guidelines. *Organizational Research Methods*, *17*(4), 372–411. https://doi.org/10.1177/1094428114548590

Nishimwe, A., & Reiter, S. (2021). Towards nearly zero-energy residential neighbourhoods in the European Union: A case study. *Renewable and Sustainable Energy Reviews*, *135*. https://doi.org/10.1016/j.rser.2020.110198

Oikonomou, E., Davies, M., Mavrogianni, A., Biddulph, P., Wilkinson, P., & Kolokotroni, M. (2012). Modelling the relative importance of the urban heat island and the thermal quality of dwellings for overheating in London. *Building and Environment*, *57*, 223–238. https://doi.org/10.1016/j.buildenv.2012.04.002

Ortiz, M. A., & Bluyssen, P. M. (2018). Proof-of-concept of a questionnaire to understand occupants' comfort and energy behaviours: First results on home occupant archetypes. *Building and Environment*, *134*, 47–58. https://doi.org/10.1016/j.buildenv.2018.02.030

Pasichnyi, O., Wallin, J., & Kordas, O. (2019). Data-driven building archetypes for urban building energy modelling. *Energy*, *181*, 360–377. https://doi.org/10.1016/j.energy.2019.04.197

Perera, A. T. D., Coccolo, S., Scartezzini, J. L., & Mauree, D. (2018). Quantifying the impact of urban climate by extending the boundaries of urban energy system modeling. *Applied Energy*, *222*, 847–860. https://doi.org/10.1016/j.apenergy.2018.04.004

Pittam, J., O'Sullivan, P. D., & O'Sullivan, G. (2014). Stock aggregation model and virtual archetype for large scale retrofit modelling of local authority housing in Ireland. In *Energy procedia* (Vol. 62, pp. 704–713). Elsevier Ltd. https://doi.org/10.1016/j.egypro.2014.12.434

Pittau, F., Lumia, G., Heeren, N., Iannaccone, G., & Habert, G. (2019). Retrofit as a carbon sink: The carbon storage potentials of the EU housing stock. *Journal of Cleaner Production*, *214*, 365–376. https://doi.org/10.1016/j.jclepro.2018.12.304

Santos-Herrero, J. M., Lopez-Guede, J. M., & Flores-Abascal, I. (2021). Modeling, simulation and control tools for nZEB: A state-of-the-art review. *Renewable and Sustainable Energy Reviews*. https://doi.org/10.1016/j.rser.2021.110851

Sbrogiò, L., Bevilacqua, C., De Sordi, G., Michelotto, I., Sbrogiò, M., Toniolo, A., & Tosato, C. (2021). Strategies for structural and energy improvement in mid-rise unreinforced masonry apartment buildings: A case study in Mestre (Northeast Italy). *Sustainability*, *13*(16), 8819. https://doi.org/10.3390/ su13168819

Schafer, J. L. (1999). Multiple imputation: A primer. *Statistical Methods in Medical Research*, *8*(1), 3–15.

Schouten, B., Cobben, F., & Bethlehem, J. (2009). Indicators for the representativeness of survey response. *Survey Methodology*, *35*(1), 101–113.

Streicher, K. N., Padey, P., Parra, D., Bürer, M. C., & Patel, M. K. (2018). Assessment of the current thermal performance level of the Swiss residential building stock: Statistical analysis of energy performance certificates. *Energy and Buildings*, *178*, 360–378. https://doi.org/10.1016/j.enbuild.2018.08.032

Tabachnick, B. G., & Fidell, L. S. (2007). *Using multivariate statistics* (5th ed.). Boston, MA: Pearson.

Tardioli, G., Kerrigan, R., Oates, M., O'Donnell, J., & Finn, D. P. (2018). Identification of representative buildings and building groups in urban datasets using a novel pre-processing, classification, clustering and predictive modelling approach. *Building and Environment*, *140*, 90–106. https://doi.org/10.1016/j.buildenv.2018.05.035

Taylor, J., Davies, M., Mavrogianni, A., Chalabi, Z., Biddulph, P., Oikonomou, E., ... Jones, B. (2014). The relative importance of input weather data for indoor overheating risk assessment in dwellings. *Building and Environment*, *76*, 81–91. https://doi.org/10.1016/j.buildenv.2014.03.010

Tejedor, B., Barreira, E., Almeida, R. M. S. F., & Casals, M. (2021). Automated data-processing technique: 2D Map for identifying the distribution of the U-value in building elements by quantitative internal thermography. *Automation in Construction*, *122*. https://doi.org/10.1016/j.autcon.2020.103478

Wang, C. K., Tindemans, S., Miller, C., Agugiaro, G., & Stoter, J. (2020). Bayesian calibration at the urban scale: A case study on a large residential heating demand application in Amsterdam. *Journal of Building Performance Simulation*, *13*(3), 347–361. https://doi.org/10.1080/19401493.2020.1729862

Wang, J., Wang, Q., & Holmberg, S. (2014). A methodology to assess energy-demand savings and cost effectiveness of retrofitting in existing Swedish residential buildings. *Sustainable Cities and Society*, *14*(C), 254–266. https://doi.org/10.1016/i.scs.?.014.10.007

Wang, Z., de Dear, R., Luo, M., Ghahramani, A., & Lin, B. (2018). The uncertainty of subjective thermal comfort measurement. *Energy and Buildings*, *181*, 38–49. https://doi.org/10.1016/j.enbuild.2018.09.041

Yi, C. Y., & Peng, C. (2019). An archetype-in-neighbourhood framework for modelling cooling energy demand of a city's housing stock. *Energy and Buildings*, *196*, 30–45. https://doi.org/10.1016/j.enbuild.2019.05.015

Zhang, J., Xu, L., Shabunko, V., Tay, S. E. R., Sun, H., Lau, S. S. Y., & Reindl, T. (2019). Impact of urban block typology on building solar potential and energy use efficiency in tropical high-density city. *Applied Energy*, *240*, 513–533. https://doi.org/10.1016/j.apenergy.2019.02.033

Index

Taylor & Francis Group
an informa business

For Product Safety Concerns and Information please contact our EU representative GPSR@taylorandfrancis.com
Taylor & Francis Verlag GmbH, Kaufingerstraße 24, 80331 München, Germany

www.ingramcontent.com/pod-product-compliance
Ingram Content Group UK Ltd.
Pitfield, Milton Keynes, MK11 3LW, UK
UKHW020156200926
475702UK00016B/2741
9781032493053